AC8.W2

THE
SUNDAY
GENTLEMAN

≫≫≫≫≫ ≪≪≪≪≪

by

IRVING WALLACE

19   65

Simon and Schuster·New York

The author is grateful for permission to quote "Elegy
for J. F. Kennedy" by W. H. Auden. Copyright ©
1965 by W. H. Auden. Reprinted from *About the
House* by W. H. Auden, by permission of Random
House, Inc.

LIBRARY OF CONGRESS CATALOG CARD NUMBER: 65–24279
MANUFACTURED IN THE UNITED STATES OF AMERICA
BY H. WOLFF, NEW YORK
DESIGNED BY HELEN BARROW

For
Sylvia
who helped to make
the Sundays possible

CONTENTS

I. Meet the Sunday Gentleman

Meet the
Sunday Gentleman

"THE BIGGEST, THE BEST, OR THE FIRST . . ."

IN THE SUMMER of 1962, when I decided to collect and enlarge the stories composing this book, I wondered what title I might give to the result. At once, a favorite little anecdote that I had heard about the great actor and wit John Barrymore came to mind. A friend of the actor's, long ailing, had finally died, and Barrymore had reluctantly attended the funeral. Barrymore had stood apart from the deceased's other cronies and had observed the burial ceremony in the cemetery with a jaundiced eye. When the service was ended and the mourners had begun to depart, Barrymore noticed that one remained behind, a doddering old man who stood near the grave, staring down into it. Barrymore considered the old man, then slowly sidled up to him, leaned over and whispered, "I guess it hardly pays to go home."

Since the book I had in mind was meant to be, in a sense, a valedictory to my magazine-writing career, a fond and nostalgic farewell to another time, when writers could write about subjects while not living under the cloud of Russian-American nuclear oblivion, I thought that I might call my book "It Hardly Pays to Go Home," adding the explanatory subtitle "One Last Look at Some Strange People, Places and Things Around the World Before the Deluge."

But when I began to work on this book, I soon realized the title that had first come to mind would never do. For the oddities and the curiosities, human and institutional, that I had observed and investigated in a span of twenty years were for the most part, not of another era but still of our time, and as alive as I was. Clearly, nostalgia and farewell were not the right notes. And then, happily, I realized what the right note was, a note less grand, less pessimistic, more personal—and I named this book *The Sunday Gentleman.*

>«<

Under the severe criminal laws of seventeenth-century England, a man in debt was liable to arrest and trial. If found guilty, and if his creditors demanded that he be incarcerated in debtor's prison for his insolvency and financial default, he could be taken into custody by the police any day of the week save one—Sunday, the Lord's Day.

As a consequence, a man wanted for debt would usually go into hiding six days of the week—but on Sunday, immune from seizure, he would appear proudly in public as safe as any solvent gentleman. He was free to breathe the free air, to mingle in the streets and alehouses with his fellows as their equal, suffering no threat from the Throne or fear of being flung into Newgate.

There were many such Sunday Gentlemen, as they came to be called, in that period, and among the foremost of these was Daniel Defoe, the pioneer newspaperman and pamphleteer, and the author of *The Life and Strange Surprizing Adventures of Robinson Crusoe, of York, Mariner*. In 1692, when his hosiery trading company was £17,000 in debt and on the verge of bankruptcy, Daniel Defoe was forced to hide from the law six days a week in a section of Bristol, emerging in public only on Sunday, to be again his own man and to stroll with dignity "accoutred in the fashion of the times, with a flowing wig, lace ruffles, and a sword by his side." This role of one-seventh gentleman was maintained until his creditors were satisfied, and then, and only then, could he be his own man and the compleat gentleman every day of the week.

During my own twenty-year career as a free-lance contributor to national magazines in the United States and Great Britain, that long apprenticeship before I could become a full-time writer of books, I too was, in a symbolic sense, such a Sunday Gentleman as Defoe had been. I would, in those lively and trying years, develop and write formula articles and stories to the best of my ability during six days of each week, to escape our modern version of debtor's prison.

I would write, in that time, short nonfiction pieces skillfully created to fill in the blank spaces between advertisements in popular periodicals, to enlighten busy and harried Everyman superficially, and to earn money for my keep and the support of my dependents. The hours were long and the pay short and uncertain. For my first published article, sold when I was fifteen years old, I received five dollars. For one of my last, when I was thirty-five, I received three thousand dollars. That was the high and the low of it, although the real low was when I received nothing at all for my speculative efforts. I recall even now, with a stab of pain that has never quite disappeared, a Wisconsin morning when I was seventeen or eighteen years old and went out to the mailbox to find in one delivery twenty manuscripts of mine that had been rejected by twenty magazines.

When I was very young, I would study various periodicals, try to determine the kind of subjects that seemed to interest them, and then dream up suitable stories—researching, organizing, and submitting the stories directly to the publications that were my targets. As many of my stories sold as did not sell, and I was sufficiently encouraged by the small payments I received, by the appearance of my name in print, by the variety of knowledge I acquired through my firsthand interviews and researches, to go doggedly on and on. In this way, I earned spending money when I was a high school student in Kenosha, Wisconsin; I supported myself in an attic room when I attended college in Berkeley, California; I managed to survive in a dingy hotel room in Los Angeles; and along the way paid for a nine-month trip of writing and exploration through Mexico, Guatemala, Honduras, Panama, Colombia, and Cuba.

Later, with more knowledge, experience, and a growing and soon obsessive desire to write well, I produced less, but struggled no less steadily, and I wrote my magazine stories with more depth of research and more care in their creation. As the important magazines began to buy and publish my articles, I changed some of my methods, but only the mechanics, not the principles behind them. Where formerly I had submitted my articles directly to editors—which was young, unprofessional, and slow, and placed me at the mercy of their autocratic decisions on what I should be paid and what I should rewrite—I now had sufficient stature to acquire a New York literary agent. He became my retailer, my middleman in the marketplace. Where I used to write an article simply because I felt it was suitable for a certain market, upon my agent's advice I began to submit one- or two-page outlines of story ideas before researching and writing them. In the end this extra step, the outlining of an idea, proved economical. It saved me days and weeks of time and energy that would have been wasted if I had written about subjects that the magazines had already published or had taboos against, or in which they were not interested.

Only when a periodical approved an outline I had submitted did I then research and write it. But even this new approach did not guarantee me a sale and an income. If the article did not live up to the promise of the outline, it was returned and I received no payment for my work. Not until the last seven or eight years of my magazine-writing career, when I had achieved a modest reputation and was being published by *The Saturday Evening Post*, *Reader's Digest*, *Collier's*, *Esquire*, *Cosmopolitan*, did I receive guarantees of payment for approved outlines. Several magazines would promise full payment, whether the article I produced was accepted for publication or not. Most magazines would promise full payment if the article was accepted, but perhaps only one-fourth payment if the article was rejected, with travel expenses in connection with research guaranteed in either case.

At the peak of my magazine-writing career, nine out of ten stories that I researched and wrote six days of the week—more for my livelihood than my pleasure, although I cannot remember ever writing a single article that did not give me some pleasure—were based on ideas I had created, and then slanted to suit the editorial peculiarities and special reading public of specific magazines. In short, I was inventing ideas which were tailor-made for a specific periodical, ideas that might have been exactly what its editors would have thought of and desired had they been inventive enough to do so.

One out of ten story ideas would come directly to me from the editors of a magazine, an assignment devised by them and one that they felt was suitable for my talents. For example, *Collier's* magazine decided, in 1946, that it would like a series of three stories on Princess Elizabeth, now Queen of England, and asked me if I would undertake the assignment. I went from Paris to Buckingham Palace to research and write the stories. On the other hand, in that same period, I suspected that *Collier's* magazine would be interested in an up-to-date article on the French Foreign Legion, an article showing that ex-Nazi Germans then dominated the French Legion's rank and file. When I suggested this idea, *Collier's* approved it with as much enthusiasm as if they had conceived the idea in their own Manhattan offices.

The point I am making is this: No matter how I obtained my assignments, the stories that I wrote six days a week were stories designed to sell to certain markets, to be published, and to earn me enough money to avoid poverty, bankruptcy, masculine failure, the twentieth-century versions of the seventeenth-century debtor's prison. Nor did I ever feel that this was literary prostitution, any more than magazine writers, newspapermen, television and radio writers and commentators today feel that they are committing prostitution. It was a respectable job to be done, just as magazine writers and journalists today are fulfilling a job in communications. It was an accommodation to a mature necessity of life, a way to survive and seek security for one's self and one's dependents. I still remember the legend on a glass paperweight, an insurance company gift, that my father used to have on his desk when I was a boy. It read: "The world owes no man a living." And so those of us who wrote on order did so because it was man's work, and we tried—as others in this position try today—to earn our daily bread with as much honor, integrity, and individual creativity as possible within the confines of the restrictive commercial world of magazines and newspapers.

There were moments of mean compromise, and aftermaths of bad conscience, of course. I often remembered a character of W. Somerset Maugham's remarking that a true artist would let his poor mother starve to death rather than write potboilers. Apparently William Faulkner read this, or subscribed to this tenet on his own, for in 1956 he told a reporter from the *Paris Review* that a writer's only responsibility in life was to his art, adding, "Everything goes by the board: honor, pride, decency, security, happiness, all, to get the book written. If a writer has to rob his mother, he will not hesitate; the 'Ode on a Grecian Urn' is worth any number of old ladies."

It was because I believed in this responsibility of the writer to his art as much as I believed that he had other responsibilities beyond writing, it was because of this ambivalent feeling toward my work, that I determined that six days a week were enough to give of myself to avoid debtor's prison. The seventh day of the week, I felt, belonged to me. And so almost every Sunday, during those twenty magazine years, I devoted to factual articles and stories that were more honest, if less commercial, because they were entirely my own. On Sundays, I wrote without any periodical or reading public consciously in mind, wrote only those articles and stories that interested me totally and interested me alone. I hoped that they would appear in print, and that I would be paid for them, but if they were not accepted and published, it did not matter. At least one day a week, I could appear to myself, and perhaps before the world, as a Sunday Gentleman.

This book then is a partial product of my twenty years of Sundays, and half of it found its way into magazines and half did not, and while it may not represent art, it does represent those reportorial and observation pieces that I wrote simply because they interested me and I wanted to write them. In these pages you will meet one writer as he wrote when he was a Sunday Gentleman—and by "gentleman" I do not mean the gentleman of the dictionaries who is "a well-bred man of fine feelings, good education, and social position"; I mean the gentleman Defoe was on Sunday, by my definition "an honest man, full of sensitivity, racked by insecurities, determined one day to be a free and independent soul, to speak and write what is in his mind and heart without fear and compromise, to write in concert with truth or his own desires."

Eventually, there came a time in my life when Sundays were not enough, when being a gentleman only once a week galled me. When that time came, I gave up writing for magazines and began writing books, because books represented to me that last refuge for the writer who wished to write as he pleased, alone, without compromising with committees, without concern for pleasing any special public. If one could write the books he wished without making concessions, and somehow derive a livelihood from them no matter how meager, I reasoned, then such a one could be a gentleman, a freeman, an independent man, not merely one day a week but seven days a week.

When I began my book-writing career, my fight for seven days of Sunday a week, I was told by book writers who had been published that I was seeking a utopia that had no existence. Few writers in America, very few, wrote books and only books and yet stayed out of debtor's prison. There were, I was told, men who wrote books and taught in schools or had working mates or mates who possessed an inheritance; and there were housewives who wrote books and had husbands with regular employment; and children who wrote books and had free board and room and weekly allowances. But any dream of an unsubsidized author writing books without compromising them, and yet surviving, was impractical and foolish. I did not believe my veteran part-time author friends. I thought that they were merely speaking out of bitterness, out of a cynicism born of defeat. I was wrong.

Actually, when I quit magazines in the hope of devoting myself entirely to books, believing it could be done, I should have known better. For, to be quite frank about it, I had never not written books. I had written them while hardly out of puberty. I had written them in high school, in college, in the army, and in the Sundays of my magazine years. But I had never had a single book accepted for publication. Looking back now, I still find myself astonished, and frightened, at the number of books I wrote in the loneliness of so many small and strange rooms, and by how thoroughly and totally (despite occasional encouragements) my books were rejected. The gravestones on my stillborn are imprinted indelibly on my memory, and when I think of them, I buy another bond, overeat, and knock wood.

When I was seventeen, I wrote half a book, *Heroes of Today*, recounting the lives of men I admired, who ranged from Clarence Darrow to Walter Reed. It was rejected, never published. When I was eighteen, I wrote half a book, *Sorry, but You're Wrong*, exploding the fallacies of popular folk beliefs. It was rejected, never published. When I was nineteen, I wrote my first complete book, *My Adventure Trail*, an enthusiastic recounting of a journey I had taken into the Honduran jungles. It was rejected, never published. When I was twenty, I wrote another complete book, *The Sunday Gentleman*—yes—a biography of Daniel Defoe. It was rejected, never published. When I was twenty-two, I wrote one-third of a book, *Roman Holiday*, a biographical account of the first twelve Caesars. It was rejected, never published. When I was twenty-two, I compiled and rewrote a book, *Etcetera*, a collection of some newly written articles together with many I had already had published in magazines. It was rejected, never published. When I was twenty-five, I wrote *Japan's Mein Kampf*, a documentary account of the infamous Tanaka Memorial. It was rejected, never published. When I was twenty-seven, I wrote a full-length book, *With Their Pants Down*, a candid memoir of celebrities I had met and interviewed in my writing career. It was rejected, never published. When I was thirty-four, I wrote two chapters of a book, *Gabrielle*, a detailed history of the pretty French murderess, Gabrielle Bompard. I was discouraged, never submitted it. In those years, I wrote at least one or two chapters of a half-dozen novels, but became doubtful about each, and never finished them or submitted for possible publication what I had finished.

This was my illustrious record when, at the age of thirty-seven, I so cavalierly left magazines to write books seriously seven Sundays a week. Actually, I had always written books "seriously." But at the age of thirty-seven, the effort was more "seriously" because I intended that my new career not be an avocation but a vocation, and I felt that I was bringing to it more experience, more understanding, more wisdom, and more passion than I had possessed when I was younger.

Between the years 1953 and 1959, I wrote and had published four books: three nonfiction books of biography and one novel. All were minor critical and minor financial successes, and combined they did not earn me as much money as I had earned, or was able to earn, in one year from other writing sources. My friends were right, after all. I could not make a living from the writing of books—a week was not meant to be made up only of Sundays—yet I had found that if I could not live from books, I certainly could not live without them.

From the first book to the fourth, I did everything I could to buy time for the next one, and to keep my wife, my two children, and others of my relations alive. I scrounged through every literary and pseudoliterary alley I could find in search of money that could buy Sundays that could mean books. I had turned my back on magazines, and so I went elsewhere for sustenance. I wrote countless tricked-up idea outlines and present-tense original screen treatments, on speculation, to submit to the film studios. I wrote numerous screenplays, on salary, for every major movie studio. At my lowest point, I wrote ten television scripts for six producers on order.

I am not complaining about this. It was a plush hell, an infernal region dominated by double-dealing, politics, feuds, pettiness, thievery, cretinism, where the writer suffered indignity, disrespect, disdain, and where he could make more money than he could possibly make in any other salaried medium of writing. There were also, in this region, good people, honest people, highly creative people, and sometimes the product of their collective talents produced a motion picture or television film that equaled or exceeded in artistic value the best current books or plays. But these talented ones, and their best products, were in the minority.

In those days, for that money, for that survival and books-in-the-future money, I worked harder and longer than I had ever worked in my magazine years. But for me, for one like myself who likes to create on his own rather than adapt, and who prefers to work alone, and rise or fall by his own efforts rather than collaborate with other writers, directors, producers, actors, it was a miserable period. I found that the big money was too costly to earn, emotionally. In the magazine world, at least, I could do a skilled craftsman's work six days a week, and know that the seventh day would be Sunday. In this frenetic, competitive world of celluloid, at least for me, there were no Sundays, none at all.

But somehow, out of all of this, some victories were gained. I did find the time (mostly nighttime, not Sunday time) to write my first four books. And I learned a good deal that I had not known before about dialogue, about scenes, about story construction (although there was also much that had been lost, and that had to be learned anew, like subjective writing, descriptive writing, inner monologues, and the necessity for story to emerge from character rather than appending characters to story). I came away with this knowledge, and the four hard-earned books, and a new determination, almost blind and savage, to write books and nothing else. In fact, I came out of this world with everything except the one thing I had gone into it for—money.

More impractical and foolish than ever, I returned to writing books with no more security than a house of my own that was not paid for, a small savings account, and a fierce desire to write a fifth book, a novel that possessed me and engaged all my senses. I wrote this fifth book. It was an immediate international best seller.

Here was the miracle I had dreamed of in my youth. At last, free, independent, confident, I wrote my next book, and my next, and my next, and my next, and each was an international best seller. By wildest luck and unbelievable good fortune, combined with a love of what I was doing and a love of the stories I had to tell, and the freedom to tell them in my own way, I had won my seven days of Sundays.

In the years since I quit magazines, and then motion pictures and television, and ever since I began to work entirely on my own as a novelist, I have become even more desirable to executives in those entertainment mediums. No month passes that I do not receive some inquiry from New York or Hollywood asking if, with few imposed restrictions, I will not write a series of articles or short stories, or produce motion pictures based on my own ideas, or create and supervise my own television show. I have always been flattered, and always declined, because my week of Sundays has been too hard-won ever to forfeit it for more money.

I might add at this point that I do not mean to say that in the various fields of writing only authors who write books are free and independent men. Usually, there are two conditions under which a man's life can be free and independent—the first is to have youth without responsibility; the second is to have maturity with sufficient savings in the bank, or earning power, to make him beholden to no one on earth. There are a handful of magazine, screenplay and television writers, I am sure, who may write as they please, but only a small handful. There are undoubtedly playwrights who are wholly their own men, too, although many of the ones I know have told me that their control of their material exists as a clause in their contract but not in its execution. If a playwright requires a big-name actor or director to get his play produced on Broadway, or needs either of these to assure his play's success, this actor or director may demand major excisions or revisions. The playwright must then choose between doing what others want him to do in order to see his play produced, or refuse to bend to compromise and face having no play performed at all. But again, in exceptional cases, if a playwright is an important name himself, and possessed of a bull's head and a backbone of iron, he may dominate the actor or director, and ultimately see his work produced exactly as he wrote it.

In the publishing world of books, there is less necessity for the creative person to bend to the wishes of others. The author has neither actor nor director to contend with, only a publisher and/or editor. Unlike the play producer, who must gamble a large financial investment, the book publisher can bring out a novel at relatively small cost, and so can afford to be less nervous about investing in a work that may be in a form that does not please him entirely.

Yet, in all honesty, I must state that complete integrity can be maintained by a book author only when the publisher needs him more than he needs the publisher. If an author has written a biography or novel on his own, and his publisher or publisher's editor insists that he radically change portions of it to suit the publisher's or editor's own critical and creative ideas, the author must often comply in order to see his beloved book in print. Of course, it is usually not quite that cut-and-dried: Writers are often permitted to retain material the publishers do not like simply because of publishers' traditional respect for the individuality and mystique of the creative artist; and often writers will eagerly make most changes suggested to them because they are insecure about the quality of what they have written, or because they feel that an experienced editor's suggestions may actually improve their work.

19

Compromises in the publishing field, minimal though they be, do exist, for reasons of an editor's personal prejudices or a publisher's economic concerns. After spending years preparing and writing my first published book, *The Fabulous Originals*, and receiving an advance of $1,000 and a beribboned contract from Alfred A. Knopf, I was stunned when he forced me to surrender a degree of my creative autonomy before my book went to press, a surrender demanded on economic grounds only. I was stunned because I had regarded Mr. Knopf as entirely a creative publisher with respect only for the well-written word. I had not realized that he was of necessity also a tough and shrewd businessman, like most other publishers. Even though my book was not unduly long, Mr. Knopf insisted that he wanted it considerably shorter, in order to make its publication cheaper and its profits (the equivalent of 9½ percent of the retail price was to be mine, I was reminded) greater. It *was* my first about-to-be-published book. Fearful that it might not reach the printer if I defended the Word against the Profit Ledger, I conceded. Of the volume's nine chapters, I was forced to pull out one chapter in its entirety, and cut out two-fifths of another. In short, I needed this publisher more than he needed me, and against my better judgment, I compromised.

Years later, when I had a good number of books in print and they were being widely read, and numerous publishers desired me more than I desired them, my new publisher suggested that my novel, *The Prize*, might be improved if I made two major changes in the manuscript before it went to press. These were not arrogant demands, but well-intentioned suggestions for literary improvement. After giving the two changes considerable thought, I rejected the first because I felt it was wrong, that it tampered with my own vision of the story, that the concession would make the book less the novel I had conceived. However, I agreed that the publisher's second suggested change was an intelligent one, worth considering as a definite improvement, and I agreed to do some rewriting. The important difference is that I was not being forced to compromise a single paragraph as a condition of publication, and the decision to rewrite was, in the end, my own. In no other field of writing have I ever encountered such absolute freedom.

Because full-time creative independence was a primary drive in my writing career, once I had achieved it with books I never again, as I have said, had any desire to return to magazine writing. Since the writing of my first published book, I have written only four magazine articles, but none of these are articles such as those I used to write six days a week, or such as those in this collection that I wrote on the seventh day. My recent articles are subjective rather than objective, and they concern the creation of my books and were inspired by an occasional need to defend or explain my novels. The only exception, perhaps, is the most recent article I have written, which is about a personal experience and forms the final chapter of this book. This article was motivated less by a desire to explain how I had researched my novel, *The Man*, than to set down on paper, more for myself than anyone else, my memory of several visits to President John F. Kennedy's Oval Office in the White House shortly before his assassination.

Looking back now on twenty years of writing for magazines as a livelihood, I think I can fairly evaluate the pleasures I derived and the difficulties I endured in that profession. I have already spoken of the most disagreeable aspect of my magazine career, the lack of opportunity to write as I pleased about subjects that pleased me. There were several other aspects of this field of writing that irritated me. There was the editorial attitude that the magazine article or short story must always be subservient to the advertisements. Of course, interesting stories were required to attract a large reading public, which, in turn, would attract advertising accounts. But if an abundance of last-minute advertising was received for a certain issue, then the stories scheduled for that issue would be coldly re-edited and slashed, without regard for the adverse literary effect or story damage this caused, to accommodate the profit picture. The last article I wrote as a full-time magazine writer—an interview I had in Essen, Germany, with Alfried Krupp—was reduced from a thorough piece to a half-intelligible pygmy of reportage due to this sort of commercial emergency. When the article appeared, I winced with pain at what had been done and what readers whom I respected would think of such an incomplete, superficial story, never knowing that I had originally written it quite differently.

Another annoyance, infrequent but terrible when it did occur, was censorship. Sometimes I would submit an article that ran counter to the magazine's editorial policy, or contained material that might be offensive to an important advertiser or to a prejudiced publisher or his wife. Then either the article would be rejected without appeal, or the offending material cut out, no matter how inaccurate this made the story or how much it threw the story out of balance. One classic example of censorship occurred to me in the summer of 1949. With a firm assignment based on an idea I had suggested, I wrote a two-part article on the controversy surrounding the Nobel Prize awards made by Sweden and Norway. In one portion of this article, I attempted to evaluate the impartiality of the Nobel Prize judges from factual voting records, and I concluded that the Nobel judges had unreasonably favored candidates of Scandinavian and German citizenship, but boycotted Russian writers and scientists, because Russia (under both the monarchy and Communism) was Sweden's historic enemy. I pointed out that Sweden had given the Russians only one and a half medicine prizes, no chemistry prizes, no physics prizes, and only one literary prize (to a White Russian, Ivan Bunin, living in exile—while Tolstoi was voted down nine times, and Chekhov and Gorki were ignored) in the first forty-eight years of prize-giving. While the editors of *Collier's* accepted this as objective reporting, the passage came to the attention of a non-editorial executive of the firm, a man who saw Red at an early age and who had never recovered. He decided that the writer of this article was a Communist sympathizer (let alone a Czarist lover) and that the article, assigned or not, must be rejected. Only after his staff prevailed upon his sense of fair play did he relent, permitting the two-part article to be accepted and published—on the condition that the factual section on the Swedish judges being anti-Russian be obliterated. It was unreasonable censorship, clear and simple, but I bowed to it in order to salvage the rest of my article and the income it would provide, after months of work. Not until I entered the freer world of books was I able to tell the whole of the Nobel story, to interweave the omitted facts with a fictional plot, in my novel *The Prize*. But that was fourteen years later.

Another form of censorship sometimes came from the subject about whom one wrote. I remember interviewing the late Raymond Chandler, the brilliant writer of hard-boiled mysteries and the creator of private detective Philip Marlowe, in 1946. I enjoyed and admired him without reservation, and found him refreshingly candid in his opinions of himself, his craft, his fellow authors. As I finished my story about him, I was particularly pleased by the following passage:

"Chandler's favorite conversational topic is the mystery story and its practitioners. He spares neither himself nor his fellows.

"S. S. Van Dine? 'I can't read him. Philo Vance is utterly detestable. He's just a second-rate imitation of the stage Englishman.' Dorothy Sayers? 'I like her as a writer, but her mysteries are lousy.' Agatha Christie? 'Her stories are phony, and worst of all, they cheat. Though *The Murder of Roger Ackroyd* was a good stunt.' Ngaio Marsh? 'I read her for a while, but now I find her tiresome.' Freeman Wills Crofts? 'A plodder.' R. Austin Freeman? 'Strictly gaslight and hansom cab, but one of my old favorites.' Rex Stout? 'Enjoyed *The League of Frightened Men*, then got weary of his work. Always liked Archie, but Nero Wolfe's eccentricities are beginning to bore me. Of course, it's hard to maintain eccentricities through a long series of stories.' Ellery Queen? 'I don't like him at all.' A. Conan Doyle? 'I never shared the great admiration everyone has for Sherlock Holmes.' Erle Stanley Gardner? 'I like the books he's written under the name of A. A. Fair, but his own Perry Mason stinks, and you can quote me. Erle is touchy, and he probably won't ever speak to me again after this.' Dashiell Hammett? 'He probably influenced me. He's tops, but I think he can be done better.' Raymond Chandler? 'His specialty is insulting people. He's a poor plotter, a bad constructionist, and he finds it easier to criticize than to create.' "

While my article on Raymond Chandler was being readied for publication, a New York columnist heard about this explosive passage and mentioned it in print. The next day, Chandler was on the telephone. He insisted that I kill that overly frank passage in my story at once. He admitted that he had said what I had written, and had said it all for publication, but now some of his fellow writers had been in touch with him and had convinced him that complete candor, in itself, was not a virtue. Reluctantly, I agreed to this censorship, and was forced to present a less candid Raymond Chandler to the magazine public.

One of the unhappiest aspects of magazine writing, a subtle but persistent dishonesty that was necessary for survival, was that of giving almost every article a strong angle. The necessity of having an angle in every article still survives in the magazine field. But it was more widely in demand, although less harshly used, during the time when I wrote for magazines. It was not enough to think of a likely subject to write about, and then write about it as one truly found it (since this might invite waste, dullness, lack of instant audience appeal). To secure an assignment, the writer had to find in advance something in a prospective subject's life that was unusual or bizarre—a "narrative hook," an "attention grabber"—and promise to prove it true and to build the story around it, as well as use an offbeat point of view or theme. Once the assignment was obtained, with this prefabricated angle pledged for delivery, the writer had to research and interview to prove the validity of the angle, to build it up, so that it could support all the remaining facts. If the writer then found that the angle really existed, and did have the importance he had claimed for it, he could use it in his prose creation and present it in full honesty. If the writer found that he had been misinformed about the truth or the importance of his angle, he could risk developing another angle (even though it did not conform to his assignment) and hope to get by with it, or as was more usually the case, he could weight the emphasis on certain facts, at the sacrifice of all his findings, to shore up his original angle. Worst of all, the magazine writer gave himself little room in which to move about during his search for truth. He had already settled upon a truth, and wearing his angle blinders, he obsessively sought it at the sacrifice of the more important facts. This partnership in sin between editor and writer usually did not produce a story that was outright dishonest, but rather one whose accuracy was distorted by reliance on predetermined opinion, by emphasis on what was desired rather than what existed.

I was, in my magazine-writing career, as guilty as my peers and colleagues of participating in this technique of angling. I offer no excuses, only apologies, and bring up one fact to mitigate my guilt. Like the majority of my colleagues, I never stayed with an angle or used it in my writing, if I found it to be utterly false. I angled my stories only when my researches proved the angles were true. But even though they were true, my angles, like those of my colleagues, were frequently distorted by editors suffering countless pressures of their own.

This happened when I wrote an article for a leading magazine about the Basques, an unusual and mysterious race ("They are neither Spanish nor French nor anything known. No one has any firm idea where they came from. Archeologists can find no clues scratched on stones or monuments; historians can locate no written records; philologists can find out little about their ancient guttural language—a frog in the throat of Europe"). This defiant people had an active underground in Spain, working out of France, battling to gain independence from Francisco Franco's oppressive Fascism. My angle was that these Basques were Catholics, yet they had defied the Vatican when they joined left-wing groups in an effort to overthrow Franco's Catholic regime. In Paris and San Sebastián, I found proof that this angle was true. I wrote about it, and submitted what I wrote, along with my proof of the angle, to the editors who had assigned the story.

The editors accepted my angle and evidence, even liked it, but appeared to be worried about international Catholic reaction. After much soul-searching, the editors began to cut and condense the material pertaining to my angle. What remained, after the article had been published, was not a story devoted mainly to a unique people who were a part of Spain and who were 99 percent Catholic, yet fought Catholic Franco, but a story concerned largely with the oddity and strangeness of the Basques as a race. The primary point of my story, Catholics in revolt against a Catholic leader, had been reduced to a passing mention in three paragraphs.

Actually, in fairness, I must add that the periodical had displayed considerable courage in publishing even that much. Still, commercial timidity had, by omission, sorely diminished the factual completeness of the Basque story. In this case, the sin, if sin it had been, was largely that of an editorial policy. But in permitting the bowdlerization, I suppose I was a minor partner to the vitiation of what had started out as balanced reporting.

But I was to learn that sometimes our compromises come home to roost. We who have sinned in even the smallest ways are occasionally made to realize the import of our transgressions when we, in turn, are sinned against. Recently, by chance, such a turnabout happened to me. With passing years, my life had changed. As I had once written stories about other men, I found others now writing stories about me. I had created controversial novels. They were being read and discussed, in different editions and many languages, by millions of people. I was fair game for the new magazine writers and editors—and their angles.

Late in 1963, my New York agent telephoned me that a leading magazine was interested in researching and publishing a biographical article about me. Would I cooperate? I agreed to cooperate because the request to be so publicized as an important personage or a zoo animal was flattering, and moreover might be valuable in acquainting many more people with my books. However, my agreement to receive the magazine's writer, who was being flown from New York to Los Angeles, was tinged with apprehension. For the magazine in question, like so many similar ones, was noted for creating stories that were sometimes based on inner editorial prejudices and half-substantiated rumors. Yet the same magazine had featured many excellent biographies of contemporary authors, and I decided that a publication so devoted to the popular novelist could not be all bad. It was my wife, more realistic than I, who first spoke the unspeakable. "What's their angle?" she said. "They must have an angle."

The magazine's young writer spent three days with me and my friends —a marathon of questions and answers—and after the first day, I could discern no angle. It was only after the second day, after he had begun to interview my friends, that the gleaming point of his angle became visible. His angle, or the magazine's angle, was to show an example of the new writing phenomenon, product of, caterer to, the new commercial age: an unliterary pasha feasting on exotic peacock tongues, caviar, champagne, surrounded by unsheathed concubines, served by relays of uniformed attendants, occasionally consulting his indexed card file of best-seller formulas in order to dash off another book on his cash register. Yet, the visiting writer confessed to me, neither I nor my mode of living fitted his publication's preconceived notions, derived from the contents of several of my novels and the publicity about my income in their files. The young writer faced the magazine writers' classic dilemma. What to do? Drop the story? Stick to the original angle and write the lie? Strike a compromise between fact and wish?

I was in France when I received a copy of the magazine that contained the article about me. My friends regarded the article as generally favorable, even affectionate in tone. Despite this, the hard angle was obvious: A group of authors existed, of which I was one, who had found the means of making a fortune from novels by writing them after a commercial formula. While this made an eye-catching angle for the story, it was (and the magazine knew it was from what I had told them) the sheerest nonsense.

If successful novelists had a formula, they would not have failures, and I know of *no* novelist who has not had a failure at one time or another. If successful novelists had only the acquisition of money for their goal, if they were motivated by royalties instead of a need for honest self-expression, they would find it expedient to give less time, less care, less inner agony to a single work, and in that way be able to produce three novels in the period that it ordinarily takes them to suffer over one. Thus, if lucky, they would enjoy two or three times the amount of income they obtained from a single carefully created book. Yet I know of no instance where an author has been influenced by this economic theorem.

In short, the angle, based on preconceived opinion, manufactured to titillate its readers, was fanciful, with absolutely no basis in fact. As a result, when my next novel appeared, about one-third of the critics, influenced by the angle in the magazine biography of me, incorporated discussions of a so-called best-seller "formula" in their reviews. While not all of this minority of critics were gullible enough to be taken in by the angle, the fact that they had even repeated it in print did have the effect of putting off some serious readers.

Neither a largely favorable press, nor the enormous circulation that this novel of mine finally achieved in the United States and abroad, could fully undo the temporary harm committed by a popular periodical's angle. As a magazine writer, I had always been uncomfortable with the demands of my employers for an angle. As a novelist, my resentment of it has been acutely intensified.

This persistent necessity for using an angle, then, as well as the lack of respect for and censorship of a writer's words that came from both magazine publishers and story subjects, and above all, the almost constant lack of freedom to write as one wished, were reasons why I left the magazine field, and I have never regretted my decision, even for a day.

Still, it would be unfair, even dishonest, of me to say that I did not derive considerable pleasure and excitement from my two decades in the magazine field. Between 1931 and 1953, I published around five hundred articles and short stories, perhaps one piece of fiction for every nine pieces of nonfiction. I suppose I also wrote an equal number of articles and short stories that remained unpublished, although some of them represented my better Sunday writing. As a youngster, before 1940, I would write for whoever would publish me: *Horse and Jockey Maga-*

zine, *American Farm Youth Magazine, Catholic Digest, Current Psychology and Psychoanalysis, For Men Only, Ken, Modern Mechanics, Thrilling Sports, Modern Screen.* Later, my markets, while still as diverse, improved in prestige and circulation: *The Saturday Evening Post, American Mercury, Esquire, Liberty Magazine, Collier's, Coronet, The Rotarian, Saturday Review of Literature, American Legion Magazine, Cosmopolitan, Literary Cavalcade, Pageant, Reader's Digest, This Week, True.*

In quest of stories for those publications and others, I traveled widely, collected adventures, knowledge, renowned and bizarre personalities, knew hours and days of thrills and experiences that would probably have been impossible to acquire in other fields of endeavor. I remember interviewing Huey Long while he, clad in silk pajamas in a New Orleans hotel suite, told me that his forebears had been blessed with great longevity, and that he expected to live until ninety-nine (this, a year before his assassination). I remember spending two grueling days climbing 17,000-foot Mount Ixtaccihuatl, outside Mexico City. I remember accompanying an expedition into the heat of the Honduran jungles to discover a freak of nature called the Fountain of Blood, and being received by the President of El Salvador for performing this feat.

I remember, the year before Pearl Harbor, secretly interviewing an American in Nanking, China, an authority on Japan's vicious policy of drugging the population of occupied China with heroin and opium, and being interrogated by the Japanese Dangerous Thought police for my curiosity. I remember, also months before Pearl Harbor, a long meeting with Yosuke Matsuoka, the Foreign Minister of Japan who had signed the Axis Pact with Hitler, and his outburst which warned me that Japan was prepared to go to war with the United States—and the reactions of President Franklin D. Roosevelt, Secretary of the Navy Frank Knox, and United States Army G-2 (waiting for me when I returned to San Francisco).

I remember Alexander Kerensky, and our conversation in a Los Angeles hotel room, and his bitterness about his failure to thwart Lenin and Bolshevism in revolutionary Russia. I remember Leni Reifenstahl, who was amiable enough to lift her skirt to her navel to display a surgical scar, and who became angry only when I suggested that she had been Hitler's mistress. I remember an afternoon with W. C. Fields at his home, and his showing me framed caricatures of celebrities he hated, several of them pornographic, each covered with chaste little curtains, and one being of Eleanor Roosevelt, and the comedian then passing out in mid-sentence from excessive drinking.

I remember the pugilist, Kid McCoy, a few weeks before he killed

27

himself, telling me how he had put the term "the real McCoy" into the language. I remember Diego Rivera, resentful and brusque because I had interrupted his painting of a nude in his studio, later coming in the rain, sweet and cooperative, to submit to an interview in Mexico City's Ritz Hotel. I remember a hushed conference with three members of the anti-Franco underground in a shaded restaurant in a suburb of Madrid, and the Resistance lookouts on the watch for headlights of the Falangist police cars. I remember Pablo Picasso's guided tour through his attic studio at 7 Rue des Grands-Augustins in Paris, as he ("looking like a prosperous Italian shoemaker wearing a beret," my notes remind me) explained his work in progress in an undertone, his eyes brimming because of the death of the wife of a friend in Switzerland that morning. I remember a Nobel judge in Stockholm, a special room inside Buckingham Palace in London, a croupier in the basement of the Casino in Monte Carlo, a monsignor in the editorial offices of *L'Osservatore Romano* in the Vatican, a legendary madam in a Montmartre bistro in Paris.

All of this is but a small portion of what I remember as the best of my two decades of magazine writing. And many of the other persons, and places, and institutions that I have not mentioned, but were a part of my magazine years, I have included in full detail in the pages of this book.

In this collection are those factual stories which I decided were the most interesting and durable of my Sunday Gentleman narratives. There are twenty of these stories in all. Of these, nine were previously published, but in abridged form. Here, they appear re-edited and in their full original length. The remaining eleven stories, which I have also re-edited, have not previously appeared in print. Of these, three were sold to magazines, but for one reason or another were never published in America.

To each of these chapters I have added an afterword or postscript which I call *What Has Happened Since,* and these vary in length from 750 words to 7,500 words. For when I began to reread these magazine articles, I became intensely curious to know what had happened to my subjects with the passage of years since I first wrote about them a decade or two ago. What had happened to the two old ladies who, in their youth, had managed the most spectacular house of ill fame in American history? What had happened to the young man who had undergone a prefrontal lobotomy? What had happened to the great sleuth who lived in Lyons? What had happened to the Nobel judge who worshiped Hitler? What had happened to the head of the geisha union? What had happened to the greatest art forger in modern times? to my favorite train, the Orient Express? to my favorite advertising column in *The*

Times of London? And so from 1963 to 1965, I traced and tracked down the subjects of my articles, to find out how they had fared from the time I had originally written about them until today. This proved to be a fascinating detective job in itself. My findings, described in twenty postscripts, add up to approximately 40,000 words written to complete this book.

For the most, these stories are a miscellany of my personal adventures with, and topical soundings of, unusual people and places that aroused my curiosity in recent years. Since subjective writing is little desired in the articles that popular magazines publish, many of the short pieces in this book are factual and objective in style. These stories are interviews, reports, impressions, made at home and abroad, on subjects that intrigued me at the time and interest me still. Why did I select these subjects at the time I did? I do not know, exactly. Perhaps my choices were always based on instinct. Or perhaps I never quite forgot what the editor of a great weekly magazine once told me. I had asked him, in the office of my literary agent in New York, to tell me what measuring stick might be used to determine whether a subject might qualify for his august periodical. He replied: "We are interested in anything that is the biggest, the best, or the first." I inquired, "Or the most unusual?" To which he replied, "Yes, or the most unusual."

While I did apply these criteria to most of my workaday articles, I did not apply them strictly to the Sunday ones in this book, unless I did so unconsciously. I wrote these stories because the subjects fascinated me and because it was fun to write about them, and now it is my hope that they will give the reader equal pleasure.

Here, then, two decades of Sundays, when one uncertain man walked "accoutred in the fashion of the times, with a flowing wig, lace ruffles, and a sword by his side," from daybreak to dusk, so briefly his own man, so briefly speaking of what he pleased and what pleased him.

» II «

The
Sunday Gentleman
at Home

» 2 «

TWO NICE OLD LADIES

IN LATE February of 1902, when Prince Henry of Prussia arrived in
New York City to accept the yacht built for his brother, Kaiser Wilhelm II, then ruler of Germany, he was asked by members of the press
what sight in America he would most like to visit. Bored reporters waited
for the expected official reply: the White House, Niagara Falls, or the
Grand Canyon. Instead, Prince Henry answered, "The sight in America
I would most like to visit? I would like to visit the Everleigh Club in
Chicago."

The members of the press were stunned with disbelief, and then alive
with delight. And thereafter, they took the prince to their bosoms. For
as they knew, and the more sophisticated male population of the United
States (and apparently Europe) knew, the Everleigh Club was neither
an attraction ordinarily discussed openly nor was it a men's club in the
ordinary sense. It was, as one periodical kindly pointed out, a club that
"no one ever joined . . . or resigned from" but it was "a Chicago
'mustn't': a house of ill—but very great—fame."

After presenting the United States government with a statue of Frederick the Great, Prince Henry of Prussia received his gift from the
United States government in return. He was escorted to Chicago, and
there, after depositing a wreath on the Lincoln monument, taking a
guided tour of the Loop, and suffering a reception at the Germania
Club, he was granted his one wish. At midnight, March 3, 1902, Prince
Henry of Prussia was the guest of honor at a great party—the local newspapers called it an "orgy"—given by two Southern sisters, who were the
madams of the Everleigh Club, and their retinue of thirty beautiful and
uninhibited hostesses.

It was a long and raucous night. Ten dancing girls, attired in fawn skins, wildly striking cymbals, amused the Prince while he solemnly discussed Schiller with Aida and Minna Everleigh, the proprietors of the internationally renowned resort. Later in the proceedings, during a moment of high hilarity, the Prince toasted the Kaiser (and the Everleighs) by drinking champagne from a girl's silver slipper, thereby popularizing a custom that would know its full flowering in the 1920's. For the Prince, the occasion had been extraordinary and memorable. For the Everleigh sisters, the royal visit had been enjoyable—and routine.

During the nearly dozen years in which it flourished, the Everleigh Club rarely went a week without the appearance of some celebrity, either American or international. In the two years before Prince Henry's visit, and for almost a decade after, famous foreigners from every nation, after making their official rounds of the stockyards, lakefront, and municipal monuments, climaxed their sightseeing with an evening in the Everleigh Club.

The club's popularity was well deserved, because few bordellos had ever existed, or existed then, that could compete with its opulence and lavish hospitality. In the time of its greatness, the Everleigh Club enjoyed constant comparison with other competing *maisons de joie* in America and abroad, but almost always to its own advantage. Typical among domestic competitors was The Castle in St. Louis, a three-story brick house managed by the plump and affable Negress, Babe Connors, whose teeth were inlaid with diamonds. In this sporting house, Paderewski once accompanied the entertainers' bawdy songs on the piano, and in its rooms a Republican national platform was once written, and from within its walls "Ta-Ra-Ra-Boom-Der-É" swept on to plebeian acceptance. Here, the young girls, octoroons, "girls in long skirts, but without underclothing, would dance on a huge mirror." Typical among the Everleighs' foreign competitors was the House of All Nations in Budapest, a $100,000 house of ill fame on Andrassy Street, where a reception parlor featured "portraits of the women, nude, from which you made your choice. You then touched an electric bell-push under the photograph and it was covered, so that the next visitor would know the lady was engaged."

Yet, despite such unique and imaginative competition, the Everleigh Club of Chicago, from its rise in 1900 to its fall in 1910, was the most renowned and unusual brothel in the world, overshadowing all similarly exotic establishments before—and since—from Paris to Shanghai.

The founders of the club—"the most famous madams in American history," Polly Adler called them—were two daughters of a successful Kentucky attorney: Aida (although the press often referred to her as

Ada) Everleigh, born in February, 1876, and Minna Everleigh, born in July, 1878. As adolescents, the sisters were enrolled in a Southern finishing school, where both excelled in elocution and playacting.

Because of their respect and affection for each other, the sisters were almost as close as Siamese twins. "Sibling rivalry" was not yet a part of the common language. And so when Minna, at the age of nineteen, fell in love with a Southern gentleman and was married to him in an expensive ceremony, it was not surprising that Aida, aged twenty-one, married the Southern gentleman's brother shortly afterward. Minna's marriage was of brief duration. "Her husband was a brute—suspicious and jealous," observed a friend. A few weeks after the honeymoon, Minna left her husband and her old Kentucky home and fled to Washington, D.C. It was only natural that within a week, for the same reasons, Aida left her husband to join her sister.

Since the Everleigh sisters had inclinations toward theatrical careers, and were attractive, they auditioned for several stock companies going on the road, and were accepted by one such company. At the time, the younger of the sisters, Minna, was the more aggressive of the pair. She was a blue-eyed redhead, slender, lively, and ambitious, with a keen business mind and a love of reading. Aida was a quiet and trim blonde, and she worshiped her younger sister.

For several months the sisters were on the road as actresses, touring the country from New York to Texas. Disenchanted by the exhausting and uncomfortable life of the road-show player, discouraged by the lack of chances for advancement, they began to look about for a more stable and ladylike means of existence. Then a series of events occurred that would soon cast them in new roles.

En route to appearances at the Trans-Mississippi International Exposition in Omaha, they learned that their father had died and had left them an inheritance of $35,000. While wondering if they could become independent by investing this money in some lucrative field, they overheard an actress friend one day drop a remark that gave them the idea for a business. The actress had complained that her parents considered the stage no better than "a den of iniquity" and the career of actress no better than that of prostitute or madam. Although the Everleigh sisters joked about it at first, they soon began to discuss more seriously the possibility of investing their inheritance in a career which, if it was considered no more respectable than acting, nevertheless might be far more profitable.

However, before investigating this new business, they decided to meet more people and learn what else was possible. In Omaha, they quit their theatrical troupe and determined to become a part of the city's commu-

nity life. Using family connections, they got themselves invited to dinners and soirées in some of Omaha's better homes. But their beauty and
gaiety were not appreciated by their married hostesses. Soon they found
themselves ostracized by the upper-class wives, and Minna began to
speak darkly of avenging herself on these wives by establishing a home
that their traducers' husbands would be only too glad to visit.

But it was not alone a desire to even the score with a handful of
snobbish wives that turned the Everleigh girls to prostitution. According
to one who was to become their closest friend and confidant, Charles
Washburn, a police reporter on the Chicago *Tribune* in that period,
what turned the Everleighs to their real career was their deep bitterness
toward males in general. "It is doubtful if Minna and Ada Everleigh ever
forgave the brutal treatment they had received from their husbands,"
wrote Washburn in an early biography of the sisters; "theirs was a stored-
up bitterness toward all males from which they could not escape. Even
though they refused to admit it, their every action indicated a score to be
settled. The way they studied men, their insight into the whims of men
and their determination to make men pawns in their parlor were the
antics of the spider and the fly."

In Omaha, Minna Everleigh made a hasty but shrewd study of the
attractions available to male customers attending the mammoth two-
million-dollar Trans-Mississippi Exposition, and she found these attractions limited indeed. She determined to improve upon the amusements
available. She bargained for, and purchased, a brothel that was doing
poorly but was situated near the exposition grounds. With what remained
of their inheritance, she enhanced the run-down house of prostitution by
adding new interior decorations, the best of foods and wines, and the
most attractive and talented of females, many of the latter recruited from
among road-show actresses she had met. Then she and Aida threw open
their doors.

The big spenders, attending the exposition in droves, quickly found
their way to the Everleigh boudoirs. By the time that the exposition
ended, Minna and Aida had increased their capital worth from $35,000
to $75,000, a considerable sum for two young girls at any time, but a
fortune at the turn of the century.

With the closing of the exposition, the Everleighs realized that they
had lost their more affluent clientele. Big money men, among the natives
of Omaha, were too few. The Everleighs looked elsewhere for a site
worthy of their knowledge and gifts. Studying their atlases and their
private notes, they could find no community not already serviced by a
house offering what they had to offer. At last, they returned to Washington, D.C., and there they sought the advice of Cleo Maitland, the most
prosperous madam in the capital city. Without hesitation, Madam Mait-

land advised the young Everleighs to do their prospecting in Chicago. The metropolis—Herbert Asbury's "gem of the prairie"—had a safe and sophisticated red-light district, of considerable dimensions, in a hedonistic political district, the First Ward, known as the Levee. For courageous investors, the growth possibilities were limitless. And above all, added Madam Maitland, there just happened to be a house she had heard of that could be had for a song.

The house available in Chicago was really two adjoining three-story stone mansions, with fifty rooms, and a broad flight of steps from the street. It was located at 2131 South Dearborn Street. It had been built in 1890 at a cost of $125,000 by one Lizzie Allen, madam, as a supplementary sideshow for visitors in search of culture at the Chicago World's Columbian Exposition of 1893. After the fair, and shortly before her death, Lizzie Allen, madam, had leased the house and sold its furnishings and inmates to Effie Hankins, madam. Now, Effie Hankins, full of years and wealth, was ready for retirement. She was also ready to deal with the Everleighs. She offered the huge seraglio at her bottom price— $55,000 for the furnishings, the girls on the premises, the good will, and a long-term lease at a rental of $500 a month.

On February 1, 1900, the Everleigh Club of Chicago had its grand opening—and on that day, for connoisseurs of joy and students of earthy Americana, its legend began. It was also the debut of Minna and Aida under the name of Everleigh. Their family name had been commonplace. Now, on the eve of history, they sought something uplifting and appropriate. One of their beloved grandmothers had always ended her letters to them, "Everly yours." So Everly it was, spelled Everleigh.

For its grand opening, the house had undergone a drastic transformation. Effie Hankins' white servants had been replaced by colored help, and Madam Hankins' hostesses (uncouth and used wenches in abbreviated costumes) had been replaced by Aida's hostesses ("comely and skilled . . . no amateurs . . . the choicest talent in the country" garbed in costly evening gowns). The kitchen was of the best, the wines were imported, the dishes and hospitality Southern, and the furnishings and decorations were unmatched by any similar brothel on the face of the earth.

To help make the opening night a festive one, a Washington senator sent flowers. The Midwest's leading wine companies and packers supplied gifts of their best food and drink. The first customers were millionaire Texas cattlemen whose party spent $300 in a few hours. Despite freezing weather, the Everleigh sisters grossed $1,000 on that historic initial evening. For fledgling madams, aged twenty-two and twenty-four, it was an auspicious beginning.

During the nearly dozen years of its heyday, following its opening night, the Everleigh Club achieved a worldwide reputation largely because of the brilliance and good taste of its proprietors, the extraordinary abilities of its prostitutes, the distinction of its service, and the splendor of its interior.

To each male seeker of escape through fleshly indulgence, this was no mean house of ill fame. Once inside its doors, the customer was quickly divested of any reservations he might have held of crass commercialism. This was at once a men's club and a great lady's home that offered culture, beauty, domestic warmth, gracious living—and expert sex encased in the thinnest chrysalis of exotic romance.

From the moment of a customer's entry into the Everleigh Club, every effort was made to seduce his senses. The fifty rooms, in buildings rising three stories high, were decorated by Minna Everleigh to represent a Midwestern Mohammedan paradise, captivating a client's eyes, ears, palate, and emotions. The rooms, decorations, niceties were not expected to satiate every facet of every man's taste. There was simply *something* available for every man, no matter what his peculiarities or needs.

On the main floor, there were twelve spacious soundproof reception parlors, and these were the Gold Room, the Silver Room, the Copper Room, the Moorish Room, the Green Room, the Rose Room, the Red Room, the Blue Room, the Egyptian Room, the Chinese Room, the Japanese Room, the Oriental Room. The Gold Room featured gilt furniture, gold-trimmed fishbowls, eighteen-karat cuspidors that had cost $650 each, golden hangings, and a $15,000 gold piano. The Copper Room was paneled in copper and brass; the Moorish Room had thick and priceless Oriental carpets and incense burners; the Blue Room had blue divans with leather pillows on which were sewn prints of Gibson Girls, and there were college pennants hung on the walls.

Then, still on the first floor, there was an art gallery with a reproduction of Bernini's *Apollo and Daphne*, a library with shelves holding one thousand books (mainly classics of biography, history, poetry, and fiction, all to Minna's taste), a vast dining room with silver dinner service, and a great Turkish ballroom with a towering water-spouting fountain centered on a parquetry floor whose woods formed mosaic patterns.

To reach the boudoirs of love upstairs, guests were led through potted palms and Grecian statuary, and up one of the two thickly carpeted mahogany staircases. In any one of the thirty boudoirs, the customer and the beautiful girl of his choice could enjoy quiet privacy and incredible luxury. The basic boudoir was furnished with a marble-inlaid brass bed, a mirrored ceiling, a shower or a gold bathtub, freshly cut roses in vases, imported oil paintings, concealed push buttons that rang bells for champagne. Yet each bedroom had its individuality. One had an automatic perfume spray over the bed. Another had a silver-white spotlight directed upon the divan. A third had a genuine Turkish mattress on the floor, covered by a white cashmere blanket. And on special occasions, Minna Everleigh, who was partial to butterfly pins on her gowns, loosed live butterflies to flutter disconcertingly about the boudoirs and parlors below.

After his first inspection of the opulent palace, Jack Lait, who was to become editor of the New York *Mirror*, exclaimed passionately (if sacrilegiously) to reporter friends, "Minna and Aida Everleigh are to pleasure what Christ was to Christianity!"

A visitor at the Everleigh Club was never rushed from the entrance to a bedroom on the second floor. He was given the illusion—at least until he received his bill—of being the guest of honor at a dinner in a wealthy home. Edgar Lee Masters, author of *Spoon River Anthology*, recalled in 1944, six years before his death, what it had been like to call upon the Everleighs. Masters, who was in his early thirties when the club was at its peak, described a visit to the brothel. He noted that, of the two sisters, Minna was "somehow the larger personality, the more impressive figure." Often, he said, "she came to the door when the bell rang. Her walk was a sort of caterpillar bend and hump, pause and catch up. She was remarkably thin. Her hair was dark and frizzled, her face thin and refined. 'How is my boy?' was her cordial salutation."

Minna's boy was soon fine. He had been given to understand that he was expected to spend no less than fifty dollars during the evening. In the Turkish ballroom, near the splashing fountain, or in one of the colorful parlors, he would order a bottle of French wine for twelve dollars (later, if he wished another bottle sent to a boudoir upstairs, the cost would rise to fifteen dollars). After exchanging pleasantries with friends he recognized, he would listen to one of the three four-piece orchestras playing, most often, "Stay in Your Own Back Yard" or the miserable tune composed by the alderman of the First Ward and one of the two dominant political figures of the Levee, John Coughlin (endearingly known as "Bathhouse John"). This song was "Dear Midnight of Love." The customer was waited upon, hand and foot, by colored valets and maids, and flirtatiously but decorously engaged by one of the club's thirty attractive girls.

If he came to the club for dinner, as well as for more desired pleasures, the guest was next escorted into the dining hall. There, on damask linen, with music still echoing in his ears, he would partake of pheasant or roast turkey or guinea fowl, served with more wine. Dinner, without wine or feminine companionship, was fifty dollars minimum. If he had brought along business associates and engaged hostesses for them, his dinner party might cost him fifteen hundred dollars.

Finally, at a much later hour, all appetites sated save one, the male guest would make his choice from those girls who were still available. The price for the enjoyment of the girl and her boudoir was fifty dollars, to which he was expected to add a generous tip. The girl gave half of the fee to the madams, and retained the other half. There was rarely, if ever, according to the documents available, any complaint from the paying customers.

Evidently, satisfaction was constant because the thirty Everleigh girls were satisfying in every way. In his 1936 biography of the sisters, *Come into My Parlor*, the Everleighs' old friend, Charles Washburn, quoted Aida on her method of recruiting the club's girls.

"I talk with each applicant myself," said Aida. "She must have worked somewhere else before coming here. We do not like amateurs. Inexperienced girls and young widows are too prone to accept offers of marriage and leave. We always have a waiting list.

"To get in a girl must have a pretty face and figure, must be in perfect health, must look well in evening clothes. If she is addicted to drugs, or to drink, we do not want her. There is no problem in keeping the club filled."

Actually, the Everleighs left little to chance. To possess beauty, good health, experience at lovemaking, was not enough to become an Everleigh prostitute. Weekly, the Everleigh sisters gave their girls instructions in makeup, dress, Southern manners, and required that they read books drawn from the club's library.

According to Charles Washburn, it was Minna who delivered the standard good-conduct lecture to new female arrivals.

"Be polite, patient and forget what you are here for," Minna would explain. "Gentlemen are only gentlemen when properly introduced. We shall see that each girl is properly presented to each guest. No lining up for selection as in other houses. . . . Remember that the Everleigh Club has no time for the rough element, the clerk on a holiday or a man without a check-book.

"It's going to be difficult, at first, I know. It means, briefly, that your language will have to be lady-like and that you will forgo the entreaties you have used in the past. You have the whole night before you and one $50 client is more desirable than five $10 ones. Less wear and tear. You will thank me for this advice in later years. Your youth and beauty are all you have. Preserve it. Stay respectable by all means. . . . We'll supply the clients; you amuse them in a way they've never been amused before. Give, but give interestingly and with mystery. I want you girls to be proud that you are in the Everleigh Club."

The girls felt like ladies, and they were proud—and so were the customers who had an opportunity to be with them. As a result, their customers came from the highest echelon of every profession and business. Understandably, some of the most celebrated customers—"a certain famous actor, a certain famous dramatic critic and a certain famous novelist," as well as a renowned aviator of the period—did not wish their names made public, and they never were. But many others were as delighted to speak of their adventures in the Everleigh Club as they were to reminisce over their best days at Harvard or Yale.

Edgar Lee Masters remembered one highly regarded Chicago attorney who spent his annual two-week vacation in the club. "Colonel MacDuff, a mighty Chicago lawyer, used to stay for days in the Club. Grown weary, to the point of madness, of trying cases, he would go to see Minna and her girls. Handing Minna $500 or so, he would retire where he could drink wine and eat fried chicken, and discuss the perplexities of life with Maxine or Gertrude or Virginia."

There were numerous other front-page figures who occasionally visited or were habitués of the Everleigh Club. Among these were celebrities of the literary world such as Ring Lardner, George Ade, and Percy Hammond; celebrities of the sporting world such as James J. Corbett and Stanley Ketchel; celebrities of the theater such as John Barrymore; celebrities of the gambling world such as "Bet a Million" Gates; celebrities of the circus such as The Great Fearlesso.

The club was a haunt for millionaires. In 1905, the thirty-seven-year-old Marshall Field, Jr., was found alone in his Prairie Avenue mansion, dead from a shot in the abdomen. Headlines, based on rumors, shouted that he had been murdered in the Everleigh Club and then removed to his own quarters, although Minna vehemently denied that he had ever visited her house and police officials stated that the fatal shot was self-inflicted and accidental.

The club's clientele ranged from gangsters to government officials. Pat Crowe, a bank robber who also kidnaped young Cudahy, was often a guest. Once, the members of an august Congressional committee arrived in Chicago from Washington, D.C., bent on investigating something or other of national interest, and after their daytime researches, the congressmen did all of their nighttime homework inside the club.

For the Everleigh sisters, it was a profitable and gay life, but it was not an easy one. Persistently, they were troubled by rival bordello owners, criminals, and reformers. In 1910, Nathaniel Moore, son of the Rock Island Railway magnate, was killed in another brothel through the use of knockout drops, and then he was robbed, and an effort was made to plant his corpse in the Everleigh furnace. But the Everleighs, forewarned of the plot by some admirers, prevented the act in the nick of time.

Once, the proprietors were held up by a dope addict who had entered the club, and only quick thinking by Aida saved their jewels. On another occasion, a guest in flannel underwear tumbled down the stairs to shout that the house was on fire. When the Chicago *Tribune* learned of this blaze, the night editor desperately tried to locate reporters to cover the story. The editor discovered that his three top reporters were already occupied in the club at that very moment.

But reformers created the greatest problem for the sisters. Some were harmless. Once, Lucy Page Gaston, head of The Anti-Cigarette League, burst into the club and cried out to Minna, "You alone can stop your girls from going straight to the devil!" Cooperatively, Minna inquired, "How, Miss Gaston?" And Miss Gaston shouted, "Make them stop smoking cigarettes!"

Other reformers were more dangerous. Gipsy Smith, the London evangelist, invaded Chicago, gathering crowds, and entreating them with fervor, "A man who visits the red-light district has no right to associate with decent people in daylight!" To acquaint Chicago's young men with the evil that was rampant in their city, Smith led a march of twenty thousand persons into the Levee for a glimpse of hell. After the march ended, at least a fourth of the males, who had never been in the Levee before, stayed behind, and the greatest number made their debuts in sin at the Everleigh Club that same evening. "We are glad for the business," Minna told the press, "but I am sorry to see so many nice young men coming down here for the first time."

In order to survive the attacks of their enemies, the Everleigh sisters openly bought police and political protection. Minna once told the police that in twelve years, the houses of prostitution in the First Ward had paid $15 million in graft. Of this sum, the Everleigh sisters had paid $120,000, plus special assessments needed to buy off state legislators in Springfield and encourage them to vote against bills unfavorable to brothels. Most of this money had gone to two colorful aldermen on the City Council, John Coughlin and Michael "Hinky Dink" Kenna, who were the political powers of the First Ward. The aldermen, in turn, had bribed the city police force and the legislators.

Despite this continuing drain on their resources, the Everleigh sisters made an annual profit (in a day when the income tax was negligible) of $120,000. While they dwelt amidst luxury, it was a business-required luxury arranged primarily for their guests. As for themselves, they were careful with their money, and invested it wisely. Before their middle years, if their business had continued as usual, they could have expected to be millionaires several times over.

But business did not continue as usual. There was a new mood in the land, a mood of growing community pride, and this infected the citizens of Chicago deeply. Churches of all denominations united to exert pressure, and the Chicago City Council was forced into establishing a Vice Commission and into allocating the sum of $5,000 to pay the investigators on this commission. In 1910, the commission issued its 399-page report. In Chicago, alone, said the report, there were 1,020 brothels occupied by 4,000 prostitutes, and managed by 1,880 madams, and among the foremost of the madams were Minna and Aida Everleigh. The commission unequivocally damned this traffic in flesh, stating, "Is it any wonder that a tempted girl, a girl who receives only six dollars a week working with her hands, sells her body for twenty-five dollars per week when she learns there is a demand for it and men are willing to pay the price?"

Little was done about this report until a new election placed in office as mayor the reform-minded Carter Harrison. At first he moved slowly, issuing a general ukase that ordered "disreputable women" moved from their places of activity and "disorderly flats" closed. He was still reluctant to shut down one of the city's most favored attractions. But then, one day, Mayor Harrison was shown an illustrated brochure that the Everleighs had published. With disbelief, he read:

"While not an extremely imposing edifice without, it is a most sumptuous place within. 2131 Dearborn Street, Chicago, has long been famed for its luxurious furnishings, famous paintings, statuary, and its elaborate and artistic decorations. . . . Steam heat throughout, with electric fans in summer: one never feels the winter's chill or summer's heat in this luxurious resort. Fortunate indeed, with all the comforts of life surrounding them, are the members of the Everleigh Club."

The blatancy of this advertising, a blot on his fair city and his regime, infuriated and finally prodded Mayor Harrison into action. He summoned his police chief and aldermen, and they came on the run. He demanded that the Everleigh Club be closed at once. He would listen to no reason, no entreaties. The Everleigh Club must vanish from the Chicago landscape and the sisters must be banished forever.

There could be no reprieve from this executive order. On October 24, 1910, Minna and Aida were informed that the end had come. Their protectors could no longer protect them . . . although possibly, just possibly, a $20,000 assessment, wisely distributed, might stay the closing order, at least temporarily. Minna would not have it. If it was over, she was ready to quit. She and Aida took the bad news philosophically. Their thirty girls dissolved in tears. And so the front door was locked to "members," the shutters fastened, the furniture draped, the servants dismissed, and the girls packed off to lesser houses in more hospitable communities.

Minna and Aida decided to go to Europe, mainly to visit Rome, and relax and absorb culture, and see if the bluenoses of Chicago would meanwhile change their minds. After six months they returned, and hearing that they would have protection once more, they opened a new Everleigh Club on Chicago's West Side. This was in August of 1912. But when, to their normal protection fee, another sum of $40,000 was added, and when the city's reform government appeared more intractable than ever, the Everleighs agreed that a comeback was impossible. They auctioned off their luxurious furnishings—all except Aida's beloved piano, and Minna's own beloved marble-inlaid brass bed, leather-bound books, favorite paintings, and several other sentimental ornaments—and they left Chicago forever.

They did not go empty-handed. In addition to furniture and artifacts worth $150,000, they departed from the Midwest with $1,000,000 cash, $200,000 in jewelry, and $25,000 worth of unpaid bills run up by trusted clients. They also took with them happy memories, no residue of bitterness, and an intimate knowledge of the opposite sex. Minna had learned, for one thing, that most men preferred to gamble with dice or cards rather than to make love to a woman. "Real men, we found," said Minna, "would rather gamble any day than gamble with women." This, she felt, was because dice were less unpredictable and less risky than women. Both sisters believed that they owed their success to married men who attended their club, and that they would have earned another million "if it weren't for the cheating married women" who competed with the club's girls. Had the madams ever indulged themselves in love affairs with their clients? Minna remained silent on this subject. Aida was always ready to speak of one wealthy young lover, who had wished to take her to New York as his wife. Why had she refused to legalize their affair? "My sweetheart took a terrible dislike to our gold piano," said Aida. "He said it was unbecoming. I couldn't forgive him for that."

In 1913, when they embarked upon retirement, Minna Everleigh was thirty-seven years old, and Aida Everleigh was thirty-nine. They wanted only peace and anonymity. At first they could find neither. The recent past trailed after them, wherever they fled. When a close friend and a former client—Big Jim Colosimo, an amiable gangster—was murdered in his Italian restaurant in 1920, supposedly by a former aide, Johnny Torrio, or by the young Al Capone, the Everleighs were found and questioned. When a skeleton was dug up behind their old property in 1923, the Everleighs were again interrogated by the police. When a prostitute who had worked for them for six years was found murdered in New Orleans, her hands cut off and her jewels stolen, the Everleighs were once more visited by the police. When Mrs. W. E. D. Stokes tried to divorce her millionaire husband, and he countercharged that she had once been an Everleigh girl, the sisters were hounded by the sensation-seeking press.

Peace, they realized at last, could be gained only through complete anonymity. And so, having given up the Everleigh Club, they now gave up its name and their name forever. Burying their past, their old identities, and calling themselves by yet another name, they became two retired, independently wealthy ladies, dwelling off Central Park in New York City.

The Everleighs disappeared from public notice so entirely that after several decades it was assumed that they were dead. And except for alumni of the old club, they were forgotten. But from time to time, there appeared in print a hint that they might still be alive. In 1936, Charles Washburn stated in his book, *Come into My Parlor*, that the sisters were very much alive and that he had visited them. He had seen the remaining marble-inlaid brass bed, the gold piano, the books and oil paintings, and the statue of Bernini's *Apollo and Daphne*. The sisters traveled extensively, he wrote, they attended the Broadway theater, and they read books and newspaper columnists. They had lost a good part of their invested fortune in the stock-market crash of 1929, but they still retained most of their jewelry. They rarely had visitors. They had purchased a radio, but except for that, they usually avoided outside companionship—and there were no gentleman callers. "They own a home in New York, free and clear," Washburn reported. "All they ask for the remainder of their lives is a roof and one quart of champagne a week."

Eight years later, there was a suggestion that they might even then still be alive. In a 1944 issue of *Town and Country* magazine, Edgar Lee Masters stated: "[Minna and Aida] knew too that the people who were throwing stones at them might well have been stoned for sins of their own. Still they kept their peace. They disappeared with smiles upon their faces, and, when last heard of, were living lives of unobtrusive gentility in New York City."

And so it was in 1944 that I made up my mind to learn whether the Everleigh sisters were really alive, and if they actually were, to learn exactly what names they had assumed and precisely where they were residing. Perhaps I was inspired by the adventure of a Bostonian, Captain Edward Silsbee, the ardent Shelleyite, who had learned, fifty-seven years after Shelley's death and fifty-five years after Byron's death, that Shelley's friend and Byron's mistress, Claire Clairmont, was still living at the grand old age of eighty-two in Florence. Silsbee had determined to meet her. And he had met her, and this, in turn, inspired Henry James to write his novelette, *The Aspern Papers*. In this, the hero-publisher learns the mistress of a great romantic poet, long dead, is still alive in Venice, and resolves to meet her. As Henry James's hero reflected, "The strange thing had been for me to discover . . . that she was still alive: it was as if I had been told Mrs. Siddons was, or Queen Caroline, or the famous Lady Hamilton, for it seemed to me she belonged to a generation as extinct. 'Why she must be tremendously old—at least a hundred,' I had said."

Thus, I, too, was inspired, and determined, to meet Minna and Aida Everleigh, almost a half century after they had reigned as two of history's foremost caterers to the pleasure of the human male.

>«

In April of 1944, while I was a sergeant in the United States Army Signal Corps, I was ordered to Washington, D.C., and New York City. Before that special assignment, I had been excited by the idea of doing a three-act play loosely based on the lives of the Everleigh sisters and their club. Nights, when I had time, I had jotted endless notes on the construction of this play. The notes were fragmentary, but among them were:

"Setting of Act I is the Golden Room of the Everleigh Club in 1905. . . . Problems and conflicts for sisters: Attractive gentleman wants to marry Aida Everleigh and take her away from it all. . . . Fictional judge, based on real Chicago attorney who took his annual vacation in club, has vacation interrupted when given information that he has been picked to head Vice Committee investigating club. . . . Minna trying to help a married client who is having troubles with his wife. . . . New and dangerous madam down the block trying to get club raided and steal Everleighs' best girls. . . . Enemies in Levee, or single reformer outside, pressing to pin responsibility for a murder on Everleighs. . . . Then last straw: Everleighs' respectable and chaste niece arriving, accompanied by her older brother, from Kentucky, to stay with her respectable aunts, the Everleighs, while she meets family of rich young man who wants to marry her (his father is a meat-packing millionaire). . . . Sisters desperate to keep little niece from knowing what they do and desperate to keep truth about their house a secret from her. Sisters must figure out how to disguise brothel and girls, maybe set up a Potemkin façade. . . . Act I curtain is, of course, arrival of niece in midst of tumultuous and embarrassing situation in club. . . . Act II curtain is when niece's potential father-in-law, the meat-packer, an occasional visitor to house, discovers the niece there among the girls. . . . Act III Minna must save impending marriage of niece as well as solve a municipal political crisis, thereby saving the club from being closed."

Since I wanted to use the Everleighs as characters, their club as the setting for the play, and some episodes from their lives, it was imperative that I discover if they were alive. If they were, I would have to obtain their permission to do this play. More important, as I have indicated, play or no play, I simply had to meet them to satisfy my own curiosity.

Now, knowing that I would be in the East on an army assignment shortly, I bestirred myself to locate someone who had known the Everleighs personally in the good old days, and who could tell me if they were still around, and if so, how they could be reached. I wrote to Charles Washburn and Edgar Lee Masters, and received no response from either. Then I remembered that Jack Lait, editor of the New York *Mirror*, had known them, and perhaps still knew them. But it would not do, I suspected, to confront Jack Lait as a stranger. If he knew the Everleighs' secret, he would be loath to share it with someone whom he did not know. And so I sought for a go-between, a friend of mine who might also be a friend of Lait's, and I found this necessary link in the person of a well-known public relations man, the late Mack Millar.

A week later, in New York, I telephoned Lait at the *Mirror* and invoked the name of our mutual friend. I told him that I'd like to see him for a few minutes about a personal matter. He invited me to come right up. I found Lait at his desk, pencil and copy in hand, looking busy and suspicious.

The moment that I mentioned why I had called upon him, he smiled and became more affable. But he was careful, also. I had to explain what I wanted of the Everleigh sisters, and what I would do with it. Lait listened, but remained noncommittal.

"Tell me one thing," I asked. "Are both of them still alive?"

"Sure they are alive. Their neighbors think they're two eccentric and retired clubwomen, with independent means. No one knows about their past. To everyone around—they're just two nice old ladies."

"I wish you'd tell me how I could get hold of them."

Lait considered me a moment longer, and then he suddenly sat up in his swivel chair. "Okay, Sergeant. You've got an honest face, sort of. Just be secretive and discreet about the whole thing, remember."

"I promise."

"Okay. Their names are Minna and Aida Lester—got that?—Lester. They own a brownstone at 20 West 71st Street, right here in New York. You want their telephone number, too? Okay. It's Endicott 2-9970. But look, I wouldn't just call them up cold. I don't think you'd get anywhere. Here's what I'd suggest. Write them a letter. You can use my name. Write them, introduce yourself, and tell them what you have in mind. And then, sit back and hope. There you have it. Now you're on your own."

I thanked Jack Lait profusely, and left. The following day, before I could either write or telephone the Everleighs, the Army Signal Corps recalled me to my station in Los Angeles.

During my first free evening in Los Angeles, I sat down and composed a long and friendly letter to Miss Minna Everleigh and Miss Aida Everleigh, and I addressed the envelope to "Miss Minna Lester, Miss Aida Lester, 20 West 71st Street, New York City 23, New York."

Less than a week later, I had my answer. It came, as all the Everleigh letters I subsequently received would come, packed bulkily into a long manila envelope, secured by silver sealing wax. The letter that was contained within was written in blue ink, in a wild and almost indecipherable scrawl, each letter of each word an inch high. This first Everleigh letter, like the correspondence to follow, was unrestrained and extravagant in its phrasing, and highly original in its punctuation. Minna, the letter writer of the pair, showed contempt for periods, commas, and semicolons, but was much devoted to dots, dashes, and exclamation points. I reproduce her first letter exactly as it was written. What follows actually covered twenty good-sized pages when written in Minna Everleigh's generous hand:

Sunday—May 7—1944—New York—
Sgt Irving Wallace

Dear Sir
    Your letter addressed to my sister Aida Lester and to me—lies on my desk . . . There is truth in the axiom that asserts "A Letter Mirrors the Soul of the Writer" . . . Your letter portrays culture, courtesy, intellect, literary and dramatic genius . . . Therefore this candid heart-prompted response . . .
Dear Sgt Wallace—
    Aida and Minna Lester's past is not linked with the Everleigh Club on South Dearborn Street—Chicago—Illinois . . . Aida Lester and I lived in Chicago during the first decade of this Twentieth Century—but in a fashion far remote from the famous sisters' exotic lives . . . Your time is precious— "brevity is the soul of wit"—suffice it to say that many times false rumors linked our puritan lives with the sensational career of the sisters referred to in your letter!!
    Aida and I travelled in Europe prior to World War I—finally returning to our own dear Land—made our home since 1915 in New York at our present residence 20 West 71st Street New York . . . Meantime rumors linked our names with the sisters of the Dearborn Street resort!!!
    Finally we took action—Aida Lester and I—we located the sisters of Dearborn Street—Chicago!!! They proved their innocence of linking their names with ours—I will not take time explaining—plotters of the South Side Levee —their enemies—had sought to cause them trouble—prompted by political

Levee gangster feuds!!! These sisters reside in New York City!!! still fearing their foes they live isolated lives— Since the panic of 1929 they have sustained severe losses from defaulted mortgage investments . . .

After receipt of your letter yesterday I visited the sisters to whom you had addressed it . . . They recall the honor of having known Mr. Jack Lait of the New York Mirror—gifted columnist—journalist—famous author . . . Sister Aida Lester and I have not had the pleasant privilege of meeting him —hope some day to have that pleasure . . . To make a long story short— dear Sgt Wallace—the sisters you addressed desire to avoid all publicity . . . (The Everleigh Sisters)— Interested in your plan to dramatize the Everleigh Club they yet ask to be forgotten!!!

I asked them if they would consider pecuniary considerations for such assistance as they might concede to you for the setting and background of their club on Dearborn Street—Chicago??—Their Answer was that they have an Album of photographs of the parlors and rooms of the Everleigh Club—They might part with those—but they must shun publicity—— Finally the Sisters agreed that they might sell their Album—for cash sum— not for financial percentage of profits after the play is produced:

Dear Sgt Wallace—I have given you a candid account of my visit to the Everleigh sisters with whom my name and my sister Aida Lester's has so often been linked . . . I enclose clippings that suggest the past should be forgotten in this swift epoch!! Forget the Everleigh Club and the haunted past portrayed in the photographs of its vanished splendor shown in the album the sisters possess!!! Did not Byron declare "The past is nothing and at last—the future can but be the past"!!

However if you still wish to have those Everleigh Club photographs—let me know ! ! ! ! Remember—the Everleigh Sisters names were Marie and Alice!!! The names Aida and Minna were borrowed from my name—and Aida Lester's when we were socialites in Chicago long ago!!!

And now—forgive this long letter—dear Irving Wallace!!! Pardon my having no writing paper that is proper size for your chic airmail envelope—so beguiling—with its special stamp!!! If you still desire that Everleigh Club Album—state so in reply dear Sgt Wallace . . . Were it mine to give it would be freely given!!!

May your heart's desire be granted!!! Let me know this message reached you!!! Truly your friend and admirer

Minna Lester

The eleven clippings that Minna enclosed consisted of an Associated Press story about a warrant officer in the South Pacific who wanted to hear the voice of his four-day-old son on the long-distance phone, and heard nothing until he instructed his wife to spank the infant; a newspaper photograph from a Mickey Rooney film; a sexy advertisement for a "Shar-Loo" slip; a newspaper photograph of Major Jimmy Stewart being decorated by a lieutenant colonel; a newspaper photograph of a radio actress; an advertisement for a newly published book on the Marines; newspaper photographs from a film called *The Hitler Gang*; a political cartoon of Adolf Hitler; three more cartoons about Himmler, Goebbels, and Hitler facing defeat; and a picture from *The New York Times* drama section showing the sheet music and the casts of five musical comedy successes created by Richard Rodgers and Oscar Hammerstein II.

I was strangely moved by this first letter from a sixty-six-year-old former madam of the world's most elegant house of rendezvous in recent times—moved by her elaborate and pathetically transparent story of having been a "socialite" who had known the real Everleighs, and knew them still. And I was touched by her lovely, banal quotations, and by her need to sell the precious album of photographs of the Everleigh Club.

I wanted to write her immediately, write her anything, but write her nicely, yet I did not—and soon I could not. I found myself traveling around the country to various army installations, researching and writing material for top-priority military films. I had neither time nor energy to devote to Minna Lester, friend of Minna Everleigh. Too, I began to have misgivings about my play project, about the possibility of securing clear-cut legal rights to use the Everleigh Club from one who was an Everleigh and yet denied it. How much of what Minna had written me, I wondered, was conscious pretense based on elementary caution and how much was the sublimation of an old lady who had come to believe in a dream identity that she had invented for herself out of Wish? Did I want to become seriously involved with such a person? I did not know. I had no time to think it out. I was on army time.

But suddenly, late in 1945, I *knew*. I was being transferred from Los Angeles to the Signal Corps post on Long Island, New York, and I would be very close to 20 West 71st Street and to the "socialites" named Aida and Minna Lester. The play that I had in mind was one thing, but the lesser one, I decided. If I could reach the real Aida and Minna Everleigh, and from them secure the rights to their story for my play, that would be fine. More interesting to me, to that persistent curiosity built into every writer, was the desire to know firsthand more about those remarkable and legendary sisters, those sweet relics of the bawdy past.

And so, shortly after my arrival in New York, on my first free Sunday —December 16, 1945—I sat down at the desk in my room in the Royalton Hotel on West 44th Street and addressed myself to "My dear Minna Lester." I had made my decision. I would join their game, on their terms.

"Perhaps you will not remember my name," my letter began. "Certainly, it is with a sense of guilt that I write you now. But if I may, permit me to refresh your memory. Early in May of last year, while I worked as a writer for the United States Army, I was briefly in New York where I obtained your address through the kind offices of Mr. Jack Lait . . ." Then, for four pages, I went on to explain why I had not been able to write the sisters in almost twenty months, how much I still wanted to create the play based on their lives, how eager I was to purchase the album of photographs of their club ("if the price is not prohibitive"), and, now that I was back in New York, how much "I should enjoy the pleasure of meeting you and talking with you."

The following evening at seven o'clock—I had just returned by subway from my army chores, and was preparing to go out for dinner—the telephone in my room rang. I lifted the receiver, and then I forgot about dinner. The voice on the other end was that of Minna Everleigh. I still have my notes, jotted down immediately after our half hour's conversation. "Minna sounds very old," I had observed. "Her voice is quavery, it goes up and down, very much the way Joseph Jefferson sounds on those pioneer recordings Linguaphone puts out. Sometimes she speaks in a shriek, but her sentences are clipped and distinct, often punctuated by shrill laughter. Her speech is staccato."

"We have your marvelous letter," Minna Everleigh was saying, "and we went to thank you for it—the most perfect letter I have ever received. Aida read it and she agrees with me that it is perfect. Now, about that matter you referred to, the Everleigh sisters—I must tell you, they just left for Florida, they are there now and will be there for several months. But Aida and I will be in constant touch with them, and we'll let them know of your requests and we'll keep in touch with you."

I told her I was deeply appreciative of the time she was giving to act as an intermediary between the Everleighs and myself.

She listened, and then she asked, "You're not a Catholic, are you?"

"No, I'm not."

"I thought not. Well, the Catholics and Puritans in this country would be against such a play as you have in mind. The Catholic Church is powerful, you know, and it's gaining strength. It has control over everything. It is against such women as the Everleighs, yet, Irving darling, when I lived in Chicago, some of the finest women I met socially were of the same class as the Everleighs, some of the very finest. . . . All this condemnation of the Everleighs. They do not merit it. I *know*. The whole thing is like those Nazis on trial for their war crimes. Many of those Nazis followed orders. I don't mean that they're not guilty. They are guilty. But they followed orders, you understand. They had to do what they did. And the Everleigh sisters had to do what they did, too."

I began to tell her that I had nothing but admiration for the Everleigh sisters, but she interrupted me.

"You know, Irving," she said, "there have been three books written about the Everleigh sisters. One is *Come into My Parlor*. It should have been called 'The Club.' Another is *The Gem of the Prairie*. And there is also *Lords of the Levee*. Most all of this is a bunch of untruths and lies. But *Come into My Parlor* is the best. . . . As to your play, I know something else you can do meantime. I've been reading four volumes written by Paul Eldridge, published by Haldeman-Julius who puts out those Little Blue Books in Girard, Kansas. Eldridge's books are not books really, but pamphlets—still, real literature you could adapt for the stage. I wrote Eldridge my opinion of his work, sheer genius, nothing like that awful novel, *Strange Fruit*. He teaches Romance languages right here in New York."

Then graphically, if somewhat confusingly, Minna acted out, over the telephone—reciting various characters' speeches with appropriate voice changes—the plot of one Eldridge book, and concluded by relating to me, briefly, the plots of the other three.

"You know, I have been writing a book of my own for seven years," she went on. "It is called 'Poets, Prophets and Gods.' I have read a lot, you know, all of the three thousand books which I have here in my home, and I went around the world twice, once in 1909 and again in 1912. I am absolutely a freethinker, no nursery stories for me. You are a freethinker, aren't you?"

"Well, yes, but—"

"My book would be heresy. I think I will have Haldeman-Julius publish it. They publish that sort of thing. I will finish it next year and you shall have an autographed copy."

"That's very kind of you."

"You may yet have your play, Irving. But really, you don't think it could actually be done, do you? Did you ever see a photograph of the Everleigh sisters?"

"No, I haven't."

"One had warm brown hair, and the other had natural golden hair, and it would be difficult to find anyone to portray them on the stage. They were very strange, not happy girls. There was so much tragedy in their lives. They left Chicago in 1911 with over a half-million dollars. They lost most of it later through investments, but don't think they are poor, because they are not. They live well, and have their jewels still. They are not poor, they are not dependent on anyone."

I was relieved about that, and wanted to let Minna know, but she was rambling on.

"We had several large parties in this house in the thirties, but in June, 1937, when the war came, we swore off parties. We only go out to the theater sometimes now. Do you think that's strange? But I do want to finish writing my book. Women friends are always calling about parties, about club meetings, about teas, but I have to refuse them. . . . We ordered eight more copies of Eldridge's books, something different for the reader, really, and I shall send you four in January of the new year. Eldridge is the modern Guy de Maupassant. . . . I saw that movie, *The Dolly Sisters*, did you? I couldn't help laughing at the picture, at Betty Grable and that other girl—I forget her name—oh, yes—June Haver. Yes. Oh dear, they were too lustful. Women in our day just weren't like that at all, but I suppose men want to see that today. Remember the old saying, 'What a man sees in a woman, he gets.' Well, nowdays, Irving, he certainly wants a hot number, that's what he wants today!"

She broke into a great peal of laughter, then suddenly sobered. "How old are you?" she asked.

"I'm thirty."

"Thirty?" She laughed nicely. "What a wonderful age." She paused, and then she said, "I will speak to the Everleigh sisters. You may yet get what you desire. But meantime, work on other things. There are more fish in the sea than are ever caught. Best wishes for the new year, darling, and thank you for the most perfect, most charming letter we have ever received, darling, and good-bye for now."

Dazed, yet stimulated, by my first personal contact with Minna Everleigh, I wondered when we would speak to one another again. The week passed without another call from Minna. But the sisters were on my mind, and so was Christmas, then fast approaching, and three days before Christmas I went to a bookstore on Fifth Avenue and bought deluxe editions of Elizabeth Barrett Browning's *Sonnets from the Portuguese* and Dickens' *A Christmas Carol* and ordered them gift wrapped and sent to Minna and Aida Lester.

The following day, a Sunday, the sixth day since Minna's first call to me, I was downstairs in the lobby of the Royalton purchasing pipe tobacco, when I was summoned to the telephone. A Miss Lester, I was told, wished to speak to me. While this conversation was briefer than our first, it was as meaningful to me, because, at last, I met Aida of the golden hair and gold piano.

At once, Minna said that she had just mailed a package to me. Her latest shipment of Little Blue Books had arrived from Girard, Kansas, and she was sending me several by Eldridge which she hoped I would consider for dramatization.

Before I could thank her, she began to reminisce about her sister and herself. "Aida and I were of a family of five," she said. "Everyone wants to be something in their life, and I was no different. Like that young actor in California we've been corresponding with. He wrote us, just as you did, under the erroneous impression that we were the Everleigh sisters. I corrected him. He now sends us snapshots of himself and baskets of fruit. He wants to be a writer as well as an actor. He writes well. I suspect he has a Semite strain. I believe the greatest poets, writers, actors were Semites. Unfortunately, Aida and I are Aryan. I wish we weren't. What are you, Irving? Are you a Semite?"

"Definitely," I said.

Minna laughed. "I love that word 'definitely.' I have a feeling you're going to go far. . . . Look, Irving, I want you to talk to my sister, Aida, also. She's ninety-nine percent more worthy than I am. I'm going to call down to her, and she'll go into the library, among all our books, and talk to you on that phone, while I stay on this one. I hope you two get along without having met. Well, hold on—"

I waited, bracing myself for Aida, the unknown, and suddenly a voice much younger than Minna's, a voice soft-spoken and well-modulated and faintly Southern addressed me. This was Aida Everleigh, and she was charming. After an introductory exchange, I mentioned the play I hoped to write. Aida said that her sister Minna usually took care of business matters. She wondered how I was enjoying my winter in New York, and she listened with interest as I related my reaction to the city.

When I was through, Aida gave me her own impressions of New York. "We've been in New York for twenty-five years, and we've seen it change. It's far too crowded now. I'm sure that's all right for the young. They like crowds. But it's difficult for us. I've been out to your Los Angeles many times. I love that climate. The last time I was there I went to see my brother. He died right after, in 1935."

Minna, who had been listening to us on the other telephone, now entered into our conversation. She did not like Los Angeles because Hollywood was in Los Angeles and Hollywood was full of actors. "I don't like actors, as a rule," said Minna. "You're not one, are you?"

"No, thank you."

"Well—actors—they all have a little of Jack Barrymore in them, you know, all of them assuming a hundred different guises. I was something of an actress myself in my youth. But now I'm writing, and I hope someone will publish what I write. Irving, you will become known with your own writing. I suppose—I suppose we all want to leave something behind. . . . Anyway, I have a feeling that a new literature is going to grow out of this war. You know, just as Hemingway and the rest came out of World War I, this second war will produce something completely new."

After a while, it was Aida Everleigh who closed the conversation. She said, "You have a lovely voice, Irving. Do you have a snapshot of yourself? If you have, please send it to us. It's wonderful to see people you've never met, people you've just spoken to or corresponded with. . . . Be sure to have a merry Christmas, and the main thing to watch out for in the new year is your health. We've managed quite well with ours. You look after yours."

Christmas Day, of that year, fell on a Tuesday. Many of us in the army were given a leave, and I had decided to spend my holiday in my hotel room, resting and reading and catching up on correspondence. At one o'clock in the afternoon my telephone rang, and as I went to answer it, I hoped that it would be Minna Everleigh. My wish was granted. She was cheerful, and she spoke to me for more than thirty minutes, and it was mostly a monologue.

"I've just finished breakfast with Aida," said Minna. "We only had coffee. We don't eat on sacred days, not even between meals, which is perhaps why I feel so good today. But on December twenty-ninth we begin to celebrate New Year's. I have a bottle of wonderful 1926 champagne, and we open it and drink it. . . . I was reading at breakfast when we received your two Christmas presents—*Sonnets from the Portuguese* by Elizabeth Barrett Browning and *A Christmas Carol* by Charles Dickens. By God, sweetheart, I'm wild about those editions. I really must apologize for the books I sent you because they're only Little Blue Books. That Haldeman who publishes them is a queer, eccentric old man. He's published one million books, and I've bought at least one thousand of them. . . . Aida came to me at breakfast, after I opened your gifts, and I said I must call you, and she said, 'Minna, you're not going to bother that Sergeant Wallace on Christmas Day.' I said that I wouldn't promise not to. But I just don't talk to anyone. I talk to you, I give you my time, Irving, because I like you. Anyway, thank you again for the books. They're cast in such a beautiful dye. I'll treasure these books until the last day of my life."

I asked her if she was going to call on anyone or have visitors this Christmas Day.

"No," said Minna, "I won't see anyone. I determined that until my own damnable book is finished and published I would live in a castle of silence. . . . Have you reread the Jesus Christmas story? You know, I believe that the two thieves that were hanging from crosses beside Jesus were really his followers who wanted to steal from the rich to help the poor. . . . I do not mind mankind's crimes, but I do mind its hypocrisy. . . . Have you been following what is going on in Europe? Anarchy is one thing, revolution is another thing, but nihilism is too much. And when people are starving and frozen—"

55

But suddenly, she was in an autobiographical mood. "Irving, did you know my father was a lawyer who spoke seven languages? It's true. And as for myself, I was able to read before I was five years old. When I was very young I got married, before I was seventeen. I married a wealthy devil of a man, but then we were divorced. Nevertheless, I have always felt that all men are my brothers, and you are one of my younger brothers. . . . Aida and I come from Virginia, you know, way back, and I consider you a brother. I lost one real brother. Aida told you, didn't she? . . . In 1679, after the Restoration in England, Charles II granted fifty-nine acres of land in Virginia to two brothers, and these two migrated to the New World. That was the beginning of our family. Those ancestors of mine, they all died of drink, insanity, and the Civil War. My grandmother was Welsh. She had a couple hundred slaves, but she loved Negroes. Yet, she would say to her Negro overseer, 'I don't believe in shipping niggers down the river, selling them off, but if I ever catch you mistreating your fellows, I'll ship you off!' . . . The last one of our family was born while my mother was dying."

In another abrupt transition, Minna began to discuss books, motion pictures, and censorship.

"I like Eldridge because, even though he is risqué, he does not use dirty language like so many of the writers after World War I. I don't believe in using coarse words, do you? . . . Still, I suppose the big fault of Hollywood is censorship. You can't censor literature and you can't censor ideas. But you can censor bawdy words, and I believe that the stage will come into its own yet and the creative artist can do more on the stage than in Hollywood. . . . Now, Irving, I'm going to do something for you that I would never do for any other man. I'm going to send you a copy of a book called *The World's Oldest Profession*. I'm going to place it at the bottom of the package. Read it—read it carefully. It'll help make you an even more tolerant and understanding person."

The following day, I was still on holiday leave and working in my hotel room when Minna Everleigh telephoned again. She and Aida were busy, she said, because they had received over one hundred Christmas cards from relatives and friends, and these had to be answered. But she was delaying this task because she still had books and writing on her mind, and she wanted to discuss the subject at greater length.

"Did you read Lillian Smith's *Strange Fruit?*" she asked me. "It's all wrong, just as that play, *Deep Are the Roots*, is wrong. I know colored women, and they would kill white women who took their men. Have you read the *Amsterdam News?* It's a paper for colored folks. There's fire there, Irving, and a new day's a-coming. I can tell you something plainly, and I know it for a fact. In his heart, every colored man hates white men. That's a reality. I don't believe in illusions. . . . I remember reading a recent novel published by Harper and Brothers. In it, the man enters the woman's room, strips off his clothes, pats his stomach, and says to the woman what you'd expect him to say. The very words, and in a Harper book! When I showed it to my typist Clara, she said, 'Good heavens, mercy, that word!' But, when you think of it, what's wrong with that word? . . . The newspapers I read and recommend are the New York *Herald Tribune* for the morning, and the *Journal-American* for the evening. That Cholly Knickerbocker is pretty bold. Every evening, for one hour, I read aloud to Aida. Reading reviews, I notice that Hollywood is shallow. What we want today is realism. Remember de Maupassant's line, 'Oh, how pale thou art compared to life.' . . . Do you know I'm related to Edgar Allan Poe? I am. You'll laugh like hell, but it's true. On my mother's side we're the same breed as Poe's mother."

Her mention of her mother brought Minna's mind to memories of other members of her family.

"I had a sister, Lula, who played the violin. Her arm became paralyzed at nineteen, and later she died. I was fifteen then. I wanted to kill myself, but Aida wouldn't let me. When I was fifteen and Aida was seventeen, Lula was nineteen, back in Virginia, and Lula started playing her violin at midnight, and she played until morning, and after that she was paralyzed. In the hotel a Negro had burned to death, and across the street in the church the white children and people laughed at his charred bones the next day. Since that time I have never been in a church, and when I die, I won't allow my body to be taken to a church. I tell this story in a part of my book called 'Realm of Dreams,' only I call Lula by the name of Lucy. Each chapter of my book ends with someone's favorable criticism of Shelley. The best is Elizabeth Barrett Browning's quotation. . . . But I was speaking of not going to church. When people tell me I ought to go to church, I say to them, 'I've read the Testaments, Old and New—but I've also read the Inquisition!' . . . Aida and I have wonderful relatives, and through them we sort of have grandchildren, too. Some we try to help financially, even though we have so little. I have one sister-in-law who is a French-Mexican girl in Los Angeles, and when she gets our allowance, she always writes me, 'You have come to me on a magic carpet again.' Someday, if I no longer have any money, if I'm broke, rather than let them put us in some Old Ladies' Home, I'll turn on the gas in this house."

Now Minna's mind darted to many subjects. She remembered the beginning of the First World War. "On August 1, 1914, in Charlottesville, Virginia, Aida and I passed a newsstand, saw the headlines, and I exclaimed, 'My God, Europe is at war.' Aida said, 'Oh, it'll be over in a couple of months.' I said, 'No, Aida, it'll be over in a couple hundred years.'" Minna spoke of her devotion to music. "I prefer orchestral music to the human voice. Look what time did to Caruso's voice, and then look what time does to a violin, improving and mellowing it. And the guitar, voice of love and passion, I worship it above all others." She spoke of her social life. "Aida and I belong to ten women's societies in New York, but since the war we have attended none of them." And finally, she spoke of men. "Irving, I love men. I esteem your sex highly."

After that, New Year's Day came and went, and so did my holiday leave, and soon I was deeply involved in my army activities. Two and a half weeks passed without a call from Minna Everleigh, and then, one evening in mid-January of 1946, returning to my hotel, I found a manila envelope in my box addressed in an unfamiliar hand. I opened it and read the following:

> *New York*
> *Saturday*
> *Jan. 12, 1946*

To Sgt Irving Wallace . . .

Greetings from Aida and Minna Lester with cordial best wishes. Since our last phone talk I have been very ill with Influenza—with severe lung congestion! Sister Aida is taking my dictation this afternoon, as I am still in bed very ill . . .

Sister Aida went to the Post Office yesterday and mailed you the promised volumes by Paul Eldridge, and the story of "the world's oldest profession"— by "Joseph McCabe." I am enclosing in this the Haldeman-Julius card and address . . . Editor and Publisher of The American Freeman . . . Devote your sophisticated mind to Eldridge's books if they appeal to you—Pardon my scrawl—I am nervous!!

Dear Irving Wallace—

You can see by the above that I am no good taking dictation!! You can phone us some day when you have received the package that I mailed you yesterday, when I hope to be able to tell you that my dear sister is quite convalescent!!

> *From yours*
> *Aida Lester*
> *Phone End 2-9970*

As soon as I could, I telephoned Minna Everleigh to learn if she had fully recovered (she had), and to inform her that I was leaving New York City in less than a week to be discharged from the army.

She was pleased that I would soon be a civilian again, and only regretted that I would be leaving her city for California. She sounded weaker than usual, and when she settled into her monologue, it was clear but disjointed.

"Even if I am a Virginian," Minna Everleigh said, "I am not intolerant. But I do know that every colored woman hates every white woman. And as for Desdemona kissing Paul Robeson in *Othello*, that I don't wish to see. . . . I have nineteen volumes of Chinese poems in my library, and I have committed seven hundred poems to memory. My favorite poet was also the favorite of Emperor Ming. . . . My mind often goes to the Boxer Rebellion, and the siege of the Embassy, when beautiful women were stripped naked and ravished by Mongols. Chiang Kai-shek is a miserable fiend, a demon. I have his entire record, that vile Tartar. Of course, you know that Stalin told F.D.R., 'I do not share your esteem for Chiang.' Hitler's father was another devil. . . . A woman needs a man's guiding hand, especially in business affairs. In 1929 and 1931 we lost a fortune in mortgages. On a half-million dollars we had invested, we got back only three cents on each dollar. I took our jewels to bolster our credit, but I was scared to go up in a skyscraper, because I feared people were following me to steal the jewels. . . . I'm glad W. Somerset Maugham is one of your favorite writers. He has a sophisticated mind. He is the grandfather of style. But I saw *Rain* on the stage, and I didn't like it. His portrait of Sadie Thompson as a cheap little prostitute, that was all bunk. And the minister who killed himself after falling into bed with her, that was bunk, too. . . . Well, Irving, so you're going to be a civilian again. What can I say, except I'll be with you in spirit next Saturday when you get your honorable discharge. Good luck, Irving, good luck."

Two weeks later I was back in California, and seven months later I was in Europe, and it was not until a year and a half later that I found the time to get in touch with the Everleigh sisters once more. I wrote them a long letter about my trip abroad. I made no mention of the play project. I mailed the letter, and waited. Almost two weeks passed, and then there arrived the bulging manila envelope addressed in Minna's fantastic scrawl. The letter inside read as follows:

Monday—August 4, 1947—New York

Dear Irving Wallace

  Your charming letter from Hollywood—dated July 24th received . . . Your cordial message came as a surprise . . . I supposed you had forgotten sister Aida and me . . . I remember you and various topics we discussed over the telephone when you were in New York in 1946 . . .

I read to my sister Aida your most interesting letter . . . We were impressed and thrilled by your eloquent recital of your adventures since last we heard from you . . . Summing these up briefly—after our last phone talk—you were demobilized from the army—you were sent out of New York —and in three days became a civilian again— You returned to your home on the Coast—rejoined your wife Sylvia—you decided to take a trip to Europe . . . You received assignments to write stories for Saturday Evening Post and Collier's—then you left by boat for Sweden—a long and thrilling trip . . . You were in Europe nine months—started in Stockholm—down by train through occupied Germany—and then to Paris—you were in Paris four months—then you went to Spain—you drove up from Madrid to the French Riviera—then drove on to Pisa and Rome . . . After that you went to Switzerland—Berne and Lausanne—then back to Paris—and finally to London . . . Sister Aida and I appreciate history and literature—dear Irving Wallace—we have travelled in Europe and Asia—we are amazed that through such exciting adventures you could as you state write stories—for magazines . . . And now you have returned home to Hollywood with your wife Sylvia!!!

Sister Aida and I read your classic serial—on the Princess Elizabeth— presumptive heiress to the British Throne and Lieutenant Phillip Mountbatten in Collier's Magazine—issued in March 1947 . . . This serial's style was superb—colossal—dear Author—congratulations!!! You have literary genius . . .

We fondly prize—two snap shot photos of yourself—dear Irving—taken on your journey—one in Paris—the other beside Raphael's painting of his mistress in Rome . . . We like them very much . . . They are handsome . . . The photo showing you smoking a cigarette resembles Jacob Weiss—whose picture I enclose [Weiss was a young member of the Jewish Irgun who was hanged by the British in Palestine] . . .

How damnable the persecution and martyrdom of the Semite peoples— earth's noblest race . . . It is the handwriting on the wall for this so-called Christian civilization!!! Satonic Russia Kipling termed—"The Bear that walks like a Man"—will destroy England and America . . .

Forgive—dear Irving Wallace—my gloomy pessimism—I have followed the Semites through five thousand years of demoniac persecution—twenty million perished in the fiendish inquisition—if the human race cannot overcome primeval savagery—let atom bombs blot out such bestiality . . . Forgive my bitter mood!!!

I meant to conceal my sadness—to answer your inspiring letter—with cheerful response—to thank you for remembering my sister and me so cordially—I felt we were forgotten—in your engrossed, absorbed life—When you visit New York again—in September or October—to consult with your various editors—you may phone me as often as you wish . . .

Concerning parties referred to in your phone conversations in 1946—I counselled you then not to waste your literary gifts on plays or books about them—however, if still resolved to write magazine serials telling stories of their lives—they still reside in New York—I will let you know their attitude to publicity!!!

Meantime—rest assured that you have our appreciation—admiration— changeless friendship . . . Let me know this response to your wonderful letter reached you . . .

Phone me when in New York—Endicott 2-9970—May life be kind to you and to your loved . . . May your heart's desire be granted in fullest measure . . .

Most sincerely—
Minna Lester

Post script—Monday—August 4—1947

Have you written stories for "The American Weekly"—one of the Hearst's New York Journal American Magazines??? Very popular—great circulation!!!

I enclose a Cholly Knickerbocker column from Hearst's newspaper—the daily Journal American telling of Phillip Mountbatten—the Prince of Greece—of his visit here in 1938—of his infatuation for Cobina Wright Jr . . . Very spicy!!! Give your impressions when you write . . .

After that, except for exchanges of greeting cards on various holidays, this was the last communication I was to have from the Everleigh sisters. I was fully occupied in my efforts to make a living as a free-lance writer, and I neglected to continue my correspondence with Aida and Minna. I was unable to visit New York, as I had promised Minna I would, and so I had no opportunity to speak to them on the telephone.

I kept meaning to write, and postponing it, and then, a year and a month after Minna Everleigh's last letter to me, I learned that she was dead.

I sent my heartfelt condolences to Aida. I added a written obituary to a number of others that had been published. Even though I had been born in Chicago after the Everleigh Club had closed its doors forever, and the sisters had left that city, I felt that I had been a part of their time and a small part of their lives. My father, my uncle, my closest male relatives had been, in their youth, in Chicago when the Everleigh sisters had also been young and renowned. These members of my family had seen or at least known of the celebrated millionaires' bagnio when princes and senators, prizefight champions and authors had enjoyed the scaled-down gold piano and fancy cuspidors, the rich library and boudoirs, the thirty beautiful girls and the sisters themselves.

I liked to believe that all of that glory and wonder had not been for our fathers and grandfathers alone. I had been one of the lucky ones to share a part of it. For I had known the Everleighs, too. True, I had known them four decades late, when they seemed to have become two characters out of *Arsenic and Old Lace*, when they had become pretenders named Lester, when they had become respectable clubwomen who belonged to ten women's societies and lived in lonely dignity off Central Park in New York City. Yet, through them, by mail, by telephone, I had become intimate with their enemies, the "plotters of the South Side Levee," with their affection for Byron and Shelley and de Maupassant, with their attitudes about women and race, with their genteel distaste for the bawdy, with their old Virginia background and family.

I had known them, and now I missed them, missed the departed Minna and wondered what would happen to Aida, poor Aida, so alone.

For me, it had been a memorable experience, that friendship with those two nice old ladies. Remembering them, I remembered a remark that Wilson Mizner, the inimitable wit, publicist, and gambler, had once made, and which has been widely quoted ever since. Said Mizner, "Always treat a whore like a lady—and a lady like a whore."

And so I knew this, finally, about my friends: No man ever had to *treat* the Everleigh sisters like ladies. Despite their place in history, they were Virginia ladies born, they were ladies in their Chicago youth, and they were two nice old ladies in New York at the time when they befriended an inquisitive and admiring writer and enlisted man from far away.

WHAT HAS HAPPENED SINCE . . .

I wrote fragments of the preceding memoir shortly after Minna Everleigh's death in 1948, and only recently reworked these into their present form. I began writing this story, so to speak, during my Sundays. I wrote it for no one else. It was for myself, until now.

To report what has happened since 1948, I must go back to the time of Minna Everleigh's death, upon which I have already remarked.

Minna's death was widely reported by the press, and it stripped away the pseudonym Lester after so many decades and left Aida and her to history as Everleigh forever. Minna died on September 16, 1948, and *The New York Times* gave her passing prominent display in a news story that I suspect she would have appreciated above all others. The story read:

"Minna Everleigh, one-time owner with her sister, Ada, of the Everleigh Club, a Chicago landmark in the period from 1900 to 1911, died yesterday in the Park West Hospital, 170 West 76th Street, at the age of 70. She had been living in the city under an assumed name for more than 25 years.

"The Everleigh Club, closed during the reform raid in 1911, was located on South Dearborn Street and drew its patronage from cattle barons, actors and royalty. It was known for its floor shows, its string music and its $100 'minimum' evening charge.

"Miss Everleigh and her sister, members of a prominent Virginia family, lived circumspectly and inconspicuously, their chief diversions being theatre-going and writing poetry. When the Club was closed, the sisters confided that they had made a million dollars and were planning to spend the rest of their lives as anonymously as possible—they wanted people to think that the Everleigh sisters were dead."

The New York *Daily News* mentioned that Minna left behind "several oil paintings, a gold piano and an estimated $100,000 worth of diamonds," and recalled that Minna had remarked several years earlier, "I like to see old friends but not old customers." *Time* magazine, headlining its obituary THE WAGES OF SIN, reported that the Everleigh Club had been "the most luxurious bordello which the U.S. ever saw," and concluded, "Last week Minna died . . . a wealthy and dignified dowager. Ada sent her body to Virginia for a burial befitting a Southern gentlewoman."

I had conveyed, as I have said, my letter of condolence to Aida Everleigh, sent it to Aida Lester at the old address. I had no idea if she ever received it. She seemed to have disappeared into thin air. Then, three and a half months later, there came an airmail envelope made out to me. The return address read, "Aida Lester, 20 W. 71st St., New York, N.Y." But the imprinted postmark, dated December 31, 1948, read, "Charlottesville, Va." Inside I found an old-fashioned holiday greeting card bearing the legend, "Best Wishes for the New Year" and a bright print of a bubbling champagne glass. Inside the card, written in blue ink, was the following message: "New Years Eve 1948. We are wishing for you a Happy and Prosperous 1949. From our Family to yours—Cordially Aida and Minna Lester."

That was all, and that was the last I ever heard from Aida Everleigh. But it made her bereavement, and her future, clear to me. To the unimaginative outside world, Minna might be considered as dead. To Aida, she would never die, and, for Aida herself, she would continue to be "Cordially Aida and Minna Lester."

After receiving Aida's card, my mind kept returning to Minna's death, and I decided to write a brief but personal remembrance of Minna for the people in show business, whom Minna had always followed and for whom she had felt (except for her loathing of actors) an affinity. In those days, a friend of mine, Irving Hoffman, a celebrated public relations man, cartoonist, intimate of the greats, conducted a lively column "Tales of Hoffman" in *The Hollywood Reporter*, a daily trade journal dispensing information to people in the motion picture and theatrical business. Hoffman had often asked me to write guest columns for him, and from time to time I had done such columns, and now I wanted to do one more. I wrote my farewell to Minna Everleigh for Hoffman's column, and he published it. I did not realize that it would bring the modern-day successor to the Everleighs into my life, but it did.

A few days after my column appeared, I received a telephone call from a person who had a deep, husky male voice. The voice, I learned in a moment, belonged to a female, and the caller was none other than Polly Adler. Of course, I recognized her name at once. Polly Adler had been a front-page figure between 1920 and 1944 when, with a handful of attractive girls who worked in a variety of magnificent apartments in New York City, she had been America's leading call-house madam. Her friends—one or two of them also were clients—had ranged from pugilists like Mickey Walker to gangsters like Al Capone, Frank Costello, and Dutch Schultz to entertainment personalities like Wallace Beery and Robert Benchley. Driven out of Manhattan in 1944, she had spent the last five years in retirement in a middle-class bungalow in Burbank, California, while she industriously attempted to acquire a college degree by attending evening classes at Los Angeles City College.

Now, it appeared, Polly Adler was completing an autobiography about her adventures as a purveyor of pleasure. In one section of her book, she had made passing reference to her foremost predecessors, the Everleigh sisters. She was not satisfied with this section, and wanted to enlarge it, but not until she read my guest column in *The Hollywood Reporter* had she known how to get the necessary information. What she wanted from me was permission to use a few paragraphs of my column to expand her own section on the Everleighs. I agreed to this at once. When Polly Adler's book, *A House Is Not a Home*, finally was published in 1953, it was a best seller and a national sensation. Acknowledgment of my own minor contribution to the Everleigh saga I found in a footnote on page 314. Polly Adler had written:

"Until Minna's death, in 1948, only a half-dozen trusted friends knew that the sisters were living the life of respectable clubwomen at a home they owned near Central Park in New York. I am indebted to Irving Wallace, one of the few who knew their secret, for this information."

After that, Polly Adler, a pudgy, Jewish middle-aged lady with a passion for knowledge, and I became fast friends. Often, I would sit in her living room, studying her voluminous scrapbooks, gorging myself on her delicious homemade chopped chicken liver, while she questioned me about the profession of writing and about the Everleighs. And when I was not eating, I would steadily interrogate her about her life as a madam—the unprintable and libelous parts that were not included in her book—and she would discourse freely on her girls, her famous clients, her philosophy about the sexual lives of men and women.

Several times, Polly Adler sought my advice on the second book that she was in the process of preparing, a sequel to *A House Is Not a Home,* a book about the prostitutes who had worked for her and what had happened to each of them. Once, I know, she traveled across the United States with a tape recorder, looking up the girls—one had become a narcotics addict, another the respectable wife of a wealthy realtor—and putting down their stories on tape. But this provocative book, like Minna Everleigh's own, was never to be published. On another occasion, Polly informed me with great glee of a marvelous evening she had just enjoyed. Alfred C. Kinsey, renowned throughout the world for his sex surveys, *Sexual Behavior in the Human Male* and *Sexual Behavior in the Human Female,* had visited Los Angeles and had wanted to meet her. And she had wanted to meet him. She had invited him over for a Jewish dinner, and he had accepted immediately. "A wonderful man, that Dr. Kinsey," she told me. "We had so much in common to discuss. But you know, I found him surprisingly prim and puritanical. One thing I will say for him. Just like you, Irving, he never left a crumb of the chopped chicken liver!"

Polly Adler followed my career as avidly as I had once followed hers. When I published my second book, a collective biography of American eccentrics and nonconformists, Polly bought a dozen copies, asked me to inscribe them, and then she wrote me:

"Thanks for autographing the books for my friends. Hustling for *The Square Pegs* is a pleasure. Too bad my time is limited. Can't do an extensive hustling job comparable to the old days.

"Your book rates it! I loved it!—Especially Victoria Woodhull [a former prostitute, advocate of free love and equal rights for women, who ran for the Presidency of the United States in 1872]—what a dame! Lucky for me she wasn't around in my day. I couldn't buck such competition."

One of the last times I heard from Polly Adler—just a few years before her untimely death in June of 1962—was on the occasion of the publication of my novel, *The Chapman Report.* The book told the story of the effects of the visit of a university sex survey team on a group of women living in a suburb of Los Angeles. Polly read it in one sitting, and telephoned me in a state of great excitement. "Irving," she exclaimed, "I adored it! Where in the hell did you pick up all that information? Why, I'll be damned, but you know more about sex than I do!" I demurred to the literary madam, but she went on, "Irving, every woman should read this book. I'm sending copies to all my old girls, and some of my old competitors." I thanked her. Then after a contemplative pause, she said, "I'd like to have sent a copy to poor old Aida Everleigh. Too bad, but maybe what happened was for the best, what with Minna so long gone." I agreed that it was too bad about Aida, and I knew in my heart that what had happened had been for the best.

For earlier in that year, after over eleven years without her sister, Aida Everleigh had died. She was eighty-four years old when she died on January 3, 1960, although one Chicago newspaper ungallantly made her ninety-four, and *The New York Times* made her ninety-three.

The news of Aida's passing was not as widely reported as Minna's had been. The Everleighs' old reporter friend and Boswell, Charles Washburn, learned of her death and wrote the primary story for the Chicago *Tribune*, and almost all other obituaries were based on his story.

Washburn's account, which appeared in the *Tribune* of January 6, 1960, began, "Ada Everleigh, the senior half of the famed Everleigh sisters and one of the most notorious madams of all time, was buried secretly Tuesday in a grave next to her sister Minna in a small Virginia cemetery not far from Washington, D.C." Then, Washburn's news story went on, "Unknown for nearly 50 years in life, she had requested to remain unknown in death. Only a few relatives attended the services. Minna died in New York City, Sept. 16, 1948." Next, the story revived some of the gaudy Everleigh Club's history, then reported, "After Minna's death, Ada returned to her native Virginia. Ada died last Sunday of old age, but no word reached this reporter until Tuesday. What few pictures she had were sent recently to the Chicago *Sunday Tribune* for safe keeping. Other evidence of her identity was long since destroyed." There was generous mention of the girls of long ago. "Everleigh Club sirens wore evening gowns and were properly introduced to the guests. The prices were $25 and up for going up the mahogany staircases. This, remember, in an age of nickel beers and 10 cent whiskey." And finally, one of the senior Everleigh's witticisms was memorialized. As the Everleigh Club closed its doors for the last time, Aida had made a farewell speech to the personnel, and her last words were "We are going from bawd to worse—retirement."

There would be no bottle of champagne in the days before next New

Year's Eve at 20 West 71st Street—or at a certain house in Virginia.

I wondered what had happened to Aida's gold piano. And I wondered what had become of Minna's manuscript, "Poets, Prophets and Gods." And then, I wondered who in New York City now had the telephone number, Endicott 2-9970.

THE AMPS

THE ARMY CAPTAIN had assured me, just before I left on the trip early that winter, that I would not have to look at surgery. "No operations, nothing of the sort," he had said. "I can't stand them, either. They make me vomit. No. This has only to do with artificial limbs. The limbs themselves, see?"

But when, after twenty hours on the train, I reached the dismal Terminal Station in Atlanta, I knew everything about this assignment was going to be bad. I had expected, somehow, that it would be a sunshiny day, but now outside it was dirty gray and the rain was slashing down and people were fringed unhappily around the depot.

I went into the cafeteria, had some milk and toast, then figured it was late enough in the morning to call. I telephoned the hospital but the colonel wasn't in yet. He had given me his residence number, so I phoned there and his wife answered. He had just left. Was I the sergeant from New York? Well, he had tried hard to find me a room, and thought that he had one at the Briarcliff. I said thanks.

I called the Briarcliff and they had something for me at five dollars and a half a day, and I thought: Christ, five-fifty a day when the Army is paying me two dollars a day for quarters. But I took it.

It was still raining. There were plenty of cabs at the depot curb, different from New York. The cabs were informal, without yellow paint and skylights, and the drivers didn't wear those caps. I got into the first cab. The driver was an angular-faced, unshaven Southern boy. He asked where to, and I told him, and he said, "That's four miles." I said I couldn't help it. He asked, "Are you new here?" I said yes. He started the car. He said, "This is the old part of town. The depot is in the old part."

I accepted the apology. We drove up the hill and away from the old part.

He settled back, observing again my uniform in his rearview mirror. "Furlough?"

I said no, then I thought I'd tell him and impress him, so I said, "I'm a writer from the Signal Corps. I'm going to be at Lawson Hospital for a few weeks gathering material for a movie."

"On the amps?"

"Yes."

He *was* impressed. "Will it be in the movie theaters?"

I wondered what he would think if I told him that the working title of our movie was *Construction and Use of Provisional Prostheses.* But I said no, it was only a training film to be shown to specialists.

After that he was disinterested.

At the Briarcliff—"Atlanta's Finest Hotel"—I promptly dispensed with my one obligatory task. I jotted messages on a half-dozen postcards, the phony, planned kind expected by friends from a Yankee on his first visit to Georgia—"I have arrived safely with my typewriter and carpetbag."

With that out of my system, I inquired how to reach Lawson General Hospital and was told it was fourteen miles out in the country. I caught a rickety trolley on Ponce de Leon Avenue, and when I asked the elderly lady behind me where I got off to transfer, she replied that she had lived in Atlanta twenty-five years but wanted to die in Long Beach, California. She had visited Long Beach last year, during the summer, and when people learned she was from Georgia they always asked when Georgia was going to join the Union. "I found out that was a joke," she said, "so I always laughed with them."

I asked her where I got off to transfer. She said where West Peachtree meets East Peachtree, and even in Long Beach everyone had heard of Peachtree Street. I thanked her, and when I rose to leave, she reminded me, loudly, not to forget that this was Southern hospitality. "We give our time to everyone. We have plenty of time, but no money."

Thereafter, during my two-week visit, whenever elderly ladies heard me make inquiries in my hard Midwestern accent, they would become solicitous. I was always being instructed by elderly ladies. The young ones, mostly with nice legs, kept their distance as if I'd come to burn Atlanta again. Always, my elderly guides, after instructions and digressions, sent me off with the local cliché, "This is just some of our Southern hospitality." When I wrote my wife, in California, about all this hospitality, she replied somewhat acidly, "Wait'll they find out you're a Jew."

At my transfer point I took a trackless trolley. After an hour, the occupants were weeded down to a handful of mothers and wives journeying to Lawson to visit between the hours of two and four. At the end of the line the mothers, wives, and I descended from the bus for our last transfer. We had our choice of waiting for a military bus that ran on an erratic schedule or taking one of the scavenger cabs that lurked nearby. The cabs charged a dime a person. It began raining again, and I stood inside a shed with the women. The women huddled together, and I stood off alone. I caught two of the women looking at my legs. It made me uncomfortable, and I finally took a cab.

Lawson General Hospital, physically, was a disappointment. I'd imagined a vast, imposing, solid stone structure, like all those city hospitals. Instead, it was a network of low-slung, insubstantial, wooden buildings sprawled along the paved highway. It seemed like a jungle of barracks, without beginning, without end. Later when I inquired, I learned from an efficient middle-aged secretary, a professional Southerner, that Lawson consisted of precisely 245 one-story buildings stretching across a frontage that covered seven-eighths of a mile.

I learned further, from a Vermont WAC sergeant who was worrying about the weight she had gained in service, that Lawson was one of seven Army hospitals handling amputees in the United States. There had been five before the war, and two were added afterward. These amputee centers, their facilities temporarily inflated, were spotted throughout the land—New York, Michigan, Utah. These hospitals had handled, or were handling, the 15,000 amputees produced by World War II. About 10,000 were servicemen who had lost a leg—or legs—mostly from wounds caused by shrapnel from enemy artillery, or by land mines.

Lawson had a bed capacity of 3,300, and during the period I was there, some 2,700 patients were registered. Most of these patients were soldiers with overseas ribbons; some few were dependents of soldiers, an additional responsibility of the army. The number of amputees was relatively small, yet their presence dominated the life of the hospital.

My initial duty at Lawson was to report to the colonel in the Orthopedic Surgery Building. His office was the first to the right, just beyond the pharmacy. The colonel was a short, slender, wiry Missourian. He was late-thirtyish. His hair gave the effect of having a crew cut, though it didn't, and his eyes were watery and distant. His profile was that of a somewhat pleasant, though emaciated Neanderthal man. His dress was eccentric only on top and on the bottom—he wore a Stillwell hat and cumbersome government-issue shoes. He had done six years of institutional and postgraduate medical work in St. Louis before the war, and had enlisted in the Army Reserve to get his year of military service over with. He had specialized in orthopedic surgery only after entering the army.

The colonel had been at Lawson four and a half years, and was a little dazed. When I first met him, which was in New York at Signal Corps motion picture headquarters, I had thought that his bewilderment resulted from being suddenly exposed to ex-Hollywood characters and their erratic manner and mystifying talk. In New York, he moved about like a Boston banker surrounded by M-G-M, and awkwardly tried to add movie terms to his own speech, which only added up to new Goldwynisms. But here at Lawson, in his own element, among his colleagues, even though he displayed brief flashes of assurance and authority, the bewilderment was still with him. I decided it was chronic.

When I first arrived, the colonel thought that he might be out of the service in four more weeks and he was quietly elated. He would take his wife and three children back to St. Louis and go into orthopedic surgery. "We had fifteen thousand amps in four years of war," he would say, "but every year, in America, there are forty thousand amp cases. For the first time, I'll be able to work with different groups, even with children, and be able to study and really take my time." Sometimes he was worried about going into private practice. "I'm a debunker now," he would say. "I tell the truth. I don't know all that fancy customer psychology. I'll probably never have a decent practice. I'll wind up selling newspapers." Then he would remember that, as an officer, he had saved enough money to buy a modest house. This cheered him. He candidly admitted that he had come into the army with a brand-new wife, one room of furniture, and five dollars.

But by the time my visit ended, his private practice was no longer a prospect. The Surgeon General's office had frozen him to his army job, frozen him overnight. He was key personnel. They had released too many medical men too fast and now they needed all remaining key personnel. After four and a half years. The colonel took it with a smile, and I liked him immensely for that, but I was sorry as hell for him, even though it is not GI for a sergeant ever to be sorry for a colonel.

After he was frozen, the colonel appeared more preoccupied than ever. Although he was a project officer, and overseer of our film, he would forget me for hours at a time if some surgical oddity reared its head. Or an unusual X-ray.

The colonel collected X-rays as other men collect artistic nude photographs or rare stamps. Any X-ray, the most pedestrian, would arrest him, and bring forth much muttering and head-wagging. Once when we were in the middle of a conference, a medical officer put his head in to say that Staff Sergeant So-and-So was being separated from the hospital.

This provoked a great show of alarm from the colonel, who promptly ordered that the staff sergeant appear at once with his complete file. When the sergeant materialized, somewhat frightened, the colonel demanded only his X-rays. "I remember you, Sergeant," the colonel said, holding an X-ray to the light. "You had a hip fractured and refractured and . . ." He drifted off into silent ecstasy over the victim's colorful breakages. Finally, after an hour of persistent tongue-clucking, the colonel selected three choice and gloomy X-rays, put them aside for his album, and sent the sergeant packing into civilian life.

On another occasion, hearing that an ex-saddler from Kentucky, who had lost both legs above the knees in the service, was being discharged, the colonel broke an important appointment just to have one last glimpse of the fellow. Later, the colonel told me that he had taken the Kentuckian into the countryside and photographed him in 16-mm color. "That boy got around pretty well for a bilateral amp," explained the colonel. "Only trouble, when I tried to get him to ride a horse again, he couldn't mount without help. He'll have a rugged time." The colonel brightened. "But I took some magnificent pictures."

The colonel's cinematic ambition, beyond our immediate project, was to make a movie about multiple amputees he had met during the war. He showed me the outline he had written. His documentary film would include the two quadruple amputees in the United States—one who had lost all four limbs when he stepped on a land mine in the Pacific theater, and who was still at Percy Jones General Hospital, and another who had suffered a winter airplane crash in Maine and lost all his limbs from freezing, and who was now a civilian. The colonel also wished to include the six triple amputees of World War II. "We have one of them right here at Lawson," he said enthusiastically. This triple amputee had been a Georgia University football end, All-American, and during the Battle of the Bulge, he almost froze to death. Three of his limbs were removed; his torso survived.

The colonel said that he wanted to make this picture a medical serial. Five years from now, he wanted the Army to send cameramen out to visit all these same amputees and film them again after their rehabilitation. The colonel asked me if I thought that this would make a good picture. I said yes.

The colonel's narrow office was also my own office during my stay, and it became for me a room out of a nightmare. It was furnished with an ordinary wooden desk, chairs, a white-sheeted examination table—and something horrible on top of the bookcase. This something was a formidable, square, glass container, filled with yellow liquid in which floated an object that resembled a dehydrated tree stump with roots streaming from it. The very first day there, I glanced at the typed label pasted on the glass. From the obscure medical language, it appeared to be the case history of a corporal from Alabama, aged twenty-eight, white, who had died in 1943. The realization hit me that this object, floating, was a part of the corporal, on display much as a writer's first rejection slip would be. It seemed impossible because the Thing resembled nothing. The pasted typed label was insistent. I finally decided it was a human bone of some kind. I was immediately nauseated.

In the days after, I was irresistibly drawn to the Thing, and I read the case history a half-dozen times, and each time was nauseated. At last I moved my project across the corridor, and took to using a WAC's typewriter.

My greatest problem of survival in the hospital was learning the native tongue. While most of the patients persisted in using the language of the barracks, and were therefore intelligible to me, the medical officers and limb mechanics, with whom I had more contact, conversed in an English more befuddling than Chaucer in the original. The two principal terms used were "amps" and "prostheses." Any patient who had a limb amputated was, quite naturally, an "amp." And the artificial limbs, ranging from arm to hand to thigh and foot (and, I was told later, false teeth might technically be included in this category), were called "prostheses" in the plural and "prosthesis" in the singular.

The vocabulary was rich and endless. Arms were referred to as "upper extremities" and legs as "lower extremities." A temporarily fitted artificial leg was a "provisional prosthesis." All amps were broken down into specialized categories—a BK was a soldier whose leg had been removed below the knee, and BE was one whose arm had been removed below the elbow. The most difficult for me to use, at first, was AK, because of its previous connotation in my vocabulary. Now it meant an above-the-knee amputee. There were others ranging from a "syme," one who had lost his foot but not his heel, to "hip disarticulation," one who was minus a leg from the hip down, a particularly limiting loss. The most revolting expression, and one bandied about constantly by the doctors, was "guillotined." When a soldier was first wounded on the field of battle, and required immediate surgery, his limb was guillotined—meaning it was sawed off straight and unceremoniously, to be operated upon again later, to shape it so that an artificial limb could be fitted.

The worst thing about the language, for a squeamish and sentimental layman like myself, was the casual manner in which it was used. The surgeons at Lawson discussed these things with less overt concern than they showed when they ordered steaks medium-well. I realized, of course, that another operation, another man without a leg, was to them as much a part of their daily life as their morning shave, and it had to be that way, but to the uninitiated it was dismaying.

Once in the evening, when most of the staff had gone home or back to the barracks, I accompanied the colonel on his last rounds. We were walking through the Orthopedic Limb Shop, and before turning off the lights in each room, he would describe some curio. In the last room, where all types of odd contraptions lay, I saw an utterly medieval monstrosity, a skeleton of leather and steel, the largest network of braces I'd ever seen. I asked the colonel about it, and he went over, and had to grunt as he lifted it. "This is the worst one," he said. "It's a prosthesis for a man who's been paralyzed from the waist down. It helps him stand. It's really not very good, but what can we do?" He set it down, switched off the lights, and as we walked out he said, "I think those paralytics would be better off if they allowed us to cut off both their legs. It might help them ambulate." I said nothing.

Another time, the colonel took me to see a hip disarticulation case. A big, blond, obliging boy, who neither smiled nor scowled, placed himself on exhibit for us with the disinterest of a sideshow freak. The boy wore a T-shirt and jock shorts and he had lost his right leg and thigh to the hip. He wore a cumbersome prosthesis, with a tremendous light brown leather socket for his hip stump, and a yellow fiber leg. The colonel asked him to walk on level floor for us, and then to negotiate a slight incline. The boy did so rapidly, professionally, but the prosthesis made him jolt when he walked. When we were through, the colonel thanked him and we left. "He has an interesting gait," said the colonel. "We'll use him for the end of our movie." Suddenly, halfway down the corridor, the colonel halted. "Sa-ay, I forgot to have him do the best thing. It'll photograph fine, show the limitations of hip disarticulation prostheses." I inquired what had been forgotten. The colonel stood there shaking his head. "I wanted to make him run for you. When he runs, he falls flat on his face!"

But the incident that affected me most was the least important. I met a lieutenant at the hospital who lived with his wife in my hotel. We became friends right off because he came from a small town near Madison, Wisconsin, and had gone to the University, and had known a football player I had attended high school with in Kenosha. He suggested that I drive back to town with him, and save myself the tedious bus and trolley ride, and I grabbed at the chance.

The first time I left with him, he was also taking his civilian secretary, a middle-aged, graying woman. As we walked to the parking lot, the lieutenant broke off his chatter to me, and turned to his secretary. "By the way, Miss Smith, I forgot to look. Do I have any surgery in the morning?" Miss Smith shook her head. "None. You're not posted." He turned back to me and kept right on talking, and as I half listened, I thought: God, in one of those shacks someone is waiting for surgery, a portion of a leg to be taken off and carted away (what do they do with the legs?); someone is waiting and his ma and pa are somewhere, away, sitting and waiting and worrying, and his girl or wife, and a couple of friends waiting, and himself before falling asleep tonight, thinking about it, his whole life standing still on this one surgery, and here I am walking with a young doctor who is asking if there is any surgery for him in the morning, he forgot to look.

When we got into the coupe, I stared at the lieutenant, a nice young guy with a handsome, beefy, red face, probably exhausted from overwork and wanting out every minute, and with his wife waiting back in the hotel and bright people coming over for dinner, a nice guy—but in one of those beds, another guy waiting for when surgery is posted. I felt lousy all the way back to the hotel.

Our picture project, which occupied most of my waking hours and a good portion of my insomnia, was divided into two parts. The first part concerned the lower extremity, and the second part the upper extremity. The first part was the more vital, since men with leg losses were twice as numerous as men with arm losses. Also, fitting the leg prosthesis was more complicated.

The earlier promise, that I would not have to witness surgery, was kept. Our picture, both parts, dealt solely with the manufacture and the use of prostheses—but always, fearfully, the surgery and the agony were just offstage.

I spent most of my time in the Orthopedic Limb Shop. This consisted, first, of a vast reception room presided over by a cheerful Irish WAC who limped. Next to it, separated by a white curtain, was the tiny measuring room, and this opened into three rooms where the construction of the artificial limbs took place.

The process was efficient and undramatic. A patient who returned from overseas with his leg missing below the knee was treated and further operated upon at Lawson. In the old days, he would have waited a year or more for a limb fitting. Now, about ten weeks after final surgery, he was wheeled into the shop. Sometimes he swung in on crutches. If the shrinkage of his stump had been uniform, and the nerves had lost their irritability, and the wound was soundly healed, he was ready. He was escorted into the tiny measuring room, and his stump placed on plain brown paper and carefully traced. Too, his good leg was traced and measured. Then he was brought into the plaster room and told to sit on a bench. His naked stump was exposed. A woolen stockinette was slipped tightly over it, plaster smeared around the stockinette, and when the cast had hardened, it was removed. The patient was also removed. From now on in, the process was out of his control.

In the shop, I met the enlisted men and civilians who manufactured the prostheses. They were a strange assortment. The boss of the plaster room, a sturdy ex-sergeant who introduced himself as *Mister* Chandler, looked like an impressive welterweight who might excel at infighting. He, for one, had been a commercial limb maker before the war. His aides were all converts. One had been a radio repairman. Another had been a garage mechanic. A bemustached corporal from Long Island had been a subway dispatcher.

In brief days, the prosthesis grew. Out of the original plaster cast came a plaster facsimile of the patient's stump. Around this plaster stump, layers of wet hide were glued. This, eventually, would be attached to the artificial leg. Elsewhere, in the shop, other items were being assembled. A willow wood foot, shaped to fit the patient's shoe size, and built so that it would bend on a rubber hinge at the ball. The willow foot was then attached to the bottom of a fiber artificial leg, usually prefabricated, and the socket to the top of that leg. A leather lacer, to hold the prosthesis to the patient's stump, and a special pelvic belt, to hold the whole mechanism to his body, were added.

The final product was always carefully aligned and fitted on the patient. The slightest irritation would send the prosthesis back through the assembly line.

When I saw my first prosthesis up close (it was a complex one built for an AK, above-knee amp), I asked, perhaps naïvely, if the men, well, went to bed wearing these limbs. The limb mechanic appeared startled, then said no, they took them off first, then understood why I inquired and added that they really weren't much trouble to take off and put on because you simply unbuckled the pelvic belt and slid out and into bed.

In New York, I had heard much criticism of these prostheses, but the only time at Lawson that their inadequacy was referred to in my presence, I brought it up. I mentioned to the colonel, as we were leaving the hospital one afternoon, that I had read a magazine article by that young Bolte who had lost a leg at El Alamein, in which he insisted that injured veterans were not getting the artificial limbs they deserved. I told the colonel that Bolte had charged that Army prostheses were too heavy, too fragile, too noisy, too crude. "It was quite an article," I said.

The colonel said nothing. He strode along beside me for about a half minute as if he hadn't heard, then he spoke. "Was it terrifying?"

I said, "No. Intelligent."

He lapsed into silence, and the subject was never introduced again, nor did I attempt to bring it up, nor did I hear anything more about it from anyone else at Lawson.

The second part of our motion picture, on the construction and use of upper extremity prostheses, was comparatively simple. The patient who had lost his arm just below the elbow, for example, knelt down before a table, placed both his stump and his good arm on brown paper, and tracings were made. From these tracings an arm cuff, leather bucket for the stump, a steel frame and joints, and a hook, were assembled and fitted. The final limb usually weighed about two and a half pounds.

My mentor, in the upper extremity department, was a thin, factual sergeant named Lukasch. He had been in the shop for thirty-seven months and he was tired. "Before comin' here," he told me, "I never saw a prosthesis. I was a metal patternmaker. Lookit me now." He meant that I should look at the long, gray ledger he pulled off the shelf and opened. He had supervised the first artificial arm made at Lawson, and the birth was in the ledger. The patient's name. The date, June, 1943. Lukasch flipped the pages. Each was filled, top to bottom, both sides, with names and dates. Lukasch slapped the ledger shut. "Seven hundred arms since I been here," he said. "That's a helluva lot of arms."

When a patient acquired an arm from Lukasch, he took it through the maze of drafty corridors to a department called "Occupational Therapy." This was three large rooms, rigged up for the most like an advanced kindergarten, and inhabited by a number of intense she-therapists dressed like nurses and some plump Gray Ladies who hovered in the background. In this department, for fourteen consecutive days, the amputee learned to live with his arm and master it.

A small, pert, brunette therapist, a good-looker from Minnesota named Miss Beardsley, eagerly guided me about and supplied the commentary. "Our job is to train the arm amp to use his prosthesis adequately," she said with a professional air. She had a wonderfully indignant quality about her. She would show small patience for an amp who pitied himself. And she would tear you apart if you did not appreciate what those boys had been through. I liked her very much.

When I looked, I could see that she was wearing an engagement ring. I thought about the type of fellow she might marry. I thought not a soldier. Then I thought yes, a soldier. An intelligent soldier who is also an amp. But I did not ask her.

She marched me over to a table. On it lay a checkerboard, with checkers that appeared to have been designed by a drunk. The checkers were as impossible as a chess set with elephantiasis. Miss Beardsley said that this was called graded checkers, and that all arm patients had to play it because the game taught them to open and close their hooks. Miss

Beardsley led me from item to item, explaining that arm patients had to learn to do everything with their hooks—to drive a car and change a tire, to dress and garden and handle a can opener, to manipulate safety pins and scissors and machinery.

I inquired if there was some activity the men participated in as a group, something we might film that would show the awkwardness of the amps without their prostheses and then their skill using their prostheses. She said yes, there was one activity—poker. "That'll make your point on the screen. They shuffle cards quite well with their hooks. Without the hooks—well, it takes two of them working together to shuffle the deck each time."

Since the prostheses were so valuable, I asked how the men themselves felt about them. Miss Beardsley wrinkled her nose. "They hate to strap on those arms," she said. "They say it's like a saddle on a filly, like a girdle on a girl. Lots of them throw their limbs away when they leave here, but they're foolish, because the limbs are helpful." I ventured that perhaps the men hated the hooks just as sailors hated those monkey suits. She said that was so, that lots of the boys discarded their hooks when they left Lawson and replaced them with cosmetic hands, which were prettier, but valueless. "The hook is functional," she said. "The boys must learn to accept it themselves, and then, even though it's ugly, they can make others accept it." I asked if there were many married men worrying about the hooks and their wives' reactions. Miss Beardsley became indignant. "Of course there are married men and of course their wives don't mind!" She pulled back the arrow and let fly. "Why, I'm marrying one of our amps in the spring!" Her amp had been a sergeant and now he was with his parents in Chicago and would be back to take her away from all this. I was happy for her. For him, too.

Miss Beardsley told me how the arm amps graduated. "On the fourteenth day, the patient is given a proficiency test. Sort of an obstacle course. The patient goes into that little room over there, by himself, and in thirty minutes he must finish each of these fourteen tasks. One of us watches him, from time to time, through a peephole. If he makes it, he graduates. He is a civilian."

She showed me the test. It was at once pathetic and Herculean. It read:

"Proficiency Test Requirements. Check each item as you complete it. The test must be completed in thirty minutes. . . . Close and lock door. Sharpen pencil. Cut meat. Butter bread. Turn on faucet. Fill glass with water. Tie tie. Wrap package. Answer phone. Put watch on wrist. . . ."

When I was leaving I saw on the bulletin board clippings of famous one-armed athletes who had lectured at Lawson. I asked if they helped morale. Miss Beardsley said no, not if they were injured in World War

I. The patients were bored with accomplishments of World War I amputees. The patients said to each other, "Hell, he's had more than twenty years to learn. Wait'll you see me after twenty years." But the amps of this war, who were already proficient, were real morale builders. One officer, who had lost both arms but now used prostheses successfully, had been brought back three times to lecture.

As much as I wanted to, in my period at Lawson, I could not avoid the amps themselves. Particularly, the legless. Wherever I went, there they were. They swarmed through the corridors, every afternoon—men in wheelchairs, bandaged stumps protruding, wheeled by members of Lawson's permanent enlisted company; or men in wheelchairs piloting themselves with amazing speed. You would go into an office, and an amp would be stretched on a table, waiting. You would walk outdoors, and an amp, already fitted, would come bobbling toward you. You would go to the PX.

The PX was the hardest to take. Every early afternoon I went down the corridor, off Ward 10A, and into the Exchange. There they would be, jammed wheelchair to wheelchair, and crutch to crutch, gathered mostly about the women's jewelry case or the smoking counters. Together, in groups, they were raucous, cheerful, profane. Together, they would scream at each other and shout wisecracks. I remember one enlisted man floundering into the PX, afraid to step on his new prosthesis, and a fat patient beside me screaming at him, "Come on, Tom, tell that leg who's boss!"

When the men were alone, I heard, it was different. Many became depressives, even serious paranoids, suffering from self-pity. Not only the endless hospitalization, a calvary, not only the maddening monotony of hours and days and bandages, punctuated with pain, but the knowledge that the limb is gone, plain goddamit gone, and no power in heaven or on earth can ever, ever in a whole lifetime, put the flesh and the bone back in that empty space.

The colonel himself was aware of the amps' psychological problems. In preparing research for our script, one day he dictated the following to me: "In the early functional use of a prosthesis, the fabric is the least important factor. More important are proper alignment and fitting . . . and even above the limb itself, in importance, stands the patient, the individual user. Upon the patient's stamina, perseverance, upon his high integrity and his will, depends his early use of the well-fitted prosthesis and his return to normal and gainful living." The colonel asked me to read it back to him. I read it back. He said, "Uh, that last phrase, change that last phrase to read 'and his return to *relative* normal and gainful living.' "

My very lowest moment with the amps occurred at the PX the afternoon I wandered in to buy a pair of short socks. I wanted a heavy pair, size twelve, light brown. The girl behind the counter said they had lots of everything except socks. I griped. But she was busy, so she said simply and as a fact, "Sarge, we just don't have as much call for socks in this PX as for other things."

Living among the amps became a horrible embarrassment to me, and with each day and each contact my misery gnawed deeper. Always before, when people wanted to know what I did in the Army, I was proud to say that I was a writer, writing propaganda and orientation and training films. I felt that this being a writer, proclaiming it, made me retain my civilian standing, my special high-level individuality. It was defensive evidence that I was not of the stupid herd, I was no part of the blurred GI image. It was my reaction to being pushed around and downgraded for three years and three months.

Now, suddenly, among the amps, I was thoroughly ashamed and miserable. I was ashamed of everything, of how far I'd been from combat, of the amount of secondhand reporting converted into celluloid I'd contributed. Most of all, I was ashamed of my legs.

My legs felt fat and luxurious when I walked on them, and I kept knowing the amps were looking at them and resenting them.

I was glad when it was over.

The train was fast going back. When I arrived at Pennsylvania Station, it was late in the evening but still there were people clustered, waiting. I rode up on the escalator, and strode through the row of shops, and outside. It was snowing, light flakes swirling around and down, and I could see the pavement was glassy. I stood a while, watching people going and coming. People hurrying home for warmth and dryness and dinner and talk.

I decided to walk up to Sixth Avenue and then to my hotel. Suddenly, in the snow and cold, the two weeks past seemed impossible, isolated like a half-forgotten event among creatures of a night's dream in a hidden valley. Here there was life, and whole people were moving, talking, rustling newspapers, laughing loudly in groups. I began moving, too, and I shivered a little in the cold. I walked faster and faster, and did not slip, even though it was slippery. Nobody was looking at my legs.

WHAT HAS HAPPENED SINCE . . .

"The Amps" was a record I wrote primarily for myself, begun in Atlanta and finished in New York City, of my last assignment as an enlisted man in the United States Army.

Of my three years and four months in the service, I spent one year in the Army Air Force writing training films, and after a transfer, the remaining period was spent in the Army Signal Corps writing orientation and propaganda films for our troops. Despite my efforts to become an overseas correspondent for *Yank*, the weekly periodical for all the services, I was never near the smoke of battle. The closest I came to combat was a credit dispute over an orientation film, waged with my superior officer, the renowned but exasperating Colonel Frank Capra.

While stationed in Los Angeles, I had done the major writing job on *Know Your Enemy Japan*, and Colonel Capra, in submitting the list of credits to Washington, D.C., omitted my name completely, giving full credit instead to several well-known civilian writers who had played only a small role in the backbreaking policy effort. There was no appeal—nor should there have been, considering what other young men had done for their country without credit. But it was irritatingly amusing to know how Hollywood standards carried over into the Army, where most of my group—including such co-workers as Captain John Huston and Colonel Theodore Geisel—lived a schizoid existence, half the time playing soldier, and half the time playing Hollywood producer or director or screenplay writer. For many of us, too, it was a schizoid existence in another way. Every day, we reported for roll call, in uniform, at a motion picture studio leased by the Army Signal Corps. There, we wrote narration for propaganda films telling our men why they were fighting and how to survive—or for what cause they might die—and then we went back to our cozy but uneasy homes at night (since there were no barracks on the post) to live as Hollywood civilians in uniform, deeply resentful of the real civilians all around us who were going merrily ahead making civilian money and who were free of the restrictions of army life. And yet all of us felt guilty about the real soldiers far away, who were suffering and dying on Iwo Jima or at Anzio, and who were unlikely to be helped one damn bit by our films.

Finally, our post in Hollywood closed down, and with intense relief I learned that I was being transferred elsewhere. On November 8, 1945, I was transferred to the Signal Corps Photographic Center on Long Island, New York, but this was little better—for on this post, which was another reconverted motion picture studio, there had been or were still such officers and fellow enlisted men as William Saroyan, Irwin Shaw, John Cheever, Stanley Kramer, Gottfried Reinhardt, Carl Laemmle, Jr., to name but a few.

In those last three months of my army career, since again there were no accommodations on the post, I lived at the Royalton Hotel on 44th Street in Manhattan. Every night, when I returned by subway from my Long Island post to the Royalton Hotel, I entered into a remarkable world. George Jean Nathan had a suite on one floor. Robert Benchley had a suite on another. And just before I left for Atlanta, Thomas Wolfe's aged mother Julia (the Eliza Gant of *Look Homeward, Angel*) registered at the hotel. I met her one evening in the lobby, introducing myself with great diffidence as "a writer" and "an admirer" of her son, and after that she talked on and on about Tom, as if he were alive and about to call for her, although he had been dead seven years. She had some unproduced and unpublished plays her Tom had written, and she was in New York hoping to arrange for either production or publication of them.

I was eager to know Julia Wolfe better—there was even stirring within me, based on her lonely visit to New York, an idea for a novel—but it was not to be. My soldier-writer existence suddenly submerged my civilian-writer existence. The Army Signal Corps ordered me to Atlanta for what was to be, although I did not know it then, my last assignment, before my discharge in February of 1946. I was ordered to proceed to Atlanta to work with a colonel from St. Louis at Lawson General Hospital on a film project to be called *Construction and Use of Provisional Prostheses*.

Altogether, I was in Atlanta for fourteen days. What the Army got out of my visit was a training film, which I wrote during my last two weeks in the service. What I got out of my assignment was the experience recounted in "The Amps," a memoir which I wrote for myself. Long after, when I came to write my novel *The Prize*, and I sought a locale for the story of Professor Max Stratman and his bruised niece, Emily, my memories of the patients' traumas at Lawson General Hospital came back to me, and I placed Stratman and Emily in Atlanta and at Lawson General Hospital.

What I lost, because of this assignment, was a chance to get to know Thomas Wolfe's mother better, and perhaps to develop a novel that might have been based on her. For when I returned to the Royalton Hotel, I learned that shortly after I had gone to Atlanta she had moved across the street to the Algonquin Hotel, and there, a few days before my return, she had died. Julia Wolfe was gone. Only Eliza Gant survived. It would be futile to attempt to show how well she had survived after "Eugene Gant's" death—when I could no longer really know.

Except for one day in 1961 when I reviewed my Atlanta experiences briefly in preparing *The Prize*, I did not reread "The Amps" until I decided to include it in this collection. Since rereading it, I have wondered what my colonel in the Orthopedic Surgery Building, then late thirtyish, now late fiftyish, had done with himself in the two decades since we had worked together. Had he remained in the service? Had he gone into private practice in St. Louis? Was he still involved with amps? It is unlikely I shall ever know, for I could not remember his name. What had happened to the Thing in the glass container in his office? Or to the triple amputee who had been a Georgia University football end? Or to those of the nation's fifteen thousand amps who were patients in Atlanta when I was there? I do not know the answers. I made no effort to learn them. I did not have the nerve.

All that I made an effort to find out, and all that I did learn, was that the Lawson General Hospital which I had seen I would never see again. The medical director of the Veterans Administration in Atlanta replied to my recent inquiry: "The Lawson General Hospital, as Mr. Wallace may have known it in 1945, has ceased to exist as a VA medical facility since 1951. In its stead, the Atlanta VA Hospital was established as a general medical and surgical facility, currently operating approximately three hundred beds for many types of acutely ill VA patients. Although amputees are often a small part of its patient population and a few prostheses are issued, it no longer remains or specializes as an amputee center."

And finally, I determined to find out what happened to the film I wrote for the Signal Corps after Atlanta, the film called *Construction and Use of Provisional Prostheses*. I do not mean that I was interested in finding out what happened to the reels of celluloid, but rather in learning what had happened in the twenty years since, to the subject I had written about—the development of artificial limbs. Had there been any progress? Had there been any major changes? Were the amputees I had known and observed, or their sons or neighbors' sons who had lost limbs in Korea and Viet Nam, any better off today (in terms of receiving an artificial limb for a real limb taken away) than their fathers were at the end of the Second World War?

Apparently, for the amps who survived the Second World War, peace was somewhat less than wonderful. Most of them "displayed keen disappointment with the artificial limbs provided them," admits A. Bennett Wilson, Jr., a member of the Committee on Prosthetics Research and Development. And then he adds, "Since they were now all familiar with extremely intricate mechanical, electrical, and hydraulic mechanisms, it was incomprehensible to them that a country so adept at turning out efficient weapons of destruction had seemed to have failed so miserably in providing substitutes for limbs lost in battle."

As a result of this disappointment felt by disabled veterans and their sympathetic physicians, severe pressure was exerted upon the military, and upon Congress, to step up a scientific program of prosthetics research. Through the Surgeon General of the Army, the National Academy of Sciences (a nonprofit organization of scientists established by Abraham Lincoln) and its National Research Council (established by Woodrow Wilson) were brought into the picture. Between 1947 and 1964, work on improving artificial limbs was vastly accelerated. By 1961, there were thirty-three "separate groups engaged in some phase of research and development related to artificial limbs." There was also a committee, with its own laboratory, that examined and evaluated new prosthetic inventions. There was even a government journal called *Artificial Limbs*.

What has been accomplished? For one thing, it appears that the hook device that served to replace a human hand has been gradually replaced by a molded rubber hand of five fingers, with three movable fingers made of aluminum and steel covered by felt. While scientists agreed that the hook device was "more functional," they also knew that the amps found it "distasteful," and they abandoned the hook in order to bolster morale.

But scientists feel that real hope for the amps lies in another direction. According to Mr. Wilson, himself an engineer: "It has long been recognized that prostheses powered by some form of energy other than from human body sources (external power) would represent the next major advance in upper-extremity prosthetics."

How advanced is "the next major advance"?

In the United States, International Business Machines had, by 1952, produced electrically powered artificial arms. Although they worked, they were rejected by the government because "the wearer was unable to operate the device without conscious thought." Since then, there has been much optimism about applying the miniature components used in guided missiles to artificial limbs, while at the same time attempting "to develop or uncover sources of body power for control of the powered units."

In Germany, at the Orthopedic Clinic in Heidelberg, an artificial arm powered by compressed gas has been developed. Brought to the United States, and modified somewhat, it was tried on 150 American amps, and of these 148 were able to use it successfully while two were not. The shortcomings of this compressed-gas arm, according to American researchers, are a "problem" sensory feedback and the fact that gas does not store as efficiently as electricity. Its virtue is that the actuators for compressed gas are lighter than those for electricity.

In Soviet Russia, there has been considerable drumbeating for an electrically powered arm of Russian design. In 1960, Dr. J. B. Reswick saw this arm in operation in Moscow. He reported to his colleagues in America that the Russians refused to reveal how the device worked, but "hinted at electromyographic control." Unable to obtain interviews with Soviet scientists, or learn more, Dr. Reswick suspected that "the device does not meet the claims made."

Perhaps the most promising artificial limb produced abroad is the so-called "Vaduz hand," an electrically powered artificial hand developed at a private limb shop in France, and manufactured in Vaduz, the capital of the Lilliput kingdom of Liechtenstein, adjacent to Switzerland. According to American scientists, the opening and closing of this hand "is controlled by muscle contraction against an air-filled plastic bladder. Feedback is provided by a force-reflecting servo. . . ." While American scientists believe that it possesses many praiseworthy features, especially its sensory feedback system, they do not feel it is ready for widespread usage because of "its complexity, apparent frailty, and limited application."

The hope for the future, the experts seem to indicate, is an electrically powered artificial limb, since electricity is most likely to integrate well with the human nervous system.

Reflecting on all of this, so many years after my visit to Atlanta, I find that I can only come to the most banal of conclusions: That there can be no satisfactory substitute for what man's mad wars take away from man, and that the only advance that will ever be meaningful to amps and potential amps will be a means of ending international violence forever.

It is this memorial that the amps deserve the most: In some near future day, standing on some high civilian bookcase, a square glass container filled with yellow fluid in which floats a repulsive object—an artificial limb, once known as a "prosthesis," a relic of an ignorant and primitive age, now no longer needed, now obsolete.

» 4 «

SAINT DETECTIVE

ON A BRISK December morning in 1946, a tall young American priest
named Father Eric O'Brien hurried through the narrow streets of
Seville toward the historic library known as the Archives of the Indies.

That morning, as on twenty-five previous mornings, Father O'Brien
was joined by his scholarly associate Father Maynard Geiger. Together
they entered the library, where Father O'Brien filled out the necessary
library slip. "Today, Señor," he told a Spanish attendant, "we wish to see
all the documents recording sailings from Spain to the New World in
1749."

The attendant disappeared into a room containing a small portion of
the 50,000 bundles of original, rare documents in the Archives of the Indies. Father O'Brien waited anxiously. After spending five consecutive
years relentlessly hunting down information on one man, Father O'Brien
was on the verge of solving a historical mystery by learning, for the first
time, from a holograph description written when he was alive, what that
man looked like.

Waiting, Father O'Brien recalled the clues leading up to this moment. He knew, first, that his subject had, in September of 1749, sailed
from Cadiz, on a ship named the *Villasota*, for Veracruz, Mexico. He
knew that, since there were no passports in those days, all travelers to the
New World were required to clear themselves through a government
agency in Seville called *Casa de Contratación*. This agency required
each traveler to state his name, occupation, business. These facts were
recorded along with the individual's physical description. The question
in Father O'Brien's mind was: Had his man, his subject, been so registered? If yes, then would his man's description be included?

86

When the bundle of precious documents arrived, Father O'Brien hastily untied it. With mounting excitement, he scanned and turned the stiff pages. Nothing, nothing . . . and then, suddenly, leaping out at him over a bridge of almost two hundred years, the name, and for the first time, in ink turned brown on paper turned yellow, an authentic description:

> JUNÍPERO SERRA, padre, almost 36 years old, of
> medium height, swarthy complexion, with black hair
> and eyes, and a sparse growth of beard.

Father O'Brien and his associate could hardly contain their pleasure. As soon as possible, they recorded the information on microfilm. It was one more powerful link in their chain of evidence.

On this day, after seven years on the trail of a man who died 164 years ago, after separate journeys ranging across California, Mexico, Portugal, Spain, Mallorca, and Italy, after 20,000 miles in airplanes and two weeks on muleback, after consulting Franciscan friars and university scholars throughout the world, Father Eric O'Brien had 8,500 pages of material to prove that a priestly predecessor and a pioneer of the American Far West, Father Junípero Serra, was a man who deserved to be a saint of the Catholic Church.

No one knows precisely how many saints there are in the Catholic Church, although one authority estimates twenty-five thousand. To this number, the Vatican is always prepared to add another, but admittance is not easy. An incredible ecclesiastical obstacle course stands in the way. "Sainthood is the climax of what has been well called the most complicated legal procedure in the world," says Father O'Brien. "The day of sainthood, with all its pomp, may mark the end of centuries of research."

Any Catholic group anywhere can nominate any person, dead one thousand years or dead one year, for sainthood. But such nomination is a waste of time unless the sponsors are fairly certain that their candidate can fulfill the three major requirements of sainthood—the deceased must have been a person of not merely ordinary virtues but of heroic virtues; the deceased must leave behind an extraordinary reputation or tradition for sanctity; the deceased shall have been gifted during his life or after his death with the power to work miracles.

If a candidate seems to measure up to these standards, his name is submitted to the Postulator General of the proper Catholic order in Rome. The Postulator General in turn appoints an expert, always a priest already residing in the vicinity where the candidate's work was done, to investigate further. This expert becomes Vice-Postulator for this evaluation and functions much like a private sleuth—in this case, a Saint Detective. Upon the clues and facts he digs up, depends the elevation of his candidate to sainthood.

When in 1941, the day before Pearl Harbor, Father O'Brien, the son of an Irish carpenter, was selected as the expert to investigate the case— or the Cause, as the Church prefers to call it—of Father Junípero Serra, he was faced with a job of detecting beside which the manhunts of the Pinkertons and the Schindlers paled. Ordinary detectives, working in an age of photographs and fingerprints, find it difficult to investigate the private lives of persons missing a day, a week, or maybe a year. Father O'Brien, by contrast, was assigned to shadow a man who had been dead a century and a half, and to prove this man, first, a human being of extraordinary virtue so that he might later prove him a saint.

In spite of the seven years' preliminary research already done by predecessors, Father O'Brien took another seven years to complete his case. That is relatively rapid. It took twenty-five years to make Mother Cabrini the first United States citizen saint. And down in Guatemala, a nominee for sainthood for two centuries is still being investigated. But Father O'Brien was able to do so thorough a job in his seven years of hunting down a legend and of bringing blurred history into focus, that today, in a special Catholic court in Fresno, California, churchmen are sufficiently equipped with facts to enable them to pass judgment on a candidate who died in August of 1784.

It all began in 1934, when the Franciscan Fathers in California decided that Father Junípero Serra was worthy of sainthood and proposed his name to the Postulator of their order in Rome. There were many who wondered then—as many must puzzle now—why Father Serra's name was proposed at all. What difference whether he became a saint? Once, in a sermon, Father O'Brien posed the question and answered it: "Why should we ask to have this man declared a saint? For God, there is the added glory of our homage to His faithful servant. For Padre Serra, there is the recognition that he shunned on earth. For us, the gain is great indeed. The Church can point him out as a guide whom we can safely follow on the road to Heaven."

When the proposal was originally made, the superficial facts known about Father Serra seemed to make him a natural choice for canonization. He was born Miguel José Serra, in November, 1713, in the village of Petra on the tiny Mediterranean island of Mallorca, or Majorca. This island today may be reached by overnight boat from Valencia, Spain, or by an hour's flight from Barcelona. At the age of seventeen, inspired by his reading of martyred missionaries in the New World, Serra took his vows in the seaport town of Palma. As is the custom, he also dropped his first name, taking in its place Junípero.

His first job was to teach Scotistic philosophy at the Lullian university on Mallorca. One day, after seven years at the university, Junípero Serra was approached by a former student, Father Francisco Palou, who wanted advice about becoming a missionary to New Spain—that is, to Mexico—where four thousand Franciscans were already at work liquidating native deities. Instead of offering advice, Serra offered to accompany Palou.

The journey from Mallorca to Cadiz to Mexico took Junípero Serra and Francisco Palou ninety-nine days. They arrived in Veracruz on December 6, 1749. Rather than ride horseback to Mexico City, Father Serra decided to emulate St. Francis and make the journey on foot. (Recently, after retracing Serra's journey but traveling by automobile, Father O'Brien admitted that the heat and mountains wore him out.) Father Serra's hike required twenty-six days. His legs not only became a mass of open sores from insect bites, but were swollen from sheer fatigue. One foot and ankle became ulcerated, and pain from this affliction plagued him the rest of his life.

In Mexico City, Father Serra attended San Fernando College, a Franciscan school for newcomers, where he learned a number of Indian dialects and more of missionary technique. After five months, he was sent with Palou to the Sierra Gorda Mountains, in Central Mexico, there to manage five missions established for the savage Pame Indians. It was one of the toughest posts in the New World. The climate was hot, damp, completely unhealthy.

Father Serra learned the difficult Pame language, and then he used it tirelessly to bring the natives into the Catholic Church. In nine years, Serra's job was done. There was not an unconverted Indian in the region.

After eight more years of crisscrossing Mexico for Christ, Father Serra, at the mellowing age of fifty-four, received his most important assignment, the job of managing thirteen missions in Baja California. He began his assignment by walking 1,000 miles in six months to inspect his Lower California missions. Soon he moved farther north into what is today the state of California. Here the prospects were discouraging. The Indians, unclothed, eating rodents and snakes, practicing polygamy, dwelling in filthy brushwood huts, believed in demons and played at war. In his first year at San Diego, Serra failed to convert a single Indian. But he was accomplishing much else. By 1769—the very year Daniel Boone on the other side of America was poking about Kentucky—Serra had founded the Mission of San Diego de Alcalá. Four years later, to obtain further funds from his superiors, he sailed from San Diego to San Blas. He then walked the rest of the distance to Mexico City and all the way back to San Diego, 2,400 miles, on sandaled feet. Five times, although racked by illness, he hiked from San Diego to Monterey, the last time when he was seventy years old.

In his fifteen years in California, hobbling thousands of miles on a crippled leg (thirty-five hundred miles in five round trips between San Diego and San Francisco alone), dealing with hostile Indians and officious governors, Serra was able to give California nine great missions and six thousand converts—a masterpiece of material and spiritual architecture that swelled, within a half century, to a chain of twenty-one missions and eighty thousand converts. He died in Carmel the afternoon of August 28, 1784, aged seventy-one. His worn body reposed on a bed of two planks, and to the end he called himself "the tepid, wicked, and useless servant of God."

These were the bare facts readily available on the candidate for sainthood. They were sufficient to convince the Postulator General of the Franciscan Order in Rome, Father Fortunato Scipioni, that Junípero Serra was worth investigating further. In 1934, Reverend Augustine Hobrecht, a California historian, was appointed to do the preliminary work, but Hobrecht was so swamped with other Church duties that he could not devote full time to the task. The Church decided to appoint someone else.

"When the Postulator General in Rome needed a new deputy," says Father O'Brien, "he asked the Provincial Superior in California to suggest someone who had studied Padre Serra's life as well as early California history. Since the work involves a great deal of time and travel, it is customary to choose a young man for the task. There were about forty thousand priests in the United States in 1941, but only seven of them had been assigned to this kind of work."

On December 6, 1941, Father Eric O'Brien, a handsome Franciscan friar, then twenty-nine years old, became the eighth.

Father O'Brien, a solid six-footer who looks like a Notre Dame halfback, was well qualified for his assignment. His Irish, Iowa-born father had migrated to California to work as cattle rancher and then carpenter. O'Brien was born in Pomona, in 1912, the youngest of nine children. Upon finishing grammar school in Los Angeles, O'Brien heard the call, and felt that he had a vocation. After four high school and two college years in St. Anthony's Seminary in Santa Barbara, and a year as a novice in the monastery at San Luis Rey, he took his vows. He now spent three years studying subjects as diverse as psychology and Hebrew, then four more years in the major seminary at Santa Barbara Mission concentrating on theology and the Scriptures, offering the Mass and other church rituals.

Father O'Brien's first assignment as a priest, in 1939, was to return to

St. Anthony's Seminary to teach Greek, Latin, and English literature. He did this for two years, until 1941, when he was appointed Vice-Postulator in the Cause of Father Junípero Serra.

Father O'Brien's first task as a Saint Detective was to prove that Junípero Serra was not only a holy Catholic, not only an extraordinarily holy Catholic, for there are many of these, but that Serra was a Catholic of heroic virtue who deserved to be held up to the entire Church as a model for imitation. Every movement of Serra's life had to be examined, and his record had to be proved spotless, if he was even to be considered for sainthood.

Father O'Brien began by doing more reading about Serra. The best source was a biography written in Spanish by Serra's close friend and onetime student, Francisco Palou. Printed in a small edition in Mexico City during 1787, three years after Serra's death, the volume was crowded with examples of Serra's fortitude and courage. There was the incident when Indians stormed Serra's San Diego camp, and he prayed none of them would be killed and thus lost for baptism. There was the time when, at Mass in a Mexican village, the wine was poisoned and Serra was carried from the altar (although modern scholars question this incident, since priests are not supposed to sip the wine, but merely lift the cup symbolically). There was the occasion when, on a ship to the New World, he argued religion with the ship's captain, an English Protestant, and though almost thrown overboard, Serra refused to accept the other's unphilosophical arguments.

There were, of course, almost endless other sources for Father O'Brien to read. The forty-thousand-book library in the Santa Barbara Mission was only his kindergarten. During the seven years following, Father O'Brien's reading ranged from an original packet of Serra's letters deposited by Serra's nephew in Barcelona in 1789 to dozens of books in the library of the Sacred Congregation for the Propagation of the Faith in Vatican City, to items on Serra in fifty-eight libraries throughout Mexico and the United States. Everything interesting or pertinent that Father O'Brien found in these books and documents, he copied or photographed on 35-mm microfilm which he later enlarged to legal-size prints.

When he and his associates finished their reading, in the summer of 1948, Father O'Brien had notes or photocopies of research amounting to 8,500 pages of material. To hunt down the original manuscripts that would authenticate this material, and even more important, to verify earlier stories firsthand, Father O'Brien made four separate trips to Mexico, and countless journeys up and down the California coast, as well as visits to Portugal, Spain, Mallorca, and Italy. Wherever, on the face of the earth, Father Junípero Serra had lived, worked, walked, two hundred years ago, there Father Eric O'Brien tried to live, work, walk today. In this way, every vague page in Serra's life was explored on the scene.

Father O'Brien spent the greatest amount of his time away from home in Mexico, a country in which he encountered his greatest difficulties but for which he developed an intense love. While he never ran into physical danger in Mexico, despite the fact that it is an anticlerical country, he did have bad moments. It is against the law in Mexico to wear clerical clothes in public, so at the Mexican border Father O'Brien took off his Roman collar. "It was kind of fun to wear a necktie again," he says. He went about in a black suit, just like the ones worn by most Mexican attorneys and physicians.

One of the least documented periods in Serra's long life was the nine years in the 1750's that he spent as a missionary in the Sierra Gorda Mountains of Central Mexico. "There were questions I had to answer, to make our case foolproof in court," says Father O'Brien. "Did anything remain there of Serra's work? What had become of the churches he built there? Were there any of his writings left? Did the people still cherish his memory? The investigation would never be complete without those answers. There were stories of robberies, murders, wild animals, poisonous snakes, diseases, bad climate. Besides, I'd not heard of a white man who had been in there since Serra. The trip was obligatory. In February, 1946, with the help of Governor Warren of California, I got special letters of recommendation from President Camacho of Mexico to the governors of the Mexican states in which I planned to work, and then I went into the Sierra Gorda."

Accompanied by Father Hugh Noonan, an army chaplain who took leave from his Puerto Rican post, Father O'Brien boarded a train from San Luis Potosí to Río Verde, the northernmost part of Father Serra's old stamping grounds. Entering their first village at dusk, the padres rode in a two-wheeled sulky, their feet up against the horse's rump, instead of in a taxi. "We rode between the pink, blue and green houses, built flush up to the street, into an eddying dusty fog, through which the tiny Japanese bulbs used for streetlights glimmered," recalls Father O'Brien. "At corners, since he had no horn, our sulky driver stuck his whip handle into the wheel spokes, creating a rattling warning noise. Long before, the old church in town had lost its Serra documents. The papers had been burned by revolutionaries. So, the next day, by station wagon, over the worst excuse for a road I ever saw, we went on to Jalpán, known as Xalpam in Serra's time, a village which had been his headquarters."

At Jalpán, which had electric lights but no telephone, telegraph, or radio, Father O'Brien found courteous natives dwelling in one-room huts of brushwood, their roofs made of palm leaves, their floors consisting of dirt. Here Father O'Brien found the largest of Serra's original five missions, with its cross-shaped Church of Santiago de Jalpán. While there was little in the church archives, Father O'Brien discovered what he believed might be a two-century-old original oil portrait of Father Serra.

"There is no title, signature or date," Father O'Brien wrote in his notes, "but the painting is very old. It shows a padre standing alone, holding a large cross. The face is youthful—Padre Serra was only thirty-six when he came to Jalpán. But there is one mystery—the padre in this painting is wearing blue, and anyone familiar with Serra's letters will recall how particular he was that Franciscan pictures for his churches show the saints as robed in gray. St. Francis of Assisi wore gray, and so did most of his followers."

The blue robe in the Jalpán painting, on a man known to have favored gray, made the whole thing seem suspect. Father O'Brien was stymied until many months later when a Serra specialist on the isle of Mallorca explained the enigmatic blue and solved the mystery in a letter to O'Brien: "Blue was the color of the habit of Mallorcan Franciscans. Blue is still worn by the Franciscan Sisters in Mallorca. This is said to have been a papal privilege, granted to the Mallorcan Franciscans, because of their devotion to the Blessed Virgin Mary."

Working out of Jalpán, Father O'Brien and Father Noonan went into the more primitive sections of the Sierra Gorda. All travel was on muleback, just as all distances were judged not by miles or kilometers but by the time it took a mule to make its way from village to village. Father O'Brien had not been on a mule in fourteen years, and the insides of his legs were bruised and painful.

The two American priests traveled over lonely trails, over steep mountains, and one night in a slashing rain they slept inside the best home in the village of Saucillo. "I'll never forget that night," says Father O'Brien. "One room filled with devotional pictures and a Singer sewing machine. Sugar-cane-frond roof, the wind howling through. Candlelight. The usual dirt floor. I tried to sleep on a bed made of rawhide strips. It was like sleeping on an oversized tennis racket. And the fleas, they had never read that DDT was supposed to be fatal."

Father O'Brien found the short, olive-skinned, Spanish-speaking natives of the Sierra Gorda courteous and considerate. With the aid of these natives, and a guide named Primitivo ("We paid him a dollar a day, which created inflation in the Sierra Gorda"), Father O'Brien located and photographed precious Serra documents, found the remains of an aqueduct Serra had built, and then visited and inspected each of the five missions constructed in the 1750's.

But if the journey to Mexico was Father O'Brien's most pleasant adventure in seven years of research, his stay inside Spain late in 1946, and his trip to Mallorca early in 1947, were his most productive. After an airplane crash in Ireland, which he survived without injury, Father O'Brien arrived in Madrid. There he lived at San Francisco el Grande, the city's largest church, which had been a Franciscan center in Serra's day.

Father O'Brien's introduction to Spain occurred when photographers representing the Madrid and Barcelona dailies crowded into his room to photograph him. No matter where he posed in the room, the photographers did not seem satisfied. They kept moving him from one wall to another, until he protested. Finally, satisfied, they shot their pictures of him. Not until later, when the pictures appeared, did Father O'Brien understand. The photographers had been attempting, and had finally succeeded, in posing him under a framed portrait of General Franco.

Father O'Brien, and his assistant, Father Maynard Geiger, head of the Serra Historical Commission in California, avoided Spanish political controversy. They found Madrid rather like Boston, while they themselves were the subject of much curiosity since *Siguiendo Mi Camino* had just finished a record twenty-week run—that was the film *Going My Way* with Bing Crosby. Between their work in Madrid and their research later in Seville (where they discovered the only written description of Father Serra extant) Father O'Brien and Father Geiger registered 2,000 pages of new material on microfilm.

The only difficulty Father O'Brien had concerning Spain occurred much later, when he agreed to deliver a lecture on his trip before the Newman Club in Santa Barbara, California. When the impending lecture was given wide publicity, Father O'Brien became apprehensive and, to be sure that he was not misquoted, had copies of his talk handed to the press.

"I have not come here to speak in favor of the Franco regime in Spain," Father O'Brien stated in his speech. "With a century of American ancestry, I love democracy as we have it, and I hate all forms of totalitarianism. . . . Some I met in Spain said that Franco was not a dictator, that the last dictator was Primo de Rivera. Others said that Franco was a dictator, but his usurpation of power was justified by the excesses committed under the Republic. Some said that while he came to power justifiably, he had long overstayed his welcome. Others said that he never had a right to power, has no right now, and never will have. . . . Because I am not a competent political observer; because I have been too taken up with my little study of one man's part in California history; and because I feel that my superficial observations of Spain would be of no real help to the indispensable need of today—international understanding—I beg to be excused from stating any such observations."

When the press, the morning following, completely twisted and misrepresented the speech, when certain reporters labeled him a Fascist, Father O'Brien vowed never to deliver another talk on the subject of Spain. And, to date, he has kept his vow.

From Valencia, Spain, Father O'Brien took a boat over the calm Mediterranean to Mallorca, the island where Father Serra was born, ordained, and where he taught until he left for the New World. Here most of the Serra documents were in the hands of private families rather than libraries. Father O'Brien had to locate these families. His most memorable experience was with an old Mallorcan marquis, who returned from his Madrid vacation to show O'Brien his eighteenth-century papers personally. "His home was unforgettable," says Father O'Brien. "One room, twice as high as our American rooms, was decorated with red damask hangings, gold-leafed mirrors, and original paintings by Goya. The room was seventy-five feet long. The living room had a pure silver charcoal heater in its center. The old marquis kept his Serra papers in the private family archives, and only he held the key. He brought down the aged documents from upstairs, then would not leave us alone, but sat stiffly across from us for hours, staring, while we took notes and made photographs."

However, the most valuable treasure was found at the Monastery of San Felipe Neri. For a long time Father O'Brien had known that as a professor at the Lullian university, Father Serra had delivered lectures on philosophy from the viewpoint of Duns Scotus. That was the clue. But for a Saint Detective, it was also a challenge. Where were those philosophy lectures? What were they about? Did they still exist? In Mallorca, Father O'Brien met priests who had found the old lecture notes, published in Latin, 1,160 pages of them, and at last he knew exactly what Father Serra had spoken about as a pedagogue.

Having proved, to his own satisfaction, that Father Serra's life had been both heroic and spotless, Father O'Brien had several other important items to investigate. He had to prove—and managed to do so—that Father Serra had never received unauthorized religious honors, such as being called St. Junípero by priests or being depicted with a halo. Next, he was required to exhume Father Serra's body and report on the findings.

Twice, since Serra's death in 1784, his grave at Carmel, California, had been opened, the last time in 1884, on the one-hundredth anniversary of his death, when a trainload of dignitaries came down from San Francisco to view the body. The third opening of Serra's grave was a long, detailed operation filled with much suspense for Father O'Brien. There were two other bodies, besides that of Serra, in separate coffins. The first was a friend from Mallorca, Fray Juan Crespi. The second was Serra's successor as *presidente* of the California Missions, Fray Fermín de Lasuén. Would Father O'Brien be able to identify one of the three as Junípero Serra? On the two other occasions when the grave had been opened, identification reports proved vague. Then there was another question mark. Was Serra in the grave at all? Historical gossip had it that the Spaniards, upon leaving California, stole Serra from his resting place by lantern light, and took him aboard a nearby ship, which was subsequently wrecked. A survivor was supposed to have recorded the incident in a stained leather-bound book. Father O'Brien tried to run down the book, and got as far as an Indian whose grandfather had been baptized by Serra. The Indian said that the book had been loaned out and lost.

On September 1, 1943, Father O'Brien, in the presence of two famous anthropologists, two United States Army orthopedists, and assorted members of the Catholic clergy, opened the grave and the coffins. While all principals were sworn to maintain complete secrecy, Father O'Brien admits absolute identification of Serra was made on the basis of some dozen arguments, some positive and others negative. The grave was kept open six days, the army took photographs for Father O'Brien, and finally Serra was returned to his rest in a new hermetically sealed copper casket.

Another question Father O'Brien had to answer was: What did people say about Father Serra before 1934, when his Cause was initiated? "This was important to our Cause," says Father O'Brien. "The Church will not consider any candidate for sainthood, unless it can be proved that during his lifetime and ever since his death, he enjoyed a reputation for holiness and miracles."

To establish Serra's reputation for holiness, Father O'Brien traveled California from top to bottom, for nine months in 1943 and 1944, interviewing members of the state's oldest families. Father O'Brien interviewed 151 native Californians, mostly Indian or Spanish, who had heard firsthand stories about Serra from members of their families. The oldest inhabitant Father O'Brien interviewed was a 104-year-old Indian lady in San Juan Bautista.

"The closest I ever came to Father Serra," recalls Father O'Brien, "was when I interviewed the ninety-year-old granddaughter of Señora Perez de Guillén de Mariner. The granddaughter, when I talked with her in 1943, remembered everything her grandmother Mariner had told her about Serra. Señora Mariner had once owned much of Pasadena and Altadena through Spanish land grants. She was born in Baja California. She came up to Father Serra's mission, was placed in charge of the mission keys as a girl, and got to know Father Serra quite well. Well, Señora Mariner lived on and on, long after Serra died. She married three times, and had a clear mind and a retentive memory even when she was over a hundred years old. She told her granddaughter many firsthand stories about Serra, and the granddaughter lived on to ninety and was able to relate them to me."

Others remembered stories passed down by great-grandparents of how Father Serra healed the sick merely by making the sign of the Cross, of how his words turned wildly charging bears away from cornered Indians, of how good crops resulted when prayers beseeched Father Serra to use his special influence with God.

Despite these verbal accounts of Serra's ability to create miracles, as well as accounts of his reputation for holiness and for virtue, Father O'Brien has today to face the last and perhaps most exacting phase of his research. He must present convincing evidence, scientific evidence, of six miracles wrought by Serra since his death.

Exactly what does the Church call a miracle? "A miracle," says Father O'Brien, "is an extraordinary occurrence which is visible in itself, and not merely in its effects, and which can be explained only by God's special intervention. Thus, there have been saints who, like our Lord, walked on the water, healed sickness by a touch, or raised the dead to life. However, most modern miracles alleged as proofs of holiness are cures from physical diseases or defects."

The hunt for these six miracles, the minimum required by the Church, a search which can go on even as the other evidence is being sifted by a series of ecclesiastical courts, may provide Father O'Brien with his most formidable hurdle. In the case of Mother Cabrini, the miracles were found and authenticated by the Church over the two decades following her death in 1917.

Since Father O'Brien first let it be known that he would investigate any miraculous cures attributed to Father Serra, he has received many helpful letters. Few, however, satisfy the rigid requirements of the Church—that the alleged miracles be substantiated by eyewitnesses, be submitted to the scrutiny of scientific investigators, and be explained only as the result of divine intervention.

About 75 percent of Father O'Brien's mail on miracles comes from people in California, the rest from twenty-six other states, as well as from Mexico, Spain, Ireland, and Australia. The average month's mail brings mostly trivia—a report from the young man in Mexico City who prayed to Serra and got his job back, from the family in Los Angeles who prayed to Serra and found a home, from the man in Baltimore who prayed to Serra and rid himself of stomach ulcers, from the gentleman in Oakland who prayed to Serra and whose weight went up from 96 pounds to 156 pounds.

Few letters merit investigation. When a letter impresses Father O'Brien, he shows it to a physician friend in Santa Barbara. If the physician agrees it is interesting, then Father O'Brien begins a correspondence. Recently, Father O'Brien's curiosity was piqued by a California woman who fell from a building twenty years ago, seriously injured both her legs, and could hardly walk. This woman went to Serra's grave, prayed, rose, and marched off, leaving her crutches behind. The physician shook his head. "Don't bother with it, Father," he said. "She suffered shock for twenty years. The visit to the grave, the kneeling, the confidence, the autosuggestion simply counteracted the shock. I don't think it's a miracle." Then, as ever, the doctor sent Father O'Brien off with his repeated advice, "Wait until something comes in that knocks your hat off, Father, something the psychologists can't explain. Then really investigate."

Once, not long ago, Father O'Brien thought he had something that knocked his hat off. A letter came in from distant Mallorca. It began, "The object of the present letter is to report to you the seemingly miraculous cure of an eye worked by Fray Junípero Serra in favor of a Franciscan Sister of Mallorca, seventy-four years old, a native of Petra and now residing in Ariany." The letter went on to explain that in April, 1945, the Sister, walking past woodchoppers, was hit in the eye by a flying splinter. After using a few domestic remedies, she went to a specialist. He said there was no hope. At least one eye had to be removed. The Sister was urged, by friends, to pray to Father Serra. "That same day," concluded the letter, "she began to invoke Padre Serra and at about three in the morning, as the pain continued very intense, she again invoked Father Serra. Suddenly the pain ceased, and at the hour for rising, she saw perfectly." When she visited her oculist, he was amazed. "Medical science cannot explain this cure!" he exclaimed. "To whom were you praying?" Upon arriving in Mallorca, Father O'Brien called on the oculist for the scientific case history that the Church requires. The oculist, fearful of what his colleagues might say, was irritable and uncooperative. "Father," he snapped at O'Brien, "when my patients need miracles, I am the one who works them." Since Father O'Brien preferred to have his miracles performed by a higher power, he took his search elsewhere.

Father O'Brien's final task, before submitting the Cause of Junípero Serra to Church courts, was to prepare a legal brief known as the *articuli*. This covered two hundred required points regarding Serra's virtue—a typical point was the heading "Faith," with twenty-one questions underneath, with other points like "Hope," "Fortitude," "Love of God," with questions underneath them. Instead of searching through his 8,500 pages of documents for his answers to include in the *articuli*, Father O'Brien had merely to consult any of his four filing cases. In these lay the cream of the 8,500 pages, each excerpt on a yellow card if Serra's own words, on a salmon-colored card if another's words, each marked with cryptic symbols like F-17 (meaning the answer to question seventeen under "Faith" in the *articuli*).

Father O'Brien finished the brief, written entirely in Latin, in August, 1948. A high Roman official, a Franciscan specialist in such matters, then traveled from Italy to California. This official spent ten days reading and discussing Father O'Brien's *articuli*. Recently, the brief was completed and submitted for trial to what is called the court of the first instance in the canonization process, that is, the Bishop's Court in the Monterey-Fresno diocese of California.

This trial, taking place in secrecy behind closed doors, sometimes before the bishop, mostly before three priests appointed as judges by the bishop, will continue until the late spring of 1949, perhaps longer. Similar trials, in the past, have been noted for their extreme length—the Cause of St. Thérèse of Lisieux, at the same stage, required 109 court sessions, each session almost six hours long, merely to determine her reputation for holiness (the evidence being recorded then, as it is now at Fresno, in longhand by a priest who covered 3,000 pages with closely packed writing).

With the evidence in, and the trial under way, Father O'Brien feels for the first time a sense of progress in his work. "The Fresno court is only a receiving station," he says. "If we run into a wall there, if we see our Cause isn't good enough, then the bishop will simply tell Rome to cancel the whole investigation. But that is unlikely. The Fresno court will probably pass on our *articuli*. If satisfied, the bishop will send, by special messenger, a sealed report on our Cause to the Sacred Congregation of Rites in Rome."

After that, in Vatican City, for possibly three years, there will follow a complicated series of legal steps including the study of Serra's writings by two theologians in search of errors against the Faith, three court hearings which will discuss heroic virtue, three more which will discuss miracles, and one final session of the Congregation before the Pope. When the candidate has thus graduated by stages from Servant of God to Venerable to Blessed, he is finally canonized in the Catholic Church's most splendid ceremony. Here the Pope celebrates a Papal Mass and commands all Catholics to honor their new saint.

When the Cause of Father Serra leaves Fresno for Rome, Father O'Brien will go with it. He will assist the theologians defending the case because so much of the material is in Spanish, a language in which he is proficient, and because so much of it deals with early California, a subject on which he is more expert than the officials in Rome. He will dwell in Rome proper, work inside the Vatican City, and fight a long running battle with his archenemy, the prosecutor, a priest expert in canon law designated as the Promoter of the Faith, but more popularly known as the Devil's Advocate. One church attorney currently fills this role in the Fresno court. Others will enact the role in Rome. It is the villainous job of the Devil's Advocate to study the briefs submitted, probe for weaknesses, and prove that the candidate in question is not worthy of sainthood. In Fresno, Father O'Brien is not permitted to argue with the Devil's Advocate. But in Rome, he will have his chance for rebuttal.

Father O'Brien anticipates the objections that the Fresno Devil's Advocate will find to Junípero Serra. "He will argue that Serra had a bad temper, that he was jealous of his power, that he used questionable tactics in ruling the Indians in California. He will search the documents and note that there were many disagreements between Serra and the California governors, and so he will try to prove that Serra was irascible. He may even say that Serra was selfish. I'm sure he'll use that hike Serra made from Veracruz to Mexico City, two hundred years ago, when Serra ruined his leg and risked his life. The Devil's Advocate will argue that the hike was headstrong, imprudent, that it was like thoughtless suicide, like flaunting the Fifth Commandment. Nevertheless, I feel Father Serra will survive these objections. If he was headstrong, he was Spanish. If he was quarrelsome, it was with good reason. He had faults, but he acted in good faith. He was, at all times, a human being, not a bloodless machine."

Today, even as he assists in the presentation of his case to the Fresno court, Father Eric O'Brien finds time to tackle a daily schedule that would give an automoton a nervous breakdown. Seven years of relentless research have hardly weakened O'Brien's energy. At the age of thirty-six, his six-foot frame is tireless as ever. Despite chaste rimless spectacles, his ruddy square face gives him the look of one who is constantly outdoors. Yet Father O'Brien is almost never outdoors.

He rises at five o'clock every morning from a cot behind his files and three statues of Father Serra. In the next two hours, after dressing, he, and the sixty other inhabitants of the mission, go to the community chapel for prayers, meditate for thirty minutes, chant the breviary, hear Mass, offer more prayers, more breviary, and then consume a homemade breakfast. The mission has its own garden, its own chickens and cows, with lay brothers to handle the cooking.

After glancing at the morning papers, Father O'Brien begins work at seven-thirty and keeps at it until noon. Following prayers in the chapel, and a half-hour dinner, there are more prayers, a chat with the other priests, a short nap, breviary, added prayers. Then, from two o'clock to five-thirty, Father O'Brien is back at his desk. In the evening, there is meditation, a half-hour supper in silence while two students alternate in reading aloud, a procession to the church for prayers, then relaxation for most, but none for Father O'Brien. From seven-fifteen until midnight, with one break for coffee and conversation, Father O'Brien toils.

What does he do in these long work periods? For seven years it was digging on Father Serra, and today there is still supplementary work on the same subject. Now there are publicity articles to be written for the Catholic press. There is the unremitting search for six miracles. There is the studying of specialized law, not taught in seminaries, dealing with canonization. There is the distribution of the pamphlet Father O'Brien has written to encourage prayers to Serra, a pamphlet which has already gone out in four languages to 938,000 people. There are the speeches Father O'Brien is required to write and deliver before organizations. He has 250 talks behind him already. He is never a peddler of platitudes. Sometimes his candor makes listeners squirm. Recently, he reminded the Native Sons of the Golden West, a California version of the D.A.R., that there were some old California families no different than "the icy dowagers who are forever harping on their Mayflower ancestry." Then O'Brien proceeded to debunk the vanity of ancestry:

"Some of the oldest and haughtiest families of this or any state are descended from persons who, if they were alive today, would be ignored or kept discreetly out of sight. The haze of time may soften, but should not distort or hide, facts. Some Spanish soldiers were notorious all over California for their immorality and cruelty. Some forty-niners made their fortunes by sharp dealings with the easygoing rancheros. This last may be the reason why so many of our oldest families seem to have an unwritten law that there must be at least one lawyer in every generation."

The most exhausting work at present, for Father O'Brien, is his correspondence. He exchanges letters with Serra scholars in Mexico, France, Spain. He also finds it agreeable to keep in touch with the other seven Saint Detectives in the United States. One of the most interesting of these was the late Reverend John J. Wynne, a Fordham University professor who devoted twenty-five years to trying to make a saint of Catherine Tekakwitha, known as the Lily of the Mohawks, who died in 1680. Among others, Father O'Brien continues to keep in touch with Vice-Postulator Father Salvator Burgio who is promoting the Cause of Mother Seton, a widow with several children who became a Catholic nun and founded the Sisters of Charity. A distant ancestor of Franklin D. Roosevelt, she died in 1821.

Even though he knows how slowly other American Causes have advanced, Father O'Brien remains confident. He is encouraged by the knowledge that, as recently as two years ago, thirty priests who were martyred in China's Boxer Rebellion were promoted to sainthood, and twenty-eight of these were Franciscans. Father O'Brien prays that the next canonized Franciscan will be his Mallorcan companion of seven intense years.

This close investigation of Serra has had a Svengali-like effect on Father O'Brien. While he does not think Serra has changed him, he feels that the old padre has affected him in one way. "He has been a constant source of reproach to me. He has made me feel that I am not doing much. He has given me the desire to have the same generosity in the service of God. I would enjoy going back to the Sierra Gorda, in Mexico, to live and work among those people, as Father Serra did, not because he did, but because I want to."

WHAT HAS HAPPENED SINCE . . .

Because I am fascinated by the highly formal and intricate, inflexible rituals of the Catholic Church—but no more and no less than I am interested in the equally involved machinery of the Communist party, General Motors, Rotary International, the Nobel Foundation—I follow the activities of the Vatican with unflagging interest. In fact, I have visited and researched inside Vatican City numerous times, and written and published stories about its Pontiff, its daily newspaper, its censorship office. But above all, I have been intrigued by the process through which the Catholic Church elevates one of its own to the universal veneration that accompanies sainthood.

As long ago as 1949, apparently, I was already possessed of this curiosity, for when I learned in that year that a friend of my wife's was working as a secretary to Father Eric O'Brien, I was instantly eager to know more about him and his activities. I spoke to my wife's friend (in the years since, she has become a nun, and we have an Easter card from her occasionally), questioned her about her work, and gained my first information about the Cause of Junípero Serra. The superficial knowledge I acquired only whetted my appetite. I knew that I must see Father O'Brien himself as soon as possible, and write about him and about the entire evolution of mortal to saint. When approached, Father O'Brien was agreeable to a meeting, and this soon took place in my living room. Stimulated by a few drinks and my own questions, the handsome, thirty-six-year-old priest exceeded mere eloquence. Following that first meeting, there were several more—one, if I remember correctly, in a room of St. Joseph's Church in downtown Los Angeles—and soon I was supplementing these interviews with additional research material gathered through intensive reading about the procedures for gaining sainthood and the life of candidate Junípero Serra.

Presently, I wrote the first draft of my story. Being a non-Catholic, I had inadvertently filled the article with minor errors and heresies, and Father O'Brien was justifiably appalled. But being a servant of Christ, and endowed with patience and tolerance, and desirous of promoting the Cause of Junípero Serra still further through me, Father O'Brien did not reject my writings. Instead, he suggested revisions and corrections of facts. These changes I dutifully made. My next submission to Father O'Brien received his approval.

The story, through my literary agent in New York, was submitted to the marketplace. It went out, and it came back. Like so many of the short pieces I wrote without assignment, but merely for pleasure, this one drew praise but no acceptance. It was seen by two or three editors, no more. They were in complete accord: It was not commercial, did not have enough popular appeal for the broadly circulating periodicals (largely read by Protestants), because it was "too special, too Catholic, too limited." I put it aside, reluctantly but with confidence that one day I should be able to include it in a book, when commercial appeal would not be the decisive criterion for my choice of subjects.

In re-editing the story sixteen years after originally writing it, I wondered—as I have wondered about the subjects of all my earlier projects—what had happened to Father O'Brien and to the Cause of Junípero Serra. I had not seen the energetic priest since 1949. From time to time, in the years after, I had read newspaper accounts that gave evidence that the Cause of Junípero Serra was still being vigorously promoted. But, I speculated, how near had Serra been raised toward the high seat that his supporters desired for him? And, indeed, what had his crusaders been up to and what were they doing today? While Serra's name was often in print, I realized that I had not seen the name of his champion, Father O'Brien, mentioned for many years. What, I asked myself, had become of that incredibly dedicated traveler-scholar of the Roman Catholic Church?

The last that I had known of Father O'Brien's activities was that he had completed his extensive legal brief, the *articuli*, setting forth in Latin the virtues of Junípero Serra, and he had presented it to the Bishop's Court in the Monterey-Fresno diocese of California. At the time, Father O'Brien had had every hope that the Fresno hearing would endorse his efforts with its approval, and forthwith submit the favorable decision to Rome. Father O'Brien expected to go then to Rome and continue the good fight.

Through recent interviews and correspondence, I have now learned that Father O'Brien's faith in the imminent progress of his Cause was not unjustified. The initial test, before the Diocesan Court, lasted eight months. Father O'Brien paraded his research and his witnesses, and when the court sessions came to an end, there were 1,260 pages of testimony. It was agreed by the Diocesan Court that Serra's heroic virtue had been satisfactorily proved. Photostatic copies of the bulky records of the trial were sent on to Rome, to be studied by the Sacred Congregation of Rites. This success was Father O'Brien's first major accomplishment after his unremitting labors for the Cause, and his victory was rewarded by a worldly bauble in the summer of 1950 when St. Bonaventure University conferred upon him the honorary degree of Doctor of Letters.

But the first triumph did not make Father O'Brien complacent. The battle had been joined, the opposition armor shallowly pierced, but the Devil's Advocate in Rome had not been unseated. Continuing his assault, Father O'Brien left his and Serra's easy, sunny California for the sophisticated, political, competitive arena that was Vatican City in Rome.

As Father O'Brien recently reported to me, he arrived in the Eternal City during September of 1950, and dwelt in Rome for almost four years. In those years he did "the historical work for the Cause." No doubt he kept a careful watch over his photostated research documents on Serra, one copy of which rested in the office of the Franciscan Order while the other copy received consideration in the office of the Relator General at the Sacred Congregation of Rites.

Father O'Brien's activity in those four years was divided—on one hand, he gave a portion of his time and energy to continuing the hunt for new facts about Junípero Serra in the archives of the Vatican, and on the other hand, he toiled at propagandizing the Cause, at making the Movers of the Vatican (and, in fact, all the world) Serra-conscious. Tirelessly, he corresponded with prelates in Latin America, and with organizations in the United States, seeking "commendatory letters" and backing for Serra. He delivered public addresses extolling the virtues and holiness of California's Apostle. In the field of promotion, his greatest achievement was arranging to give a series of twelve talks on Serra, to an international audience, over Vatican Radio.

In April of 1954, Father Eric O'Brien left Rome and returned to the United States. When he arrived in California, his role as leader and Vice-Postulator of the Cause came to an end. Whether or not he requested to be relieved of his arduous position, whether or not the Church removed and replaced him as a matter of rotating policy, I do not know. In any event, what he had begun as an eager young priest of twenty-nine was, so far as his part was concerned, ending in his forty-second year. He had done the pioneer work. He had traveled widely, read deeply, written ceaselessly. He had delivered an impressive total of 500 speeches on behalf of the Cause. His Franciscan brothers gave him their supreme accolade in print. Of Father O'Brien they said: "For sixteen years the zealous Friar dedicated his talents to tracing around the head of Padre Junípero Serra the halo of a Saint. Inasmuch as one man can be credited with the present happy status of the Serra Cause, that individual is the former Vice-Postulator."

After relinquishing his leadership of the Cause in 1954, Father Eric O'Brien moved into the Serra Retreat in Malibu, California, and there he dwells at present, devoting his peaceful, contemplative days to retreat work, such as giving time to lay Catholics, and to writing. His writing, of course, concerns his old friend, Junípero Serra. According to a recent issue of the *Apostle of California*, a quarterly bulletin that keeps all Serrans informed of the advances being made in the Cause for the Canonization of Junípero Serra:

"The ascetical stature of the candidate presented for canonization is the most important consideration in the eyes of the Sacred Congregation of Rites. This particular aspect of Padre Junípero Serra has been the specialty of the Rev. Eric O'Brien, O.F.M. It is his intention to compose an ascetical 'life' of California's Apostle. The friends of the Cause not only wish him every success in this distinctive endeavor, they pledge their prayers . . ."

Meanwhile, the Cause goes marching on. The players change. The goal is the same. Not until four years after Father O'Brien had gone into his ocean-side retreat was there an official replacement named for him. In July of 1958, the Reverend Noel F. Moholy was appointed the new Vice-Postulator of the Cause. Father Moholy, a wiry, middle-aged native of San Francisco, was not a stranger to Junípero Serra. After being ordained a priest in 1941, Father Moholy taught languages and theology in California, did graduate work in Quebec, and then resumed teaching— but for five of those years he had collaborated with Father O'Brien. During the entire period that Father O'Brien had been in Rome, and for more than a year afterward, Father Moholy had served as his American administrator of the Serra Cause.

Upon succeeding Father O'Brien as the main leader of the Cause, Father Moholy applied himself to promotion of sainthood for the California Apostle with as much vigor as his predecessor had shown. Working out of the Old Mission Santa Barbara—which he had helped restore and expand through his fund-raising campaigns—Father Moholy threw himself into writing, and appeared on radio and television, in a further effort to impress upon the Vatican and the world the Serra Cause.

In 1961, Father Moholy took on as an aide the scholarly Father Florian Guest, sending him to Rome to continue the historical phase of the work. In Rome, Father Guest found that the next hurdle to be overcome was the requirement that all the basic Serra findings be translated into Italian. Father Guest accepted the challenge, but before he could proceed very far with the project, he fell ill. A little more than a year after entering Rome, the ailing Father Guest was forced to return to Los Angeles.

Today, under the guidance of the new Vice-Postulator, Father Guest, who is attached to St. Joseph's Church in Los Angeles, is slowly going ahead with the Italian translation of the voluminous Serra case.

As Father Guest explained to me: "The historical work for the Serra Cause is to be completed in two volumes, both in Italian. The first is to contain a translation of all the most important documents bearing on the Cause, together with a critical introduction to them. The second is to include the historical proof that Junípero Serra practiced heroic virtue. When these two volumes are completed and approved, Serra's Cause will have been canonically introduced. Partly because of the large number of Causes being considered by the Sacred Congregation of Rites, the work may be prolonged for several years. The Franciscan Order alone is promoting the Causes of 190 candidates for the honors of the altar."

Because of the competition from the large number of other candidates for sainthood, because six proved miracles are needed for Serra's beatification and for his canonization, some supporters of the Cause believe that it may be another ten years before the California Apostle is presented for the final judgment in Rome.

But the promoters of the Serra Cause have been trained in patience. They remind themselves that it took more than five hundred years for Joan of Arc to be made a saint. They know that it took forty years for Pope Pius X to be so recognized. Yet, most encouraging is the fact that Mother Elizabeth Seton—the remarkable New York-born Protestant convert to Catholicism, who bore her husband five children before she was widowed, and who died in Baltimore in 1821—required only twenty-three years to attain beatification, the almost certain prelude to canonization. Mother Seton's Cause was introduced in 1940, and she was beatified and praised by Pope John XXIII in 1963.

The Serrans know the odds they must overcome. Since the founding of the Church of St. Peter, the Vatican has raised perhaps twenty-five thousand of its own to sainthood. In the three and a half centuries since the Church began listing its saints, there have been fewer than three hundred who have been canonized. Despite these awesome odds, despite the fact that there are nearly 1,200 candidates, including five popes and thirteen cardinals, contending for sainthood in Rome at the moment, despite the fact that there are 190 of their own order among these candidates, the California Franciscans remain confident that Father Serra will ultimately be so honored.

One hundred and eighty years have passed since Father Junípero Serra, that "useless servant of God," as he characterized himself, died in Carmel, California. Only thirty years have passed since the Franciscan Order first undertook to prove that Father Junípero Serra was worthy of international veneration and prayer. Ten more years of effort seem little enough when weighed against the magnitude of the success in sight. Then, if the human race has survived, there will be time enough for those who are believers to enjoy the guidance and pray for the miracles they hope the vision of the lame, old, courageous padre, Mallorcan and Californian, with his hard-won halo, will provide. Amen.

5

EVERYBODY'S ROVER BOY

ONE DAY in the year 1890, Miss Nellie Bly, of the New York *World*, came roaring into Brooklyn on a special train from San Francisco. In a successful effort to beat Phileas Fogg's fictional 80 days around the world, Miss Bly, traveling with two handbags and flannel underwear, had circled the globe in 72 days, 6 hours, and 11 minutes. Immortality awaited her.

Elsewhere that same year, another less-publicized globe-girdler made his start toward immortality. He was Mr. Burton Holmes, making his public debut with slides and anecdotes ("Through Europe With a Kodak") before the Chicago Camera Club. Mr. Holmes, while less spectacular than his feminine rival, was destined, for that very reason, soon to dethrone her as America's number-one traveler.

Today, Miss Bly and Mr. Holmes have one thing in common: In the mass mind they are legendary vagabonds relegated to the dim and dusty past of the Iron Horse and the paddle-wheel steamer. But if Miss Bly, who shuffled off this mortal coil in 1922, is now only a part of our folklore, there are millions to testify that Mr. Burton Holmes, aged seventy-six, is still very much with us.

Remembering that Mr. Holmes was an active contemporary of Miss Bly's, that he was making a livelihood at traveling when William McKinley, John L. Sullivan, and Admiral Dewey ruled the United States, when Tony Pastor, Lily Langtry, and Lillian Russell ruled the amusement world, it is at once amazing and reassuring to pick up the daily newspapers of 1946 and find, sandwiched between advertisements of rash young men lecturing on "Inside Stalin" and "I Was Hitler's Dentist," calm announcements that tomorrow evening Mr. Burton Holmes has something more to say about "Beautiful Bali."

Burton Holmes, a brisk, immaculate, chunky man with gray Vandyke beard, erect bearing, precise speech ("Folks are always mistaking me for Monty Woolley," he says, not unhappily), is one of the seven wonders of the entertainment world. As Everyman's tourist, Burton Holmes has crossed the Atlantic Ocean thirty times, the Pacific Ocean twenty times, and has gone completely around the world six times. He has spent fifty-five summers abroad, and recorded a half million feet of film of those summers. He was the first person to take motion picture cameras into Russia and Japan. He witnessed the regular decennial performance of the Passion Play at Oberammergau in 1890, and attended the first modern Olympics at Athens in 1896. He rode on the first Trans-Siberian train across Russia, and photographed the world's first airplane meet at Rheims.

As the fruit of these travels, Burton Holmes has delivered approximately 8,000 illustrated lectures that have grossed, according to an estimate by *Variety*, five million dollars in fifty-three winters. Because he does not like to be called a lecturer—"I'm a performer," he insists, "and I have performed on more legitimate stages than platforms"—he invented the word "travelogue" in London to describe his activity.

His travelogues, regarded as a fifth season of the year in most communities, have won him such popularity that he holds the record for playing in the longest one-man run in American show business. In the five and a half decades past, Burton Holmes has successively met the hectic competition of big-time vaudeville, stage, silent pictures, radio, and talking pictures, and he has survived them all.

At an age when most men have retired to slippered ease or are grounded by high blood pressure, Burton Holmes is more active and more popular than ever before. In the season just finished, which he started in San Francisco during September, 1945, and wound up in New York during April, 1946, Holmes appeared in 187 shows, a record number. He averaged six travelogues a week, spoke for two hours at each, and did 30 percent more box-office business than five years ago. Not once was a scheduled lecture postponed or canceled. In fact, he has missed only two in his life. In 1935, flying over the Dust Bowl, he suffered laryngitis and was forced to bypass two college dates. He has never canceled an appearance before a paid city audience. Seven years ago, when one of his elderly limbs was fractured in an automobile crack-up in Finland, there was a feeling that Burton Holmes might not make the rounds. When news of the accident was released, it was as if word had gone out that Santa Claus was about to cancel his winter schedule. But when the 1939 season dawned, Burton Holmes rolled on the stage in a wheelchair, and from his seat of pain (and for 129 consecutive appearances thereafter), he delivered his travel chat while 16-mm film shimmered on the screen beside him.

Today, there is little likelihood that anything, except utter extinction, could keep Holmes from his waiting audiences. Even now, between seasons, Holmes is in training for his next series—150 illustrated lectures before groups in seventeen states.

Before World War II, accompanied by Margaret Oliver, his wife of thirty-two years, Holmes would spend his breathing spells on summery excursions through the Far East or Europe. While aides captured scenery on celluloid, Holmes wrote accompanying lecture material in his notebooks. Months later, he would communicate his findings to his cult, at a maximum price of $1.50 per seat. With the outbreak of war, Holmes changed his pattern. He curtailed travel outside the Americas. This year, except for one journey to Las Vegas, Nevada, where he personally photographed cowboy cutups and shapely starlets at the annual Helldorado festival, Holmes has been allowing his assistants to do all his traveling for him.

Recently, one crew, under cameraman Thayer Soule, who helped shoot the Battle of Tarawa for the Marines, brought Holmes a harvest of new film from Mexico. Another crew, after four months in Brazil last year, and two in its capital this year, returned to Holmes with magnificent movies. Meantime, other crews, under assignment from Holmes, are finishing films on Death Valley, the West Indies, and the Mississippi River.

In a cottage behind his sprawling Hollywood hilltop home, Holmes is busy, day and night, sorting the incoming negative, cutting and editing it, and rewriting lectures that will accompany the footage this winter. He is too busy to plan his next trip. Moreover, he doesn't feel that he should revisit Europe yet. "I wouldn't mind seeing it," he says, "but I don't think my public would be interested. My people want a good time, they want escape, they want sweetness and light, beauty and charm. There's too much rubble and misery over there now, and I'll let those picture magazines and Fox Movietone newsreels show all that. I'll wait until it's tourist time again."

When he travels, he thinks he will visit three of the four accessible places on earth that he has not yet seen. One is Tahiti, which he barely missed a dozen times, and the other two are Iran and Iraq. The remaining country that he has not seen, and has no wish to see, is primitive Afghanistan. Of all cities on earth, he would most like to revisit Kyoto, once capital of Japan. He still recalls that the first movies ever made inside Japan were ones he made in Kyoto, in 1899. The other cities he desires to revisit are Venice and Rome. The only island for which he has any longing is Bali—"the one quaint spot on earth where you can really get away from it all."

In preparing future subjects, Holmes carefully studies the success of his past performances. Last season, his two most popular lectures in the East were "California" and "Adventures in Mexico." The former grossed $5,100 in two Chicago shows; the latter jammed the St. Louis Civic Auditorium with thirty-five hundred potential señores and señoritas. Holmes will use these subjects again, with revisions, next season, and add some brand-new Latin American and United States topics. He will sidestep anything relating to war. He feels, for example, that anything dealing with the once exotic Pacific islands might have a questionable reception—"people will still remember those white crosses they saw in newsreels of Guadalcanal and Iwo Jima."

Every season presents its own obstacles, and the next will challenge Holmes with a new audience of travel-sated and disillusioned ex-GI's. Many of these men, and their families, now know that a South Sea island paradise means mosquitoes and malaria and not Melville's Fayaway and Loti's Rarahu. They know Europe means mud and ruins and not romance. Nevertheless, Holmes is confident that he will win these people over.

"The veterans of World War II will come to my travelogues just as their fathers did. After the First World War, I gave illustrated lectures on the sights of France, and the ex-doughboys enjoyed them immensely. But I suppose there's no use comparing that war to this. The First World War was a minor dispute between gentlemen. In this one, the atrocities and miseries will be difficult to forget. I know I can't give my Beautiful Italy lecture next season to men who know Italy only as a pigsty, but you see, in my heart Italy is forever beautiful, and I see things in Italy they can't see, poor fellows. How could they? . . . Still, memory is frail, and one day these boys will forget and come to my lectures not to hoot but to relive the better moments and enjoy themselves."

While Burton Holmes prepares his forthcoming shows, his business manager, a slightly built dynamo named Walter Everest, works on next season's bookings. Everest contacts organizations interested in sponsoring a lecture series, arranges dates and prices, and often leases auditoriums on his own. Everest concentrates on cities where Holmes is known to be popular, Standing Room Only cities like New York, Boston, Philadelphia, Chicago, Los Angeles. On the other hand, he is cautious about the cities where Holmes has been unpopular in the past—Toledo, Cleveland, Indianapolis, Cincinnati. The one city Holmes now avoids entirely is Pomona, California, where, at a scheduled Saturday matinee, he found himself facing an almost empty house. The phenomenon of a good city or a poor city is inexplicable. In rare cases, there may be a reason for failure, and then Holmes will attempt to resolve it. When San Francisco was stone-deaf to Holmes, investigation showed that he had been competing with the annual opera season. Last year, he rented a theater the week before the opera began. He appeared eight times and made a handsome profit.

Once Holmes takes to the road for his regular season, he is a perpetual-motion machine. Leaving his wife behind, he barnstorms with his manager, Everest, and a projectionist, whirling to Western dates in his Cadillac, making long hops by plane, following the heavier Eastern circuit by train. Holmes likes to amaze younger men with his activities during a typical week. If he speaks in Detroit on a Tuesday night, he will lecture in Chicago on Wednesday evening, in Milwaukee on Thursday, be back in Chicago for Friday evening and a Saturday matinee session, then go on to Kansas City on Sunday, St. Louis on Monday, and play a return engagement in Detroit on Tuesday.

This relentless merry-go-round (with Saturday nights off to attend a newsreel "and see what's happening in the world") invigorates Holmes, but grinds his colleagues to a frazzle. One morning last season, after weeks of trains and travel, Walter Everest was awakened by a porter at six. He rose groggily, sat swaying on the edge of his berth trying to pull on his shoes. He had the look of a man who had pushed through the Matto Grosso on foot. He glanced up sleepily, and there, across the aisle, was Holmes, fully dressed, looking natty and refreshed. Holmes smiled sympathetically. "I know, Walter," he said, "this life *is* tiring. One day both of us ought to climb on some train and get away from it all."

In his years on the road, Holmes has come to know his audience thoroughly. He is firm in the belief that it is composed mostly of traveled persons who wish to savor the glamorous sights of the world again. Through Burton, they relive their own tours. Of the others, some regard a Holmes performance as a preview. They expect to travel; they want to know the choice sights for their future three-month jaunt to Ecuador. Some few, who consider themselves travel authorities, come to a Holmes lecture to point out gleefully the good things that he missed. "It makes them happy," Holmes says cheerfully. Tomorrow's audience, for the most, will be the same as the one that heard the Master exactly a year before. Generations of audiences inherit Holmes, one from the other.

An average Holmes lecture combines the atmosphere of a revival meeting and a family get-together at which home movies are shown. A typical Holmes travelogue begins in a brightly lit auditorium, at precisely three minutes after eight-thirty. The three minutes is to allow for latecomers. Holmes, attired in formal evening clothes, strides from the wings to center stage. People applaud; some cheer. Everyone seems to know him and to know exactly what to expect. Holmes smiles broadly. He is compact, proper, handsome. His goatee dominates the scene. He has worn it every season, with the exception of one in 1895 (when, beardless, he somewhat resembled Paget's Sherlock Holmes). Now, he speaks crisply. He announces that this is the third lecture of his fifty-fourth season. He announces his subject—"Adventures in Mexico."

He walks to one side of the stage, where a microphone is standing. The lights are dimmed. The auditorium becomes dark. Beyond the fifth row, Holmes cannot be seen. The all-color 16-mm film is projected on the screen. The film opens, minus title and credits, with a shot through the windshield of an automobile speeding down the Pan-American Highway to Monterrey. Holmes himself is the sound track. His speech, with just the hint of a theatrical accent, is intimate, as if he were talking in a living room. He punctuates descriptive passages with little formal jokes. When flowers and orange trees of Mexico are on the screen, he says, "We have movies and talkies, but now we should have smellies and tasties"—and he chuckles.

The film that he verbally captions is a dazzling, uncritical montage of Things Mexican. There is a señora selling tortillas, and close-ups of how tortillas are made. There is a bullfight, but not the kill. There is snow-capped Popocatepetl, now for sale at the bargain price of fifteen million dollars. There are the pyramids outside Mexico City, older than those of Egypt, built by the ancient Toltecs who went to war with wooden swords so that they would not kill their enemies.

Holmes's movies and lectures last two hours, with one intermission. The emphasis is on description, information, and oddity. Two potential ingredients are studiously omitted. One is adventure, the other politics. Holmes is never spectacular. "I want nothing dangerous. I don't care to emulate the explorers, to risk my neck, to be the only one or the first one there. Let others tackle the Himalayas, the Amazon, the North Pole, let them break the trails for me. I'm just a Cook's tourist, a little ahead of the crowd, but not too far ahead." Some years ago, Holmes did think that he was an explorer, and became very excited about it, he now admits sheepishly. This occurred in a trackless sector of Northern Rhodesia. Holmes felt that he had discovered a site never before seen by an out-sider. Grandly, he planted the flag of the Exporers Club, carefully he set up his camera, and then, as he prepared to shoot, his glance fell upon an object several feet away—an empty Kodak carton. Quietly, he repacked and stole away—and has stayed firmly on the beaten paths ever since.

As to politics, it never taints his lectures. He insists neither he nor his audiences are interested. "When you discuss politics," he says, "you are sure to offend." Even after his third trip to Russia, he refused to discuss politics. "I am a traveler," he explained at that time, "and not a student of political and economic questions. To me, Communism is merely one of the sights I went to see."

However, friends know that Holmes has his pet panacea for the ills of the world. He is violent about the gold standard, insisting that it alone can make all the world prosperous. Occasionally, when the mood is on him, and against his better judgment, he will inject propaganda in favor of the gold standard into an otherwise timid travelogue.

When he is feeling mellow, Holmes will confess that once in the past he permitted politics to intrude upon his sterile chitchat. It was two decades ago, when he jousted with Prohibition. While not a dedicated drinking man, Holmes has been on a friendly basis with firewater since the age of sixteen. In the ensuing years, he has regularly, every dusk before dinner, mixed himself one or two highballs. Only once did he try more than two, and the results were disastrous. "Any man who drinks three will drink three hundred," he now says righteously. Holmes felt that Prohibition was an insult to civilized living. As a consequence of this belief, his audiences during the days of the Eighteenth Amendment were often startled to hear Holmes extol the virtues of open drinking, in the middle of a placid discourse on Oberammergau or Lapland. "Sometimes an indignant female would return her tickets to the rest of my series," he says, "but there were others, more intelligent, to take her place."

This independent attitude in Holmes was solely the product of his personal success. Born in January, 1870, of a financially secure, completely cosmopolitan Chicago family, he was able to be independent from his earliest days. His father, an employee in the Third National Bank, distinguished himself largely by lending George Pullman enough cash to transform his old day coaches into the first Pullman Palace Sleeping Cars, and by refusing a half interest in the business in exchange for his help. Even to this day, it makes Burton Holmes dizzy to think of the money he might have saved in charges for Pullman berths.

Holmes's interest in show business began at the age of nine when his grandmother, Ann W. Burton, took him to hear John L. Stoddard lecture on the Passion Play at Oberammergau. Young Holmes was never the same again. After brief visits to faraway Florida and California, he quit school and accompanied his grandmother on his first trip abroad. He was sixteen and wide-eyed. His grandmother, who had traveled with her wine-salesman husband to France and Egypt and down the Volga in the sixties, was the perfect guide. But this journey through Europe was eclipsed, four years later, by a more important pilgrimage with his grandmother to Germany. The first day at his hotel in Munich, Holmes saw John L. Stoddard pass through the lobby reading a Baedeker. He was petrified. It was as if he had seen his Maker. Even now, over a half century later, when Holmes speaks about Stoddard, his voice carries a tinge of awe. For eighteen years of the late nineteenth century, Stoddard, with black-and-white slides and magnificent oratory, dominated the travel-lecture field. To audiences, young and old, he was the most romantic figure in America. Later, at Oberammergau, Holmes sat next to Stoddard through the fifteen acts of the Passion Play and they became friends.

When Holmes returned to the States, some months after Nellie Bly had made her own triumphal return to Brooklyn, he showed rare Kodak negatives of his travels to fellow members of the Chicago Camera Club. The members were impressed, and one suggested that these be mounted as slides and shown to the general public. "To take the edge off the silence, to keep the show moving," says Holmes, "I wrote an account of my journey and read it, as the stereopticon man changed slides." The show, which grossed the club $350, was Holmes's initial travelogue. However, he dates the beginning of his professional career from three years later, when he appeared under his own auspices with hand-colored slides.

After the Camera Club debut, Holmes did not go immediately into the travelogue field. He was not yet ready to appreciate its possibilities. Instead, he attempted to sell real estate, and failed. Then he worked for eight dollars a week as a photo supply clerk. In 1902, aching with wanderlust, he bullied his family into staking him to a five-month tour of Japan. On the boat he was thrilled to find John L. Stoddard, also bound for Japan. They became closer friends, even though they saw Nippon through different eyes. "The older man found Japan queer, quaint, comfortless, and almost repellent," Stoddard's son wrote years later. "To the younger man it was a fairyland." Stoddard invited Holmes to continue on around the world with him, but Holmes loved Japan and decided to remain.

When Holmes returned to Chicago, the World's Columbian Exposition of 1893 was in full swing. He spent months at the Jackson Park grounds, under Edison's new electric lights, listening to Lillian Russell sing, Susan B. Anthony speak, and watching Sandow perform feats of strength. With rising excitement, he observed Jim Brady eating, Anthony Comstock snorting at Little Egypt's hootchy-kootchy, and Alexander Dowie announcing himself as the Prophet Elijah III.

In the midst of this excitement came the depression of that year. Holmes's father suffered. "He hit the wheat pit at the wrong time, and I had to go out on my own," says Holmes. "The photo supply house offered me fifteen dollars a week to return. But I didn't want to work. The trip to Japan, the Oriental exhibits of the Exposition, were still on my mind. I thought of Stoddard. I thought of the slides I'd had hand-colored in Tokyo. That was it, and it wasn't work. So I hired a hall and became a travel lecturer."

Copying society addresses from his mother's visiting list, and additional addresses from *The Blue Book*, Holmes mailed two thousand invitations in the form of Japanese poem-cards. Recipients were invited to two illustrated lectures, at $1.50 each, on "Japan—the Country and the Cities." Both performances were sellouts. Holmes grossed $700.

For four years Holmes continued his fight to win a steady following, but with only erratic success. Then, in 1897, when he stood at the brink of defeat, two events occurred to change his life. First, John L. Stoddard retired from the travel-lecture field and threw the platforms of the nation open to a successor. Second, Holmes supplemented colored slides with a new method of illustrating his talks. As his circular announced, "There will be presented for the first time in connection with a course of travel lectures a series of pictures to which a modern miracle has added the illusion of life itself—the reproduction of recorded motion."

Armed with his jumpy movies—scenes of the Omaha fire department, a police parade in Chicago, Italians eating spaghetti, each reel running twenty-five seconds, with a four-minute wait between reels—Burton Holmes invaded the Stoddard strongholds in the East. Stoddard came to hear him and observe the newfangled movies. Like Marshal Foch who regarded the airplane as "an impractical toy," Stoddard saw no future in the motion picture. Nevertheless, he gave young Holmes a hand by insisting that Augustin Daly lease his Manhattan theater to the newcomer. This done, Stoddard retired to the Austrian Tyrol, and Holmes went on to absorb Stoddard's audiences in Boston and Philadelphia and to win new followers of his own throughout the nation.

His success assured, Holmes began to gather material with a vigor that was to make him one of history's most indefatigable travelers. In 1900, at the Paris Exposition, sitting in a restaurant built like a Russian train, drinking vodka while a colored panorama of Siberia rolled past his window, he succumbed to this unique advertising of the new Trans-Siberian railway and bought a ticket. The trip in 1901 was a nightmare. After ten days on the Trans-Siberian train, which banged along at eleven miles an hour, Holmes was dumped into a construction train for five days, and then spent twenty-seven days on steamers going down the Amur River. It took him forty-two and a half days to travel from Moscow to Vladivostok.

But during that tour, he had one great moment. He saw Count Leo Tolstoi at Yasnaya Polyana, the author's country estate near Tula. At a dinner in Moscow, Holmes met Albert J. Beveridge, the handsome senator from Indiana. Beveridge had a letter of introduction to Tolstoi and invited Holmes and his enormous 60-mm movie camera to come along. Arriving in a four-horse landau, the Americans were surprised to find Tolstoi's estate dilapidated. Then, they were kept waiting two hours. At last, the seventy-three-year-old, white-bearded Tolstoi, nine years away from his lonely death in a railway depot, appeared. He was attired in a muzhik costume. He invited his visitors to breakfast, then conversed in fluent English. "He had only a slight accent, and he spoke with the cadence of Sir Henry Irving," Holmes recalls.

Of the entire morning's conversation, Holmes remembers clearly only one remark. That was when Tolstoi harangued, "There should be no law. No man should have the right to judge or condemn another. Absolute freedom of the individual is the only thing that can redeem the world. Christ was a great teacher, nothing more!" As Tolstoi continued to speak, Holmes quietly set up his movie camera. Tolstoi had never seen one before. He posed stiffly, as for a daguerreotype. When he thought that it was over, and resumed his talking, Holmes began actual shooting. This priceless film never reached the screen. Senator Beveridge was then a presidential possibility. His managers feared that this film of Beveridge with a Russian radical might be used by his opponents. The film was taken from Holmes and destroyed. Later, when he was not even nominated for the presidency, Beveridge wrote an apology to Holmes, "for this destruction of so valuable a living record of the grand old Russian."

In 1934, at a cost of ten dollars a day, Holmes spent twenty-one days in modern Soviet Russia. He loved the ballet, the omelets, the Russian rule against tipping, and the lack of holdups. He went twice to see the embalmed Lenin, fascinated by the sight of "his head resting on a red pillow like that of a tired man asleep."

Although Holmes's name had already appeared on eighteen travel volumes, this last Russian trip inspired him to write his first and only original book. The earlier eighteen volumes, all heavily illustrated, were offered as a set, of which over forty thousand were sold. However, they were not "written," but were actually a collection of lectures delivered orally by Holmes. The one book that he wrote as a book, *The Traveler's Russia*, published in 1934 by G. P. Putnam's Sons, was a failure. Holmes has bought the remainders and passes them out to guests with a variety of inscriptions. In a serious mood he will inscribe, "To travel is to possess the world." In a frivolous mood, he will write, "With love from Tovarich Burtonovich Holmeski."

In the five decades past, Holmes has kept himself occupied with a wide variety of pleasures, such as attending Queen Victoria's Golden Jubilee in London, chatting with Admiral Dewey in Hong Kong, driving the first automobile seen in Denmark, and photographing a mighty eruption of Vesuvius.

In 1918, wearing a war correspondent's uniform, he shot army scenes on the Western Front and his films surpassed those of the poorly organized newsreel cameramen. In 1923, flying for the first time, he had his most dangerous experience, when his plane almost crashed between Toulouse and Rabat. Later, in Berlin, he found his dollar worth ten million marks, and in Africa he interviewed Emperor Haile Selassie in French, and, closer to home, he flew 20,000 miles over Central and South America.

Burton Holmes enjoys company on his trips. By coincidence, they are often celebrities. Holmes traveled through Austria with Maria Jeritza, through Greece with E. F. Benson, through the Philippines with Dr. Victor Heiser. He covered World War I with Harry Franck, wandered about Japan with Lafcadio Hearn's son, crossed Ethiopia with the Duke of Gloucester. He saw Hollywood with Mary Pickford, Red Square with Alma Gluck, and the Andes with John McCutcheon.

Of the hundreds of travelogues that Holmes has delivered, the most popular was "The Panama Canal." He offered this in 1912, when the "big ditch" was under construction, and news-hungry citizens flocked to hear him. Among less timely subjects, his most popular was the standard masterpiece on Oberammergau, followed closely by his illustrated lectures on the "Frivolities of Paris," the "Canals of Venice," the "Countryside of England" and, more currently, "Adventures in Mexico." Burton Holmes admits that his greatest failure was an elaborate travelogue on Siam, even though it seemed to have everything except Anna and the King thereof. Other failures included travelogues on India, Burma, Ethiopia, and—curiously—exotic Bali. The only two domestic subjects to fizzle were "Down in Dixie" in 1915 and "The Century of Progress Exposition" in 1932.

All in all, the success of Holmes's subjects has been so consistently high that he has never suffered seriously from competition. One rival died, another retired eight years ago. "I'm the lone survivor of the magic-lantern boys," says Holmes. Of the younger crowd, Holmes thought that Richard Halliburton might become his successor. "He deserved to carry the banner," says Holmes. "He was good-looking, with a fine classical background, intelligent, interesting, and he really did those darn-fool stunts." Halliburton, who had climbed the Matterhorn, swum the Hellespont, followed the Cortés trail through Mexico, lectured with slides. "I told him to throw away the slides," says Holmes. "He was better without them, his speech was so colorful." When Halliburton died attempting to sail a Chinese junk across the Pacific, Holmes decided to present an illustrated lecture on "The Romantic Adventures of Richard Halliburton." He used his own movies but, in the accompanying talk, Halliburton's written text. "It was a crashing failure," sighs Holmes. "His millions of fans did not want to hear me, and my fans did not want to know about him."

For a while, Hollywood appeared to be the travelogue's greatest threat. Holmes defeated this menace by marriage with the studios. He signed a contract with Paramount, made fifty-two travel shorts each year, between 1915 and 1921. Then, with the advent of talking pictures, Holmes joined Metro-Goldwyn-Mayer and made a series of travelogues, released in English, French, Italian, Spanish. In 1933, he made his debut in radio, and in 1944 made his first appearance on television.

Today, safe in the knowledge that he is an institution, Holmes spends more and more time in his rambling, plantation-style, wooden home, called "Topside," located on a hill a mile above crowded Hollywood Boulevard. This dozen-roomed brown house, once a riding club for silent day film stars, and owned for six years by Francis X. Bushman (who gave it Hollywood's first swimming pool, where Holmes now permits neighborhood children to splash), was purchased by Holmes in 1930. "I had that M-G-M contract," he says, "and it earned me a couple of hundred thousand dollars. Well, everyone with a studio contract immediately gets himself a big car, a big house, and a small blonde. I acquired the car, the house, but kept the blonde a mental acquisition." For years, Holmes also owned a Manhattan duplex decorated with costly Japanese and Buddhist treasures, which he called "Nirvana." Before Pearl Harbor, Holmes sold this duplex, with its two-million-dollar collection of furnishings, to Robert Ripley, the cartoonist and oddity hunter.

Now, in his rare moments of leisure, Holmes likes to sit on the veranda of his Hollywood home and chat with his wife. Before he met her, he had been involved in one public romance. Gossips, everywhere, insisted that he might marry the fabulous Elsie de Wolfe, actress, millionaire decorator, friend of Oscar Wilde and Sarah Bernhardt, who later became Lady Mendl. Once, in Denver, Holmes recalls, a reporter asked him if he was engaged to Elsie de Wolfe. Holmes replied, curtly, No. That afternoon a banner headline proclaimed: BURTON HOLMES REFUSES TO MARRY ELSIE DE WOLFE!

Shortly afterward, during a photographic excursion, Holmes met Margaret Oliver who, suffering from deafness, had taken up still photography as an avocation. In 1914, following a moonlight proposal on a steamer's deck, he married Miss Oliver in New York City's St. Stephen's Episcopal Church, and took her to prosaic Atlantic City for the first few days of their honeymoon, then immediately embarked on a long trip abroad.

When his wife is out shopping, Holmes will stroll about his estate, study his fifty-four towering palm trees, return to the veranda for a high-ball, thumb through the *National Geographic,* play with his cats, or pick up a language textbook. He is on speaking terms with eight languages including some of the Scandinavian, and is eager to learn more. He never reads travel books. "As Pierre Loti once remarked, 'I don't read. It might ruin my style,' " he explains.

He likes visitors, and he will startle them with allusions to his earlier contemporaries. "This lawn party reminds me of the one at which I met Emperor Meiji," he will say. Meiji, grandfather of Hirohito, opened Japan to Commodore Perry. When visitors ask for his travel advice, Holmes invariably tells them to see the Americas first. "Why go to Mont St. Michel?" he asks. "Have you seen Monticello?"

But when alone with his wife and co-workers on the veranda, and the pressure of the new season is weeks away, he will loosen his blue dressing gown, inhale, then stare reflectively out over the sun-bathed city below.

"You know, this is the best," he will say softly, "looking down on this Los Angeles. It is heaven. I could sit here the rest of my life." Then, suddenly, he will add, "There is so much else to see and do. If only I could have another threescore years upon this planet. If only I could know the good earth better than I do."

WHAT HAS HAPPENED SINCE . . .

Only a small portion of Burton Holmes's wish for "another threescore years upon this planet" was allowed him. After my story about him appeared in *The Saturday Evening Post* during May of 1947, Burton Holmes lived on for another eleven years and one month. However, there was little new that he ventured or achieved in those eleven years to alter the story I had written about him.

For one year, after I met and wrote about him, Burton Holmes actively continued to present his beloved travelogues in person. After that, he quit the public platform and legitimate stage to serve an organization, Burton Holmes Travelogues, in an advisory capacity. Not until two years before his death did he submit to complete retirement from work.

During almost six decades, he had been Everybody's Rover Boy. And for doing what he enjoyed most in life, he had earned five million dollars. But at the age of eighty-eight, no longer able to leave his hill above Hollywood Boulevard, he was ready for that one last journey. He died in July of 1958, and he was cremated at his own request. His mortal remains, his ashes, were deposited in a favorite Siamese urn, one which he had cherished.

But Burton Holmes left more than ashes behind in 1958. He left behind a Name, a vast audience who responded to that name, and an organization to represent that name by proxy in order to hold onto the vast audience. Several years before his death, Burton Holmes, person, had become Burton Holmes Travelogues, corporation. When the person was no more, the corporation remained to carry on.

Today, the corporation, promoting the Burton Holmes name, consists of four people, all of whom were close to Holmes before his death. The most dominant member of the corporation, yet now the least active, is the Great Traveler's widow, Margaret O. Holmes, who had been his spouse for forty-four years. At the age of eighty-six, Mrs. Holmes still lives on in "Topside," with two companions. Although she keeps an eye on the corporation, Mrs. Holmes's retirement is largely devoted to basking in the memory of the old glories, and to occasionally strolling about her three acres or, if the weather is hot, taking a swim in her pool. The only times she emerges from seclusion, and descends from "Topside" into the bewildering new world of freeways and television antennas, is when a Burton Holmes Travelogue series is being presented in Los Angeles. Then she attends each film and lecture. Sometimes, too, she will go forth to see what the competition is doing, quietly slipping into an auditorium where some young lecturer with new film is attempting to challenge the corporation and the Name.

The active head, heart, and limbs of the Holmes corporation consist of three lively, energetic gentlemen, who, because they knew and respected Holmes, possess a shrewd understanding of what was valuable in the past—as well as what is necessary in the present and the future. The president of the corporation is a Phi Beta Kappa named Robert Mallett, a former foreign correspondent who once interviewed Sir Winston Churchill and Charles de Gaulle. Mallett's main concern is the business side of the corporation. But sometimes, when the fever is on him, he will take to the boards. Recently he personally narrated the descriptive lectures for travelogues on Sweden and Japan. The least publicized member of the corporation, who managed the travelogues before Holmes died and who manages them today, is Walter T. Everest. The most colorful member of the trio, André de la Varre, bears an uncanny resemblance to the Master. The Burton Holmes trademarks—"Vandyke beard, erect bearing, precise speech"—may all be found in de la Varre, who had made 120 travel short subjects for three motion picture studios and had won a Motion Picture Academy Award before joining Holmes. Today de la Varre produces many of the corporation's films, and presents some of them (such as the ones on Italy and Switzerland) in person. These men consider the Holmes organization to be the leading producer of travelogues in the United States.

If the shade of Burton Holmes were to return to earth, it is likely that he would be satisfied with the way his heirs have perpetuated his travelogues. Basically, little has changed. Had Holmes's shade visited the Academy of Music in Philadelphia to attend the Holmes Seventieth Anniversary series, consisting of five different subjects presented during four weeks in January and February of 1963, he would not have been disappointed. At a top price of two dollars a seat for a single evening, or the bargain rate of eight dollars for all five shows, he would have been able to see Robert Mallett presenting "Today's New and Progressive Japan," then "America's Wonderland: the Pacific Northwest," then "Grand Tour of Delightful Sweden." On alternate nights, Holmes's shade would have seen Andre de la Varre presenting "Playground of the World: Switzerland" and "Sicily and Byways of Italy." And Holmes's shade would have been happy to know he was part of a full house.

Yet Holmes's heirs, while adhering to certain Burton Holmes traditions—such as projecting the sharp original Kodachrome film and not prints or copies, delivering narration live while standing beside the film being projected rather than succumbing to sound tracks, and making all their appearances in white tie and tails—have tried to keep pace with our fast-moving, ever-changing times.

For one thing, five absolutely new films are presented every year. There are no reruns of the old Burton Holmes reels, which are preserved in storage. When I asked a member of the corporation if any of Holmes's original material was usable or ever used today, I was told, "We frequently utilize short film segments from the footage Burton Holmes shot in the early days of motion pictures." When the heirs recently made "Roundabout London," they could not resist including film shots of Queen Victoria, which Burton Holmes had once taken. When the heirs produced "Lands of the Nile," they spliced in some 1933 scenes of Emperor Haile Selassie's coronation in Ethiopia, taken by the only motion picture photographer present—Burton Holmes himself. Occasionally, too, the heirs will lift an appropriate excerpt from Holmes's old lectures to use in one of their modern-day narrations.

Besides using glossier new film, the heirs have made other changes in the travelogues. When I reminded them that Burton Holmes had told me there were two ingredients he had studiously avoided in his films— adventure and politics—I got the impression that the heirs (who insisted that Holmes's policy was "still in effect," but admitted that "this does not mean we avoid showing a country in true perspective") were not averse to injecting a little adventure and politics. I suspected that here and there they had conceded that life was real, life was earnest, and that romanticism and escape finally had to make their compromises with the grimier and grimmer realities of the Nuclear Age.

One member of Holmes's organization was more candid about a change that had taken place. "Last year we presented a film on Hong Kong," he said, "and this not only showed the usual tourist attractions but included treatment in depth of the housing problems and the menace of the Red China border a few miles away. It is our feeling that the public is considerably more interested today in world affairs and getting to know the citizens of another country than they were prior to World War II. It is not enough to present a picture-postcard approach to a subject any more. There was a time, of course, when color motion pictures alone were novel enough to satisfy an audience. This is no longer true. . . . However, we do continue to inject a feeling of taking a trip by the use of scenes showing tourists boarding trains or planes, and enjoying the attractions of the country. Basically, our audiences are people who have already traveled extensively or hope to in the future. Our narrations always include helpful suggestions to the would-be tourist."

Remembering that Burton Holmes had told me he was less popular in Cincinnati, Cleveland, Indianapolis, and Toledo than elsewhere, and that he avoided Pomona, California, completely, I wondered if there had been a geographic shift in the popularity of his travelogues after his death. The heirs would only comment that "bad cities" were the result of "bad local management and support," and that most big cities were "good cities," including Philadelphia which was one of their best. They felt that they often did well in cities where the ethnic origin of the community paralleled the subject of the film—in other words, Scandinavian subjects did wonderfully well in Minneapolis, and German subjects were popular in Chicago and environs.

The Burton Holmes team admitted that they are faced with two problems that the Master had not had to contend with in his day. The first problem is the cost of producing a travel motion picture today, a major burden being the rise in the price of transportation and living abroad. The second problem, a more serious one, is the population shift in the United States, which has directly affected the Burton Holmes audiences and the lecture itineraries. Audiences are moving from the city to the country. "Many patrons," confessed a Holmes heir, "find it unattractive to drive scores of miles from an outlying community to the center of a large city. In some large Eastern cities, older patrons have been discouraged from going out at night by newspaper reports of crime and violence." To combat this urban exodus, the Burton Holmes corporation made the decision to follow its audience into suburbia. Today, while the Chicago box office has shown a decline, this loss has been balanced by profits from travelogues offered in the outlying suburban communities of Greater Chicago.

One enemy, with whom Burton Holmes himself had never really competed, was the dragon that I felt most endangered his heirs. This dragon had not been mentioned. I mentioned it. I used the dread word —"television."

I asked, "Why should people continue to come out of their homes and pay to see and hear a live travelogue when free television, in their homes, shows them the wonders of the world for nothing? Burton Holmes had no such competition. You have. What are you doing about it?"

The heirs appeared unconcerned. Television travel films, they said, are ruined by poor prints and by the frequent advertising spiels interjected into the half-hour or hour-long programs. The true travelogue aficionado would not have his Kyoto or Taj Mahal or Matterhorn sullied by constant talk about the newest detergent or filter-tip cigarette. The true aficionado prefers the beautiful original film to the grainy print, the original with its illusion uninterrupted by grating pitchmen. Paid television, without commercials, is another thing. This, I gathered, the heirs would not try to lick but try to join. "We are following with great interest the development of pay television," I was told. "This would seem to be the perfect answer to our problem of reaching the vast untapped audiences in smaller cities across the country."

Well, despite these reassurances of the hearty future of the live travelogue, I found myself concerned and apprehensive. Perhaps the Burton Holmes corporate heirs are doing the best that can be done in this field in the United States. Perhaps they have tuned in to the times, and the mechanics of their filming and projection are better than in the past, and their subjects possess the fresh dimension of timeliness. Still, I suspect, in order to compete with free television presentations, the live travelogues require a single dynamic, persuasive, and colorful personality around which to build a cult. When a travelogue comes to a legitimate theater today, it is one more diversion, not an event. In the old days, when Burton Holmes appeared, it was an event, like the rare visit of the rich and wise uncle from faraway who, alone, could afford to see and do everything, and was ready to share with his poorer relatives the marvels he had enjoyed.

I miss Burton Holmes, as do his audiences, I am sure, just as we all miss Count Leo Tolstoi, Admiral Dewey, the Emperor Meiji, who peopled that other day when life was simpler and safer and the world still kept its secrets from the Many. I recall that when Burton Holmes died in 1958, *Life* magazine offered him a two-page pictorial obituary. There we saw the man who had been so much a part of our younger days, and was no more—Burton Holmes, Vandyke and all, immersed in a Japanese bathtub, Burton Holmes in Seoul wearing Korean traditional mourning attire, Burton Holmes dressed as a Greek soldier in Athens.

Without this Burton Holmes, I fear the travelogue will not survive this generation. And it is not the loss of Holmes himself or the expansion of television that may sound the death knell, but the contraction of the planet on which we live.

Before the Second World War, the world was still large, and its marvels—the pyramids of Egypt, the Colosseum of Rome, the Acropolis of Athens, sacred Fujiyama of Japan—were still faraway. Most men could enjoy them, and their promise of adventure and romance, only secondhand, through reading or viewing films or listening to tales spun by the travelogue lecturer. And so millions of persons paid money to escape their workaday worlds and enjoy vicariously the more exotic worlds offered by the travelogue lecturer. As a result, the Burton Holmeses flourished.

After the Second World War, most of this changed. During the war, the sons and daughters of the Burton Holmes audiences had been uprooted from their insular existence and transported to the aged cities of Europe, to the sands of Africa, to the islands of the Pacific, and they had seen these faraway places through the cynical eyes of reality. They had been where the travelogue lecturers had been, and what these young people had seen and lived was, for the majority, neither romantic nor adventurous. Disillusioned, they had returned home, and for a long time after, most of them had little patience with glossed-over narratives delivered by professionals, or with the crusted credulity of their parents who did not know better.

By the 1950's, the faithful old audience of the travelogue lecturer was dying off. Its heirs had not been converted to this form of escapism, and the new generation appeared more interested in a do-it-yourself philosophy, since a revolution in transportation had made this possible. Members of the new generation and their growing offspring had little inclination to listen to adventures related from a platform or to do their sightseeing by watching colored celluloid, when, in little more time than it took to attend a travelogue, they could visit in person, by jet-propelled aircraft, and often at cut-rate prices, the Mosque of St. Sophia in Istanbul, the Blue Grotto on Capri, or the Parsee Towers of Silence in

Bombay. The wonders of the world were suddenly accessible to anyone with a small savings account or an active credit card.

In short, I am suggesting that an international war and the turbojet, added to free television and the absence of a Big Personality, may be the graveyard of the travelogue as it was invented and popularized by Burton Holmes.

Happily, this was not to be Burton Holmes's graveyard. He lived long, but he died soon enough—certainly soon enough to avoid the ignominious end of fading into obscurity. Burton Holmes did not outlive his audience, and so he escaped the cruel fate of becoming an anachronism. Instead, like Nellie Bly, he became an American legend, and as a legend, if not as a corporation, he will enjoy immortality.

6

PARAGON OF THE
PAPERBACKS

I T IS UNLIKELY that you will find Gilbert Patten's name in many biographical dictionaries, or serious studies of literary criticism. Yet his pen, perhaps the most prolific in the whole of American authorship, was inspired to create a character whose name became part of our living language and whose feats encouraged a great proportion of today's eminent male Americans to strive for success.

Gilbert Patten, who rarely wrote under his own name and never received a penny in royalties for most of his 648 published books, died a half-dozen years ago, a forgotten man at seventy-eight. But the character he created lives on, immortal, for Gilbert Patten gave birth to Frank Merriwell. And it was through the fictional Frank Merriwell, exponent of the clean life and chivalrous act, master of the ninth-inning home run, that Patten made his indelible imprint on American thought and action, by influencing countless leaders who today direct and guide American life.

Christy Mathewson, Woodrow Wilson, and Babe Ruth were early and fanatic Frank Merriwell followers. O. O. McIntyre, Al Smith, Floyd Gibbons, and Wendell Willkie worshipfully regarded Merriwell as a beacon for good, ranking behind only Church and Mother.

Today, John L. Collyer, president of the B. F. Goodrich Company, admits that he went to college, and on to success in industry, because of encouragement found in reading Frank Merriwell. James Knott founded his chain of hotels, Jed Harris became a renowned Broadway producer, and Eddie Eagen gave up professional pugilism for Yale and fame, all because of the early inspiration derived from Gilbert Patten's hero. It was Frank Merriwell "who shaped my ambitions for clean living and athletic supremacy," Eagen confessed in his autobiography. "Merriwell's superhuman virtues were to me precedents far more impressive than the Ten Commandments." In much the same vein, Jess Willard, Jack Dempsey, Rudy Vallee, Franklin P. Adams, Fredric March, and even a congressman from Maine publicly admitted their debt to the paragon of the paperbacks.

In the fifty-five years of his make-believe life, Frank Merriwell has served the citizenry tirelessly and well in an entertainment decathlon of dime novels, magazines, syndicated columns, comic strips and radio. To-day in Hollywood, a major producing company, the Frank Merriwell Enterprises, assisted by Patten's surviving son, will soon project the perpetual Frank on television—and a whole new generation of red-blooded Americans, who no longer read his books, will derive from him the same inspiration their fathers did and will in turn strive ever Onward and Upward.

Clearly, Frank Merriwell has become as much a part of our national heritage as Huck Finn, Paul Bunyan, Tarzan, and Mickey Mouse. But even as his fame is renewed, the name of his creator recedes with passing years. Yet, to know Merriwell, one must know his genesis, must know the long-neglected, colorful hack who conceived and developed him under fantastic pressure.

William Gilbert Patten was born in Maine, during 1866, the son of ardent pacifists. His father, who was six feet four and had met Lincoln, hoped Gilbert would become a carpenter; his mother hoped he would become a minister. In a literary sense, Gilbert became both. He hated school, where his teachers regarded him as somewhat retarded, but he read omnivorously at home, especially Dickens and Hawthorne. He wanted to write a novel as great as *The Scarlet Letter*, and, at sixteen, started a baseball novel which he soon laid aside. Actually, he was led into this early sedentary life by his stature and his parents' pacifistic convictions. A gangling six-footer, he was not permitted to fight the other boys. His sole diversion, beyond pushing a pencil, was managing the Camden baseball team, a member of the Knox County League, to a pennant. In wet-nursing these bush-leaguers, Patten incubated at least a half-dozen players for the major leagues—as well as the peerless Merriwell.

While still in his adolescence, Patten started a weekly newspaper, *The Corinna Owl*, and within a year had acquired $900 in debts. Fortunately, his weekly had cut into the circulation of a rival paper, and when they offered to buy him out, he grabbed. Still eager to write, he talked about free-lancing. His father gave him a month to put up or shut up. Challenged, young Patten, in four frenzied days, wrote two short stories—"A

Bad Man" and "The Pride of Sandy Flat"—and sold them to a New York weekly for three dollars each. Elated, he finished his old baseball novel, sold it for fifty dollars, and followed it with another which brought seventy-five dollars. After that, he forgot about college, married a Corinna girl friend who had helped him with his grammar, and was soon earning $2,700 a year grinding out dime-novel detective and western stories.

Raising his sights, he went to Broadway to become a playwright. He wrote a drama about a nagging wife, *Men of Millions,* which opened and closed in New Haven, hissed into oblivion by Yale students. This catastrophe invited others. After being evicted from his walk-up for nonpayment of rent, and finding himself suddenly burdened by an invalided father and mother, in addition to a wife, Patten reluctantly returned to dime novels. He did not mean to stay in the field; he just wanted a few easy dollars to tide him over. He scribbled western after western for Beadle and Adams, under the name of Wyoming Will, at $150 an epic. Quitting the Beadle firm over an argument involving a ten-dollar advance, he turned to doing boys' adventures for Street & Smith.

Patten's new publishers liked his work and suggested a juvenile series built around a single character who "should have a catchy name, such as Dick Lightheart, Jack Harkaway, Gay Dashleigh." The publishers suggested that the hero become involved in escapades while attending a military academy, then inherit a "considerable sum of money" and temporarily leave school. "A little love element would also not be amiss," the publishers wrote Patten. "When the hero is once projected on his travels, there is an infinite variety of incident to choose from. After we run through twenty or thirty numbers of this, we would bring the hero back and have him go to college—say, Yale University; thence we could take him on his travels again to the South Seas or anywhere."

Patten gave the assignment some thought. Then, in four days, he whipped out his first 20,000-word novel under the pseudonym of Burt L. Standish. The hero, introduced on the very first page—"His face was frank, open and winning, but the merry light that usually dwelt in his eyes was now banished by a look of scorn"—was none other than the one and only Frank Merriwell. The date was April 18, 1896.

"I took the three qualities I most wanted him to represent—frank and merry in nature, and well in body and mind—and made the name Frank Merriwell," recalled Patten later. While the character was fictional, some of Merriwell's more spectacular talents were carefully fashioned after the fabulous Indian athlete, Louie Sockalexis, who had played baseball under Patten in Maine and could dash one hundred yards in ten seconds in full uniform. Sockalexis, educated at Holy Cross, was signed by the big-league Cleveland Spiders, who thereafter became the Indians. Persuaded by well-wishers to forsake his milk diet for bourbon, the prototype of Merriwell was finally dropped by the major leagues for his extended bouts with alcohol. He wound up as a street beggar in Hartford.

Patten gave Frank Merriwell the Indian's prowess, but none of his personal problems. Merriwell neither smoked nor drank. "I wanted," said Patten, "a boy who had no vices, but who didn't act as if he had no vices." And again, "When I conceived Frank, I think I hit on approximately the boy that every kid would like to be. Not, mind you, the boy that every kid ought to be. That was the Horatio Alger idea—a moral in every story. But my boy pointed no moral; he was just every boy's ideal picture of himself."

Frank Merriwell was introduced to America as he stepped down from the train bringing him to Fardale, his prep school. In the opening paragraph he saw a bully, Bart Hodge, kick a dog and cuff a young popcorn vendor. Promptly, Frank spoke his first of a million words to follow: "That was a cowardly blow!" The battle was under way. Merriwell floored the bully with a smashing right to the jaw. With that electric punch, all young America took Merriwell to its heart.

Like Byron, Merriwell woke up to find himself famous. The first nickel *Tip Top Weekly*, with its colored cover, featuring "Frank Merriwell; or, First Days at Fardale," was a complete sellout. No sooner had young readers had a taste of Merriwell overcoming the heavy's efforts to keep him out of Fardale, Merriwell rescuing the wealthy, brunette Inza Burrage from a mad dog, Merriwell escaping from a locked cemetery vault, than they loudly clamored for more. Within three months, *Tip Top Weekly* soared to a circulation of 75,000, then 100,000, and Patten estimated that actually over 500,000 boys were reading the stories every week. Hundreds of adults, after glimpsing the stories, hopefully named their newest offspring Frank Merriwell Smith or Inza Jones. Thousands of Rand McNally geography texts camouflaged Merriwell paperbacks in the country's classrooms, causing one educator to remark wryly, "We're now teaching readin', writin', 'rithmetic, and Merriwell."

Gilbert Patten, when he started the series, had hoped to devote no more than four or five days a week to the Merriwell potboilers, and give the rest of his time to more mature creative efforts. But the sudden popularity of the character, the public's insatiable demand for more plots, characters, variety, overwhelmed him. Merriwell became a triple-threat Frankenstein's monster, consuming all his waking hours and energy.

Patten was contracted, at $50 a week, to deliver a complete 20,000-word adventure every seven days. Seventeen years and twenty million words later, he was still delivering his weekly quota, though his salary had been upped to only $150. His pen name, his hero, his stories belonged solely to the publishers. Patten never collected a royalty during this literary marathon.

After two years of Merriwell, his fingers became calloused and cramped from the unceasing physical labor of writing, and Patten switched to dictating. During mornings and through lunch periods, he paced the equivalent of five miles as he dictated four hours daily to a stenographer; during afternoons he revised, researched, and jotted notes on new backgrounds. He plotted thirteen different Merriwell stories at a time. He had so many characters entering and exiting that he kept an index file of them. "Now and then I did forget a character and made a slip," he once recalled, "and a thousand youngsters immediately jumped on me. Once I killed Inza Burrage's father in Africa. I forgot to cross out his name in the card index. A year later, I brought him to life. Indignant letters flooded me. Luckily, I hadn't described the scene in which her father was killed, so in my next story I was able to explain that it was all a mistake and he wasn't dead after all."

Almost all the Merriwell sagas were written under pressure. When he worked in Maine, Patten sometimes delivered his uncorrected manuscript, at a dead run, to the clerk aboard the passing mail train to New York. Once, to obtain a week's vacation, he manufactured 50,000 words in seven days. But he liked to point out that he was painstaking when compared to several of his contemporaries. Ed Wheeler, to make a deadline, once did a 30,000-word Deadwood Dick novel in forty-eight hours, and Colonel Prentiss Ingraham once topped this mark by completing a 33,000-word Buffalo Bill story in twenty-four hours.

But if Patten was not the fastest, he was surely one of the most prolific scribes of all time. True, Alexandre Dumas, *père*, turned out 1,200 books, but he employed a factory of hired hands. Patten, single-handed, ripped out 208 of the 245 Frank Merriwell paperbacks (each book containing four of the *Tip Top* stories), 415 other nickel novels featuring characters like Lefty Locke and Bill Bruce of Harvard, and 25 hardbound volumes—in all, about 40 million words, half of them devoted to Merriwell, and with an estimated total circulation of 137 million copies.

Patten's publishers were constantly fearful that he might fall ill or for some other reason one day fail to meet his weekly deadline. To protect themselves, just as play producers hire understudies for their leading actors, Patten's publishers kept a stand-in writer in the wings, with three pseudo-Merriwell stories written and ready to go. The stand-in, who was never needed, and who went on to create his own Merriwell in Lanny Budd, was Upton Sinclair.

The constant grind, the seventeen-year search for new situations, kept

Patten in hot water. The prep school days at Fardale were relatively easy. Frank Merriwell, when he had time off from boxing, wrestling, track, football, and his outstanding sport, baseball, was busy converting enemies into friends. Bart Hodge, whom Merriwell had floored at the railway station and whose life he later saved, as well as Jack Diamond, who still recognized the Confederacy, and Bruce Browning, a tough Goliath, were all bullies who succumbed before Merriwell's missionary tactics.

Early in the series, young America gradually learned of Merriwell's past. His father had been a wealthy mine owner, addicted to gambling, who had disappeared in the wild West. Merriwell's inheritance consisted of a school allowance, a ring bearing peculiar scratchings, and an eccentric guardian named Professor Scotch. In Fardale, a mysterious group of mobsters tried to abduct Merriwell and steal his ring. Needless to say, Frank outwitted the thugs.

In due time, Merriwell was matriculated in hallowed Yale. The Ivy League had seen nothing like him before. He played only in the last minutes of football games, and won them all, especially when pitted against Harvard. During track season, he was constantly being kidnaped, rendered unconscious, and tied down, only to appear miraculously in time to gallop off with a victory in the last lap of the critical relay. But baseball was his specialty. Great hurlers have come and gone since Merriwell—Matty with his fadeaway, Faber with his spitter, Hubbell with his screwball, Feller with his fast one—but none ever mastered, or came near mastering, Merriwell's untouchable double-shoot (it curved in two directions on its way to the plate).

For game after game, though drugged by the blackest villains, Merriwell would escape some distant barn or dungeon to capture and foil the heavy and his henchmen, and to return to the diamond in time for the last of the ninth. Usually as he staggered on the field, to thunderous acclaim, Yale had the bases loaded, two outs, and trailed helplessly by three runs in the last of the ninth. Dark day for Old Eli, and then Merriwell strode to the plate. A pitch. A swing. A mighty home run. *Merriwell!*

Sometimes, though, to break the monotony, Patten would permit Merriwell only an ordinary single, as witness:

"Coulter tried to fool Frank with an outcurve on the next delivery. He believed Merriwell would bite at it, and he was right. But right there Coulter received a shock, for Merriwell leaned forward as he swung, assuming such a position that the ball must have hit him had it been a straight one. It had a sharp, wide curve, and passed at least ten inches beyond the plate. Passed? Not much! Merriwell hit it and sent a daisy-cutter down into right field, exactly where he wished to place it."

Merriwell won so many athletic contests for Yale that Heywood Broun was moved to recollect, years later: "After the first eight or ten years, some of the readers began to complain. They said that, even though he was a fictional character, Frank shouldn't be allowed to stay in college so long. Eight years is a long time for a man to play on a varsity football team—even at Yale." This criticism brought an immediate and indignant rebuttal from Patten, who insisted that Frank had never gone to Yale a day over four years and he could prove it. As a matter of fact, Broun's memory was faulty.

But keeping Merriwell in college for the proper four years—yet busy for seventeen years—required literary juggling that eventually led Patten into a nervous breakdown. When the series was at its popularity peak, Merriwell was already a junior. Fearful of allowing Merriwell to graduate too soon, thereby making him ineligible for further college sports, Patten had racked his brain for a solution.

Suddenly inspired, Patten made his hero drop out of college. The scratchings on Merriwell's inherited ring proved to be a map of a gold mine in the West. Transferred to paper, the map fell into the hands of Frank's enemies. Merriwell left Yale, and raced his rivals toward the mine. After surviving an ambush, and other inconveniences, Frank staked out his rightful claim. Thereafter, he remained on the loose. He went to work on a railroad and settled a strike. He routed train robbers. He plunged into Darkest Africa to slay a lion and save blond Elsie Bellwood, attractive daughter of a sea captain. He sought Inca treasure in the crags of Peru. He hurried to Europe to engage a depraved French adversary:

"Frank Merriwell's movements had been equally as swift as his adversary's. The instant the light went out, he swung his body far to one side and thus it happened that Bruant's hands grasped nothing when he made that savage clutch across the table. But the violence of his spring flung the table against Frank, who was unable to extricate himself, and over they went with a crash upon the floor. A curse escaped the lips of the strangler. He caught hold of Merry, and it was wonderful how swiftly his hands leaped up to the throat of the young American and fastened there. Frank felt that the supreme moment had come. . . . Judging well where to hit, Frank Merriwell struck Bruant down in the dark. He found his way across the room to the door, flung his shoulder against it, and burst it open. The old man in the front shop stared at him open-mouthed. 'Monsieur,' said Frank quietly, 'the man in the back room needs the services of a skilled surgeon.' "

Returning to Yale in time to clout another winning home run against Harvard, Merriwell learned that his father had remarried before dying, and left him a half brother somewhere in the Rockies. Merriwell's college days were almost over, and the half brother, Dick, had been planted by Patten to perpetuate the paperback series. After a hair-raising odyssey, Frank finally located the wild, unruly Dick, a fifteen-year-old who could converse with animals and who was being raised by an Indian. After enrolling his half brother in Fardale, Merriwell graduated from Yale, barnstormed the country with his double-shoot, took over the Bloomfield Home for Wayward Boys (the boys resented Frank at first, but learned to love him), and finally married and produced Frank, Jr.

The energy expended by Merriwell in these acrobatics would have required in any normal citizen the constitution of a Hercules supplemented by an ample supply of Benzedrine. Merriwell needed neither. Conditioning was the major factor in his success. For one thing, he avoided liquor. "Though, once I had him take a drink," Patten has recorded, "just to prove to my millions of readers that he was not an insufferable goody-goody. A gasp of horror swept across the nation that week."

Too, Merriwell despised cigarettes, and warned his half brother off coffin nails, thereby inspiring the impressionable Dick to sermonize to a roommate, "Tucker, you're a jolly chap, and I like you, but I wish you'd cut those little paper-wrapped devils out of your list of friends supposed-to-be." Merriwell also frowned on cursing. The strongest expletive ever to cross his lips was "Gosh hang it all." His lone weakness, inherited from his father, was gambling, a vice which, happily, he finally conquered.

Patten always resented remarks that his brainchild was too much the Galahad. "They laugh about Frank's bravery," he once told an interviewer, "but, as a matter of fact, he wasn't so brave. He was scared often. Much more important was his loyalty, something that boys esteem more than anything else. No matter how hard pressed Frank might be, he never played anybody a dirty trick. Of course, it was my business to see that he was hard pressed in every story. He was always getting into jams, so that if he would only turn against his friends he could make a million dollars. Of course, he never did it."

Merriwell, as any middle-aged reader will remember, had a lively, if unsubtle, sense of humor. He was a practiced ventriloquist, and turned his bewildered cronies into swivel-heads. Once, he placed a turtle in the bed of a jumpy friend, and rolled on the floor in glee at the result. And he never failed to double up at the speech of his sidekick, Harry Rattleton, a word-mangler, who would say, "I seel filly—I mean, I feel silly."

As for the ladies, Merriwell was a gay dog when the occasion demanded. True, he rarely had time for anything more demonstrative than saving them from runaway horses or massive abductors, but he did manage to kiss Inza Burrage twice during the Fardale years. For a long time, he could not decide between the spirited Inza and the softer Elsie. Patten was about to have Merriwell wed Elsie, when a storm of protest halted the marriage. "I liked Elsie better," Patten admitted. "But I got so many letters from readers favoring Inza, that I had to have him marry her instead. The readers seemed to like the girl who went out and did things, as Inza did, rather than the clinging-vine type like Elsie."

In 1913, Patten ended what he had begun in 1896, ended what he liked to call "the longest serial story ever written." After he switched to writing for another pulp magazine, Street & Smith assigned three writers to carry on the Merriwell saga. The half brother, Dick Merriwell, who had not mastered the double-shoot and was somewhat windy, and Frank, Jr., who was merely a pallid edition of his famous father, pushed on for three more years of trial and tribulation at Yale, before they were suffocated by the novelty of the nickelodeon.

Patten had made little more than a livelihood out of Merriwell. Now he turned his back on his old friend, to see what he could do on his own. Patten became, successively, a magazine editor, a Hollywood scenarist for Norma Talmadge, a free-lance writer. Worried that he'd been typecast by Merriwell, eager to prove he could write on other subjects, he began producing successfully for *True Story* magazine and *Saucy Stories*. "That stuff made me pretty sick," he admitted, "but it convinced the editors and won me a new market." Meanwhile, he returned to his first love, playwriting. A whodunit, *The Invisible Power*, was accepted by Sam Harris, shelved by an actors' strike, and never revived.

Finally, with the bases loaded against him, Patten called Merriwell in from the bullpen for one last fling. Actually, Merriwell had never been out of Patten's thoughts. He had hovered over his brainchild like an anxious mother hen. Once, an editor of the Junior Literary Guild had blasted the Merriwell series. "They are too easy to read. They pander to all our outworn and shoddy old shibboleths, have almost no content, are sentimental and sensational." Patten had defended his character then as "honest, manly, patriotic" and insisted he had never heard of a single criminal who'd read Merriwell.

Obtaining, at last, the copyright on Merriwell, Patten put him to work again in comics, columns, and on the radio. And in 1941, at a publisher's request, he wrote a modern, full-length novel called *Mr. Frank Merriwell*, in which his hero, now middle-aged, dwelt in a bungalow called The Nest, with matronly Inza. Merriwell had two children, the presidency of the Town Improvement Society, and the desire to rescue America from isolationism. He was the old dependable, true-blue Merriwell, roaring at a crooked lawyer, "Neither browbeating nor cheap mockery will get you very far, Judge Grimshaw." In this novel Merriwell thrashed four ruffians with a cane, and turned on those who would frame him with, "Get out of here, you filthy tools of a vile master!" In the end, the villain, who could never "restrain a corner of his thin upper lip from lifting sneeringly," was soundly subdued by the aging Merriwell.

The book caused hardly a ripple in the sea of American letters. But one review, in the New York *Herald Tribune,* warmed the old author's heart. "You may have, if you want them, all the slick novels about pretentious society females, whose souls are riddled with neuroses that would make a small-town high school girl blush with shame, but for good, clean heartthrobs and unsuppressible tears down the cheek, give us Frank Merriwell every time."

Although Gilbert Patten, a handsome, athletic, six-footer, looked like Merriwell until the very day of his death, at seventy-eight, in 1945, he was anything but his hero in private life. He married three times. He was a chain smoker and a poker fiend. He was never quite sure he cared for the young boys who were his audience. He hated travel. Twice he started West to get color for his stories, only to turn back once at Omaha, and the next time at Denver.

He liked Mark Twain, but not Tom Sawyer. He enjoyed reading Deadwood Dick, but thought his greatest competitor, Horatio Alger, was poor at plotting. He regretted, above all else, that he'd never gone to college. He regarded laughter as the greatest of medicines. "I believe in one hearty laugh a day. It's my safety valve." He enjoyed almost every day of his life. "Life has always been a grand adventure for me, even at its dullest. It's still the greatest invention I know of."

Several years before his death in California, someone asked him if he had ever really cared for Frank Merriwell. He thought a moment, then replied, "Did I love Merriwell? Not at first. Those early stories were more of a joke to me than anything else. But when it got so that a half million kids were reading him every week, I began to realize that I had about the biggest chance to influence the youth of this country that any man ever had. Yes, I loved him. And I loved him most because no boy, if he followed in his tracks, ever did anything that he need be ashamed of."

WHAT HAS HAPPENED SINCE . . .

When I was a boy growing up in Wisconsin, the Frank Merriwell stories were still available, but had declined sharply in popularity. In those days, I recall, I was devoted to a more scientifically oriented hero named Tom Swift. I was also reading *The Red-Headed Outfield* by Zane Grey, *Tarzan of the Apes* by Edgar Rice Burroughs, *Pitching in a Pinch* by Christy Mathewson—until, still in preadolescence, I graduated to *The Hound of the Baskervilles* by A. Conan Doyle, *Twenty Thousand Leagues Under the Sea* by Jules Verne, and *Of Human Bondage* by W. Somerset Maugham.

Yet, somewhere in between I had finally gone over to Gilbert Patten's Frank Merriwell. The dime novels, as I have said, were still around. Patten had ceased writing them three years before I was born, but his stories could be bought on Main Street in my hometown at Becker's Tobacco Store, and I bought them and read them voraciously. The invincible Merriwell was an idol of my grammar school period, and idols of one's formative years die hard. But as I grew older, matured, I saw, in retrospect, that he was quite impossible. Yet, I could never satirize or dismiss him, any more than I could derogate the best moments of my youth—and it was with difficulty, when I finally wrote about him, that I found the objectivity to chide his purity and perfection.

I always knew that I would write about him, and about the unappreciated literary giant who created him, but for many years I could not find the time. I did set up one file folder, among the many others, labeled "Merriwell-Patten," and from time to time I deposited appropriate clippings or notes in it.

One day in 1952 I learned that an acquaintance of mine, a film agent named Ira Ure, had gone into partnership with a film producer named Tony London, and they had acquired the rights to turn the Frank Merriwell stories into a television series. I spoke to the partners, told them of my interest, and learned that they had a considerable amount of factual information on Patten and Merriwell, obtained from the author's family. I told them I would like to add this material to my own and write a story about Patten for a major periodical. From their point of view, this was a wonderful idea. Merriwell had receded into obscurity, and any published story would advertise their projected television series. From my point of view, the possibility of a television show gave me a timely peg on which to hang the Merriwell saga, and gave me the excuse to write a story I had always wanted to write.

I asked *Reader's Digest* magazine if they were interested. They were very much interested. And so, enjoying every minute of it, I wrote "Paragon of the Paperbacks," and it appeared in the January, 1953, issue of *Reader's Digest*. Its appearance flushed out the fact that there were numerous ardent collectors of the Gilbert Patten dime novels throughout the land. Even one friend of mine, the late Horace McCoy, author of *They Shoot Horses, Don't They?*, telephoned me in a fever of ecstasy.

"My God, Irving, that was a wonderful article about Patten," he said, "and about time someone did it. Here we've known each other all these years, and I didn't know you were interested, and you didn't know I have a complete collection of every Frank Merriwell story ever published!"

While the publication of my story endeared me to Merriwell devotees, and was apparently read by millions who enjoy the curiosities of Americana and literature, it made no impression on the executive pioneers of television. The Merriwell series never developed, and the producers moved on to other projects.

However, one of the disappointed producers, Tony London, remained friendly with the widow of Patten's only son. Her name was Mrs. Harvan Barr Patten, and she dwelt in Vista, California, and her basement was an unexplored repository for what was left of her father-in-law's literary estate. Since London's interest in Patten and Merriwell did not diminish in the ensuing six years, it was to him that Mrs. Patten turned in 1959. She was about to move and had to determine how to dispose of her father-in-law's old manuscripts, which were still stored in several boxes in her basement. London agreed to review this material, which had remained unopened for eighteen years.

Not long after he had explored Mrs. Patten's basement, I received a telephone call from Tony London. I had not spoken to him more than a few times since the publication of my Patten article six or seven years earlier, and I was surprised to hear from him. There was repressed excitement in his voice. At last, he blurted out the reason for his call. By a fantastic stroke of luck, he said, he had uncovered a minor literary treasure.

What he had found, while poking through the manuscripts in Mrs. Patten's basement, was an autobiography that the creator of Frank Merriwell had written but never published. The manuscript was filled with fresh and little-known, or heretofore unknown, information about Gilbert Patten, and was written with a good deal of candor, even when treating with his personal life. Patten revealed that he was forced into his first marriage, which lasted twelve years and produced his only son; that his impulsive second marriage to a lively Southern girl ended because, among other things, she was flirtatious; that his third wife, Carol, daughter of a Union officer and educated abroad, gave him his happiest times. Interestingly, although he lived until 1945, Patten brought his autobiography up to only 1918. However, he had added a section on his third wife, which ended all he would ever write of his life: "Our honeymoon lasted more than twenty years. Carol died the twenty-first of August, 1938."

There was much more detail about the dime novel era and the saga of Merriwell, but I had heard enough to know it was a valuable find. When London finally posed his question—"Could this be published as a book today?"—I replied without reservation, "Yes." Of course, it would require an editor, as well as a writer who could bring the story along from the time the autobiography ended, when Patten was fifty-two, until the time his life ended, when he was seventy-eight.

Because of my own interest in Patten and Merriwell, because I had already published five books (three of them biography), because one of my books, *The Chapman Report*, was enjoying a popular success at the time, Tony London inquired if I would be interested in preparing Patten's autobiography for publication. I told him that at another time I would have undertaken it, but my mind had turned to the creation of fiction, and that I would have to pass up this opportunity. But, I added, I was still interested enough to see if I could help get the autobiography into print.

After numerous inquiries among my author friends, I was able to direct London to a writers' organization, and through this organization the Patten story fell into the able hands of Harriet Hinsdale, a Los Angeles playwright and novelist. In 1964, *Frank Merriwell's "Father"* as edited by Harriet Hinsdale, assisted by Tony London, was published by the University of Oklahoma Press. In its pages I learned that, according to the American Bible Society, the Holy Book had sold 545,214,000 copies in the United States in 143 years. "Yet in the short span of less than 20 years, it has been estimated by the publishers, that of the Merriwell books alone, about 500,000,000 were printed."

The literati may make what they wish of those figures (now being increased by the appearance of a new series of juvenile paperbacks featuring Frank Merriwell, Jr.). As for myself, I am gratified to have contributed, in however small a way, to a brief revival of the noble, intrepid, and flawless Frank Merriwell in the dark age of the anti-hero.

7

THEY CUT AWAY HIS
CONSCIENCE

P ERIODS OF MENTAL DEPRESSION—"the blues," as most people like to
call them—are as much a part of every human being's heritage as
death and taxes. Normal persons, however, are able to snap out of these
spells readily and regularly. Usually, a stiff drink, a fresh experience, a bit
of good news, a short trip, or even a new day, will turn the trick.

But these simple cures, unfortunately, do not work for everyone. Often, the causes of depression are too deep-rooted, and the results too
acute, for the victim to function normally. When this happens, the family doctor is prescribed, or a psychiatrist, and possibly insulin or electric
shock treatments. Sometimes, however, even these measures do not help,
and the patient becomes too morbidly depressed and psychopathic to
perform the most ordinary workaday tasks of living.

The illness can take many forms. The patient may become obsessed
with worries, agitated by countless fears, haunted by agonizing anxieties.
He may reach a purgatory of the mind: he cannot live, and he cannot
die. He may become sufficiently psychotic to require confinement, or
become insane, or, wishing he were dead, attempt suicide.

When a human being reaches this stage, and all obvious cures seem to
have failed, there still remains a treatment of the last resort. This is a
drastic operation which, though relatively safe and painless, has been
performed about 20,000 times throughout the world, on poor and prominent alike. It is a form of psychosurgery known as prefrontal lobotomy.

During the operation, a thin knife is used to sever the tissue of the
frontal lobes of the brain, which govern a person's social behavior, from
the thalamus, at the lower rear of the brain, an area considered to be the
center of a person's emotions. The frontal lobes, the gray matter behind
the forehead, are generally conceded to be the storehouse of a human's

foresight and insight, his imagination, self-consciousness, anticipation, which when tinged by painful emotion, become the seat of his apprehension and anxiety. By disconnecting these frontal lobes from the rest of the brain centers, the pressure of worry and mental pain is permanently removed.

Prefrontal lobotomy, first tried in 1936 in Lisbon by an elderly Portuguese neurologist, who won a Nobel Prize for his accomplishment, is probably the most radical method so far invented in modern times to relieve mental distress. The operation is no mere opening of flesh and bone to remove some tangible malignancy. Actually, the operation seems to make an incision into the very stuff of Life.

The fact is, the man who submits to a prefrontal lobotomy comes out of the anesthetic a different person. He may appear the same physically, but his personality is changed, often totally. There are those who feel this is a good thing, since he couldn't live with his old self, anyway. There are others who insist this is a bad thing, an unpredictable infringement on the Creator's work.

Thus, in the years since its inception, prefrontal lobotomy has been the center of a heated, worldwide controversy. The neuropsychiatrists who favor the operation can back up their stand with the fact that prefrontal lobotomy prevents insanity and suicide and alleviates pain by reducing anxiety and removing worry. Thus, they can show that it usually makes men happier. Two of the foremost exponents of this school, physicians connected with an eastern university, strongly favor the operation. "Prefrontal lobotomy is an operation of last resort," they write. "It should be performed only on those patients who no longer have a reasonable hope of spontaneous recovery. It should be done only in cases of threatened disability or suicide, and only after conservative measures have failed. It should be done with the full appreciation of the changes in personality that will inevitably be brought about. . . ." Once the operation is performed, say these advocates of lobotomy, and the patients find themselves freed of their old tensions, they learn the surgery has made "life particularly agreeable to them and they enjoy it to the fullest."

On the other hand, there is the school of thought that can prove, also from factual evidence, that prefrontal lobotomy converts patients into docile, inert, often useless drones, stripping them of their old powers, giving them convulsive seizures, making them indifferent to social amenities, filling them with aggressive misbehavior, and impairing their foresight and insight. Then, there are those who feel the operation tampers with the God substance, who feel that if it cuts out a man's cares, it also cuts out his soul and his conscience. But the greatest number of critics are less opposed to the operation itself than to its indiscriminate use. Dr.

Nolan D. C. Lewis, director of the New York State Psychiatric Institute, says, "In recent years, early cases are being subjected to the operation in ever increasing numbers, often without adequate psychiatric examination. Such widespread application of a radical surgical method should be limited, until there is more proof of what the actual results involve."

Neither side, in the disagreement, is able to marshal adequately decisive statistics as evidence—although, currently, the Veterans Administration Psychiatric Division, which has performed 1,200 of these lobotomies, is in the process of making a survey of the results. Their findings may, one day, help evaluate the operation's merits and settle the controversy. But, while surveys may seem to show whether or not the results justify the attendant changes in personality, it is doubtful if statistics will ever actually be able to solve the human equation involved. For, in trying to determine if an operation has been good or bad, what absolute measuring stick or standard can be used to judge? And from whose point of view can judgment be made? From the point of view of the patient? Or from the point of view of those around him? Or from the point of view of the doctor in the case?

Out of the 2,000 to 3,000 prefrontal lobotomies performed in the United States since 1936, I have had the opportunity, in the last few years, to come in particularly close contact with one case. From the details of this single case, perhaps, the reader may be able to judge for himself the moral and medical rights and wrongs involved in psychosurgery. But before setting down the events in the life of Larry Cassidy, as I shall call him, I must remind the reader that these things happened, that the incidents here put down are fact, not fiction.

>«

One might say that the real story of Larry Cassidy began in 1943 when, at the age of twenty-nine, he began to have headaches, sudden unaccountable fits of crying, terrible attacks of depression, and a growing inability to work or play. Actually, though, as even the most amateur psychiatrist may guess, and as Larry himself learned quickly enough from professional analysts, it had all begun back in the dim shadow of remembrance that was his childhood.

Larry's father was a big barrel of a man, a naturalized citizen, well-educated, hot-tempered, given to ranting when angry, and righteousness when controlled. He owned a small, prosperous weekly newspaper in New York City, which adequately provided for his large family. Larry's mother was a tentative creature, hovering in the background, gentle and cowed, beloved by father and sons alike.

There were five boys. Next to Tim, Larry was the oldest. Of the others, the one who would remain the closest to Larry and play the most important role in the drama that lay ahead was Jack, the youngest, born when Larry was already eleven. From his earliest years, Larry, alone, re-acted strangely to his father's severity and bursts of anger. If one of the boys committed mischief, and the culprit hid behind silence, Larry would usually step forward to take the blame. When he was punished, he took it stoically. The others would let out normal yelps and shed normal tears when spanked. But no one remembered that Larry ever cried.

The boys had one thing in common. They resented their father, each for a different reason, and they all constantly trooped to their mother for consolation and soothing. Each was, in his own way, bright, but Larry was brilliant. By the age of nine, he had devoured most of the classics. On Sundays, when the family sat around and listened to symphonic music, and the boys took turns imitating Toscanini with a ruler for a baton, it was Larry who was the most expert and feverish conductor.

When Larry was thirteen, his father suddenly became blind. The elder autocrat remained fiercely proud. He dressed himself, and shaved himself, and continued to go about his business as if nothing had happened. No one in the family ever dared mention his blindness in front of him.

Shortly after Larry entered high school, at fourteen, he broke out in a rash and became mildly ill. The family doctor said that the boy had been studying too hard, was run down, and just needed a little rest and he would be fine. However, despite his illness, in high school Larry ex-celled in his studies, played tennis and swam with efficiency, enjoyed watching the New York Yankees, liked to browse through the Museum of Modern Art, or attend an occasional movie recommended by *The New Yorker* magazine. He seldom dated. And when he accompanied his brothers and friends to a dance or a bar, or around town to raise hell in general, he was always with the group but not a part of it. Occasionally, he forced himself to participate. But he preferred to observe.

Larry wanted to become a college professor, since he thought he could do well in this field. (His father objected, saying that there wasn't any money in it, and he expected Larry to begin taking over the weekly paper when he finished school.) At the time he entered Princeton, in 1932, at the age of eighteen, Larry was a shy-mannered, pleasant-looking young man of middle height. He was gentle, kind, unselfish, given to introspec-tion and to never expressing an opinion until he had read all sides of a subject, and even then he would usually say that he was not sure what he thought. He roomed with a clever, more energetic young man named Burt, the son of a wealthy New York magazine publisher, who became his best friend and remains his best friend today.

During his freshman year, Larry wrote a letter home, the first of many to follow, on the uselessness of life. The family did not take it seriously. "That Princeton punk," a relative said with amusement, "he's just found Schopenhauer." But Jack, the youngest brother, still remembers the impact of the letter on his own immature mind. "It was brilliantly written, terribly logical, and at the time seemed practically unanswerable."

Larry majored in English. He planned to become a professor, even though his father continued to regard this as an impractical whim and still expected him to take over the weekly paper. Except for playing tennis and golf, Larry buried himself in books and avoided campus social life. His I.Q. was over 150, in the "near genius" category, as compared to the more common I.Q. of between 85 and 114 possessed by 66 percent of the population. An essay he wrote won him a $300 university prize. He became a Phi Beta Kappa, and when he graduated from Princeton in 1936, was among the top ten in his class. He was the only member of his class who did not bother to show up for the commencement exercises.

After Princeton, despite the elder Cassidy's insistence about the family newspaper, Larry took a job with Burt writing detective stories and movie features for the pulp magazines published by his roommate's father. The work soon bored him, and he quit. He obtained a job in the New York *World-Telegram* advertising department, but this bored him even more, and he quit again. Finally, he went to work on his father's weekly newspaper. He kept irregular hours. Usually he went to the office at ten in the morning, and called it a day at noon. He had no patience with the work, even though what he did he did well. After the two hours in the office, he spent the afternoon home reading. He rarely left the house. By eight in the evening, he was in bed.

This was 1939. And during that year Larry's mother suddenly died. It was a crushing blow, not only to Larry but to his father and brothers. His father had loved his wife deeply. And for the boys, it seemed the one light in the house had gone out. For a full year after her death, the six men, blind father and five sons, met at the dinner table and exchanged hardly a word. The only smiling face in the house, during that period, was Harriet's. She was the housekeeper, a rather plain, simple girl, in her middle twenties, who had never gone beyond the fourth grade in school and who had come to New York from a small Ohio farming town located near Dayton. She was given to easy laughter and quick enthusiasms. She worshiped Larry.

About a year after their mother's death, the boys left home to go their separate ways. Larry and his youngest brother, Jack, stayed on with their father several months. Larry was increasingly erratic about performing his job on the weekly newspaper. He spent more and more time alone at home with his books, skimming three or four a day, and he became more and more morose. He began suffering attacks of nausea. He could not hold food in his stomach. For a period after each meal, he would regurgitate.

Presently, almost naturally, the threesome broke up. Jack was placed in a boarding school. Larry, accompanied by Harriet who insisted upon nursing him, went to Albuquerque to join his older brother. Larry still thought that he might become a schoolteacher. Meanwhile, the elder Cassidy had given up the old family house and moved to a hotel. There, though blind, he lived in brooding silence, stubbornly taking care of himself and his room. Daily, he made his way to the hotel restaurant by himself, always on time, always taking the same place at the same table.

In Albuquerque, despite the devotion of his brother Tim and Harriet, Larry became more and more ill. He continued to vomit after meals. He became gloomier. He suffered a multitude of aches and pains. But he steadfastly ignored suggestions that he visit a psychiatrist. Although advanced in many subjects, Larry was backward in this one. He stubbornly insisted that the causes of his condition were physical, not mental—and he obstinately believed that psychiatry, still a world war away from being fully popularized, was for the idle rich and the near insane.

With the Japanese attack on Pearl Harbor, Tim enlisted in the army. On impulse, Larry tried to enlist with him. He was rejected because of high blood pressure. Left alone with Harriet, Larry was now more nervous than ever. Gradually, watching Harriet, fascinated by her good humor and tenderness, he got the notion that he wanted to marry her. In the years when she had been the family servant, he had hardly noticed her. All the brothers, Larry included, had playfully taken her to ball games and movies. In the previous weeks in New Mexico, even though they were close and he was dependent on her cheer, Larry had never suggested that their relationship be anything more than friendly. In fact, he had never once formally dated her. Abruptly, he proposed marriage. And she, long secretly in love with him, accepted. They were married by a justice of the peace early in 1942.

Harriet was good for Larry's frame of mind, but not good enough. Her zest for living, her animal spirits, her constant curiosity, stimulated him briefly. But presently the vomiting and depression returned. Finally, one morning, short weeks later, he emerged from the bathroom, razor in hand. "I'm going to kill myself," he said. She hurried him to a doctor, a nearby general practitioner. The doctor diagnosed a few physical ills, a bad case of hypertension, and prescribed regular shots and a long rest.

In July, 1942, Larry was notified by his draft board to report for an army physical. When he appeared, he was in much worse shape than when he had been rejected a half year earlier. But if he was in worse shape, so was the army. The doctors ignored his condition and passed him.

Larry was in the United States Army almost six months. He did not see one day of active military service. During his first morning, after induction at Fort Bliss, Texas, he suddenly broke down, falling into a fit of uncontrollable crying. He was promptly transferred to a Texas army hospital, and placed in a ward with violent mental cases. Today, his family feels that if it was a single experience that was responsible for shoving Larry over the line, this confinement in the mental ward of an army hospital might be regarded as that experience.

Harriet, who kept up their apartment in Albuquerque and worked in a five-and-ten-cent store, visited Larry as regularly as possible. He complained to her constantly of the insensitivity of certain officers and army nurses. Once, he came up for discharge. But someone noticed his I.Q., the highest in the hospital, and he was turned down. An officer remarked, and the remark was passed along to Larry, "His I.Q. is too damn high. He's officer material." In desperation, Larry secretly stored his barbiturates. He decided, if he were not discharged soon, he would commit suicide. In December, 1942, he was discharged.

Larry returned to Albuquerque and Harriet. The army had given him some mild drugs to relieve his pains. He took these, then resumed taking shots from the young doctor he'd been seeing before he had been drafted into the army. He spent his days reading and working crossword puzzles. A few weeks later, he received word that his father, aged sixty-three, had died on New Year's Day in a violent accident precipitated by his blindness. The father, who had dominated him all his life, was gone. At last, Larry was free. But it was too late. When Larry received the news, he hardly blinked. He simply returned to his crossword puzzles.

Now, Larry became dangerously ill. Each morning was a calvary. He could hardly get out of bed to face the day. Once out of bed, he feared each thought, each pressing moment. "Days torture me," he told Harriet. "Thoughts come. I can't blot them out." He continued to weep irrationally. He constantly wanted to scream. His body perspired and his palms were always wet. He changed shirts as often as six times a day. In desperation, Harriet sent for his younger brother, Jack.

With Jack's arrival, there began a running battle with time. Each day had to be made to pass swiftly. Jack encouraged Larry to stay up late, reading. This was easy, since Larry dreaded sleep. Larry would read until three in the morning, then sleep until one the next afternoon. In the afternoons, Larry, avoiding any volumes that might provoke introspection, would rent three or four mystery books from a nearby library, and read them through the rest of the day and night. Before he left Albuquerque, he had read the entire wall of mysteries in that library. He saw every new movie that opened, played golf daily, until he could chip a ball into a tin can at thirty feet.

Meanwhile, the young doctor, who had been giving him shots and pep talks, finally realized the source of his ills. Larry had been begging the doctor for drugs. "Give me anything to stop the pain," he pleaded. "Give me morphine, heroin, opium, anything. I just want five years of peace, and then death." Finally, the doctor told him, "Larry, your pain may not be from physical causes at all. Either try shock treatments, or try psychoanalysis. Matter of fact, there's a great psychiatrist right here in Albuquerque."

Larry went to the great psychiatrist. As a result, he was on the couch three or four times a week for eight months. The first day was the worst. After an hour with the analyst, Larry returned to the apartment to meet Jack. He walked into the apartment unsteadily, face white, and suddenly broke into racking sobs. Jack rushed to him, alarmed. "What's happened, Larry?" Larry pulled a sheet of paper out of his pocket and handed it to his brother. Jack remembers it was a crude sketch of two telephone switchboards. One switchboard had the circuits properly plugged in, the other had its cords all tangled. The psychiatrist had explained to Larry that the human mind was like the first telephone switchboard, with the plugs ordinarily all neatly in place. But in Larry's mind, the cords had gotten badly mixed up and needed straightening out. "From that day on," Jack remembers, "he began to understand, for the first time, that his sufferings were not physical but mental. He began to look upon himself as a hopeless mental case. He became obsessed by this and seemed to deteriorate steadily."

During this time, there was only one bright period. That was during the seventh month of his analysis. And it had nothing to do with his treatments. Harriet became ill with flu, and was put to bed for two weeks. Larry attended her hand and foot. He appeared happier than he had been in years.

Shortly after Harriet recovered, and returned to her dime store job, Jack left to join the Air Transport Command in California. Larry quickly lapsed into his old black rut. Meanwhile, the psychiatrist was making a little progress. It was established that Larry was suffering from a manic-depressive psychosis, with overtones of anxiety. He was being suffocated by melancholia. The root of this, most likely, was father domination. Too, he had a strong Oedipus complex, as evidenced by his marriage to Harriet, who was older than he and in whom he saw his adored mother.

The psychiatrist knew what was wrong with Larry, and how his psychosis was being evidenced, but was extremely doubtful whether analysis could lead him back toward normality. It was one afternoon, in the latter stages of treatment, that the psychiatrist mentioned a new operation known as prefrontal lobotomy. Had Larry ever heard of it? He had not.

But soon, reading voraciously, Larry knew a great deal about it. He learned that, before 1935, medical men understood little of the function of the frontal lobes in the human brain, though they realized that whenever these lobes were damaged or removed in tumor operations, the mental makeup of the patient changed. A celebrated case, concerning a middle-aged member of the New York Stock Exchange, had been reported on by Dr. Richard M. Brickner, a New York neuropsychiatrist. In this case, while removing the patient's brain tumor, both frontal lobes, a quarter of a pound of tissue, had been cut away. Recovering, the patient underwent a complete personality change. Though his intelligence was unimpaired, he lost his ability to reason as logically as before, lost his feelings of self-consciousness, became an abnormal braggart and became indifferent to his earlier illness and to worries in general.

Meanwhile, in 1935, a group of Yale research scientists, headed by Dr. Carlyle F. Jacobsen and Dr. John F. Fulton, had given a chimpanzee a series of tests, before and after removing its frontal lobes, with significant results. According to one medical report of this experiment, "Before operation, if the animal made a few mistakes, he would scream with rage, urinate and defecate in the cage, roll in the feces, shake the bars and refuse to continue the experiments. After the operation the same animal would continue in the experimental situation long beyond the patience of the examiner, making mistake after mistake, without the least indication of being upset emotionally."

In 1936, a distinguished Portuguese neurologist, sixty-one-year-old Dr. Egas Moniz, appeared in Paris to report to the Academy of Medicine that he had devised an operation to help psychotic patients, an operation called prefrontal leucotomy or lobotomy. Dr. Moniz, a professor at Lisbon University, the author of three hundred medical papers, and one-time Foreign Minister of Portugal, working with an associate, Almeida Lima, had bored buttonlike holes in the foreheads of his patients, inserted a slender, needle-thin scalpel, and cut through brain tissue and nerve fibers connecting the frontal lobes with other parts of the brain. He had found this technique fairly successful in paranoia or persecution mania cases and in schizophrenia or split personality cases. He had found that while the operation seemed to cut away the patient's ability to imagine and anticipate, it also cut away his cares and anxieties. In 1936, Dr. Walter Freeman and Dr. James W. Watts, of George Washington University, Washington, D.C., began performing Dr. Moniz's prefrontal lobotomy in the United States, and by the end of the year had performed twenty such operations. On learning that Drs. Freeman and Watts were the foremost lobotomy specialists in the United States, Larry tried to read all he could about them and their cases. In the Albuquerque library, he located an issue of *Time* magazine, published late the year before, that had the most recent report on the team of psychosurgeons. "Of their 136 cases," he read, "Drs. Freeman and Watts regarded 98 as greatly improved, 23 as somewhat improved, 12 as failures. Only 13 patients are still in mental hospitals; most are back to their jobs or housekeeping after one to six years of psychotic incapacity."

When he finished his reading, Larry's decision was made. He could not go on as he was, any longer. His mind had become his enemy. It told him that he had no right to relax, to enjoy himself, to live. It entombed him in fear, fear of the next day, of the world around him, of himself. He would cut himself free of this mind. He would go East, at once, and have a prefrontal lobotomy.

Accompanied by Harriet, he went to New Jersey and lived with one of his brothers, who was eager to be of help. Together they consulted two psychiatrists, one in Philadelphia and one in New York City, about the wisdom of a prefrontal lobotomy operation. Both psychiatrists firmly advised against it as "too drastic at this time." Larry was confused. He had been afraid to live, afraid to die, and the lobotomy had presented itself as a lifebelt, with which to survive as long as fate decreed. Now the lifebelt was being withheld from him and there seemed no other choice. Then, suddenly, overnight, there were a half-dozen choices, and Larry, snatching at anything and everything, began his Dantesque journey through Hell.

While Harriet remained with his brother in New Jersey, Larry entered the special mental clinic of a major New York hospital, in January, 1944. He lived inside the walls of the hospital for one unrelieved year, without once venturing outdoors. He was assigned a woman psychiatrist. It was felt that the change in the sex of his analyst might be beneficial. But after several months, the woman psychiatrist pronounced him beyond the help of psychoanalysis. She, after calling in other doctors for consultation, decided upon insulin and electric shock treatments. The doctors administered sixty shock treatments to Larry. The hospital claimed that they had never before given a patient so many. Before going downstairs for each shock treatment, Larry would stiffen with fright. Yet, after it was over, he never remembered having had it. As time passed, the hospital became Larry's entire outer world. He occupied himself with reading, Ping-pong, oil painting. He did some handicraft work. And he sank deeper and deeper into his manic-depressive anxiety state. At year's end, the hospital admitted that no similar case had been confined so long. At year's end, there was no real improvement in Larry, despite his momentary periods of high elation. He finally left the clinic and rejoined Harriet in New Jersey.

Now, acting on every new suggestion made, Larry began riding a mad merry-go-round of therapy. There was the German refugee psychologist-religionist, a Jew possessing a library of perhaps six thousand books and pamphlets on Jesus, who tried to infuse him with faith in the future and in God. There was a new psychiatrist in Kentucky. And a kindly, perceptive young analyst in East Orange, New Jersey, whose medical summary of Larry read, "He was in an extremely agitated state. He paced about the room, wept, distorted his face grotesquely and complained bitterly about obsessive thoughts. Everything was 'a torture to me—your shoe-laces, your tie, that dresser scarf—the very thought torments me.' It was felt that he was possibly suicidal, although his anxiety was by far the predominant feature of his mental picture. After four months, we began to change our diagnosis. We felt that the illness was considerably more malignant than a diagnosis of anxiety state would indicate. His illness came to be thought of as Pseudoneurotic Schizophrenia."

Finally, there was even a miracle man in New England, who worked wonders by inserting strange tubes and rubbing secret compounds. After Larry visited the miracle man, he enjoyed a relatively good period. He even felt, briefly, that the miracle man might save him. But, in the end, it turned out to have been only his manic stage, and when his depressive stage arrived again, with its private hell of crying spells and perspiration baths and twisting abdominal pains, and he threatened suicide, the miracle man was quickly abandoned, as had been all the rest before him.

Larry's limited social life was equally frustrating. Once, double-dating with an old acquaintance in New York, Larry, in a deep downbeat mood, discussed the ethics and pleasures of suicide. This not only threw a wet blanket on the evening, but infuriated Larry's friend, until he finally told Larry that he was a fake. If he wanted to commit suicide, why didn't he? He was just playing on everybody's sympathy, trying to get attention.

"Harriet later told me how Larry argued back," Jack says. "The friend just didn't understand. Most people didn't. They could look at a man who'd lost an arm or a leg and realize his incapacity. But they couldn't understand a mental cripple. They couldn't grasp that, like a man who's lost a limb, Larry had lost something in his head. They'd see he looked healthy, and that he was smart, and they'd say all he needed was to snap out of it. It was like telling a man without legs to get up and walk. After that there were no double dates."

It was late in 1945. Since abandoning the miracle healer, they had run out of doctors, and Harriet suggested that another change of scenery might do him good. From that moment, they were constantly on the move. They went to Tucson, Arizona, to visit Tim, who had been discharged from the army. The train ride was a nightmare, with Larry in a constant state of terror, shouting, "Kill me! Kill me!" Few onlookers understood his illness. In Tucson, Larry borrowed Tim's coupe and went out driving alone, to return hours later, soaked with sweat. He had pushed the little car to eighty miles an hour, hoping it would skid off the road. It had not, and he had not let it.

Next, they went to the farming town in Ohio where Harriet's large family lived. Larry was accepted with simple affection, but, soon tired of reading and of rides on his brother-in-law's delivery truck, he began speaking wildly of suicide again. They pushed on to New Jersey, to live with another of Larry's brothers. The East Orange psychiatrist took over again, gave Larry about thirty-five insulin and shock treatments, then refused to give any more. One night, Larry had convulsions and the doctor had to be summoned on the run. As analysis plodded on, without success, Harriet and Jack (who had just been discharged from A.T.C.), suggested hypnosis. The psychiatrist flatly rejected this. In desperation, the family confined Larry to the Veterans Hospital at Lyons, New Jersey. Larry was there several months, unable to keep his mind off himself, steadily growing worse.

In the end, it was neither Larry nor Jack, but a doctor at this Veterans Hospital, who brought up the subject of prefrontal lobotomy once more. The doctor sent a recommendation for lobotomy, along with Larry's case history, to the Veterans Administration. The VA turned the recommendation down.

Meanwhile, another doctor, in the same hospital, made an off-the-record suggestion that the lobotomy be performed on the outside by private doctors. He recommended an experienced psychosurgery team in the East. For ethical reasons, I shall refer to this team under the fictional names of Drs. Leon Goldsmith and Raymond Rogers, and locate them in Boston. The army doctor thought that Goldsmith and Rogers were among the best, and least expensive, in the country, for the particular job at hand. In desperation, Jack and Harriet asked the opinions of seven different doctors on the advisability of lobotomy. Four were against it. Three were for it.

Who was to make the decision? Larry was too ill, too torn by pain, to care about anything. His wife Harriet was too upset and bewildered to decide. And so, the major weight of the decision devolved upon his brother. Inexperienced though he was, Jack weighed both sides of the matter carefully. Doctors, obviously, could not give him a clear-cut answer. Their opinions on lobotomy were split almost down the middle. But there was still one more thing to ask them. Without lobotomy, was there any hope for Larry's recovery? The answer was unanimously no. A miracle might happen, of course, but they had no statistics supporting miracles. On the other hand, Larry might one day succeed in killing himself, although they held this unlikely. "He'll soon go into a completely psychotic state," they agreed, "and have to be institutionalized for the rest of his life."

This promise of Larry's future, combined with his relentless decline, suddenly panicked Jack. Lobotomy was useful only if a patient still had his grip on reality. Larry was rapidly losing his grip and might soon be beyond lobotomy. Time had become a factor. Jack could see no other choice. There appeared no less drastic treatment left. Lobotomy was relatively painless, even less uncomfortable than having one's tonsils extracted, they said, and it was relatively safe, with a record of only a 3 percent fatality. Whatever else it might do to Larry, lobotomy would relieve him of anxiety. Larry was consulted. He was almost beyond coherence but agreeable to anything, even euthanasia. Harriet and the other Cassidy brothers were consulted, and reluctantly they all agreed that there was nothing else to do.

During the last week in March, 1947, Jack and Harriet journeyed to Boston to consult with Drs. Goldsmith and Rogers. Jack and Harriet waited in a reception room with seven or eight other people, mostly relatives of patients. However, there was one actual patient, a robust, middle-aged woman, who kept conversing with her husband, speaking at the top of her voice. Since everyone else in the room was silent, her loudness made them stare. Once, she stared back at the others, then yelled, "Don't worry, I'm fine! Look at me! I'm happy! I feel wonderful!" Jack glanced at Harriet, apprehensively. The woman's husband caught the glance, and later managed to sit down beside Jack. "She really is doing quite well, you know," the husband explained. "Since her lobotomy, she's taking an interest in housework again. She even does the dishes occasionally."

Presently, Jack and Harriet were ushered in to meet Dr. Goldsmith, a serious, bespectacled, middle-aged man, gaunt and lanky. In preparing for the lobotomies, he was the psychiatrist of the team. He diagnosed the illness and plotted the operation. Dr. Rogers, a heavyset, easygoing Iowan, was the surgeon.

When Jack finished his recital of Larry's ills and previous treatments, he asked Dr. Goldsmith one question. "Will the operation do Larry any good?" Dr. Goldsmith reassured him that they were most successful in handling cases of Larry's type, that is, anxiety cases. Dr. Goldsmith said that prefrontal lobotomy would definitely free Larry from his fears and anxiety, but he reminded Jack and Harriet that the operation might also make Larry lose his sense of responsibility, as well as his knowledge of social graces. For example, shortly after the operation, he might urinate while in the living room, instead of going to the bathroom. Also, he would lack initiative and have a confused sense of time. He would remember his nervous illness, but it would be a faraway thing. He would remember the lobotomy itself, but only when reminded, and only as something that seemed to have happened to someone else. Finally, he would never be able to do creative work, like writing, again. At best, he might succeed at holding a clerical position.

Doggedly, Jack reiterated that they all wanted the operation performed at once, before Larry went insane or committed suicide. Dr. Goldsmith promised to let them know as soon as he was free, as soon as a scheduled operation was canceled. The very next day, in New York, Jack received a telegram stating that a cancellation had come through.

Two weeks later, during the late morning of April 14, Larry, accompanied by Harriet, Jack, another brother who dwelt in New Jersey, and his old roommate, Burt, boarded a Boston-bound train in Newark. As the train sped on, Larry became more and more agitated. They all took turns sitting beside him, trying to distract him. But his mind kept coming back to the operation. He was afraid to have it; he was afraid not to have it. "I'll wind up an idiot," he kept muttering. Burt tried to reassure him. "Larry, this operation is the most wonderful thing in the world." Larry shrugged. "I don't care, don't care if it kills me. Anyway, if it doesn't, at least I won't have to be myself any more."

They reached Boston in the afternoon. It was an overcast day. They took a taxi to the hospital, where a bed had been reserved for Larry. The hospital telephoned Dr. Goldsmith. Before the doctor arrived, the others in the party were permitted to see Larry once more. They tried to give him pep talks.

It was early evening when Dr. Goldsmith appeared, carrying photographic equipment. Dr. Goldsmith was alone with Larry for an hour. Later, they were joined by Dr. Rogers. Talking to the doctors, Larry was severely depressed. He alternately cried, perspired, and choked out his desire to die. When the talks were ended, Dr. Goldsmith set up his photographic equipment and took several shots of Larry. The portraits showed a fearful, haunted man.

The next morning, it rained. Burt had returned to New York to go to work. Jack, Harriet, and the other brother, who had spent the night in a hotel across the street, were in the waiting room of the hospital early. Dr.

Goldsmith and Dr. Rogers had a prior lobotomy scheduled for nine o'clock. Larry was second on the list. At eleven o'clock, the first operation was completed. At eleven-fifteen, Larry, head shaved, drowsy under a basal anesthetic, was swiftly wheeled past his wife and brothers into the operating room.

Harriet gasped, then began weeping. She cried almost steadily during the next two hours. The worried brother from New Jersey watched her in stunned silence. Jack fought tears, as he saw Larry disappear into surgery. Jack remembers, to this day, the thought that went through his mind that last, helpless moment. He thought: I will never see him again as I've known and loved him all my life. He will soon be returned from that room, the same name, the same face, the same body, but a different human being, forever, for the rest of his life and ours.

While the three sat in dreadful silence, in the lonely waiting room, Dr. Goldsmith and Dr. Rogers bent over Larry inside the operating room. Dr. Rogers had marked out areas on Larry's shaved scalp for the trephine openings. These areas had been injected with Novocain. Nothing that followed physically hurt Larry. The localized anesthetic, as well as the fact that the human brain is insensitive to pain, fortified him. Following his earlier markings, Dr. Rogers made the necessary incisions at each temple, above the ears. A button of bone, smaller than a dime, was removed on each side of his skull and now the brain lay exposed. Silver clips were applied to bleeding vessels, as excess blood was sponged away.

Now Dr. Rogers probed inside the holes in Larry's forehead with a special type of cannula rod. This done, he inserted another instrument, the leucotome, a long thin dulled knife. He moved the knife in a fan-shaped arc, downward, then upward, slicing into the nerve fibers that connected the frontal lobes with the thalamus to the rear. As Dr. Rogers made his drastic incision, Dr. Goldsmith talked continuously with Larry, who lay drowsily awake. Dr. Goldsmith kept questioning Larry, who tried to answer as best he could. This question-and-answer session, during the operation, was part of the technique. From Larry's answers, Dr. Rogers could tell when he was sufficiently disoriented, when the cutting was deep enough and should be halted. As the operation proceeded, Dr. Goldsmith asked Larry, "Why are we operating?" Larry answered, "I don't know." Dr. Goldsmith asked, "Where are you now?" Larry answered, "Baltimore." Dr. Goldsmith asked, "Do you know who I am?" Larry squinted up, saw the gaunt face, and replied, "Yes, you're Jesus Christ."

The cutting was done. The prefrontal lobes had been sufficiently disconnected from the other brain centers. The cutting had been deep—a profound lobotomy—and Larry would no longer be dominated by fears and anxiety. The thin knife had removed his worries. It had also removed his old personality. After the wounds were given a final check, to be sure all bleeding had stopped, the buttons of skull were replaced and the flesh stitched. The prefrontal lobotomy was over.

It was now afternoon, ten minutes after one. The operation had taken almost two hours. Dr. Rogers emerged first. He went directly to Harriet, Jack, and the other brother, and said, "It's all done. It went well." Harriet and the brother both cried. Jack turned away, walked hurriedly down the corridor to the men's lavatory, pushed inside, leaned against a wall and sobbed for twenty minutes.

A short time later, they had all composed themselves. They waited anxiously to see Larry. He was wheeled out of the operating room. He was asleep and his head was bandaged. They could tell nothing. They returned to their hotel until evening, then crossed back to the hospital again. Larry was awake now, and they were admitted to his room. They stared down at him. He opened his eyes, met theirs, then averted his eyes. They were led out of the room. The following morning, Jack went in to see Larry first. He looked at Larry, who still seemed faraway, then asked, "Who am I?" Larry's eyes fastened on him a moment, then he whispered, "Hello, Jack."

Larry, attended by special nurses day and night, was in the hospital two weeks in all. Jack and Harriet visited him twice a day, and though he never spoke unless spoken to, he gradually became more responsive. His docility shocked Jack, who could not forget his wild agitation of a few days before. Jack thought that he seemed entirely too disinterested, but Dr. Goldsmith explained that Larry's mind was disoriented and that it would take some months to reintegrate itself.

Jack says he first fully realized the remarkable change that had come over Larry when, a week after the operation, he tried to converse normally with him. During the years of Larry's illness, Jack had adopted a bantering manner. Also, before ever saying a single word, Jack had learned to censor his conversation automatically. "I was careful never to say anything that might upset or depress him, or make him moody," Jack recalls. "I learned never to ask him, 'How are you feeling mentally, Larry?' Well, when I saw him in the hospital, I was still conditioned by the past. I said, 'How's about a set of tennis, Larry?' I'd wanted to ask how he felt, but from habit suppressed it. When he didn't react to my patter, I suddenly realized that I didn't have to be evasive. On impulse, I asked him, 'How do you feel mentally, Larry?' He simply nodded, quite normally, and replied, 'Fine, fine.' Then, the full impact really hit me. I knew he was a changed person."

On the day that Larry was released, Jack and Harriet were waiting for him. Dr. Goldsmith photographed him before he left. Without urging, Larry gave the camera a broad smile. The resultant photograph, of a relaxed, cheerful young man, seemed incredible when laid beside the photograph snapped two weeks earlier, with its tortured, emaciated face. Before the three departed, Dr. Goldsmith warned Harriet that Larry's home care was important, that he must not be allowed to drink alcoholic beverages, that he would have to be retaught personal habits of cleanliness like shaving, bathing, and remembering to use the toilet.

As they left the hospital, Larry seemed to be in a good mood. His head was unbandaged, and the scars, on both temples, were clearly visible. They would be concealed, however, when his hair grew back. Larry's face was pleasantly animated, and he appeared at peace with the world. Harriet was taking him back to her family in Ohio, where he'd have care while recuperating. There were several hours before the train left, and Jack and Harriet debated how they could best occupy them for Larry. They decided to visit the State House on Beacon Hill, and then sit in a park and rest. At first both Jack and Harriet were very restrained with Larry. They could not relax. They kept expecting him to become annoyed by something they'd said. It was not until they went into a restaurant for breakfast, that they realized almost nothing could annoy him. In the restaurant, Harriet asked Larry what he would like to eat. He glanced at the menu without reading it. "Anything," he said finally. "It doesn't matter." He ate heartily, and after the meal, Jack asked him how he felt. "Just fine," he said, good-naturedly.

While Jack went back to New York to find a job, Larry and Harriet boarded the train for Ohio. They lived with her family again. The family only dimly comprehended what the whole thing was about. They were not sure why or how Larry had been ill, or what the operation with the funny name involved, but he was Harriet's husband and he had been sick and that was enough. They treated him, as they had before the surgery, with consideration.

The operation and care had cost between $1,000 and $1,500, and there was only a small share of Larry's inheritance and of Harriet's savings left. Harriet invested this money in opening a neighborhood bakery. Larry lacked the patience to help her. When he visited the bakery, he was only in the way. He took to accompanying his brother-in-law on the delivery truck again. Sometimes he hung around a nearby confectionery store, playing the pinball machine or glancing at newspaper headlines. Dr. Goldsmith had thought that he would read comic books. He never picked one up, although he loved movies, anything and everything, indiscriminately. Nor did he ever urinate outside of the bathroom.

Often, Larry went on long walks for mile after mile. When he returned to the house, Harriet found large blisters on his feet. He said he had not felt them. He seemed immune to pain. Once, when it was very cold, he wandered outdoors in his shirt-sleeves, oblivious to the weather. Harriet's mother chased him, calling out, "Larry, why don't you put your jacket on?" He halted, then said, "Why yes, good idea." He ran back into the house for his jacket.

He had no interest in his personal appearance. Harriet always reminded him to shave. When he prepared to shave, and had turned on the faucet, he would frequently stand staring at the running water for a half hour or more. He usually thought that he had been there only a minute or two. Harriet had been warned that most lobotomy patients lose their concept of time, and many are fascinated by water. He never drank whiskey. Harriet told him he could not, and he never disobeyed her. He was satisfied to sniff her beer, when they were out.

He was difficult in many ways. He seemed to have lost a certain social awareness. In the street several times, he abruptly confronted strangers with his hands raised in a pugilistic pose, and threatened, "Want a fist full of knuckles?" He was always good-natured about the way he did it, actually kidding, never aggressive, but people did not know that and they were constantly startled.

Harriet's family had a five-year-old boy in the house. Larry played juvenile games with him and enjoyed teasing him. He'd make funny faces, and invent fantastic names to amuse the boy, saying "Look out for Goofus Gerhardt, the bear! He's under the bed!" Then he'd steal the five-year-old's ball from him, and when the boy complained, Larry would playfully pinch him. When the family, irritated, protested, Larry would tease them, too. Everyone's nerves began to fray. Meanwhile, Harriet's bakery, which had done wonderfully the first month, steadily declined. Harriet was forced to give up and sell. She'd lost most of their money in the ten months that had passed. She decided that a change might do them both good, and so she took Larry to New York.

Jack, informed of their coming, rented a room for them from a French landlady in Manhattan. After they were settled, Jack and Harriet twice took Larry to see Dr. Goldsmith. In Larry's presence, Harriet related some of his difficulties and habits. She could not understand the things he did. Still in Larry's presence, Dr. Goldsmith replied, "Well, Larry is only three and a half years old socially." Jack thinks he said this merely to test Larry's reaction, but Larry did not react. Later, as the conversation continued, Dr. Goldsmith turned to Larry and said, "Certainly you can shave yourself, Larry." Larry stared at him a moment, then suddenly spoke. "I'm three and a half years old, doctor. How could I possibly know how to shave?" The doctor blinked, and Harriet and Jack were agape.

In New York, to support Larry and herself, Harriet took a job in a Schrafft's kitchen. It was heavy work, hard work, from seven-thirty in the morning until four o'clock in the afternoon. She went about, daily, in a daze of exhaustion. Larry, with no one to look after him full time, was constantly in trouble. One day, alone, he went into an expensive restaurant and ordered the best meal. When he was done, he told the manager that he could not pay. The manager was decent about it, and there was no incident. A little later, Larry ran into an old acquaintance and invited him to lunch. They both ordered expensive meals. When the check came, Larry admitted that he did not have a penny.

Once, Harriet returned home to find Larry nursing a black eye and bruised cheek. She wanted to know what had happened. "I met a man and called him a sonofabitch and he hit me," Larry explained proudly. "He knocked me down." Harriet was aghast. "What did you do after you got up?" Larry answered seriously, "I didn't call him a sonofabitch any more."

Also, he had taken to bragging. Before the surgery he had been gentle, shy, self-effacing, never once mentioning his educational attainments. Now, if he met someone, and chanced to get into a discussion or friendly argument, he would suddenly terminate it by shouting, "I'm a Phi Beta Kappa man! You're just a shoe clerk!"

When Harriet returned from Schrafft's every day, she was physically depleted. Yet she had to prepare dinner, look after household affairs and Larry's clothes, and give him a bath. She had to face the aftereffects of his latest escapades, and listen to his complaints. In the evening, though she was half asleep on her feet, he would want her to go walking with him until two or three in the morning. Sometimes she tried. Usually she could not, but if she could not, she would toss in bed wondering what was happening to him. They had been married six years, and in those six years she had not had a single full night's sleep.

She could not take it any more. When she had first come to the Cassidy household so long before, and even when she had married Larry in Albuquerque, she had been a happy, bouncy, enthusiastic extrovert, full of health and hope. Now she was thin, jittery, thoroughly crushed in spirit. She confided to Jack that she had reached the end of the road. She was leaving Larry. She would not divorce him, since she was Catholic. She told Larry that she had to leave. He was upset. But not deeply. He was incapable of deep feeling or hurt. He told her that she was inconsiderate. And two days later he had forgotten the whole matter. She moved to New England, where she now lives and works. Larry rarely speaks of her and never writes.

After Harriet left, Jack took Larry into his own walk-up for a week. He had intended to keep him longer, but it was impossible. Jack, working as an insurance salesman, would allow Larry to accompany him on his rounds. When they would reach a call, Jack would say, "I'll only be five minutes, Larry. You wait right here for me. Don't move." Larry would nod agreeably. When Jack would emerge, five or ten minutes later, Larry would be gone. He would be at least six blocks off, in any one of four directions, strolling aimlessly.

At the time, Jack was in love with a pretty, saucy model named Susan, who had time to spare and tried to give Jack a hand. She took Larry to movies, museums, walking in Central Park. But this was not enough. Jack, and his brothers, who had been kept informed, felt that Larry needed full-time care. They arranged for his readmittance to the Veterans Hospital in Lyons, New Jersey. Larry accepted his new address with complete docility. After several months in Lyons, Larry was transferred to the Veterans Hospital in Roanoke, Virginia, where the Veterans Administration was carrying out a special program for the rehabilitation of lobotomy cases.

Early in 1949, Jack married Susan, and they decided to try their luck in California. On the way, they stopped over in Roanoke to see Larry. He wanted to go along with them. His reasons were not sentimental. "I want to write again," he said. "I want to write Alan Ladd movies for a hundred thousand dollars." Jack promised to have him transferred to California, and this was accomplished in the summer of 1949.

Larry has been in Los Angeles ever since and lives there now. He is committed, by his own signature, to the Brentwood Neuro-Psychiatric Hospital, which is connected with the Sawtelle Veterans Hospital. He was first kept in an open ward, which was neither guarded nor enclosed, but after two attempts to run away, he was more closely confined. The first time, having saved his veterans' disability checks, he left in the middle of an afternoon for San Francisco, but soon returned voluntarily. The next time, he took off without funds for Phoenix, where his brother Tim lives.

Like most of the inmates in Sawtelle, Larry keeps army hours. He sleeps in a room with other patients, rises at dawn, now shaves promptly and efficiently, almost never bathes or showers in the hospital, and carelessly wears the same clothes day after day. There are work therapy groups and various classes for the patients, but Larry is disinterested in them. Once, he promised the doctors and his family that he would attend classes. He went for two days and never returned to them. Because he had the highest I.Q. in the ward, he was made a library attendant. He stayed on the job two hours and then wandered off. "We don't want to force him to do anything," a hospital psychiatrist told Jack. "This isn't a penal colony."

There are two things that Larry is faithful about—movies and food.

Regularly, without fail, he goes to the two movies shown weekly and sits through them both. And he is always on time for meals and cleans his plate. Since the lobotomy operation, his appetite has been enormous. He is actually capable of eating six or seven full-course meals a day. But he has little patience for other activities. He used to enjoy golf. Recently, when Jack led him to a pitch-and-putt green, he took a couple of pokes at the ball, on the second hole tried to hit it using one hand, and finally threw down his clubs and walked off to sit in the parked car. He still carries two or three paperback books in his pockets all the time, a hangover from his old reading days, but he rarely does more than scan them. What he likes to do most, still, is walk. He tramps the hospital grounds constantly, tirelessly. Jack estimates that Larry must cover thirty miles a day. He never thinks much, when he walks, or if he does, he never remembers what he was thinking about.

He has few friends in the hospital. He likes only the patients and doctors who respect his intelligence, believe his claims of suffering petty persecutions, and who accept his own high opinion of himself. When another lobotomy case doubted that Larry had ever gone to Princeton, Larry refused to speak to him again. He likes to say that he is smarter than the doctors, because after all he is a Phi Beta Kappa. In arguments with other patients, he propounds flash opinions formed from glancing at a headline, and is extremely dogmatic about them. He likes to give advice to other patients. When he observed one patient being considerate of another, Larry interrupted, "Don't be so damn considerate, mister. Look where I wound up being considerate—in a booby hatch." He likes to call the hospital a booby hatch or a nut house.

He has mingled contempt and respect for the hospital staff. When the family noticed that his teeth were bad, though he suffered absolutely no pain from them, he refused to visit any army dentist. "Those guys," he said contemptuously, "I can buy and sell them ten times." One day, he regards the hospital staff as so many dedicated Arrowsmiths, and thinks he will write an epic movie dramatizing their courage. The next day, down on them for some fancied slight, he mutters threateningly of the book he will write. "It'll make *The Snake Pit* look sick," he says. "It'll blast the Veterans Administration apart. It'll let everyone know how they treat their patients." The harassed army doctors, aware that Larry needs some way to work off his constant if momentary grudges and aggressions, accept his mutterings with good-natured tolerance.

Larry has long forgotten his dream of becoming a teacher. However, he still wants to write. When Burt, who is editing a Hollywood quarterly published in New York, heard this, he sent Larry a simple assignment. He sent him material about a famous film star and told him to write it up into a five-hundred-word picture caption. Larry managed to finish the task and send it to New York. The caption had to be completely rewritten, but Burt mailed him a check, nevertheless. For months after, Larry refused to cash the check, keeping it instead, to show to the patients and doctors as proof that he was a writer. Whenever Jack and Susan visit him, he promises to deliver at least a paragraph of a story by the following week. But he never does. "I don't want to write in this nut house," he says. "I want to do screenplays for Alan Ladd. I'll go over to Paramount one day and tell them I'm Larry Cassidy, and you watch and see if they don't roll out the red carpet."

Most every weekend, either Susan, who now writes about interior decorating, or Jack, who works for a large public relations office, picks Larry up at the hospital and brings him to their newly purchased bungalow in the San Fernando Valley, about a twenty-minute drive from Hollywood. Often, when the weekend begins, Larry is angry with Jack. For a while, it was because he remembered that Jack did not invite him to his wedding in the East. "You were afraid Susan would like me better," he told Jack. More recently, he felt that he was being confined in the hospital because Jack feared that Larry might take his public relations job away from him. When he suffers these brief delusions of persecution, he will wag his fist in Jack's face, until Jack says, "But, Larry, I'm your brother. I love you." Then Larry will lower his fist, and break into a childish grin. "That's right, Jack," he'll say, "and I love you, too."

During these weekends, Jack is able to see the degree to which Larry has changed, for better or for worse. Dr. Goldsmith had promised that Larry's behavior would level off after three years, and however he was then would probably be the way he'd remain for the rest of his life. Today, at thirty-seven, with four years behind him since the lobotomy operation, Larry's new personality has probably solidified.

Unquestionably, today, he is happier than he was before the operation. His face is round, young, cherubic, and he's getting plump about the middle. He is never depressed, rarely moody, and when moody, only for fleeting moments. Emotionally and physically, he is free of pain. His occasional complaints of persecution, his pretended belligerences, and his continued social impatience do not alter the fact that he is carefree, irresponsible, happy-go-lucky.

The price of this contentment, of course, has been the loss of many of his old powers. His intelligence is still high, but this brilliance is erratically mixed with terrible streaks of childishness and unreality. When he has bright periods, behaving as of old, and his family begins to think he is recovering, he suddenly lapses into irrelevant fantasy or moronic soliloquy. In his pre-lobotomy days, he used to listen to the radio program

Information, Please, and in several years missed only one or two questions, a record which matched John Kieran's. He knew, for one thing, the most obscure passages from Shakespeare. Recently, when someone asked him to recite the routine "To be or not to be" passage from *Hamlet,* he was unable to recall it. Yet, a few days after that, walking with Jack past a library, he read the Latin inscription etched above the entrance and accurately translated it. On another occasion, when Jack was writing a publicity story about a burlesque queen, and trying to remember a synonym for striptease that had something to do with insects, Larry looked up and said, "Ecdysiast, just call her that." Jack went to his Webster's and found "ecdysis" defined as the "act of shedding an outer cuticular layer, as in the case of insects, crustaceans, etc."

Now the family has learned neither to underestimate nor to overestimate Larry's intelligence. They accept the fact that he has stupid days and smart days, without rhyme or reason. They also accept gratefully the fact that his sense of humor seems largely unimpaired by the operation. One afternoon, driving in Beverly Hills, Jack committed a minor traffic infraction. A motorcycle policeman rolled up alongside and bawled Jack out. The moment the policeman left, Larry exclaimed, "Somebody ought to give that cop a lobotomy." Around the hospital, arguing politics, he will often get steamed up at the national administration and say that the President ought to have two lobotomies a week. Leaving the hospital for his weekend recently, he realized that he had forgotten something, and blurted in exasperation, "Gee, I should have my head examined." Then, looking about the hospital corridor with quick humor, "Matter of fact, I'm in a great place for it!"

While his mind still has roots in the past, his memory is badly scrambled. Infrequently, he recalls his lobotomy operation. "I'm glad I had it done," he will say. But if someone asks him if he ever talks to the other lobotomy cases in his ward, he will snap, "Who can talk to those idiots?" He remembers all his relatives and friends, though without much depth of feeling toward them one way or another. He still regards Burt as his best friend, and writes him a letter every week. Occasionally, he remembers special days and is exceedingly thoughtful. On Jack and Susan's last wedding anniversary, he quietly rose at dawn, hiked from their Valley bungalow the many miles into Hollywood, found a store that was open on Sunday, selected and bought a pair of beautiful bookends, and hiked all the way back with the gift.

People who meet him for the first time, and have not heard of his lobotomy operation, always accept him as a perfectly normal citizen. They regard him as intelligent, jovial, although somewhat egotistical and impatient. After they meet him a second or third time, they begin secretly to suspect that something is wrong with him, that perhaps he's a little eccentric. His continued impatience, irresponsibility, and lack of restraint are usually the final giveaways.

For months, for example, Larry had spoken of going to Ciro's, an expensive night club. Jack and Susan decided to surprise him on his birthday. They brought him in from the hospital. They peeled his old suit off him and forced him into the bathtub. They presented him with a new suit. Then, with a party of friends, they took him to Ciro's. After ten minutes, he was ready to leave. He had no patience even for Ciro's. Later the same night, an incident occurred that revealed his attitude toward the opposite sex. He had long begged Jack to line him up with a lusty woman, and Jack had obligingly paired him off at Ciro's with an uninhibited redhead. After they had driven the redhead home, Jack and Susan settled down in the car for a long wait, while Larry led her up to her door. In two minutes, he was back. Jack was amazed. "Why so fast? Didn't you even kiss her?" Larry was genuinely shocked. "Kiss her? Do you think I'm a cad?"

Larry's lack of social control, above all else, causes those around him constant consternation. He is not supposed to drink, even though in recent months he has been permitted an occasional sip. One Sunday morning, when Jack and Susan were out, some neighbors down the block spotted Larry out walking. They invited him to join them in an early morning drink. He gulped down one shot, then two, then three. The whiskey tasted like tea to him, and by the time Jack located him, he had had six and was thoroughly potted. Jack put him to bed, and when he woke up, Jack lectured him. "They're nice people," Jack said, "but I don't want you drinking with them. They're dipsomaniacs and that's not for you." The following Sunday, Larry was on his eternal walk, when the same neighbors saw him and invited him in again. Larry was agreeable. They inquired if he would like to join them in drinks again. He primly refused. "My brother says I can't," he announced. "He says you're a couple of dipsomaniacs and I mustn't drink with you!"

That same Sunday, a few hours later, Larry again exhibited his lack of restraint. Susan, who is Catholic, took him to church with her. He sat beside her in perfect silence throughout the sermon. When it was done, he broke into wild applause. The priest looked startled, and everyone in the church turned and glared. Susan blushed, and whispered that he must not applaud in church. "Why not?" he asked. "That guy makes a lot of sense!"

This is Larry Cassidy today. How typical is his post-lobotomy personality? While results vary from individual to individual, it is evident that everyone who has undergone a lobotomy has much in common with

Larry. For evidence on other lobotomies, Drs. Goldsmith and Rogers cite the findings of fellow psychosurgeons, especially pioneers like Drs. Freeman and Watts of Washington, D.C.

After performing prefrontal lobotomies on over 400 persons, with whom they kept in contact, Drs. Freeman and Watts came to certain conclusions. "Patients who have been operated on are usually cheerful, responsive, affectionate and unreserved. They are outspoken, often critical of others and lacking in embarrassment. . . . They tend to procrastinate, to make up their minds too quickly and to enunciate opinions without considering the various implications. The most striking and constant change from the pre-operative personality lies in a certain unselfconsciousness, and this applies both to the patient's own body and to his total self as a social unit. The patient emerges from the operation with an immature personality that is at first poorly equipped for maintaining him in a competitive society; but with the passage of time there is progressive improvement, so that in about one-half the cases earning a living again becomes possible."

The fact that psychosurgery is supported by a large proportion of the medical profession is evident from its widespread acceptance and usage. In August, 1948, when the First International Conference on Psychosurgery was held in Lisbon, 8,000 lobotomy cases were reported on by doctors from twenty different nations. Lobotomies are being performed today in countries as disparate as India, Sweden, Czechoslovakia, New Zealand, and Japan.

Those who support lobotomy stand on its record. The English Board of Control, checking the results of 1,000 lobotomy cases in forty-three hospitals in England and Wales, found 35 percent could be discharged into regular life (of these, 242 were able to earn a living or keep house) and 32 percent were improved in their hospital adjustment. Drs. Freeman and Watts have reported, at different times, that after lobotomy about one-third of the patients recover, one-third improve and one-third fail to improve. "There are variations from one investigator to another and from one disease to another," Drs. Freeman and Watts conclude, "but the results are sufficiently good to warrant the use of prefrontal lobotomy on a large scale for the relief of the very serious and chronic forms of mental disease that keep the back wards of the psychiatric hospitals filled to capacity and beyond."

However, the critics of lobotomy are equally numerous. Dr. Stanley D. Porteus, who studied fifty-five cases in Kaneoke Hospital, Hawaii, decided, "Undoubtedly, if everyone in the world was to be simultaneously lobotomized, it would spell the end of all progress. Industry, except at the simplest levels, would cease. A population of cheerful drones could hardly carry on the complex business of modern living." Dr. Nolan D. C. Lewis feels lobotomy patients should be carefully selected and operated upon only as a last resort. "Meanwhile the *furor therapeuticus* continues with an enthusiasm that may prove dangerous," he says, "unless an accurate stock of the situation is soon taken and made known." A prominent Philadelphia psychiatrist regards lobotomy as "disuseful" in beginning cases, but of value if no other therapy has improved the condition of a serious mental case.

Dr. G. Rylander has quoted the families of lobotomy patients, who are stunned by the personality changes produced by the psychosurgery. One wife, whose husband had a lobotomy, protested, "Doctor, you have given me a new husband. He isn't the same man." The mother of a girl who had a lobotomy complained, "She is my daughter, but yet a different person. She is with me in body, but her soul is in some way lost. Those deep feelings, the tenderness, are gone." There are other objections, too. Some Catholics, like Dr. R. O'Rahilly, feel lobotomy is morally wrong. And, since the announcement that lobotomy has been tried on criminals, Dr. D. H. Winnicott has argued, "What guarantees have we that a Bunyan in prison will be allowed to keep his brain intact and his imagination free?"

Because he has always felt that he played a major role in deciding upon Larry's lobotomy, Jack Cassidy keeps abreast of this medical controversy. He still does not know whether he did the right thing by Larry or not. On Saturday nights, when Larry is staying over for the weekend, and is asleep in the spare room, and Susan has gone to bed, Jack will often settle into the big living-room chair, and try to read the Sunday papers. But invariably, he admits, his mind returns to Larry. Listening to Larry's heavy breathing, Jack finds himself automatically reviewing the events of the past years.

If they had waited a little longer, he will reflect, maybe a miracle would have happened after all. Or maybe one of the newer operations would have been better. They are still using prefrontal lobotomy, he knows, but they are also experimenting with all kinds of offshoots and variations like topectomy, gyrectomy, and transorbital leucotomy. Then, thinking about it, he remembers something else. He remembers Larry's face before the operation. He remembers the agony on that face, and how Larry wanted to die. He is sure Larry would have wound up in an asylum, suffering for the remainder of his life, or possibly insane, or even a suicide. Besides, there was the time element. If they had waited, it might have been too late even for lobotomy.

Thinking about it, Jack tries to rationalize. Sure, it hurts to see what has become of Larry. Why, Larry had been practically a genius, even though his genius was of little value. Now he is dulled, no longer the person that they once knew. On the other hand, some of him is still that same person. And the rest of him is happier, and enjoys certain pleasures, and does not mind what he has become. Perhaps that is better than nothing.

About this time, on Saturday nights, Jack is always tired, and he reaches up to turn off the lamp. He walks through the darkened house to his room, with Larry's heavy breathing following him. Were they right or wrong? Jack will never know. Anyway, it is a hell of a thing to try to answer at two in the morning.

After all, Jack asks—"What would you have done?"

>‹‹

WHAT HAS HAPPENED SINCE . . .

When I submitted the foregoing story to *The Saturday Evening Post* in May, 1951, the editors were fascinated by it, but concerned about its strangeness and the moral and religious considerations involved. An associate editor was assigned to learn if lobotomy was really an acceptable surgical procedure, and if I had presented the clinical aspects of Larry Cassidy's case with accuracy. Among the several psychiatric experts consulted on lobotomy, the most important was a doctor on the faculty of the University of Pennsylvania. He assured the associate editor on the telephone, "Lobotomy is of help to many who are in a hopeless condition, living at a purely instinctive level, trying to kill themselves or someone else, and existing like caged lions."

The associate editor reported this conversation to Ben Hibbs, then the editor of *The Saturday Evening Post,* and recommended that my story be evaluated by "an unbiased psychiatrist," such as the one on the University of Pennsylvania faculty. Mr. Hibbs agreed, and a copy of my Larry Cassidy story was sent to the unbiased psychiatrist. One week later this psychiatrist replied, in writing, to Mr. Hibbs:

"Psychosurgery in the form of lobotomy, lobectomy, under cutting (topectomy) or transorbital lobotomy, etc., is a recognized treatment procedure and has a definite place in psychiatric therapy. This place in relationship to the general problem of psychiatric treatment can be likened to the role that heart surgery plays in the problem of the treatment of cardiac disease or that the role of total removal of a lung plays in a case of tuberculosis. There are neither psychiatric objections nor moral nor religious arguments against the procedure. Lobotomy as a procedure is definitely accepted. The author describes incidents of behavior on a patient's part that are fairly typical. . . ."

Immediately, *The Saturday Evening Post* accepted "They Cut Away His Conscience" for publication.

First, however, I was asked to make some minor revisions and major cuts. The average *Post* article, at that time, was eighteen manuscript pages. The story I had submitted was fifty-four manuscript pages. I had not given a damn about formula or length when I wrote the story, for I was determined to present Larry's saga on my own terms. Now a compromise was effected. The editors of the *Post* agreed to run the story as "a double-length feature," that is, thirty-six pages in length. I agreed to make the painful excisions. (When re-editing the story for inclusion in this volume, I decided to restore at least a thousand words that I had been forced to put aside in 1951.) On July 8, 1951, I delivered to *The Saturday Evening Post* the cut-down version, and it was accepted with enthusiasm.

So emotionally devoted was I to the story, that I could hardly await its appearance in print. At last, in *The Saturday Evening Post* dated October 20, 1951, it saw the light of day. There was one change. Because my title, "They Cut Away His Conscience," was considered too controversial, a new title was used. It had become, safely, "The Operation of Last Resort."

The immediate public response to the story was unexpected. Despite what the reader may have heard to the contrary, authors who write fiction or nonfiction for popular periodicals generally receive little acknowledgment from the vast faceless population of magazine buyers and subscribers. A writer's short story or article is only one of a dozen or more appearing in a single issue of a magazine. So even if his tale makes some impact, its identity is usually suffocated by the surrounding stories and advertisements. Also, his contribution in a single issue of a weekly has a brief life span, because the next issue is too quickly at hand, offering newer marvels. A writer fades quickly into oblivion in the pages of a magazine.

But there are exceptions. And for me, the appearance of my story on Larry Cassidy was such an exception. Whereas an average article or essay might bring me a half-dozen letters from appreciative or critical readers, the travail of Larry Cassidy inspired a small mountain of mail. Much of the mail was congratulatory; readers were deeply moved. Some of the letters, from physicians and clergymen, questioned or discussed the wisdom of Larry's psychosurgery. Other letters came from parents or relatives of mentally ailing persons, tragic, heartrending letters, asking for more factual information, inquiring for the real names and addresses of

Dr. Leon Goldsmith and Dr. Raymond Rogers. The editors of *The Saturday Evening Post* advised me that the double-length feature had drawn a record amount of mail, and was, in this respect, among the two or three most provocative stories they had published in a decade.

The day after publication, from Los Angeles, I was prompted to write my New York literary agent, Paul R. Reynolds: "The response, out here, to 'The Operation of Last Resort' has been overwhelming and gratifying."

The responses of some of the leading players in the story interested me most of all. Larry's best friend and former roommate at Princeton, Burt, worried at his publishing desk in New York that the story did not tell enough and might give the impression that Larry's case was satisfactorily solved. Larry's younger brother, Jack, was pleased that Larry's terrible odyssey and his own dilemma were out in the open, and pleased also to have a portion of my earnings from the sale of the article to help support his charge.

And Larry Cassidy, the lobotomized hero still in the Sawtelle Veterans Hospital, how did he react to the publication of his story? Knowledge of its appearance was not kept from him. He was exhilarated by the biography of himself, even though he had been given a fictional name in the narrative. It gave him real identity in the hospital, and supported his own contention of his superiority over the other patients. During 1951, he marched through the halls of the ward, brandishing a copy—*the* copy —of *The Saturday Evening Post*, waving it under the noses of fellow inmates and psychiatrists alike, bellowing, "See, here it is in print, here is the whole truth—I went to Princeton, I'm smarter than all of you! Look at it! *The Saturday Evening Post* doesn't publish articles about idiots!" And in the years immediately after, speaking or writing to his friend Burt, he would constantly announce that the author of that article was as great a man as Burt, or Dwight David Eisenhower, because the article had made Larry "world-famous!"

Of course, Larry's former physicians around the nation read the popular biography and recognized in it their onetime patient. One doctor in particular, who had been fairly cooperative about supplying information during the early stages of my writing the article, later resented the final form of the case history. When I showed him a copy of the manuscript, he was appalled and angry. He felt that I had relied too much on the Cassidy family for material and consequently had given "a one-sided presentation." He demanded that his real name be removed from the story, and ended a letter to me with the quotation, "If you can see your words twisted by knaves to make a trap for fools . . ." After that pronouncement on my knavery, and the startling statement that Larry had been an unsatisfactory lobotomy result ("in the lowest 5 percent of rating of results of lobotomy"), this doctor withdrew further cooperation from me.

But after the story appeared in print, and its reception was favorable, this same doctor did a complete about-face. Unashamedly, he wrote his knave asking for assistance in placing for publication a popular medical article that he had written. I felt little charity then—I might feel more today—so I dropped his literary request into the wastebasket and did not reply to him.

I have since tried to analyze my irritation with this one doctor, and I believe that it comes to this: The doctor had been disappointed in the result of Larry's lobotomy, which he had advocated, and wanted to bury forever his own contribution (one among many) to that result, and so, figuratively, he had disowned his patient. But when my story, in a conservative periodical, had briefly made Larry a national personality, accepted by a vast public of judges as an object of interest and sympathy, the doctor seemed suddenly to regain a measure of pride in his neglected stepchild. I do not say that this is what happened, but it is my only guess. It was as if, until then, by not responding at top level to recommended psychosurgery, by losing too many of his powers, Larry had failed this doctor and all physicians associated with the case. It was as if Larry had remained a walking rebuke to the doctor's presumably invincible magic. Larry had failed this doctor, and the doctor had washed his hands of him. When, by an accident of circumstances, Larry had become a public figure, much discussed and debated, the doctor had reconsidered, perhaps decided that in some way his operation had succeeded, and that Larry had been a success, also. In a sense, the doctor permitted Larry to join the club again, mounted his addled but celebrated brain on the medical mantelpiece, and said all was forgiven.

Well, that was in 1951, when Larry Cassidy was thirty-seven years old, and his lobotomy personality was four years old—and since then we have had the long tension years under President Eisenhower, President Kennedy, and President Johnson—and today, Larry Cassidy is fifty-one years old and his lobotomy personality is eighteen years old. How has the passage of time affected Larry? What is he today?

Following the appearance of the story, I had no further personal contact with Larry. Shortly after becoming "world-famous," he had removed himself from Los Angeles, and only occasionally, through his friend Burt or his younger brother Jack, did I hear what he was doing. But what I did hear, usually in the form of some singular Kafkaesque anecdote, made it clear to me that his incredible odyssey in search of peace, first from his demon mind, and then from his altered conscienceless mind— tragicomic sometimes, outrageous often, pitiful usually, and, finally today, somewhat remarkable—was continuing without respite. When I decided to include Larry's story in a book, I also determined to find out, if I could, what had happened to him in the last fourteen years. I have now found out.

In 1951, Larry Cassidy had already spent two years in the Brentwood Neuro-Psychiatric Hospital, located in West Los Angeles. It will be remembered that twice he had attempted to run away from this institution. His weekends with his brother Jack, whom he approached with hate and love, and his sister-in-law, Susan, were not solace enough for him. He was still a ward of the government, technically imprisoned among those whom he considered his inferiors, and he chafed against his commitment and agitated to become a free citizen of his country again. Perhaps what happened next was triggered by the appearance of my story and its effect upon him. This story gave him concrete evidence of his importance, and possibly made him even more resentful of having his unique genius caged. In any event, Larry persistently begged for freedom from the hospital, but nothing came of it. Then, one day in 1952, a shrewd fellow patient in the ward said to Larry, "You know, you're too smart to be in here. It's unfair. Why don't you get out? Even though Jack put you in here, he can't have you held. Legally, you committed yourself. You signed yourself in. Why don't you sign yourself out? No one on earth can force you to stay here."

The sudden realization that he was self-committed spurred Larry into immediate action. He applied for release. And he signed away his right to government care and maintenance in return for liberty and independence. When his brother Jack learned of this, learned that Larry's discharge was already being processed, he rushed to an official of the Veterans Administration. "You can't let him out," Jack implored. "He's irresponsible. He can't make a living. You've got to hold him here." The official shook his head. "We can't hold him, if he doesn't want to be committed. We need beds for people who want to be here. He doesn't want to be here. That's the way he feels." Jack replied angrily, "He's not in a position to feel that way or any way about himself. Can't you see that?"

The government could not see that. It saw nothing except the law. Preparations for Larry's release from the Neuro-Psychiatric Hospital went on. In a desperate effort to stave off what he feared would be a catastrophe, Jack made up his mind to battle the United States government. He retained an attorney, and went to court. Informed of Jack's move, Larry spent much of his hoarded veteran's pension to hire a lawyer of his own.

The legal action was brief. The law was the law, and Larry won his case. In 1953, he received his discharge from the Neuro-Psychiatric Hospital. Harboring bitterness against the Cain who he fantasied was jealous of him, Larry left Los Angeles. In New York, he was sure, he had a better friend in Burt, his long-ago, wealthy Princeton roommate, who was now a successful magazine editor. Burt, Larry decided, understood his creative abilities, and would help him make use of them and help him make his mark in the world.

Although apprehensive upon Larry's arrival, Burt was sympathetic and useful. He settled Larry in the first of a series of inexpensive one-room apartments. Because he wanted to bank Larry's monthly pension check for him, Burt allotted him a weekly allowance out of his own pocket. Perhaps it was Larry's handling of this weekly allowance that made Burt remember his friend's condition. Each weekly allowance evaporated in a single day. Larry's sense of responsibility had been left in a surgery room in Boston six years before. Thereafter, Burt doled out Larry's allowance on a daily basis, a four-dollar check every morning.

Now began the epic of Larry Cassidy, Wage Earner. Larry's grandiose dreams of obtaining high-salaried executive positions were quickly deflated. From that beginning in New York City, and for ten years after, and to this day, Larry's career story has been the story of small jobs found and small jobs lost. The lobotomy had stripped him of the necessary faculties of compromise and competitiveness. In no single year has he ever earned more than $300. Largely, he has lived on Burt's charity and his veteran's pension. His pre-lobotomy personality, with an I.Q. of over 150, a Phi Beta Kappa key, a desire to become a professor, and a wish to commit suicide, all this that had been good and bad, had been permanently removed. Now, as a post-lobotomy product, possessing a shallow belligerence as well as freedom from anxiety, he was left with an intelligence so erratic that it could not cope with a profession. In fact, it became quickly evident to Burt that Larry could not manage even menial jobs. Variously, he was a night watchman, a delivery boy, a salesman. Yet, he was none of these for more than three or four days at a time. He was fired, most often, because he antagonized employers by flaunting his superior educational background and complaining about his demeaning work, because he appeared eccentric and unstable in his behavior, and because he lacked the ability to concentrate on a task or stay in one place for any length of time.

Aside from his endless wanderings about Manhattan, Larry's social and recreational activity consisted of visiting Burt and Burt's family once a week. An hour or two before dinner, Larry would appear, disheveled and filthy, for he had no one to care for him and had no interest in caring for himself. Burt would run a tub of water, strip him, get him into the bath, then rush his clothes through the washer and dryer. While the clothes were being ironed, Burt would shampoo Larry's hair, scrub his back, and cut his fingernails. Once Larry was clean and dressed, he would, said Burt, "wait like a Pavlov dog for the dinner bell to sound, all the while pacing up and down, talking constantly." His best monologues were in praise of Burt, his patron, of the President of the United States, of the armed might of America that could crush any opponent on earth, of recent books he had read. Occasionally, the somnolent belligerence would awaken. Larry would suddenly halt his pacing, strike a pugilistic stance, and then chuckling, he would address his unseen enemy. If the unseen enemy was young, Larry would tell him, "I am going to hang one on you. I wouldn't urinate on you if you were on fire." If the unseen enemy was aged, Larry would growl, "I'll urinate on your grave." Who were the unseen enemies? They varied from the Veterans Administration officials to hospital patients he had known to his brother Jack to Dr. Goldsmith and Dr. Rogers. But the hostility lacked depth. Quickly, the pacing while waiting for dinner would be resumed, and Larry would be discoursing on the level (low) of culture in American society.

For five years, this pattern, the briefly held jobs, the endless walks, the visits to Burt, were the confined Andorra-like boundaries of Larry's life. Then there occurred a dramatic change. For some time, stimulated by newspaper advertisements and his own fancies, Larry Cassidy had been demanding a trip abroad. Burt turned his friend's pleas aside as long as he could, but at last, with dire misgivings, he gave in, praying the change might give his lobotomized ward some stimulation and joy. Burt planned the first of what was to become three foreign trips with care. Using some of Larry's pension savings, taking advantage of off-season rates, Burt went to a reliable New York travel bureau. He arranged for every step of the itinerary in advance, for every flight, hotel, meal, sightseeing trip. And then he packed Larry off with two small bags of clean clothes and a booklet of travelers' checks.

The first Grand Tour, which included Great Britain, France, and Italy, went well. There was only one misadventure. According to Jack, Larry's belligerence landed him in a Paris jail overnight. According to Burt, it was Larry's irresponsibility that caused the trouble, and that did not land him in jail. Rather, he had spent all his available funds, and was unable to pay his Paris hotel bill. There was an unhappy scene, but in the end the Paris hotel merely held on to Larry's luggage, which was sorely in need of fumigation anyway. Aside from that one incident, and some mild confusion about Larry's destination when he took to exchanging flight tickets, both Larry and Europe survived his visit, and he returned to New York enriched and intact.

Encouraged by the results of the first trip abroad, Burt permitted Larry a second one the following year. This sojourn was uneventful, until Larry arrived in England. Still possessed of some foxed fragments of literary knowledge, Larry joined an overnight round-trip bus tour from London to Stratford-on-Avon. On the bus, he found himself seated beside a small, shy, not unattractive, middle-aged English woman, a secretary full of romantic readings, on a holiday. Her name was Nellie. Their brief encounter in the mellow English countryside—they were travel companions no more than forty-eight hours—became love, for each of them, at first sight. For Larry, this incredible sweet bird of a woman, so reticently English, so ingrown, yet warm and sympathetic, filled the void left by his Catholic wife, Harriet, who had abandoned him as a matter of self-preservation almost a decade before. For Nellie, her vision filtered through her own neuroses, Larry was a handsome, dashing, knowledgeable visitor from the New World, interested and interesting, as unrealistically romantic and erratic as herself, and portending good prospects. When the pair returned to London, they exchanged addresses and promises. Nellie went back to her parents, to hope, and Larry returned to New York and Burt, to wage a campaign that would conquer his Maid Marian.

Larry wooed his love by airmail correspondence. His passionate letters to Nellie poured out daily. Because lobotomy had deprived him of restraint, his letters were earthy. Nellie was not dismayed, except when her parents saw the letters and confiscated them as "pornographic." Her own daily letters had a different tone. As a friend of theirs told me, "Her letters were on the Elizabeth Barrett Browning level of love, and his were on the men's-room-wall level of love. Her letters savored more of a cry from the soul, his from the groin." Yet, to them, their semantics were not so far apart, but conveyed a commonly understood yearning.

A year of correspondence with his beloved Nellie was all that Larry could endure. He was determined to visit her in her native habitat, to show her family that he was not a lecher, and to request her hand in marriage. Without disclosing to anyone his ultimate plan, he asked Burt to help him travel to England once more. Burt agreed, and put him aboard an eastbound French liner, destination Southampton.

On the first westbound French liner out of Southampton, Larry was back in New York City. He had neither set foot on English soil nor laid eyes on his fevered and waiting Nellie. The British immigration authority, it appeared, had refused to allow Larry to land. Had Nellie's disapproving parents or Larry's disapproving brothers intervened? On checking, Burt learned it was not any relative who had prevented Larry's landing. Larry had been the cause of his own undoing. Handed a routine

British entry questionnaire, before disembarking, he studied the question, "Have you ever been committed to a mental institution?"—and he answered, "Yes." Immediately, the British immigration officials summoned him for an interview. What met their eyes was a bewildered, unshaved, unkempt, foul-smelling passenger, who admitted to having no money and was unable to remember that all his expenses had been prepaid. Promptly, his visiting privileges were rescinded. The undesirable alien was sent home, while Nellie grieved on the dock.

Love thwarted became love intensified. Larry confessed his plan. He must marry Nellie. Burt and Larry's brothers, Jack and Tim, tried to dissuade him. The leucotome, the knife that had once severed Larry's prefrontal lobes, had dulled Hamlet but not affected Romeo. He wanted Nellie, and she wanted him, and if he could not go to her, he would bring her to him.

Horrified at the prospect of Larry and the poor, unsuspecting Nellie under one roof, as mates, Burt took the decisive step. He wrote Nellie the truth. He revealed all of Larry's history, including the clinical facts about his prefrontal lobotomy operation, and was certain that that would end the love affair. Burt was wrong. Blandly, Nellie wrote back that she was familiar with lobotomy cases—during World War II she had volunteered to serve in a military mental institution, and had helped handle the more hopeless lobotomy patients—and now she was even more eager to join Larry and care for him. Stunned, Burt wrote more letters to her, and enlisted other old school friends and relatives of Larry's to write to her. All of this negative propaganda failed. Nellie remained adamant: She was determined to abandon her family, her job, her country, to answer Larry's summons and love.

In one final effort to disenchant Nellie, Burt telephoned London—he remembers, wryly, that the toll charges came to $125—and he spoke to Nellie, spoke interminably. He played down Larry's good points. He emphasized Larry's hostilities, relating how he had once slapped his landlady, how he most resented people who tried to help him, how he was incapable of holding a job.

When Burt had finished presenting his case, Nellie, choking with emotion, cried out over the transatlantic cable, "I don't care what you say! I must be with him! I'll commit suicide unless I can come to America to be with him!"

For Burt, there was no more to say. After he had hung up the receiver, he was as torn about his own role in Larry's future as Jack had been, so many years before, on the eve of the decisive prefrontal lobotomy operation. Recently, recalling that period, Burt said to me:

"After that transatlantic call, I was *forced* to play God. In fact, I wasn't playing God. I *was* God. I knew that Nellie was a disturbed person, and that lots of disturbed persons *do* commit suicide, as she had threatened. I knew further that if she *could* help Larry, it would be an incredible blessing. He was living alone in a filthy, filthy slum. Aside from seeing me once a week, he had almost no human contacts (though plenty of inhuman ones, with landladies and neighbors). Larry was rotting. The years ahead presented a frightening prospect. And, meanwhile, Nellie kept assuring me that love could move mountains.

"There were enormous pressures on me from both camps. My own family and Larry's family were outraged at the idea of my helping Nellie come over here. You see, her coming here was in my hands, for she needed letters from me promising she would never become a ward of the government. At the same time, Nellie was talking about suicide, and Larry was rotting. It was a genuine dilemma. You know how I decided, and only the real God above knows whether I decided right or wrong."

What Burt finally decided to do was to cooperate fully in bringing about the reunion of Nellie and Larry.

Nellie's troubles began the moment she walked down the gangplank in New York City. So overwhelmed and nervous was she, that she was unable to face Larry during her entire first day in the United States. Presently, the reunion was effected by Burt, and Nellie set up housekeeping in Larry's wretched apartment. She could not be his legal wife, or even his common-law wife, because Larry still had a wife somewhere, named Harriet, who was too religious to divorce him. And, since Larry was legally incompetent, he could not sue for a divorce. From their first domesticity—as in the years after, and today—Larry and Nellie lived in gentle sin.

A friend, who saw them in their first weeks together, told me, "It was almost as if the two of them were trying to get out of a bog, Larry using her as a stepping stone, and the higher Larry rose out of the muck, the lower Nellie went in." Suddenly, it seemed, Larry's story became Nellie's story. He leaned on her, and was supported, but like her predecessor, Harriet, she slowly began to collapse under the burden.

Nellie's initial shock came when she faced the conditions of her new life on New York's West Side. She had been catapulted from a neat, whitewashed, antiseptic, tightly efficient English atmosphere into a neighborhood crowded with impoverished and angry immigrants. She had moved into an apartment, half-furnished, primitive and dirty, crawling with bedbugs. There was not even the illusion of romantic privacy. The walls that sheltered them might have been of Japanese rice paper. In the day, the toilet sounds came through. In the night, the bed sounds tortured her. The next cause of shock was her companion, who wanted a nurse not a mistress, who was at once intelligent and unintelligible, whose habits were often as civilized as those of a roving animal.

Yet, she loved him and he loved her, and she determined to mold what was left of Larry into an acceptable member of the human race and into a good provider. He had once dreamed of being a professor, and had confided his dream. She would, she determined, make him a teacher, at least, a respectable pedagogue, and together they would escape this hell-hole. Larry applied to Long Island University, to study in the school's education department, and he was accepted. Nellie, working on what was left of his Princeton I.Q., studying with him, for him, got him through the required classes. With her help, he managed to become an accredited teacher. This had cost them $500, but now Larry, the teacher, was ready. He applied for positions. He was interviewed. Alone, without his collaborator, he fell down every time. The keen-eyed buyers of teacher-minds saw that his was not a dependable mind. He had the credentials, but no job.

Anguished over their defeat, Nellie insisted that at least they escape the slum. They moved to a cleaner apartment in a small New Jersey town, which was near the residence of one of Larry's brothers. Nellie was still determined that Larry should make his own way. More of his savings were withdrawn, and he was enrolled in the Graduate School of Library Service at Rutgers University. Diligently, Nellie coached her charge, but to no avail. Larry failed his tests and was dropped by the school. Because money was needed, he obtained employment as a night manager in a movie house. Under Nellie's soothing encouragement and guidance, he held the job for two months. Then he was dismissed.

Friends came to the rescue. There was an opening in the Princeton University Library. Larry was recommended, and accepted for the job subject to an interview. In high spirits, he invested a fifty-dollar deposit on a modern new apartment in Lawrenceville, to be near his library, and then he had his interview. Shortly afterward, a member of the library called Larry—apologetically, to be sure—to explain that the opening was no more, because its former occupant had decided to return. In short, in his interview, Larry had talked too much.

There was something about a possible post-office job in Philadelphia, so Larry and Nellie moved to Philadelphia. Once more, Larry bent to his books, and Nellie hovered over him, and finally he took his civil service examination. His grade was passing, but low. Jobs were given on the basis of grades received. Impatiently, Larry waited to be called. Once more, funds were needed, and Nellie went to work. This, then, became their life, Nellie, frail and fading and fearful, working, and Larry, agitated and angry and aggrieved, waiting. It was eighteen months before the Philadelphia post-office summoned him. Once more, the fateful interview. Once more, Larry talked. Once more, he remained unemployed.

At last, in Philadelphia, reality caught up with Nellie. She came to the knowledge that dreams are for the sleeping and not the waking hours. She came to see what her life with Larry truly was, and what it could truly never be. The weight of this disenchantment, atop her own neuroses, broke her down completely.

A friend who was with them in Philadelphia told me the next of Nellie: "The Seven Plagues of Egypt were visited on her frail and quaking little body and suffering soul. There were protracted periods of sweats, chills, insomnia, violent and alarming tachycardia. She had depression to the point of nausea. Then there was severe pyorrhea, to add to all else, or because of it, that cost one thousand dollars to repair. Inevitably, the total nervous breakdown. She was committed to the Philadelphia General Hospital. After three weeks she was released as possibly cured. But she was still in black despair. Then followed private treatments—ten electric shock treatments—and this helped her considerably."

All of that was 1962, a year that ended with one more job prospect for Larry, on one more far horizon. The prospect was in Sacramento, California, and so Larry and Nellie left Philadelphia and moved to the West, and the full circle had closed for Larry. He was back where he came from, in effect, but this time not committed to a hospital.

The job prospect in Sacramento did not work out. However, there was temporary employment, very temporary, as a salesclerk in a department store. And then, more important, there was something better. After ten years of resenting and missing his younger brother, Jack, Larry was reunited with him in the early part of 1963.

The years had not been easy on Jack since he had fought the Veterans Administration in a Los Angeles court to keep Larry institutionalized. True, in terms of career, he had grown and become successful. While still a struggling young publicity man, he had determined to risk going into business on his own. He established a talent agency. Because of his ingenuity and drive, he had prospered enormously. But there had been difficulties. One major problem was with his wife, Susan. Another was with his own neuroses, coupled with his guilts and uneasy conscience about consenting to Larry's lobotomy.

For Jack, his marriage became untenable, and he and Susan drifted apart, until at last, in 1959, they were divorced. Now his guilts had become unbearable, and finally, on advice, Jack acted to make himself happier. Psychosurgery, especially lobotomy, had fallen into disrepute, and the new medical age was experimenting with, even favoring, mind-changing drugs such as LSD, mescaline, psyilocybia, and tranquilizers such as reserpine and chlorpromazine. Jack decided to undergo LSD treatments. He received nine treatments in all. As he told me, "When I went into LSD, I was filled with self-recrimination. All of Larry locked up inside me poured out. Other things poured out, too. And at the end of my treatments, I was a new person. It was the most remarkable and wonderful thing that ever happened to me."

Freed from tensions by his divorce and his LSD therapy, Jack Cassidy married a lovely fashion model, had a son and daughter by her, expanded his business firm, and thus fortified, determined to see Larry for the first time in ten years. Early in 1963, Jack flew to Sacramento to face Larry and meet Nellie. He recounted the reunion to me. "I had not seen Larry in so long. I was full of apprehension. Then there he was before me, and when I saw him, the dam burst, burst wide open. We embraced and kissed, and there were tears in his eyes, and I don't mind admitting I cried. He was so very proud of his baby brother who had made good among the film stars. He was sweet, and all the old hostility was gone."

Jack was thrilled at the transformation he thought he detected in Larry. "His face was cherubic and peaceful," said Jack. "And he looked youthful. He is eleven years older than I am, but he seemed at least three or four years younger." The several times that they saw each other, Larry was clean-shaven, and although his clothes were frayed and worn, they were immaculate. And the small apartment in which Larry and Nellie lived, while sparsely furnished, was neat and comfortable. Before returning to Los Angeles after his first visit, Jack bought the couple a television set, and also a shelf of books since Larry had become a voracious reader again. Jack promised to find a medically oriented hypnotist, to help Nellie, and before departing, he promised to see them from time to time, to write regularly, and to assist them with money.

Larry and Nellie still live in Sacramento. Larry devotes his days to reading fiction, favoring mysteries, and to hunting for jobs. Most recently, he was trying to become a printer or an editorial assistant. At night, Larry and Nellie sit mesmerized before the new television set, so now both have an outside social life in their own living room. Financially, they struggle along on the monthly veteran's check, the regular checks from Burt and Jack, and the income from the occasional job.

Larry receives no extraordinary medical attention. From time to time he will hear from Dr. Goldsmith, who writes from Boston to inquire about Larry's progress, mainly for the psychiatrist's statistical records. Larry hates the psychiatrist, and rarely replies to him. Once, Larry wrote him to try to borrow money, but received no answer. Larry informed Burt, "I wrote to Dr. Goldsmith to tell him I'm now in Sacramento, and to ask him for advice on jobs. His only suggestion was that I should apply for a job as a garbage collector!"

And so, Larry today. I asked the two men closest to him, his friend Burt in New York, and his brother Jack in Los Angeles, what they think of his present and his future. While Burt tends to be mildly pessimistic, and Jack mildly optimistic, both are in full agreement that Nellie has improved Larry, brought him closer to the company of men.

According to Burt:

"Is Larry's progress real or specious? I can't be certain. I am no professional (if such there be, which I purely doubt), but I'd lean toward specious. Take Nellie away from him, take away the humanizing restraints she places on him, the proprieties she insists upon, and he might lapse within a week. In my opinion, it's all Nellie. Because I suspect his lobotomy personality is still there. She is the one who keeps it contained. She is the supporting cast that enables him to play the role I'm sure he would have enjoyed playing in New York before her time, had he been able to find someone to play opposite him. He knows what words like status and respectability mean. He likes them. He wants status and respectability, but not if he has to do anything to get them. So Nellie does the job for him.

"Was I wrong to bring Nellie to him? I've come to this. It was an eye for an eye. Larry is vastly better off, and Nellie vastly worse. Have I any final judgment to pass on Dr. Goldsmith and Dr. Rogers and their lobotomy? Certainly not. As between the wretch who spent his days sweating and screaming, before the lobotomy, and the wretch who now has brought someone else down to his former level, but himself knows no pain, who can choose? Anyway, he wanted her, and she was ready to die without him. And that's the way it is."

According to Jack:

"Of course, today Larry's handicaps remain, the same inability to get and hold a job, the same inability to sustain interest in anything, the same necessity to talk incessantly. Yet, in a sense, this is a story with a sort of happy ending, if it can be called that. I believe this. The life he lives would not be a meaningful or normal or happy life to you or to me. It is too limited. But for him, in relation to what he had been before, it is now better and happier than it has ever been since he became an adult. From his point of view, he has a life he can live with, thanks to Nellie.

"As to the lobotomy to which I gave my consent in 1947—well, I've come a great distance since then. I've learned to live with my part in deciding about his life. I get along with it now. . . . But you know, often, so often, I say to myself—maybe if we had waited, just waited a little longer . . ."

The Sunday Gentleman Abroad

» 8 «

TOURIST'S BIBLE

EARLY IN World War II, when Hitler assigned Hermann Goering the job of blasting Great Britain from the map, Goering cast about for an accurate list of targets. He did not have to look far. On his bookshelves rested the one source that he trusted even more than his costly intelligence reports. He pulled down his red-covered copy of Baedeker's *London and Environs*, studied it, then officially commanded the Luftwaffe to "destroy every historical building and landmark in Britain that is marked with a star in Baedeker." Thus began the thunderous Nazi air attacks which came to be known to the English as "the Baedeker raids."

It was not surprising that Goering owned a set of Baedeker guidebooks. Up to the outbreak of war, over two million other persons residing in every civilized nation of the world had bought the eighty-seven different titles of the famous peacetime guidebooks published in Leipzig. Most of these readers, however, used their Baedekers for more constructive purposes.

Unlike Goering, the mass of Baedeker owners were ordinary tourists, who reverently regarded the guidebook as their sightseeing bible. They relied upon its pioneer system of rating sights by stars to save them time in travel (Two stars, "must see," the Louvre, the Kremlin, Niagara Falls; one star, "see, if possible," the Jungfrau, Yale University, street scenes of Cairo; no stars, Tolstoi's home, the Chicago stockyards, the Albert Memorial). Tourists counted upon Baedeker for capsule culture ("China's Great Wall, completed towards the end of the 3rd century B.C. as a protection against inroads by Huns. Constructed mainly of bricks and is in a ruinous condition. No stars"). Readers drew heavily on its practical advice (In Naples, "Iron bedsteads should if possible be selected as being less infested by the enemies of repose").

But above all, sightseers depended almost fanatically on Baedeker's accuracy. Their faith was mirrored, some years ago, in a German cartoon depicting a father and his family studying a castle and a waterfall. In the father's hand, a copy of Baedeker shows the scene reversed, waterfall and then castle. And the father is complaining, "Why, this scenery is all wrong!"

In a century and a quarter, Baedeker's hypnotic influence over readers grew so strong that its subjects often took Baedeker's descriptions as seriously as did the sightseers. Once, when Kaiser Wilhelm was in a critical conference with his ministers in Potsdam's palace, the wall clock struck noon and the palace band began forming outside for its daily concert. Immediately, the Kaiser rose. "With your kind forbearance, gentlemen," he said, "I must excuse myself now to appear in the window. You see, it says in Baedeker that at this hour I always do."

More recently, an innkeeper located in the Black Forest, a mile north of the main highway, was horrified to learn a new edition of Baedeker had mistakenly placed his inn a mile *south* of the highway. When his business began to fall off, he filled the highway with signs pointing out the right direction to his inn. But tourists ignored his signs and stuck to their Baedekers. At last, in desperation, the innkeeper uprooted his entire establishment, moved it from its position north of the highway, to a mile south, exactly where Baedeker had located it.

Such devotion by readers, and submission by sites, to the judgment of a travel volume—the first to make a fetish of infallibility—soon made the name Baedeker an international synonym for guidebook. Nothing in the travel field, published before or since, has ever attained the renown of Baedeker—with its thirty volumes in English and fifty-seven in French and German.

Yet, despite its historic popularity, it appeared for a time that Baedeker might not survive World War II. For Goering, by perverting the guidebook's use, almost caused its downfall. The British, enraged by "the Baedeker raids" and determined to destroy Baedeker's presses and great store of maps, retaliated. In 1943, the RAF struck at Leipzig, unloading tons of bombs on the Baedeker printing plant, reducing a century and a half of painstakingly prepared records, maps, plates to rubble.

As if that were not enough, Baedeker was beset by an even greater menace in postwar Europe and America. While Baedeker, trying to replenish its records, trying to raise financing, wavered between continuing or quitting, the world's tourists were suddenly bombarded by a new type of guidebook. The new guides, written or edited by Fielding, Sutton, Joseph, Ogrizek, Clark, Fodor, were, for the most, "modern"—i.e., casual, cute, wisecracking, bright. Often, facts were smothered under personal opinion and prejudice. In some, photographs and art had completely replaced scholarship. Several were insensitive to culture and history. While all strove for accuracy, and a few attained it, still, it was not the dogged, detailed, checked and rechecked Teutonic accuracy provided by the old Leipzig plant.

That was enough for the elders of the Baedeker clan—old Hans and Dr. Dietrich Baedeker, grandsons of the founder. No one, they felt, had yet successfully replaced them. No one, they decided, had yet given their vast footsore public what it most desired. They made their decision. Baedeker bounced back into the postwar battle for the world's sightseers.

But still it was not easy. On resuming publication, seventy-three-year-old Hans Baedeker, because of lack of funds and backlog of material, decided to stick close to home with his first book. Working in Communist-controlled Leipzig, he obtained Russian approval for a guidebook on that city. He was forced to let the Communist mayor of Leipzig write the preface, and forced to publish it through a Communist printing plant. But he would not compromise on detail or accuracy. Because all Germans, at one time or another, had to visit the Russian Kommandatura Building, Hans plainly located the building on one of his maps. The moment Baedeker's *Leipzig* was released, the Soviets saw the map and arrested Hans for committing a breach of security. He got off with his life, but had his publishing license revoked. In despair, Hans quit, and disappeared into the anonymity of the Russian zone with his brother Dr. Dietrich Baedeker.

But old Hans had a nephew, Karl, and Dr. Dietrich had two sons, Hans and Otto, all three dwelling outside of Leipzig. These young Baedekers, physically free of Russian restrictions, fired by the popular reception to the family's first postwar guidebook, pledged themselves to keep the firm alive. Karl Baedeker, a handsome, forty-four-year-old army veteran, established new headquarters in the British zone, outside Hamburg, using his father-in-law's thatch-roofed cottage for a publishing office. Young Hans set up shop in Stuttgart, while aristocratic, twenty-eight-year-old Otto went to work in London.

Slowly, steadily, in the seven years since, the dry, factual, oddity-crammed, red-covered books, still stressing accuracy, have crowded their way back into the world's bookstores. After Baedeker's *Leipzig* came a whole series of German travel guides on Munich, Frankfurt, Northern Bavaria, and Schleswig-Holstein—and, finally breaking out of Germany, Baedeker's *London*, which had first been issued in 1862, and was now republished simultaneously in Hamburg, London, and New York City.

Although the *Saturday Review* detected in the Northern Bavaria guidebook, an "undercurrent of nationalism"—because the Baedekers, though never pro-Nazi, harped on the Allied bombings of Germany—the general reception was enthusiastic. *The New York Times* spoke of Baedeker's "enviable standard of scholarship," and the Cincinnati *Enquirer* admitted, "when you come right down to it, there is no more satisfactory guidebook than the Baedeker type."

Encouraged, the three Baedeker great-grandsons are today preparing more popular volumes on Paris, Switzerland, and Italy. But they agree even guidebook makers must have a guide. Theirs is the original Karl Baedeker, who founded the firm 126 years ago. The great-grandsons speak of him as if he were still alive, their active senior partner, as well he might be—since it is his name that continues to appear as author of the books, even though he died in 1859.

While researching for their most recent editions, the three young Baedekers like to remember that the original Karl, one April night and morning in 1854, spent thirteen and a half hours alone in the Père Lachaise cemetery of Paris, searching out famous gravestones and noting their inscriptions and positions. The modern Baedekers like to remember, too, the old man's honest admission, in a guide on Austria, that he could not describe a certain stretch of countryside because he had "travelled over it by night only." Above all, they like to remember the founder's warning, "A good guidebook is always in the making and never made."

Karl Baedeker the First, a printer's son born in Essen during 1801, entered Heidelberg University at the age of sixteen to major in philosophy and history, and later went to Berlin to study bookmaking. The most important part of his schooling, however, took place outside the classroom. Fellow students regarded Baedeker as an eccentric because he constantly wandered off on lone sightseeing hikes, during which he filled dozens of notebooks with historical facts, statistics, impressions. At twenty-six, facing the necessity of earning a livelihood, he opened a bookstore in bustling Coblenz, capital of the Rhine Province of Prussia, a city which harbored the first Rhine steamship line, already heavily used by English vacationists en route to Switzerland.

Bored with his bookstore, intrigued by the Rhine, Baedeker began to spend more and more of his time exploring its banks, jotting down notations of the sights. One afternoon in 1827, when neglect had brought his bookstore to the verge of bankruptcy, Baedeker was rowing a dinghy along the river. Suddenly, he saw a small dog tumble into the water. The dog's master stood helplessly on shore, calling for help, as the animal floundered. Baedeker rowed to the dog's aid and rescued it. The grateful owner of the animal, a Dr. Wilhelm Klein, explained that he was author of a new guidebook, Klein's *Rheinreise—The Rhine Journey; A Hand-*

book for Travellers in a Hurry—prepared for rushed tourists using the new river steamboat service. Dr. Klein presented Baedeker with a copy of the guide, and later Baedeker was able to tell him, "I only saved your dog—but you saved my future with that little book."

Reading the Rhine guide, Baedeker saw that it was useful, but incomplete. He felt that he could improve upon it a hundredfold. And at once, he knew what he wanted to do—combine his knowledge of bookmaking with his love for sightseeing and fact-gathering. Learning that the ailing Dr. Klein was prepared to liquidate his business, Baedeker set about raising money. He got rid of his bookstore, borrowed money from his father, and took over Klein's guidebook. He rewrote it completely, drawing heavily upon the notes he had made during his Rhine excursions, and adding detailed maps. He retained Dr. Klein's name on the new edition, had it published, and waited. He didn't wait long. It was a sensational sellout within three weeks. Baedeker was ecstatic. He had found his vocation. He looked about for new worlds to conquer.

Baedeker realized that while guidebooks were nothing new (pilgrims had used them in the Middle Ages), there was a desperate need for the special kind of volumes he had in mind. The Napoleonic Wars were over, and ordinary citizens, so long locked in, were eager to travel. There was only one Continental guide available, a handbook to the Lowlands and Germany, brought out by John Murray, the English publisher. But this guide, like the lesser ones, was designed to serve travelers who possessed money, leisure, and education. It was taken for granted by these guidebooks that those who traveled had available luxurious carriages, previous knowledge of Europe's capitals, and socially prominent friends abroad.

But what about the middle-class tourist? The shopkeeper who had only four weeks? The student with limited means? The eldest daughter who'd never been outside her home and didn't know a soul? For them, nearby foreign countries were as impenetrable as the African jungles. Toward travelers without money or contacts, every hotel porter, every restaurant owner, every guide acted like a beast of prey. There were no big travel agencies to arrange protective group excursions. There were no newspaper columns or magazine articles offering handy advice and tips. If these travelers dared venture forth, they were bedeviled, exploited. It was this growing army of the world's timid tourists that Karl Baedeker determined to help. He would make each and every one of them, he decided, "independent of hotel keepers, commissionaires, and guides."

But he realized that, to accomplish this, he must learn firsthand if it was really possible to travel quickly, cheaply, comfortably—and yet see everything of importance, and understand what had been seen. Immediately, he embarked upon his first swing through Europe. Thereafter, unceasingly for thirty-two years—leaving his wife Emilie, four sons, and two daughters behind—he moved about Europe, observing, experiencing, recording. He traveled by foot, on bicycle, on horseback, and in stagecoach. He even took the first railroad journey across Belgium, covering a whirlwind six miles in three-quarters of an hour, and excitedly reported to his father, "What a thrill! Objects near the track seem to merge!"

Throughout the Continent, his serious round face, with its wide forehead, piercing eyes, full lips, set atop a barrel of a body, became a familiar sight. On the road, he usually wore a shawl over flannel shirt, rough breeches, old boots, and he always carried a knapsack. On hot days he would open an umbrella or shield his eyes from the sun with green crepe paper. In cities, he often changed to long black coat and black cravat. His prejudices became as renowned as his appearance. He liked rooms with a southern exposure, beer, horse racing, mountain views, Paris by night, and Honesty.

In his guidebooks, he placed Honesty next to Cleanliness. He went to great lengths to ferret out all who conspired against tourists, and tourists appreciated this and consequently trusted him. Assuming shabby, frayed attire, and a country-cousin manner, he would often register in some swank Zurich hotel. If the management proved snobbish, relegated him to an overpriced room, treated him to the companionship of bedbugs, he would promptly remove the hotel's star from the Baedeker guidebook. At various recommended restaurants in Vienna, he would sit down to dinner incognito. If he received watered soup, another star fell.

Although essentially a kindly man, he could be exceedingly blunt. In the beginning, he severely censured slipshod hotels. When France retaliated by banning his books for a brief period, he changed his policy to one of criticism by omission, remarking drily, "Hotels which cannot be accurately characterized without exposing the editor to the risk of legal proceedings are left unmentioned." Sometimes, however, he was unable to contain himself, as in his comment on a Belgian restaurant, "The waiter's arithmetic is occasionally at fault."

Besides dishonest hotelkeepers and restaurant owners, the other villains mentioned in his volumes were bandits who drove carriages, guides who overcharged, and pickpockets. He was equally firm about opposing handouts to beggars, overtipping, and missing a two-star sight. And as for those who were embarrassed to be recognized as tourists, who fought to get off the beaten path, he was positive this attitude was overrated; hence his constant cautioning against out-of-the-way lodgings: "The Traveler is warned against sleeping in chalets unless absolutely necessary. Whatever poetry may be theoretically in a fragrant bed of hay, the cold night air, the ringing of cowbells, the grunting of pigs hardly conduce to refreshing slumber."

Despite his trials on the road, he never lost his enthusiasm for sight-seeing. "Europe is for me like a wonderful garden with many lovely flowers," he wrote a friend. "I try to be a good gardener." That he was a good gardener became evident from the public clamor for his meticulously detailed guides on Belgium and Holland, Germany and the Austrian Empire, Switzerland, and finally, the last one he wrote himself four years before his death, on Paris. In these books, poetry walked hand in hand with practicality, as in his advice on Lourdes: "The torchlight procession presents a fairylike scene (Beware of pickpockets)." Or again, in discussing hiking trips, "Over all the movements of the walker, the weather holds despotic sway (West winds usually bring rain)."

Not only the general public, but eventually members of royalty and celebrities, adopted Karl Baedeker's little red books. Countless famous people like Elizabeth Barrett Browning, Thackeray, Hawthorne, Carlyle, Ruskin, Dickens, Henry James, Mark Twain, Theodore Dreiser, made the Grand Tour, Baedekers in hand. The greatest number of these readers favored the volume on Switzerland, with the Rhine following closely, and Paris just behind. It is a tribute to old Karl that Baedeker's *Switzerland* still remains the top best seller of all time on the firm's large list.

Baedeker's *Switzerland* appeared first in 1844. Its immediate success, and continuing popularity for over a century (it went into twenty-eight editions), was due not only to the attraction Switzerland held for the middle-class tourist, not only to Karl's elaborately detailed advice and suggestions, but also to the attention he gave to the interests of outdoor enthusiasts. "The maps alone were the most expensive and valuable the firm ever produced," says Otto Baedeker, old Karl's great-grandson in London. "Each map showed accurate mountain climbing routes, almost all tried out by Karl himself. These map plates were destroyed during the war, and now have to be replaced from scratch."

Old Karl was at his best in this volume. Nothing was too minor to be overlooked. "A light rucksack suffices to contain all that is necessary for a week's excursion," wrote old Karl. "A pocket-knife with a corkscrew, a drinking cup, a tin-opener, a pocket flash, stout gloves, a compass, and a pocket first-aid outfit should not be forgotten. Useful, though not indispensable, are a pair of binoculars, sewing materials, a piece of cord, and an electric torch." But before the climber took off, old Karl stayed him a moment, admonishing, "The enthusiast must curb his ardours at the outset." For countless problems had to be anticipated. The climber's feet, for instance. For an overdose of "ardour," Karl suggested, "The feet may be rubbed morning and evening with brandy and tallow. Soaping the inside of the stocking is another well-known safeguard against abrasion of the skin." As to meals: "Glacier water is dangerous and cold milk is also prejudicial. A little cold tea, slightly sweetened, or a dried prune now and then, will suffice." As to the inevitable diarrhea: "Fifteen drops of a mixture of parts of tincture of opium"—though later Baedekers took a dimmer view of opium, and finally dropped the medical suggestion from the book.

As tourists continued to scramble and puff up Jungfrau and the Matterhorn, Karl prepared them for real dangers. Perhaps a slip, perhaps an avalanche. In that case, "Distress signals may be made by waving a flag or handkerchief on the end of a stick, by shouting, whistling, or by showing a light (lantern, fire, etc.)." In the event of a thunderstorm, "it is best to seek refuge from the lightning in some sheltered spot, carefully avoiding single trees and other prominent objects, while on the open mountain it is sometimes advisable to lie flat on the ground." Finally, after achieving the summit and making a safe return, the greatest danger of the entire excursion: the tip. But old Karl, ever watchful for his purse-poor reader, surmounted it nobly. "Among the Swiss mountains the judicious traveller knows well when to make the tender of his cigar-case or spirit flask."

When Karl, aged fifty-eight, his immortality secure among those afflicted with wanderlust, lay on his deathbed in Coblenz, he gathered his four sons about him. "I have shown my fellow men Europe," he told them. "I leave you to show them the rest of the world."

Two of the sons, Fritz and Karl II, undertook this task. But when Karl II suffered sunstroke in Egypt, and retired, Fritz Baedeker carried on alone. While old Karl had established the firm, and set the high standard for its continued excellence, it was Fritz who made Baedeker truly international. He insisted that his employees think not as Germans, but as world citizens. Toward this end, he quickly introduced the French and English language editions. One of his most pleasurable moments occurred on the occasion when he sat in a depot rereading Baedeker's *Switzerland* in German, and an American lady tourist, noticing the book, exclaimed, "Oh, you have the translation!"

As the automobile and the railroad supplanted the stagecoach, enabling tourists to cover more ground, and as more and more vacationers went to the Near East, Africa, the Orient, Fritz Baedeker's job became increasingly complicated. He realized that the guidebook was no longer a one-man job. He began to hire foreign editors to prepare the volumes on their native lands, professors and other experts to assist with specialized chapters, and "spies" to deliver lesser material. In preparing his first

book on London, in 1862, he hired cab-drivers and street sweepers to report to him, and was then able to write in the guide, "The stranger is
warned against going to any unrecommended house near Leicester
Square, as there are several houses of doubtful reputation in this local-
ity." In preparing his *Sweden and Norway* in 1879, his Scandinavian
"spies" reported on certain discomforts in their vicinity, and Fritz passed
them on to his readers: "Visitors to Lapland and the Swedish Norrland
should also be provided with veils to keep off the gnats."

In Coblenz, and later in Leipzig where the firm established larger
headquarters, Fritz employed as many as twenty assistants to help him
coordinate the information that poured in.

In the years that Fritz headed the firm, Baedeker blanketed the world.
Not only was London covered, but such widely varied localities as Palestine, Egypt, Italy, Sweden, North America, Spain, Canada, the Riviera,
Constantinople, India, and Russia. Where his father had given Baedeker
its first big best seller in *Switzerland*, Fritz supervised the company's
most distinguished later volume, which was on Egypt, and was regarded
by the *Manchester Guardian* as "one of the most astonishing guidebooks
ever put together."

Baedeker's *Egypt*, first published in 1878, went into eight editions, the
last appearing in 1929. The special editor assisting Fritz Baedeker was
Professor Georg Steindorff, an Egyptologist from Leipzig University who
eventually moved to New York. The 495 pages of the guide ranged
through a potpourri of subjects such as Arab cafés, Egyptian dialects, the
Nile, Mohammedan manners and customs, the major Egyptian deities
and sacred animals. Full chapters were devoted to hieroglyphics and Is-
lamic architecture.

But though it was a scholarly masterpiece, and everywhere regarded as
a work of art, at no time did Fritz Baedeker forget his primary audience.
One hundred and six maps and town plans filled the book, and the
Great Pyramid was covered to the satisfaction of the most retiring tourist. "The ascent of the Pyramid, though fatiguing, is perfectly safe,"
Fritz assured his readers. "The traveller selects two of the importunate
Bedouins and proceeds to the N. E. corner. Assisted by the two Bedouins,
one holding each hand, and, if desired, by a third (no extra payment)
who pushes behind, the traveller begins the ascent of the steps." Often
the guides rushed the tourist. But Fritz advised, "The Traveller should
insist on resting as often as he feels inclined. 'Quiet, or you shall have no
pay' is a sentence that may often be employed with advantage. All requests for bakshish should be refused, and it is well to keep an eye upon
one's pockets." As to exploring the interior of the pyramid, Fritz warned:
"Travellers who are in the slightest degree predisposed to apoplectic or

fainting fits, and ladies travelling alone, should not attempt to penetrate into these stifling recesses. The floor is often very slippery and the air smells strongly of bats."

If Fritz fathered Baedeker's greatest guide, he also helped produce a number of others that held lesser records of distinction. Baedeker's *India*, published in 1914, was the most difficult and wearisome volume the firm ever put together. It took four years to prepare, and sold poorly, because of the lack of tourist traffic in India. Baedeker's *Palestine and Syria*, first published in 1875, fared somewhat better, even though it helped defeat Fritz's homeland in World War I. For General Allenby, a Baedeker fan, used his 1912 edition of *Palestine and Syria* in his fight against the Turks and the Central Powers.

Baedeker's *Italy*, published by Fritz in 1872, proved to be the most controversial volume on the firm's list. Fritz found Naples wanting in cleanliness, oppressively hot in September, and swarming with beggars (who, he wrote, could best be dismissed by "a slight backward movement of the head, accompanied by a somewhat contemptuous expression"). The Naples Chamber of Commerce protested, officially, to the German government. At the same time, the Italian pharmacists in Rome threatened legal action because Baedeker advised tourists in the Eternal City to confine their medical shopping to drugstores owned by Americans and British. The gondoliers of Venice felt similarly put upon. Baedeker, they screamed, assaulted their gallantry (he had merely said that they often insulted ladies, and advised the sensible escort not to push the offenders into the canal but simply to "lodge a complaint"). Baedeker, they wailed, deprived them of their livelihood (he had merely suggested caution in stepping out of a gondola, "steps slimy," then added the death phrase, "gratuity not obligatory").

Baedeker's *North America*, prepared at a cost of over $100,000 and published in 1893, was the firm's first venture into the New World. Great care was taken with the guide. Viscount James Bryce, British Ambassador to the United States, was hired to write an entire chapter on the United States Constitution. Baedeker found much to recommend in America. Two stars were awarded Yellowstone National Park, the Morse Collection of Japanese Pottery in Boston, and Niagara Falls ("perhaps the greatest and most impressive of the natural wonders of America"). On the other hand, there was much that disturbed Baedeker. Public toilets were lacking in New York City, San Francisco architecture was abominable, and the Chicago stockyards could interest only those "whose nerves are strong enough to contemplate with equanimity wholesale slaughter and oceans of blood." Other barbarisms were duly noted, but happily, in the 1909 edition, Baedeker was able to add:

"Throughout almost the whole country travelling is now as safe as in the most civilised parts of Europe, and the carrying of arms is unnecessary."

The present Karl Baedeker admits that the firm's greatest financial failure occurred in that period. "At great expense, Fritz Baedeker prepared and brought out a guide on Russia. It appeared in 1914, on the eve of World War I. The war, and new Communist government, quickly outdated our book. We lost a fortune."

Nevertheless, Baedeker's *Russia—with Teheran, Port Arthur and Peking—A Handbook for Travellers* remains a fascinating curiosity of recent times past. There was no Iron Curtain before 1914 ("the visa is good for six months"), and Baedeker researchers were able to prepare 40 detailed maps, 78 town plans, and 590 pages of exact information. Still, tourists were warned of difficulties. "Passengers are strongly advised not to send their luggage in advance. Unprinted paper should be used for packing, to avoid any cause of suspicion." Fritz found only one hotel in Moscow, the National, worth even a single star. As to historic sights, there were few musts. One of the few was the Kremlin: "In the centre of the city, on a hill rising 130 feet above the Moskva and dominating the whole of Moscow, rises the Kremlin [two stars], in which all the reminiscences of Moscow's past are united. For the Russians the Kremlin is a holy spot." Even though few tourists ever found use for this volume, one purchaser found it invaluable. During World War I, the British General Staff bought up all available copies to guide its officers on the customs, manners, and favorite landmarks of the Russians.

After Fritz Baedeker's death in 1925, his son Hans took over until 1946, when his retirement was enforced by the Communists. Since that time forty-four-year old Karl Baedeker, in partnership with cousins Otto and Hans, has headed the firm. The present-day Karl was drafted into the German Army during World War II and stationed with the occupation forces in the Balkans. He was assigned to take his fellow soldiers on tours of Greece, where he gave learned lectures on the two-thousand-year-old Parthenon (two stars). Like his great-grandfather, he jotted down notes on everything he saw. And, with an eye to the future, he investigated certain sites. He remembers scaling a 13,000-foot Yugoslavian mountain five different times to discover the safest and most scenic route to recommend in a future guidebook on the Balkans.

Today, Karl Baedeker works on limited funds out of his in-laws' private residence near Hamburg, where he lives with his wife and two children. He admits the going is difficult. "We put so much money into our guidebooks, the profits are small," he says. "We've had many offers from rich backers, but we've refused them all. They want fast profits, which would force us to lower our standards. That we could never do."

As Karl, Otto, and Hans carefully prepare their new Baedekers on Paris, Switzerland, and Italy, they continue to adhere rigidly to the formula laid down by the founder. While they are not sure that they like the old star system, they are maintaining it. "This star system is a sore point with us," Otto Baedeker says. "Too many tourists, in a hurry, feel they must see anything with two stars, even if it bores them. Once bored, they blame us. But why go to an art museum, if you hate art, simply because it has two stars? Why not, if you love science, go to a science museum, though it has no stars at all?"

In the new Baedeker on London, such old standbys as the Tower of London, the Rosetta stone, Windsor Castle, all continue to hold their two-star rating. In future volumes, Rome's Colosseum, St. Peter's, and the Louvre are promised two stars. But the Baedeker family insists that stars are something that can only be added or removed after a few decades of reflection. In the guidebook on Germany, in 1861, the Amalienburg, outside Munich, wasn't even mentioned. Ten years later it was not only mentioned but awarded two stars. The Austrian Army Museum, in 1896, had a star; by 1929 it was starless. And Vienna's Maria-Theresa Memorial, in 1888, had a star; by 1918, that star was gone, too.

The present Baedekers are also following the firm's historic policy of criticizing by omission. "It is not our business to criticize man's work or God's work," says Otto. "Nothing is really all bad. If we don't like something, we speak of it mildly. More often, we don't mention it at all." Actually, this policy was made a firm house rule shortly after the publication of Baedeker's *Palestine and Syria*. In that volume, referring to a restaurant that proved to be a clip joint, Fritz Baedeker wrote, "Proprietor Arab; fix prices beforehand." Filled with indignation, the Proprietor Arab sued Baedeker for defamation and libel. He won a large settlement. Baedeker then set its new policy of omission, and dropped the Arab's restaurant from its next guidebook. The Arab was stunned by the omission. As his clientele dwindled, he finally forced himself to write Fritz. He offered to repay all the money that he had won in the lawsuit if he could be reinstated in Baedeker. Fritz refused.

Actually, what causes the biggest headache for the Baedeker family is not criticism but fact-gathering. The pitfalls are countless. "After all," says Otto, "what is a fact? It's all in the point of view. Who won Waterloo? It depends on what you read and where you live. The English say Wellington. The Germans say von Bluecher. It was over a point of view that we fought our biggest lawsuit when two Belgian cities sued us in 1933."

This famous lawsuit was provoked by two historical statements in the 1930 edition of Baedeker's *Belgium*. First, Baedeker remarked that citizens of Aarschot had killed a German colonel who was commanding the forces occupying the town in 1914, and in retaliation the Germans had executed 158 Belgians and burned the town. Second, Baedeker remarked that inhabitants of Dinant had fired upon German troops entering the city, and in return the Germans had executed 669 citizens. Enraged by what they regarded as falsification of facts, the municipalities of Aarschot and Dinant pooled funds, hired two former Belgian Ministers of Justice to represent them, and sued Baedeker.

The case was fought out before the Tribunal of Brussels. The Belgians argued that the German colonel in Aarschot was murdered, not by their citizens, but by his own men, and that the Germans entering Dinant were fired upon, not by Belgians, but by retreating uniformed French. Baedeker replied that the guidebook accounts were based on war archives in the Reich, that there had been guerrilla warfare in the Lowlands, that the firm was only interested in promoting understanding between nations. The judgment was against Baedeker, which was forced to pay the costs of the suit plus the costs of printing the verdict in ten European newspapers. Baedeker protested to *The Times* of London and the League of Nations, but finally submitted to the Belgian decision. Ever since, Baedeker editors have been wary of two-faced facts.

The Baedekers admit that in preparing their new guides they try to be sensitive to changes in tourists' tastes. Each generation looks upon a historic monument with different eyes. Usually, there is agreement between sightseers of the past and those of the present. But when there is not, Baedeker feels this must be detected and recorded. Members of the firm cite the Albert Memorial in London as the perfect example of tourist fickleness. In Baedeker's *London and Environs*, 1878, the Albert Memorial was given a half page, leading off with "To the S. of Kensington Gardens, between Queen's Gate and Prince's Gate, near the site of the Exhibition of 1851, rises the Albert Memorial [one star], a magnificent monument to Albert, the late Prince Consort (d. 1861), erected by the English nation at a cost of 120,000 pounds."

By 1930, the Albert Memorial was reduced to one-quarter of a page, and was no longer "a magnificent monument" but only "a gorgeous monument." By 1951, the Albert Memorial was cut to five curt lines, stripped of its one star, and, though still "gorgeous," Baedeker had to confess, "it does not arouse universal admiration."

But though the living Baedekers agree that they are changing with the times, trying to catch the modern temper in their little red books, they remain inflexible about one tradition. They insist that each new Baedeker guidebook must be as accurate as those published by old Karl over a century ago. They quite agree with A. P. Herbert's lyrics written for a

Paris tourist scene, in an English musical comedy called *La Vie Pari-sienne:*

> For kings and governments may err
> But never Mr. Baedeker.

WHAT HAS HAPPENED SINCE . . .

I had always been tantalized by the Baedeker legend. Early in 1953, when I suggested to *Reader's Digest* that I do a story about the founder of the firm, his family, and their guidebooks, I was immediately given the assignment. In the summer of 1953, I traveled to England to visit with Otto Baedeker, one of the three great-grandsons of the founder. Otto, who was then twenty-eight years old, was on temporary leave in London, working in the editorial department of Allen & Unwin, the publishing firm. He was there mainly to improve his English and increase his knowledge of publishing techniques in England and the United States, and since Sir Stanley Unwin, one of the heads of the company, was an old friend of the Baedeker family, Otto was being generously instructed.

I ransacked many sources on the Continent for the material in the preceding article, but it was Otto Baedeker in London who proved to be my most valuable source. The story that I wrote for *Reader's Digest* was well received by its staff. Yet it appeared only in their German edition, because Germany was the one country in Europe in which Baedeker guidebooks had already made a full comeback in the postwar years up to 1953.

My affection for the Baedeker legend never waned, and when I decided to include my Baedeker story in this book, which would be its first appearance in English, I began to wonder what changes had taken place in the old German firm during the passage of years since 1953. In 1964, I located Otto Baedeker, who had returned to his native Germany, and in 1965 I carried on an interview by correspondence with him. What I learned was that my original story was still valid and accurate, and that the only significant changes concerned some members of the family, the location of the firm, and the expansion of the publishing house.

In 1953, ten years after the destruction of the main plant in Leipzig, the eldest of the three great-grandsons, Karl Baedeker, was doing business out of a house owned by his wife's parents in Malente, a health resort in Schleswig-Holstein. When it became apparent that the Baedeker guidebooks were as much in demand as ever, and when the first of the postwar revised editions began to sell, Karl decided to put the firm back in business in a big way. In 1956, he established the publishing house—Karl Baedeker Verlag—in the university city of Freiburg, in southwest Germany, where it is flourishing today. While Karl, now fifty-six years old, presides over this plant and its subsidiaries, he has delegated to his forty-year-old cousin, Otto Baedeker, control of both editorial content and production of the English language editions.

The third of the present-day Baedekers, thirty-five-year-old Hans Baedeker, is editorial and technical supervisor in a Stuttgart branch of the firm known as Baedekers Autoführer-Verlag. This enterprise is the result of a partnership that the Baedekers formed with Dr. Volkmar Mair, who had been the foremost European publisher of automobile maps and atlases. The Baedekers control the editorial policy of this subsidiary, which brings out Baedeker's *Touring Guides*. According to Otto Baedeker, "This new venture has proved very successful. The *Touring Guides* are, in a way, streamlined guidebooks, intended mainly for motorists and for travellers who do not stay very long in one place, but rather undertake a quick tour of a whole country."

These condensed guides for automobile tourists are the Baedeker family's major recent concession to the jet age. As a Baedeker brochure explains, "When the first Baedeker was published, travellers went by stagecoach, averaging 50 or 60 miles a day. Now you can fly with your car to the heart of Europe in a few hours." These special guidebooks for the automobile tourists tend heavily toward maps, routes, distances, lists of recommended wayside hotels. Since 1953, there have been English editions of these guides for France, the Low Countries, Italy, Scandinavia, Spain, Switzerland, Austria, and Germany. The most popular of these English editions are the guides to France and Spain. The most popular German editions are those to France and northern Italy.

Wondering what the elder Baedekers, who thought a train was a daring adventure, would have said about all this, I asked Otto what had happened to the elders. I recalled learning in 1953 of the father of the present-day Karl, seventy-three-year-old Hans Baedeker, and the father of the present-day Otto and Hans, Dr. Dietrich Baedeker. Together they had tried to revive the firm in Leipzig after World War II, had suffered seeing their publishing license revoked by the Russians after an editorial faux pas, and, as I had written, they had "disappeared into the anonymity of the Russian zone." I now learned that the senior member, Hans Baedeker, had died at the age of seventy-nine in 1959. I also learned that Dr. Dietrich Baedeker was still alive, but retired.

I wondered how actively the sons were publishing since they had taken over the firm and moved its headquarters to Freiburg. I remembered that between 1827 and 1953, there had been thirty Baedeker guidebooks published in English and fifty-seven published in French and German. What had happened since?

"Since the firm started up again after the last war," said Otto Baedeker, "thirty-eight German and eighteen English titles have been issued, most of them running into several editions. From 1827 until 1964, ninety-two German, thirty-three French, and forty-five English titles have been published. This may not seem a large number, but it must be remembered that each title runs to a certain number of editions—some of them well over forty editions—and that each new edition is completely revised, and more or less constitutes a new book. The number of these editions may therefore be more relevant: 740 German editions, 268 French editions, and 311 English editions—1,319 editions in all. If you further take into account that all new titles and most new editions have passed through the hands of a Baedeker, this must give you some idea of the work accomplished by four generations."

Using the same exhaustive research techniques that I had described in my original article—except, as Otto stated, "the very-quickening pace of this post-war world has made a greater amount of research necessary"—the younger Baedekers have recently published, in English alone, new guidebooks on Italy, France and Corsica, Southern Bavaria, Yugoslavia, Scandinavia, as well as others devoted to such special cities as Cologne, Frankfurt, Munich, Salzburg, Berlin.

Karl Baedeker the First, one imagines, would have had no criticism of the guidebooks produced by his great-grandsons. Few concessions have been made to tourists interested in speed and condensation. The New York *Herald Tribune* praised the Baedekers' "traditional accuracy and thoroughness" and considered the new products "a model of what the guidebook of today ought to be." When Baedeker's *Italy* appeared in 1963, *The Listener* of London called it "still the best, and, ultimately, the most economical . . . the most lavish and scholarly of guides." And in New York, the *Saturday Review* added, "The first, and apparently still the last, word in guidebooks . . . leaves no sight unseen, no church uncharted, no fact unfathomed in its relentless pursuit of everything," objecting only that "its mass of information makes it somewhat difficult to curl up with in front of a fire on a cold winter's night."

While two recent English-language Baedeker guides to Yugoslavia and Scandinavia, have had only—according to the American publisher—"a modest success in this country," reader resistance could be attributed as much to the fact that Yugoslavia and Scandinavia are not favorite tramping grounds for American travelers as to an American impatience with Germanic thoroughness.

Elsewhere around the world, and especially in Europe, the sale of Baedeker guidebooks is booming once more. The latest success is Baedeker's *Berlin*, published in German text early in 1964. So detailed was its exploration of Germany's greatest city that the president of the House of Representatives in Berlin gave a copy to each and every member. "Within one year of publication," said Otto Baedeker, "over ten thousand copies were sold, a great part actually to Berliners. The latter illustrates the two tasks which the handbooks have to perform: firstly, to aid the tourist; secondly, to serve as works of reference."

Today, Baedeker is going all out to capture the eyes, minds, and dollars of American tourists. In the next decade, there will be Baedeker guidebooks in English on Great Britain, and on the cities of London, Paris, and Rome. And supplementing these, there will be automobile guides to Germany, Turkey, and "the whole of Europe" in English.

For me, only one question remained. Would the historic system of rating sites by stars continue to be used—and if so, were any changes or modifications in the star system contemplated?

To this, Otto Baedeker replied at length:

"No, the star system as such has not been changed or modified within the last decade, and it will not be changed. Of course, some stars may disappear in the course of time—a particular painter or painting may have been held in high esteem at the turn of the century, but today is no longer looked upon as important. Or a building which at the time of its construction was a great feat of engineering is no longer outstanding in this respect. But these are gradual changes, which do not affect the star system as such."

Otto Baedeker was eager to illustrate how the star system was kept up-to-date. "The prehistoric drawings in the Altamira cave in Spain now have two stars, whereas before the war they had only one, because at that time the interèst in archeology was perhaps not as great as it is today. A new two-star item is the Television Tower at Stuttgart, which was the first building of its kind and represents an outstanding engineering achievement."

Then, as he had so many years ago in London, Otto Baedeker reminded me that the star system must not be overemphasized. "We naturally take the greatest care in awarding stars," he said. "But we would be the last to suggest that 'he who has seen the stars has seen it all,' and that the culture and scenery of a country could be summed up by a list of starred objects. I am saying this because we have at times been reproached for inducing people to rush from one star to the next. This, we think, is rather unfair. Firstly, we try to provide accurate and well-balanced information, and to point out what in our opinion is important. But we cannot be held responsible for the use people make of this

information. Secondly, it is only natural that American tourists, for example, with a limited time to spend in Europe, should restrict themselves to what is outstanding."

I was satisfied. With Baedeker, little had altered since 1953, or even
since 1827. In a new time of flux, a bewildering time of illusive horizons,
many of us yearn for the finite, the known, the dependable. Death, yes.
Taxes, oh yes. And Baedeker, always. In my book, still, Baedeker shall
have its two stars.

» 9 «

INTRIGUE EXPRESS

O NE NIGHT in the late winter of 1930, the crack international train, the Simplon-Orient Express, hurtling through Turkey on the final lap of its regular run from Paris to Istanbul, ran into a blinding snowstorm. As first sleet and then swirling snow blanketed the rails, the Orient Express slowed, and at last, somewhere in the vicinity of Tcherkeuy, came to a full stop.

About the immobile train, the storm grew in intensity. Within a matter of hours the snow was piled many feet high, and by early morning it almost obscured the windows of the Wagons-Lits coaches. The thirteen passengers—most of the other travelers had been dropped at previous stops in Lausanne, Milan, Belgrade—found themselves trapped within a fortress of white. These thirteen passengers, according to Wagons-Lits personnel who swear to the fact, represented exactly thirteen different nationalities. One was a sleek Italian countess who wore low-cut dresses, another was a young British diplomatic courier, the third was an American corporation lawyer, and among the several couples there was an ex-Prussian officer with his pretty Swiss bride.

The employees of the Simplon-Orient Express (or plain Orient Express, as they and everyone else preferred to call it), engineers, conductors, cooks, led by the *chef de train*, immediately held a council of war in the restaurant car. Several had been snowbound for as long as four days on previous trips, and they knew that this present imprisonment might last even longer. Their first concern was for the passengers who, sealed in by a wall of hard-packed snow and representing all types of nationalities, might become irritable, troublesome, even dangerous. A rule was made, promptly announced, and as far as possible, strictly enforced. Passengers must not discuss politics with each other. They might discuss, nostalgically, their homes, friends, experiences, they might discuss art, literature, sex, sports, but absolutely no politics. This was a sage rule that Orient Express personnel, themselves representing seven nationalities, observed on their hectic trips three times weekly between Paris and Istanbul, and it had prevented friction on the run for almost a half century.

With this censorship established, all hands settled down to mingled boredom and hope of rescue. As it turned out, there was no boredom, and rescue proved long deferred. The first cook was given complete dictatorship over rations. Instead of three sumptuous meals a day, he ladled out only one meager repast, since the train had been almost at the end of its journey and the cupboards were practically bare.

On the sixth day, disaster seemed unavoidable. The food ran out. And late in the afternoon, just as in the most improbable of adventure stories, wolves began howling. The seventh day was not a day of rest. The snow melted and receded slightly, and the weary passengers, peering from their windows, could see the wolves at a distance, erratically circling the train. The conductors found three guns, and stood guard, in shifts, on the open platforms between the coaches.

The food problem now approached desperation since there was no means of communication with the outside world and no way of knowing when help might arrive. Soon the coal was gone, and the train became bitterly cold. The passengers sat huddled and hungry in their compartments. When the water supply ran out, all optimism went with it.

The personnel of the Express did not despair. The second cook, with the ingenuity of Robinson Crusoe, solved the water situation. He began melting snow and boiling the water from it, and that helped. Meanwhile, others of the Orient Express personnel tried to burrow a tunnel through the snow, but the first two tunnels collapsed after a dozen yards. A third tunnel was begun. Reinforced with the train's furnishings, the red plush seats, the silk armchairs, the dismantled berths, it held, and on the ninth day they broke out into daylight at the foot of a shallow bank. Conductors, armed against the wolves, climbed into the open and after brief exploration found semisolid footing. They knew by checking their timetables that the village of Tcherkeuy was nearby. That was their only hope. Two conductors, lightly dressed, often slipping and sinking waist-deep in snow, set out on foot for aid. For another day, the passengers, in their snowbound train, alternately paced and prayed.

And then the break came. The conductors, driven by a Turkish farmer in a primitive sleigh, returned. They had found the village and bargained with the villagers for sheep and coal, and there would be roast lamb for dinner. And they had telephoned of their plight, and learned that help was already on its way from several directions.

On the fifteenth day, Turkish soldiers, in horse-drawn sleighs, arrived with food, clothing, first aid. On the following day a snow sweeper arrived from Switzerland. Shortly thereafter, its latest misadventure at an end, the famed Orient Express, two and a half weeks overdue, limped into Istanbul and disgorged its baker's dozen of exotic, long-suffering passengers.

Occurrences such as this, although regarded as strictly routine by the sophisticated personnel of the Orient Express, are the stuff of which thriller fiction is spun. For example, five years after the incident at Tcherkeuy, Agatha Christie, who often accompanied her archeologist husband on the Orient Express to diggings in the Near East, wrote a suspense novel entitled *Murder in the Calais Coach*. Her mystery, if not based directly on the incident at Tcherkeuy, was at least compounded of several such near catastrophes that have befallen the Orient Express.

"High in the mountains of Yugoslavia," states a blurb on the dust wrapper of Miss Christie's novel, "the Orient Express, speeding northward, was halted by heavy storms and huge snowdrifts. One compartment of the Calais coach was occupied by one of the most delightful of all detective characters, Hercule Poirot. In another lay the body of a murdered man!" Among those also stranded in Miss Christie's Orient Express were a British colonel returning from India, a Belgian director of Wagons-Lits, a young English lady from Baghdad, an American commercial traveler, a White Russian princess, a Hungarian diplomat, a German maid, a female Swedish missionary—and, of course, the knifed body.

To those who like their stories straight, Miss Christie may seem to have been spreading it on a bit thick. But the most jaded world traveler will quickly confirm that the Orient Express is one institution that does not disappoint—it offers an authentic romantic experience, one of the few left available, where fact and fiction merge.

For, what the Orient Express sells is glamour. It has none of the standard attractions. It is neither as fast as the Super Chief or the City of Los Angeles ripping across the United States, nor as old a scheduled train as the Royal Scot running from London to Edinburgh, nor does it travel as long and as far as the Trans-Siberian chugging from Moscow to Vladivostok in nine days. In place of records for speed, longevity, or distance, the Orient Express, the world's first and foremost international train, offers romance.

In a single journey of two days and three nights, the Orient Express crosses seven foreign frontiers, more than any other train in the world. It is the only train in existence whose passage from country to country has been arranged by diplomatic treaty among governments, rather than by mere contracts between railways. Most important, it links two worlds. In connecting Paris, metropolis of Western Europe, with Istanbul, colossus of the Near East, it promises that, for the price of a one-way ticket, the twain shall meet—three times a week.

More than its physical journey, more than its highly advertised luxuries, it is something else that makes the Orient Express the most colorful and dramatic rolling stock on earth. It's the people you meet.

Even though the Orient Express, like its more mundane counterparts in America, carries its share of traveling salesmen (conductors refer to the late Sir Basil Zaharoff, a regular passenger, as "that salesman"), the specialty of the house is still, as it has been since 1883, female secret agents swathed in mink, bearded men in monocles, inscrutable heads of armament cartels, pretty girls in distress, royalty in flight. "Ah, if I had but the pen of a Balzac, I would depict this scene," an Agatha Christie character sighs, observing the assortment of passengers boarding the Orient Express. "All around us are people, of all classes, of all nationalities, of all ages. For three days these people, these strangers to one another, are brought together. They sleep and eat under one roof, they cannot get away from each other. At the end of three days they part, they go their several ways, never perhaps to see each other again."

No journey on this train is without its strange drama. The cast of characters, especially before World War II, often included Franz von Papen, King Michael of Romania, Greta Garbo, Toscanini, King George of Greece, W. Somerset Maugham, Pierre Laval, Sonja Henie, Edda Ciano, King Gustaf of Sweden, Philippe Petain, Lily Pons, Baron Edouard de Rothschild, King Boris of Bulgaria, the Duchess of Kent, Maurice Chevalier, the Duke of Windsor, King Alfonso of Spain, Marlene Dietrich.

Personnel of the Orient Express affectionately remember Pope Pius XII, when he was Cardinal Pacelli, as a frequent passenger. He would chat with the conductors, or fellow passengers, in perfect French, often probing into their lives and hearing out their problems. Sometimes he would retire to his compartment, leave the door ajar, and could be seen pecking away on a pure white portable typewriter. The 244-pound Aga Khan, direct descendant of Mahomet's daughter Fatima, is remembered by the personnel with less affection. The Aga, an owlish mountain of flesh, was always remote, uncommunicative, and he devoted hours to lolling back listening as his male secretary read aloud to him from a book or newspaper. Many times there were ex-King Carol and his redheaded, pudgy Pompadour, Magda Lupescu. Since they never lived openly together in Romania, they remained equally discreet on the Orient Express, riding in separate compartments.

The majority of passengers, however, were not celebrities, but they were no less provocative. There was the cameo-faced French girl, gowned by Schiaparelli, dripping with orchids, who kissed her elderly French husband good-bye, cried a little, boarded the Express and, as it pulled out, joined a young Czech artist in his compartment. There was the French countess who traveled on the Orient Express monthly, picked up wealthy industrialists in the diner, and lived on the expensive gifts she obtained from them. There was also the cute Italian actress, all ingénue, who stole jewels and was finally apprehended. Most memorable of all, there was the quiet little Englishman, with unruly rust hair and quick smile, who, as the Orient Express was moving across a bridge high in the Swiss Alps, was seen suddenly plummeting from the train to his death thousands of feet below. The French Sûreté, in the best manner of Vidocq and Bertillon, later combed the train and its luggage for a clue, questioning everyone, but never learned whether he fell, jumped, or was pushed.

It is because of such incidents, because everything (and everyone) happens on the Orient Express, that writers of international tales of intrigue like Agatha Christie, Eric Ambler, Leslie Charteris, Georges Simenon, Graham Greene, persist in starring the intrigue train in their fiction. For the same reason, Hollywood producers have used this mobile Grand Hotel as inspiration for settings of suspense, while some of the classic English adventure films (like Alfred Hitchcock's *The Lady Vanishes* and Carol Reed's *Night Train*) have played all their action on the Orient Express, or a reasonable facsimile thereof, even though they have taken a necessary dramatic license and attached crowded day coaches to the Express (a proletarian liberty its proprietors would never permit in the lush prewar days), so that their strange characters might all be depicted before the camera together.

When World War II broke out, and the Orient Express, in September of 1939, made its last full run from Paris to Istanbul and back again—"with only four of us in the diner on that last ride," a newspaperwoman representing the Istanbul *Vatan* recalls, "and two were Americans eating chicken"—it was feared by the train's owners, the French and Belgian officials of the Wagons-Lits company, that the old train might never be the same again. Their fears, stemming from the knowledge that Herr Hitler had his eye on the famed Express and its luxurious equipment, were well justified. When Hitler marched into France, he confiscated most of the glittering coaches and baggage cars of the Orient Express for the use of German officialdom and its military hierarchy. However, while it is difficult to hide a train, the French managed to salvage a handful of the Orient Express coaches by the process of sending them to the cities of Lyons, Vichy, and Dijon as temporary shelters for war refugees. During the war, these coaches of the Orient Express, along with other Wagons-Lits cars put out to pasture, managed to house more than 58,000 persons.

With the dawn of V-E Day, the Wagons-Lits people began collecting and reassembling the remnants of their stock. They brought coaches back from Germany, the Lowlands, the Balkans, and from every corner of France, and by September, 1945, they had a shabby, makeshift edition of the Orient Express traveling from Paris to Innsbruck. At last, after months of steady repair work and reupholstering, after two international conferences at Lugano and Montreux, it was officially announced that the Orient Express was ready to go three times a week as far as Milan, while its numerous sister trains were ready to proceed to Vienna and Prague. With that announcement there was the merest hope among the romantics that glamour might again be had for the cost of a $138 one-way ticket.

Today, if ever before they entertained doubts, the romantics may rest easily. Despite endless complications—the Russians creating difficulties for branch coaches of the Express passing through Austria, the Greeks declaring they could not possibly repair bridges for several years, Marshal Tito refusing the Express permission to traverse Yugoslavia unless he might have his way about loading the train with Yugoslav conductors and obtain a better share from the money exchange—the Orient Express, in January of 1947, with too much makeup and too much fuss, and creaking at the joints like an actress who has come out of retirement once too often, again got up steam for its historic run into the Near East. The usual staff of multilingual employees bustled about, but instead of the old label-plastered leather luggage, there was a dismaying preponderance of barracks bags and briefcases, and most of the first passengers were staid businessmen, army officers, and French railway officials. With this cargo, the Express puffed out of the chilly Gare de Lyon en route through broken Europe.

Today, again, the conductors walk down the corridors chanting, "Paris . . . Lyons . . . Lausanne . . . Milan . . . Trieste . . . Ljubljana . . . Zagreb . . . Belgrade . . . Sofia." Now, three times weekly, five coaches of the Orient Express roll as far as Sofia, Bulgaria. Then the passengers tumble out, climb into Turkish sleepers, and continue overnight across a corner of Greece and into Istanbul.

Today, the Wagons-Lits company—in preparation for the 300,000 American tourists the American Express Company has predicted will visit Europe this year, in preparation for the dollars these tourists will spend, according to the promise of the U. S. Department of Commerce—has printed timetables and travel folders for the old-fashioned, undiluted trip from Paris to Istanbul, without the Bulgarian change-over, and Wagons-Lits has officially announced that this trip will be resumed in the next few months.

While a prewar first-class ticket from Paris to Istanbul could be purchased for $138, today's American tourist will find that the purchase of through passage is no longer simple, nor is the price quite so definite. In Paris, the average tourist will visit the five-storied Wagons-Lits Cook building in the Place de la Madeleine, or the American Express offices in the Rue Scribe, wait in line an hour, learn that he must make his reservations at least twenty-eight days in advance, and be advised that he cannot purchase or pay for a through ticket. Because of the eccentricities of money-exchange control regulations, the tourist can buy, with French francs, rail tickets and sleeper reservations on the Orient Express only as far as Italy. There, in American dollars, he must pay for extensions on his ticket to Belgrade, and in Belgrade, using Yugoslav currency, he must pay for an added ticket to Sofia. The whole process will cost him $134, more or less, depending upon the fluctuations of exchange, and at journey's end he will be an economist or a madman.

In return for these financial acrobatics, the tourist will have the finest railroad accommodations in Europe today—although veteran travelers will assure him that, comfortable as they are, the Orient Express just is not what it used to be. At least, not yet. While the 57-ton sleeping coaches, each containing eleven private compartments, are still paneled in mahogany, and expensively carpeted, the added touches are missing all down the line. In the palmy days, for example, there were showers on the train. They are no more. Also, before the war, the Orient Express featured a de luxe special compartment for dogs only. Now passengers must keep their Pekingese, Scotties, and Russian wolfhounds on the floors of their own compartments.

In the good old days, the Orient Express diner, gleaming with silver, sparkling with bone china and mirrors, abounding in deep leather chairs, was a mobile mess for epicures. Now, though still physically attractive, it is simply a mess.

The Orient Express often changes dining cars four times on a single run. It starts with a French diner, staffed by French chefs, switches to a Swiss diner, then to an Italian kitchen, and finally to a Yugoslav one. Before the war, the first and second chefs, in white uniforms, supervised six cupboards on each diner, each cupboard representing a nation through which the Express passed and containing the choice delicacies and vintages of that country. Because each European nation had its food restrictions and drink monopolies, all cupboards were kept securely locked, except the one containing the food and drink of the land through which the Express happened to be moving. As the Orient Express left Paris, the chefs extracted French wines from the French cupboard, and waiters in silk breeches and buckled shoes served these in Belgian crystal goblets during the two-hour evening dinner period. When the train crossed into Switzerland, a French customs official boarded it, locked the French cupboard with its array of wines and liqueurs, then a Swiss customs man came on and unlocked the Swiss cupboard with its chocolates, cheeses, and jams. When the train entered Italy, a Swiss customs man came on, sealed the Swiss food cupboard, and an Italian official followed him and opened the Italian cupboard. And so it would go through Yugoslavia, Bulgaria, and Turkey.

Today, these cupboards are anything but a gourmet's delight. No longer can the Orient Express chefs prepare, and the three train waiters (sporting immaculate white gloves) serve on rich silver platters the old menu of eight hors d'oeuvres, omelets, fish, a choice of four meat dishes, and a selection of the best white and red wines in the Old World. Now, due to shortages and government rationing, the dinners are frugal. When the Orient Express goes through France, the dining car features, for 150 francs or $1.25, a set menu of soup, a choice of fish or meat, two vegetables and, for dessert, an apple. The best meal to be had on the journey, if the passenger will rise before dawn, is breakfast in Switzerland, where everything may be ordered from high-grade coffee and fresh eggs to real butter and white bread. After that, in Italy and on through Bulgaria, the quality and quantity of the food deteriorate and the local chefs shrug, and in their awkward French invariably explain, "*C'est la guerre.*" Payment for these various meals is as complex as the food is simple, since payment must be made in the currency of the country in which the food happens to be served.

The Orient Express still carries two baggage cars. Only the contents of these cars are now different. Ten years ago there would have been an exotic assortment of trunks bearing brightly colored labels, at least one bantam automobile such as a German Opel or an Italian Fiat, crates of gold being transferred from a French bank to a Serbian bank, and poking out above all this, like porcupine quills, dozens of skis and alpenstocks. Once, at the time when the late dictator of Turkey, blond Kemal Ataturk—who had converted mosques into granaries and put an end to polygamy—decided to westernize his country further by abolishing the traditional fez, the Orient Express was called upon to transport its strangest cargo. Ataturk was deadly serious about his ban on the fez; he even slapped the Egyptian minister for daring to wear one. Consequently, all males in Turkey were desperate for some kind of substitute headgear. The clothing stores and bazaars of Istanbul and Ankara put out a hurried SOS to the clothiers all over Europe. Overnight, the Orient Express baggage vans were loaded down with the most improbable, high-priority shipment they ever carried—London bowlers, German homburgs, Basque berets, Polish visor caps—all for the unprotected pates of Turkey.

Today the luggage reflects the times. One baggage car will carry hundreds of food packages, secondhand bicycles, several baby carriages, endless bundles of clothes. The few trunks, with the remnants of their Monte Carlo and St. Moritz stickers, have seen better days. The second baggage car is devoted entirely to mail, delivering the bulk of land communications from Western Europe to the Near and Far East. In this car, all the postal clerks, by international agreement, are Frenchmen.

However, for the American tourist, the most unusual thing about the Orient Express will be the minor ways in which it differs from his own de luxe streamliners at home. While almost all first-class American trains have green- or rust-curtained sleeping berths lining both sides of a center aisle, the Orient Express has none. Every cushioned seat on the Orient Express, when converted into a berth at night, is enclosed in a private room, similar to the bedrooms and compartments on American Pullmans. Today, the officials on the Express are embarrassed by a temporary exception to this advertised privacy. Due to the acute European transport shortage, the train has been forced to drag along, at its rear, six ordinary day coaches. This appendage for the peasantry, regarded as a sort of steerage class, is not discussed openly by the officials of the train.

While the Express now has central heating, its windows are not hermetically sealed as they are in similarly expensive American trains, but may be pulled down at will by passengers. Once, the Express experimented with a single coach, equipped with sealed windows, but the idea was quickly abandoned when the Continental fresh-air fiends complained they were being suffocated. The individual compartments, with directions printed usually in French, German, and English, lack the individual concealed toilets of the American streamliner. Nor do the coaches have separate lavatories for men and women. Instead, there is one community water closet at the end of each car. And while there is usually a pitcher of drinking water above the washbasin in each compartment, this is regarded as an American barbarism, and travelers are expected to have wine served in their rooms by the conductor when they are thirsty. Most surprising of all, perhaps, for the American traveler is the absence of Pullman porters. The brown-uniformed conductor doubles as the ticket collector and the attendant who makes up berths.

The private car, so often attached to the Orient Express, is an institution that will provide further amazement for the traveling American. Of course, Americans know all about private cars and can brag about building some of the world's best. Many Americans will cite how Death Valley Scotty came out of the California desert, hired a luxurious private Pullman coach, and rode to New York in it, flinging gold pieces and greenbacks to the populace all along the way. Others will relate the extravagances of Mrs. Marjorie Post Davies, largest stockholder in the General Foods Corporation and wife of Joseph E. Davies, ex-Ambassador to Russia, who bought her own railroad Pullman, hired herself a private porter, and had the car fumigated before each trip. And almost every American knows about the highly advertised Presidential Pullman, so often used by F.D.R. and to a lesser extent by President Truman. But the use of the private car in the United States is still the exception, whereas in Europe, on the Orient Express, it is a routine thing.

The private car most frequently attached to the Orient Express is a special gray salon coach built for the Presidents of France and for foreigners of equally high station. The most recent personage to travel in it was Farida Zulfikar, Queen of Egypt, the wife of King Farouk I. Her government applied for its use through the protocol section of the Élysée Palace, and it was promptly offered, along with a staff of police from the Sûreté Nationale, by the French government and the Wagons-Lits company. The queen was astonished by its luxury. She discovered the coach interior was paneled with mahogany, inlaid with exquisite Lalique glass, and the car illuminated by indirect lighting. The entire car was divided into only four rooms—a large bedroom, with a real bed instead of a berth, for the queen's use; a private bathroom; a tiny room for her maid or secretary; and the remainder a comfortable living room furnished with deep sofa, bureau, and easy chairs.

Run-of-the-mill celebrities and millionaires, however, are not permitted to use this car, but instead must hire a first-class coach of their own. The stunning Marina, Greek widow of the late Duke of Kent, always hired a private coach when she journeyed from London to Athens. The most frequent users of private cars have been Indian maharajas who cross over from India to Turkey and take the Orient Express to Paris. Once, a particularly wealthy maharaja even hired a private restaurant car to trail his sleeper.

Another rich Indian potentate bought out an entire Wagons-Lits coach, all twenty-four berths, at a cost of around $3,500, to take, in complete privacy, the most curious collection of passengers the Orient Express ever carried from Istanbul to Paris. M. Bortolotti, a Frenchman and twenty-year veteran of the Express, was *chef de train* on that trip, and he recalls it with relish. "This Indian, a maharaja or whatever he was, hired the private coach with the provision that all other passengers and Express personnel be barred from entering it except myself. I couldn't wait to get in, to see what he was hiding. And then when I went in for the tickets and passports, I saw. What a sight! He had his whole harem on the Orient Express! There they were, seven of them, and don't let anyone tell you modern harems aren't pretty. All seven girls were young and beautiful, Indo-European types, gorgeous figures. Each wore a veil, but the veils were thin and you could see right through them. Each girl had a tiny diamond set on the right side of her nose and one in her right ear lobe, as beauty marks, I imagine. These diamonds didn't look grotesque at all, but shone from behind the veils and were very exciting. I tried to act nonchalant. After all, we on the Orient Express are supposed to be used to everything. But I couldn't help staring, and the girls kept giggling at me until I finished my business with their husband and left."

The personnel of the Orient Express, men like M. Bortolotti, with their stock of fantastic stories, form the most unchanging part of the train. Of those who worked on it before Hitler, most are back on their old jobs again. Only the German conductors are now missing. The boss of the Orient Express, on each journey, is the blue-uniformed *chef de train*, whose position is like that of a purser on a ship but whose authority is greater. He is in charge of the conductors, solves special problems for passengers, keeps in contact with various stations en route, and at trip's end hands in a log of the journey to the Paris office. He often knows six languages. Bortolotti, for example, besides speaking his native French, has taught himself German, Dutch, Italian, Yugoslav, and English.

The conductors who are under the *chef de train*, one in each coach, are predominantly French and Swiss, and each must, as a minimum, know three languages. The service language of the train is French; all must speak it. The other two tongues are optional, but are usually German and English.

Constant travel between two worlds has made sophisticates of the Orient Express conductors, and surprise is an emotion they rarely feel. The conductors assigned to the subsidiary Orient Express, traveling only to Vienna and back, must guide their flock through four military zones. Conductors state that American MP's, who invariably come on the train singing, create the greatest consternation. They usually chew gum, and since many Balkan passengers have never seen gum, conductors must patiently explain the ingredients. On this same trip, farther down the line, across the river Enns, bearish Russian soldiers emerge from wooden barracks to inspect military passes. According to the Express conductors, the Russian soldiers from Leningrad and other big cities are bright boys, but those from Asia often hold passengers' military permits upside down as they pretend to read them, and then approve them if they are colored red. These Russians are rotated weekly, probably so that their thinking may not be sullied by the decadence in evidence on the Orient Express.

Conductors are expected to fulfill almost all passenger requests without batting an eye. Sometimes a conductor will be asked by a prominent Frenchman in Paris to deliver personally champagne or caviar to someone in Sofia. Once, Fritz Kreisler absently left one of his priceless violins in the Austrian Embassy in Warsaw. He remembered the oversight after boarding the Orient Express, and asked the conductor to take care of the matter. The violin reached Kreisler safely a week later. Another time, when there was plenty of space available, a millionaire from Bucharest came on the train and asked the conductor to sell him three compartments so that he might have one for sleeping, one for working with his secretary, and one in which to smoke. And there was the occasion, according to the story, when Josephine Baker—the renowned colored entertainer, who left St. Louis to thrill Paris with her dance performed in a G-string of bananas—woke hungry at two in the morning on the Orient Express, and demanded cheese sandwiches and beer. When she was told by the conductor that this request was somewhat unreasonable, she asked to be taken to the sleepy-eyed chef and then proceeded to promise him that if he would go to work at this hour in the kitchen for her, she in turn would perform for him. The chef eagerly agreed, delivered the repast, and *la Bakhair* danced for it in her nightie, in the diner aisle, as the Orient Express rolled into the dawn.

Because they extend such special services, the personnel of the train is able to supplement its salary with generous tips. In fact, the subject of tips is the topic most thoroughly discussed and debated by the conductors when, after each journey, they meet amid the oyster baskets and wine bottles of the railroad café, Au Depart, across from the Gare de Lyon. As a result, the subject of tipping on the Orient Express has a thoroughly documented history. The conductors enjoy breaking down tipping into categories. For instance, they classify tippers according to nationality. Most conductors seem to agree that, before the war, the highest tippers were the German travelers, not only industrialists but officials like von Papen and Funk. On the other hand, conductors regard South Americans, particularly Argentinians, as the most tight-fisted of all passengers. "Perhaps the rich men from Argentina don't know any better," said one conductor, "or perhaps they are just stingy." Most conductors feel that, as a class, pre-1914 royalty like the Grand Duke of Russia or the Queen of Austria or a random Esterhazy tipped most handsomely.

All personnel on the Orient Express, from the highest operational official to the youngest conductor, unanimously agree that the best modern tipper among the bluebloods and, in fact, the most colorful character ever to travel the Orient Express, was King Boris III of Bulgaria. Before the war, King Boris, a gentle, charming man in his late forties, who once listed as his pet hobby "locomotive driving," would invite train person- nel into his compartment for tea and discuss every aspect of the Orient Express as if it were his very own toy. He was, in truth, in love with the train. For years, on every trip between Sofia and Paris, after becoming bored reading his stack of newspapers in six languages, he would leave his wife, Queen Giovanna, the Italian Princess of Savoy, knitting in their compartment. He would work his way forward, through car after car, to the engine, and at the first stop, crawl in beside the two French engi- neers and take over the throttle. This went on for countless trips, over many years, until the word got around that the Orient Express was being driven by the King of Bulgaria. When various diplomats heard this, and then authenticated the fact, they raised a furor. The governments of France and Italy formally advised King Boris that he must not drive the train through their territories, endangering both train passengers and the citizenry. On his first Orient Express excursion after the ban, King Boris sat glumly and slept restlessly through France, Switzerland, Italy, and Yugoslavia, but when the Express reached the Bulgarian border where his own word was law, he left his compartment, pulled on a pair of clean overalls, walked to the engine and took over the throttle to Sofia. More than any other passenger lost in the war, the conductors miss Boris. They insist that he did not die naturally in 1943, that they have inside infor- mation he was poisoned by the Gestapo when he refused to turn the Bulgarian Army over to Hitler.

Among plebeians, the most fabulous tipper ever to ride the Orient Express was a Mr. Capile, an Italian shipbuilding millionaire from Genoa. "He was a wonderful man," recalls one conductor. "He enjoyed the train. At the end of each trip he would go into the kitchen, among the kettles, compliment the chef, tip him and his assistants, and then he would tip the *chef de train* and then the conductor. One time, in two days on the train, he tipped a thousand dollars."

Some of the Orient Express conductors have become celebrities in their own right. Perhaps the most famous is seventy-three-year-old Jean Bonnefoy who, in his thirty-five years on the train, hobnobbed with the world's greats. Today, in his anecdotage, he remembers that Queen Amelia of Portugal would always inquire first if he were on the Orient Express before making her reservations. He recalls, too, how once he stopped the train to rescue the Duke of Windsor when, as a lad, he was left stranded on a platform in Dijon. Bonnefoy's fame grew as a result of poetry he wrote during long, lonely nights on the Express. One volume, *Visions of Rome*, brought him a personal letter from Benito Mussolini and he was made a Knight of the Crown of Italy. Thereafter, he was the only decorated conductor on the Orient Express.

Today, on pension, Bonnefoy longs for the good old days. "Before the First World War," he says, "the Orient Express was really luxurious, the upper halves of the compartments painted white, the lower halves built of teakwood. And all personnel, conductors as well as waiters, had to wear white gloves. Things have gone downhill since." Sometimes, just before ten-fifteen in the evening, Bonnefoy will walk from his flat down into the Gare de Lyon to watch the great train pull out. He will stand in the drafty station and snort at the lack of festivities. As recently as 1939, when the Orient Express took off, it was like a ship embarking on an ocean crossing—great, gay parties to see friends off, singing from compartments, champagne corks popping, all the high bustle and excitement of a bon-voyage celebration. Today, the departure is quiet and efficient. Most people aren't traveling in Europe for fun. They are going about their business, and there's usually nothing to toot tin horns about.

When the train pulls out slowly—it will later clip along at 80 kilometers an hour (it used to go 100 an hour, but now there are weak bridges and poor rails)—Jean Bonnefoy will remark, "Ah well, so it is not the same, but there are two things that are the same as ever—the scenery, the glorious sights in all those countries—and the organization that makes seeing the sights and the whole trip itself possible."

Most of the Wagons-Lits personnel, either for political reasons or because they are genuine converts, like to extol the unseen organization which they serve. However, except for recognizing their immediate superiors, most know little about who owns and runs the Orient Express. For that matter, outsiders know even less. Yet this organization, like an enormous hidden perpetual-motion machine, has sent the Orient Express catapulting from Paris to Istanbul and back again, with precision and without a hitch, for exactly sixty-four years. Actually, the Orient Express is owned by Compagnie Internationale des Wagons-Lits, located in Brussels, and operated out of a large branch building in Paris, where the messenger boys are outfitted as train conductors. The Orient Express is under the complete authority of a wealthy Frenchman, René Margot-Noblemaire, whose father is manager of the French National Railways. The Noblemaire family has dominated French railroading since the late nineteenth century.

The Wagons-Lits company was conceived in 1872 by a Belgian engineer named Georges Nagelmackers, who had visited the United States, seen the world's first sleeping cars, and wanted to set up facsimiles of the Pullman in Europe. Nagelmackers' idea of luxurious sleeping cars was met with derision throughout Europe, and he had almost abandoned the idea when he was summoned by King Leopold II of Belgium to discuss it. The king was enthusiastic and within a year the first Wagons-Lits sleeper—carrying a dozen bunks, heated by burning briquettes, and lit by oil—was placed on the run from Ostend to Berlin. The sleeper was a success, and in 1876 the Wagons-Lits company was organized into its present form. King Leopold was one of the first stockholders, and with the prestige of his name, the company was capitalized to the sum of 4 million Belgian francs.

That was the beginning. Seven years later the company produced a complete train—boiler engine, two sleeping cars holding a total of twenty-eight persons, one diner with twenty-four seats, two baggage cars —guaranteed to transport pioneers via the historic route used by the Celts, Huns, and Crusaders, from France, running north of the Alps, across Bavaria, down along the Danube, to Turkey. On June 5, 1883, the world's first international luxury train made a trial run from Paris to Munich to Budapest, to deposit passengers on a steamer that crossed the Black Sea from Varna to what was then Constantinople, in 81 hours and 40 minutes.

Exactly four months later, the Orient Express was officially inaugurated. Speeding along at 55 miles an hour, it went from Paris through Strasbourg, Stuttgart, Munich, Salzburg, Vienna, and Budapest. Everywhere there were festivities to greet the passengers of Europe's Iron Horse. At Szeged, Hungary, the furnishings of the diner were pushed aside while a band of eleven gypsy musicians came on and played Viennese waltzes and czardas for two and a half hours. "When the band attacked the 'Marseillaise,'" reported a nineteenth-century correspondent, Opper de Blowitz of *Le Temps*, "our bearded French cook rushed out of his kitchen and, hand on his heart, with flaming eye and ecstatic face, poured it forth in deep and sonorous voice. We finally had to send him back to his stove to prepare lunch. The gypsies left the train at Temesvár."

In Bucharest, the Orient Express was held over while the passengers were taken to the Romanian Royal Palace to be received by King Carol I. At Giurgiu, a tiny Romanian town on the Danube, the passengers left the Express, were ferried across to Ruse, on the Bulgarian side, and then proceeded on another section of the train to Varna. This section of the journey was particularly hazardous since the rails were not protected from animals by the usual metal fences and the locomotive swept cows and oxen aside with a vast iron grating, or cowcatcher, attached in front. At Varna, on an inlet of the Black Sea, the passengers sloshed across a muddy field on foot to embark on a small steamer which, despite a choppy sea, brought them in 15 hours to minareted Constantinople. The East and the West had met, and the total time had been 77 hours and 49 minutes.

To arrange this trip, the Wagons-Lits company had conferred, earlier in 1883, with railroad people and royal diplomats of the Duchy of Baden, the Kingdom of Württemberg, and of Bavaria, Austria, and Romania. In the sixty-four years since that first treaty, the Wagons-Lits company, in arranging the various frontier crossings and routes of the Orient Express, has acted more like a sovereign state than a mere railroad corporation.

In 1888, to give one instance, a manager of the Wagons-Lits company, M. de Richemont, was rushed to Sofia to negotiate with Prince Ferdinand of Bulgaria about a new line that would bypass the Black Sea steamer trip and take the Orient Express straight overland into Turkey. Due to haste, M. de Richemont arrived in Sofia with only two business suits. He was advised by the prince's aides that he could not enter the palace in ordinary clothes. He made inquiries and, learning that a uniform was considered formal attire, he promptly sent his train personnel into the streets to find anything that resembled one. The men returned with a Bulgarian police captain, who consented to rent his uniform. But this was not enough. To it, M. de Richemont added the accessories of the Wagons-Lits conductor—from cap to service ribbons—and in this way, having satisfied the demands of the prince's advisers, he entered the Royal Palace and bowed stiffly before Ferdinand. The prince took one look at the outlandish uniform, grinned knowingly and confided, "Isn't this the damnedest country!" After that, the agreement was easily made, and a year later the Orient Express went directly from Paris to Constantinople by land and reduced the time of the journey by 14 hours.

Year after year conferences were held between Wagons-Lits and the various European governments to settle the problems of passports, currency exchange, luggage, and conductors. It was agreed that if a conductor committed a minor crime, he could not be summarily pulled off the train but enjoyed the status of an extraterritorial and came under the jurisdiction of the Geneva Court. If he committed a major crime, it was determined that he was subject to the laws of the nation through which the train was passing at the moment of the crime—that is, hypothetically, if an Italian conductor strangled an English duchess while the Orient Express was racing through Yugoslavia, he would have to submit to the trial and judgment of a Belgrade court.

In 1919, at the Versailles Peace Conference, the Wagons-Lits company signed a series of international treaties and contracts, the most important of which provided that the train should cut its time to Istanbul by passing through the longest tunnel in the Alps, the Simplon Tunnel. Because it steamed through this hole, entering at Valais, Switzerland, emerging in Piedmont, Italy, the old Orient Express was officially renamed the Simplon-Orient Express, a name the Wagons-Lits people now use in documents and advertising, but which Continental travelers persistently ignore.

Other treaties have been concerned mostly with namesakes of the Orient Express. An American traveler in Europe who believes there is but one Orient Express will, after a few days at travel bureaus, be sadly confused by the repetitions of the name, applied to a variety of trains which seem to go in every direction at once. The fact is, there is not one Orient Express, and there never has been. There are a half-dozen or more different trains going back and forth to the Near East, three times a week, and all are rightly called the Orient Express. Then, too, in normal times, there are special sleeping coaches that go and come from Rome, Athens, and Berlin, on other trains, and are eventually attached to the Orient Express en route. They then proceed with it either to Paris or to Istanbul. Just before the war the special Orient Express sleeper, brought down from Berlin to meet the main Express, often carried disguised Jews with false papers, escaping the wrath of Hitler, and Nazi secret agents going into the Balkans and France. For security reasons, the German car was kept isolated, by means of a locked door, from the rest of the Express. Today, also, there is an Orient Express that goes from Paris, through Munich, to Vienna and Bucharest, and there is a sister train, the Arlberg-Orient Express, that goes through Zurich, Switzerland, to Vienna in 34 hours. Added to all this confusion, there is another luxury train, the Taurus Express, that picks up some passengers the Orient Express drops off in Istanbul and takes them to Cairo or Baghdad.

But these trips remain sideshows beside the three-ring circus provided by the Paris-to-Istanbul train. Starting at night, from the hangarlike Gare de Lyon in Paris, the Orient Express speeds through Dijon, crosses the French frontier station of Frasne, and chugs into the mountains of Switzerland. With the dawn, it runs through Lausanne, skirting the north shore of Lake Geneva, the most spectacular of Switzerland's 1,484 lakes, passes Montreux, and goes through the Simplon Tunnel, over twelve miles long. With the new day, the Orient Express swings past Lake Maggiore toward Milan. The American tourist, having missed France and Switzerland in the night, will still see a good part of northern Italy. All the first day, the Orient Express rides through or pass such cities as Verona, Venice, Trieste and, with the second night, leaves San Pietro del Carso and enters Yugoslavia.

The passenger, sleeping through Zagreb, capital of Croatia, will have breakfast his second morning in Belgrade, while coaches arriving from Ostend, Berlin, Prague, Vienna, and Budapest are attached. Listening to the newcomers, he will hear plenty to write home about—that Lidice is now a flourishing wheat field, that Princess Gabrielle Esterhazy now runs a Budapest furniture delivery company, that the current anti-Russian joke making the rounds of the Balkans is that "Joe Stalin made two big mistakes—in showing Europe to the Russians, and the Russians to Europe."

Passing from Yugloslavia to Bulgaria, conductors will point out their favorite oddity, the small island of Ada-Kaleh in the middle of the Danube, which still belongs to Turkey because diplomats forgot about it. All the second day the Express moves through Bulgaria, reaching Sofia before nightfall. The passenger, if he stays up late, may dine when the train goes through Dikea, Turkey, but he will certainly be asleep as the train crosses Pityon, Greece. In the early morning, puzzling over piasters, assaulted by dragomen who wish to show him the Mosque of St. Sophia and the ninety-two streets of the Grand Bazaar, the tourist will alight in Mohammedan Istanbul.

But long after the sights seen between Paris and Istanbul have become as unreal as a picture postcard, the American tourist will remember, vividly, the best sight of all—his fellow travelers on the journey, both the world-famous and the nonentities, and he'll remember what they did and what they said.

Before the war, Pierre Laval, Philippe Petain, and Field Marshal von Rundstedt once traveled in the same coach of the Orient Express at the same time. Singers and musicians frequently jammed the train. Lily Pons and Grace Moore would ride it, and be heard warbling each day on their way to engagements in Italy, and Bruno Walter and Toscanini would go regularly on it to Salzburg. Paderewski, just before his death, was a frequent and favored passenger. In the dining room, whenever he sat to eat, fellow passengers would be treated to a silent recital; as he talked in French to tablemates, Paderewski would drum the table with the fingers of one hand, playing passages from various piano works, and it was always a favorite sport among observers to try to identify a particular composition.

Anthony Eden is remembered as the train's most elegant passenger. He would have a compartment for himself, another for his wife, a third for the rest of his family. He would wear a freshly pressed suit every day, melt female passengers with his manners, and talk politics to the train personnel. The late Cardinal Luigi Maglione, Secretary of State of the Vatican, was equally elegant, handsome, and much more awesome. "I'll never forget the cardinal," said one passenger, "very severe and stiff, all

Jesuit, constantly nodding over his Bible. And when he looked at you, well, you tried to remember the last time you'd been to church." Maurice Chevalier often traveled the Express in those days, and while many passengers liked him, the conductors generally detested him for his bad manners. "Once there were some Americans on the train," recalls one conductor, "man, wife, children, good solid people. They had admired Chevalier's old Hollywood films and they sent their card by me inviting him to dine or have a drink. He just tore the card up, threw it back at me, and refused to reply. So I made up a nice excuse for the Americans, but it was rude of him." Another entertainer, Marlene Dietrich, traveled on the Orient Express from her earliest days with UFA, the Berlin film company. Male passengers drooled over her, and mash notes were slipped under her compartment door, but she remained smilingly aloof.

Government representatives regarded the Orient Express as their personal conveyance. Dr. Eduard Beneš, the unsmiling President of Czechoslovakia, usually devoted fifteen hours a day to working on notes, his bulging briefcase beside him, but on a few trips he mingled with other passengers and expounded his ideas on disarmament and a United States of Europe. But mostly there were kings—rulers of nations like King Michael of Romania, who always took first-class passage instead of a private coach, and rulers of finance like the endless European Rothschilds, who were regarded variously by the employees of the train (the French Rothschilds considered too class-conscious and cold, the Austrian Rothschilds considered charming, friendly, and handsome tippers). King Gustaf of Sweden, annually on his way to Monte Carlo via Paris to play tennis under the pseudonym of Mr. G., would delight other passengers with his stories of hunting in Sweden. King Ferdinand of Bulgaria, father of the late King Boris, is remembered as having the biggest appetite ever seen on the Express. He would eat his way through five courses, following them up an hour later with five more, and often awarded Bulgarian decorations, for extraordinary services to the crown, to chefs and conductors.

The numerous coaches usually attached to the Orient Express at Belgrade brought their share of celebrities, characters, and stories. The most prolific coach for anecdotes was the one switched on from Berlin. Karl Fürstenberg, the German banker, was a regular passenger. Once, for privacy, he bought both the lower and upper of a compartment. The train was crowded, and a new arrival asked old Fürstenberg if under the circumstances he might use the empty upper for the night. Fürstenberg, who was making an overnight trip, sniffed and said, "Sir, I always make it a rule to sleep on my decisions. I'll let you have my answer in the morning."

The Berlin coach of the Express was always a beehive of smuggling.

All sorts of persons were trying to get their possessions out of Germany, under the noses of the Gestapo. One Romanian artist, now in Hollywood, a Jew who had incurred Hitler's anger by marrying the German girl selected as "Germany's most typical Aryan beauty," knew that he must get out while the getting was good. His life's savings were on his person, but he realized they would be confiscated when his train left Germany. Carefully, the Romanian made a study of all trains leaving Berlin and then selected, for his flight, the Berlin coach of the Orient Express simply because it had the only possible place he might successfully hide his money. This was a metal sign, with some instructions to passengers, screwed onto the compartment wall. This, the Romanian felt, was the one foolproof place, unlikely to occur to anyone searching. He worked for hours in desperation, unscrewing the sign with a penknife, fearful every moment the Wagons-Lits conductor might discover him. At last, it was loose. He shoved his bank notes behind it, screwed it back into place, and then sat down to wait. The German frontier was reached. The customs officer came on. The Gestapo came on. He was searched. Every inch of his room was searched. But the Nazis overlooked the metal sign, and they left, and in a moment the train was out of Germany and the Romanian's money was safe. As they passed the frontier, the Wagons-Lits conductor stuck his head in the door. "Hope you had no trouble with your money, sir," he said. "Best place to hide it is behind that metal sign up on the wall. Everyone does, and it always fools those pigs." And he winked and walked down the aisle.

Before the war, the nonentities on the Orient Express were often more fascinating than the celebrated travelers. A Wagons-Lits inspector, Mr. Lebrun, traveling up from Istanbul to Paris, noted his fellow passengers in the same coach, on a single journey. They included one Japanese returning from Iraq, a Berlin tailor who had been to Baghdad to take measurements of wealthy customers there, a Pennsylvania professor returning from a jaunt through the Near East in which he tried to follow the footsteps of Alexander the Great, and a Spanish nobleman. The only celebrity in the coach was the relatively sedate and bemused Mr. Lloyd George.

But those were the good old days, the Wagons-Lits people say now, and though it was less than ten years ago they make it sound like a century. They insist that most of the people traveling today are dull businessmen going to Zurich, or Italians who have wangled passports, or French traveling in search of better meals, or Chinese UNESCO representatives. They complain that the newly rich, "the bloodsucker black marketeers" as they label them, who used to travel third-class, now clutter the Orient Express. "You should see," says an Orient Express controller, "how these new rich put their feet on the opposite seat, litter the car, spit on the floor. But we catch them and make them pay for everything soiled or broken."

This Orient Express controller is a cherubic, elderly man, most zealous about his job, and several weeks ago he took me down into the Gare de Lyon to watch the Orient Express pull in from faraway Sofia. As the passengers stepped off the train and came walking through the steam vapors, dodging baggage trucks, the controller intercepted the blue-uniformed *chef de train*, a skinny, toothy fellow, and said to him, "I have a writer here. Tell him the kind of people who have just been on the Orient Express with you. I have been warning him that the old glamour is gone."

The *chef de train* nodded, glanced down at his passenger list, then, in a matter-of-fact voice, said:

"It was a quiet trip. I would estimate 40 percent of our passengers were dealing in the black market or just smuggling. It's the usual thing. Our conductors must resist those devils all the time. You remember what happened in June? No? Jean-Pierre Coateval, a gangster, was arrested for using fourteen of our men on the Orient Express as smugglers for gold, jewels, foreign exchange, and drugs like heroin between countries. The whole syndicate got rid of 300 million francs' worth of goods. Well, that was cleaned up, and our conductors are above reproach now. But our passengers continue, four out of ten of them, to deal in these shady activities.

"Who else did we have? Oh, the everyday thing. Government officials, and two diplomatic couriers with padlocked pouches—they are not touched by customs. A colonel who had come up all the way from India. Those two walking over there, they came on from Bucharest. Jews. Terrorists from Palestine. I hear one is going into England to direct sabotage of public works.

"Oh, yes. One more thing. Most amusing. A little Turkish governess. She got on at Sofia. A very nervous girl. In Yugoslavia, she pulled the emergency cord, held up the whole train at night for five minutes. She said a man wearing a coat had been in her compartment, but she screamed and scared him off. Ridiculous. We couldn't even get into her compartment—it was bolted from the inside—until she opened the door. The conductor says he saw a mystery novel by her berth. We had that once before, you know, an English girl who had read and heard too much about the Orient Express, all the fantasies, the nonsense, and got hallucinations one night about stranglers, and she pulled the cord. But if you wish to write stories about the Orient Express, monsieur, you have certainly picked the wrong time. It is nothing now. Come, have a brandy with me at the café, and I will tell you about the old days and the real types."

We turned to go, and I almost bumped into her. A dark-eyed, tall, slender brunette with a slow smile. She had just come off the train. She was wearing a mink coat. In one hand she had a mink muff, and in the other a gold cigarette holder. The man behind her, wiping a perspiring, beefy face, was saying, "Countess, it's wrong—"

I could not hear the rest, because the *chef de train* of the Orient Express, striding along beside me, was chattering too shrilly. "Yes, monsieur," I could hear him saying, "yes, you should have been down here in the good old days, just before the war. . . ."

WHAT HAS HAPPENED SINCE . . .

Shortly after the preceding story was published in the July 12, 1947, issue of *The Saturday Evening Post*, I ran into my friend, Joseph Wechsberg, the well-known author and gourmet. He congratulated me on my story about the Orient Express, and told me that he thought one day he would write about it, too. And one day, not many years later, he did.

Following the publication of Wechsberg's Orient Express article, we had a reunion at the apartment of a mutual friend in Los Angeles. Our mutual friend and host said:

"I am glad both of you are here, because I am puzzled about something that you can perhaps clear up. You have both written about the very same subject, yet your versions are completely contradictory. Except that you both agree as to statistics and history, you might have written about two entirely different Orient Expresses, although you both insist it is the same one. Irving's Orient Express, for him, was attractive, exotic, exciting. Joe's Orient Express was, for him, unattractive, dull, boring. Irving's Orient Express offered the reader of his article adventure and the promise that the train will live up to its legend. Joe's Orient Express offered the reader a guarantee of tedium and disappointment. Which of you has the facts right? Which of you is telling the truth?"

There was a lively discussion, and, as best as I can recollect, it was agreed that both Wechsberg and I had the facts right, and each of us had told the truth. The Orient Express that we both had known was one and the same. The difference lay in the psyches and attitudes of its two passengers. I had ridden a romantic Orient Express because I was, to some extent, a sentimentalist and optimist; Wechsberg had ridden a dreary

Orient Express because he was, to some extent, a sophisticate and cynic. There was no answer to our host's question: Which of you is telling the truth? There was none then, and there is none now, for we both told the truth—though perhaps we told more about ourselves than about the famous train. I have since remembered a quotation, source unknown: "Truth has many faces, and any one of them alone is a lie."

My article, then, is the one face of the Orient Express that I saw.

In the eighteen or nineteen years since I first rode on the Orient Express and wrote its biography, I have traveled on it and enjoyed its wonders more times than I can remember. I have gone from Paris to Milan and Venice on the Orient Express, and from Paris to Berlin, and from Paris to Vienna on its sister trains, and returned on them, and they have never failed me. Perhaps at times I chafed at, or even deplored, certain things wanting in the accommodations—the lack of air conditioning and Diesel engines, the lack of private bathrooms, the lack of community lounge cars. But these omissions, I found, were far outbalanced by what was available there, and on no other train—the incredible variety of scenery, the delicious foods and wines, and above all, the people I met on every journey—the beautiful, flirtatious young Austrian dancer returning home from the Orient, the stocky Yugoslav businessman hunting for his son who had disappeared two days before in Italy, the Wagons-Lits conductor who told everyone I was Edgar Wallace, the French inventor who alluded to some mysterious meeting in Zurich, the Russian diplomat who pretended that he did not understand me when I spoke to him, but permitted my young daughter to play with his daughters and then questioned her in excellent English.

Therefore, it was with sadness that I read the news of what was happening to the Orient Express—at least, what was happening to it, according to certain stories in the press. On a May evening in 1961, the Orient Express with ninety passengers aboard supposedly made its last run from the Gare de l'Est in Paris to Budapest. This final public appearance was widely publicized. Two reasons were given for the train's retirement. One was that the jet airplane had taken most of its wealthy passengers away. The other was that Communist customs men and frontier guards in their continuing search for fleeing refugees or smuggled goods were partially dismantling the train every time it crossed through the Iron Curtain. This caused delays and discomforts that discouraged passengers, as well as the Wagons-Lits company. Shortly after May, it was announced that the Arlberg-Orient Express, going from Paris to Bucharest, had also been retired from service. And finally, in July of 1962, it was announced that the Simplon-Orient Express, going from Paris to Venice to Zagreb to Sofia to Istanbul, had made its final journey.

Even as I lamented the loss of the world's most exciting train, I failed to understand its being abandoned. For, despite the competition from airlines and the interference of Communist officials, it seemed to me that the Orient Express still represented one of the few adventurous experiences that could be purchased in Europe today. After checking on events connected with the train since I wrote about it in 1947, it became clear to me that intrigue had continued to travel with it year after year. In 1948, a United States military attaché disappeared from the Arlberg-Orient Express. His corpse was found in a tunnel of the Austrian Alps. As recently as 1962, Communist agents found and apprehended several Yugoslavs trying to escape their country by hiding in the metal battery boxes beneath the Wagons-Lits coaches.

Despite such continuing wonders, my friend Joe Wechsberg was one of the many to write the train's obituary: "The fiction of the elegant Orient Express had become a bad joke. . . . The Orient Express had lost much of its initial speed, most of its pretense, and practically all of its onetime elegance. It was just a cheap, slow train." A newsmagazine elaborated, in the obituary it published: "Under cold-war conditions, the Orient Express . . . no longer could maintain its once superb service. The train windows began to rattle; the cars became dirty; train personnel forgot what a really fat tip looked like. In addition, the ubiquitous airplane began carrying anyone—spies and all—faster and more comfortably."

My old friend Art Buchwald, the syndicated columnist and satirist, who is a secret romantic like myself, deplored the stories debunking the Orient Express as much as I did. When, just before the train's demise, a traveler (just off the Orient Express) told Buchwald not to take the train because it was no longer glamorous, Buchwald was distressed.

Said Buchwald, "But if these things are true, then the great books we've been brought up on, such as *Orient Express, The Lady Vanishes,* and *Istanbul Train* are all lies, and we've been deluded."

Replied his friend, with great sagacity, "Not necessarily, Virginia. No matter what they say, there is a little of the Orient Express in all of us. We must believe in the Orient Express. As long as there is one mystery book to be written, one movie to be made, one television program to be shown, the Orient Express will continue to capture our imaginations. Not believe in the Orient Express? You might as well not believe in Santa Claus. The Orient Express lives and will live forever. A thousand years from now, nay ten thousand years from now, it will continue to roll along the tracks of Europe."

Truer words were never spoken in a jest.

And yet, one last mystery: Is the Orient Express really dead? It is not, despite its obituaries. It lives on not only in the hearts of romantics—but in timetables and Eurail passes. From my journal entry under Venice, dated August 24, 1964, I find the following: "Took a motor launch from the Hotel Danieli to the Venice depot. The Orient Express, in from Athens, was waiting. We had two compartments. Orient Express left Venice at 12:10 P.M. and headed for Milan, Lausanne, Paris. . . . Orient Express brought us into Gare de Lyon, Paris, at 6:20 morning."

Recently, to straighten out the confusion caused by the announcements of the train's death, and its obvious resurrection, I consulted Olivier Chermiset, an executive of the Compagnie Internationale des Wagons-Lits in Paris. According to M. Chermiset, the obituaries published in 1961 and 1962 were misleading. What had come to an end was not the life of a train, but rather the train's old route. The main Orient Express no longer goes from Paris to Vienna to Budapest to Istanbul. It simply goes to Vienna, and no farther. The Arlberg-Orient Express, which used to travel to Bucharest and Athens, now winds up its run at Vienna, too. And the Simplon-Orient Express, instead of passing out of existence in 1962, suffered only a name change. It is now called the Direct Orient Express, and for $136—the price of transportation and a first-class compartment—the adventuresome traveler may board it in Paris, ride it through Lausanne, Milan, Venice, Trieste, Belgrade, Sofia, and still alight at Istanbul. Only when M. Chermiset began to speak of plans to make the Orient Express more democratic and modern—lower-priced compartments with berths for three, snack bars and cafeterias instead of diners—only then did I flee. For I had heard all I wanted to know: that there would be, as there had been in 1964, an Orient Express waiting for me again another summer in Venice.

Yes, Virginia, there is an Orient Express. You can ignore the obituaries and pallbearers. They are the lie. And one more thing, Virginia. Ignore the debunkers. Listen to me. I was up at three that last morning, in the aisle of the Orient Express as it sped through Switzerland and France—and you know what? There *was* a lady in distress. True, she was only on her way to the bathroom. But she *was* swathed in a long mink coat, a mink coat and nothing else, *nothing else*, Virginia. When that happens on an airplane, I'll turn in my Wagons-Lits ticket and fly. But not before. No, never.

THE AGONY COLUMN

U NTIL THAT DAY in 1933, when he picked up his copy of *The Times* of London and as usual began to read the classified advertisements in the Personal column, Mr. Peter Fleming, a slender, dreamy young Englishman, had lived a relatively dull and sedentary existence.

Fleming's background consisted of Oxford, a stint with BBC, and a brief job in Wall Street in New York. Now, as literary editor of the London *Spectator*, he was immune from all dangers but that of writer's cramp. He sometimes played squash, but his favorite indoor sport consisted of musing over the Personal column of *The Times*. Here, in the small type of the world's first and most famous Personal column, which for a century and a half had been nicknamed the "agony column," Peter Fleming found his escape.

"What strange kind of a creature can it be whose wolf-hound—now lost in Battersea Park—answers to the name of Effie?" he would reflect, as he read. "Why is Bingo heart-broken? And what possible use can Box A have for a horned toad?"

On that particular day in 1933, when Fleming, as was his habit, read through the mysterious and romantic classified advertisements, he stumbled suddenly upon one that made him sit up. It announced:

> Exploring and sporting expedition, under experienced guidance, leaving England June, to explore rivers Central Brazil, if possible ascertain fate Colonel Fawcett; abundance game, big and small; exceptional fishing; ROOM TWO MORE GUNS; highest references expected and given. Write Box X, *The Times*, E.C.4.

For the first time, Fleming did not idly speculate or let his fancy play over an advertisement. Instead, he answered it. As a result, within a few months, he was transported into the middle of the primitive Matto Grosso jungles of Central Brazil. There, led by an American whom Fleming chose to call Major Pingle, he found himself wading through piranhas, brushing off stinging insects, dodging wild animals, hiding from hostile natives, and constantly searching for traces of the renowned Colonel Fawcett, who had disappeared in 1925 while in quest of the fabulous City of Gold.

After completing this excursion, Peter Fleming wrote a humorous best seller called *Brazilian Adventure*. Besides the fame and wealth that he soon acquired, he also became an explorer in Tartary and a traveler in Russia, China, Japan. He even married Celia Johnson, who would later attain cinema stardom in the film *Brief Encounter*.

Anonymity, daydreaming, the dull sedentary life were far behind—all because of a brief ad in the agony column of the London *Times*.

Of course, this unusual case history is not meant to suggest that the agony column, in steady doses, is a sure cure-all for monotony. But certainly, on the basis of past performances, the agony column of *The Times*, like all Personal columns modeled after it, remains one of the last modern outposts of hidden romance and adventure in a weary realistic existence made unhappy with the atom bomb, inflation, and Communism.

Few readers of the agony column ever actually succumb to its classified invitations. Peter Fleming was one of these few, the rare exception. Most readers prefer to enjoy their adventures vicariously, in the armchair, on the bus, and their number is legion. It is a known fact that William Hazlitt, Charles Dickens, Thomas Hardy, and Cardinal Newman were Constant Readers. So was Disraeli, and so was Queen Victoria.

Today, the Queen of England, studying her special royal edition of *The Times* printed on rag paper, is an agony column fan. Among world leaders, the late Benito Mussolini once admitted that he followed the column. Winston Churchill, as well as dozens of others in politics, has found relaxation in perusing the agony ads.

Perhaps the most celebrated reader of all was Sherlock Holmes—for whom mail, addressed to No. 221 B Baker Street, is still received daily by the London post office. In "The Adventure of the Engineer's Thumb," the faithful Dr. Watson reports that "Sherlock Holmes was, as I expected, lounging about his sitting-room in his dressing gown, reading the agony column of *The Times*." Again, flinging his newspaper aside, Sherlock Holmes confesses, "I read nothing except the criminal news and the agony column. The latter is always instructive."

For detectives and criminals alike, the agony column has, indeed, always been instructive. In 1916, Anna Maria Lesser, the beautiful Fräulein Doktor of the German Secret Service, invaded England during World War I posing as an Irishwoman, brogue and all. Following up a rumor that the English had invented an ironclad machine to break the trench deadlock on the Western Front, Fräulein Doktor moved into a little village near Hatfield Park. Here she got rid of the local scoutmaster, volunteered to take his place, and used her innocent boy scouts to spy on secret experiments being held before King George V and Lord Kitchener. One of her scouts watched an entire experiment from a tree, and described in detail the first invented tank to Fräulein Doktor, who, in turn, transmitted the intelligence to Germany. When things got hot, the Fräulein used the agony column at least twice to communicate her findings to other spies bound for the Continent. It is a known fact that several German graduates of Elzbeth Schragmuller's infamous Antwerp spy school kept in constant touch with one another and with their leaders through the agony column, where strange ads, no matter how cryptic or curious, excited no suspicion.

In World War II, Nazi agents in England tried to repeat the successful use of the agony column by their World War I predecessors. British Intelligence admits such attempts were made, and quickly adds that every means was employed to block such use of the agony column by enemy spies. Odd or suspicious advertisements, as recently as two years ago, were submitted by the London *Times* to the official government censor. Cryptic messages, from persons who had not advertised in the agony column before, were often rejected. In many cases, either *The Times* or British Intelligence quietly investigated the background of advertisers.

Today, Scotland Yard uses the column as an unconventional arm of the law when hunting for murderers, thieves, blackmailers, and adventurers. While *The Times* does not permit a Personal advertisement to appear in a foreign language, curiously it allows ads to appear in code or cipher. Several times Scotland Yard has secretly solved code messages in the ads and thus learned what criminals were communicating with one another. In one case, Scotland Yard detectives, after breaking a blackmailer's code, composed a dummy ad in the same code and planted it in the agony column. The trick worked. The blackmailer was trapped, and arrested.

Scotland Yard, however, is not the only code breaker. Often ordinary readers, who regard the column as a diversion superior to crossword puzzles, will try to find the key to a cipher. This game proves as stimulating as opening someone else's mail. Occasionally, a prankster among these will write and insert a false ad in the same cipher, and shatter a budding romance. One such case occurred as far back as ninety-four years ago, and with sad consequences.

Two lovers were holding fervent clandestine meetings in the agony column. Their notes to one another were in cipher. On February 11, 1853, one contacted the other in the agony column as follows:

> CENERENTOLA. Jsyng rd mifwy nx Xnhp mfaj ywnji yt kwfrj fs jcugfitynts Kwt dtz gzy hfssty Xngjshj nx xfsjxy nk ymf ywzj hfzxj nx sty zxzujhyji; nk ny nx tgg xytwnjx bngg gj xnkyji yt ymj gtyytr. It dtz wjrjrgiw tzw htzn'x knwxy uwtutznynts: ymnsp tk ny.

The villain in the piece, apparently the girl's father, noticed the ad, suspected his daughter and her lover, and decided to teach them a lesson. He set to work studying ciphers, and found that this one was quite elementary. It was based on a primitive code used by Julius Caesar. With solution in hand, the girl's father, determined to show the errant pair that he knew what was up, translated the ciphered ad and openly published it in the agony column. It read:

> CENERENTOLA. Until my heart is sick have I tried to frame an explanation for you, but cannot. Silence is safest if the true cause is not suspected. If it is, all stories will be sifted to the bottom. Do you remember our cousin's first proposition? Think of it. N pstb Dtz.

Except for correcting some atrocious typographical errors, the father made only one addition. He added the three last words, written in the very code he had broken—"N pstb Dtz"—meaning "I know you."

But the irate parent wasn't through. Having solved the coded ad, and published his solution, he now answered it with vigor in an ad of his own. On February 19, the father addressed the lovers in the agony column as follows:

> CENERENTOLA. What nonsense! Your cousin's proposition is absurd. I have given an explanation, the true one, which has perfectly satisfied both parties, a thing which silence never could have effected. So no more absurdity.

This was the last word. No more cryptograms were exchanged between the couple. Obviously, Irate Parent had won, and the Constant Reader was obliged to return sadly to the more pedestrian Personal ads that begged prodigal sons to return home or suggested "tonight, same hour, same place."

Today, though an established English institution, the agony column is by no means confined to the British Isles. The agony column has imitators in the newspapers of every civilized nation on earth and in every state of the United States. The American who, for his armchair adventure, picks up his New York *Daily News* or Chicago *Tribune* or San Francisco *Chronicle*, to turn with relish to the classified ads and run through the Personals, is reading only variations on an idea started by *The Times* of London as long ago as 1785. One American, the short-story writer O. Henry, acknowledged that he derived many of his ideas for fiction from his habit of reading these paid notices.

The Personal column, as a form of inexpensive amusement and a springboard for glamorous daydreams, is now as much a part of the American scene (and with about as much promise of escape) as the activities in print of Mr. Dick Tracy and Mr. J. Edgar Hoover. *The New York Times* alone receives as many as 2,500,000 classified ads a year, and a goodly number of these are in the best agony-column tradition. Recent ads included a request for "a haunted house" in Manhattan, and for buyers interested in 60,000 clean chicken wishbones. A typical *New York Times* ad, not long ago, requested that "Anyone knowing whereabouts of Robert Charlton, last heard of in New York 1900, or his descendants, communicate with Gilbert Charlton (brother), address 15 Brighton Street, Petersham, New South Wales, Australia." A month later *The New York Times* learned that the brothers, separated almost a half century and by thousands of miles, had incredibly been reunited through this Personal notice.

At the other end of the country, the Los Angeles *Times*, in its Personal column, carries numerous provocative ads beginning, "Lonely? Plain sealed details free." Other ads hold out a variety of rare promises. For those who want money, "Cash for diamonds." For those who want their loved ones, "Missing persons traced." For those who demand less, "Good home desired for good boy 12."

Because of its reader-amusement value, as well as its revenue potentialities, the Personal column has spread from newspapers to popular magazines and even trade journals. One American weekly, the *Saturday Review*, features some of the best agony ads in the business. Here, in an average issue, we find an "unusually stupid, utterly untalented charmless harmless male" eager to meet "similarly endowed female." Here we find a "woman, weary of city's drabness, invites correspondence from green hills far away." Here, too, we find a Hawkshaw prepared to ferret out "information discreetly" on "any matter, person, problem, anywhere."

But these American versions of the agony column, while good, are not the best. The best is still the original Personal column of *The Times* of London. Because it outranks all its imitators for sheer entertainment, drama, and eccentricity, the agony column of *The Times* has become the center of a growing legend. Earl Derr Biggers, before inventing Charlie Chan, used the agony column as the subject and title of a murder mystery. Both Edgar Wallace and Sir Arthur Conan Doyle drew upon it regularly for their fiction. Researchers into curiosities of human nature referred to the agony column. Only a few years ago, two American psychologists excerpted ads from the column to help illustrate character differences for their weighty tome, *Plots and Personalities*.

Today, the agony column appears daily on the front page of the staid London *Times*. This front page, with its seven columns of small type, is the only front page in London, and one of the very few in the world, devoted entirely to classified advertisements. The third column from the left, the one nicknamed the agony column, is headed with its formal name—"Personal." Beneath this heading is a brief passage from the Bible (the *Times* personnel call it the Text), and a different quotation submitted by readers is used each day. A typical Text, which appeared in a recent edition, read, " 'As ye would that men should do to you, do ye also to them likewise'—St. Luke vi, 31."

The ads themselves occupy the rest of the column. Many persons submit ads thirty and forty lines long, but these are returned, since an ad needs an exceptional reason to be allowed more than five lines or thirty words. A five-line ad costs ten dollars and must be written in prose. Ads containing poetry are rejected. Display ads, ditto. The taboo against display ads was broken only once—"in the interests of justice"—and that was back in 1845. A wealthy gentleman had received three threatening letters, each in a different handwriting. He wanted to publish facsimiles of these letters, along with an offer of a $100 reward to anyone identifying their sources, in the agony column. The police thought that it was a good idea, and so *The Times* relaxed its policy and ran the display ad.

The man in charge of the agony column is a small, gray-haired, reticent advertising veteran named Mr. L. Canna. He looks like an elderly Bob Cratchit. He has been handling classified ads for *The Times* for over thirty years, and two years ago was made the head of the agony column. His domain consists of a somewhat ventilated room (it was damaged by a hundred-pound Luftwaffe bomb during the Blitz) in *The Times* building off Printing House Square in London. The room has a counter and post-office-style grilles, before which most advertisers appear in person with their insertions. A small percentage of ads are submitted by mail, and some of these come from the United States. Americans like to send ads offering to sell Englishmen their old clothes, but Mr. Canna cannot accept these ads because of British currency control.

Mr. Canna's main problem is postwar censorship. "The agony column does not advertise adoptions," he says. "It does not advertise political grumbles, and it does not accept lonely-hearts or matrimonial advertisements." During the war, according to Mr. Canna, the agony column was swamped with matrimonial ads sent in by American GI's stationed in England. "The American boys usually described the English girls they wanted to marry. They wrote out the color of eyes preferred, the height and weight preferred, and in several cases suggested that if the female applicant had a little capital it would go a long way in her favor. The majority of GI's also sent in photographs of themselves to go with the ads. We returned all, explaining that *The Times* does not handle this sort of advertisement."

Mr. Canna is constantly on the alert for other transgressions. If a man wishes to repudiate his wife's debts in the agony column, the ad must be submitted through an attorney. If a housewife wishes to advertise the sale of her furniture, she must prove her identity and give her address, since *The Times* does not like to have retail dealers use the column. If, after a robbery, the victim submits an ad stating that anyone returning the stolen goods "will be rewarded" and "no questions asked," Mr. Canna must reject the ad since its publication would put *The Times* in the position of aiding and abetting a crime.

Many source books have vainly attempted to analyze the character of those ads that finally appear in the agony column. The august *Encyclopaedia Britannica* describes the agony column as one devoted to "announcements of losses or bequests . . . a medium also for matrimonial advertisements." Mr. Canna shakes his head over this. "Entirely inadequate and entirely incorrect," he says. Mr. Canna likes to read from a brochure on the agony column, issued by *The Times*, which defines the column more dramatically. "The largest human reading is found in our Personal column. Here, speaking in accents uncouth, is found the Average Man himself."

Most members of *The Times* feel that the essence of the column was best caught by Constant Reader Peter Fleming. "The world of the Agony Column is a world of romance," wrote Fleming, "across which sundered lovers are for ever hurrying to a familiar rendezvous ('same time, same place'): a world in which jewellery is constantly being left in taxi-cabs with destinations which must surely be compromising: a world of faded and rather desperate gentility, peopled largely by Old Etonians and ladies of title . . . a world in which every object has a sentimental value, every young man a good appearance, and only the highest references are exchanged: an anxious, urgent, cryptic world: a world in which anything may happen."

Indeed a world in which anything may happen. A world in which the following advertisement (which was permitted to exceed *The Times'* length restrictions), a novel in itself, a motion picture scenario certainly, recently appeared:

> Middle-aged peer and peeress, energetic, capable, former with military and business experience, good linguist (French, German); latter good organizer, two and one-half years general nursing experience (London and military); desire suitable employment together with accommodations; no salary. London or near south or southwest England preferred.

The stream of dramatic and curious ads, in recent years, has been endless. Mr. Canna's favorites include the ad offering to sell a tiny island off the Spanish Main, and another offering an isle in the Bahamas at a reduced price. Mr. Canna also remembers the man who advertised in the agony column for a parrot—offering to pay four dollars for every word the parrot could speak. Mr. Canna often clips his favorite ads, and one of these reads: "Wanted to hire. A full-grown forest-bred Bengal Tiger. Very active."

The agony column has carried insertions offering a batch of lion cubs for sale, a request for miniature monkeys ("I will pay $4 per ounce for the monkeys"), an inquiry for mustache cups, and an offer to purchase all Aeolian harps that could be had. Sometimes cryptic ads appear from Inland Revenue acknowledging the receipt of money—published at the request of persons who, having once evaded income tax, guiltily, anonymously, send in conscience money.

Recently, when I visited the London *Times,* I went through innumerable files of Personal columns. A typical advertiser had a "used Rolls-Royce" to sell or "an evening gown, worn once." Mostly there were ex-servicemen seeking "remunerative posts," including the lieutenant colonel "with high-powered car," and the "ex-RAF wing commander, suffering from overdose of political inertia."

Then there was the young accountant who lacked money to support his wife and two daughters and wished "to contact a Gentleman with desire to arrange mortgage on my house." There was the person with

"Nelson relics for sale, American offers are welcome." There was "the advertiser wishing to free himself from the tyranny of possessions, will sell car, pictures, camera, stamps, guns." And, as in prewar days, the "titled lady and Oxford man willing to take small party young people on educational tour of France, Switzerland, Italy, Portugal."

In these columns I met the most interesting people. The "gentlewoman" who "takes paying guests in her beautiful country mansion." The "young married ex-officer" who "requires practical experience of mushroom-growing." The "stammering [gentleman]" who "wishes to meet another gentleman suffering from similar disability with view to discussing means of improvement." Here, too, I met the "lady, aged 25" who "wishes to see the world," the "ex-Major, aged 29" who is "despondent in today's world of moribund commercialism," and the "lady, 46, suffering acutely from Head Noises."

Other ads intrigued with their half-told dramas:

> Decidedly NO. Too dogmatic. Lack sympathy. Nothing in common between us—O.

> C.A. You should remain steadfast whatever the cost. —Heartbroken mother.

> Home wanted for Gentleman subject to alcoholic bouts. Supervision required.

> Grateful thanks to the Lady of Lourdes.—H.B.

> Susan. Please tell me how you are and what you are doing. Time isn't changing anything. Love always. —Jon.

> Hong Kong Resident whose library was looted during the Japanese occupation, wants to negotiate for replacement.

> Articulated skeleton required.

But if today's ads appear to have dramatic possibilities, they are but minor intrigue compared to some of the pathetic, villainous, and zany ads of the past. Although the first Personal column of *The Times* saw light in 1785, occasional ads of this type were printed years earlier when the paper was known as the *Daily Universal Register*. And even before, bizarre Personal advertisements were being published, such as the one that appeared in London during 1749, as part of the design for a gigantic practical joke.

In that year several celebrated persons, including the Duke of Portland and the Earl of Chesterfield, were seated in their London club discussing the question of human gullibility.

"I will wager," said the duke, "that let a man advertise the most impossible thing in the world, and he will find fools enough in London to fill a playhouse and pay handsomely for the privilege of being there."

The Earl of Chesterfield objected. "Surely, if a man should say that he would jump into a quart bottle, nobody would believe that."

It was a tough challenge, but the duke stuck to his guns. He insisted that people would be gullible enough to believe it and made the wager.

The two wrote out a Personal advertisement:

> AT THE NEW THEATRE IN THE HAYMAR-
> KET, on Monday next, the 16th instant, is to be
> seen a Person who performs the most surprising
> thing—viz, He presents you with a common Wine
> Bottle, which any of the spectators may first exam-
> ine; this Bottle is placed on a Table in the middle of
> the Stage, and he (without any equivocation) goes
> into it, in the sight of all the spectators, and sings
> in it; during his stay in the Bottle, any Person may
> handle it, and see plainly that it does not exceed a
> common Tavern Bottle. Tickets to be had at the
> Theatre. To begin a half an hour after six o'clock.

The appearance of the advertisement created a sensation in London. There was a great rush for tickets priced from two to seven shillings, and on the scheduled night, the pit seats, the boxes, the galleries were packed with people. They waited patiently, until the appointed hour came and passed, and then they began to boo and catcall. The theater manager appeared, bowed, apologized for the delay, and announced that he would refund the money if the performer did not appear in fifteen minutes. Fifteen minutes came, went—thirty minutes, an hour. The galleries began to hiss ominously. A nobleman threw a lighted candle from his box onto the stage. Then, as one, the audience rose, began ripping up seats and benches, began tearing down fixtures and curtain. Inside, the entire theater was gutted. Outside, its furnishings were transformed into a huge bonfire. In the chaos, someone stole off with the box office receipts.

And the Duke of Portland won his wager.

Thereafter, and for 162 successive years, the agony column dominated the game and offered a field day for its readers. High romance was afoot as early as August 20, 1795, when the following notice appeared in the Personal column of the ten-year-old *Times:*

> If the Lady who, on Tuesday morning last, between 12 and 1 o'clock, was addressed by a Gentleman near the top of King Street, Covent Garden, when they afterwards walked together in that neighborhood, and an unexpected separation abruptly happened, would favour that Gentleman with a few lines, directed to A.B. at the Turk's Head Coffeehouse, in the Strand, to remain till called for, and mentioning any morning, place and hour, when and where he may have the satisfaction of meeting her again, he would esteem himself much obliged.

One's imagination soars. Who was the ardent Gentleman? Up from the country, no doubt, or he would have been walking in a better part of town and would not have accosted an unattended Lady. And the Lady? "Who was the unknown fair who had made such an impression on the gentleman who accosted her?" muses an editor of *The Times*. "Ladies encountered by chance in Covent Garden, unaccompanied and of none too difficult access, were not generally the type for the renewal of whose acquaintance one would insert eager appeals in *The Times*. What was she? Clarissa Harlowe or Moll Flanders? A Countess incognito? A masquerading lady's-maid (the 18th century was much too full of these)? A beautiful distressed émigré from across the Channel?" And how did their unexpected separation come about? The Lady's guardian, her husband— who or what frightened her? And, after the Personal ad appeared, did she write, did they meet again? What tragicomedy followed?

The agony column merely posed the questions, started the game. Each reader supplied his own answers. But other provocative advertisements overshadowed that one. In 1795, came a simple, somewhat terrifying announcement. "A most capital, superb, and valuable assemblage of jewels, late the property of Madame la Comtesse du Barry, deceased." Madame du Barry had lost her head, in France, two years before. And in 1798, when matrimonial advertisements were still permitted, a touch of humor. A gentleman requests a wife. "I am of excellent and unimpaired constitution, but afflicted with an incurable weakness in the knees, occasioned by the kick of an Ostrich." And, in that same year, another amusing advertisement. "Two pigs found swimming in the Thames, near Westminster Bridge. Now safely lodged, awaiting a suitable reward, at the Swan, by Lambeth Church."

A whole series of mundane patent medicines and new inventions ushered in the 1800's. In the agony column "a Medical Man" offers for sale his newly invented "Patent Coestus," an elastic steel belt, "used in my own family above 15 years, preserves the vital organs from pressure and retains the figure in that beautiful oval form so remarkable in Grecian sculpture." Another ad features "Soyer's Magic Stove" which "enables a Gentleman to cook his dinner in his pocket." And of greater moment, the first announcement, by some genius, of braces or suspenders. "New invented gallowses or breeches suspensors, for keeping up the breeches without girting them tight around the waist, but, on the contrary, keep them well up and loose."

Between 1848 and 1900, an endless number of eccentric and unrelated ads dot the agony column:

> You could not speak. It was so sudden. I am a good rider. Green is my favorite color. I want money.

> Small House. Danger. Cross the sea.

> Since Friday morning I die hourly. Where are you and when will you return?—J.S.

> My colours are nailed not tied to the masthead. T.

> Hampstead Heath Enclosure. Something's up.

> If the youth that left Islington on Sunday evening can remember that he ever had a mother, he is informed he will soon be deprived of that blessing, except he immediately writes with particulars, or personally appears before her.

> Cloves. Many things have forced themselves upon me. From the past let us gather strength. T wants to meet Bird. Infelix.

> I entreat you to keep your word, or it may be fatal. Laws were made to bind the villains of society.

However, the most intriguing ads in the Victorian era ran in series, the interested parties corresponding through Personal ads. Readers followed these as avidly as Dickens' serials. For example, between July and November of 1850, the following advertisements appeared:

> The one-winged dove must die unless the Crane returns to be a shield against her enemies.

Somerset, S.B. The mate of the Dove must take wing forever unless a material change takes place.

It is enough. One man alone upon earth have I found noble. Away from me forever. Cold heart and mean spirit, you have lost what millions, empires, could not have bought, but which a single word, truthfully and nobly spoken might have made your own to all eternity! Yet you are forgiven, depart in peace. I rest in my Redeemer.

The mate of the Dove bids a final farewell. Adieu to the British Isles, although such a resolution cannot be accomplished without poignant grief. W.

The most mysterious series consisted of three cryptic ads in three different years. On March 24, 1849, this appeared in the agony column: "No doormat tonight." One year later, March 28, 1850, the message was: "Doormat and beans tonight." More than a year later, May 28, 1851, only: "Doormat tonight." Students of the agony column have speculated for years on this series. What did the key word "doormat" mean? Did it mean the absence of a stern father or a jealous husband, or did it point to the victim of a murder? History provides no answer but the reader's own.

The longest single series of advertisements in the agony column ran fifteen years, from 1850 to 1865, and was inserted by an eccentric millionaire named E. J. Wilson. There appeared a steady bombardment of ads, written (when *The Times* had as yet no ban on foreign languages) in French, German, and English. These advertisements tell a sad little story. Wilson worked in the British Customs Office, had a private fortune, married, and produced a daughter. He became involved in some smuggling scheme; his wife objected and left him. For fifteen years, through the agony column, he tried to woo her back. His advertisements followed her when she traveled to Stockholm and to Paris. His paid notices eventually accused her openly of having a lover. She replied, in the agony column, to this charge. "You are deceived. I foster none, but am true to ties of happier days. Open to me a communication and a public investigation. Mary." Many of Wilson's ads were in code: "ACHILLES has got the lever. Corruption sinks and virtue swims. E.J.W." Finally, in October, 1865, having lost his job, his fortune, and his health, Wilson arranged a meeting with the wife whom he had not seen in a decade and a half. The time and place of the meeting appeared in an ad in the agony column. Whatever the outcome of this meeting, Wilson had placed his last advertisement.

And today, others take up where Wilson left off. In the tiny print of the agony column, in a vocabulary replete with words like "desperate" and "brokenhearted," parted lovers continue to meet, schemes for easy millions continue to materialize, beautiful old Paisley shawls continue to sell, and escapists desiring "any sort of remunerative adventure, would risk all" continue to defy the ever-more-crowded columns of Mortgage Investments, Legal Notices, Business Offers—and Births and Deaths.

>«

WHAT HAS HAPPENED SINCE . . .

I became interested in the agony column of *The Times* of London while I was living at the Athenaeum Court off Green Park, and later at the Savoy Hotel, in London during the bitter winter of 1946 and 1947. The city was still suffering from the aftereffects of the Second World War, and there were food shortages, and rationing was still in existence. The standard price for an austere postwar dinner was five shillings, although if you were in a better-class restaurant, then two to six shillings extra was added as a "house charge." Lunch was always an omelet made from powdered eggs, and tea. Dinner was usually three courses, a soup thick with potatoes, chicken patties and brussels sprouts, and a sweet. If the diner wanted bread with his meal, he had to give up one of his three courses. Since I was a compulsive bread eater, and there was no bread with the regular meals, I was constantly famished. In fact, the highlight of that visit to London occurred when an English newspaper correspondent, connected with Buckingham Palace, appeared at my hotel room on New Year's Day of 1947 with an overwhelmingly generous gift —a loaf of bread that he had purloined from his own mother's ration.

During those London evenings, as I contemplated my receding navel (I lost seventeen pounds in that period), I would often try to take my mind off my stomach by reading the London *Times*. Since I was not interested in cricket or bird-watching or Labour's latest program, this was not particularly diverting—until I discovered what I had for several weeks overlooked: the agony column. This discovery was a major enchantment. And from that time on, I read the agony column as religiously as the Archbishop of Canterbury read his daily Scripture. I lost my interest in the staff of life because I now had what a writer needs most of all—food for thought.

Before leaving London, I began to research the agony column, questioning the oldest employees of *The Times* and spending hours poring over back editions of the newspaper. Later, in Los Angeles, in 1948, I wrote my story of the world's foremost Personal column. I wrote about it for pleasure, as one writes about an unusual hobby like collecting porcelain buttons or locks of human hair or epitaphs on tombstones. I then filed away my precious story, awaiting some future time when the immediate postwar tensions and the atmosphere of all-work-and-no-play would be supplanted by a new era of leisure and well-being. While preparing this book, I decided that such a day had dawned. Many Americans who sought escape from the harsher aspects of life, who wanted mental diversion and fleeting peace of mind, were turning more feverishly to crossword puzzles, Double-Crostics, mathematical games, and James Bond. Surely these were the ones to be reminded of the stimulations, challenges, amusements, and ultimate contentment available to them every day through their local Personal columns, heirs to the honored agony column of *The Times* of London.

As a matter of fact, in recent years I have found that more and more Americans are reading, and later reciting their favorite items from, the Personal columns of their own favorite newspaper. Every so often, lately, I find myself reading a newspaper report or feature about a Personal advertisement in some other city that has led to the arrest of a criminal, the reunion of a long-separated family, the location of a missing heir, the exposure of an espionage ring, or the beginning of an exotic adventure.

In October of 1962, the Hearst newspaper chain carried the story of a Personal advertisement that had appeared in the San Francisco *Examiner* six months earlier, and which had led to a denouement that few authors of fiction could equal, let alone improve upon, in their most fertile imaginings.

The circumstances that fostered this dramatic Personal advertisement were these: In 1954, an elderly antique dealer named Clarke was found dead in his shop. He had been tortured, then slashed to death. In his shop were also found two ornate swords bearing bloody fingerprints. In 1960, the Federal Bureau of Investigation came across fingerprints of a steelworker named Robert Lee Kidd, who was living in Gary, Indiana. His fingerprints matched those on the swords in the shop where the antique dealer had been murdered six years before.

The authorities learned that Kidd, a former sailor, and a heavy drinker, and his devoted wife Gladys, had lived in San Francisco at the time of the crime. A year later they had moved to Gary, where Kidd found steady employment and settled down. Kidd was charged with the murder, brought back to California for trial, tried, found guilty, and sentenced to the gas chamber. After the state Supreme Court reversed the verdict on a technicality, a second trial was held. This resulted in a hung jury. When a third trial was scheduled, Gladys Kidd, by now totally impoverished, passionately certain of her husband's innocence, became desperate. What she wanted was a topflight criminal lawyer, who believed in her husband's innocence as firmly as she did. Without knowledge of such an attorney, or funds to hire him if she found him, she wondered what could be done for her mate. The critical trial was only eight weeks off. At almost the last minute she struck upon the idea of inserting a brief advertisement in the Personal column of the San Francisco *Examiner*.

Gladys Kidd wrote her ad, paid for it, and in the normal process of events it appeared in the classified section of May 2, 1962:

> I don't want my husband to die in the gas chamber for a crime he did not commit. I will therefore offer my services for 10 years as a cook, maid or housekeeper to any leading attorney who will defend him and bring about his vindication. 522 Hayes St. UN 3-9799.

The drama inherent in the routinely printed advertisement sent Gladys Kidd's plea and offer vaulting onto front pages of newspapers throughout the country. Five prominent attorneys immediately came forward and offered to serve her. She selected Vincent Hallinan, one of the most gifted and colorful attorneys in San Francisco, a city filled with great lawyers. Hallinan set out to prove that Kidd was a decent human being, and at the same time to imply that the police had done a poor job of investigation and to cover up their failure had built a shaky case against Kidd.

In the third trial, the defense attorney interrogated a University of California criminologist, who stated that neither of the swords in the victim's antique shop had been employed as the murder weapon. Kidd's attorney then interrogated an antique specialist, to show that such swords were sold, bought, resold frequently, and the same ones turned up in shop after shop. Finally, the attorney interrogated Kidd himself, and revealed that Kidd and a friend had often browsed through San Francisco antique shops, and had once visited a shop where they had come upon these same swords, picked them up, and engaged in a playful duel during which Kidd's fingers were cut, which accounted for his bloodstained prints. Apparently the weapons had found their way to Clarke's shop, although Clarke had not been murdered with either weapon. The jury deliberated, and after eleven hours announced that Kidd was not guilty. But when it was time for payment, attorney Hallinan declined to accept Gladys Kidd's offer of ten years' bondage.

Once again, a Personal column had served not only dreamers—but justice.

Yet, it is unlikely that this Personal column, or any others in America or the rest of the world, would have existed to serve people like the Kidds had not the agony column of the London *Times* made such advertisements fashionable and popular.

Recently, I wondered if the situation of the original agony column, and the rules under which the column was conducted, had been altered in any way during the seventeen years since I had written about it. I made inquiries of the managers of *The Times* and soon had my answers.

Since 1962, *The Times*, as well as its advertising offices, has occupied quarters in a new building, unscarred by bombs. Mr. Canna, the advertising veteran of thirty years who had been in charge of the agony column when I had been in London in 1947, had retired from *The Times* and relinquished his supervision of the column in 1952. *The Times* appeared loath to mention his successor by name, informing me: "These days no one individual has sole charge of the Personal column. . . . It would be misleading to introduce personalities."

The placement and format of the column remain immutable against the changes often demanded by progress—the front page and tiny type are as ever. Today, customers cannot submit an ad of less than two lines, for which they are charged eighteen shillings and sixpence per six-word line. However, in seventeen years, many old restrictions—such as those against political ads, foreign-language ads, matrimonial ads, and ads longer than five lines—have broken down. An executive of the London *Times* defined the new and more liberal policy for me as follows: "There are now no restrictions on size or language (provided that we are sent a translation for our own records); we do however still exclude all forms of display advertising from these columns. Political advertisements are generally acceptable; so, within the bounds of reason and good taste, would be lonely-hearts advertisements—although I do not recall any instances of such advertising. Adoption advertisements are illegal in this country."

But the most outstanding attraction of the agony column, its colorful contents, remains unspoiled by time. In studying the Personal notices for 1962, 1963, 1964, and 1965, I was relieved and pleased to see that the column was still a parade ground for the dramatic, the provocative, the bizarre, the comic, the romantic, the mysterious.

Only a few new trends disturbed me. While *The Times* always permitted the agony column to serve as a marketplace for the wares of individuals, they had also always sternly rejected any invasion from retail dealers. However, unless I misread certain ads, this commercialized invasion has slyly begun. In an issue of *The Times* for September, 1964, I was at first heartened, then disillusioned, by the following:

Deirdre—Fly at once. All discovered—Hugo. Everyone knows about us! All agree you must leave London now! Come and work out of town with me. If
your firm won't go, you must. Tell your fiendish
bosses lots of new offices going up in Essex, Herts,
etc. Get him to write to Mr. A. Galbraith at the
Location of Offices Bureau . . .

To the true agony-column addict, this deceptive realty salesmanship is
deplorable. All purists must regard such invasions of the column's function as beastly.

However, I must quickly add that individual sales of personal wares, or
inquiries after objets d'oddity, are as tantalizing and satisfying as they
have ever been. I need only quote a sampling of advertisements concerning goods that appeared between 1962 and 1964, to reassure fellow
devotees:

Honeymoon tent, brand new and unused; cost 42
pounds, will accept 34 pounds. Write Box K 160.

Lordship of Manor. Ancient documents and right to
use the title "Lord of the Manor" 13th century
origin; will only be sold to British residents with
good references. Write Box E 1470.

Covered Waggon Or Suchlike. Will any person who
abominating seeing children left outside, while parents are drinking, lend any two large covered vehicles to use during the rebuilding, as a temporary
children's play place.

Regretfully, too, I found some indication, in a certain type of new
advertisement, that England is fast becoming a land of many Scrooges.
"A large number of people," an executive of *The Times* told me, "have
been putting ads of holiday greetings in the Personal column instead of
sending Christmas cards."

More or less typical of these were the persons who, in the Christmas
week of 1962, placed this ad in the agony column: "C.T.P., N.J.S.L.,
T.A.M.E., I.M.O., D.I.A.H. are too idle and too broke to send Christmas cards"—and then offered their best wishes, wholesale, to one and
all.

Happily, in Christmas week of 1964, another English couple recanted
a similar heresy, when they advised the agony column readers, "Mr. and
Mrs. Frank Muir will not be making an announcement in *The Times*

this year. Instead they will be sending their friends Christmas cards."

As always, no week passes without some English subject advertising his gratefulness (for whatever intriguing and undisclosed personal benefits he has received) to the Maker and the Son and all the Heavenly Hosts. Glancing through the agony columns of recent years, I found F. M. T. proclaiming, "Many Thanks to Almighty God that we are justified by Faith alone," and J. B. calling out, "Grateful Thanks to Our Lady of Fatima, St. Jude, and St. Anthony," and J. A. N. flatly stating, "Many Thanks for Religious Freedom in Protestant England," and J. P. pathetically imploring, "Saint Martin de Porres, half-caste and illegitimate, cure us of intolerance."

The balance of the Personal columns of the last four years I found brimming with gems of dramatic promise, casual little advertisements ready to send a hundred Peter Flemings into a hundred strange adventures. Some recent examples from the agony column of *The Times* are:

> Darling Rita—most beautiful 20-year old for the next 365 days—My love always, John.

> Madame Serphoui Mendillian seeks her son, Antranik Mendillian, born . . . Turkey, 1910. Would anyone having any information concerning his whereabouts please contact Mme. Serphoui Mendillian . . . Marseille, 15c, France.

> Married Couple in late 30's would like to join lively party for Christmas, please reply to Box S 651.

> Crocodile Hunting. Advice wanted, good dinner offered. Write Box P 1896.

> A lady of title would like to chaperone debutante. Every advantage. Write Box M 1307.

> A Persian passport was left in a train on Saturday 5th December; if found please return it to Embassy.

> MacGreen—Would Mrs. MacGreen of London, who had in her care, Victor Rober Liukkonen from Finland, about year 1899, please contact Mrs. Jenny Lind, Helsinki Liisankatu 17 C 19 Finland.

Finally, on May 13, 1965, the Personal column of *The Times* received a unique curtsy of homage from an American visitor. On that date, the agony column carried the following advertisement:

New York—Extremely reliable and competent young woman, 25-35, needed to look after girl of seven and boy four in New York City; English or French native language. Telephone, Hyde Park 3808 or 9666, between 10 and 12.

The advertisement had been placed by Mrs. John F. Kennedy.

Confident that there will always be an England, I am satisfied that there will always be an agony column and a world (minimum two lines, no display ads) of infinite wonder.

» 11 «

MILLIONAIRE'S CHARIOT

WHEN in February of 1945, Franklin D. Roosevelt offered the magnificent gift of a fully equipped C-47 to King Ibn Saud of Saudi Arabia, international diplomacy was challenged. Winston Churchill, for one, felt that his country must not be outdone by the United States' effort to butter up the old Arab war-horse. Yet, what could austere Britain offer to match F.D.R.'s airplane?

Then Churchill hit upon it. While he knew Ibn Saud owned five hundred automobiles, varying widely as to age and pedigree, he also knew that the Arab did not possess that ultimate luxury which Churchill, the British people, and most of the world's leaders regarded as England's foremost product. Churchill promptly offered Ibn Saud a Rolls-Royce.

As it turned out, Churchill's gesture proved to be as impractical as it was enthusiastic. For while F.D.R. was able to make good his offer by immediately delivering the C-47, Churchill found on his return to London from the Summit Conference that the Rolls-Royce factory in Crewe —as well as those in Derby and Glasgow—was still (by his own order) turning out engines for Spitfires, Hurricanes, and Lancasters. Nary a Rolls-Royce limousine had been manufactured since the outbreak of the war. For Churchill, it was an embarrassing position in which to be caught, and the loss of diplomatic face incalculable. Churchill consulted with his Ministry of Supply, and the Ministry, in turn, huddled with the harried directors of Rolls-Royce. In the end, it was decided that Ibn Saud's limousine must be given the highest priority.

Under pressure, and in almost no time at all, a single dazzling Rolls-Royce was produced, assembled entirely by hand and under the severest handicaps. Veteran Rolls-Royce experts were pulled off airplane engines to produce the chassis, while designers at Hooper and Company, which works with Rolls-Royce, turned out the body. The result was a touring limousine model, which retailed at $18,787 (purchase tax included), and it was a Sunday driver's dream, customed to a king's taste.

The body was painted metallic green, with contrasting darker green fenders. The running board was very wide, so that three of Ibn Saud's slave-bodyguards could stand erect on either side of him while the car was in motion. There were also a siren and a searchlight for the body-guards to operate. Inside, the leather upholstery and the cabinetwork were in metallic green. Dominating the rear was a sterling silver bowl that could be filled from a copper water tank, equipment for Ibn Saud's Mohammedan ceremonial ablutions. After use, the water could be emp-tied out through a drain in the car floor. Other back-seat accessories included an electric fan to combat the desert heat, a super radio set, three built-in alabaster thermos flasks, and a chest containing three brushes and a comb. "We were careful," explained a Rolls-Royce designer, "to have the brush bristles made of Nylon, since the king, being a Moslem, would not use hog bristles." The entire rear seat of the car was built like a spacious royal throne, for one person, sufficiently broad so that Ibn Saud could sit on it cross-legged in Arab fashion.

Now, when Ibn Saud makes his annual journey to Mecca, he orders out his entire caravan of five hundred automobiles. Most of them—since they are transporting his three Moslem wives, many of his 150 divorced wives, and his vast harem of non-Moslem Armenian, Sudanese, and ref-ugee Russian girls—have window shades drawn to hide the veiled women. At the head of the caravan rides the only Rolls-Royce England produced during its six war years, and in the rear seat, alone, sits Ibn Saud with no window shades to hide his obvious pleasure and pride.

"And he darn well ought to be pleased," one Rolls-Royce director told me. "Because even if he doesn't know that Winnie interrupted our war effort to make the automobile for him, he should know by now that he has the best car in the whole world."

This boast—"the best car in the world"—which the Rolls-Royce peo-ple use in all their chaste literature, has very little absolute meaning. Being the best car in the world implies being better than one's competi-tors, but the Rolls-Royce is not meant to be compared with ordinary mass-produced vehicles. It stands by itself, in a special field of its own making, offered at a price that makes no pretense of competing econom-ically with other cars. Its very name has become a part of the language, and is used by every business from vacuum-cleaning concerns to Yo-Yo manufacturers as a synonym for the word "luxury." It is to other cars as a yacht is to a rowboat.

To Englishmen, the Rolls-Royce is not a crass piece of merchandise; it is an institution, wrapped in a carefully constructed tradition. Next to the royal family, next to the liner *Queen Elizabeth,* it is the fabulous Rolls-Royce and the list of international celebrities (ranging from maharajas and presidents to captains of industry and spiritual prophets) who own the car, that give most Englishmen their greatest feeling of national pride.

Englishmen will tell you, and there are few who would disagree, that with his green Rolls-Royce, Ibn Saud became a member of one of the world's most exclusive fraternities. It is a matter of fact that very few persons have ever owned new Rolls-Royces who were not famous or wealthy or both. Czar Nicholas II of Russia, whose income was about a million dollars a month, was one of the early buyers. In May, 1914, he purchased two seven-passenger Rolls-Royces, both upholstered in silk, from the company's Paris salesroom and had them shipped to Moscow. The czar used one for himself, and gave the other to his wife and Rasputin. About the same time, Hirohito's insane father, Emperor Yoshihito of Japan, regained just enough sanity to purchase a Rolls-Royce for his state limousine. It was painted cherry-red and black, with the imperial chrysanthemum hand-painted in gold on either door, and when it rolled down the streets of various Japanese cities, attendants sprinkled fresh sand before it.

But the most famous Rolls-Royce, during World War I years, was driven by a commoner. He was Colonel T. E. Lawrence, the enigmatic Lawrence of Arabia. The British government loaned him nine Rolls-Royces for his Arabian guerrilla campaign against the Turks. In a single day, using three of them, Lawrence wiped out a Kurdish cavalry regiment, captured two Turkish outposts, and blew up two bridges.

Once after the war, Lowell Thomas asked Lawrence, "Is there anything on earth to be bought with money that you can't afford but would like to have?" Lawrence smiled. "Perhaps it is childish," he replied wistfully, "but I should like my own Rolls-Royce car with enough tires and petrol to last me all my life."

It was this kind of postwar reverence for the luxury vehicle that inspired the friends of Woodrow Wilson to chip in and buy him a new Rolls-Royce as a get-well gift, when the tired ex-President was suffering his last illness in the house on S Street.

The Rolls-Royce is possessed by rulers and millionaires in almost every corner of the globe. On the Riviera, the Aga Khan, spiritual leader of the ten million Moslems known as Ismailis, owns an ornate Sedanca model Rolls. In Siam, the royal family possesses a pale blue, chromium-plated, community Rolls-Royce. It was purchased originally by King Rama VI, whose love for Things English also extended to his translating Shakespeare into Siamese. In Japan, Hirohito, like his father before him, has a Rolls-Royce to go with his maroon German Mercedes. In Mexico, President Alemán bought one of a recent shipment of Rolls-Royces to the New World for $13,000, a bargain since the price was raised to $18,787 a few weeks later. In Iran, Mohammed Reza Pahlevi, the reigning shah, drives about in a spacious, elderly, completely bulletproof Rolls-Royce. The shah's late father, an opium-smoking despot, bought the car when he took over the throne of Iran in 1925, always drove it at the head of a sixteen-car caravan—and, incidentally, upon staying overnight in a village had all the local dogs shot so that their barking might not disturb his sleep.

Even though the automobile is international, Englishmen, loyal to a home product, remain its best customers. King George VI, of course, has a Rolls-Royce. As a matter of fact, so do almost all other members of the royal family. Lord Louis Mountbatten, the last viceroy of India, has the most magnificent Rolls-Royce in the family. It is a $20,000 convertible, with a chauffeur enclosure that can be removed in London's rare moments of balmy weather. When the car was built, Lord Louis hovered over it like an expectant father. He supervised the decision on every dimension, demanding extra room both for his outstretched legs when reclining and for sitting upright when he wore a top hat, and he insisted that map cases be installed in the walnut paneling in the rear.

Other Englishmen emulate the royal family. Sir Alexander Korda bought an all-silver-colored Sedanca model. Sir Malcolm Campbell purchased a complete Rolls-Royce merely so that he could remove its engine, install this in a racing car, and, flashing over the Bonneville salt beds in Utah, become the first person to drive more than five miles a minute. Lord Derby, an invalid, had a Rolls-Royce uniquely custom-built to suit his infirmity, by having the back seat cut in half, one part removed, and a chromium-fitted wheelchair slipped in. To disguise the wheelchair from passersby, its upholstery exactly matched that of the car. Today, when he must attend a public function, Lord Derby snaps his chair loose, and glides down a specially designed ramp which his chauffeur has extracted from the trunk.

Second only to the popularity of the Rolls-Royce in England is the demand for it in the United States. Even before World War I, the Rolls was selling mightily in America and the directors of the company looked with new eyes upon the old colonies. In 1919, Rolls-Royce decided to expedite the delivery of cars in the States by setting up the Rolls-Royce of America, Inc., plant in Springfield, Massachusetts. The company, using skilled United States mechanics in addition to three hundred Crewe veterans, started with a capital of $3,200,000. Customers were assured that they were getting a genuine Rolls-Royce (with only the gears and carburetor modified), while paying a smaller price, since it could now be sold duty-free. But American customers did not bite. They wanted the real McCoy imported from England. After a few years, the Rolls-Royce invaders folded their tents and stole back to the sceptered isle, where they have remained ever since.

A large portion of Manhattan's high society crowd own, or have owned, the English car. Mrs. Cornelius Vanderbilt still rides in a 1913 model, painted in the traditional Vanderbilt maroon. The late J. P. Morgan had a Rolls-Royce, and now most of the Wall Street Morgan partners follow his lead and faithfully drive their own. Mrs. Otto Kahn gets about in an antique one that resembles a fugitive from a family album, a 1911 edition. One of the Woolworth girls has a Rolls-Royce discreetly furnished with a $3,000 vanity case and a $1,200 electric clock.

In Hollywood, the senior Douglas Fairbanks was one of the first Rolls-Royce owners. After him, the deluge. In the filming of Moss Hart's lush *Lady in the Dark*, a technicolor dream sequence resembling a cross between Mohammedan Heaven and Santa's Workshop required an appropriate dream automobile. The Countess di Frasso, a movieland butterfly, promptly loaned Paramount her Rolls-Royce at a rental of $240 a day. This chariot, which had cost around $28,000, had an all-aluminum body welded into a single unit. Another Hollywood figure, Constance Bennett, often picked up pin money renting studios her equally sumptuous but older Rolls-Royce, a $40,000 beauty. Before the war, Norma Shearer, Marlene Dietrich, Jack Warner, and Joseph Schenck all bought themselves $24,000 Rolls-Royces in New York or Paris.

Sundry other Americans have similarly indulged their automotive whims. The Smith brothers, kings of the coughdrop, long had an ancient Rolls-Royce in their garage. George Baker, once tried for lunacy in Georgia, better known to the faithful as Father Divine, had a $22,500 Rolls-Royce limousine that he had purchased secondhand in 1933 for $150.

Among the most fabulous Rolls-Royces ever owned by an American were the two town cars that eighty-four-year-old William Randolph Hearst purchased in Paris to join his Rembrandts, zebras, Egyptian mummies, private three-coach railway train, and million-dollar swimming pool at San Simeon. Each Rolls-Royce possessed, proportionately, as many mirrors as Versailles. In the rear, for the passenger, was a duplicate dashboard inlaid in walnut, several built-in thermos bottles, gold vanity cases filled with compacts and combs, a tiny wooden rolltop desk, a miniature table to be pulled out at mealtime, and a portable bar.

But such pleasures pale beside the automobile luxuries regarded as necessities by the princes of India. In their incredible toylands, these modern monarchs drive in Rolls-Royces that might have been designed for the tastes of a Midas or a Haroun al Raschid. The most majestic Rolls-Royce owner in India is the seventh Nizam of Hyderabad, richest man in the world with an estimated two and a half billion dollars in rubies, diamonds, and gold. Instead of a herd of elephants, the Nizam has fifty Rolls-Royces. His favorite is a canary-yellow model, furnished with elevated throne instead of a rear seat. It is thirty-six years old, which is impressive since the first Rolls-Royce was brought out only forty-three years ago. Despite its longevity, this Rolls-Royce has been driven only 400 miles. The Nizam's enemies say its owner is too stingy to drive it, since learning it consumes a gallon of gas every eight miles; the Nizam's friends say that he just has no place to go. According to the Rolls-Royce people, the most luxurious car they've sold the Nizam is "a London-Edinburgh chassis fitted with a special body for state drives." The special body is made of solid silver. The top of the car consists of a domed roof. The interior is decorated with old-gold brocade uphostery and lace curtains. The seats fold back into daybeds. And there are special drawers in the rear for shoes. The price paid for this mobile palace is unknown, but it is the most incredible Rolls-Royce, and probably the most expensive four-wheeled vehicle, on earth.

A good share of India's remaining 661 princes have Rolls-Royces custom-made to fit their own eccentricities. According to the Rolls-Royce company, the greatest quantity purchaser has been the thirty-four-year-old Maharaja of Patiala, a black-bearded giant who heads the ferocious Sikhs. While one maharaja bought five Rolls-Royces at once (presenting his used one to his favorite jockey), and while another maharaja bought six at one time (and sent them all back to be redecorated), the Maharaja of Patiala recently purchased thirty-five new Rolls-Royces. The maharaja, who owns a kennel of four hundred dogs, a private racetrack, and by budgeting keeps his household expenses down to $500,000 a year, has his Rolls-Royces furnished with handmade Swiss clocks, built-in medicine chests, gold-plated dashboards, seats upholstered in costly broadcloths and floors covered with lush beaver rugs. One car is used exclusively for hunting. It has special headlights designed to dazzle tigers, a sliding roof that allows the maharaja to stand and aim his gun, and steel-mesh windows to keep out attacking big game.

That the Rolls-Royce has become a standard plaything of the world's rulers, celebrities, and wealthy citizens is plain enough. But what are the characteristics that distinguish it and contribute to its popularity among the so-called upper classes?

A paramount factor behind its success is a carefully nurtured exclusiveness. From the very beginning, the founders of Rolls-Royce realized that, since almost anyone making a decent livelihood could afford an attractive mass-produced car, there must be a yearning among the landed gentry for exotic vehicles that would set them apart from the mobile peasantry. Toward this end, only 22,800 Rolls-Royces were produced between 1904 and 1939. Today, a mere 20 Rolls-Royces are made each week. The Detroit-style assembly line and mass production are unknown in Crewe. When American mechanics visited the Rolls factory before the war, they were amazed to find no conveyor belts. The chief engineer of one great American automotive company, after studying the Rolls-Royce motor, exclaimed, "Why, it's made like a wristwatch!" The Rolls is as close to being handmade as a car sold to the public can be.

The exorbitantly high price set on the car gives it further snob appeal. Of the four different models of Rolls-Royce made today, the cheapest, tax included, is $16,998, and the highest $18,787. In other words, the price of one new Rolls-Royce would buy several top-category American automobiles. Obviously, the restrictive price keeps out undesirable elements—like people who don't have their first million.

Rolls-Royce confines itself to making the chassis for these models and, by special arrangement, retains three famous coachmakers, Hooper and Company, H. J. Mulliner, Park Ward and Company, to build the bodies. In the near future, to keep the price down, Rolls-Royce plans to make its own bodies, allowing its coachmakers to fill only special orders.

Rolls-Royce, Ltd., makes great sacrifices to preserve the vehicle's exclusiveness. Several years ago, in the secret experimental chambers at Crewe, a handful of technicians invented a small, 15-horsepower vehicle that passed the 20,000-mile road test in a breeze. This new auto was the king-sized Rolls-Royce reduced to a compact, and was intended to be sold for one-tenth the big car's price, the poor man's dream. But in the final analysis, the board of directors, though they knew its production would bring them a considerable profit, vetoed the bantam. They felt its low price would enable anyone to own a "Rolls-Royce," thus destroying the exclusive appeal of the trade name. So the experimental model was dismantled and destroyed.

Another factor in the car's appeal, especially to hedonists, is its irresistible air of luxury. The four standard Rolls models vary only slightly in design. The Sedanca model has an open-air front seat for the chauffeur. The sports saloon makes the greatest concession to streamlining, with a curved instead of squared top and a slight torpedoing of the fenders. The touring limousine and the enclosed limousine are immense, heavy, rich, and square wagons. The standard Rolls-Royce, a six-cylinder car which holds seven passengers and 18 gallons of gas, and has four speeds plus reverse, is built with an aluminum body instead of steel to prevent paint trouble or rust, and is "tropicalized" to prevent fungus growth or deterioration in damp weather. The Rolls-Royce is equipped with a windshield defroster that melts ice, a warning light on the dashboard that signals when the gas supply is low, a right-hand-drive steering wheel, and hydraulic lifting jacks on the sides operated by a power pump hidden beneath the hood.

All this may be had at the regular cost of no more than $18,787. But the real promise of luxury is found in the following line in the Rolls-Royce catalogue: "Quotations can be supplied for bodies of other designs to suit customers' special requirements." Most Rolls-Royce buyers have "special requirements" and no objection to added costs. While many other automobiles, the earth around, are custom-built for a variety of eccentric and expensive tastes, none are specially equipped so frequently and daringly as the Rolls-Royce. One English lady had the rear of her Rolls-Royce fitted out with concealed washstand, chamber pot and cupboard, and blinds that could be pulled down. An English industrialist had a Chubb safe built into his car. One Indian prince had his steering wheel made of two tusks of ivory he sent from India, another prince had the windows of his car of a special blue glass which would enable his harem wives to look out without being seen, and still another prince had an electrically operated perfume spray constructed beside the rear seat. The Gaekwar of Baroda had his car interior upholstered in hand-embroidered silk which cost $32 per yard, while his wife sent a sample of her nail polish from India to London with the request that her Rolls-Royce limousine be painted in the same color. A wealthy African family, who had their Rolls-Royce roofed in canvas, requested holes for them to put their heads through so they could look about. A Middle East ruler had a small seat built on each running board to seat his lackeys. One Rolls-Royce boasted a collapsible bathtub in the rear; another, shown at the New York World's Fair, featured a revolving cocktail bar which rotated when an electric button was pushed, and countless Rolls-Royces have been equipped with built-in bags for golf clubs and special holders for skis.

But despite all of these added baubles, most of them hidden from sight, the Rolls-Royce is probably still the most conservative car on the market. Not only those who love exclusiveness and luxury buy it. It is also the car for those who worship tradition, longevity, and solidity. Perhaps this, rather than any other factor, is the car's greatest appeal. The Rolls-Royce has never completely submitted to the craze for streamlining. It remains, like the Englishmen who make and drive it, ancient, square, strong, unobtrusive, and dependable. While the car has undergone many modifications since its invention, two things stand unchanged. The basic outline of the car, a sleek, rectangular candy box, has not been forsaken in forty-three years. And the radiator grille remains today exactly as it was in 1904. This grille has provoked much argument within the firm. The younger Rolls engineers feel its square shape is an aesthetic eyesore and the design outmoded. They feel, also, that the shape creates continued difficulties in manufacturing—the welding of the sharp corners is a tricky task, and special machinery is necessary to make the silver plating perfectly flat. The opposing school of thought, which includes the directors of the firm and the agents who sell the car, doggedly declares, "There is something solid and permanent about the radiator, and though fashions and cars come and go, the Rolls-Royce is always the same."

The Silver Lady mascot, on the radiator cap, is another bait for lovers of tradition. She is over thirty years old. Some owners treasure her so much that they have her unscrewed and brought in with them when they dine away from home, to prevent theft. This has given rise to the story that the Silver Lady is made of pure silver, and worth a large amount of money. The Silver Lady is made of chromium and nickel-plating, nothing more, and her value is purely sentimental.

These unchanging factors of design, radiator grilles, and mascot serve to give the Rolls-Royce the appearance of timelessness. The Rolls people say that, while the life of the average automobile is seven years, it is not unusual to see fifteen- and twenty-year-old Rolls-Royces gliding about and appearing quite in style. As a matter of fact, Rolls-Royce was able to keep one unchanged model, the Silver Ghost, in production for nineteen years, longer than that of any other car model in history (including the Model-T Ford, which was in production for only eighteen years). The Silver Ghost model came out in 1907, and no change was made in it until 1925-26. Even in the twenties, according to Rolls engineers, this model did not seem old-fashioned, because its original design had been so far in advance of the times. After nineteen years, it still had the fastest pickup of any car in the world—from a standstill, it was able to attain a mile-a-minute speed in eighteen seconds. And in a day when most automobiles had the repose of a hula dancer, it was possible to balance a penny on the Rolls-Royce's hood with the engine idling.

One final factor serves to keep the Rolls-Royce popular on the blue-blood circuit. This is the unique three-year guarantee that accompanies each new car. If anything goes wrong in the first three years, repairs or replacements are made entirely free of charge. The directors of the company like to say they can make this guarantee because of the high quality of work done by their ten thousand employees. As the auto's creator, Sir Henry Royce, once remarked, "It's impossible for us to make a bad car—because the doorman wouldn't let it go out."

Only the Rolls-Royce factory at Crewe makes automobiles (the others at Derby and Glasgow turn out airplane engines), and here the work is painstaking. Some parts are tested as many as eight times before leaving the shop. No chassis leaves Crewe without traveling fifty miles in a trick saloon body, so built that it amplifies every unwarranted sound in the engine and transmission. The final test of a new model consists of 20,000 consecutive miles of rough driving through the Derbyshire hills, through London traffic, over the *routes nationales* of France, and into the Alpine passes of Switzerland. As a result of this care, Patrick Balfour, author of *Grand Tour*, was able to drive a Rolls-Royce to India without any trouble, and Humfrey Symons was able to drive a Rolls-Royce from London to Nairobi, Kenya, and back again, without adding "a single drop of water to its radiator."

In order to maintain the car throughout the world, and to facilitate spare-part replacement, Rolls-Royce, Ltd., has small service depots in Brussels, Rome, Zurich, Oslo, Lisbon, Copenhagen, New York, Bombay, and, "in season only," at Cannes and Biarritz. To work in these depots, English boys must go into apprenticeship at fifteen, become specialists at twenty-one, and only then are shipped to duty in some distant corner of the world. The technical heads of the depots are required to return to Crewe periodically, like old boys returning to Eton, to keep in touch.

Rolls-Royce, Ltd., is run more like a men's club than an automotive firm. This does not imply a disdain for profits. The firm has continually made money. Anyone farsighted enough to have invested $28,000 in Rolls stock over forty years ago could sell out for $250,000 today. (But this is admittedly only a drop in the bucket, compared to growth in stock value realized by less conservative companies.) Much of the Rolls-Royce company profits are reinvested to preserve the amenities of life—and the reputation of the car. There is a London School of Instruction over twenty years old for owners, their families, and their chauffeurs. Any Rolls-Royce driver may attend the school's lectures on correct lubrication and maintenance, and the lab demonstrations explaining the chassis, which last for twelve days. Upon completion of the course, the owner or chauffeur is rewarded with a sterling-silver badge.

Another club touch is the inspection service. During the three-year guarantee period, a Rolls-Royce representative ("usually public-school") calls upon the new owner annually. "Good day, Your Grace," the Rolls inspector will begin, "how are the pheasants this fine morning?" After an hour spent discussing the unpredictability of pheasants, the terrors of the local golf club, the scandalous conduct of Labour leaders, and the prospects at Aintree, the inspector will tactfully inquire as to the health of the automobile. Usually at this time the Rolls man will extract an immaculate set of overalls from his attaché case, pull them on, crawl under the car and examine it, then take the owner for a spin and gently point out how the car is being mishandled or neglected.

The chumminess with which Rolls-Royce, Ltd., approaches its customers is also practiced on its employees. Within the giant new auto factory at Crewe, in the airplane plant at Derby, and in that London turning, off Regent Street, where the main sales offices stand at 14-15 Conduit Street, the men who rule Rolls-Royce behave to each other like so many subdued Rotarians or Eagles. Every company executive and department head, no matter how important or unimportant he may be, addresses every other executive by initials. This was begun over two and a half decades ago, when many members of the firm who had been knighted by the current king were embarrassed at having their old co-workers call them "Sir." The General Works manager at Crewe, Ernest Hives, who started as a test driver and is now more directly responsible for producing the car than any other single executive, is known as "E. H." But the man who really guides the company today is "R."—Sir Henry Royce—dead fourteen years, but still the boss.

In 1947, the board of directors held a critical meeting in London. They were debating a technical change, a radical innovation in the postwar Rolls-Royce. The majority favored the change, but the minority refused to give in, and there resulted a stalemate. Finally, one dissenting director rose and said, "Most of you favor the change, but the important thing is—would Henry Royce have done it?" After a few moments, each man present agreed that Henry Royce would not have done it. Promptly, the majority switched their votes, and the innovation was unanimously dropped.

Royce was a powerful personality, brilliant and dogmatic, and most of the executives who run the firm today are his devoted disciples. Through them the impact of his person is still felt. Another factor which enables Royce to rule the company from the grave is "the bible."

Before World War I, Royce suffered a severe breakdown from overwork. He was given three months to live. He survived for twenty years. But he never again went within a hundred miles of the Rolls-Royce plants. Instead, he dwelt in a villa in southern France, in a seaside English-type house, surrounded by a permanent staff of three company designers and two personal secretaries. Royce ran the factory by correspondence, accurately remembering and discussing even the position of various machines. In 1915, after Royce had produced a flood of letters concerning his first airplane engine, the directors of the firm reverently collected all his correspondence and printed it as a 301-page book. Only six copies of the leather-bound volume were run off, and each was stamped on the blue cover "Strictly Private and Confidential." These six copies were distributed among the heads of the designing and engineering staffs to be used as reference volumes. Today, kept under lock and key, these books are called "the bible," and company executives like to murmur, "It is one of the most secret engineering documents in the world."

Frederick Henry Royce, the son of a miller, was born in 1863. After only one year at school, he found it necessary to work as a newsboy, telegraph messenger, railway apprentice, toolmaker, and electricity tester, until he invented an improved dynamo at the age of twenty-one, made money, and was able to marry. Enjoying his sudden prosperity, he bought a French car, but was dissatisfied with it, took it apart, found its faults, and decided to build a better car. On April Fool's Day, 1904, he tested his first handmade automobile. He drove it the fifteen miles from his workshop in Manchester to his home, followed by another car in case his creation broke down. But it did not break down, and thus the first Rolls-Royce was born. In this automobile, Royce did not try to give the world something new. He wasn't a trailblazer. Instead, he tried to give the world something improved, something better. In days when automobiles rattled, screeched, whined, and shook, Royce produced a quiet, gliding, 10-horsepower, two-cylinder, luxury buggy.

That same year, Royce was introduced to a young man named Charles Rolls, third son of a wealthy baron. Rolls, a daredevil balloonist, as well as a cycle and auto racer, had joined with a friend named Claude Johnson, a cultivated bibliophile, to open one of London's largest automobile salesrooms. Rolls and Johnson sold Panhards and Minervas, but when they went for a ride in Royce's new car, they were smitten. In March, 1906, Rolls-Royce, Ltd., was formed with a capital of $240,000. The new car, with models selling at from $1,580 to $3,560 each, was to be called Rolls-Royce-Johnson, but that was too cumbersome, and in the end it was called Rolls-Royce because that name had the sound of "quality, luxury, and something British."

In 1910, after being taken up for his first airplane ride by Wilbur Wright at Le Mans, France, Charles Rolls forgot about the new automobile that he was backing. He bought a Wright Brothers plane of his own, and in July of that same year, at the age of thirty-three, was killed while trying to pull it out of a steep dive. In the early twenties, Claude Johnson died. And so Henry Royce, surviving his own illness, ran the growing company alone via penny post.

Royce was a fantastic character. He was an engineer with no knowledge of mathematics. "I never use a slide rule," he said; "I can do simple arithmetic." His sense of touch was nearly perfect. Purely by feel, he once filed a brass hubcap into an exact-fitting hexagon. He took to playing the flute because he was interested in its sound waves, and he stopped going to church because, he insisted, "You can't be an engineer and still keep going to church." He hated waste and inefficiency. Once, observing a laborer awkwardly sweeping a shop floor, he yanked off his coat, grabbed the broom, and demonstrated how to use it properly. He abhorred golf and tennis because they were nonproductive pastimes, and advocated gardening instead. When he died in 1933, he left the surprisingly small estate of $450,000.

As a result of his death, one change was made in the Rolls-Royce car. The front nameplate, a small metal plaque on the radiator grille, had always been made of silver with the RR in red. The year of Royce's death, the RR was changed from red to mourning black. It has remained black until this day.

Today, it is the airplane engine—the first of which Royce finished in 1915—rather than the car engine, that brings the company its greatest amount of revenue. Rolls-Royce aero engines have made history. They fought the dogfights over France in World War I. They helped Alcock and Brown become the first humans to fly the Atlantic in 1919, eight years before Lindbergh. And during World War II, Rolls-Royce turned out 20,000 engines per year or one million horsepower per week, the only engine to fight against the Luftwaffe and help win the crucial Battle of Britain. Today, planes powered by Rolls-Royce hold every world's record set for piston and turbine engines.

But while the airplane engine brings in the big money, the men of Rolls-Royce spend most of their time coddling the automobile. It is their first love. All of their energies are devoted to the Rolls-Royce they are building for tomorrow. "The chief change in the postwar car," says W. A. Robothan, head engineer at Crewe, "will be in making it simpler. Today, the owner-driver is largely predominant, and only 5 percent are chauffeur-driven. We are going in for increased durability. Our target for the postwar car is that it should run 100,000 miles without a major overhaul, which on the average means ten years of life."

Recently, an English journalist most accurately summed up the wonder of Rolls-Royce, Ltd. "It is as British as the weather," he concluded. "It stands for the highest grade precision work, yet can turn its hand to mass production. Its name means civilian luxury, yet its products won the aerial dogfights that saved Britain and mankind. It serves the elite, yet is run by promoted laborers in soft collars.

"No one understands Britain who does not understand Rolls-Royce."

WHAT HAS HAPPENED SINCE . . .

A slightly shorter version of this story on Rolls-Royce appeared in *The Saturday Evening Post* for November 8, 1947. When I had researched the story in London, a half year before, I had found the Rolls-Royce people friendly but somewhat less than fully cooperative. As *Inside Information*, the house organ of the Curtis Publishing Company, explained it at the time:

"To Wallace, brought up like all other Americans on a diet of promotion and advertising, their reluctance came as a surprise. He learned that Rolls-Royce gives practically no information to British magazines and absolutely nothing to the newspapers.

" 'They were very stuffy about it and did not approve,' he says. 'I was unable to get any cooperation in doing research, and none of the officials would talk about the cars they were manufacturing for Indian princes and such.'

"The writer patiently set out to explain to the Rolls-Royce management that their business would not be hurt by a magazine article, that undoubtedly many people in the United States had mistaken ideas about the company and the high prices it charged for its motorcars. Perhaps Wallace's own use of advertising and promotion techniques impressed them; in any event, their air of aloofness became one of friendly—though a trifle reserved—cooperation.

" 'When I broke them down, finally, the word got around London fast,' Wallace says. 'A few evenings later the editor of a big London daily telephoned me at the Savoy Hotel. He had heard, he said, that I was doing a piece on Rolls-Royce for *The Saturday Evening Post* and that I was getting material.'

"Then the editor asked Wallace, 'Could I have a reporter come around and interview you, old chap?'

" 'But why interview me?' Wallace replied. 'I'm not a story.'

" 'Well, you see, it's the only way we might find out something about Rolls-Royce!' the editor told him."

The point of the published anecdote was, indeed, correct. In fact, a year later, the English magazine, *John Bull*, had to come to me in the States to request permission to reprint my story in order to inform their readers about one of their great English institutions.

Less accurate, however, was another anecdote in *Inside Information*:

"Wallace, by the way, does not own a Rolls-Royce. We thought it might be of interest to have a picture of him with his own bruised automobile by way of contrast with the subject of his article.

" 'Unfortunately,' Wallace told us, 'the idea won't work very well with my car—I own a Cadillac. If you go out in the streets in Hollywood in anything less, they stone you.' "

That the editors had hoped to pose me with my own jalopy, as a telling contrast to the car I had written about, but had then canceled the idea with dismay when they learned I owned a Cadillac, was true. But the final quip, that I owned a Cadillac out of fear that I would be stoned if I drove anything less, was sheer flippancy. I owned a Cadillac (and drove beyond my means) because when I had learned to drive, I'd dreaded the whole business of having to learn to use a clutch and hand shift. I wished it were possible to learn to drive in a vehicle that had eliminated complicated shifting by hand. Then to my amazement and delight, I learned that there *was* such a car. General Motors had just produced a Cadillac with a new, completely automatic shift. In short, you could drive it—and look, no hands. I begged, I borrowed, perhaps I even stole. But that is how I came to the Cadillac—and how *Inside Information* lost its picture.

In the years following my own difficulties with the Rolls-Royce management, I kept an eye on the company's promotional activities. I was able to observe a gradual change in its relationship with the press and the public. To survive in the new world, half Communistic, half democratic, where royalty and billionaires were fast becoming curiosities, Rolls-Royce had to become a people's car—a rich people's car, to be sure, but a people's car nonetheless—instead of a car merely for the pedigreed. As a consequence, the Rolls-Royce management had to unbend, open its doors, seek the people, meet the people, sell the people—and yet not destroy their snob appeal. Apparently, Rolls-Royce straddled the fence successfully. If they found as many businessmen, physicians, and attorneys buying Rolls-Royces as were the diminishing ranks of royalty, it did not mean that the car's image and exclusivity had been tarnished. It only meant that there now existed a new, broader-based, moneyed elite. Rolls-Royce had let down its hair—and was no less attractive for having done so. A Rolls-Royce dealer in San Francisco remarked with pride, and in justification, recently: "As yet we haven't sold many to people who wash their own cars."

The promotional turning point in modern Rolls-Royce history—if one must pinpoint a date—probably occurred in 1958. In that year, the Rolls-Royce management retained advertising man David Ogilvy, along with the other partners in his firm, to help increase sales of the luxury car in the United States. Ogilvy, educated in Edinburgh and at Oxford, had become a New York advertising legend. He had given "the man in the Hathaway shirt" an eye patch, and had made the New World conscious of such necessities of the good life as Schweppes and Beefeater. The

Rolls-Royce management recruited him to do what he could for their motorcar.

After a brief study, Ogilvy decided that what was wrong was the static Rolls-Royce image. The image, he suggested, should be altered. For one thing, chauffeurs were passé. The Rolls-Royce had to become a vehicle for do-it-yourself drivers. Dukes and duchesses, maharajas, and Middle East billionaires who reclined in the well-appointed back seats, were out. The Rolls-Royce must become an acceptable vehicle for highly solvent behind-the-wheel republicans and citizens. Baronial castles and Mediterranean yachts were going, and would soon be gone. The Rolls-Royce must take the family to the beach or picnic, and afterward be lodged beneath a carport or inside a garage attached to an unpretentious, modern American house. The old snob sell used in previous advertisements—"The Best Car in the World"—had become obsolete. The new sell should emphasize comfort, durability, and long-range economy.

And so Ogilvy created a fresh advertising campaign for the Rolls-Royce, with the memorable headline: AT 60 MILES AN HOUR THE LOUDEST NOISE IN THIS NEW ROLLS-ROYCE COMES FROM THE ELECTRIC CLOCK. This was an enormously effective sales technique with the buying public. But —even though the story may be apocryphal—I have been told that the publicity was not appreciated by a dedicated Rolls-Royce engineer in Crewe, who, upon reading the new advertisement, took it as a personal rebuke. The engineer thought that he'd better have another look at that damn clock. Now the electric clock, too, is silent.

The plebeian appeal in advertising has continued. An advertisement in *The New Yorker* during 1965 included the following copy:

"Myth has it that Rolls-Royce is very aloof about who can buy a Rolls-Royce or Bentley car—and that if you are lucky enough to buy one of these cars, it will be taken away from you if you don't take proper care of it. Nonsense! Rolls-Royce is as anxious to sell its products as any manufacturer is. It's *easy* to buy a Rolls-Royce. . . . Many women tend to shy away from driving the Rolls-Royce—until they get in it, drive it around a bit, discover that the Rolls-Royce is a *family* car—and give their husbands an ultimatum to buy one by such and such a date *or else!*"

Other recent Rolls-Royce advertising, while still emphasizing that the car can be equipped with such luxuries as a miniature bar, now mention accessories of more practical use to the family. In the four-door saloon model, potential buyers are reminded that the Rolls-Royce now offers "built-in mineral water rack and special reading light," as well as "built-in picnic tables." All well and good, those picnic tables, but one feels that King Ibn Saud of Saudi Arabia and the Nizam of Hyderabad would have been aghast.

When I set out recently to investigate what had happened to Rolls-

Royce since 1947, I found that this altering of the image was one change that had taken place. As a corollary, the management had become considerably more receptive to publicity. When I made inquiries of the management about the latest developments concerning the automobile, I received immediate and direct replies. When I wanted to read what had been written about the car since I had written about it, I was pleased to find no dearth of articles in periodicals and newspapers of recent years. But I also found out something else that was quite gratifying: My story about the motorcar, like the car itself, had suffered little depreciation across the years. An article about an American automobile, written in 1947, would be entirely out of date today. My article on Rolls-Royce, except for very minor changes and modifications, was as accurate in the mid-sixties as when it had been written.

Today, the Rolls-Royce remains the most expensive automobile in the world. While there is a simple four-door model that may be purchased for around $18,000, the Rolls-Royce convertibles and limousines sell for prices varying from $27,000 to $30,000 each. The only car nearly as costly is Rolls-Royce's sibling, the Bentley, which has a model that sells for $26,000. Below that, for the more insecure rich, I found a German Mercedes-Benz that sells for $20,500, an Italian Maserati that sells for $16,-300, a French Facel that sells for $15,500, and an Italian Ferrari that sells for $14,200. The most expensive American cars are the Lincoln Continental convertible, which may be purchased for $6,940, and the Cadillac convertible, which may be bought for $6,630.

In 1947, I related how Rolls-Royce had built an economy edition of their big car, an experimental model, which they considered putting on the mass market. But at that time, they rejected the idea because they felt that it would destroy the exclusiveness of the big car. In 1964, the Rolls-Royce management finally decided to go after the mass market with a smaller, cheaper vehicle which was still, at least in part, a Rolls-Royce. Collaborating with another company, the British Motor Car Corporation, makers of the Austin and MG, Rolls-Royce produced a small automobile known as the Vanden Plas Princess "R"—the "R" being the Rolls-Royce part of it. The only portion of the car that is genuine Rolls-Royce, actually the most important portion, is the engine, a modification of one used in Rolls-Royce trucks. This hybrid baby Rolls, which can attain a speed of 112 miles per hour, sells for $5,600.

One major change that took place at the Rolls-Royce plant in Crewe was that, in 1949, for the first time, the company began to produce a complete motorcar. At the time I had written about Rolls-Royce, its makers had never made a car with a body. The makers did not believe in bodies, because they felt that they were engineers and not carpenters.

In those days, while Royce assembled its perfect chassis, one of Great Britain's three leading coachbuilders prepared a customed body. But in 1949, the engineers ceased looking down their noses at the carpenters. Rolls-Royce, Ltd., bought out and absorbed one of the most venerable coachbuilders in England, Park Ward, Ltd., and began to produce not only a chassis but a body. However, for elaborate custom-made bodies, the services of either 250-year-old Hooper and Company, or Mulliner, are still retained.

I was pleased to note that, despite all its concessions to a plebeian consumer public, Rolls-Royce has remained the darling of the royal, the wealthy, and the renowned. However, it is true, as I have indicated, that the changing world has made itself felt. A member of the Soviet Russian hierarchy, Anastas Mikoyan, has had a Rolls-Royce for a dozen years, one which he drives to the Kremlin himself. *The New York Times* has pointed out that when, in another age, the Maharajah of Patiala purchased six new Rolls-Royces in one day, it was front-page news. But in 1960, an American family in Indianapolis bought six Rolls-Royces in a single day, and the event was hardly mentioned in the press at all. Furthermore, there are now American firms who lease Rolls-Royces by the month or rent them by the day—to *anyone*. One New York City car rental company has twenty-eight Rolls-Royces, and each is rented out for nine dollars an hour. And *The New York Times* found a Harlem chauffeur who possesses his own big Rolls-Royce—fitted inside with stocked liquor cabinet and French walnut desk—which he rents out along with his own services daily to such visiting celebrities as Vice-President Hubert Humphrey, Aristotle Onassis, Margot Fonteyn, and Lana Turner.

The elite, however, continue to patronize Rolls-Royce. Not only does Queen Elizabeth own a special large model assembled exclusively for royalty and heads of state, but Princess Margaret and the Duchess of Kent have similar models. Wealthy and mysterious financiers like the Armenian oil billionaire, Nubar Gulbenkian, and celebrities like Gregory Peck, the actor, are Rolls-Royce owners. Today, one could not travel far through the Near East or India without seeing the familiar Silver Lady mascot on a radiator. Last summer, I stood outside the Monte Carlo Casino one weekday evening and counted five brand-new Rolls-Royces in the parking area.

Despite the fact that the Rolls-Royce continues to be a vehicle designed mainly for a privileged class, its management persists in fighting down the image they once so carefully built. When *The New York Times* repeated the oft-told story about Rolls-Royce, Ltd., paying $15,-000 to buy back an old Rolls-Royce that was about to be converted into an ordinary taxicab, the company's promotion personnel in New York immediately declared the story false. I have their release before me. It reads:

"It has been rumored that Rolls-Royce has paid up to $15,000 in the U.S. to prevent the use of one of its cars as a taxicab. . . . No modern-day manufacturer would attempt to prescribe ways in which a car might or might not be used. It is unlikely that a door-to-door huckster might use a Rolls-Royce in his daily rounds, and Rolls-Royce executives might inwardly wince if they saw a Rolls-Royce being used as a blatantly commercial vehicle, as would any maker of a quality product. However, most of those who buy Rolls-Royce will inevitably display discretion and taste. Otherwise they probably wouldn't buy a Rolls-Royce in the beginning."

Going on with my investigation of the changes in the Rolls-Royce since 1947, I learned that the number of Rolls-Royces produced in ensuing years has not increased dramatically. The Rolls-Royce has never been, and probably will never be, an assembly-line car turned out by the hundreds of thousands. In an average year, there may be 1,200 Rolls-Royces sold in Great Britain, and 600 sold in the United States.

Since the Rolls-Royce is crafted and assembled by hand, no more than thirty-five a week, or 1,800 a year, are produced at Crewe. On the other hand, there are 150,000 Cadillacs produced annually in Detroit. Where it requires only five minutes to assemble a Cadillac, it takes almost ten weeks to assemble a Rolls-Royce.

In 1964, the managing director in charge of Rolls-Royce production was a gray-haired Doctor of Philosophy named F. Llewellyn Smith. Under him there were seven thousand persons devoted to making the Rolls-Royce. Since the company still guarantees mechanical repairs on a Rolls-Royce for three years (American-made cars generally carry guarantees of three months), and since the average Rolls-Royce is expected to have a vigorous lifetime of fifteen years and cover 150,000 miles without a major repair (one Rolls-Royce is said to have covered 500,000 miles, and is still as active as ever), the standards of production are as rigorous today as I found them to be in 1947.

The company takes pride in the durability of its product, and to dramatize this aspect of the automobile's value, the company permitted Metro-Goldwyn-Mayer to make, and release in 1965, a motion picture bearing the title *The Yellow Rolls-Royce*. The star of the film, the lemon-colored car, is seen as it affects the lives of three of its owners during thirty years, one owner a British diplomat, another an American gangster, another an American millionairess who smuggles it to the Yugoslavian underground during World War II. Although Ingrid Bergman and Jeanne Moreau appeared in this ode to an automobile, one film reviewer was moved to write, "The Rolls-Royce is probably the most elegant thing in the picture. And if nothing else, the film is a testimonial to its endurance."

To assure this longevity for each 4,650-pound Rolls-Royce, experts spend three weeks and $700 in testing each individual motorcar. Once a Rolls-Royce leaves the assembly section of the vast one-story eight-acre factory in Crewe, it goes across the road to the testing department. After running each car for forty miles on rollers, and then driving it hard over 150 miles of country roads, it is brought back for an analysis of its weaknesses and for adjustments. Each Rolls-Royce must pass ninety-eight separate tests. If the test driver hears so much as a faint whine in a rear axle, an expert will go after that whine with a stethoscope, until it is located and muffled. Each door is opened and closed 100,000 times by an automatic rig to determine if it is correctly fitted and quiet. Silence is an obsession in Crewe, as always. The Rolls-Royce passengers are expected to be able to carry on a conversation in a normal tone of voice, even when the car is going 110 miles per hour.

As far as I could learn, the variety of modern Rolls-Royces is as luxurious and individual as ever. The wood used for the dashboard, door interiors, and folding table in a Rolls-Royce is cut from a single walnut log approved by the company. No car leaves the plant without at least fourteen, and sometimes as many as nineteen, coats of paint. Rolls-Royces continue to be ordered with unusual and eccentric accessories, just as they were ordered by the wealthy in the old days—recently an elderly arthritic English Dame had a small elevator attached to the running board of her Rolls; another customer ordered a Rolls with a collapsible bathtub inside and window shades; one maharaja ordered his Rolls with a built-in safe. Cecil Michaelis, the English painter, ordered his Rolls-Royce with an artist's studio in the rear, and received one with built-in easel, movable roof and side panels to give him ample light and a view of the passing landscape, and seats that converted into a daybed.

The best illustration of the traditional Rolls-Royce, surviving unchanged, is its radiator grille with the mascot on the radiator cap. The design and shape of the grille today are exactly what they were in 1905, only the grille is somewhat larger than in 1905, because the motorcar itself is larger. In the beginning, Henry Royce, learning what the radiator grille cost to make, had railed against it as "a rather stupid luxury"— but allowed it to remain, because he was seduced by its classic beauty. And so the radiator grille, made of burnished stainless steel, soldered by the nation's foremost tinsmiths, has remained. And so has the Silver Lady mascot adorning the top of the grille. Every Rolls-Royce leaving the factory has featured the Silver Lady on her prow—except one.

Queen Elizabeth of England had her Rolls-Royce ornament replaced by a sterling-silver mascot representing St. George and the Dragon, designed by the royal silversmiths, who smashed the mold after pouring a single cast.

However, the motorcar produced by Rolls-Royce, Ltd., today is no more than the company's toy and symbol of prestige. The real profits come from the company's airplane works in Derby and Glasgow. Eighty-five percent of the company's sales are related to aircraft production. While 7,000 employees continue to concentrate on the motorcar, there are 42,000 others who are dedicated to airplane research, design, and manufacture. Today, more than half of the world's airlines are flying planes propelled by Rolls-Royce jet or propjet engines. And in 1964, Rolls-Royce announced that it was developing an airplane that would hurtle through space without any engine at all. As Rolls-Royce executives told the press:

"A new method of propulsion known as surface burning involves no combustion chambers, no air intakes, and no compressors or turbines. Virtually all that remains is the fuel. . . . The idea is to use the shock wave produced by a wedge shape at very high speeds to compress the air behind the wedge so much that, when fuel is injected into it, it explodes. The burning fuel produces a forward thrust. In principle, surface burning could be used for flying at speeds between about five and fifteen times that of sound."

But despite the successful advances made by the company in the field of aviation, I suspect that the name Rolls-Royce, at least in our time, will continue to be synonymous with the most luxurious of automobiles.

Wondering how the Rolls-Royce rates today, speculating on its strengths and its weaknesses, I consulted a number of automotive writers and their published works. The pro and con about the Rolls-Royce seem to be as follows:

In its favor: Unexcelled materials, craftsmanship, roadability, driving pleasure, quietness, comfort. The Rolls-Royce depreciates less in cash value than any other car. The Rolls-Royce bestows social prestige. No American car, said Ken W. Purdy, the automotive authority, provides "that air of utter solidity—a manor-house-on-wheels effect—that Messrs. Rolls-Royce achieve by design, finish, masses of walnut and leather, back-seat cocktail cabinets with cut-glass decanters, and so on."

Against it: Behind the times in mechanical improvements and design. The Rolls-Royce still uses old-fashioned drum brakes instead of advanced disc brakes, and old-fashioned non-independent rear suspension. It lacks safety devices, such as a padded dashboard. Its sitting room and luggage space are too confined. But above all, just not enough of those modern innovations.

For the first time in its history, Rolls-Royce is being compared to other automobiles in its own class, and occasionally to its disadvantage. Several British car experts have admitted that certain American automobiles drive more quietly than the Rolls-Royce. And Purdy recently committed major heresy in automotive circles by announcing that the Mercedes-Benz 600 sedan was one "deluxe motorcar mechanically more advanced than the Royce." According to Purdy, the Mercedes-Benz was "more comfortable than a Rolls-Royce, safer, faster, better handling. It will lack but one thing: the inimitable *cachet*, the tapestried legend of the Rolls-Royce."

To all such criticism the members of the Rolls-Royce management reply with unrelenting firmness. They will not introduce disc brakes, until they can eliminate any accompanying brake squeal. They will not change their rear suspension system, until they can find a means of doing so without bringing on "a wholly unacceptable transmission of road and axle noise and transmission jerks." Rolls-Royce will not change its mechanical apparatus or design simply to give its salesmen something new to promote. As the managing director, Dr. Smith, said to a London reporter: "Innovation is not merit in itself, you know. . . . Most innovation in motorcars nowadays is just gadgetry."

» 12 «

THE MAN WHO SWINDLED
GOERING

LATE IN MAY of 1945, shortly after the American Seventh Army had located the late Hermann Goering's five-hundred-million-dollar art collection in Germany's subterranean vaults, special Allied teams led by United States Army's Monuments and Fine Arts Division arrived at the Field Marshal's villa south of Berchtesgaden to recover and classify the plunder. The collection of twelve hundred paintings, most of it representing Nazi loot taken from the major galleries of Europe, was dazzling. None of the investigators, knee-deep in Raphaels and van Goghs, regarded the oil *Christ and the Adultress*—signed by Jan Vermeer, the seventeenth-century Dutch painter—as anything more than another of Goering's numerous "acquired" masterpieces.

The Allied investigators could not foresee that very soon this Vermeer painting would start a curious chain reaction of exposures that would first explode in Holland, and then rock all the art capitals of Europe. They could not know that their routine discovery would generate an artistic controversy that would rage through the remainder of 1945, through all of 1946, and give promise of being extended, amid intrigue, violence and high passion, into 1947.

Yet the most dramatic and fantastic art scandal of modern times, exposing a crime (which started as a practical joke) involving over three million dollars, and more important, involving the reputations of some of the world's leading art critics and experts, began exactly on that day the Allied investigators learned Goering possessed a Vermeer. The springboard for the scandal, however, was not Goering's possession of the Old Master, but rather, the discovery of his means of obtaining it. Had it been merely pilfered, like so many of his objets d'art, like the Rubenses and Rembrandts lifted from Amsterdam museums, it could have been quietly returned to its rightful owner and the case closed. But strangely, this oil was one of a small group that had not been stolen.

A zealous Dutch expert, assigned to one of the Allied investigating teams, stumbled upon the fact while glancing curiously through Herr Goering's private papers and documents. The Dutch expert found a receipt, made out to Goering from Amsterdam, marked "Paid." It was a receipt for the Vermeer. It proved, conclusively, that someone in the Netherlands had coldly sold the great painting to Goering's art procurer, Walther Hofer, in 1943 for 1,600,000 gulden. Someone had carried on a business collaboration with the number-two Nazi.

The Dutch expert, studying his evidence, was profoundly shocked. The audacity of it made his outraged patriotic and aesthetic sensibilities swim. For the sale of a Vermeer to an enemy was not an ordinary act of collaboration. Thousands of Dutchmen had cooperated with the Germans, and been caught, and duly blotted out. But if collaboration was a run-of-the-mill crime, the mishandling of a Jan Vermeer was a warped and horrible act. Jan Vermeer, born at Delft in 1632, was and is, like Rembrandt, a Dutch national hero. There have been few internationally great Dutchmen, and of these few, a great percentage were painters. Vermeer is among the foremost of these. Numerous streets and public squares in Holland bear his name. His statue decorates public buildings, and his three dozen authentic works are carefully reproduced and hung in even the poorest homes. His obscure personal history is studied religiously in Dutch classrooms, even as General George Washington is studied in American classrooms. Each of Vermeer's yellow-and-blue oils is a state treasure—and the sale of one to an enemy is a crime of treason comparable only to the possible kidnaping and sale to an enemy of that other more bulky state treasure, Queen Wilhelmina.

Enraged at his find, the Dutch expert collected the Vermeer painting, the available evidence and scurried back to his government in The Hague. There was a brief meeting, a discussion, and then swiftly the wheels of justice began turning.

The Dutch authorities went directly to the home of the man in Amsterdam who had sold the picture to Goering's agent. This man was Aloys Miedl, a Bavarian, who had moved to Holland from Germany after marrying a Jewish girl. He had been an old friend of Goering's, and during the war had sold the Nazi many lesser Dutch objets d'art. But the Dutch authorities did not find Miedl at home. He had fled, weeks before, to Spain. The Dutch then learned that Miedl had acquired the picture from an art dealer in Amsterdam. They hurried to this art dealer. He insisted that he was not to blame. He had only handled the picture on commission for another. And who was the other? A little man named Reinstra. The authorities went after Reinstra. He was a professional go-between, a man who lived by his wits, often persuading artists to permit him to sell their works through dealers on commission. He vehemently disclaimed any knowledge of collaboration. He had obtained the picture from someone else. The authorities were becoming impatient. From whom had Reinstra obtained the Vermeer? From van Meegeren, he said. Hans van Meegeren, an artist in Amsterdam.

The authorities went to van Meegeren. He proved to be a gray little man, high-strung, childish, with a half-foxy, half-humorous face. He dwelt, with the unhappy second wife whom he had divorced the year before, in a huge, glittering marble-halled mansion that squatted on a canal. He was wealthy, owned fifty houses, two nightclubs, and two original Old Masters (one a Franz Hals). He had made his grubstake, three million dollars, by selling his collection of six Vermeers. Five he had sold to great museums in The Hague, Rotterdam, and Amsterdam. The sixth Vermeer had been *Christ and the Adultress*. The authorities were curious about only the sixth, the one that had been sold to Goering. Where had he got it? From a collection he had bought in Italy. The authorities jumped at this. He had bought from Italian Fascists? And sold to German Nazis? He was promptly arrested.

Van Meegeren spent three weeks in jail. These weeks were a torment. He was not permitted his bottles of gin. He was not brought his sleeping pills. He became hysterical. He sank into melancholia. He suffered epileptic fits. Then, without being given a reason, he was released. A few days later, just as he was beginning to recover from the experience, the Dutch police reappeared. They arrested him again, and took him to the central station in Amsterdam. There, they began to bombard him with questions. Through midnight into the morning, they grilled him. They wanted him to admit he was a collaborator, to admit he had sold a sacred Vermeer knowingly to the Nazis. He refused. They hammered. Then, as dawn broke, van Meegeren cracked.

"You idiots!" he shrieked at the police. "You fools! I sold no national treasure to the Germans. I sold no Vermeer. I sold a van Meegeren! I sold a Vermeer forged with my own hands!"

Van Meegeren rapidly dictated his confession. He had faked six Vermeers between 1937 and 1943. The first he had sold, as an original Vermeer, to the Boyman's Museum of Rotterdam. The last he had sold, as an original Vermeer, to Hermann Goering. He had received eight million Dutch gulden, $3,200,000, for these hoaxes. He ranted on that he had fooled respected museum heads who had purchased the paintings, the art historians and scientists who had tested and expertized them, and above all, dozens of European and American art critics who had written glowing reviews of the spurious Vermeers. He had proved, he boasted, that he was as good as the old masters and that the critics who had so long harassed him were asses. He could not be a collaborator, because he had sold no state treasure to the Nazis, only one of his own forgeries.

His police confession was blazoned in print throughout the Netherlands the next morning, and thereafter in newspapers throughout the world. His confession began:

"Driven by the psychological effect of being disappointed in not being acknowledged by my fellow artists and critics, on a fatal day in 1936 I decided upon proving to the world my value as a painter and resolved to make a perfect seventeenth-century painting."

The Dutch police were confused. If the man's confession was correct, and he was simply a forger, then certainly he could not be a collaborationist. One way or the other, he was guilty of a crime. But the crimes were leagues apart. If he had sold original Vermeers, and was a collaborator, then the case was open and shut, a local affair. On the other hand, if he had painted his oils in the manner of Vermeer, signed the master's name, and palmed them off as genuine, he was not a collaborator but a faker whose act had international implications. The Dutch police decided to summon the leading Dutch art experts. The police did not have to go far. The art experts were already on hand, at once anxious and indignant. The police asked their opinion. The Vermeers that they had once judged and accepted, they insisted, were still absolutely authentic. Their reputations and livelihoods were based on the authenticity of these Vermeers. They dared not be made fools of now. Van Meegeren, they chorused, was a drunken scoundrel for claiming the authorship of such classics. He had not forged and sold fake Vermeers. He had obtained and resold authentic Vermeers. Their opinion was unanimous, and they were stuck with it.

The controversy raged in the press, the cafés, the homes of Holland. It fanned out into London, Paris, Rome. It trickled into New York and Chicago. One way or the other, Hans van Meegeren was a criminal. That was clear. But again that was not the important point. The important point was that the oft-debated question of the absolute knowledge and integrity of experts, upon whose judgments museums and private collectors were dependent, and of critics, upon whose opinions the layman was dependent, stood on trial. For if van Meegeren was a forger, he had proved that, while there were numerous honest and competent men in the world of art, there were also those who judged too hurriedly and impulsively, those who praised too often according to signature and not merit, those who did not know what was true and what was false. To

make this point against his own critics, a point which he claimed provoked his gigantic hoax, van Meegeren begged to be declared guilty of
forgery. And on the other side, his rivals, the dealers, essayists, museum
heads, art detectives, the whole camp intimately involved and
committed, fought bitterly to have him proved not guilty of this charge.

Were the six Vermeers, hanging in great museums and galleries, were
they by Jan Vermeer (1632-1675) or by Hans van Meegeren (1889-?)?

The Netherlands authorities debated. Then one minor official, inheri-
tor of the mantle of Solomon, made a suggestion. Why not let Hans van
Meegeren paint, under police supervision and in full view of all concerned, a new forgery in the manner of Vermeer? This seventh portrait
might prove, once and forever, whether he was capable of forging an old
master so magnificently or whether he was merely trying to save himself
from collaborationist charges. The proposition was made. Van Meegeren happily agreed. The experts unhappily agreed. The newspapers,
elated, printed banner headlines—ARTIST PAINTS FOR HIS LIFE!

Less than a year ago, van Meegeren began his peculiar labor of defense. The authorities requisitioned a large studio, but barred its windows like a prison. The authorities permitted him to acquire all the necessary canvas, oils, other materials, but refused to allow him the months
of planning and study he claimed he had found necessary in the past.
The authorities presented him with a daily ration of Burgundy wine,
extra packs of scarce cigarettes, a bottle of sleeping tablets, but they left
insensitive police guards to hover in his studio night and day.

"I'm enjoying it," he told a friend who visited him at work. "But it is
difficult. I do not have the exact oils and I do not have the time to think.
They rush me. And they look over my shoulder when I work. Still, I
believe it will be beautiful. But outside, they are against me. They've
already judged this work. They will stare at it, and knowing it is not a
Vermeer, they will cluck their tongues and say well done, well done, but
really, it is not Vermeer. They will find tiny flaws now to prove this is
not a seventeenth-century work, and they will say that a madman could
not forge an Old Master."

As van Meegeren's oil took shape, it proved to be a depiction of the
Child Christ in the Temple of the Elders. Six figures on a broad canvas.
All the famed Vermeer trademarks were in it—the exquisite rich yellows
and blues, the refinement of technique, the pointillé touch. Physically,
the work was foolproof—seventeenth-century linen used for the canvas,
the paint overheated exactly as Vermeer and Rembrandt had overheated
their paints, the brushes made of badger hair the same as the brushes
wielded by artists of the 1600's.

At last the job, Exhibit A, was done. The Dutch authorities appointed
a special jury of international art experts, including authorities from Ox-

ford University, Harvard University, and the Rijks Museum of Amsterdam to study it. Van Meegeren's fate would depend entirely on the jury's report. A decision would be reached in May, 1946. But the month of May came and went, and the jury reached no conclusion. A new date was announced. A decision would be made public in September, 1946. This month came and passed. Still the jury studied, meditated, debated, wrangled.

Few who followed the case were surprised at the delay. They pointed out that determining the origin of a really well-done oil, which stood on trial for forgery, was often as difficult as deciding the guilt of a defendant, on circumstantial evidence, in a nearly perfect murder. Many remembered the bitter battle, seventeen years before, surrounding the authenticity of a second *La Belle Ferronnière* by Leonardo da Vinci. On that occasion, a Mrs. Andrée Hahn, who'd had the da Vinci in her family for years, was frustrated in her effort to sell it to the Kansas City Art Institute for $250,000 because the English expert, Sir Joseph Duveen, judged it a fraud, a mere student's copy of the alleged da Vinci original that hung in the Louvre. Mrs. Hahn haled the English expert into court. For almost three weeks, expert argued against expert. Sir Joseph contended that the da Vinci in the Louvre had been in the possession of France for four hundred years and was unquestionably by the master's hand and that Mrs. Hahn's painting was a copy. Mrs. Hahn's rebuttal was spearheaded by George Sortais, who arrived from Paris to insist that the da Vinci in the Louvre was an inferior copy made by Beltraffio and that unquestionably Mrs. Hahn's was the original. In the end, no conclusive decision was reached on which da Vinci was the original and which the copy, although it was announced in print that Mrs. Hahn withdrew her suit against Duveen "in return for an indemnity of $60,-000."

Today, as in the case of many such precedents, the van Meegeren controversy is, understandably, still at a stalemate behind locked doors. A special gallery in Amsterdam, with all of van Meegeren's six Vermeers and his fateful seventh decorating the walls, is the headquarters of the jury. Some members, befuddled, have withdrawn. New experts are promptly appointed when this happens. Constantly, from all over Europe, fresh critics and art detectives are brought in as consultants. Meanwhile, Dutch authorities have announced they do not expect any final decision before the spring of 1947. Amsterdam reporters, who have long covered the case, feel there will never be a clear-cut decision. "There can't be," said one, "because all the judges now know the works are fakes, that they were all fooled for ten years, yet they just can't bring themselves to admit it."

Meanwhile, fifty-eight-year-old Hans van Meegeren is permitted limited freedom. He lives at home, but is not allowed to discuss the case with outsiders. He goes to his favorite bar daily and drinks steadily. In one recent afternoon, he gulped down fifty-two shots of straight gin in six hours. A short time ago, a close friend of his, a Dutch journalist working for Algemeen Nederlands Persbureau, was able to see him alone. They had lunch, and at last the journalist said to him, "Hans, we have walked, dined, drunk together dozens of times, we have been friends for years, and for all that, I still don't know if you did or did not paint those Vermeers." Van Meegeren stared at his friend, then said quietly, "I painted them." The subject was not discussed again.

The Netherlands government's official information service agreed with van Meegeren's confession from the outset. "There can be no doubt," it stated, "that this mad genius did paint the pictures attributed to Vermeer." Of eight art authorities consulted by this author in Holland, most of them disinterested in van Meegeren as a person, all eight agreed, separately—several reluctantly, several under the condition that their names not be used—that van Meegeren had certainly forged the Vermeers.

One of these men, M. M. van Dantzig, a caustic and peppery little art detective who had just published a volume in Dutch on Vermeer, masochistically admits van Meegeren fooled him at the outset. "But now, after careful study, it is quite obvious his Vermeers are fakes," says van Dantzig.

Incidentally, van Dantzig's favorite indoor sport consists of haranguing his fellow experts with the statement that 60 percent of the paintings owned by museums and collectors are, like van Meegeren's Vermeers, fakes. Van Dantzig arrived at this somewhat arbitrary figure through a private alchemy, which none of his friends understands. His colleagues have long ceased to argue with van Dantzig about his percentage, which they regard as preposterous and beyond proof, but they do agree wholeheartedly with him that there is a large number of fakes floating about in high places. As one Dutch critic, reviving the old art witticism, jested, "Of the 2,500 paintings done by Corot in his lifetime, 7,800 are to be found in America." Other critics, more seriously, cite evidence ranging from the two copies of Gainsborough's *Boy Blue*, which produced international consternation, to the recent exposure in Paris of a forgery factory turning out Picassos and Utrillos by the dozen. So expert were the latter that Utrillo, called in by the gendarmes, had to look twice and accept the advice of a Sûreté specialist before disowning the oils forged under his name.

"There are many reasons for fakes in collections," explains van Dantzig. "For one, it was quite proper and fashionable in the seventeenth century for an apprentice to make copies of his master's work or his style and sign his name and sell the copies as the master's originals. The so-called art experts are often unable to discriminate between copy and original. A masterpiece is accepted as genuine because others before insisted it was genuine, and so the legend builds. But really, you cannot simply glance at an oil and say it is authentic. Van Meegeren's forgeries prove this once and for all. You must look through a painting to the personality behind it. In an old master's original, the color, composition, all elements go together. That is because the originator does it all at once, creatively, in one fresh stroke. The copyist, the forger, does each thing separately, because he isn't inventing and creating, but rather thinking, analyzing, imitating. But many experts do not see this, and that is why many collectors own masterpieces no more authentic than van Meegeren's Vermeers."

Other Dutch authorities, off the record, agree that the van Meegeren case places a question mark before acquisitions in many famous collections, especially the younger collections. It shakes the confidence of the broad art public, many of whom may wonder about the authenticity of the accepted Vermeers now hanging in The Hague, Edinburgh, Berlin, Vienna, New York, London. Are they real or not, since some contemporary experts have been proved thoroughly gullible? And what about other works of art? "The number of pictures bought and sold, at one time or another, as Rembrandt's," Dr. Maximilian Toch, the Manhattan art detective, has remarked, "is six to ten times as great as the maximum number that Rembrandt can have painted, and there is a much larger discrepancy in the case of other artists, like Anthony Van Dyck, with some two thousand attributed to him but perhaps only seventy executed by his hand."

And what about the numerous "originals" by Raphael? Millet? Rubens? Ingres? Are they all authentic? And who determined that they were?

To these troublesome questions, now pumped to life in the cafés and art circles of Europe, the supporters of van Meegeren add one more: If van Meegeren's false Vermeers were passed upon and bought and praised as originals, then is not every creative forger who has worked in the style of another, and who has hoodwinked the experts even for a time, a special kind of genius in his own right?

There is a whole cult in Holland that thinks so, that thinks Hans van Meegeren is a perfect example of this kind of genius. They remind you that their hero did not copy a single "known" masterpiece, but rather created brand-new masterpieces in the manner and style that the old master might have used had he been around longer. They call it "creative" forgery in the Netherlands, and they say it is not crime but Art, and that van Meegeren is perhaps one of the greatest painters in this category in all art history.

Van Meegeren, at present, is less interested in being regarded as a genius than in proving that his mortal enemies, the art critics, are wrong. "I could fool them again, if it were kept secret," he insists. "If I had time to study Rembrandt carefully, to learn exactly how he mixed his paints, I could fool those idiots with forged Rembrandts—and they would see the signature, the style, the cracked canvas, and exclaim, 'Ah, a new undiscovered Rembrandt, the most magnificent yet!'"

Hans van Meegeren began sketching seriously in grammar school, at an age when other young men were playing with Erector sets and dropping live turtles down their sisters' backs. But by the time he went to Delft, the university town near Rotterdam, he was determined to make a sane living as an architect. This resolve did not last long. Delft was the birthplace and home of Jan Vermeer, and the background for many classical Dutch landscapes, and Hans van Meegeren soon fell under its spell. He abandoned blueprints for an easel. While living in Delft, he supported himself by teaching art history and drawing at the Delft Institute of Technology, but he devoted every moment of his spare time to his own painting.

In 1914, one of van Meegeren's oils won a major prize in a competition sponsored by the Academy of Art in The Hague. That was van Meegeren's beginning as an artist. By the 1920's, he had achieved a minor reputation, but had earned little money. It was a period when he was in desperate need of money. In 1912, he had married Anna de Voogt, and she had borne him two children, Inez and Jacques. He had the support of this family to worry about. Then, in 1923, having fallen in love with Jo van Walraven, a half-Dutch, half-Spanish divorcee and actress, van Meegeren divorced Anna to make off with Jo, whom he did not marry until 1929. But by then, his financial situation had begun to improve. Two books of his line drawings and black-and-white studies were published in Holland, and he was receiving commissions to paint members of the nobility in London and several American millionaires on the French Riviera.

About this time, van Meegeren began his bitter feud with Dutch critics and contemporary Dutch painters. They resented his independence, his barbed wit, and his growing financial success. Too, they resented his refusal to play ball. In prewar Holland, the press was sometimes quite as venal as it was in nearby France. When Dutch critics approached him with the routine offer of good reviews for his exhibits if he would pay for them, van Meegeren indignantly refused. So the critics wrote bad reviews. They roasted and scalded him. They labeled him a second-rater. The feud continued for five years, and at last, in 1936, when he could bear the criticism no more, van Meegeren determined to get even. He conjured up several plans, and in the end, it was the most difficult and most decisive that gripped his imagination.

The critics and experts were always fawning over and prattling about the Old Masters, he reflected, and everything was great for them when it had the guaranty of the signature and tradition. "The more I thought, the more I knew they would even swallow my own work if they were sure it was important and had the right signature," van Meegeren told a friend later. "It was a terribly difficult undertaking, and tricky, but I was furious with them and wanted to make them ridiculous. So I decided I would have my joke. I would paint an Old Master and have them accept and praise it."

Van Meegeren laid the groundwork for his hoax carefully. He weighed against one another the Old Masters that he might imitate. He considered da Vinci and Rembrandt first, then discarded them. Finally, he selected Vermeer. Why Vermeer? "Because I had a great admiration for him," he says now, "but I could have just as easily taken any other. Also, there were other reasons. His style was easiest for me, and most adaptable. And much of his personal life was cloaked in mystery, which would make the discovery of a new Vermeer more reasonable."

Although he already knew much about the artist of his choice, van Meegeren spent added months studying Vermeer thoroughly. He went to contemporary accounts for fragments about the master's personal life. He learned that Vermeer had been married as a youth, had had eight children, and had lived a very respectable life in Delft. He learned Vermeer had been a prosperous artist—one visitor to Vermeer's studio recounted that he could not find a single oil for sale, all had been sold, and the visitor was forced to buy his Vermeer from the neighborhood baker. In reading further, van Meegeren found evidence that Vermeer had toiled as a student or apprentice under the immortal Rembrandt. In fact, Rembrandt had had twenty apprentices at the time, who helped fill in the backgrounds of his more detailed oils.

In his researches, van Meegeren learned also that Vermeer had been forgotten for almost two hundred years after his death simply because he had quarreled with the Dutch historian Houbraken, who thereafter refused even to mention him in his *The Great Theater of Dutch Painters,* which became a bible for critics. "Because he was not mentioned in that book, he was neglected and forgotten," says van Meegeren, "and probably many of his finest pieces were lost through neglect because his name was not well known. It shows you how critics judge greatness." In 1865, an exiled Frenchman named Burger-Thore became interested in the obscure Vermeer, chased his paintings about the world, publicized them, and laid the foundation for Vermeer's current fame.

With this information in his head, van Meegeren began to study Vermeer's actual paintings. Some catalogues named thirty-six authentic Vermeers, others named thirty-seven and forty. Van Meegeren confined his study to a handful of paintings of undeniable authenticity (whose provenance was established by contemporary accounts) that hung in Amsterdam and The Hague. He observed Vermeer's sense of color, his brush stroke, his square touch. He noticed his weaknesses in drawing heads, and his genius at portraying still life. He absorbed Vermeer's trademarks —infallible as fingerprints—the repetition in many paintings of the lion-headed chair, the rumpled rugs, the stained-glass windows in the backgrounds.

Van Meegeren's last step in his preparation was a technical one. The painting must be physically foolproof, something right out of 1670. The experts, of course, would test the effect of alcohol on the colors, would inject hypodermic needles to find the chemical content of the paint, would employ X rays and infrared rays to photograph the canvas, would employ quartz lamps to penetrate the overlays. All this, van Meegeren anticipated.

He dug out contemporary seventeenth-century manuscripts and learned that Vermeer and Velasquez utilized for colors gamboge, a gum resin used as yellow pigment, lapis lazuli, a blue obtained from the powdered stones, and white zinc instead of white lead. To obtain real lapis lazuli, van Meegeren paid as high as $2,000 a tube. "The one stumbling block," van Meegeren recalls, "was the oil to be used in paint mixtures. Moderns use linseed oil for mixing. That's no good. Use it and your paint will never get hard and old. Luckily, I discovered in an old manuscript exactly the oil Vermeer used. I used it, too, and it hardened my paint and made it foolproof against all alcohol tests."

No detail was too small to van Meegeren. He overheated his paints because Vermeer had done so. He learned that the masters used badger hair in their brushes, instead of hog's bristles which are used today. Van Meegeren knew that when the experts found some of the seventeenth-century-type hairs in the oil of his painting they would be positive of its authenticity.

When he was ready, van Meegeren took his knowledge, his materials, his wife, and moved into a barnlike villa in Nice. He devised, for his Vermeer, an inspiring portrait of Christ breaking bread with his disciples at Emmaus—De Emmausganger. He toiled, meticulously, untiringly, hour after hour, day after day, for seven consecutive months on this painting. Not even his wife knew what he was up to. When it was done, he went over it again, point by point. Everything was there—even to the old cracks in the surface. He had learned that in the years before Vermeer, the paint broke in large cracks, but the paint in Vermeer's oils (like the paint in the oils of Vermeer's contemporaries) broke in smaller, chainlike cracks, so van Meegeren's own imitation cracks, created by scratching them out in pattern and then baking them apart in a kitchen stove, were exactly in the manner of the master. There was only one last touch. Vermeer's signature. Van Meegeren daubed it on, and the deed was done.

Now, from his knowledge of Vermeer's life, he invented the story of the "discovery." He knew that Vermeer had worked side by side with Italian student-painters. The Italians had painted Christ at Emmaus. They had taken their products to Italy. Most likely, then, Vermeer had done Christ at Emmaus, and most likely, in the unrecorded years of his life, he had traveled in Italy. Very well. This new Vermeer would be found in Italy. Van Meegeren would learn of it through a friend, purchase it cheaply, and then resell it.

Thus fortified, he went with his handiwork to Amsterdam. Before putting it up for sale, he knew he must obtain a certificate of authenticity. Van Meegeren approached one of Holland's great art historians and experts, ninety-year-old Dr. Abraham Bredius, a doddering ancient who dwelt in obscurity and who was a year away from death. Van Meegeren showed Dr. Bredius his discovery. The old expert, flattered that someone was consulting him again, blinked at it through dim eyes, submitted it to spectroscopic, X-ray, and alcohol tests, and then gave his enthusiastic seal of authenticity and approval.

Still excited by the "masterpiece" that he had authenticated, Dr. Bredius published an article about it in *Burlington Magazine*, an English art review. Full of unrestrained praise for the newly discovered Vermeer, Dr. Bredius wrote: "It is a wonderful moment in the life of a lover of art when he finds himself suddenly confronted with a hitherto unknown painting by a great master, untouched, on the original canvas and without any restoration, just as it left the painter's studio! . . . We have here a—I am inclined to say *the*—masterpiece of Johannes Vermeer of Delft."

Succeeding steps were routine. In late 1937, the members of the Rembrandt Association, after hiring four more experts to test the Vermeer with chemicals and rays and having found it authentic, paid van Meegeren half a million gulden—$200,000—for his treasure, and then presented it to the august Boyman's Museum in Rotterdam. Its first public exhibition took place in September, 1938, when it starred in a showing of 450 Netherlands masterpieces gathered to celebrate Queen Wilhelmina's Jubilee. Critics from The Hague, from London, from Paris swarmed to view it. So great was their reverence that they demanded the museum floor be carpeted about the Vermeer to prevent noise while they contemplated. The museum obliged. Several critics wrote ecstatically that it was far and away Jan Vermeer's greatest effort.

Van Meegeren was delighted. He had proved his mortal enemies idiots and made himself rich. The following year, he decided to make a second Vermeer. This too he sold, for an even higher price. The next year, he made a third. In all, he produced six. The public prosecutor of Amsterdam feels this was his biggest crime. "Had he painted his first one, and made fools of the critics, well, all Holland would have laughed and he would have been a great hero. But no, he couldn't stop. He wanted to get rich quick. He turned his little joke into a big business. That is his crime."

Van Meegeren disposed of all his forgeries except the sixth. Not needing the money it represented, and since he rather fancied it, the painting was kept on the wall of his house beside an authentic Franz Hals he had recently bought. Then came his downfall. An agent, the go-between Reinstra, appeared and persuaded him to permit its sale. Van Meegeren explains that he did so only reluctantly, and with the provision that it not be sold to the Nazis, who were then occupying the country. Three weeks later, after competitive bidding by a Dutch syndicate, the picture went to Hermann Goering in exchange for 150 of his paintings, valued at 1,600,000 gulden or $600,000 (at the 1943 rate). Out of this sum, $250,000 was passed down to van Meegeren, and the rest was retained by the agent in commissions. So delighted was Goering with the deal that he wrote thanking van Meegeren and addressing him as "my painter laureate." Van Meegeren remembers the incident sadly. "I was indignant when I learned it had been sold to Goering. But I took his money, and that was the beginning of the end."

Today, a year and a half after his confession of forgery, Hans van Meegeren is a tired and broken man. The only thing that keeps him going is his burning desire to prove, beyond all doubt, that he faked the Vermeers and tricked the high priests of art. Constantly, he brings forth new evidence to prove his guilt. He points to the Vermeer heads. Vermeer painted life-sized heads. In his own pictures, van Meegeren purposely drew all human heads six centimeters larger than Vermeer's, because he had a pet theory that they looked more lifelike when enlarged. This, he says, is only one of many proofs of his forgeries. But his enemies glibly reply that this un-Vermeer-like touch is not proof of forgery but merely proof that this newly discovered series of Vermeers is unique and different.

Undaunted, van Meegeren presents other proofs. The chairs on which Christ sits, in the first and sixth pictures, are drawn after the fairly modern chair in his own studio. And Christ's hands are not modeled after Vermeer's type of hands but after van Meegeren's own hands. And his paints: He displays receipts from dealers in London, where he purchased the more expensive tubes. Recently, van Meegeren recalled that he had left a remnant of the rare seventeenth-century canvas he had used lying on the floor of his French villa. He felt that this would be irrefutable proof of his forgery. He demanded that the strip of canvas be brought to Holland. The Dutch government dispatched two police officials to van Meegeren's villa in France. The police ransacked the villa. There was no seventeenth-century canvas. Van Meegeren was crushed, and now insists that his enemies got there first and destroyed it.

While van Meegeren has many friends, he has few who dare to come out in the open and defend him. One who does defend him, while thinking very little of his artistic talent, is van Dantzig, the Amsterdam art detective. Van Dantzig insists there is no question that van Meegeren is a forger. "There are dozens of pieces of evidence that van Meegeren perpetrated a hoax," he says. "Take one single thing. The brush stroke. That is one of the most individual, subconscious acts of a creative artist. Some strokes are long, some short, some thick, some thin, some curved at beginning and at the end, and made with a quick motion. Jan Vermeer used small strokes, putting down flecks of color and dots of reflected light in sharp decisive movements. He was creating and knew where each one went. Van Meegeren's strokes are slower, more careful, his flecks and dots much more studied, as if done by one who had to think where and how to put them down. Or take the human hand. Vermeer's hands are broken, knuckled like living hands. Van Meegeren's hands are blobs and his fingers lifeless sausages. Or take the human hair. You can feel Vermeer's hair. It grows. Van Meegeren's hair is a mop, stuck on, manufactured. And so on. There's no end of evidence."

Nevertheless, even though short on ammunition, van Meegeren's enemies continue to do battle. They constantly try to embarrass him with questions. They ask him to produce his living models for the Vermeers. He retorts that he had no models, needed none, that an artist who has done three thousand figures in his lifetime can dispense with models. His enemies then divert their attack to his alleged collaboration with the Nazis. Not long ago, a Dutch journalist in Berlin found a book of van Meegeren's reproduced black-and-white drawings bearing the inscription, "To my beloved Fuehrer, with best wishes, Hans van Meegeren." His enemies broadcast this news throughout the Netherlands and the Continent. Van Meegeren countered at once. He recalled that during the occupation a German officer, an aspiring artist, had asked for his autograph in a book of his drawings. He obliged with his signature only. He insisted the German officer must have written in the inscription to Hitler over his signature, and sent it on to Der Fuehrer. Van Meegeren demanded that the signature and inscription be studied by Dutch handwriting experts. This was promptly done. The handwriting experts reported that van Meegeren was right, the signature was his own but the inscription to Hitler was by another hand. Van Meegeren asked for the volume itself. He wanted it for evidence in his trial. When the police tried to produce it, it was gone—no one knows where.

So the intrigue and word-baiting continue in Amsterdam. What will be the legal result? Opinions vary widely. A minority feels the case will be dropped in the next year or two, and that van Meegeren will be given his freedom. The majority feels the international jury will be forced to admit that the Vermeers are clever fakes. If so, van Meegeren will most likely be jailed for a period of two to six years or fined two million dollars. This, incidentally, would be a somewhat stiffer sentence than he would have got as a Nazi collaborator.

But Hans van Meegeren wants the stiffer sentence. It will vindicate his honor and blast the complacency of art critics. He also wants to buy his six paintings back. He has had an offer of eight million dollars, a sum widely publicized in Europe, for the lot from a well-known American millionaire. Van Meegeren will not reveal the name of the American.

But van Meegeren does not think that he will ever live to see his victory and collect this new fortune from the United States. "If I should die tomorrow," he says quietly, "the dealers, museums, critics would be much relieved. The thorn would be out of their side. The case could be dropped, the Vermeers I forged declared authentic, and the experts would never be bothered again. As long as I live, they are on the spot. There is much at stake in my life. Millions of dollars in cash, and years of art-dealer prestige. They know all of this, and they are desperate. That is why I am very careful on the streets these days. When I see a car driving toward me very fast, I duck into a doorway. It would be a shame if an accident happened to me at this stage, wouldn't it?"

>«

WHAT HAS HAPPENED SINCE . . .

When I arrived in the Netherlands in September, 1946, intent on obtaining material about the Hans van Meegeren saga, I was told by members of his intimate circle that I was the first writer to make an effort to present his story in depth through a large-circulation periodical. Before my investigation into the Vermeer forgeries, there had been numerous brief newspaper accounts of the raging art controversy, but these had not attempted to assess van Meegeren's personality, or consider his full role in the series of hoaxes, nor had they shown the fantastic dilemma his case presented to the authorities.

I was unable to spend time with van Meegeren himself. He was ill. He was also under strict police surveillance and control. Consequently, a considerable amount of my material was acquired through my friendship with M. Petzoldt, a clever Dutch journalist in Amsterdam who was well acquainted with and trusted by van Meegeren. Not only did Petzoldt answer any questions I had to ask, but he acted as a go-between, taking my more personal inquiries to the ailing painter and bringing back van Meegeren's frank replies. Also, the Amsterdam art expert, M. M. van Dantzig, gave generously of his time and cooperation. And there were at least a dozen other sources in Amsterdam that I eventually tapped for information on van Meegeren.

When I had what I wanted, I moved on to Paris. There I wrote my story, which I called, "How to Be an Old Master." Before leaving for Madrid, I sent the completed draft to my New York literary agent, Paul R. Reynolds, who immediately placed it with *The Saturday Evening Post*. They published it under a more provocative title, "The Man Who Swindled Goering," in their issue of January 11, 1947. Even before the story appeared, the *Reader's Digest* had purchased it for a lead reprint, and ran it in their issue of March, 1947.

Few short pieces that I have written have received as much attention as did the van Meegeren story, from those interested in acquiring dramatic rights. I was overwhelmed by inquiries about motion picture, play, and radio rights. Of some interest was a serious inquiry from Edward Gross, who had successfully produced *Chicken Every Sunday* on Broadway, and who wanted me to convert my van Meegeren article into a stage drama. I agreed to try to do this. I still have a clipping from the February, 1948, theatrical page of a New York daily, which begins: "Edward Gross will cast Irving Wallace's play, 'Masterpiece,' on the Coast. Gross plans to open it in Los Angeles this spring and then tour east to Broadway." The announcement was accurate but premature. I had, indeed, entitled van Meegeren's story *Masterpiece* for the stage version, and I had written an outline and almost one full act, when I was forced to abandon the project. I no longer remember exactly why this was, although I suspect that a major reason was that I had run out of eating money just when I had become a father for the first time, and was forced to revive my bank account by becoming a salaried screenwriter.

But if movie and play interest in van Meegeren came to nothing, there was a third source of interest in the dramatic rights, and this one did develop successfully. On January 1, 1948, Paul Muni starred as Hans van Meegeren in a national network radio adaptation of "The Man Who Swindled Goering." And in 1953, my story was acquired by a television company, and somewhat later was shown coast-to-coast as *The Hoax,* featuring Herbert Marshall and Paul Henried.

Unfortunately, Hans van Meegeren did not live to know how widely his fame—or notoriety—was publicized, not only through the radio and television versions of my story on him, but through the great amount of literature concurrently growing up around his legend. To my limited knowledge, there have been at least one dozen, perhaps two dozen, books published since his death which are devoted entirely or in great part to his life and his acts of creative forgery. Merely glancing at my nearest bookshelf, I can see such volumes as *The Master Forger* by John Godley, *Vermeer—van Meegeren: Back to the Truth* by Jean Decoen, *Van Meegeren's Faked Vermeers and De Hooghs* by Dr. P. B. Coremans, *The Art of the Faker* by Frank Arnau, *The Mystery of van Meegeren* by Maurice Moiseiwitsch.

When I left van Meegeren in Amsterdam in the autumn of 1946, he was still awaiting the decision on the seventh Vermeer, the one which he had deliberately forged for a jury of international art judges. Based on this *Child Christ in the Temple of the Elders,* the art judges would determine if van Meegeren should be tried by the state as a man who had perpetrated fraud by faking six Vermeers and swindling Goering with one, or if he should be tried as a political collaborator who had faked none of them but simply sold real Vermeers, and one of them to a wartime enemy.

After I departed from Amsterdam, Hans van Meegeren lived on for another fifteen months. It was in the early autumn of 1947 that the international art judges came to their decision. They voted that Hans van Meegeren had, indeed, fooled all of them, and their learned colleagues. The seventh Vermeer, done by van Meegeren on assignment, had convinced them that the other six Vermeers were fakes. The key evidence, aesthetic considerations aside, was that presented by one of the judges, Dr. P. B. Coremans, director of the Central Laboratory of the Belgian Museums, who stated that laboratory investigation proved van Meegeren's seventeenth-century Vermeers contained in their paint a synthetic resin, which had not even been discovered until 1900. Despite the fact that a Swiss chemistry professor dissented—"the microchemical analyses on which Coremans has based his findings yield no evidence that any synthetic resinous products are present in the layers of paint"

—the other art judges reluctantly agreed with Coremans that although the signatures on the six Vermeers bore the master's signature, "I.V.M." (for I. V. Meer), the paintings had been executed by the impossible Hans van Meegeren.

And so, on October 29, 1947, Hans van Meegeren went on trial before the District Court of Amsterdam. To his delight, he went on trial as a George Psalmanazar, as a Thomas Wainewright, as a William Ireland, admirable fakers and impostors all, and not as a commonplace collaborator. The evidence of forgery was heard in a single day. Van Meegeren did not contest it. The state prosecutor demanded that van Meegeren receive two years' imprisonment for his fraud. The court adjourned for two weeks to consider the sentence it should deliver. On November 12, 1947, the court reconvened. Hans van Meegeren, frail and ailing, awaited the sentence. Because of his ill health (and, perhaps, because of the sympathy of the Dutch public, so appreciative of one who had so daringly tweaked the noses of critics and authorities), the prosecution's demand for two years' imprisonment was not heeded. Hans van Meegeren was sentenced to only one year in jail.

Van Meegeren returned to his great house at 321 Keizersgracht to await his official removal to a prison cell. No one came for him. He lived a Kafka nightmare. He waited and waited, and still no one came. There were countless legal actions against him. Those who had bought his forgeries as Vermeers were pressing suits to recover all money paid him. The government wanted back taxes on this disputed income. There were court costs. Van Meegeren's assets dwindled swiftly. Bankruptcy proceedings were begun.

Among collectors of paintings there was a carnival interest in van Meegeren, the kind of curiosity that lures people to the freak exhibits. From London, New York, Paris, there were orders for portraits, for book illustrations, for new oils "in the style of Vermeer." Van Meegeren desired to resume with brush, palette and canvas, but was unable to begin. His resolve and wasted body were weak. His impending imprisonment hung over him daily.

In those days of waiting, he had nurses, he had a few friends in, he had regular visits from his son Jacques. Since there were no police to stop him, he took to walking along the canals in the afternoons, greeting and accepting the compliments of the populace. In the evenings, he often attended his favorite café. He drank heavily. He slept lightly, poorly, despite the drugs. He got weaker. After five weeks in limbo, he collapsed. He was rushed to the Valerius Clinic in Amsterdam. During the evening of December 30, 1947, he suffered a severe heart attack and died.

Two days later, Paul Muni dramatized his life, based on my story, for listeners the length and breadth of the United States, and perhaps on that evening Hans van Meegeren had his resurrection, and his real legend began.

Today, the legend is stronger than ever, the legend of warped genius.

Van Meegeren's last word to posterity was encompassed in his prison confession. It was, according to a 1964 dispatch by the Reuters news agency: "that he had produced work intrinsically as good as that of the great masters. It gave equal pleasure and therefore did not defraud anybody. The only difference, he said, was the signature."

Two posthumous judgments would have appealed to him. One concerned his talent, and the other concerned his critics.

In 1949, in London, there appeared Dr. P. B. Coremans' judgment of Hans van Meegeren's gifts:

"Van Meegeren was indisputably the greatest forger of all time. As an artist, he achieved the best and the worst since his natural gifts were warped by the line of least resistance, the lust for gain and luxury. These same characteristics are evident in his fakes. An immense conceit and contempt (if not hatred) of the official art world made him create the beautiful painting of the Disciples."

In 1951, in Rotterdam, there appeared Jean Decoen's speculation about van Meegeren's critics:

"One thing remains a mystery to me. It is the attitude of all those who, in 1938, by their statements and writings, announced to the world one of the greatest masterpieces of Dutch art of the seventeenth century. And the qualities, which this work possessed, and which everyone could see, do they no longer exist? Do qualities that go to make a masterpiece exist only in the minds of men, and have they no real foundation? Does everything evaporate because the name of the artist and period in which the painting was made have been changed? It is therefore Name, not work, which possesses this sympathetic magic. . . . Of all van Meegeren's forgeries examined from distance or close quarters, none can be compared with the Disciples, and I reiterate that if van Meegeren is the maker of it, I take off my hat to him and forgive him all the forgeries that he ever made."

Here it was, then, the critics' surrender:

"The greatest forger of all time"—creator, in the twentieth century, of "one of the greatest masterpieces of Dutch art of the seventeenth century. . . . I take off my hat to him."

Somehow, I cannot believe that Hans van Meegeren would have been displeased with these critics. He had proved that the species could harbor fallible fools. To their credit, the majority of critics, humbled, had recanted from their belief in their omniscience. But there will soon be a new generation of them to renew and perpetuate their exclusive hold on Infinite Wisdom and Final Judgment. For them, the legend of Hans van Meegeren should tower as a disturbing reminder of human fallibility. One can hope.

13

MONSIEUR BERTILLON

At the turn of the century, an enterprising New York publisher traveled to Paris to offer the world's greatest living detective one dollar a word for his memoirs. Though potentially the offer far exceeded his salary as director of the French Sûreté's Identity Department, Alphonse Bertillon firmly refused it. "To write the whole truth for you," he told the publisher, "I would have to tell secrets, which might be useful to criminals. If I skipped the secrets, I would cheat the public."

Undaunted, the publisher promptly offered to pay the same rate if Bertillon would disguise his facts in a fictional detective novel. "Surely you would have no objections to the detective novel?"

"On the contrary," said Bertillon, "I love detective stories. I would like to see Sherlock Holmes's methods of reasoning adopted by all professional police. Yes, perhaps I will write a mystery story one day when I retire, if I retire. But now I have no time. It is such a pity. I have so many wonderful stories to tell!"

When at last he died, in harness, just thirty-five years ago, Alphonse Bertillon had still not found time to write his mystery book. But, in his incredible record of achievements, in the scientific advances he willed to criminologists the earth over, in the very life he lived, were more "wonderful stories" than any that he might have invented.

Today, every time the FBI corners a Dillinger, every time Scotland Yard catches a Crippen, every time the French Sûreté traps a Landru, they are paying silent tribute to Alphonse Bertillon. Instead of memoirs, Bertillon left behind countless weapons of detection with which the law can evenly pit itself against the wit and savagery of outlaws and killers. He gave the world its first successful means of identifying and classifying criminals, thus catching repeaters. He discovered a method of seeing through aliases, disguises and plastic surgery. He invented police photography. He was among the first detectives to use psychology on criminals successfully. He was the first detective to solve a crime through fingerprints. He was a pioneer in scientific sleuthing.

But it was not easy. Once, when Bertillon was guiding old Louis Pasteur on a tour of the Sûreté, the scientist halted, gazed thoughtfully at the detective, and asked, "Was it difficult, Monsieur Bertillon, getting the government to recognize your discoveries?" Yes, Bertillon admitted, it had been terribly difficult, and added, "But I never despaired. When they resisted, I became more aggressive." Pasteur smiled. "Ah, then you know—the difficulty is less in discovering than in having discoveries understood and adopted."

In the beginning, Bertillon's most arduous case was in solving Bertillon. He, who would discover so much, could not find himself. Born in 1853, the second son of a Parisian doctor whose hobbies were studying skulls and physiological statistics, Alphonse Bertillon was the family disgrace. He failed to do satisfactory work at three different schools, and lost a half-dozen jobs, varying from banker to schoolteacher, in France, England, and Scotland.

Then came a job he could not lose. He was drafted for compulsory military service, and, as a private, was stationed with the 139th Infantry Regiment in Clermont-Ferrand, France. There was plenty of leisure, and out of sheer boredom young Bertillon began taking night courses in the medical school of the local university.

Suddenly, for the first time, he found something that interested him. His father's old hobby—human skulls. Now, fascinated, he began studying them, measuring and classifying hundreds. Soon his interests expanded to the 222 bones of the human skeleton. He made a personal discovery. The skulls and bones of no two human beings were exactly the same. Bertillon began compiling statistics, but before he had enough to substantiate his theory, his military service was ended. He was home, again unemployed. His father was pleased with the statistics, but realistic. "To be a disinterested scientist is well and good, Alphonse, but to be fully disinterested the scientist must make money first. I am going to try just once more to get you a job."

In March, 1879, through his father's contacts, Bertillon went to work as a lowly auxiliary clerk in the French Sûreté headquarters in Paris. His duties, inside his tiny, cold cubicle, were dull, monotonous and, he felt, quite stupid. Several times he was tempted to quit, but something about the work returned him to his desk. His job consisted of recording descriptions of criminals arrested during the day, just in case the same criminals should ever turn up again. But the descriptions consisted of generalities that were impossible to file accurately, and so they were never used. The pointlessness of the method was what bored Bertillon, and yet challenged him. To make his job more interesting, he decided to improve on the primitive system of catching repeaters.

Just a half century before, he learned, the only means of checking on whether an offender was an ex-convict was by seeing if he had been branded with a red-hot iron. When branding was abolished by law, the police in France, as well as those in other nations, were limited to age-worn tricks. They would plant a detective, dressed as a prisoner, in the new convict's cell. They would offer bonuses to detectives who located repeaters, and they would write lengthy descriptions, too vague to be classified. It was a farce. A man had only to change his name or features, however crudely, to avoid being recognized as a previous offender. Habitual criminals were constantly turned loose for lack of concrete identification. The police were helpless. Crime had a holiday.

And then Alphonse Bertillon remembered his human skulls: that no two were alike. An idea struck him. Age, hunger, sickness might alter a murderer's flesh but not his bones. His study of statistics had told him that between the ages of twenty and sixty, certain parts of the human body do not change. The width of a man's head, his right ear, his left middle finger—all three normally remain the same size. Bertillon checked and rechecked. The ear alone, he calculated, was enough to identify thousands of criminals. There were twenty distinctive parts to a single ear. A killer might dye his hair, bob his nose, lift his chin. But unless he cut it off, the ear remained the same, difficult to disguise, easy to observe.

Thus, within eight months of the day he had joined the Sûreté as a lowly clerk, thirty-one-year-old Alphonse Bertillon had conceived his revolutionary system of classifying and trapping criminals by measuring certain unchangeable parts of the human body. He called his invention "anthropometry" or body measurement, and it consisted of making a composite chart of a criminal's eleven unalterable features.

Enthusiastically, he presented his system to Police Prefect Andrieux. He waited for congratulations. Andrieux scanned the outline of the system, and then threw it back at Bertillon. "You are a lunatic," said Andrieux. "Get out."

Bertillon was confused. Back in his office, he reread his presentation of his system, took it apart, put it together again, made subtractions, additions, finally rewrote it in more detail. Once more, he submitted it to the police prefect. This time Andrieux completely lost his temper. "So now clerks tell us how to run the Sûreté! I will teach you a lesson!" Andrieux dashed off a note to Bertillon's father stating that the young man was mentally unstable, and that he would be fired if he persisted in expounding his cracked theory.

Exasperated, the elder Bertillon summoned his son for a final showdown. Alphonse appeared, not with contrition but with the summary of his system in hand. In an hour, anthropometry had its first convert. Excitedly, the elder Bertillon appealed to the prefect, but to no avail. The Sûreté chief refused to reconsider. It had become a matter of saving face.

Alphonse Bertillon returned to his clerical desk. He dared not mention his system. A single word, and he would be fired. He wanted to remain in the Sûreté desperately now. So he played dumb, and waited. He waited one year, two years, three years. The future seemed hopeless. And then, suddenly, Andrieux was out, and a new police prefect named Camescasse was in.

Once again, Bertillon presented his revolutionary system. The new prefect listened with a tolerant smile, admitted that he realized the importance of what Bertillon was trying to do, admitted also that he had not the slightest comprehension of how Bertillon planned to do it. But he was impressed by the young clerk's enthusiasm. "Monsieur Bertillon, you shall have your chance. I will give you exactly three months. If in three months your identity system has caught one recidivist, the Sûreté will permanently adopt it. If in three months it has caught none, you are to drop it forever and never bother us again. That is the gamble I offer. Are you satisfied?"

Three months did not seem enough. Bertillon hesitated. But it was this or nothing. "I accept, sir. You shall have at least one criminal because of my system in three months. And, thank you, sir!"

On the morning of December 13, 1882, Bertillon introduced the world's first scientific system of classifying criminals. Bertillon began by forcing each offender into a revolving chair, which is still used at the Sûreté today, and taking a series of 24-by-30-inch glass-plate photographs. Until that date, the Sûreté had photographed about 60,000 criminals, stiff, full-faced, unrevealing portraits. Bertillon changed all that. He introduced, despite the difficulties presented by time exposure, a pioneer form of candid photography. Convicts were photographed informally, in natural poses. Bertillon played down the standard full-faced picture, which he felt distorted the appearance, especially of the nose. Instead he concentrated on profiles, which he felt gave police a more honest view of a man's brow, nose, chin. Also, he snapped close-ups of prominent facial features.

Next, Bertillon applied his system of recording physiological statistics. Each man's head, right ear, left middle finger, left forearm, and left foot were carefully measured and noted. The measurements were taken three times and averaged, except in the case of the head, where all three measurements had to agree exactly. There were other measurements: left index finger, arm spread, chest girth, height. Physical oddities, like moles and scars, were jotted down. Even the exact shade of the eyes was recorded; Bertillon felt the color of adult eyes never changed. All of this was placed on an index card, and, with the photographs, classified and filed according to a clever system of size groupings Bertillon had created. The file which Bertillon inaugurated that first day, sixty-seven years ago, may still be seen in the Sûreté Identity Department, above the Summary Courts of the Palais de Justice in Paris—except that, today, these files contain ten million cards, with names now classified phonetically instead of alphabetically, each record being kept on file for ninety years.

As the first day gave way to the first week, and then to the first month, Bertillon recognized the unavoidable flaws in his system. Juvenile delinquents or aged criminals, whose bone structures were changing, growing, deteriorating, were not represented in his file. Then there was the human element involved in measuring. Some Sûreté operators measured a convict in a slipshod fashion, some so carefully as to exaggerate reality. Nevertheless, Bertillon felt that his identification method was accurate enough to catch most repeaters. Yet, at the end of two months, he had failed to identify a single one.

It was on a dreary afternoon, in late February of 1883, that a stocky young man, about thirty years old, stood before Bertillon. He said his name was Dupont. Bertillon snorted. This was the day's sixth Dupont, a name which in France is often used as a fictitious name, as Americans use John Doe. The man had been arrested while committing an act of burglary. As a first offense, this was not so serious. As a second offense, they could throw the book at him. Dupont insisted that this was his first crime. Bertillon took his measurements, and then began checking his new files. He came up with two cards. The statistics on one did not completely correspond with Dupont's. The other card bore the measurements of a man named Martin, who had been arrested for burglary eight weeks before. Martin's measurements, from ear to fingers, and forearm, were exactly the same as Dupont's!

Trembling, Bertillon confronted Dupont. "Do you recognize these photographs, Monsieur Martin? They were taken on your last visit here."

Dupont stared. "He looks like me, but his nose is longer."

"Exactly. You altered your nose. But you could not alter your bone structure. Read the measurements for yourself!"

Faced with the facts, Dupont surrendered, admitted that he was Martin, and confessed to a half-dozen previous offenses.

Bertillon had won his long-shot gamble. In less than three months, his new system had succeeded. The sensation it created was tremendous. The prefect promoted him. The Sûreté honored him. The press pestered him. There was an avalanche of requests for interviews, speeches, and banquet appearances. But Bertillon was busy. In the first year, 7,336 criminals were measured, and 49 repeaters caught and jailed. In the second year, 241 repeaters were caught. Before ten years were up, Bertillon's identification system would place 3,500 dangerous criminals behind bars in France alone. In 1885, the Sûreté officially adopted anthropometry, and three years later Bertillon was promoted to chief of the new Identity Department with a sizable raise in salary.

The individual cases solved by Bertillon's system were spectacular. A body, swollen and distorted by immersion in water, was fished out of the Marne River. The shirt was monogrammed P.C., the key ring initialed J.D. Bertillon took measurements, consulted his files, identified the body by its large skull, found the victim's previous history, and through it the clues that led to the murderer. Another time, a bricklayer named Rollin disappeared. His wife and friends identified him as one of three corpses in the morgue. Bertillon wasn't sure. An hour before the funeral, he measured the corpse, found it to be the body of a famous criminal and not that of Rollin. Later, Bertillon proved that Rollin was still alive.

Then there was the case of a tall, blond German known as Hiller who had committed a cold-blooded murder outside of Lyons. Witnesses thought that they had seen a tall, blond man hurriedly catch a train to Paris, only the man had appeared to be French, not German. Fortunately, there was a Bertillon index card on Hiller, which included the notation, "Roman nose with turned-down base, triangular ears; he habitually gnaws at his nails." Sûreté detectives watched the exits of the Gare de Lyon. A tall, blond, Roman-nosed foreigner came striding through. The detectives started, but halted. This man's nose base was straight, his ears round. The detectives made a quick decision. A commotion about the wrong man might scare off the real fugitive. The detectives waited. And then, seconds later, came another tall, blond man. The Sûreté ignored his French clothes, concentrating only on his face. Roman nose with turned-down base. Triangular ears. The detectives swarmed over him. When they pulled off his gloves, they saw that his nails were bitten. At headquarters, his measurements coincided with Hiller's. He *was* Hiller. And he confessed to the killing.

But skeptics wondered if Bertillon's system could penetrate a really professional disguise. To prove that it could, Bertillon dramatically caught an absconding bank teller, who had managed to change himself from a plump, bushy-haired, popeyed businessman to a skinny, bald, rheumy-eyed tramp, caught him by the unchanged appearance of his ears.

These cases gave Bertillon prestige inside France, but his methods were still little understood by the world at large. This was remedied by the antics of Michel Eyraud and his pretty, twenty-one-year-old mistress, Gabrielle Bompard. One evening in July of 1889, Gabrielle Bompard lured a well-off government official named Gouffé to her Paris apartment with promises of love; then, as she disrobed, she teasingly slipped the cord of her dressing gown around his neck. That moment, she signaled Eyraud to step from behind a curtain and yank the cord tight. The murdered official was robbed, stuffed into a trunk, and the trunk dumped off a road near Lyons.

In search of a prosperous new life, Eyraud and Bompard sailed for Canada, spent time in Montreal, and then in San Francisco, and finally went into the wine business in the small community of Saint Helena, California. Meanwhile, a month after the crime, the French Sûreté had located Gouffé's corpse and the trunk. By November, 1889, based on clues unearthed by a brilliant inspector named Goron, and through use of Bertillon's system of identification, the Sûreté decided that the murderer had been Eyraud, and his accomplice had been Gabrielle Bompard. Two Sûreté detectives, Huillier and Soudais, were sent on a fantastic chase across Canada, the United States, Mexico, hunting for the fugitive pair. However, on her own, Gabrielle Bompard, and a new male companion she had acquired, returned to Paris, where she surrendered herself to the Sûreté. And shortly after, Eyraud was trapped in Havana, and brought back to Paris. The pair were turned over to Bertillon, who photographed them, measured them three times, and filed their statistics away with others in his growing list of criminals. After a sensational trial, in which Gabrielle's susceptibility to hypnotism became the cornerstone of her defense and received headlines throughout the world, the two were found guilty of premeditated murder. Eyraud was sentenced to death, and executed on the guillotine in 1891. Gabrielle was sentenced to a jail term, and not released until 1905. The international publicity that Bertillon gained from his minor role in this case, as well as added publicity that he obtained from measuring the battered face of an anarchist named Ravachol, who had blown up the home of the Paris public prosecutor, helped familiarize other nations with the new identity system.

Bertillon's fame spread. Among the first of the foreign cities to adopt his system was Chicago, after Major R. W. McClaughry, warden of the Illinois State Penitentiary at Joliet, translated Bertillon's methods into English and became his foremost disciple. In New York, the crack detective, Inspector Thomas Byrnes, who worked under Police Commissioner Theodore Roosevelt, adopted Bertillon's criminal photography and in-

vented an album whose nickname was soon to become a byword in the
United States, the "Rogues' Gallery." The International Association of
Chiefs of Police organized a global clearinghouse of Bertillon records in
Washington, D.C. Bertillon himself never found time to visit America.
Instead, as his ambassador, he sent his brother Jacques, who amazed him
by reporting back that even a railroad porter in Philadelphia recognized
the family name. The only concession Bertillon made to help spread his
gospel was his attendance at crime congresses throughout Europe. He
was terrified of speechmaking, and when forced to speak in public, wrote
out every word in advance. At the International Prison Congress, in
Rome, he satisfied detectives of every nation with a thorough ninety-
five-page report on his system.

His name became a part of the language. People spoke of "bertillonage." In the nightclubs on Montmartre's hill, in Le Lapin Agile and in
Moulin de la Galette, painted ladies sang topical tunes about Bertillon's
"l'identification anthropometrique." Czar Nicholas II sent him a gold-
and-pearl clock, and Queen Victoria sent him a medal, for helping with
identity work in Russia and Great Britain. The future King Edward VII,
Victoria's son, came to see the Sûreté laboratory, and requested Bertillon
to measure two criminals before him personally. Fourteen foreign governments, including Sweden and Austria, honored or knighted him. His
name and his invention were everywhere, and the world was becoming a
safer place in which to live.

With his system apparently established, Bertillon restlessly searched for
new crime problems. Intrigued by so-called perfect crimes, he risked his
reputation by going into the field to solve them. And in these efforts, he
gave law enforcement one of its earliest tastes of modern psychology and
deduction.

A robbery suspect was jailed with only the weakest evidence against
him. Bertillon felt sure of the man's guilt, but he could not prove it. Privately, using his police as actors, he reconstructed the crime as he deduced it had happened. At last, satisfied with his theory, Bertillon prepared to verify it. One night, he slipped into the burglar's cell. Then,
pencil and pad in hand, he sat patiently beside the sleeping man. At
dawn the man woke, yawned, was about to turn over, when he saw
Bertillon making notes beside him. He sat up with a shriek. "What are you
doing here?" Bertillon waved his notebook. "Taking down your full confession, monsieur. You talked in your sleep. You told me every detail of
your crime. Ah, you do not believe me? Very well. I shall read your confession from my notebook." Bertillon looked down at the blank pages in
his notebook and pretended to read. Step by step, he described the man's
crime as he had earlier reconstructed it. The criminal gave up any

further resistance. He signed a formal confession of guilt. Bertillon's deductions had been correct to the most trivial detail.

Again, a wealthy, well-known European figure, Baron Zeidler, was found dead in his stables. Nearby, neighing and kicking, was his newest hunter. The baron was examined, and hoof marks were found on his face and skull. He had obviously been knocked unconscious and then kicked to death by the unruly horse. It was a terrible accident. Bertillon, strolling in and about the stables, asked to see the deceased baron's face. He studied the hoof marks thoughtfully, then announced, "Gentlemen, this was not an accident but murder. Very clever. Well planned. But the murderer slipped. You see, the horseshoe marks on Baron Zeidler's face are at the wrong angle. He'd have to have been standing on his head when the horse kicked him to receive the marks in this fashion." Bertillon's deduction was accurate. After a brief investigation, the murderer was caught. He had summoned the baron to the stables, and then battered him about the head and face with a heavy club to which a pair of horseshoes was tied.

Bertillon believed that too much police evidence depended upon eyewitnesses ("Most people look without seeing," he would say), too much depended upon hearsay, guesswork, and not enough upon cold scientific factual evidence. He had turned the Sûreté into a mammoth, machine-like laboratory. His enemies, conservative, old-fashioned, at home and abroad, challenged some of his scientific innovations. Bertillon's reply was to point to the Tellier case.

Here, it appeared, was the perfect crime. The body of a man, clubbed to death, then doubled over, tied tightly with rope, and wrapped around with tar paper, was discovered in the Bois de Boulogne just outside Paris. There was absolutely no clue to his identity. Or at least there was none until Bertillon appeared on the scene. Gravely, he listened to the reports of his detectives. Then, silently, with his traveling microscope, he went to work. A half hour later he gathered his men around him.

"The victim was an accountant or an office clerk," he began. "His hands show no sign of having done manual labor. His right shirt-sleeve is cleaner and newer than his left. Accountants and clerks protect the sleeve on their writing hand with a special cuff. This keeps the sleeve almost new. The victim was hit on the head from behind with a club. He was murdered in a large wine cellar, dragged into a second room filled with sawdust, sand, and coal, and then temporarily hidden in a third room—a pitch-black room with absolutely no windows. This was all done in a house beside the Seine."

The Sûreté detectives were dumbfounded, but quickly Bertillon explained. "My microscope located, on the back of the victim's shirt collar, two opaque, blind parasites, a rare species of blind arthropod which can only live in a pitch-black room. On the victim's coat and vest are bacilli causing alcoholic fermentation, proving these garments were in a room near stores of wine. The grains of sawdust, sand, and coal on the body indicate a cellar room where there are such deposits. The sand also makes it probable that the killing occurred in a house near the Seine."

Briskly, Bertillon gave his orders. "First we will look for a recently missing office worker. That will give us the identity of the corpse. Then we will look for a house near the river, with cellars containing wine barrels, loose sand, and a very dark room filled with blind parasites. Find these and we find the murderer."

After three days of intensive hunting, the Sûreté found a firm near the Luxembourg Gardens that admitted its veteran bookkeeper, Charles Tellier, had been unaccountably missing from his desk for over a week. Tellier's rooms were searched, his friends and associates thoroughly questioned. The trail led to his bookie, Monsieur Cabassou, beloved and genial proprietor of a restaurant on the Seine.

Bertillon questioned Cabassou, and his beautiful redheaded wife, Marcelle, and learned that they both had known Tellier. But there was no cellar. Later, before dawn, at great personal risk, Bertillon returned, searching again until he found a trapdoor, and a staircase leading into a secret cellar. There was a large room filled with wine barrels, and on the wall a bloodstain. A door led to a second room, its floor covered with sawdust and cut logs, sand from the river, and pieces of coal. And finally, through a trick entrance in the cellar wall, Bertillon entered a pitch-black third room. A flashlight showed thousands of parasites on the walls and ceiling, and the microscope revealed that they were blind, colorless arthropods. Cabassou, realizing his game was up, tried to escape, was caught, and confessed. Having learned his wife was in love with Tellier, he had lured the bookkeeper into the cellar on the pretense of inviting him to sample the wine, and then murdered him. An almost perfect crime—solved because of one clean shirt-sleeve and two sightless insects. Bertillon had shown diehards the value of deduction and the power of science.

At his peak, Bertillon was the embodiment of today's detective. A great, stern, bewhiskered man, he was unsentimental in his work, tough, explosive. His foremost student, Dr. Edmond Locard, France's leading detective today, affectionately remembers him as "a bad-tempered werewolf." A Sûreté technician, recalling him, says, "He was a perfectionist. We feared him. Silence was his best praise."

Bertillon never forgot an offense. Juan Vucetich, the Argentine police scientist who did pioneer work in fingerprinting, once ridiculed Bertillon's system. Later, when Vucetich came to Paris, he asked to see the Sûreté Identity Department. Unsmiling, Bertillon met him at the entrance. "Monsieur," said Bertillon, "you attempted to harm my system" —and then he slammed the door in the South American's face. More often, however, he resolved his feuds good-naturedly. When a Paris columnist named Sarcey ridiculed Bertillon's photographic methods in print, Bertillon invited him to the Sûreté. As they strolled through the laboratories, the columnist explained that he doubted if anyone could photograph a man candidly if the man did not wish to be so photographed. Bertillon listened in silence, and then, at the end of the tour, handed Sarcey ten remarkably true photographs of himself—all automatically snapped by hidden, secret cameras that caught the columnist whenever he passed through a Sûreté door.

Unquestionably, Bertillon's personal genius made the Sûreté what it is today, and through the Sûreté, made the FBI and Scotland Yard what they are today. "Ask yourself two questions about every premeditated murder," Bertillon would say. "Who profits by this crime? Where is the woman?" He proved 90 percent of major French crimes have a woman involved in them. He cautioned his detectives, "I distrust a man who always smiles." When grilling a suspect, Bertillon always made him take off his shoes. "A man without shoes is less arrogant," he would say. He taught his colleagues that women are usually the killers of little children, that men are almost always the forgers, and women the blackmailers.

The French claim Bertillon first discovered a criminal's height could be determined by his stride marks, and that he was the first to insist on photographing the scene of a crime. He enjoyed putting criminal photography to odd and new uses. When the *Mona Lisa* was daringly stolen from the Louvre by a little Italian named Perugia in 1913, and later recovered in Italy, it was Bertillon's enlarged photographs of the brush strokes that identified the disputed oil as the fabulous original.

Friends and enemies alike knew Bertillon solely as a brilliant human bloodhound. But there was another side. One afternoon in 1882, while crossing the Rue de Rivoli, he had met a young blonde with a Viennese accent. She had turned to him and asked: "Sir, would you help me across the street? I am nearsighted, and have forgotten my spectacles." That was how he met Amelie Notar. She had come to Paris from Austria, and was teaching German for her keep. Bertillon found that the only way he could woo her was by taking German lessons from her. After his identity system had succeeded, Bertillon married Amelie.

Suzanne Bertillon, a niece who now resides in Paris, remembers the marriage as a wonderfully happy one, and recalls that her uncle was far less a terror at home than at the Sûreté. "On summer Sundays he loved to fish, swim, go boating," Suzanne recalls, "but on winter nights we would all sit around the dining room table, under the petroleum lamp, in the family place in the Place du Trocadéro. Bertillon would frighten us with horror stories, but they always ended in a funny way. Perhaps so that we would sleep. He had a great taste for fun."

Bertillon's favorite form of relaxation, which he indulged in regularly at his summer country house on the Marne, was to meet with three colleagues: Lacassagne, the laboratory expert from Lyons; Reiss, the German crime photography wizard; and Minovici, boss of the Bucharest police. The quartet would exchange wild crime experiences by the hour, ranging from the killing which Reiss had solved by analyzing the substance scraped from under a human nail, to the strange clue Lacassagne had found in Lyons, the fingerprints of a pair of large monkeys trained to rob.

Bertillon enjoyed conversation on all subjects, but there were two subjects he did not like to discuss. One was the Dreyfus case. While this case was in its earliest stages, he had been called in to study examples of handwriting, a subject with which he was less familiar than with most other techniques of crime detection, and he had unequivocally reported that his analysis proved Dreyfus the author of the treasonable document in question. Later, when the scandal over evidence forged by Major Henry (who committed suicide) broke into the open, Bertillon was among the many experts proved wrong. Ignoring the decision of the Supreme Court of Appeals, Bertillon refused to retract his analysis, insisting it had been correct and scientific.

Bertillon was even more stubborn about his identity system, anthropometry. It was his brain baby, his life, and he refused to listen to the growing clamor about another identity system—fingerprinting.

Today, many persons believe that Bertillon invented fingerprinting. This is not true. Today, many specialists think Bertillon had nothing to do with fingerprinting. This, also, is not true. To begin with, fingerprinting as an identification method is not a recent discovery. The Chinese were using thumbprints for signatures fifteen hundred years ago. In 1856, an Englishman in India, Herschell, who was entrusted with the job of paying Indian moguls their pensions, learned that many undeserving recipients were collecting under false names. In one particular case, a pension had been doled out to the same name for two hundred years. So Herschell conceived the idea of fingerprinting all Indians who came to collect their pensions. But fingerprinting did not become popular outside of India until Sir Francis Galton, the great English scientist, devised a workable dactyloscopic system in 1892.

The exponents of the fingerprint system bombarded Bertillon and his adherents with a series of spectacular statements. Human fingers always are perspiring lightly, they argued, so they cannot touch a smooth surface without leaving behind a telltale mark. Fingerprints never change, they argued. The adult pattern exists in a foetus at four months. And clear prints can still be taken from stuffed monkeys, and from Egyptian mummies five thousand years old. Fingerprints are not affected by race, class, or intelligence. They are made by savages and anthropologists, geniuses and idiots, queens and prostitutes, in related and recognizable patterns. When the fingertip is injured or cut off, the newly grown skin assumes its original pattern (sensationally proved, in our time, in the case of John Dillinger, who had a doctor alter his fingertips; yet, after his death, the FBI found that his new prints already had over three hundred points identical with the old ones). Above all, according to various experts, the odds range from sixty-four million to one, to a ratio of novemdecillion to one, against the probability that two human beings would ever have exactly the same fingerprints.

Bertillon snorted. He had found, he said, twin brothers whose fingerprints bore thirty marks of exact resemblance. He respected, he said, the efforts of his friend, Sir Francis Galton, but fingerprinting was too new, too untried. Had it ever caught a murderer? Solved a crime? On the other hand, his own anthropometry, while more cumbersome, was surely tried, proved, and infallible. Suddenly, one day, an incident occurred in the Federal Penitentiary, Leavenworth, Kansas, that shook Bertillon out of his complacency.

A criminal, Will West, had been committed to Leavenworth, and given prison number 3426. As he was being photographed and measured according to the Bertillon system, one of the operators remarked that he appeared familiar. He asked Will West if he'd been there before. West said that he had not, that this was his first offense. Brought before the chief identity clerk, West still claimed that he never before had seen the inside of a prison. The clerk said, "West, you are lying, you've been here. We have your photographs and measurements. I'll show you." The Bertillon files were quickly consulted. Sure enough, there were photographs and an index card marked "William West, Number 2626." Will West admitted the photographs looked like him, that the measurements tallied with his, but violently insisted he had never been in Leavenworth before. Annoyed, the clerk flipped the identity card over, and read on the back, "William West. Committed to this institution September 9, 1901. Murder." The clerk blinked. If this was true, it meant the William West on the card was already in a cell of the prison. The second Will West was summoned. In ten minutes the two men stood side by side: Will West, Number 3426, and William West, Number 2626. They were not twins, not even relatives, but their faces were the same, their bodies, and their Bertillon measurements were exact in five out of eleven points, and differed only a fraction of an inch on the other six points.

The West case caused an eruption in police circles. Bertillonage had not been discredited, but it had been severely shaken. Several years before, Bertillon himself, to please Galton, had added four fingerprints to each of his measurement reports. But he remained an enemy of fingerprinting. Now, his basic honesty asserted itself. Still the scientific man, he suddenly did an about-face. He would prove that he was not too old to change, to accept new ideas, to accept and *improve* upon new ideas. At once, he had the Sûreté fully adopt fingerprinting. To his own measurements of each new criminal, he had all ten fingerprints added.

In a frenzy, he decided to make up for lost ground. His enemies had insisted that he was suppressing the growth of fingerprinting by the prestige of his opposition. Now he would show them. He invented fingerprint photography. He perfected a white powder for picking up prints. He experimented with a new classification system. But one thing bothered him. Fingerprints had solved no major crime.

On an October night in 1905, an unknown person broke into the home of a Parisian dentist. The criminal smashed a glass case, removed some valuable antiques, and then, apparently, as he was about to escape, was confronted by the dentist's servant. From the wreckage, it appeared a wild battle had been fought. In the end, the servant had been floored, kicked unconscious, and then battered to death. Bertillon came to study the crime. There seemed to be no clues. Bertillon poked through the debris, carefully collected pieces of broken glass, and returned with them to his laboratory.

"On one fragment of glass, he noticed four clear fingerprints," says Suzanne Bertillon. "Powder was not necessary. The prints were plain enough to be photographed and enlarged. In great excitement, Bertillon hurried to his files and began poring over them. At last, he came up with an index card. It belonged to a hardened ex-convict named Scheffer. The prints on it exactly matched those on the broken glass! Immediately, Bertillon sent out a description of Scheffer, based on photos and measurements in his files. All European police were notified. In three days, the killer was trapped. Scheffer, a sort of Jekyll-and-Hyde personality and a homosexual, had planned his crime as a murder and tried to make it appear like robbery. He had gone to kill the dentist's servant, whom he had lost as his boy friend. He was sure he had escaped successfully. He had not reckoned with Bertillon.

"This was the first time in world history," said Miss Bertillon, "that a murderer was caught through fingerprints. It created an international sensation in police circles. It helped popularize and establish the new system of fingerprinting. And, in the end, it was Alphonse Bertillon who did it!"

Bertillon died February 13, 1914, aged sixty-one. His funeral, three days later, was a national event. Because he lived, thousands of criminals died by the hemp, under the blade, or in the electric chair. Because of him, the earth's two billion men, women and children, from St. Louis to Singapore, from Rio to Rome, sleep more safely tonight.

WHAT HAS HAPPENED SINCE . . .

I had not yet determined to do a story about Alphonse Bertillon that late summer afternoon in 1949, when the detective's niece, Suzanne Bertillon, came to call upon me at my Paris hotel. I will never forget my first sight of her: a tiny gnome of a woman, middle-aged, full of vitality, pedaling a bicycle up the Rue de Berri to the California Hotel where I was waiting. We went into the bar for a drink, and there she presented me with a copy of *Vie d'Alphonse Bertillon,* the biography she had written about her illustrious uncle, published by Gallimard eight years earlier. I suppose it was my conversations with Miss Bertillon about her uncle, and the reading of her biography, as well as my visit to Alphonse Bertillon's great admirer in Lyons, Dr. Edmond Locard, that made me decide to undertake the writing of "Monsieur Bertillon."

Until then, what had made me resist a project that held enormous interest for me was the scarcity of research materials. In his lifetime, Bertillon had produced thirteen scientific papers and books, all highly technical, and none revealed anything of the man himself. There had been a work on him written jointly by Dr. Locard and Professor Lacassagne, published in Lyons, and another work published in Belgium, but neither offered the kind of material I desired. The truth about Bertillon had to be excavated from beneath a mound of sensational and often inaccurate newspaper clippings in several languages, scientific treatises, and popular memoirs written by other detectives who had known and admired him. Could a story be derived and constructed from these fragments? I was doubtful. And so I had held back, until Miss Bertillon's biography in French, her wonderful anecdotes in English, supplemented by additional colorful material from Dr. Locard, made the story possible.

I wrote "Monsieur Bertillon" late in 1949. It was published in the January, 1950, issue of *True* magazine, and reprinted in the February,

1950, issue of the *Reader's Digest* under the title "France's Greatest
Detective." I had enjoyed writing the story, but I had expected it to
have a short life after its publication, inasmuch as I felt that few Americans would identify with a French hero. I was wrong. As a direct result
of my story, millions of Americans first became acquainted, or became
better acquainted, with the life and exploits of Bertillon. For, as chance
would have it, the television rights to my story were acquired by *TV
Reader's Digest*, which produced it as a half-hour television film starring
Arthur Franz in the role of Alphonse Bertillon. The television film was
shown coast-to-coast in the United States. And even in recent years, it
has continued to be replayed on television.

And what has happened to the reputation of Alphonse Bertillon in the
last fifteen years? The fact is that his name has gained ever wider popular acceptance. On my reference shelves, I find that he is cited in the
Encyclopaedia Britannica as one who "invented the system of identification of criminals, known as Bertillonage"; in Webster's Biographical Dic-
tionary as the "French anthropologist and criminologist" who "devised
system of identifying criminals by anthropometric measurements"; in the
Encyclopedia Americana as one who "is widely noted as the founder of
a system of identification of criminals . . . he established his system of
measurements which were remarkable for their precision."

Six years after my magazine story was published, Bertillon's reputation was further enhanced by the appearance of the first book ever written in English on the French detective. This was *Alphonse Bertillon,
Father of Scientific Detection*—by Henry T. F. Rhodes, an Englishman
with a good knowledge of French apparently. In this volume, Bertillon is
given his full due. Affectionately, Rhodes quotes from Professor Lacassagne's memorial to his friend, that "Bertillon was a man above the common sort" who "had lived to realize in his maturity a dream of his youth."
And again, Rhodes quotes Dr. Locard who said that Bertillon "was a
genius" because he created "a new technique" which, for the first time,
introduced science into law enforcement, and led to a marriage between
the two which has endured ever since. Rhodes concludes that "Bertillon's discoveries were an historical event of the first magnitude. His anthropometry met a social as well as a technical need, and it thus gave a
new form and shape to judicial processes and events."

However, to my mind, the happiest monument to the genius of Alphonse Bertillon is to be found in a classic of detective fiction. The
reader may remember that at the outset of my story, I quoted Bertillon
as telling an American publisher, "I would like to see Sherlock
Holmes's methods of reasoning adopted by all professional police." Well,
recently, I was rereading A. Conan Doyle's *The Hound of the Basker-*

villes, and to my delight, in the very first chapter, I came across what I had not noticed before—clear evidence that Sherlock Holmes, the foremost detective in fiction, had obliquely repaid Bertillon's respect by bestowing upon him the greatest compliment one man can confer upon another—that of jealousy.

A Mr. James Mortimer, having just met Sherlock Holmes, admitted that he was faced with an extraordinary problem. Then Mr. Mortimer, still addressing Sherlock Holmes, went on:

"Recognizing, as I do, that you are the second highest expert in Europe—"

"Indeed, sir! May I inquire who has the honour to be the first?" asked Holmes with some asperity.

"To the man of precisely scientific mind the work of Monsieur Bertillon must always appeal strongly."

"Then had you not better consult him?"

"I said, sir, to the precisely scientific mind. But as a practical man of affairs it is acknowledged that you stand alone. I trust, sir, that I have not inadvertently—"

"Just a little," said Holmes. . . .

This display of Holmes's jealousy, actually an accolade from the greatest sleuth in fiction to the greatest detective in fact, was published in 1902. How very much Alphonse Bertillon must have appreciated and enjoyed it.

14

THE
FRENCH SHERLOCK HOLMES

FOR FIVE YEARS, terror gripped the town of Tulle, France. The anonymous letters, printed crudely by hand, appeared sporadically at first, then swept over the community like a dreadful plague. In all, there were three thousand poison-pen letters written, an average of a dozen a week. Toward the end of the affair, with two persons already dead because of the letters, the town was in a frenzy of fear, friend suspecting friend, neighbor suspecting neighbor.

These vicious letters, most of them directed at public officials, told one popular civil servant that his great-grandfather had been a notorious swindler, another that his grandmother had borne an illegitimate son, a third that his mother was a kleptomaniac, a fourth that his son was homosexual. The revelations arrived in curious and terrifying ways. Some were mailed by ordinary post, some pushed under office doors; others were dropped on the sidewalk of the main street, several were slipped into housewives' shopping bags, and once, one fluttered down into the middle of a festive outdoor gathering. Little was done about the assault until two of the letters had left death in their wake.

A city official, informed by an anonymous letter that his ailing wife was the perpetrator of the crimes, had a heart attack and fell dead. Then his best friend, who also worked in the city hall, learned, through a similar communication, that his wife was having a tawdry affair with a younger man. This husband suffered an apoplectic fit and died.

The local police did their blundering best. Investigations revealed that every employee in the Tulle city hall had received anonymous letters except one — a handsome Frenchman named Maury. The police learned, too, that Maury and his pretty wife were the only persons praised in the letters received by others. Throughout the town, feeling ran high against Maury. In fact, one city hall worker, Jean Laval, made himself spokesman for the community and fearlessly denounced Maury to the police. When the police, confused, failed to act, they too received anonymous letters blaming them for slackness in not arresting Maury.

At this point, the local prefecture contacted the Sûreté Nationale in Lyons, and promptly Dr. Edmond Locard, France's foremost criminologist, was assigned to the case. From the moment Dr. Locard entered Tulle, events sped to a swift climax.

After examining the evidence, Dr. Locard dismissed the popular villain, Maury. Instead, he began to investigate the victimized peoples' spokesman, Jean Laval, as well as his relatives and friends. At once, interesting facts came to light. Dr. Locard learned that a year before the letters began plaguing the populace, Jean Laval had helped his sister obtain a job in the city hall. Here the sister, Angèle Laval, worked side by side with a Miss Fioux, in an office run by Maury. Both women, it appeared, had set their sights on Maury, competed coquettishly for him, and after a close contest, Miss Fioux had won. Maury married Miss Fioux, and Angèle Laval was left loveless and embittered.

"There we have our motive," Dr. Locard told his colleagues. "Angèle Laval hated Maury for marrying Miss Fioux. Angèle decided upon revenge. She began the anonymous-letter barrage. With the help of her mother, she had enough malicious gossip and half-truths to throw the town into an uproar. She committed a terrible crime, and then tried to point the finger of guilt at Maury by not sending him any letters, by complimenting him in her letters to his neighbors, by whispering suspicions to her brother, who consequently accused him. Yes, I am sure it is Angèle Laval. Now comes the most difficult part. We must prove it."

Unable to obtain samples of Angèle Laval's handwriting, Dr. Locard summoned the frail young lady to his office and bluntly accused her of the crime. She denied everything. Dr. Locard ordered her to take dictation, while he read aloud from various of the anonymous letters. Calmly, slowly, Miss Laval wrote on the paper. Dr. Locard compared her block lettering to the printing of the anonymous notes. They did not match at all. Either she was disguising her printing or she was not guilty. How to discover which?

Then, Dr. Locard had the inspiration which has since become legend in police circles. Miss Laval was pulling on her gloves, preparing to leave, when Dr. Locard halted her. "One moment, Miss Laval," he said, "we are not quite through. You have given me one sample of your hand. It is not enough, I must have more."

Dr. Locard stacked a hundred sheets of blank paper and two dozen sharpened pencils before Miss Laval, and commanded her to print as he dictated. He gave her no rest, no pause. When she protested, he grimly dictated faster, pressed her harder. One hour passed. Two hours. Page after page was completed. Angèle Laval hunched, quivering, her face flour-white, her cramped hand rapidly printing sentences on the pages. Three hours. Four hours. She was shaking, gasping, scribbling automatically now, without feeling or thought or deliberation.

Suddenly, abruptly, Dr. Locard stopped. The third degree by penmanship was over. He snatched up the last dozen pages she had filled. He compared them to the anonymous letters. They were exactly alike.

"*Voilà, simple!*" Dr. Locard told his colleagues later. "She was writing too slowly, deliberately changing her true handwriting. I knew if I could break her down, tire her, prevent her from thinking before she wrote, she would reveal her natural hand. When she became exhausted, she could not fake. So she signed her own confession of guilt."

Sent home with a policeman for her belongings, Miss Laval managed to escape with her mother through the rear door of the house. At a deep swimming hole called Gimel the two women tried to commit suicide, but woodcutters plunged into the water after them. The mother was drowned. Angèle Laval was rescued, quickly placed on trial, quickly found guilty. Since it had all begun as an affair of the heart, a factor which has a persistent melting effect on the hard objectivity of French jurors, the terror and the deaths were overlooked, and Angèle Laval was sentenced to a short jail term and a stiff fine.

The affair at Tulle was ended, but not without an unexpected and pleasant aftermath. For as it turned out, this celebrated case—which occurred twenty-seven years ago, and which inspired a French movie called *The Raven*, a great success across the United States—became the pivotal point in the remarkable career of Dr. Edmond Locard.

"I am grateful to that Laval woman," Dr. Locard likes to say today. "After I trapped her, my name became known everywhere. Look, here is the front page of a Texas newspaper. You see how far away it was publicized at the time. Well, sir, after that I began to get more and more cases outside of France, crimes from Germany, England, Africa, South America. At that moment I became an international criminologist."

Dr. Edmond Locard was forty-five years old when he solved "*l'affaire Laval.*" Today, at seventy-two, he is still as active as any renowned private eye on the screen, and certainly one of the few great man hunters in the world, if not the greatest of them all. Of course, there is no precise scale by which one can rank men who solve crimes. No real record is kept of their times at bat, their hits, their errors. But if such an average could be kept, Dr. Locard would undoubtedly be the Ty Cobb or Babe Ruth of criminology.

It is unlikely that his versatility, ingenuity, success, and scope of operation have ever been matched in law enforcement history. The United States has had its share of wizards, from Pinkerton and Burns to Leonarde Keeler and Raymond Schindler. However, most of those men were, or are, specialists. Some excel in fieldwork, others in the laboratory; some are good with a gun, others with a microscope. Dr. Locard is one of the few who can do all these things, a man with as many talents as the god Siva has arms. He is not merely a human bloodhound or a laboratory technician. "Dr. Locard is not a detective as we understand the term," says H. Ashton-Wolfe, an Englishman who studied under him in the twenties. "He is an expert on crime. He is in real life the embodiment of Sherlock Holmes and Dr. Thorndyke. He is psychologist, doctor, chemist, and criminologist." And he is equally at home in crimes involving arson, forgery, swindling, smuggling, or murder.

Today, although at the ripe age when most men are spending portions of their pension checks on nurses, canes, and grandchildren, Dr. Locard is at his peak of activity and popularity. His twenty books on solving assorted methods of extinction by violence, the most important of which is the seven-volume encyclopedia he wrote called Book of Criminology, are now studied by detectives and police scientists throughout the world. Several weeks ago, a French movie short subject on Dr. Locard's methods, starring the old man himself, was playing in Paris cinema houses, and this film will eventually be shown in London and Rome. Fellow criminologists, like Rochat in Geneva, continue to consult him on enigmatic cases—just as Lombroso, the brilliant Italian Jew at Turin University, and Nelcher, the Berlin police head before the advent of Hitler, and Percival Frazer, the New York City laboratory expert, used to consult him when they were alive before the Second World War. Embryonic sleuths, from as far off as Singapore, make their way to France to study for a few months under Dr. Locard.

Most impressive of all, though he remains by choice in the relatively remote city of Lyons, are the world's harried victims of crime who beat a path to his door. Movie stars from Hollywood, politicians from Paris, millionaires from Cairo are included among his recent or current clients. Dr. Locard is in the curious, and somewhat enviable, position of being able to take on cases that are official as well as unofficial. That is to say, he works for the Sûreté Nationale as well as for individuals—just as if J. Edgar Hoover, besides his work for the FBI, were able to take on assignments as a private detective.

"I work for the French police, with ten government experts under me," Dr. Locard explains, "but I contribute my services to the government free, without salary. Therefore, I am able to accept private cases and investigations. You would be surprised at how many wealthy husbands suspect their wives are slowly trying to poison them, and want to hire me to investigate first before going to the police."

Despite the fact that he is officially director of the Lyons Laboratoire de Police, with its one million criminal charts—police headquarters for the Rhone district of France—and even though he works with the colorful French Sûreté, which is said to be the oldest law enforcement agency in existence, Dr. Locard prefers to think of himself as crime consultant to the world.

In his private cases, almost nothing surprises Dr. Locard any more. Recently, he received a half-dozen poisoned arrows which had killed a trader in Africa and which the colonial governor of the resident foreign power wished examined. Once, Dr. Locard was hired by the President of Brazil for a special criminal investigation assignment. Another time, a wealthy Egyptian family retained Dr. Locard to untangle a one-million-dollar inheritance case, which had been complicated when dozens of forged wills turned up. It was Dr. Locard's longest case, requiring one year and two months to solve.

Not many years ago, he admits, he was involved in apprehending a New Caledonian multiple murderer with cannibalistic tendencies. While he prefers not to discuss this case, he concedes that he cooperated with German authorities in convicting Haarmann, who murdered from thirty to fifty German boys to sell their effects, and in catching Grossman, who slaughtered twenty-five young ladies and practiced cannibalism on their remains. In telling about Grossman, Dr. Locard likes to produce a photograph showing the murderer's twenty-fifth victim, an attractive brunette, lying on a sofa quite extinct and very nude, but still in one complete piece when the authorities caught the criminal.

Two years ago, faked Picasso and Utrillo oils were floating about, and sold at enormous prices. The paintings were such excellent forgeries that Utrillo himself was not sure which of the street scenes bearing his name were actually his own and which were copies. Dr. Locard, retained to settle the matter, proved that when Picasso or Utrillo sign their works, they just sign in a natural manner. In the case of the forgeries, the swindlers, to be certain that the signatures were exact, first traced on the name of Picasso or Utrillo in pencil and then painted over it. Dr. Locard revealed the faint pencil markings, and helped smash a million-dollar racket.

He even had his finger in the prosecution of the Lindbergh kidnaping case in the thirties, a case that he regards as the most fascinating criminal investigation in American history. "It will become a classic, a legend," he says. "There is so much to it. I examined the evidence and delivered an expertization on the wooden ladder to Colonel Lindbergh. I also checked and corroborated the findings of the American experts. Of course, they were right. Bruno Hauptmann was unquestionably guilty."

When Paris police officials, or victims of crime, wish to consult Dr. Locard, and do not wish to trust their problems to correspondence, they usually board a train in Paris, and reach Lyons, which is about half-way to Marseille or the Riviera, seven hours later. For foreign visitors, Lyons, France's third city, squatting between the Rhone and Seine rivers, more industrial and French than is Paris, holds few attractions beyond Dr. Locard. The foreigners hurry across a concrete-and-wooden bridge to the towering Palais de Justice. There they are directed to the rear of the courthouse, to a tiny crowded street called the Rue St.-Jean. Just beyond the entrance to the Sûreté Nationale is a grilled gate-way bearing the sign LABORATOIRE DE POLICE. Going through this en-trance, and then up four flights of cement stairs (there is no elevator), they reach Dr. Locard's headquarters. His private office, files, and labora-tories occupy the entire top floor.

He sits at the far end of a huge wooden table, his pretty, plump secretary across from him, a green-shaded lamp hanging down from the ceiling over him, a full wall of crime books and documents in seven languages behind him, and built-in metal files of his various investiga-tions elsewhere surrounding him. Visitors, prepared to meet a man of seventy-two, usually expect a shrunken invalid in a wheelchair, and are dumbfounded when he rises briskly to greet them. Of medium height, slender, electric, Dr. Locard appears a young fifty-five. His white hair is short and rumpled, his eyes at once penetrating and amused, his nose hooked, his mustache full. He claims to know a dozen major languages. In our several talks, he would switch absently from his native French to German or Spanish or Russian. His English vocabulary, however, was limited, and somewhat exotic.

Visitors are often surprised to find that a man so scholarly can have a sense of humor. Dr. Locard, after finishing a long dissertation on some complex aspect of murder, usually likes to reward his guests or students with a light anecdote. His favorite, which he insists is true, involves the gentleman who developed a silent hatred of his old friend and room-mate and finally decided to dispose of him. At the opportune moment, this gentleman massaged his roommate on the skull with a flatiron, and after making certain that rigor mortis had set in, he tried to think of a way of getting rid of the corpse. As a last resort, he dissected the body, neatly divided the pieces between a hand trunk and two small cartons, and then went outside with his load. As he staggered down the avenue, an inquisitive acquaintance watched him, then came alongside and in-quired, "That's quite a load. What are you up to?" The gentleman re-plied, "Oh, I am only helping move a friend."

When foreign visitors, impressed by his versatility and acumen, inevitably compare him to Sherlock Holmes, Dr. Locard beams. He likes to think of himself as a Gallic edition of the fictional English detective. At the first mention of Sherlock Holmes, Locard dips into his desk and whips out a youthful, rather pensive, photographic portrait of himself trickily superimposed on a silhouette of Sherlock Holmes. Recently, when a woman was found murdered in a French hayloft, the leading suspect alibied that he had spent the night sleeping by a roadside. Dr. Locard vacuumed the suspect's pockets, dug out the grit under his fingernails, and analyzed the minute particles. This revealed not the minerals in road dust, but organic hay dust. The suspect was convicted and guillotined. "Sherlock Holmes was the first to realize the importance of dust," Dr. Locard explains. "I merely copied his methods."

Besides copying the master's methods, and besides forcing his disciples to read all the Sherlock Holmes short stories and novels, Dr. Locard carries his Baker Street fetish even further. In one classic story, Sir Arthur Conan Doyle has Sherlock Holmes remark that he had written a monograph "Upon the Distinction Between the Ashes of the Various Tobaccos, An Enumeration of 140 Forms of Cigar, Cigarette and Pipe Tobacco." While the treatise may have been fictional when Sherlock Holmes spoke of it, Dr. Locard has since made it a fact by writing a learned paper on the identification of tobaccos through a study of ashes left at the scene of a crime.

Dr. Locard likes to say that he personally caught the killer who, in real life, almost extinguished Sherlock Holmes before his time. This killer was a thirty-five-year-old Frenchman named Jules Bonnot, whom Dr. Locard regards as the most daring and resourceful murderer he ever squared off against. Bonnot, a mustached man with a pleasant concave face, ran wild in France just before the First World War. Working out of an innocent-looking motorcycle repair shop, which he used as a cover and as a storehouse for his artillery, Bonnot committed almost every crime in the book. He forged documents, counterfeited money, kidnaped, robbed, committed arson, and performed twelve brutal murders. His most spectacular murder was that of a Société Générale bank messenger, whom he waylaid, killed, and robbed of half a million francs. Bonnot was well-traveled, and had adopted criminal techniques from every European nation. The Sûreté suspected any number of gangsters, but narrowed their hunt down to Bonnot and one other person on information provided by an informer. But, until the police obtained real evidence, Bonnot was safe. Then, in Lyons, a risky safecracking job was attempted. The Sûreté, acting on another tip, broke in on the thief. In the dark, unseen, Bonnot slipped out of the net and escaped. He even managed to take his torch and tools away with him. Dr. Locard, examining the damaged safe, discovered telltale traces of marks left by the tools. With photographs of this evidence, Dr. Locard secretly made his way into Bonnot's repair shop, and compared the marks to the tools lying about. In ten minutes, Dr. Locard had found the instruments that fitted the marks. Bonnot was apprehended, almost fought his way free from his captors, but was finally jailed. Under muscular questioning, he confessed to all of his previous sins. The French police bypassed the aristocratic guillotine to execute Bonnot by a firing squad composed of giant African Zouaves.

One day, a short time thereafter, Sir Arthur Conan Doyle stopped off in Lyons to chat with Dr. Locard. Eager to play proper host to the creator of his beloved Sherlock Holmes, Dr. Locard escorted his visitor to the three private rooms in his laboratory which only his friends and celebrated guests are ever permitted to see. In these three rooms, his crime museum, Dr. Locard keeps mementos of crimes solved: weapons, tangible clues, and a pictorial gallery of rogues he has brought to justice. As he guided Sir Arthur through the rooms, explaining the offenses committed by the owners of the various profiles in the photographs, he suddenly heard his guest gasp. Dr. Locard turned. Doyle was staring ahead at a large photograph of Bonnot. "Why, I know that fellow!" blurted Doyle. "He was my chauffeur for two months in London. What in the devil's he doing here?" When Dr. Locard told him what Bonnot was doing here, the creator of Sherlock Holmes shivered. "Actually shivered," says Dr. Locard. "It was quite a coincidence. That is why I always say that I caught the man who might have abruptly ended Sherlock Holmes's career. Bonnot chauffeuring Sir Arthur Conan Doyle. The flesh creeps. Think how close we came to not having all we do have of Sherlock Holmes!"

Dr. Locard possesses a large rectangular ledger in which he records every criminal assignment that crosses his desk. In forty years, he has scrawled 9,253 entries in this ledger. He has not solved them all, but his successes are fantastic. He enjoys a clever crime, and he likes to solve it in a subtle way. "The great difference between crime in the United States and in France," he says, "is that American murders are usually merely physical and violent. Here in France our killers tend toward finesse. They always prefer to mix their murder with a bit of forgery or with a swindle or with melodramatic trickery."

Dr. Locard is never aroused by a straight unimaginative homicide. When Vacher, a runty Frenchman who looked exactly like a sweet little Arab, but had slaughtered twenty-nine farmers and shepherds, was caught while opening the stomach of his thirtieth victim, Dr. Locard considered the catch routine. "Vacher was merely mad," he says, in a masterpiece of understatement, "and therefore thoroughly uninteresting."

Another crime which Dr. Locard regarded as routine, but which had Paris in an uproar, began when one Charles Weber accused his sister-in-law, Jeanne Weber, of strangling his year-old son while baby-sitting, as well as of murdering her own children and her two nephews. The bodies of the youngsters were promptly exhumed, but autopsies revealed neither strangulation nor poison. Several months later, a hysterical neighbor reported to the police that her only child had died in the night while Jeanne Weber was baby-sitting. Again, autopsy revealed neither strangulation nor poison. In subsequent months, more youngsters died in the night, and though people referred to Miss Weber as "the Ogre of Goutte-d'Or," there was not a shred of evidence against her. At last, deciding to employ a dangerous strategy, the police found a friend of Miss Weber's who felt that she was absolutely innocent and who was willing to risk his two offspring with her for a night. As the friend left the house, Miss Weber was placidly baby-sitting with his two-year-old boy and ten-year-old girl. But when the police broke in shortly after midnight, they found the little boy almost dead of suffocation. His sister quickly came out of hiding to describe how Miss Weber, in an uncontrollable fit, had climbed atop the child, and pressed both hands down on his chest until he could not breathe. At her trial, Jeanne Weber provided a field day for Freudians when she stated that since childhood she could not stand the sight of a youngster. "When I am near one, I hear a voice telling me to kill. Before I know what I am doing, I have killed." After she had served a few weeks of her twenty-year term, Miss Weber completely lost her sanity. "It was a *crime sans cause*," says Dr. Locard. "Terrible, but it involved cleverness on neither her part nor ours."

Dr. Locard prefers his crimes to be unusual and challenging. He likes to remember the murder near Tours which he solved by observing the pattern of a corduroy jacket smeared on a dust-covered marble slab; or the criminal that he caught through tooth prints because the famished culprit had bitten into a pastry from which a plaster cast could be taken; or the fugitive who was found because he fell on a sandy beach while fleeing the police—the clear impression of his copper-buttoned vest, which was left, brought him to justice in three days.

One of Dr. Locard's favorites involves the robber who, leaping from the first-floor window of a villa, fell to his knees, rose and escaped. "I examined the spot where he fell," recalls Dr. Locard, "and found two clearly visible knee marks. They showed he wore striped velvet trousers. One set of stripes seemed broader, proving to me that one of his knees had a patch of slightly different material. This gave us a perfect picture of the man. We had him in twenty minutes."

Another time an engineer was found murdered in a meadow outside

of Lyons. There were no clues. Dr. Locard studied the immediate, surrounding terrain with the greatest of care. The day following, when suspects were paraded in and out, Dr. Locard was about to dismiss a burly
man when he noticed a tiny seed clinging to the suspect's sleeve. "I
identified the seed. It was *scorzonera lumilis*," says Dr. Locard. "That was
one of the plants beside the corpse in the meadow. Of course, our man
confessed. He was guillotined."

One of Dr. Locard's most highly prized crimes occurred thirty-seven
years ago. A sixty-five-year-old prostitute named Coco-la-Chérie was
found in her tiny room, her throat cut, her body a sieve of stab wounds.
She had had countless clients, so the suspects were many. "When we
examined her corpse we found hordes of rare parasites attached to her,"
says Dr. Locard. "I thought I'd take a few of these insects. Perhaps the
criminal would have had enough contact with Coco to have caught
them. The second day after the murder, a drunkard was brought in. He
was one of those who'd slept with Coco on the fatal night. He thought
he might have killed her, but he wasn't sure. He'd been too drunk. I
examined him, found parasites, but of an entirely different kind. We
released him. The third day another suspect, a boy of twenty named
Mayor, was brought in. In his hair I found the same rare parasite Coco
had on her person. Mayor denied the crime. But when his fingerprints corresponded with those in her room, he confessed. He had killed
her, and then stabbed her thirty times in a fit of fury, because she
wanted fifty centimes for sleeping with him instead of the thirty-five
centimes he offered. Incidentally, the fingerprint that convicted him was
the prettiest I have ever found. In France we require that twelve points
on a suspect's fingerprint correspond with prints found at the scene of
the crime, in order to convict. Well, this fellow Mayor's print had one
hundred corresponding points. It was delightful."

Often, employing the same methods, Dr. Locard is able to disprove a
crime. Not many years ago, a spinster businesswoman named Lea Camelin was found on the floor of her train compartment, gagged and drugged
with ether. Recovering, she explained that near Brotteaux, two men had
attacked her and stolen her wares. Dr. Locard, studying the bottle of
ether, found only one set of fingerprints on it. He was not surprised to
learn that they were Miss Camelin's own prints. She had invented the assault because, she confessed, she was unhappy and wanted to commit suicide, but since she was Catholic she had to make the suicide look like
murder to be buried in hallowed ground.

When a French general, on a hunting party in occupied Germany,
was shot through the head, the military authorities requested Dr. Locard
to find the murderer. Dr. Locard studied the general's skull, hair, and the

fatal bullet. Then Dr. Locard proved that the killing was not a murder, but an accident. Someone had shot at a wild pig, and the bullet had ricocheted off the pig and penetrated the back of the general's skull. The proof was simple. The coarse pig bristles were still imbedded, along with the general's hair, on the bullet.

Above all, however, Dr. Locard relishes an exotic case. It may deal with murder, or with a lesser crime, but if it is sufficiently weird, Dr. Locard will give it all of his energies. For instance, he glows when he recalls the events that led to the capture of Dr. Pierre Marain, of Venissieux. The good doctor, experimenting with quack cancer cures, used his wife as he would a laboratory mouse. When the robust lady died suddenly, and Dr. Marain prepared to collect handsomely under her will, the police became suspicious. Dr. Locard moved in on the case, and located two wills. In one, dated 1913, the deceased had left her money to her church. In the other, dated 1917, she left this money to her husband. Using intelligence, and ultra-violet rays, Dr. Locard went after the second will and proved that the 7 in 1917 had formerly been a 1, which Dr. Marain had forced his wife to alter. Then, even more sensationally, an invisible sentence in the will—"I died murdered by my husband"—was brought to light. It had been written, apparently, with a hairpin dipped in milk. This ended the career of Dr. Marain.

Sometimes Dr. Locard has his fill of gore, and then he enjoys nothing more than relaxing over some case that requires only giving his authoritative opinion. Recently, a rich Parisian, whose hobby is collecting authentic strands of hair from the heads of historical personalities, nervously appeared with a single hair enclosed in a velvet box. He had bought this tiny hair for 20,000 gold francs. It was the prize of his collection, a hair purported to be from the head of Napoleon Bonaparte. Now that he owned it, the collector wanted a certificate of authentication to show his friends. Dr. Locard studied the strand of hair intensively, and came up with his report. The hair did not come from Napoleon. It came from a cow.

But Dr. Locard is not infallible. Even though, in forty years, he has rarely fumbled, he has once or twice failed in a tricky experimentation, or found himself stumped by a brilliant swindle. Dr. Locard and the Sûreté eventually trap most swindlers. But occasionally, a gang will come along that operates successfully for years.

"The slickest couple I've ever run into," says Dr. Locard, "pulled off their fanciest job in the Rue de la Paix in Paris. A gentleman with an appearance of extreme wealth visited a famous jeweler in the Rue de la Paix and shopped for a diamond. He selected a small but rare item, priced at $4,000, but insisted that he also wanted a matching diamond, and would pay a higher price for the second. The jeweler said the diamond was an oddity, and would be difficult to match; however, he would do his best. In three days, the gentleman reappeared, explained that he was eager to get the matching diamond since he wanted to present the pair soon as a birthday gift, and even though he'd paid only $4,000 for the first, he offered to pay as high as $15,000 for the second one. The jeweler again said he would do his best. After only two days had passed, the gentleman appeared a third time, demanding the second diamond. The jeweler confessed that he had had no luck yet. Providentially, two weeks later, a young lady, whose clothes were good but shabby, wandered in, red-eyed, with a story that her husband had left her, and that since she had no money, she would have to sell her diamonds. She brought out several. The jeweler examined them, and to his amazement and delight, he discovered one stone that was the exact twin of the diamond his client was trying to match. The young lady asked $10,000 for it, and would not take a sou less. Although the jeweler had sold a similar diamond for only $4,000, he reminded himself that he could get $15,000 for this twin. Here was an easy profit. Quickly, he bought the diamond, cheerfully paying the $10,000.

"The following day, the jeweler went to call personally on his wealthy gentleman client at the address he had been given. There was no such gentleman at the address. There never had been. The jeweler studied the diamond he had bought for $10,000, and, too late, realized it was precisely the one he had sold for $4,000. When he came to us with his story, we showed him our gallery of swindlers. He identified the couple at once. They had a long record of more flagrant crimes. Of course, we did not catch them, and never have. Perhaps they are trying the same trick today in Rome or in New York."

Dr. Locard credits most of the successes he has had in his 9,253 cases to the thorough education he received under his old mentor, Professor Alexander Lacassagne, who taught legal medicine at the University of Lyons. Professor Lacassagne, a short, handsome man with a vast white mustache, preceded Dr. Locard as head of the laboratory in Lyons, until he was killed by an automobile in 1924. Lacassagne became a legend in France for his work in helping such Sûreté stars as Bertillon and Goron solve the first internationally publicized trunk murder, one committed by the pretty Gabrielle Bompard and her hypnotist lover Michel Eyraud.

Dr. Locard dates his own interest in crime from an incident that occurred one afternoon in Lyons when, as a lad of twenty-two, he accompanied Lacassagne on an assignment to treat an injured workman. Returning home, the two were caught in a windstorm, and sought refuge in a hallway. "We had nothing to do but twiddle our thumbs," Dr. Locard remembers. "I happened to have a Spanish magazine in my pocket. Even then I knew many languages. I gave it to the professor to read. Since he knew only French, he asked me to translate aloud to him. So as we stood there in the hallway, I translated aloud from a Spanish book review about a volume dealing with fingerprinting in South America. It was fascinating. When I had finished translating the review, I began to discuss fingerprinting, and crime in general, with the professor. At that moment, I decided to specialize in criminal investigation."

Dr. Locard spent time, as a student, in police laboratories in Lausanne, Berlin, Turin, and Rome. He even worked in Paris under Alphonse Bertillon, founder of the world's first system of criminal identification. "He was the greatest genius I've ever met," says Dr. Locard. "He concentrated fiercely. He did not like to explain things. One had to learn by watching him."

Dr. Locard officially became a member of the French police on January 10, 1910, and eight years later he was sent on a trip around the world to study advances made in work on fingerprints, palmprints, footprints, as well as on teeth, hair, and anatomy, in other nations including even far-away China. In 1918 he visited San Francisco, Chicago, and New York. Of his only visit to the United States, he remembers most fondly not the skyscrapers but the case of a New York doctor who solved his mother-in-law problem by slipping typhoid bacteria into her food.

By 1922, Dr. Locard was famous enough to be invited to serve on an international committee headed by General Pershing, to oversee an election in Arica, Chile, an area then claimed by both Chile and Peru. Dr. Locard was assigned to detect ballot forgeries. In the years following, his reputation grew so rapidly that he was appointed editor of the *Revue Internationale de Criminalistique,* a trade paper to which detectives of every land contributed their most noteworthy crime cases and discoveries, written in their own tongue.

During World War I, Dr. Locard was a member of the French secret service. In the Sherlock Holmes tradition, he would amuse Allied dignitaries by glancing at a muddy soldier and the soil stains on the man's uniform, and then announcing exactly in what area he had been fighting. Once, during this period, Dr. Locard was almost assassinated. Late one night, a French *femme fatale,* a spy in the pay of the Germans, worked her way into Dr. Locard's private office and began going through top-security papers. At this moment, Dr. Locard walked in on her. Immediately she hurled herself at him, brandishing a knife. Acting on instinct, Dr. Locard kicked her in the wrist, knocking the dagger to the floor, and then he pinned her to the wall until his men took her away. Today, Dr. Locard keeps the blade on his desk as a good-luck piece and likes visitors to feel its sharpness.

During World War II, Dr. Locard refused to budge from his desk although the Nazis occupied Lyons. He was interrogated three times by the Gestapo. He says they did not rough him up, but they tested all the weapons, even the antiquated ones, in his private museum, and they tapped his telephone. Once, when the Gestapo was about to limit his activities, the chief of the Gestapo came to him with a problem. The chief complained that twice his wallet had been robbed. He was anxious to catch the culprit. If Dr. Locard would help him, he would give Dr. Locard complete freedom to continue his work. Dr. Locard gave the German a powder to spread on his wallet, telling him that it would turn anything that contacted it a deep violet, and that the more one washed and scrubbed at the violet, the deeper its color grew. "A week later the Gestapo chief noticed that his German chauffeur's fingers looked like a bishop's glove," says Dr. Locard. "After that I was not bothered by the Nazis."

In his forty years of detective work, Dr. Locard has made many lasting contributions to law enforcement. One of his most popular discoveries resulted from his radical theory that the fingerprint is old-fashioned because it is often limited. Dr. Locard argued that the pattern made by any number of two thousand tiny pores of a single fingertip was as valuable as the entire fingerprint. To prove his point, he perfected, in 1929, poroscopy, a technique which required only one-twentieth of a man's single finger to trap him. Using this method, he solved a dozen cases in the next years. In one instance, a burglar used a candle instead of a flashlight during a robbery. He left no fingerprints, but Dr. Locard discovered that a piece of wax from the burning candle had fallen, bounced off the thief's finger, and dropped intact to the floor. Through use of microphotography, Dr. Locard made out the criminal's overall pore pattern on the wax drop. In a week, the criminal was identified and convicted.

While he believes, perhaps more strongly than the majority of his colleagues, in the power of the criminal laboratory, Dr. Locard does not feel that the detective talents and individuality of modern sleuths should be completely buried under test tubes, files, and business machines. Today, everywhere, the machine is winning, but if Dr. Locard has his way, there will still be a few inspired detectives in the world. Toward this end, in a one-man effort to perpetuate such a species, he works the year around with human bloodhounds sent him by other nations. Besides routine techniques, Dr. Locard tries to hammer all kinds of shortcuts and bits of odd information into his students. He reminds them that the most damaging evidence is often found on the bottom cuff of a man's trousers, since this is a place usually overlooked by the criminal when he brushes himself off.

When searching for evidence to back up his deductions, Dr. Locard prefers one faded bloodstain, one droplet of fat, one speck of dust, to a dozen witnesses. "Certainly witnesses are important," he tells his students, "but they are too often unreliable. They subconsciously exaggerate, because they are human and want to make themselves look important." In revisiting the scene of a crime, to search for a body or for hidden wealth, Dr. Locard advises detectives to walk close beside the suspect and hold his arm lightly. "Always hold his arm, because then you will feel his reaction. The trick never fails. And often, without knowing it, the criminal will guide you toward what you are searching for." Dr. Locard warns his young students that murderesses present the greatest problems. "They react differently than do men. They are always surprised to be accused, they deny everything, they are shocked and affronted and insulted. They appeal to your sentiment, your weakness as males. When you have them, when they can no longer deny the facts, then they blame men for their downfall; they blame a husband, a lover, a father, a brother, a man who misled them. *Cherchez la femme*, gentlemen, but when you find her, beware of her!"

Despite this intense distrust of women, Dr. Locard has been married, has a grown son with the Lyons police, and owns a comfortable house in the suburbs. He has three forms of relaxation. One is conversation. He used to enjoy long scientific arguments with the late Dr. Alexis Carrel, the Nobel Prize winner. He used to discuss crime by the hour with his friend Nelcher, of the Berlin police, who fled Hitler's wrath. Nelcher had proved that the Nazis themselves had entered the German Reichstag in 1933, through an underground heat tunnel from Goering's house, and had used chemicals to start the historic Reichstag blaze that vaulted Hitler into power and set the entire world aflame.

Another of Dr. Locard's pastimes is his collection of autographed letters dealing with crime. He owns letters handwritten by Vidocq, the celebrated rascal who founded the modern Sûreté, and by Mata Hari. One letter is addressed to Washington, D.C., and is an application for an engineering job. The signature is that of an ex-convict named Latude, who spent a record thirty-five years in the Bastille for the practical joke of having included a bomb in a thoughtful bouquet to Madame de Pompadour.

Dr. Locard's most passionate form of relaxation is attending the movie theater. He sits in a darkened cinema, laughing, crying, agonizing with hero and heroine. Neither rain nor storm (nor murder) keeps him from his weekly film. Recently, at the end of a busy afternoon, Dr. Locard was called out to a villa which had just been robbed. It was a routine affair. There was only one complication. When Dr. Locard entered, he found that the criminal was still there. The two parties were equally surprised. The criminal smashed Dr. Locard on the jaw with an uppercut, and Dr. Locard went down. "I was unconscious for ten minutes," he says, proudly. Later, after the criminal had been caught and jailed, and Dr. Locard's glass chin repaired, the police led their venerable chief to his home and forced him to lay his fragile frame on his bed.

After his staff left, Dr. Locard quietly got out of bed, dressed, and drove swiftly back to Lyons. He was barely in time to catch the last showing of his weekly movie. "I just couldn't miss it," he says sheepishly. "It was a Humphrey Bogart picture."

WHAT HAS HAPPENED SINCE . . .

In 1949, while I was visiting New York City en route to Paris, I met with a new editor on *Cosmopolitan* magazine, who was interested in my suggestions for some factual stories. When he told me that he wanted to give his publication more masculine appeal, I immediately thought of a story I had wanted to do for years, an interview-biography of Dr. Edmond Locard, of Lyons. Dr. Locard was reputed to be one of the world's foremost living detectives, although he was relatively unknown in the United States. The editor thought that this was a fascinating idea, and he gave me the assignment.

Once in Paris, I telephoned Dr. Locard in Lyons. He proved ready to cooperate with me. I took a night train from Paris to Lyons, and there spent several days chatting with Dr. Locard. Aside from the time I spent with the great detective, who was friendly and colorful, I found Lyons a bore. It was dismal, lacking in charm, and a municipal tomb after nine o'clock in the evening. I am a night person, and I have always shunned cities that go to sleep early. New York and Paris are night cities; Zurich and Vienna are not. Lyons was the worst of all. Except for Dr. Locard, the place was impossible.

I hastened back to Paris not only with the inner relief of one who has been liberated from a mausoleum, but with the excitement of one who has collected material for a good story not yet told. I wrote this story, sent it by airmail to *Cosmopolitan*, and a week later learned that the periodical had again changed its policy—it now wanted stories of feminine appeal, anything with masculine appeal was taboo. My unhappiness was alleviated somewhat by the fact that I had met a remarkable man in Lyons —and considerably more by the fact that I had on hand a completed story that I knew I would one day publish.

In 1953, when I returned to Paris, I took rooms as always at the California Hotel in the Rue de Berri. There the bartender, concierges, and telephone operators knew all my business as I knew theirs (they had known, four years earlier, of the purpose of my side trip to Lyons), and I heard from one of them that Dr. Locard was dead. I was not surprised by this, since he would have been seventy-six years old in 1953. But I was surprised that I had not read about it in the news. I asked my French informant—a knowledgeable telephone operator, as I recall—if she had read Dr. Locard's obituary in the press. She could not be sure. She believed that she had learned about it on the radio or had seen it in a newsreel. Well, I thought at the time, Good-bye, dear Dr. Locard, perhaps one day my story will be your obituary.

A full decade later, in 1963, when I decided to assemble the material for this book, I made the decision to include this story of Dr. Locard among my favorite published and unpublished articles. But a sense of incompleteness troubled me. To cap the story of Dr. Locard's life, I must have the exact place and time and circumstances of his death. I wrote to a friend of mine, a correspondent in the Paris bureau of *The New York Times*, and asked him if he could supply the information I needed. I assured him the task would be simple. It turned out to be anything but simple.

I kept getting memorandums from my correspondent friend in Paris, each one more exasperated than the last. He had gone to the files of *France-Soir*. There was "a big dossier" on Dr. Locard. No obituary. He had gone to the files of Agence France-Presse. No date of death. He had consulted the French *Who's Who* for 1961-62. There was a birth date, but no death date.

In desperation, my friend visited the Paris bureau of *Progrès de Lyon,* and what he heard in reply to his inquiry sent him running to a telephone. As he wrote me that evening of April 10, 1963:

"Herewith a surprise for you: Dr. Locard not only is not dead, but I talked to him over the phone just a half hour ago!"

Dr. Locard, at the age of eighty-six, was still alive in Lyons. The resurrection of one whom I had unfairly buried ten years before shocked me, then excited me, and finally spurred me into action. Quickly, I reviewed what I had written about the great detective in 1949, and now, in 1963, I fired off ten questions to Lyons to learn what had happened to him in the interval of fourteen years. The old crime hunter replied promptly, and for the most part frankly. But since he was evasive or cryptic on certain points, I was forced to fill in some answers from material found in various archives in Paris, after I arrived there in June of 1963. Here, then, is the compleat Dr. Locard to date:

For almost two years after I met him, Dr. Edmond Locard remained on active duty for the Sûreté Nationale in Lyons. In that short period, Dr. Locard was directly involved in 1,652 criminal cases—in other words, during his entire career for the Sûreté Nationale, he was involved in a total of 10,905 criminal cases, a formidable record.

I have the impression, however, that in those last two active years he was receiving more public attention as an author than as a government sleuth. Only one case in that time was found worthy of mention by the Paris press. This investigation occurred in December of 1950, and concerned two physicians, brothers-in-law of a dead man, whom the government suspected of having made some revisions in the deceased's will. Since 50 million francs were at stake, the authorities called upon the expertise of Dr. Locard. I did not learn what Dr. Locard accomplished, only that he was brought in and that his effort was publicized. Although only this single case, of the 1,652 cases which he covered between 1949 and 1951, was mentioned in the newspapers, there were numerous references to Dr. Locard in his capacity as criminologist-author and to the variety of his writings for the same period.

In 1950—a prolific year for our aging hero—Dr. Locard published a revised edition of his seven-volume Book of Criminology, a single-volume work entitled *Defend Yourself Against the Criminal*, and several magazine articles and essays. One of the latter received special attention. It was a provocative piece in the journal *Médecine 50*, called *La défense du crime*. As Dr. Locard told curious reporters, "I should really have called it 'In Defense of the Criminals.' After all, we are all perfectly capable of being criminals."

As Dr. Locard's advanced years began to make retirement an imminent probability, the French government decided to decorate him for his services to his country. In France, there are five grades of decoration, omitting the *Grand Cordon*, which President de Gaulle alone holds. Of these five, in November, 1950, Dr. Locard was awarded the third-highest. He was given the rank of *Commandeur de la Légion d'Honneur*.

After that, there was little else for Dr. Locard to do but step out of government service. And so, on February 21, 1951, after automatically being made "honorary director of the Laboratoire de Police" in Lyons, Dr. Locard retired from the Sûreté Nationale. He was seventy-four years old. He had been in the Sûreté's service for forty-one years.

One thing that made retirement easier for Dr. Locard was that he was replaced in the Lyons laboratory by his own son, Dr. Jacques Locard. But there is a sad note here, for his son served only one year and nine months. When I asked Dr. Locard about his son, he replied curtly, "Died 24th of November, 1952. He was succeeded by Professor Bouret."

But retirement from his official position did not mean retirement from work for Dr. Locard. At seventy-four, he felt young and therefore was young. He rented offices at 5 Rue Mercière in Lyons, and he did not resume but rather continued his activity in all aspects of criminology. Soon he was off to North Africa on a lecture tour of Tunisia, Algeria, Morocco. He had always been interested in motion pictures, but mainly as a spectator. Now, returning home, he decided to become a film writer and actor. Late in 1952, he delivered the completed manuscript of a scenario entitled "Crime Never Pays" to Henri Lepage, the French film director. Perhaps recalling his apprehension of Jules Bonnot, A. Conan Doyle's former chauffeur who had committed twelve murders, Dr. Locard's cinematic villain indulged in similar crimes in Lyons' Chinatown and deposited the corpses in the Rhone River. The hero, an elderly professor-detective, whom Dr. Locard lovingly created for his own film debut, identified the villain from a silk thread clinging to a rope found in the culprit's house, a thread of the same material as that of the blouse of a female victim. The hero then closed in on the murderer after finding a wax droplet from a candle the killer had used to make his way, corpse on his back, to the river. Unhappily for Dr. Locard, if not for cinema audiences, the scenario was never made into a film.

In the fifteen years following his retirement from the Sûreté, Dr. Locard continued to devote himself to his twin passions—writing about crime for periodicals and in books, and using the laboratory for detection. His prolific international correspondence with other detectives and prospective clients and admirers suffered. He had time, he told me, to correspond regularly with only "a few famous lawyers and a few criminals."

The hours taken from private correspondence, apparently, went into his public writings. When he retired, he had told the local press, "I will now be able to write that great work that is so close to my heart—a complete general catalog of the lichens in France." Since the relatively inoffensive lichen is a symbiotic plant that thrives on bark or rocks, Dr. Locard's questioners were understandably confused by this odd enthusiasm. His explanation of this interest gives us a minute insight into a traumatic moment of his youth. When he was in school, he explained, taking a botany examination for his baccalaureate, he was unsure of one important test question—on lichens. He asked a fellow candidate for the correct answer, misunderstood his friend's whispered reply, and as a result put down the wrong answer. He received a poor grade. Then and there he determined to compensate for his failure by becoming an expert in botany. When I inquired, a dozen years later, if he had overcome the lichen and exposed it in print, he replied tersely, "Book not finished."

Other books, however, were finished. Dr. Locard wrote and published *Les Causes Célèbres*, a popular and dramatic nonfiction book about famous criminals including Mata Hari and Angèle Laval, the latter the poison-pen letter writer whom he had apprehended in Tulle and who had made him world-famous. In 1961, the French publisher of scientific books, Payout, brought out Dr. Locard's more serious study, *Expertises de Documents Écrits*. Not unexpectedly, Dr. Locard was frequently approached about writing his memoirs. He had neither the interest nor the time, but at last he permitted Robert Corval, a Paris newspaperman, to collaborate with him on his autobiography, which appeared in France in September of 1957. There is no evidence that it was widely read.

Meanwhile, Dr. Locard continued to occupy himself with other aspects of creativity. He wrote and published his scientific papers and his popular articles. He edited a magazine, which I have never seen, called *Androcles*. And he contributed to the "Letters to the Editor" section of such newspapers as *Figaro* of Paris.

From time to time, through the years of so-called retirement, he made himself available to interviewers from Paris. When a journalist from the late *Samedi-Soir* asked him if the violence reported in mass-circulation newspapers had effected the increase in crime, Dr. Locard replied that he doubted if the press contributed to crime at all. Then he turned against an old love. The motion picture, he said, was far more dangerous, because films often gave potential criminals graphic illustrations—"ideas" —of how to commit their crimes. Dr. Locard went on to castigate his old enemy, the anonymous letter writer. He felt, he said, that there was no difference between a writer of anonymous letters and a murderer who killed by poison. And as to the poisoner, Dr. Locard added, lax colleagues who believed that any evidence of arsenic in a crime was absolute proof of premeditated poisoning were jumping to conclusions. Said Dr. Locard, "Arsenic is everywhere, even to be found in the armrests of easy chairs, and finding it does not prove anything."

But above all, in recent years, Dr. Locard has remained active as a private detective. I asked him in 1963, "Since your retirement, have you accepted criminal investigations in a private capacity?" He replied, "Yes. Especially in cases involving forgery and anonymous letters." He was often engaged, he said, in cases concerning the forgery of rare stamps. "And there is not a day that passes," he went on, "that someone doesn't send me, for one reason or another, a specimen of hair to examine Generally, it is just hair from dogs."

While reluctant to discuss in detail any specific criminal cases he had handled since he left the Sûreté Nationale, Dr. Locard made it clear to me, when he wrote me in April of 1963, that he was as occupied in the fight against crime as ever. "I put my signature this morning underneath crime report Number 11,704." This meant that, in his years of private practice, he had been involved in 799 criminal cases.

It is plain that Dr. Edmond Locard needs no further spectacular investigations or front-page publicity to secure his place among the great detectives of all time. What Sherlock Holmes suggested as possible in fiction, Dr. Locard transformed into reality. What France's Minister of the Interior wrote to him upon his leaving the Sûreté holds true today:

"In an era when the most current means of convicting people were the confession and witnesses, you, Dr. Locard, undertook to place in the first position research and scientific precision in establishing material traces and indices as essential objective proof of crime. This method has progressively become a classic approach in all judicial inquests of democratic countries."

When I last heard from him, Dr. Locard was still enjoying the comforts of his old house in a suburb of Lyons. He was not wanting in companionship. "I have fifteen grandchildren," he told me, "the oldest of whom is soon to get married." Although in good health, he no longer was going out to attend his weekly movie. One might imagine he has been too busy with his work or with that newer diversion—television. But I suspect another reason for his neglect of the cinema. There has been no one to replace his beloved Humphrey Bogart.

When I asked him if he had any ambition or wish for the future, Dr. Locard replied that he had but one. "To die in peace," he said. "At eighty-six, that is the unique perspective."

15

TYCOON

A‌T SEVEN-THIRTY every morning, a lean, tall, somewhat hunched and preoccupied man, with receding hairline, shaggy eyebrows and angular Teutonic face, hurriedly leaves his modest seven-room house in suburban Werden, Germany, folds himself into a small Porsche sedan, and speeds toward the industrial city of Essen.

By eight o'clock, he is piloting his tiny car through the gray, grubby, broken streets of the Ruhr metropolis, past a wildly jagged landscape etched by 275 Allied bomber raids, to the rubble and ruin surrounding a towering office building at 103 Altendorferstrasse, the headquarters of the world-famous Krupp works. Parking his Porsche before the building, he quickly strides inside, catches the open-faced cubicle of a nonstop rotating elevator, and is carried up to the third floor.

As he moves toward his office, his eyes are introspective and worried. His face is furrowed beyond his forty-six years. His brown suit is undistinguished. To the busy employees who brush past him in the corridor, he looks like just another anonymous minor executive, rushing to reach his overcrowded desk on time. Passing him, few recognize him—yet all know and fear his name, depend upon him as serfs once depended upon feudal lords, and speak of him as one of the few hopes for a reborn and virile Fatherland.

For the name of this seemingly pedestrian figure is the name of the most powerful man in Germany today, one of the strongest men in all Western Europe, one of the richest human beings on earth—and the center of a great storm of international controversy. His family name—synonymous with the wholesale merchandising of death—has hung over generations of Americans and Europeans, like a massive dagger. It is

Krupp—and he is Alfried Krupp von Bohlen und Halbach, of Essen.

Commonplace though his appearance may be, and his habits, his background is incredible. His great-grandfather made cannon for Bismarck, his grandfather made U-boats for the Kaiser, his father made Tiger tanks for Hitler. His mother, Bertha, still dwelling near him in Essen, gave her name to the Big Bertha gun, which shelled Paris in World War I. Alfried Krupp himself was raised in a home with 117 rooms—the guest house had 60 rooms—and the family was attended by 125 servants. Often, as many as 600 guests came to dinner. Ten years ago, when he took over "the works," as he likes to call the family factories, it covered five square miles, employed 160,000 laborers, and kept the Reich's war machine rolling.

At war's end, Krupp was imprisoned, tried as a war criminal (for planning aggressive war, plundering captive nations, using slave labor), and sentenced by three American judges to twelve years in Landsberg prison (where Hitler wrote *Mein Kampf*). Two years ago, after serving only half his term, Krupp was pardoned, all his wealth—and power—returned to him. Except for having to give his promise to stay out of coal and steel production, he was back in business as usual.

Once again, Krupp controls his shipyards in Bremen and Kiel, as well as his factories in Essen which produce locomotives, Diesel trucks, tools, home fixtures; his real estate holdings which embrace 10,000 houses; his chain of hotels; his 120 food shops; and in addition, any moneys to be received from the enforced sale of nine Ruhr coal mines and five iron mines. His coal mines, which produce 7,000,000 tons a year, and his steel plants, which produce 1,500,000 tons a year, would gross him about fifty million dollars if they are sold. His other property is worth about ninety-five million dollars, and it now enriches him with a profit of three and a half million dollars each year.

When his fortune was returned to Krupp, the great controversy began —and rages still. In commuting Krupp's sentence and restoring his property, John J. McCloy, then United States High Commissioner in Germany, stated, "I can find no personal guilt in the defendant Krupp sufficient to distinguish him above all others sentenced by the Nuremberg courts." Immediately, from Moscow, Russia's *Izvestia* screamed, "The release of the Nazi leader once more confirms that the American aggressors are recruiting Fascist specialists in mass murder to help prepare a new war. Washington is no longer satisfied with using Wehrmacht generals for drilling Eisenhower's divisions. They need the Fascist manufacturers of gas vans, the builders of the devilish ovens of the Auschwitz, the merchants in guns, bombs and poison gas." From France, the newspaper *Franc-Tireur*, after alleging that Krupp had remarked, "There are good and bad moments in life," commented, "But the good moments for a Krupp, let us add, correspond to the bad moments for the people."

From England came the most mixed reaction. Six members of Parliament, Labourites, regarded Krupp's return to the family business as "a betrayal of the men and women who laid down their lives in two World Wars. It will encourage the re-emergence of Nazi elements." On the other hand, a correspondent for a staid London daily reported, "United States officials claim that the present danger is not that Krupp may sneak back into arms manufacturing, but that he may refuse point blank to do so. Allied officials here in Germany take the view that the production of arms in the Ruhr would not only add to the military security of Western Europe, but would also divert dangerous German competition from overseas trade and markets."

Even now, Krupp continues to remain a subject of disagreement among the Western Allies. Actually, the United States is firmly resisting the use of Krupp in the European armament race—fearing his factories, rebuilt for arms, might one day fall into the hands of the onrushing Reds.

On the other hand, Great Britain feels Krupp should make guns and tanks, but only under rigid controls. As one British official explained, "The sooner Krupp pitches in to do his share in rearming against Russia, the better. We don't like to see Krupp capturing all the civilian export markets, while the rest of us struggle to produce arms for the common defense."

As the Allies debate their future policy toward him, Alfried Krupp insists he is fully honoring his agreement. He is cooperating in arrangements for the eventual sale of his entire coal and steel holdings. He is avoiding armament production. "I will repeat what I said two years ago," he told me. "I am not interested in producing armament." There are some cynics who question this statement—feeling he will jump at the opportunity to make guns, if we permit him to—and will one day make them anyway, even if we don't permit him. They point to the activities of his father, who promised the Allies not to help Germany rearm after World War I—but later bragged that he had "duped" the Allies by milking money from the United States for his "peace industries." Actually, he was designing rockets and setting up a dummy submarine firm in Holland that drafted blueprints for U-boats, which later saved the Nazis "from two to four years" in production time.

But, at the moment, there is every evidence Alfried Krupp is engaged solely in peaceful pursuits. His factories in Essen are again booming. He is occupied with supplying South Africa with five million dollars' worth of locomotives, India with thirty-one million dollars' worth of blast furnaces, and Yugoslavia with expensive mining machinery.

While United States government representatives in Western Germany continue to confine Krupp to locomotives and blast furnaces, there are certain American Army men who agree with the conservative British elements. They want to see Krupp helping us rearm Europe against Communism. And they regularly make overtures to Krupp—unofficially.

Recently, the United States Army asked Krupp to repair American tanks. He flatly refused. Angrily, an American ambassador reminded Krupp that he could be forced to cooperate. Blandly, Krupp replied, "First you put me in jail for making arms, and now you threaten me if I don't make them. What do you want me to do?"

American officials don't know what they want Krupp to do—simply because they don't know the real Krupp at all. They don't know if they can trust him. They don't know if he is honest. They don't know what he thinks, feels, or believes. For that matter, the majority of people in Europe do not know anything about him, either.

Few important men in our time, possessing so fully the power to affect the futures of so many the earth over, remain as little-known and mysterious as Herr Krupp. Primarily to solve this mystery—to learn the kind of security risk Alfried Krupp really is, to learn if the dynasty that made cannons for Bismarck and Hitler should be encouraged to make them for the democracies—I traveled the road to Essen, Düsseldorf, Frankfurt-am-Main. I observed, questioned, listened—listened to the elusive Krupp himself, to his second wife, his attorneys, his workmen, his friends, his American overseers, his British and French critics.

I realized, immediately, that to understand Herr Krupp one must understand his colorful ancestry. The Krupps of Essen, I discovered, have always been a dynasty dealing in death. It all began in 1587, when a wine merchant named Arndt Krupe married a wealthy German girl whose family made suits of armor. In the years after, Krupe became Krupp and prospered mightily due to the Thirty Years' War. By 1812, when the United States was locked in its sea conflict with Britain, the Krupps had begun to produce modern arms and feed them to Napoleon for his invasion of Russia. After Waterloo, the Krupp fortunes waned.

In 1850, Alfried's great-grandfather, a stern, towering, spade-bearded gentleman, perfected a formula in Essen for casting steel cannons. At once, the family's wealth was re-established. In 1866, Krupp cannons were cheerfully sold to both sides during the Austro-Prussian War, and in 1870, Krupp cannon backed Bismarck's blood-and-iron Reich in the Franco-Prussian War.

By 1902, the Krupp family had monopolized German armament production. When the patriarch of the family died that year, the Kaiser himself walked behind the coffin.

At the outset of World War I, the legal head of the firm was a female, Bertha Krupp. Ten years earlier, in Holland, Bertha had met a German career diplomat, Gustav von Bohlen, whose grandfather had fought for the North in the American Civil War and whose cousin is Charles "Chip" Bohlen, United States Ambassador to Russia. At the age of nineteen, Gustav von Bohlen had served in the German Embassy, at Washington, D.C., in Peking, and in Vatican City. After marrying Bertha in 1906, he served Krupp.

In 1909, holding power of attorney from Bertha, and ordered by Kaiser Wilhelm to adopt the Krupp name, he took over management of the booming Krupp works. As World War I progressed, he produced the first U-boat, a great quantity of battleships, the most lethal mortar in the world (which he named "Big Bertha," after his wife—the Allies later applied the same nickname to the outsized cannon that bombarded Paris), and seven heirs, the eldest of whom was named Alfried Krupp von Bohlen.

Alfried was raised in the ancestral home of the Krupp family, a mammoth mausoleum outside Essen called Villa Huegel, which was built at a cost of one and a half million dollars by his grandfather in 1871. Alfried rattled about the 117 rooms of the three-story pile, riding the silent elevators, using the indoor swimming pool, poking about the electric kitchens. "It wasn't built for comfort," a friend of the family commented. "Old Krupp built the villa as a showcase. He was in the export business, and his business depended upon international good will. He didn't trust the stiff-necked Prussian government to entertain foreigners properly. He thought he could do it better under his own roof. Often, when Alfried sat down to dinner, there were between four hundred and six hundred persons at the tables. He met kings, ambassadors, bankers, celebrities of every kind. He still remembers meeting and worshiping Henry Ford. And in the villa he met the Duke of Windsor, who remains a close friend."

Recently, it was announced that Alfried Krupp had given up Villa Huegel and was donating it to various German scientific and cultural societies. I asked him why he had done this. "Because it's too big," he said. "People just don't live like that any more. The upkeep is enormous. Good servants are impossible to get. Besides, it's not an agreeable place. I was raised there, but it never felt like a home. I always dreamed of having a small modern house in the garden of the estate. And now I have it, and I'm happier."

Until he was fourteen, Alfried had private tutors. He remembers learning French before German. Then, after three years at a private school in Essen, he attended the University of Munich, specializing in meteorology. He graduated a Diploma Engineer. Had he ever thought of any other career? "No," he admitted. "I'm a fifth-generation Krupp. I was educated to take over the works. I joined the firm in 1936, as a junior executive, signing letters. But I didn't enjoy management, and was transferred to the technical end."

Alfried's father, Gustav, did enjoy management, but faced countless political difficulties. Today, the Krupp family maintains that in 1933 Gustav contributed over a million marks to von Hindenburg in an effort to defeat "that upstart" Hitler. This may be true. On the other hand, records prove that Gustav, in that same year, definitely contributed to Hitler's election fund. Through the years, he continued to back Hitler. In 1941, Gustav wrote and published an article which stated, "After the assumption of power by Adolf Hitler, I had the satisfaction of being able to report to the Fuehrer that Krupp stood ready, after a short warming-up period, to begin the rearmament of the German people without any gaps of experience." During World War II, besides serving as Hitler's main source of armament production, Gustav manufactured armor for the highly effective Tiger tanks and created the Sevastopol gun, the world's largest mortar which hurled seven-ton shells at the Russians. Early in 1943, Gustav von Bohlen became half paralyzed and wholly bedridden. Bertha insisted that he retire. In April, 1943, Alfried Krupp was promoted to chairman of the board and, early in 1944, assumed full control of the works.

A year and a half later, as the Nazi war machine disintegrated and the Allies closed in on the Berlin bunker, Hitler ordered Krupp to report to him. Krupp refused. Hitler sent the Gestapo to arrest him. The Allies got to Krupp first. Krupp recalls that he was in the villa, pacing, waiting, the night Germany surrendered. Krupp gave himself up to a British Tommy. He was kept locked in the villa for thirty days, then shipped to Frankfurt-am-Main, where he was placed in a military guardhouse. Shortly thereafter, he was delivered to Nuremberg, to be tried as a major war criminal.

Actually, it appears that the Allies had intended to prosecute Gustav, as head of the Krupp firm. They had spent two years preparing a case against him. Since the old man was now ill, three nations sent doctors to examine him. They reported him incompetent. (He died five years later, at seventy-nine, in a servant's cottage on his Austrian hunting estate.) The new reigning head of Krupp, Alfried, was substituted for his father. Justice Robert H. Jackson agreed that, while Alfried must be tried, he could be tried only as a minor war criminal. Although Alfried's offenses were committed in the British zone of Germany, the British refused to touch him. Consequently, the United States was left to do the job. In

August, 1945, Krupp, along with eight of his company's directors, went on trial before United States Military Tribunal Number 3 in Nuremberg.

Since Krupp was going on trial before three American judges—the presiding judge was H. C. Anderson, of Jackson, Tennessee—he demanded the right to hire an American attorney. This the authorities refused. Meanwhile, two Americans, a civilian and an army officer, promised Krupp that they could get him proper representation. He retained them and waited.

The efforts of the two enterprising Americans came to the attention of Earl G. Carroll, an army captain in Frankfurt. Carroll, a beaky, kindly, middle-aged lawyer, had prosecuted the accused in the Kronberg jewel robbery, and Colonel Kilian in the infamous Lichfield case. Carroll accused the Americans of "out-and-out fraud" and said that he was going directly to the Krupp family.

The night before the trial, Carroll advised the Krupp family that they could expect no help from the Americans they had retained. At once, Alfried's younger brother, Berthold, asked Carroll himself to represent the family. "I told him I'd try," said Carroll. "A special permit was required in order to represent war criminals in court. I applied for the permit. I was turned down. I then filed a notice of appearance. Immediately, the Army sent over an armed guard. I was hustled to an airport and flown out of Frankfurt. I then had my partners in Hayward, California, Tom Foley and John Purchio, apply to defend Krupp. They, too, were rejected. So Krupp went on trial without an American attorney, without any attorney of his own choice. The court foisted a young German named Gunther Geisler on him. In arguing over a legal point, Geisler got angry, refused to apologize to the judges, walked out, and was therefore barred from the courtroom. So Krupp had no real representation at any time."

Case Number X, at Nuremberg—*United States vs. Krupp*—lasted forty-six days. The prosecution, led by Joseph W. Kaufman, of New York, turned up 85 witnesses. The defense presented 141 witnesses. To the first charge—of planning aggressive war—Krupp replied, "As a member of the fifth generation which produced steel, the fourth generation which forged weapons, I should like to add one thing. Never in my parents' home did I hear one word or experience one act which welcomed or promoted any war, at any place, or at any time. The symbol of our house does not depict a cannon, but three interlocked wheels, emblem of peaceful trade." On this first charge, Krupp was acquitted.

Next, Krupp was accused of spoliation—looting and plundering of captive nations. A prosecution witness recalled a scene in 1940—like an exaggerated moment out of an old pacifist play—when he saw Gustav von Bohlen, and three other German industrialists, seated about a large table studying a map of Europe, while a radio blared forth news of German Army advances through Holland and Belgium. The witness said old Gustav pointed to locations on the map, and announced, "We will arrest this owner here, and take his three factories. Over there, I will take over. You will have the other one, and you the third." On this charge, Krupp was found guilty.

In the final count, Krupp was accused of harboring and abusing slave labor. The prosecution revealed that the Krupp works had accepted and used 55,000 displaced persons, 18,000 prisoners of war, and 5,000 inmates from concentration camps. Many of these forced laborers had suffered cruelly. In one case, a captive Russian laborer had tried to pick up a crust of bread instead of metal scrap and had been shot to death by a guard. Later, a Krupp director congratulated the guard.

Krupp replied that he had been forced, against his wishes, to take on slave labor. Goering and Speer had delivered the prisoners, and moved seventy-five Nazi officials into the works to supervise them. Krupp insisted that he and his father, appalled by the condition of the laborers, had set up special kitchens to feed them.

In its judgment, the tribunal decided that Krupp employed slave labor "in armament production plants and in unhealthy and dangerous occupations, a number of whom suffered mistreatment in that housing, food, air-raid shelter and medical care were inadequate and that certain physical mistreatments occurred." On this count, also, Krupp was found guilty.

The American judges sentenced Krupp to twelve years in the prison at Landsberg. It was at this time that Earl Carroll, returned to Frankfurt as a civilian attorney, re-entered the picture. He approached General Lucius D. Clay, United States High Commissioner in Germany, and asked permission to visit Krupp in prison. Permission was granted. Carroll saw Krupp in 1948, and was retained by Krupp to plead his case further.

Carroll wrote a brilliant 230-page brief requesting executive clemency for Krupp.

The lawyer summarized, to me, his reasons why the Americans prosecuted Krupp. "First, American isolation made us ignorant of Germany. The only people in America with any knowledge of Germany were refugees, bitter, filled with hate. We sent them back to administer for us. Three of the Krupp prosecutors were German or Austrian nationals. One admitted that members of his family had been gassed at Auschwitz. I don't condemn their hate. In their place, I would have felt the same. But, from a purely judicial point of view, there was too much prejudice in Krupp's trial. Second, in meetings with the Allies, Stalin had insisted that war criminals be punished. And he included industrialists as war criminals. Naturally. As a Communist, he wanted to get rid of as many capitalists as possible. Third, the case against Krupp was prepared two years before the war ended, against Gustav, who was then alive. When Gustav couldn't be tried, his name was crossed out, his son's substituted, and this son was accused of the same crimes, even though the accusations made little sense."

To the argument that Krupp was lily-white, and railroaded into jail in his father's place, the prosecutor, Joseph Kaufman, recently replied, "Alfried Krupp was found guilty on the basis of his own personal misdeeds, not his father's. By special Hitler decree in 1943, Alfried became owner and head of the entire Krupp empire; not even his father enjoyed such ownership, which was vested in his wife Bertha. Alfried voted for, approved and signed a Krupp resolution to establish a plant at the notorious Auschwitz so that the Krupps could directly employ the slave labor available there. The five hundred Hungarian Jewesses, who were later to disappear and never to be heard of again, except two or three who managed to escape, were slave laborers at Essen itself, where Alfried actively maintained himself as head of the firm."

When Carroll presented his defense brief, appealing for clemency, to General Clay, the High Commissioner agreed that clemency was deserved. But before he could set up a board to act, he was replaced by John J. McCloy. "I went to McCloy," said Carroll. "He studied the brief, and also agreed Krupp deserved clemency. But he felt that he was too new to his appointment to grant it immediately. A year passed. And finally, McCloy released Krupp."

Krupp had been a prisoner for six years. "In prison I read a good deal," Krupp told me. "Whatever they gave me. Mostly American history and biography. I worked in the locksmith shop making ashtrays and crosses. I had learned this art when I was a student."

Immediately after his release, Krupp returned to the Villa Huegel. He took an inventory of the 117 rooms, and then announced that American GI's and British Tommie's had "liberated" from his home one and a half million dollars' worth of furnishings. He requested that the FBI and Scotland Yard return an assortment of old masters, Gobelin tapestries, Ming vases, Persian carpets, and sterling silverware. No sooner had Scotland Yard begun the hunt than it was revealed that $750,000 worth of Krupp's belongings had been pilfered by six Germans, who had used the villa as an air-raid shelter. The London press was furious. Roared one English daily, "For impertinence, gall, and unmitigated crust in high places, let the undisputed heavyweight championship be awarded to that scaly millionaire, Mr. A. Krupp."

Meanwhile, Krupp, flanked by Carroll and another American attorney from New York, Joseph G. Robinson, went after bigger game. In 1951, Krupp began negotiating to recover his factories. After months of legal gymnastics, Krupp won back his one-hundred-and-fifty-million-dollar empire. The Russians wanted Krupp's holdings confiscated. The British and Americans did not. Justice Jackson had disapproved of confiscation of property, saying, "We have no such penalty, and for historical reasons, that would be extremely unacceptable to the American people."

Krupp was returned his empire, on the condition that he get rid of his coal and steel holdings. "Alfried doesn't get a dime from coal and steel today," explained Carroll. "What he will get is the proceeds of the forced sale of securities. A banking group has been given five years to liquidate the coal and steel. If they don't find buyers, the whole thing goes on the auction block."

While the lengthy negotiations proceeded, Krupp had a great deal of time on his hands. "I have been active in the works only since March of this year," he said to me. "In the two years before, while negotiations were going on, I was permitted to do nothing. Once, just to see the extent of the devastation to my factories, and to let my employees know I was alive, I visited the works. The next day, my manager was called to Duesseldorf by the Allies and ordered to explain what in the devil I had been doing in the plant."

On the social side, Krupp was more active. In May, 1952, in the mayor's office at Berchtesgaden, he married attractive forty-year-old Baroness Vera von Hohenfeldt, an American citizen. It was Krupp's second marriage and Vera's fourth. She had come to the United States in 1939, the wife of a German movie director named Frank Wisbar, who now makes television films in Hollywood. She became an American citizen in 1946, and divorced Wisbar three years later. She then went to work as a receptionist for Dr. Sigfried Knauer, a Los Angeles physician, married him, and divorced him in 1952, five months before returning to Germany to marry Krupp. Once, she had sold cosmetics in a Los Angeles department store, and roughed it in a small apartment. After marrying Krupp, she wrote her friends in Hollywood, "Now I carry out no more garbage cans!"

This year, as his wife busied herself furnishing their new California-style home in the shadow of the old villa, Krupp returned to manage the works. Except for business appointments, he has refused to see outsiders. Especially, he has avoided the foreign press. For two months I tried to contact him from Paris, but received no reply. Just when I had about given up hope of his granting an interview, I received a telegram: WOULD BE PLEASED TO SEE YOU NEXT WEEK AT MY OFFICE ESSEN ALTENDORFER-STRASSE 103. ALFRIED KRUPP BOHLEN.

It was a Tuesday morning when I saw Krupp. There were four of us in the spacious room—Krupp, tall and serious; his wife Vera, bright and brisk in a brown suit; myself; and a large stately oil portrait of great-grandfather Krupp. We gathered at one end of a long directors' table, and sat and talked through the morning. Krupp's English was labored but accurate. He said that he had learned it in his German school, during a brief stay in England, and from his American attorneys, since their German was limited to *auf Wiedersehen.*

His wife, on the other hand, spoke a breezy American English. She was proud of her American citizenship, said that she visited the States regularly, and that she voted in the last presidential election. She begged me not to refer to her as "a former actress." She had never been an actress, she said. A girl friend had once got her a bit part in a German movie. In Hollywood she had not acted at all. She went on to say that she had met Krupp twenty-three years before, "at someone's home in western Germany."

During my talk with Krupp, Vera constantly and gently interrupted her husband, elaborating on or revising statements he made, fearful that everything he said would be misinterpreted. Usually, Krupp ignored her interruptions, and went doggedly on with what he was explaining. I had the overall impression of a man who, right or wrong, was extremely candid. He dodged no questions. I will give one startling example.

While I was determined to ask him about Adolf Hitler, I was afraid that he would not be direct with me. When the average German is questioned about Hitler today, he assumes an expression which seems to say, "Hitler? How do you spell it?" I expected Krupp to suffer similar amnesia. Consequently, I did not ask him if he knew Hitler. Instead, I told him that I had been reading a book, recently published in London, that recorded all of Hitler's luncheon conversations, taken down at the command of Martin Bormann. Had Krupp read the book? He said that he had not.

"Well," I went on, "this book quotes Hitler as saying that he used to enjoy greatly coming down to Essen to see the works and to see you."

Immediately, Vera interrupted. "Hitler visited all the plants in Germany, not only Krupp!"

Krupp did not look at her. He stared at me a moment, then he said, "Of course, I knew Hitler. I would see him when he came here. He was very smart about industry, about technical problems, and about new weapons. He knew absolutely nothing about economics. He had one obsession. With him, everything had to be not just big, but the biggest. I think that is why he liked me, liked to come to Essen. My plant was the biggest. My cannons were the biggest. My villa was the biggest. I remember once in Berlin, he pointed out the Olympic Stadium, which had held the 1936 games, and seated over a hundred thousand people. 'You know,' he said to me, 'if I had built that, I'd have made it really big!' "

Krupp and I went on to discuss politics. I had a clipping from a London paper. In it Philip Noel-Baker, a Labourite, had objected to Krupp's release, remarking that it was dangerous: "The Krupps have never been able to keep their hands off politics." What did Krupp have to say about that? He shrugged. "It is exaggerated, as those things always are. We are a large firm, so of course we must watch politics, become involved in politics. But we have never been active. Personally, I am not a bit interested in politics. I remember when the Americans were interrogating me at Nuremberg, one of them said, 'The trouble with you, Krupp, is that you should have been *more* interested in politics!' "

Once during our conversation, Krupp rose and led me to a large window, overlooking the battered blocks surrounding his present plant. The works were only one-fourth their former size. There had been 275 air raids on Essen, and 55 direct hits on the Krupp works. These had caused complete devastation in 33 percent of the area, and heavy damage in 29 percent.

"The greatest damage came after the war was over," said Krupp. When the Russians and British moved in, they began dynamiting and dismantling. The Russians carried off 130,000 tons of valuable machinery, even carting away the entire Borbeck Smelting Plant, which weighed 75,000 tons. They removed the originals of all of Krupp's steel patents, and enough industrial blueprints and diagrams to paper 30,000 square yards. The British made off with 150,000 tons of scrap iron. "We are limited now," said Krupp. "We have room for only sixteen thousand workers instead of the prewar 160,000. Still, we will manage."

Krupp himself is the complete boss of the works. He explained that he had a large family, however, and that their ties were close, and so all participated in the firm's earnings. Krupp's mother, Bertha, now sixty-seven, has returned from Salzburg to live in Essen. Of his four younger brothers, two were killed during the war. Klaus, a Luftwaffe lieutenant and holder of the Iron Cross, was shot down over the Hürtgen Forest in 1940. And Eckbert, attached to the Italian Army, lost his life in action outside San Marino, Italy, in 1945. Another brother, Haarold, is still a prisoner of war in Russia. "He was sentenced to twenty-five years at hard labor for espionage in Manchuria," said Krupp. "He's never been in Manchuria. We send him a parcel every month, and occasionally receive Red Cross cards from him."

Krupp spoke at length about his tastes. He dislikes opera, has no time for movies or nightclubs, but enjoys playing host to a few guests at his home. He used to hunt a good deal, and sail (he won third prize in the 1936 Olympics), but no longer has time for either. His only hobby is photography. He has visited Egypt and Israel, but has never seen the United States. He expects to visit it one day soon.

His enemies distrust him, his employees fear and respect him, and many Germans worship him. I have heard him called a Nazi, a monster, a scoundrel, a liar; and an Englishman said, "Krupp is harder than the steel he makes." His attorney Carroll loyally insists that Krupp is misunderstood. "I've known lots of German industrialists. This man is different. He never commands. He never pushes people around. He spends half his workdays talking to laborers, marking down complaints and problems in the notebook he carries. And, big as he is, he is really modest. He traveled down to Frankfurt once to confer with me. We talked all day. By night, it was raining. He did not feel like returning to Essen. He said, 'Do you think I can get a room at the Frankfurter Hof?' That's the best hotel in town. I smiled. He reached for the phone, called the hotel. He asked for a room, never told them his name. The clerk said that they were all filled up. Krupp turned to me. 'They're all filled up. Can you think of another hotel?' I did not believe that they were filled up. I told my secretary to call them back. She did. She said, 'Herr Alfried Krupp von Bohlen wants a room.' Immediately, three clerks were on the phone shouting, 'Krupp? How many rooms does he wish?' But he'd never think of telling them his name."

This picture of a modest, diligent, peaceful Krupp can hardly be the whole truth. For truth is two-sided. And on the other side is the historical fact that cannons are in the Krupp blood.

The enigma of Krupp is buried in coal and steel. Would Krupp make coal and steel again? He had told me no, flatly no. I asked his attorney. "Coal and steel?" said Carroll. "Look, he's had his chances. Both Mexico and Brazil offered him free land, if he'd come over there and build steel factories and manufacture. He could have done it. He did not. He feels that he must stay in Essen. He has an obligation to his workers and to his family."

Still, I was not satisfied. Would this obligation continue to anchor him to Essen? Would he or would he not be back in armament again—with American permission or without it? Carroll considered the question, then blinked at me, and slowly replied, "Remember one thing. Alfried Krupp is not allowed to produce coal and steel inside Germany. But it's a big world. And he *is* permitted to go anywhere in the world, even to the United States or South America, and produce coal and steel again. This is permitted. And this he may do again—one day."

WHAT HAS HAPPENED SINCE . . .

Twelve years ago, I asked Earl Carroll, Krupp's attorney, if his client would one day be back in armament production, with or without American permission. Carroll had replied equivocally that even if Krupp could not produce coal and steel inside Germany, he could do so anywhere else in the world. "This is permitted," Carroll had said. "And this he may do again—one day."

Today, I have a more exact answer to the question I asked Carroll. The "one day" came swiftly. Now, a dozen years later, Alfried Krupp is producing coal and steel not only elsewhere in the world, but inside West Germany as well. And somehow, I must confess, thinking back to my meeting with Krupp, I am not surprised at all.

Recently, William Manchester, who had visited Alfried Krupp in 1964, said that he thought Krupp looked like "an unemployed English actor" or "an eccentric Midlands beekeeper," but not at all like "gentry" and certainly not like a munitions tycoon. My own description of Krupp, after I had seen him in 1953, was that he resembled "another anonymous minor executive." I can still recall that I thought him diffident, introverted, more the thinker than the doer, yet refreshingly direct and forthright in his conversation. At the same time, there had seemed to be some quality about him—and I think I might have sensed this even if I had not known his name and legend—that was strong and sure. I was left with the conviction that should this man have an ambition, he would somehow, by hook or by crook, satisfy it. I retain today my memory of this quality in him, and therefore I am not surprised that he has entered, in open defiance of the directive of his country's conquerors, steel production where he was not to be permitted to try it again, as well as doing what his attorney had said was permissible. Evidently, the inner Krupp might be represented by the symbol of the traditional mailed fist in the velvet glove. His determination and his uncanny ability to play on the weaknesses and fears of his legal custodians (in this case the Western promoters of expediency in a world of uneasy coexistence with Communism), have made Alfried Krupp probably the richest single individual in the world today.

I had traveled from Paris to Essen, checked into the hotel known as the Kaiserhof, and taken a taxi to my meeting with Alfried Krupp during a morning in June, 1953. When I finished talking with him, I had returned by train to Frankfurt-am-Main, been driven to a house at 24 Rheinstrasse, and had enjoyed my talk with Krupp's colorful American attorney. Not long ago I read that Carroll received an alleged two and a half million dollars as his legal fee for obtaining clemency for Krupp, for getting Krupp out of prison after he had served only six years of his twelve-year sentence as a war criminal, and for helping Krupp recover his shattered and dispersed manufacturing empire. I do not know if this figure is correct, but if lawyers are entitled to charge not only what the traffic will bear but also for the results of services rendered, I feel that Carroll deserved at least that large a sum.

After my researches had been completed, I wrote a 5,000-word story about Krupp. *Collier's* magazine accepted it and an editor wrote me, "The Krupp story couldn't be better." My literary agent wired me, COLLIER'S DELIGHTEDLY BUYS KRUPP. NOW FOR A BOOK."

The last was in reference to the fact that I had decided that I had had enough of playing the Sunday Gentleman, that the Krupp story was to be my final magazine piece, and that I had decided to do what I had always wanted to do, to write books, and was in fact already writing my first book. I finished this book in October, 1954, and it was published under the title of *The Fabulous Originals* in October, 1955.

But even as my first book was being prepared, my last magazine article was published. The Krupp story appeared in the issue of *Collier's* magazine for October 30, 1953. Although it excited a considerable amount of favorable comment, it was a disappointment to me. *Collier's* had planned to feature my entire 5,000-word article in a later issue, but suddenly, for some reason, they had to replace another shorter article that was scheduled to go to press, and they were desperate for a substitute story. My Krupp story was on hand. Hastily, *Collier's* slashed it to about half its length, and shoved it into the gaping hole left by the canceled piece. My article came out bowdlerized, as vapid and safe as an innocuous Victorian debutante. However, the Krupp story preceding this postscript is the full Krupp story, exactly as I wrote it following my visit to Essen.

After I had decided to follow Alfried Krupp's footsteps from the moment I had left him at the third-floor elevator in the Krupp works in 1953 until 1965, I found myself astonished at how far he had traveled, and how much had happened to him along the way, in the interval of a dozen years. This, then, is a brief report on the high spots of Krupp's rise and progress in the years since I saw him, and on his situation today.

At the time I saw Krupp, he had hired, only nine months before, a new general director for all of his enterprises. This recent addition to the firm was a hard-hitting, thirty-nine-year-old Pomeranian businessman named Berthold Beitz. The new director's biography was splendid. He had resisted joining the Nazi party. He had survived the Second World War by managing oil fields in Poland for the Reich. After the war, he had served as an oil company executive, a banker, and the moving force behind a prospering insurance firm. While I was in Essen, hardly anyone mentioned Beitz to me. Presumably, the impact of his energy had not yet been felt. But in the years since, Beitz, whose annual salary is $300,000, has been the dynamic force behind Krupp's fantastic revival and expansion.

Someone once remarked that it was Beitz who introduced Alfried Krupp to the twentieth century. I would suggest that Beitz did not "introduce" but rather, to phrase it inelegantly, "dragged" Krupp into the twentieth century. Beitz, breezy, unceremonious, daring, contemptuous of bowing and heel-clicking, affectionate toward first names and New Orleans jazz, was not unexpectedly nicknamed "the American." It was Beitz who conducted the day-to-day affairs in the works; it was Krupp who made the final decisions. As a result of this collaboration between the forty-eight-year-old Berthold Beitz and the fifty-eight-year-old Alfried Krupp, the Krupp works are today bigger, more influential, more powerful than they have ever been in their entire dramatic history.

Recently, I had a look at a Krupp sales catalog of products and services. There were over four thousand of these items to be found within a patent-leather-covered book as large as a good-sized telephone directory. If an interested customer wanted to buy a locomotive, an oil tanker, a prefabricated city, a set of false teeth, a heavy truck, a child's toy, a harbor, a crane, a dredge, a time clock, a suspension bridge, he could find one and all in the Krupp catalog.

As his attorney reminded me, Krupp could go anywhere on earth to produce or sell his wares. In these past years, he has done this. Krupp has sold Diesel engines to Brazil, built a twenty-five-million-dollar steel plant in Pakistan, sold trucks to Arabia, licensed and supervised an eight-mile-long monorail in Japan, constructed an oil refinery in Greece, dredged up a pharaoh from the mud of the Nile in Egypt, guided the hunt for uranium in Australia, and erected a steel factory—together with a city to house 100,000 laborers nearby—in India.

Even Soviet Russia, Red China, and the United States have become cautious Krupp customers. Krupp sold a synthetic fiber and chemical plant to Russia, sold industrial equipment to Red China, and in a single year did thirty million dollars' worth of business with the combined Communist nations. To show his political impartiality, Krupp also, to use his own words, "built a carloading facility for the Chesapeake and Ohio Railway at Presque Isle" in the United States. In a recent interview, Krupp stated that 55 percent of his exports went to the free nations of Europe, 10 percent to Latin America, 7 percent to the United States,

9 percent to Asia, 7 percent to India, 1 percent to Russia and Red China, and the other 11 percent elsewhere. Krupp predicted that in years to come, most of his export trade would be with Africa, India, Latin America, and Indonesia.

However, the real strength of Krupp's power remains in his domestic production of coal and steel. This may seem confusing to the reader who has just finished my 1953 article, in which I explained that Krupp was released as a war criminal under the condition that he sell his "entire coal and steel holdings." At the time of our interview, Krupp had said to me, "I will repeat . . . I am not interested in producing armament." Yet, today, Krupp has not only failed to divest himself of his coal and steel holdings; he has enlarged them. Chronic skeptics may not be surprised. Big money has its own private planet, its own international citizenship, its own code of morality, and its own super-laws which transcend mere national governments. The language of this super-one-world is profit— profit made possible by the frailty of lesser mortals who believe in expediency and self-preservation. This may sound old-fashioned. Nevertheless, I suggest it is still true. Yet even the most cynical may wonder—how did Krupp do it?

Well, it was quite simple, really. In 1953, after his release from prison, Alfried Krupp signed the "Mehlen Accord" with the Western powers. He agreed to break up his coal and steel empire and sell off his various holdings at "a fair price," and all within five years. To promote good will, Krupp grandly sold a number of his companies to relatives and friends, among the latter his munitions colleague, Dr. Axel Wenner-Gren, the Swedish industrialist. But as his vast remaining coal and steel holdings increased in value, Krupp complained to the Allied commission that he could not find buyers outside of his family who could afford his coal and steel plants. After five years, he still possessed them, and began to apply to the Allies for time extensions on their sale. Annual extensions were granted, and have continued to be granted ever since.

There is little doubt that the charitable attitude of the United States, and its European friends, was dictated by political concern. Post-Hitler West Germany had become an ally of the West, one that must be strengthened, not weakened. To keep Krupp intact and muscular was a means of keeping a new ally intact and muscular. The Allies had come to agree with West German chancellors and economic ministers that the old sell-off order was now "out of date." By 1964, Alfried Krupp again owned the Westfaelische Draht Industrien, the last segment to be repurchased of the coal and steel empire Krupp had begun to dismember. The pretense remains that "no qualified buyer" has ever appeared. Divest himself of his coal and steel? Never. As the Associated Press reported not long ago: "The expectation prevails that no serious attempt will ever be made to force Mr. Krupp to comply."

Further evidence of Krupp *über* the Allies was submitted by the North American Newspaper Alliance, in a story from West Germany published in February of 1965:

"Bonn government officials say Krupp's general manager was able to convince the Johnson Administration that nothing could be gained by forcing Krupp to divest itself of its steelmaking capacity—but that a great deal could be gained for the Western cause by helping Krupp pioneer 'captialist-communist' production partnerships.

"Beitz . . . had appointments in Washington with Vice-President Humphrey, Undersecretary of State George Ball, Sen. Robert F. Kennedy and other top Administration figures. In Germany, there is amazement—and relief—at his enthusiastic reception in Washington."

In *Holiday* magazine, Manchester quoted "Alfried's chief lieutenant"—presumably Beitz—as saying that Krupp would never liquidate his coal and steel holdings, for a Krupp without steel and coal is like "a woman cut off at the navel." On this anatomical truism, both Soviet Russia and the United States appear, for once, to be in full agreement.

Encouraged by all this benign permissiveness, Alfried Krupp has gradually begun to involve himself more directly in armament manufacture, or at least in manufacturing products that may one day lead to his again making weapons of destruction. In 1963, Krupp, already active in building up a West German air force for NATO, joined with United Aircraft and two other companies to acquire the Focke-Wulf aircraft company of Bremen. Besides making fighter planes, Krupp specialists have completed an atomic reactor and engaged themselves in the burgeoning space program. Will Krupp produce nuclear weapons? Only if he must, Krupp said recently. And then he added, "We must not forget reality."

Krupp's comeback is complete. His works in Essen, and his subsidiary firms, are worth over a billion dollars. His annual profits are so enormous that he is said to retain a million dollars a year for his own support and limited pleasures.

Except for his family situation, there have been few important changes in Krupp's personal life in the last dozen years. He still refuses to live in his one-and-a-half-million-dollar ancestral castle, Villa Huegel, but uses it instead for large social functions such as receptions for one or two hundred guests or the entertainment of notables like the King of Greece, the President of Brazil, the Chancellor of Germany, and assorted American ambassadors. He dwells modestly in a fifteen-room house near the villa. He still drives a Porsche to the office early every morning, and returns home late.

When I saw him, Krupp was confining his activities largely to Essen. Today, he has become mobile. He travels abroad two or three months of each year. He makes these trips in his private plane, which he often pilots himself. In the last decade, he has visited Canada, Venezuela, Turkey, India, Egypt, and Australia (where, alighting in inhospitable Melbourne, he was met by pickets carrying signs emblazoned with "Butcher" and "Jew-killer"). And, although convicted war criminals are banned from entry into the United States, a news magazine announced in 1957 that Alfried Krupp's passport had at last been approved to receive an American visa.

Barring travel, his pleasures are as austere as ever. An airplane, yes. A schooner, still. But, mainly, after hours and on weekends, he devotes himself to photography, card games, Scotch, and solitary meditation. He is a stranger to books.

Nor does Krupp find solace in a large and closely knit family. One of his two surviving brothers, Berthold, who had been an artillery officer in occupied Romania during the Second World War, spends much of his time with his wife and offspring in an old castle on the Rhine River. Alfried's other living brother, Haarold, whom he had told me about when I was in Essen, remained a Russian prisoner of war in the Urals for two more years after our talk. Through the intervention of West Germany's President Adenauer, Haarold was released by the Russians in 1955, after serving eleven years of his twenty-five-year sentence. Haarold is now a partner with brother Berthold in a German chemical company, and also in a German automotive-parts firm. One of Alfried's sisters, Irmgard, lives with her six children in Bavaria; the other sister, Waldtraut, has acquired a new mate and a new home in Argentina.

While these five children of the elder Krupp have survived, the family ranks have nevertheless been reduced by two. In the years since I saw him, Alfried Krupp has lost both his mother and his wife. His legendary mother, Bertha Krupp, died at the age of seventy-one in Essen during September, 1957. His second wife, Vera von Hohenfeldt Langer Wisbar Knauer Krupp, onetime "actress," naturalized American citizen, had already left him in 1956.

I was surprised to learn the last, recollecting how loyal to her husband Vera Krupp had appeared to be during my interview. I can see now, more clearly than I did then, that her attendance at our meeting had not been motivated by Krupp's social dependence upon her but by his desire to have another American in the room, one who was on his side.

Krupp is now a bachelor again, and perhaps he was always meant to be one. His first marriage, which had taken place in 1937, was to Anneliese Bahr, the daughter of a German manufacturer. She had been a divorcee, and Krupp's dominant father had disapproved. Obediently, Krupp had divorced her in 1941. He had been more his own man when he married for the second time in 1952. I am told that Vera quickly found Essen too restricting and boring, found her mother-in-law too much in evidence, found that the works were her husband's only real interest, and after four years her attorneys informed Krupp that she wished a divorce. According to Norbert Muhlen, a Krupp biographer, "it was hinted that she could disclose quite a few secret foreign accounts and even more secret political schemes of her husband." At any rate, there was a settlement made behind closed doors—Krupp's biographer says that Vera received a five-million-dollar settlement and a $250,000-a-year income for life. Thereafter, Vera Krupp, free agent, cropped up in the more frivolous gossip columns from time to time as a glamorous female personage reportedly being escorted by male celebrities to social affairs at fashionable resorts, and to the intimate gatherings of café society. Eventually, Vera found her way to Las Vegas, Nevada, where she was said to have invested $185,000 in the New Frontier Hotel. When last heard from, she was living on a 400,000-acre ranch outside Las Vegas.

Since the Krupp works have never been a publicly owned corporation, or even a limited partnership, but entirely a one-man business, and remain such today, it is natural to speculate on the royal line of succession. Who are Krupp's heirs? The direct blood heir is his handsome, tall son Arndt, presented to Krupp by his first wife in 1940. Arndt Krupp was educated in Switzerland, attended Albert Ludwig University in Freiburg, and later studied business courses at the University of Cologne. After he had indulged in his brief postgraduate fling at nightclub life with German beauties, Arndt was shipped off to Japan in 1959 for indoctrination in a Krupp subsidiary. Recently, he was at work for his father in São Paulo, Brazil.

Today, Krupp remains alone, sole master of what H. G. Wells characterized as "Kruppism, this sordid, enormous trade in the instruments of death." Perhaps Krupp's main love and only family are the 100,000 laborers upon whom he bestows a lavish paternalism and who, in turn, have never staged a strike against him. He has their devotion and loyalty completely. They will defend him, unto death, against all enemies, and they will defend his humanity, present and past. As William Manchester remarked in 1964: "They insist that he was jailed only because Krupp made guns; the fact that Krupp also supplied dog whips and steel truncheons to drive spindly chattels through the streets of Essen is passed over in silence."

But not passed over in silence by Alfried Krupp. I was relieved to read the other day that Krupp has agreed to compensate the Jewish slave la-borers who survived their sentences to the works. It seemed a little late, this gesture, but it was nice because it was so in character. It proved that Alfried Krupp is still his father's son: a tycoon who can tell himself money *is* everything, and there is no man who cannot be bought, not even a broken one, not even a dead one.

16

THE SEVEN SECRET
PRISON CELLS

S EVERAL WEEKS AGO, a taxi bumped over the uneven cobbled pavement of the Wilhelmstrasse, in the outskirts of Berlin, and came to a halt before the towering red-brick walls of the most heavily guarded and most highly secretive prison in the world.

The German cabdriver turned from his wheel. *"Hier ist was Sie suchen, mein Herr.* Spandau Prison!"

The American reporter, in the rear seat, stepped out of the taxi. *"Danke schoen.* Hold it a few minutes. I want to look around."

Crossing the street, the American saw four large brick houses facing him across the narrow thoroughfare. These were the permanent billets for the director, wardens, and guards from Soviet Russia, Great Britain, France, and the United States, the four powers in charge of running the incredible German jail. Directly behind the houses rose the prison itself, with its blue-steel entrance door, and its medieval-styled twenty-foot-high walls.

Determined to have a closer look, the American reporter walked around one of the billets to the sidewall of Spandau. A sign, in both English and in German, greeted him:

WARNING—DANGER—DO NOT APPROACH THIS FENCE. GUARDS HAVE ORDERS TO SHOOT.

Between the sign and the prison proper, he saw a series of obstacles that made Alcatraz and Devil's Island seem, by comparison, invitingly accessible. A massive roll of concertina wire lay coiled and menacing in front of a wickedly barbed barrier about ten feet high. Behind this, fiendishly modern, gleamed an electrically charged fence set in a cement base. To the rear of that stretched another roll of concertina wire, and then three yards of green grass, and finally the crimson-colored giant solid wall enclosing the buildings of Spandau.

Atop this wall, on a wooden platform fitted out with two immense searchlights and a cubicle with three large glass windows, an unsmiling British Tommy, rifle slung over his shoulder, moved slowly round and round.

Studying the layout of the block-square prison, the American reporter counted six of these sentry lofts perched along the high wall. He jotted, on the back of an envelope, a note about this and other penal refinements. Then, stuffing the envelope in one pocket, he pulled a camera out of the other and brought it up to his eye.

That moment, the roof fell on him. Or so it felt.

For in a split second, the entire area seemed to swarm with wild life— wild-eyed life, that is. Two large, angry men, one in civvies, one in a blue uniform, came charging out of the prison toward him. Two other men, even larger and angrier, tumbled out of the brick building beside him. The total effect, the American reporter recalled later, was that of being run over by a stampede of charging rhinoceroses.

There was a brief, silent, panting skirmish over the camera. The two from the prison heatedly crowded the American, while the two from the building held back, watching and listening sullenly.

"You're in trouble, brother," the blue-uniformed guard was saying. "This is a security area. Top secret."

"Nothing in that sign says you can't look or take pictures—from the outside."

The guard was not interested in technicalities. "Two more steps and you'd have been shot dead. What's your nationality? What are you doing here?"

The American handed over his green passport, and his army travel orders for Berlin, three of them written in English and one in Russian. A vigorous fifteen minutes of argument followed. The air was blued, the notes studied, the camera film confiscated.

"Lucky for you we're Americans," the guard said. "The others wouldn't have let you off." He lowered his voice. "See those two over there. The ones from the building. They're two of the eight permanent Russian guards here. They spotted you from an upstairs window. They reported to the prison that you were taking notes. At the same time, the British sentry up there phoned back that you looked suspicious. Listen, pal, this is a four-power jail. Inside, we've got seven of the biggest criminals in the world. We can't be too careful. Haven't you heard about Spandau? No pictures. No stories. No outsiders. No *nothing*. Get it? We hate to talk to you like this, but we've got to. As it is, those Russians are taking in everything—they know you're an American, and we'll have to explain about you at the next four-power prison directors' meeting. So take off fast, while you can. Last week, a German photographer did what you were doing. He's still in jail."

The American reporter prudently beat a hurried retreat. Looking back once, he saw the two Russian guards arguing with the two Americans.

I can vouch for the accuracy of what happened to that American at Spandau—because I was that American.

But what happened to me, I later learned, was only a repetition of what had happened to inquisitive visitors many times before. In the almost two and a half years since Spandau had become an active international prison, at least two dozen other curious journalists of varied nationalities had been jailed, roughed up, or chased, all for daring to snoop in the vicinity of the red-brick walls. Despite this, several overly enthusiastic journals have advertised that their representatives have penetrated Spandau. None of these claims can be classified as nonfiction. For the fact is, no outsider, journalist or visiting fireman has seen the inside of Spandau Prison, in Berlin, since July 1, 1947. Why this super-security? Why the hush-hush?

The answer lies in the nature of the criminals incarcerated. Of the twenty-two top Nazis tried at Nuremberg, only seven escaped paying the death penalty. These seven, today, are in Spandau Prison. The most infamous of the group is fifty-three-year-old Rudolf Hess, Hitler's personal deputy, who was sentenced to life imprisonment. The other two lifers are seventy-three-year-old Erich Raeder, the Nazi admiral, and fifty-nine-year-old Walther Funk, boss of the Reichsbank after Schacht. The two youngest and healthiest Nazi prisoners in Spandau, the ones with the greatest likelihood of surviving their twenty-year sentences, are forty-two-year-old Albert Speer, an architect who became Minister for Armaments, and forty-two-year-old Baldur von Schirach, the youth leader who wrote poems to Hitler. The remaining two are seventy-six-year-old Constantin von Neurath, once Hitler's Foreign Minister, who is serving a fifteen-year sentence, and fifty-eight-year-old Karl Doenitz, head of the Nazi Navy and seven-day ruler of Germany after Hitler perished in his bunker, who is serving only ten years.

These seven are guarded in this fantastic manner, not because they might manage to escape but because they might be forcibly liberated. It is highly unlikely that Doenitz, for example, could get out of his cell-block, past the three hundred or so guards, soldiers, and general employees dedicated to keeping him in, over the wall and through the fences to freedom. But it is possible that, among the 60 million surviving Germans who followed, and in some cases worshiped, these men, there are several hundred or more armed fanatics who might one night try to storm Spandau.

The four-power brain trust charged with securing Spandau is at present most worried about Baldur von Schirach. The moon-faced, boyish von Schirach, whose great-grandfather was a Union officer at Bull Run and whose mother was a Philadelphia girl, was the Reichsjungenfuehrer or Reich Youth Leader. It was von Schirach—whose home Hitler so often visited—who spent busy, frenzied days over the years visiting every German village and city, instilling in German youngsters between the ages of five and nineteen a belief in the party ranking above God, in *Deutschland über Alles*, in the superiority of the pure German "Aryan" to Jews and mongrelized peoples everywhere. As one Spandau official told me, "This von Schirach was really the idol of all German kids. There are still millions of them, now strong, smart young men, burning with a desire to rescue their hero. One day, they may get together and try to pull it off. It hasn't happened yet. But it could happen tomorrow. Anyway, we're not taking any chances."

Another reason for the security surrounding the prison is that the four guarding powers do not want Spandau to become a mecca for the Fascist faithful. A tough American officer, speaking to me in a Berlin bar one evening, explained, "We want the Germans to forget those bastards. We don't want the Germans to keep thinking about these seven, then about the good old days, and then start squirming and giving us headaches. We don't want these seven to be turned into living martyrs." As a matter of fact, it was for this reason that Spandau, which is almost outside of Berlin and flanked by a field on one side and an orchard on another, was selected over several other sites. There was less traffic here, fewer citizens residing in the vicinity.

At one time, when the Allied powers were searching for a prison, they seriously considered the cement-and-steel antiaircraft Flak Tower or Tiergarten Bunker, in Berlin. This tower, built to house thirty thousand persons underground, was the place where the SS made its last stand against the onrushing Soviet troops. It was a perfect prison, so perfect that when the British tried to blow it up with the latest of explosives recently, they succeeded only in twisting it and thereby lost face in front of the smiling German population. Despite its strength, this Flak Tower was not acceptable, because too many Berliners passed it daily to and from work. "Can't you picture thousands of Germans hiking past it every day," said the American officer, "staring at it, thinking to themselves, 'Seven great men are in there. One day we must have men like that again, other gods like them to restore our dignity and prosperity.' No, that wasn't the way to make the Germans forget."

Yet, inconsistently, while the four powers keep Spandau isolated from publicity in order to make Germans forget their late gods, the powers are at the same time permitting newspapers, magazines, book publishers in Germany to bring out story after story written by people who had been close to Hitler. Recently, *Die Abendzeitung* told its Frankfurt readers, "These naïve memoirs of valets and adjutants, secretaries, mistresses and chauffeurs tend to leave one with the impression that after all Hitler wasn't so bad; a little violent but very generous. He drove millions of Germans into death, but basically he was a good fellow, fond of children and flowers. . . . These publishers count on their readers' stupidity, but leave out of account the others who use such publications to their advantage, the *Bleibtreus* [those who 'remain true' to the Nazis] who are awaiting their chance to persecute our people again."

There was yet another reason, I learned, for the blanket of secrecy over Spandau. It was less dramatic than the others, more practical, and one that could any day explode into an international scandal. As one high-level source put it bluntly, "It's not only that we want to keep information on Spandau away from the Germans. We want to keep it away from our own people back home. And believe me, all four powers feel exactly the same way. Imagine what the American taxpayer back home would say if he knew what it was really costing him to keep those seven in this fancy prison!"

Reliable sources reveal that it is costing five governments—the four powers and Germany—exactly $252,000 a year to run Spandau Prison. Since there are only seven prisoners in the mammoth jail, this means $36,000 is being spent annually to feed, house, and guard each one of the Nazis. That is more than 150 times the amount spent on the average German convict. Of the total sum, the West Berlin government pays the largest amount, 450,000 German marks, roughly $135,000. Next highest is the United States, which contributes $60,000 a year. Russia, Great Britain, and France contribute slightly more than $20,000 each.

The Germans are very bitter about paying such a heavy share of the budget. As a Berlin magazine, the *Insulaner*, remarked, "The German administration has no opportunity to hire laborers for Spandau or dismiss them either. It can only pay." Off the record, German officials like to imply that much of their money is going for graft, to supply the four-power guards with luxurious living quarters and expensive foods. These insinuations are, of course, utterly untrue. As a matter of fact, the Germans, who are trying to reduce their share of the burden by $35,000, have been remiss in furnishing Spandau with many necessary supplies, ranging from office equipment to toilet paper, and the Americans have been quietly furnishing these items out of Uncle Sam's pocket.

No, the reason for this nightmarish expense is not graft, or even mismanagement, but rather the simple fact that Spandau is a kind of Mad Hatter's castle. Originally built for 132 convicts, it had been overcrowded with 600 prisoners before the four powers requisitioned it. Emptied, and then rebuilt for Nazi war criminals, the prison that last held 600 men now holds merely seven. Of the 132 cells, 125 are empty. And, because the four powers managing the prison often cannot agree, expenses are quadrupled. There are, for instance, four kitchens instead of one, just as there are four guards' barracks instead of one. Little wonder the four powers want to keep Spandau out of the limelight.

As a result of the super-security, few American taxpayers know what they are getting for their money. They do not know that powerful efforts are this moment being made behind the scenes to get Albert Speer legally pardoned and out of jail, his lobbyists arguing that he alone defied Hitler's scorched-earth policy and that he once planned to gas Hitler through the ventilators of the Chancellory bunker. They do not know that Doenitz wears silk underwear (he has ten sets), that Hess alone still mentions the Fuehrer out loud, that von Neurath is expected to die very soon.

More important, as a result of this security, too few Americans know that with the exception of the air safety center in Berlin, Spandau Prison remains the only four-power institution in all Germany. For although the Soviets no longer meet with the British, French, and Americans anywhere in Germany to discuss mutual problems, they still permit their Spandau director to confer weekly with the directors representing the three Western powers. At these weekly meetings, the Russians have fought for solitary confinement for the seven Nazis, and lost to the British on that point; have fought against any religious worship in Spandau, and lost to the Americans on that point; have fought against publicity on the prison, and successfully defeated the French on that point.

Yet, despite the fact that no one can get into Spandau Prison, authentic information does get out. This report, perhaps the most complete made public since the prison became top secret, was obtained from firsthand sources. Which sources? That will have to remain this writer's own top secret for the present.

The present use for Spandau Prison was conceived one month before the Nuremberg trials ended. On September 7, 1946, the Allied Control Council circulated the highly restricted Directive 35. The fifth paragraph of this directive ordered the four Allied elements of the Berlin Kommandatura, which was that city's version of the bigger Control Council, to find and prepare a suitable prison in the Berlin area "for all persons sentenced" to prison at the Nuremberg trials. It was estimated that about one hundred Nazis would be sentenced in the series of four-power trials.

After an intensive search, the investigators came upon Spandau, located deep in the British sector of Berlin. Constructed in 1881, Spandau had been used as a military prison for German soldiers sentenced by court-martial. During World War I the Kaiser converted it into a civil penitentiary, and when that war was lost the prisoners broke out and rioted in the streets. During the Hitler regime, it was nicknamed Rote Schloss or Red Castle and was used to hold political prisoners before they were shipped to concentration camps like Sonnenburg. One prominent prisoner in that period was Paul Lobe, a president of the Reichstag under the Republic.

When the four-power representatives visited it in 1946, there were 600 common criminals inside, the convicts crowded five to each one-man cell. However, Spandau seemed perfect for this new purpose. It had the right number of cells. It was strongly built. It was isolated. Without dissent, the Kommandatura agreed upon the investigators' choice.

To guarantee security, Spandau was promptly renovated. The 600 resident criminals were moved out, most of them being transferred to Moabit Prison in the French sector. Seven houses surrounding the prison were torn down, wire and electrical barriers erected, a half-dozen sentry perches added, entrances and cells reinforced, the old Nazi guillotine and gallows removed. But meanwhile in Nuremberg, something went wrong.

The first trial, before the International Military Tribunal, ended in violent discord. The Soviet judge, I. J. Nikitchenko, dissented on the acquittal of Schacht, von Papen, and von Fritsch. Furthermore, he objected to the life sentence given Rudolf Hess. "Taking into consideration that among political leaders of Hitlerite Germany Hess was third in significance, and played a decisive role in the crimes of the Nazi regime," said the Soviet judge, "I consider the only justified sentence in this case can be death." Quietly, the Russians withdrew from Nuremberg, insisting that thereafter they would try their own war criminals in their own way, and let the Western nations try theirs in their way. As a result, unexpectedly, this trial of twenty-two Nazis at Nuremberg was the first and last four-power trial.

Spandau was ordered to prepare for seven prisoners, instead of one hundred. And, because they were the only four-power prisoners, special and extraordinary precautions were taken. The main jail inside the Spandau walls was three stories high. A new ceiling was added, plastering off the upper two floors. Seven of the thirty cells on the first floor were given new solid steel doors, each door built with a slot at eye level.

Inside the seven cells, all glass and all electrical installations were removed. By January, 1947, Spandau was ready for the seven. Yet it remained empty for six months, while the four powers wrangled over how to run the prison and how to handle their criminals.

The four nations, sitting together in the Kommandatura headquarters at 16 Kaiserwerther Strasse in Berlin, agreed almost at once on details for the administration and protection of Spandau. By cumbersome compromise, they agreed that everything about the prison would be completely quadripartite. Each nation would contribute one director, a military man, who would have under him one civilian warden and seven civilian guards. The four directors, to be called the Prison Governorate, and the four wardens, and the twenty-eight guards, would constitute a permanent interior personnel. However, the exterior or outside guard of the prison would be rotated monthly. The first of every month, one of the four powers would supply sixty armed soldiers to patrol the outer wall of Spandau. Thus in December, sixty Americans, armed with M-1's, will replace the Russians and guard the outside of Spandau. The first day of January, the British, bearing Sten guns and mounting machine guns, will take over from the Americans in a colorful ceremony. In February, the French will police Spandau. And in March, it will be done by a platoon of Russian soldiers.

But although everyone got together amicably on Allied personnel problems, sparks flew in the Kommandatura headquarters when Hess and his playmates were mentioned. The Russians were particularly bitter about Hess, probably because they still remembered that in 1937 he had worked with Trotsky to overthrow Stalin. "From the start, the Soviets disagreed with us on almost every point," one American member of the Kommandatura revealed to me. "The trouble was that our mentalities were so different. The Russians went at every point with a kind of Slav logic, literal, unimaginative. I don't say their logic was worse or better than ours. I only say it was different. In Directive 35 there was a clause reading that the prison would be under 'full quadripartite administration.' Let me invent an example to show how this clause was interpreted. Say Admiral Raeder was to be shaved. To the Americans 'full' administration of the shaving meant the four powers would agree on one man to do the job. But to the Russians, the word 'full' meant an American slapped the lather on Raeder's chin, an Englishman wielded the razor, a Frenchman sprinkled the talcum, and a Russian applied the wet towel. To them that was full administration of Spandau!"

The greatest four-power arguments raged over the style of confinement, communal work, religion, freedom of speech, and exercise. The British, leaning over backward to be fair, wanted Hess and company treated as ordinary German criminals, which meant that they would be permitted to dwell behind barred cells, yet be free to go into the prison yard and work together, exercise together, worship together, and talk together. The Russians strongly opposed this leniency, insisting that the seven were not ordinary but extraordinary criminals and that they should be kept separate, silent, and in permanent solitary confinement.

When the question of outdoor exercise was being debated, the Soviet representative argued that all seven could get sufficient exercise inside their cells. The British doubted this. The Russian leaped to his feet, paced forward three steps, pivoted, paced back three steps. "That is exercise if you do it long enough!" he bellowed. As to religion, the Americans pointed out that German lifers in all German prisons are permitted to go to services on Saturday or Sunday. Replying to this, a Russian general rose and said, "So you want to give them religion on Sunday, do you? Very well. What religion? Tell me, who was their god? The only god they know is the god of war. Where will you find a clergyman who will represent the god of war?"

On the issue of free speech within Spandau, the British argued that if Funk wanted to stand up in the garden and lecture to the other six Nazis, he should be permitted this privilege. The Russians said if he so much as opened his mouth, he deserved punishment. At last, on this issue, as on most of the others, the French and Americans effected a compromise. There would be neither full silence nor full freedom of speech. Funk could talk to Hess about duties at hand, but not about outside matters. Funk could say to Hess, "Help me lift this wheelbarrow," but he could not say, "Tell me, Rudolf, what did you and the Fuehrer really discuss before you flew to Scotland?"

After six months the rules were agreed upon, and on July 18, 1947, the RAF flew the seven Nazis from Nuremberg to Gatow Airport outside Berlin, and then, behind lorried infantry, they were driven the three miles to Spandau Prison.

Since that day the four directors of Spandau have continued to meet weekly around a single table. While interpreters translate their conversation, and secretaries take down every spoken word for superiors in Moscow, London, Paris, and Washington, the four men continue to rehash and arbitrate all aspects of Spandau life. "Of course, they still disagree," one witness to their meetings told me. "They are four different personalities. Major Roger Smith, who used to be General Frank Lee Howley's adjutant in Berlin, is an outspoken earthy American from Maryland with nineteen years in the army behind him. The British director comes from the Isle of Guernsey. The Frenchman is from Metz. The Russian director comes from an unpronounceable place in the U.S.S.R. Haggling is inevitable. Their backgrounds and educations are different. The American argues with the Frenchman as often as with the Russian. Put it this way. Find yourself any four grown men. One wants to go to a cricket match and insists the other three must come along. Well, two of the others want to see naked women, and the fourth wants to get drunk. How can they get together and choose one amusement for all four? It's not easy. But the four directors are managing to do just this. In fact, relations with the Russian director were never better than at recent weekly meetings. Right now, they're having a great argument about memoirs. Two of the seven Nazis want to spend their spare time writing memoirs. The Russian director says the result would be a couple of *Mein Kampf's*. Two of the three Western directors think the Nazis should have such freedom to write, since the four powers can censor every word anyway. The disagreement has been passed up as high as the Berlin Kommandatura, which now contains only three powers, and to the Russian military in the East Berlin zone."

However, there are no disagreements whatsoever among the four-power employees who guard the interior of Spandau. The American and Russian guards, when they bull-session in German, the official prison language, never argue the merits of capitalism versus Communism or of their respective atom bombs. "We get along swell with the Reds," an American guard recently told a friend. "On the other hand, if they get along too good with us, they're yanked out fast and replaced by new boys."

There are supposed to be thirty-two guards, including four wardens, inside Spandau. Actually, there are twenty-eight. Only the United States has not filled its quota. Russia, Great Britain, and France have each supplied eight men, but the United States has supplied only four. "It's because too few want the job," said an American official. "The guards get sick of being enclosed. They become bored, ambitionless, introspective, morbid, until they're feeling like Rudolf Hess himself."

The four American guards, paid $3,619 a year each, fill the minimum qualification of having been army noncoms for two years, or members of the Navy, Marines, Coast Guard, or a civilian police force for three years. Like their fellow guards, they all speak and understand German fairly well—even though they are not permitted to talk to the seven Nazi prisoners, except when giving orders.

All of the guards—warders, the Prison Governorate prefers to call them—are supposed to be civilians. But, according to an inside source, the eight Soviet Russian guards and the Russian warden are not really civilians, but Red Army soldiers pretending to be civilians. Of all the guards, the British are the most experienced in prison work, and the

Americans the least. Seven of the British guards worked together before the war, in a Hong Kong colonial prison. After being interned by the Japanese, and eventually released, they accepted the same kind of employment again in Berlin.

These four-nation interior guards, wearing loaded .45's or their equivalent, attired in specially designed blue uniforms (with outer flap pockets, resembling the British flight officer's uniform), which were made by the German government, work a constant and rugged schedule. Two guards, always representing different nations, slowly patrol the first-floor cellblock that holds the seven Nazis. Every three minutes, one of these guards is supposed to peer into each cell to see what the occupant is doing. While there have been no suicide attempts yet (because the seven have even less opportunity to obtain and hide potassium cyanide vials than did Goering), the guards are still not supposed to take any chances. The fact is, the guards, by unspoken consent, have agreed that the peek-once-every-three-minutes routine is too tiring, and they now take a look about every fifteen minutes.

The guards work in shifts of four, employing a pattern that is complex but effective. While two of them are patrolling the cellblock, a third guard naps in the warden's austere office nearby, and a fourth toils at the entrance reception office checking various other prison personnel in and out. In a two-week period, each guard works three separate sets of hours —from eight in the morning until four in the afternoon for three days, from four in the afternoon until midnight for two days, from midnight to eight in the morning for three days, with two to three days off between each change of hours.

The guards who are bachelors are billeted in the brick buildings in front of the prison; the married guards have apartments requisitioned for them closer to the center of Berlin. The food inside the prison changes every month. For with the start of each new month, as the exterior platoon of guards changes, the new director in charge brings in his own mess. The permanent personnel in the kitchens, which includes several Dutchmen, a Czech, a Hungarian, a Finn, and a Pole, but no Germans, is prepared to cope with anything. During the Russian month, most of the guards drink vodka, during the English month they drink ale or gin, during the French month they have wine or cognac, and during the American month, Cokes or Scotch. The Russian food, which leans heavily on borscht and pork, is the most unpopular. The English mess, roast beef, kidneys, mutton chops, is considered the skimpiest, the French mess the tastiest, and the American mess the healthiest.

The seven prisoners rarely share their captors' food. The prisoners' meals are prepared in a special kitchen adjacent to their cellblock.

Each receives 1,680 calories a day, precisely the same ration that two out of every three Berliners receive. The Berlin government reluctantly pays the prisoners' food bill. Most of the food comes from American army stores—for such security purposes as preventing poisoning. Sometimes the meals are supplemented by leftovers from the guards' mess. The prisoners' main dish is usually prepared in a large stewpot, which the cook leaves inside the door of the cellblock. Each week, one of the prisoners takes a turn at KP duty. As the warden watches (sometimes glancing between the three slices of bread on each plate for messages or poison), the prisoners are released from their cells, one at a time. The first prisoner marches to the end of the cellblock, accepts his food on a tin plate, accepts a spoon (no forks or knives permitted), and returns to eat alone and in silence behind his closed door. The others follow in turn.

"The portions of food are usually equal," one gastronomic observer remarked to me. "They had better be. Hess knows that even if he is sore at Raeder, he cannot cheat him out of his full share of food, because if he does, Raeder will remember and get even when it is his turn at KP." The only one of the seven with a special food allotment is Doenitz. Because a French army doctor noted that he was severely underweight, he now receives 510 grams of extra butter every two weeks. When gossip of this leaked out, the Berlin *Neue Zeitung* commented bitterly, "Many Germans on the outside wish they could be as well off with their meals as Doenitz." The slow method of serving the food usually means that the last two prisoners will find their helpings cold when they return to their cells. To overcome this, the Americans once tried to introduce a speedier method of feeding—but the Russians vetoed it.

There are thirty cells in the main block. The cells across from, and on either side of, each prisoner are kept empty. Walther Funk's cell, six feet by nine, is typical of the rest. The door is made of solid steel, but has a small slit at eye level. Inside, the cell is furnished with an army cot, wooden stool, small table, and toilet. There are four plaster walls, no windows. Having received permission, Funk, like most of the others, has pasted up several photographs of his family, as well as sacred pictures of Jesus and of Mary.

Funk and his six companions wear round gray hats that match their light gray jackets and trousers. Their shoes, designed years before by Albert Speer for the Reich's slave laborers, are wooden. Once, while trying to do double time in the shoes, Speer ruefully remarked to a guard, "If I had known I would ever have to wear them, I'd have put a little leather in them." Doenitz alone has been granted the luxury of silk underwear because of a skin allergy. None wears a belt, for the obvious reason. Instead, they use ordinary elastic suspenders, which—for the same obvious reason—have been cut in half and then sewed together again with just enough thread to hold up their trousers.

The prisoners rise at six every morning, dress, soap and scrub their cells, then remove their shirts and wash. Once a week, they are led to hot showers, two at a time, while an armed guard watches. Von Neurath is the only one not well enough to take his weekly shower. There is a daily shave given by the prison barber, a Dutchman, and a daily medical inspection by the prison doctor. Once a week, two of the prisoners spend four hours doing the laundry for all seven.

After breakfast, a nine-hour work period begins. Activity is divided among the potato garden outdoors, and indoors the pasting together of paper envelopes, and the making of straw shoes for the German economy. Speer seems to enjoy the garden most. On warm days he strips to the waist before he digs and plants, and he is the only one with a generous suntan. It was in the garden that a classic incident occurred, one which the German press picked up and spread throughout the Reich. Rudolf Hess, who along with Doenitz still has moments of humor, was laboring in the garden one morning when an American guard walked over with a hose. "Here," said the guard, "water the plants." Hess looked up, then suddenly grinned. "Give it to Admiral Doenitz," he said in pointed English. "He knows all about water."

While all of the seven have been docile since their imprisonment, there remain stringent penalties for any one of the group who gets out of line. According to the official four-power agreement on Spandau, "Punishment for offenses committed in jail may consist of cancellation of privileges, and may include the cutting off of light in the cell for a period of up to four weeks, reduction of food which will be replaced by bread and water, deprivation of furniture and clothing, and, in special cases, fettering."

The privileges the seven possess consist primarily of smoking, letter writing, and reading, during the two-hour evening rest period between dinner and lights-out at ten o'clock. Each receives a package of tobacco a week, but may smoke only after meals or during the evening rest period. Hess occupies much time just pacing, and on several occasions has broken into a crazy goose step. Sometimes he will sit for an hour and stare at the wall. Several times he has been caught talking earnestly to himself. Hess is the only one of the seven who speaks of Hitler, referring to him still as the Fuehrer. The bald Funk, too, utilizes the privacy of his cell, alternately weeping out of self-pity and whistling jazz tunes as he beats time on the wooden stool.

Most of the other five devote their nights to reading. An extra empty cell has been converted into a miniature library, with several shelves of carefully chosen books (public library discards) and quiet, cold, old-maidish Admiral Raeder is librarian. All of the volumes, which are in German, are either classical fiction or unprovocative nonfiction. There are volumes by Goethe, Shakespeare, Schiller, Mark Twain. There is nothing that discusses modern war or European politics. Once, by accident, a history of the Russo-Japanese War of 1904-05, which dramatized Russia's crushing defeat, found its way into the library. Before any of the Nazis could borrow it, the Soviets discovered the volume and destroyed it.

Speer tries to read everything related to architecture, von Neurath reads and rereads anything dealing with mineralogy, and Doenitz favors English poetry. Von Schirach is the confirmed bookworm. He prefers such French authors as poet Francis Jammes. Once, in an expansive mood, von Schirach told a prison psychiatrist that reading had warped him, and now he hoped that it would straighten him out. He claimed that reading articles in Henry Ford's newspaper about the "Eternal Jew" and the "Protocols of the Elders of Zion" in his youth had helped make an anti-Semite and a Nazi out of him, and it was not until Nuremberg that he learned Ford had long before backtracked on his stand and that the "Protocols" were a long-discredited forgery.

None of the prisoners is permitted access to either German or foreign newspapers and magazines, or to radios. The only periodical they read is a weekly religious paper, printed in German, which the French pastor distributes on Saturdays. No news whatsoever of the outside world is supposed to enter Spandau. Yet one afternoon von Schirach turned to his guard and inquired, "Tell me, how long is the airlift to Berlin going to continue?" On another occasion, a French guard was quitting to return to Paris. During his last morning, each prisoner solemnly shook hands with him and said good-bye. How did von Schirach know about the airlift? How did all seven know about the Frenchman's departure? Probably by overhearing the four-power guards gossip in German outside the cells at night.

Each prisoner is allowed to write one letter a month not exceeding four pages in length. This letter is closely censored by all four powers. Only one incoming letter a month is permitted, but usually extra business letters from family or lawyers, discussing liquidation of property or local trials, are let through. Last year, Hess's attorney wrote him that he was going to attempt to reverse his client's sentence (on the grounds that the Japanese war criminal trials proved that war activity before 1939 was not a crime). Sometimes, gift packages arrive. One prisoner's family sent him a box of cookies, tobacco, and soap. The directors threw away the cookies, but allowed the tobacco and soap to remain in the supply room until the next ration of these was due. Then the prisoner received his family's tobacco and soap instead of the prison's routine supply.

Although the Russians strongly opposed it, each prisoner is permitted one visitor every two months. The visitor may be an old friend, relative, or attorney. In the case of immediate family, one visitor can mean several members of one family. All seven Nazis have living relatives. Von Schirach has a wife, Henny Hoffman, the daughter of Hitler's photographer, and he also has three young sons; Raeder has a wife who just fled from the Russians; Hess has a forty-nine-year-old wife, Ilse, who was just cleared by a denazification court in Munich, even while telling the judges that Himmler was a "good" man.

When one of the prisoners' wives arrives at Spandau, she rings a bell and announces herself through a tiny grilled opening in the metal door at the front entrance. She is admitted by one of the interior guards, checked, searched, then led across an open area to the jail. From the warden's office, a guard escorts her into another room where she meets her husband. The meeting is limited to fifteen minutes and is anything but private. Representatives from Russia, Great Britain, France, and the United States gather in the room. All understand German. All take shorthand notes on the conversation.

On Saturdays, a French pastor, an army chaplain, comes to Spandau to perform religious services. He works without salary. Six out of seven of the prisoners congregate in the narrow prison chapel. Hess alone refuses to attend. "I want nothing to do with religion any more," he recently told the pastor. During the Protestant services, five sing hymns while Funk accompanies them on the organ. The prisoners are permitted visits from the pastor during the week, but only von Neurath takes advantage of this.

All legal German holidays are recognized inside Spandau, but the biggest holiday is Christmas. This coming Christmas, their third in Spandau, the seven will sing carols in the cell which is their chapel and will have slices of cake in addition to potato stew and bread.

"But don't let that pathetic picture of those seven lousy bums get your sympathy," one Spandau administrator growled to me. "Just remember some of the other Christmases they celebrated, shooting defenseless GI's in the snow during the Battle of the Bulge, building bonfires out of screaming old women and little children in Poland and Czechoslovakia. I wonder how many lonely widows and frightened orphans there are, who won't sing carols this Christmas, because of them. Walther Funk likes to whine that he was only a banker. Sure. He's the guy who kept those gold fillings, from the teeth of murdered Frenchmen,

Englishmen, Russians, in the vaults of the Reichsbank. Von Neurath makes like he's just a pleasant old diplomat. Says he. Like when he was Protector of Czechoslovakia. Have the folks back home forgotten Lidice already? And Hess. Just an addled old boy. But he's the one who took down *Mein Kampf* when Hitler dictated it, and he's the one who personally broke the heads of Jewish kids in Munich. Millions dead, maimed, miserable this Christmas because of those seven and their buddies. Sure, we should let them eat cake this Christmas, but we should also show them some movies. A triple feature. Dachau. Belsen. Buchenwald. I say let 'em rot here, those dirty bastards."

How long will they rot in Spandau? Insiders feel that only Albert Speer and Baldur von Schirach may survive their sentences to emerge free men in seventeen years. As for the others, they are aging and ailing. Von Neurath is on his last legs. Erich Raeder has been seriously ill. When he feared strangulation from a twenty-year-old hernia, the Americans, who were in charge of Spandau at the time, suggested moving him to the American Army Hospital. The Russians said no. So one room of the prison was converted into a makeshift hospital by German workmen (among the first Germans admitted inside Spandau), and there Raeder successfully underwent surgery lasting thirty minutes. Funk had one attack of bleeding hemorrhoids, but was pulled through when British exterior guards donated their blood.

The Egyptian-born Rudolf Hess, who twice before Nuremberg tried to kill himself, is the sickest of the seven, mentally. Nine psychiatrists have examined him, and agree that he has a split personality with delusions of persecution. He still cannot believe Germany lost the war. He thinks that his jailers are trying to poison him. According to Douglas M. Kelley, who spent five months interviewing and testing Hess, "Diagrammatically, if one considers the street as sanity and the sidewalk as insanity, then Hess spends the greater part of his time on the curb. . . . Hess will continue to live always in the borderlands of insanity."

When I passed on these psychiatric reports to an American who sees Hess daily, the American laughed. "Tell those psychiatrists they're twice as nuts as Hess. Believe me, he's saner than any of us." Despite this, the professional evaluations are probably the more accurate.

Meantime, agitation continues inside Berlin for a smaller, more economical prison. The German government feels that the seven Nazis should be committed to an ordinary Berlin jail along with hundreds of other felons. The four-power directors are against this, because they worry that fellow convicts might either slaughter the seven or assist them in escaping. But, driven by fear that their costly organization may one day create a scandal, the four powers insist they are constantly searching for a more economical prison. To date, they have not found one. And, since Soviet Russia, Great Britain, France, and the United States must all again agree on the jail, it is unlikely that they will ever find another. So Spandau remains, a gigantic $252,000 Red Castle for seven mass murderers, per capita the most expensive, per setup the most incredible, perhaps the most secret, and positively the most strongly guarded man-made prison in all the world.

WHAT HAS HAPPENED SINCE . . .

I had been fascinated by the world's strangest maximum-security prison, and by its unusual administration and unique prisoners, from the first moment I had heard a few details concerning it. When I realized that no major story had been written about Spandau, I suggested such a story to the editors of *Collier's* magazine. They were enthusiastic. In September, 1949, I traveled by train from Paris to Berlin—the train sealed during the East Germany portion of the journey—and was housed for two weeks in a suburb of Berlin by the United States Army Press Center.

The Spandau story was almost as difficult to penetrate as Spandau prison itself. There had been some sketchy newspaper accounts in several languages, and I had read them. But firsthand information appeared impossible to acquire. When I went by taxi to 23 Wilhelmstrasse to see Spandau for myself, I was almost arrested, and my camera film was taken from me, as I have related in my account of the adventure. However, my unexpected reception at the prison, instigated by the Russians, had its good result, and this was what really opened up the story for me. A day or two later, a high-ranking United States Army officer connected with Spandau found me at the Press Center, apologized for the rough treatment I had received, returned my camera film, and said that he was sympathetic to my assignment. He felt that the American taxpayers who were supporting Spandau should know something about it. Through this high-ranking officer I made other contacts, one of which was with a former guard in Spandau, another with an attorney connected with the legal division of the prison (a man I had known in my own army years), and from these three I acquired much inside knowledge of the red-bricked fortress. There were other sources, German and French, but these three Americans were the principal ones.

After returning to Paris, I wrote "The Seven Secret Prison Cells," encouraged and elated by the realization that I had an exclusive story containing material as yet untouched by the international press. In October, 1949, *Collier's* magazine purchased my story. With rising excitement, I waited for my story to appear in print. I waited and I waited, and it never appeared. What had happened was that, a month after acquiring my story, and even as they were preparing to go to press with it, the editors of *Collier's* were dismayed (as was I) to learn that a rival publication was publishing a Spandau story of its own. When the rival periodical's Spandau account appeared, it proved to be a thin memoir written by an American doctor who had been in and out of Spandau, and was now capitalizing on his experience by selling it to a magazine. Since *Collier's* felt that my own story was far more thorough, the editors decided to go ahead with its publication. But, for some reason, they never did so.

Recently, when I reread my story, I realized that I could publish it at last, because—even after the passage of sixteen years—it would still stand as the most complete account of Spandau yet to appear in print. In investigating the prison, its administration, its guards, its prisoners today, I found that little had been altered since 1949. There had been some minor modifications of the rules, there had been some minor intrigues, but the only significant difference was that the huge Teutonic Bastille now held three Nazi war criminals instead of seven.

After sixteen years, the administration of Spandau Prison remains unchanged. Small disagreements among the representatives of the four controlling powers continue, but they are rarely serious. If anything, the Russians are said to be more tractable than ever. The only important area of altercation is a basic one: The United States, France, and England, supported by West Germany, want to close down Spandau and transfer the surviving prisoners to any other German prison, preferably a small one, such as a specific one that exists about a mile from Spandau; Russia refuses to close down Spandau as long as one Nazi war criminal breathes within its walls. Otherwise, as an American foreign correspondent reported recently, Spandau stands as "a model of harmonious East-West cooperation."

In 1949, I was told that it was costing the four powers and West Germany $252,000 every year to maintain Spandau. By 1956, numerous economies had been introduced, and the operating cost had dropped to $107,000 annually. Today, it requires a budget of $66,000 a year to run the prison. However, as the West German government has pointed out, if the three remaining prisoners could be moved to an ordinary German prison, the total cost for housing and guarding them would be only $800 a year.

Other changes are infinitesimal. When I was in Berlin, each of the four powers was allowed to provide eight guards inside the prison. Now, each power provides five guards. When I was in Berlin, each imprisoned Nazi was allowed one outside visitor a month for fifteen minutes, and each was permitted to write and receive one letter of no more than four pages in length once a month. In 1952, this was liberalized, and today each prisoner may have one visitor a month for thirty minutes instead of fifteen, and each may receive four letters a month instead of one.

I learned that Spandau is still a maximum-security prison, still inhabited by nearly three hundred military and civilian personnel controlled by the four powers, still heavily guarded and fortified, still impenetrable and secret. This vigilance continues because all four of the controlling powers, but largely and most persistently the Russians, continue to fear that one day some outside political group may try to rescue one of the Nazi prisoners by force. For the Russians, this fear seems to be a permanent obsession.

From what little I could observe and learn during recent visits to West Germany, this fear seems to be groundless. There are fanatical bands of former Nazis, to be sure, old men who dream of the old glories—and there are young men who would like to restore to Germany the philosophy espoused by Hitler—but I doubt if enough of these zealots are willing to give their lives to liberate one decrepit historical figure from Spandau, especially since two of the three left in the prison will soon be legally released. Rudolf Hess, serving life, would then be the only captive they could rescue, and in his present mental condition he is hardly worth such drastic action.

However, the Russians may be completely right in fearing a rescue plot. Occasionally in the last sixteen years, evidence has appeared, and rumors have been heard, that such a rescue operation was in the making. In the late 1950's, there was said to have been a plot instigated by the onetime SS strongman, General Otto Skorzeny, who so dramatically rescued Benito Mussolini from the Allies in Italy. The plot was that Skorzeny would lead an armed, lightning-fast task force into Spandau by air. He was to land two helicopters in the Spandau prison yard at the exact moment that Rudolf Hess was puttering in his potato garden. While one helicopter would disgorge fanatics with automatic hand weapons to hold off the Spandau guards, the raiders in the other helicopter would grab Hess and waft him away to a secret hideout, from which he could be held up as a living inspiration for the faithful. Apparently this plot—if it ever truly existed—was uncovered by the four-power intelligence agents, and several conspirators were arrested. From time to time since, there has been a rumor that a group of diehard Nazis, in heavy tanks, was planning to appear out of the night, ram and batter down a Spandau wall, and bring Hess to freedom. These rumors have never materialized into fact.

In Berlin during 1949, I was told that it was Baldur von Schirach, the former Nazi youth leader, who might be the object of any such rescue attempt. He alone, it was felt, represented the hope of a militant Germany Resurrected to the German youth. In 1962, the weekly newspaper, *The National Observer*, discounted von Schirach as being of any value, because he had "deteriorated mentally," but cited Albert Speer as "a possible danger." However, today, all sources regard Rudolf Hess as Spandau's only property of value to fanatics.

The first of the seven to gain release and freedom was Hitler's onetime Foreign Minister, the elderly, ailing Constantin von Neurath. It is alleged that his family, which in earlier days had maintained a close friendship with the British royal family (von Neurath himself had once been ambassador to England), appealed constantly to their high-placed English cousins. They pleaded that the old man, no longer a threat to anyone, be paroled so that he might receive proper medical care, and eventually be buried in the family plot instead of an unmarked grave.

These appeals on von Neurath's behalf at last reached Winston Churchill, and the seventy-nine-year-old Churchill, personally conscious of the infirmities that go with advancing years, went before the House of Commons one day in 1954 to plead for a fallen foe: "I certainly have felt for several years that the conditions in Spandau were very hard and inhumane, and in this case we are dealing with a man of eighty-one years which, I can tell you, is quite a lot, and who is suffering from illness."

The four powers controlling Spandau heard Churchill, and respected his wish. Late in 1954 Constantin von Neurath, who had served almost half of his fifteen-year sentence, became the first of the seven to walk out of Spandau, to return to his family, his family doctor's care, and at last to burial in the historic family cemetery plot at Enzweihingen in August, 1956.

And now there were six.

Admiral Erich Raeder, in his eighties, and banker Walther Funk, in his sixties, were both almost as ill as von Neurath had been. The four powers met and agreed to parole Raeder and Funk from Spandau because of "age and illness." Both Raeder, who was released in 1955, and Funk, who was released two years later, died in 1960.

And now there were four.

Admiral Karl Doenitz, who had ruled Germany for one week after Hitler's death, had been sentenced to ten years' imprisonment. All but one year of this sentence was served in Spandau, which he detested more strongly than did any of his colleagues. He survived his sentence in relatively good health, and received his release in October, 1956. Spandau definitely did not break him. Shortly after gaining freedom, Doenitz was invited to lecture to the student body of a school outside Hamburg. He accepted, and in his speech he defended the Nazi party and its military conquests with pride, and he bitterly attacked the Allied prosecution of Nazi war criminals. His speech generated such a mixed storm of protest and acclaim, and consequent embarrassment for the West German government, that the professor who had invited Doenitz to speak promptly committed suicide. Doenitz himself went into retirement, devoting himself to writing his memoirs, which were published in 1959 under the title *Memoirs: 10 Years and 20 Days*. He also offered an occasional public utterance. His last one, made in 1964, criticized the Allies' demand for Germany's unconditional surrender in World War II. Doenitz told the Associated Press, "The demand for unconditional surrender was a grave political mistake of the Western allies and led to a senseless prolongation of the war. In addition to the Germans, the entire free world suffers today from this mistake." Doenitz was severely castigated for his statement until, later in that same year, ex-President Dwight D. Eisenhower publicly agreed with him. No doubt there were those connected with Spandau who regretted ever having permitted Doenitz's release.

And now there are three.

By 1965, two of these three, fifty-eight-year-old Albert Speer and fifty-eight-year-old Baldur von Schirach had served nineteen years of their twenty-year sentences, eighteen of those years inside Spandau. Von Schirach's life has altered little in the sixteen years since I wrote about him. True, his wife, Henny Hoffman, divorced him, retaining custody of their children. But one of his sons visits him every month. Otherwise, von Schirach has devoted himself to intellectual and aesthetic pursuits, perusing more French novels, studying music, memorizing poetry, and constantly disowning Nazism and Hitler. Early in 1965, von Schirach, for the second time in three years, was removed to a British military hospital outside Spandau's walls, this time to have the detached retina in his right eye corrected. The operation was reported as "not too successful," but nevertheless, the patient was returned to his Spandau cell, where he is now planning his autobiography which he expects to write upon his release.

With even more determination than von Schirach, Albert Speer has refused to let Spandau destroy him. Instead of brooding or indulging in self-pity, Speer has concentrated upon developing himself as an architect. Year after year, Speer has kept himself abreast, within the reading limitations imposed by Spandau, with architectural advances, and he has produced hundreds of original designs.

Both von Schirach and Speer will have completed their twenty-year sentences in 1966, and after that they will enjoy freedom. It is unlikely that either one will suffer any financial difficulties. Von Schirach has told guards that he has inherited a considerable sum of money from a deceased American relative, and that this will maintain him in comfort. Speer will be reunited with the six children he hardly knows any longer, one of them a daughter who was educated and raised by an American family in Westchester County, New York. There is little doubt that Speer will prosper in some West German firm of architects.

One suspects, by all accounts, that it is not freedom from Spandau alone that these two will enjoy, but freedom from the oppressive daily presence of the erratic—and for them, unbearable—Rudolf Hess.

From all that I could learn, Hess today is much like the Hess I learned about in 1949, only more so in every respect. By now, at the age of seventy-one, he has been in one jail or another for twenty-four consecutive years, and over eighteen of those years have been spent in Spandau. Physically, he is a gray-haired, hollow-eyed, wrinkled, hunched and bony scarecrow. As an American officer in Spandau told the Associated Press in 1964: "He looks a strange sight as he shambles around in an old German army ski-cap and a long military overcoat that flaps around his ankles. His mental state has not improved with the years. Some nights he howls like a wolf in his cell."

Prison psychiatrists consider Rudolf Hess still psychotic but not insane. Recently, Dr. Maurice N. Walsh, a psychiatrist associated with the University of California at Los Angeles, admitted that he had examined Hess in the presence of fifteen witnesses during 1948, but had been told to keep his diagnosis secret, for fear of irritating the Russians during the tense days of the Berlin airlift. According to Dr. Walsh, "I determined that he was a latent schizophrenic, a man in and out of psychosis. But I found him in no immediate danger of suicide."

Today, Hess's condition remains unchanged. His hypochondria has deepened, and he weeps over imaginary ills. He begs his guards to break rules to extend him special favors, and when a softhearted one complies, Hess informs on the guard to his superiors. Sometimes when guards hear him screaming, they will scream back at him. Often they will find him stretched out on his cell floor, in a partial trance, babbling to himself.

Hess's interests are few. He looks forward to his daily session of gardening. He enjoys writing his regular letters to his wife Ilse, who manages a resort lodge near Munich, and to his twenty-six-year-old blond son, Wolf-Ruediger (a graduate of the University of Munich and an engineer), who is loyal to the memory of his father. However, Hess has never once permitted his wife or son to visit him at Spandau. According to his wife, "He could not stand for us to see him living like a caged animal."

Just after New Year's Day, 1965, Hess received the first visitor that he had ever invited to call upon him inside Spandau. At that time, he summoned his attorney, Alfred Seidel, and the two men spent most of their half hour together drafting the terms of Hess's will. Later, Seidel told the press that Hess did not want him to fight for a pardon, that he hoped to be paroled when von Schirach and Speer were freed, and that he wished no further visitors, not even members of his immediate family. According to Seidel, Hess is anything but insane. "His memory functions superbly. Hess especially wanted to know how his family lives. He is worried about the economic existence of his wife and son."

His one unflagging interest is his nostalgia for the Nazi past, when he was Hitler's deputy Fuehrer and third in command. More often than before, the guards of the four nations can observe him goose-stepping in his tiny jail cell. And sometimes they hear him singing, in a cracked voice, the "Horst Wessel" song. His memory, fairly clear about events that happened up to May of 1941, frequently seems to have been arrested at that date. That was the period when Hess—knowing that England was in desperate straits, knowing that his Fuehrer wanted to make peace with England before striking at Russia but could not reach Churchill with a peace offer—determined to take matters into his own hands. Although it meant defecting from Germany, Hess flew a Messerschmitt to England, landed in a cow pasture, and eagerly offered to present a peace plan to the Duke of Hamilton and others. He never had a chance to discuss his offer. He was clapped into an English jail where he languished until Germany was defeated. Even though Hitler declared Hess insane at the time of his defection, and tried to obliterate his name from records of the Third Reich, there are scholars who now believe that Hitler was aware in advance of Hess's flight, and even encouraged it. Hitler disowned Hess, and disavowed knowledge of the flight, only because the mission proved a dismal failure.

But all of that is in the past, where Rudolf Hess spends so many of his hours and days, a past more agreeable to him than his present situation in Spandau. When von Schirach and Speer are gone, Hess will be alone in Spandau, and one doubts that he will be unhappier, since he always resented their repudiation of Hitler, their judging Hitler as a lunatic, their sharing of Hess's privileges as a martyr of the Third Reich.

And so, with the other two gone, there will be only one.

Incredibly, there will be three hundred specialists, from four powerful governments, guarding one deranged old man, the relic of a political regime that no longer exists, in a burdensome German St. Helena.

And when Hess dies, or is murdered, there will be none. And at last, the seven secret cells will be empty, and the warders will go home with their stories, and Spandau will belong to the historians—and the makers of fiction.

» 17 «

THE MAN WHO LOVED
HITLER

THE TALL, blond clerk at Fritzes, Stockholm's leading bookstore, did not think that I should see Dr. Sven Hedin for a possible magazine story. "He is our national disgrace," said the clerk.

But as far as I could observe, Dr. Hedin's disgrace—he had embarrassed the neutral Swedes by supporting Nazi Germany in the Second World War, and Germany had lost—was not often discussed in public. In a small land, where great international names are few—Swedenborg, Strindberg, Nobel, Lagerlöf, a handful more, also dead—they do not relinquish their heroes easily or prematurely. At the age of eighty-one, Dr. Sven Hedin was still well-known throughout the world, and so any ostracism by his countrymen was both occasional and reluctant. However, for the great majority of Swedes (only a small minority had been as pro-Nazi as Dr. Hedin), their hero stood as an uncomfortable reminder that their nation had traded with Hitler's Germany throughout the Second World War.

Dr. Hedin's numerous thick books on his explorations of Inner Mongolia and Tibet, printed in Swedish, German, and English, crowded the shelves of all Stockholm's many bookstores, including Fritzes. As explorer, hydrographer, cartographer, and travel writer, Dr. Hedin had visited the Forbidden City of Lhasa in 1896, and had returned to Tibet in 1906. From 1927 to 1935, traveling out of Peking, he had led a caravan of twenty-seven men and three hundred camels on the greatest expedition ever attempted into Central Asia. As a result of these adventures, he had become Sweden's best-known explorer. I found him listed in a recent government publication as one of Sweden's twenty great scientists of the preceding three hundred years, and he was given more

371

space than any other living Swede. And only the week before I arrived in Stockholm, he had dined with Count Folke Bernadotte, the busy nephew to the king.

Clearly, despite a certain amount of antagonism toward him by a variety of Swedish citizens I had met, Dr. Sven Hedin was not to be counted out. My curiosity about Dr. Hedin mounted. I wondered what had happened to a member of that unclassified species, the neutral-nation Nazi, after the war was over. To satisfy my curiosity, I sent Dr. Hedin a note. Promptly, he replied to it with an invitation to tea.

The two modern apartments which he kept, one above the other, were located on the Norr Mälarstrand, overlooking the quiet canal waters and white ferryboats of the Mälaren. Dr. Hedin met me at his door, a quick, shrewd-eyed gnome of a man, wearing thick spectacles, gray scrub mustache, stiff winged collar, and pin-striped suit. He grasped my hand in both of his. How good to see me! Ah, he had not been to America since 1932, when he had supervised construction of a replica of Jehol's Golden Pavilion at the Chicago World's Fair. An electric land, America. He had lunched with Henry Ford. Good man, Ford, even though Ford had refused to back a Hedin expedition into China, and was interested only in new roads for American automobiles in Russia. Did I know that Dr. Hedin had a letter from the late Franklin Delano Roosevelt? Oh yes, yes indeed.

Talking steadily, Dr. Hedin guided me into a narrow room, with built-in files on both sides, the files jammed with the correspondence of sixty years. He began opening files. The Roosevelt letter, the letter, ah, here, from the White House, Washington, D.C., 1933, a polite thank-you for some Chinese stamps and an invitation to drop in sometime.

We went into the parlor for tea. Dr. Hedin introduced me to his elderly sister, Alma, a tall, wary, watery woman in blue. She collected stamps, had founded the Flower Fund ("It's barbaric to waste flowers on the dead at funerals, so I make our people spend the same money on apartment houses for old folks"), and was now writing her autobiography. She had published one book, *My Brother Sven*, and it had been brought out in Germany recently.

Next, Dr. Hedin introduced me to his niece, Ann Maria Wetterlind, a compact blonde who spoke British English. She had been traveling these last years as Uncle Sven's secretary, and she had adored Berlin most of all. Those good times in Berlin, those parties, those wonderful people Emmy and Hermann, and Adolf's marvelous anecdotes. They were all such gentlemen, except Robert Ley, head of the Nazi Labor Front, he alone repelled her.

Ann Maria was now occupied taking care of eighteen refugees from

Poland and Estonia. There were 98,000 refugees in all, in Sweden, and many were very ill. They had suffered horribly in concentration camps. Mentioning the last, Ann Maria did not hide her confusion. These refugees claimed Emmy and Hermann and Adolf had put them there, in those camps, and yet Ann Maria had met Emmy and Hermann and Adolf and found them charming. Where was the lie?

We sat around a large, low coffee table, and with the first ceremonious pouring of tea, Dr. Sven Hedin took over. He seemed faintly concerned that I did not know enough about his importance in Sweden. Did I know that he was a Nobel Prize judge, and the only judge to vote annually on three of the four categories that Sweden controlled? I had not known, and was impressed, and showed it.

Feeling surer now, Dr. Hedin proceeded to elaborate upon his Nobel Prize connections. He had, he said, been a member of the Royal Swedish Academy of Science since 1905, and every year since then had voted for the laureates in physics and chemistry. In fact, in 1924, because of seniority, he had been president of the Academy of Science. During his membership, Dr. Albert Michelson, Dr. Guglielmo Marconi, Dr. Max Planck ("Five years ago, when he was eighty-five, he wrote me he had climbed the Jungfrau, up and down, in a single day"), Dr. Albert Einstein had been honored in physics, and Dr. Ernest Rutherford, Dr. Marie Curie, Dr. Irving Langmuir, Dr. Otto Hahn had been honored in chemistry.

Back in 1913, Dr. Hedin continued, he had been elected to fill a vacancy among the eighteen who composed the Swedish Academy, and thus, as one of the august eighteen, he had also become a judge to vote on the annual Nobel Prize for literature. Today, he was one of the three eldest of the eighteen. Oh, he went back a long way. He had personally known Alfred Nobel himself. "Knew him quite well. A nice man, and kind, but not like other men. An eccentric. Very definite in his ideas and opinions. His famous last will was scratched out on a half sheet of paper, because he had torn off the blank bottom half to save for other writing. He backed an early expedition of mine."

Dr. Hedin discussed some of the Nobel literary awards for which he had been, at least in part, responsible. Since he had become a literary judge, Romain Rolland, Knut Hamsun, Anatole France, George Bernard Shaw, Thomas Mann, Eugene O'Neill had all received the prize. Dr. Hedin explained that he and Selma Lagerlöf had been jointly responsible for swinging the Nobel award to America's Pearl Buck in 1938. Oh yes, it was a fact. He had admired Pearl Buck's work, her interest in China, and he and Selma had opposed and overcome the resistance of their fellow judges. "Pearl Buck and her husband published my last book, a biography of Chiang Kai-shek. They gave me too little money for it, and to think how I got her the Nobel Prize!" Not many days before, Dr. Hedin had heard from Pearl Buck's husband, who published under the John Day imprint, recommending Lin Yutang, one of his authors, for the next Nobel Prize. Dr. Hedin was doubtful about Lin Yutang ("His work is not broad enough"), but he would read more of his books and reconsider.

I asked Dr. Hedin how a relatively unknown writer, like Gabriela Mistral, the Chilean poet, who had won the Nobel Prize the year before, had gained a majority vote. "Well, that was interesting," said Dr. Hedin. "One of our judges, Hjalmar Gullberg, a very great poet here, had read Miss Mistral's poetry in the original Spanish and was enthusiastic. He nominated her, as did someone from South America. She had never been translated into Swedish or English, so none of us knew her work. To convince us, Professor Gullberg went to work translating Miss Mistral's best verse into Swedish. He had it published, and sent all of the judges a copy. It was a beautiful translation, and we voted her to be the laureate for 1945. But do not have the wrong impression. There are no politics in the awards."

I asked Dr. Hedin why certain prominent authors had not been honored. I named names, and Dr. Hedin had an explanation for each rejection. Maxim Gorki had died too soon. "His name came in second several times, and he would have got the prize eventually." H. G. Wells had been considered. "Too minor and journalistic." W. Somerset Maugham had also been considered. "Too popular and undistinguished." And James Joyce? Dr. Hedin seemed puzzled. "Who is he?"

By now confident of my interest in him, Dr. Hedin turned to what he regarded as a more important topic of conversation—world politics. Germany was in a terrible condition, he said. Germans had no place to live. Their homes had been destroyed by American bombers. Germans were starving. They would die in droves this postwar winter. Field Marshal Milch's wife had written him a pathetic letter begging for food packages. Dr. Hedin regarded me hopefully. Surely, I would tell America of this. Surely, America would help. After all, in the next war, a democratic United States of Germany would be America's best ally. The German people were one people, and no artificial zones could ever divide them. Had not Walter Lippmann written that today the Germans were the strongest people in Europe? Did I not think William Bullitt was America's most intelligent man?

Dr. Hedin told me that he had studied in Germany in 1889. It had always been his second homeland. He had been recognized there, feted, fussed over. The Kaiser and von Hindenburg had been his dearest friends. (Of course, he added, Pope Pius XI, King George V, Czar Nicholas, Emperor Meiji, Theodore Roosevelt had also been his friends.) And his books had always sold better in Germany than in the United States or Great Britain.

In 1927, Dr. Hedin went on, Dr. Junkers, the German airplane manufacturer, had sent him to Central Asia to see about establishing an air route from Berlin to Peking. The Chinese government had refused permission for such an airline. The expedition had then been refinanced and redirected by Dr. Hedin's friend, King Gustav of Sweden, with a strictly scientific objective. When Hedin's Swedish funds had run out, the Chinese took over his project and converted it into a pioneer highway-mapping enterprise. Dr. Hedin's explorations in Central Asia had consumed eight years. On returning to Sweden, Dr. Hedin had undertaken to produce an encyclopedic series of books on his findings in Central Asia. Thirty-one volumes had already been published in Stockholm, and Dr. Hedin was in the midst of collaborating on the twenty-five remaining books in the series. He expected this would leave him little time for any more exploring in the future.

He had also written, he added proudly, about 500 manuscript pages of another book, one that had nothing to do with his exploring. "I will call it 'Germany's Last Years,' " he said. Instantly, his sister protested. "They were not Germany's last years. Germany is not dead, Sven." Dr. Hedin blinked behind his thick lenses. "Alma, I mean it will tell about Germany's recent years." It would relate the entire story, he said, of his countless visits with the Nazi leaders. Although himself one-quarter Jewish, Dr. Hedin had been extremely friendly with Hitler and Goebbels, and whenever he dined and chatted with them, he would, upon leaving their presence, scurry back to his suite in the Kaiserhof Hotel in Berlin and transcribe every word he had heard. He felt that his position, as an unbiased listener from a neutral country, had been unique, and he had been then, even as now, possessed of an acute sense of history.

I wondered exactly how friendly he had been with Adolf Hitler. In reply, Dr. Hedin nodded to his sister, who rose, disappeared, and then returned with a large red velvet box. She opened it with care. "We keep it hidden now," she said softly. Deep inside the box, embedded in solid silver, the silver etched around with miniature swastikas, reposed a full-length picture of Hitler, a photograph affectionately autographed to Dr. Hedin.

After removing the framed picture, sister Alma extracted an oversized envelope. Dr. Hedin opened the envelope, pulled out a letter, typewritten, three pages long, dated "Oct. 27, 1942," signed by Hitler.

There was a story about this letter. Dr. Hedin had published, in Leipzig, a book entitled *Amerika im Kampf der Kontinente*. Hitler, who rarely had time to read books himself, retained a man to read books for him, and then recount them in oral synopsis to him at bedtime. Yet, Hitler had found the time and been impelled to pick up Dr. Hedin's book one evening at nine o'clock, and read straight through it until three o'clock in the morning. He had then dictated this affectionate letter to the author, discussing the book, and passing along the tidbit that he had attacked the Soviet Union only because he had learned the Bolsheviks were making secret preparations against him.

I asked Dr. Hedin about the others in Hitler's inner circle. Dr. Hedin recalled that he had attended Goering's fiftieth birthday stag party, and enjoyed it. He considered Goering a sweet, overgrown child. He reminded me that Goering's first wife had been Swedish, and that had she lived, she would never have permitted him the outrageous vanity of flaunting all those medals. Dr. Hedin said that Himmler had been a kind, inoffensive person. Once, Dr. Hedin had got into a violent political argument with Himmler. To conclude it, Himmler had remarked, "Sven, your Sweden is no problem for us. A nation that has had no war for a hundred and thirty years is weak." Dr. Hedin remembered how this had infuriated him, and how he had snapped at Himmler, "We are not weak but civilized. We have in our museums more flags and standards taken from other nations in victorious battle than you have in all Germany and Austria. We have four thousand captured trophies in one museum alone!" The argument ended, said Dr. Hedin, when he quoted the Fuehrer's statement that Germany's aim and goal was peace, something that Sweden had already achieved. After that, Himmler had fallen into silence.

Dr. Hedin's only real grievance was against Walther Funk. It appeared that in 1936, Dr. Hedin had delivered a series of 150 lectures, during which he traveled the length and breadth of Germany, and then he had returned to Stockholm to write a book about the Third Reich. He had been promised that 260 German organizations would buy copies of his book and publicize it. "I would have made a fortune," said Dr. Hedin. "As a matter of routine, I sent the manuscript in advance of publication to Funk, who was to approve the contents. He liked the book, but he insisted that five of the three hundred pages I had written must come out. These five pages were critical of the Nazi policy toward the Jews. I refused to cut out the five pages. Then there ensued a vehement correspondence between Funk and myself on Germany's Jewish policy. He wrote me eight letters in all. I have them here. But the book was never published."

Dr. Hedin said that he had last heard from Adolf Hitler two months before Berlin fell and the Fuehrer disappeared. This communication had arrived on Dr. Hedin's eightieth birthday. Hitler had sent a long telegram of congratulations, as had Keitel, Schacht, Raeder, von Ribbentrop, and Rosenberg. "I suppose Hitler is dead," said Dr. Hedin, "but I would not bet my head on it."

I made some oblique reference to Dr. Hedin's awkward position in Sweden today. Before he could comment, his niece spoke up. She said that at the start of the Second World War half of the Swedish people were for Germany, and half against. During the war, Hitler's invasion of neighboring Norway had made the majority of Swedes anti-German. Dr. Hedin interrupted his niece. "Today, it is changing back, so that more and more of our people are again sympathetic toward Germany. Right now, I am in disrepute here, but that will change, too." He stared at me. "I am perhaps also a black sheep in the United States now, no?" I did not reply.

Our genteel tea had taken four hours, and outside it was dark. I came to my feet, and thanked the three of them for their hospitality. When I moved toward the door, Dr. Hedin almost trotted beside me. In a rapid monologue, he told me that he was working night and day to save General von Falkenhorst, who had been sentenced to death by the British. After assuring me that von Falkenhorst had been "a humane man," Dr. Hedin added that he was enlisting the aid of the Swedish royal family in an effort to save the general.

I opened the door to leave, but Dr. Hedin continued speaking. He had just read that General Eisenhower was returning to Germany. "A good German name, Eisenhower," said Dr. Hedin. "I think he is going to Germany to make preparations against Russia." I said nothing. Dr. Hedin looked at me. Then, suddenly, he said, "I have done all the talking and answered all of your questions. Now you must be kind enough to answer one for me." I said that I would be glad to do so. Dr. Hedin weighed his question for a moment, then he formed it, and asked it. "Tell me, what do you think is the date for the war to start between the United States and Russia?" I stared at him, wordless for an interval of seconds, unable to speak, able only to shake my head. At last I said good night, thanks again for the tea, and then I walked downstairs and out into the cool, fresh neutral air.

WHAT HAS HAPPENED SINCE . . .

After three and a half years as an enlisted man in the United States Army Air Force and in the Army Signal Corps, I was honorably discharged from the service on February 3, 1946, at Fort Dix, New Jersey. While I had made writing tours through Mexico, Central and South America, Japan, and China, I had never been to Europe. I was determined to go as soon as possible. I obtained a series of writing assignments from three national magazines, my wife resigned from her editorial position on a motion picture magazine, and six months after my return to civilian life we were aboard the Swedish liner *Drottningholm*, bound for Göteborg, Sweden.

We reached Stockholm on September 3, 1946, and soon found ourselves settled in a regal corner suite of the Grand Hotel, the hotel that annually played host to the Nobel Prize winners. The cost of the suite was $13.44 a day, utterly beyond our means, but worth it for the view from the third-floor living room overlooking the Strömmen canal and the Royal Palace.

From the first day, I was constantly out in the cold, wet northern city, running down clues to possible stories, questioning, listening, observing, taking notes. I wrote a story on the Swedish National Theater, which was published, and several more stories on a variety of subjects, which were not published. Among the latter was the little adventure with Dr. Sven Hedin.

I had always known of Dr. Hedin. His books of travel and exploration, *The Conquest of Tibet, Across the Gobi Desert, The Silk Road*, were as familiar and romantic to me as the lighter works of Richard Halliburton and Carveth Wells. As I moved about Stockholm, I was surprised to hear his name mentioned often, not only at the King's bookstore, Fritzes, but almost everywhere I went. The reason this surprised me was that Hedin's conduct during the Second World War had been scandalous, yet his countrymen rarely referred to his specific activities. Germany's role in the Second World War had ended little more than a year before, and although many so-called neutral Swedes had been sympathetic toward the Third Reich, Dr. Sven Hedin had been almost the only internationally prominent Swede to announce such a sympathy. Indeed, he had called Adolf Hitler "one of the greatest men in world history." Since Germany had lost the war, and the Nazi concentration camp horrors had been brought into the open, most Swedes, while admiring Dr. Hedin's international stature, were embarrassed by his continued loyalty to Hitler's memory.

I decided that I must meet Dr. Hedin. I was curious. I sensed a story. I had no assignment, in fact no specific story angle or publication in mind, but I had to see the Scandinavian villain. I saw him on a sunny Sunday afternoon, September 8, 1946, and what occurred during our meeting I wrote down a week later, entitling it "Dr. Hedin's Disgrace."

Beyond the mere experience of meeting Dr. Hedin, there was something else that happened to me during our conversation, or as a result of it, an inspiration, an idea, that would have a lasting effect upon me as a writer—even though it would find no tangible expression until sixteen years later.

When Dr. Hedin had told me that he was a Nobel Prize judge, I had been quite startled and, indeed, impressed. I was impressed because, to me—to most, I am sure—the Nobel Prize in any category is the earth's foremost accolade given by man to man. And here was I, informally chatting with one of the august judges. And, I repeat, I was also startled. What startled me was the fact that this person I was interviewing was a cobweb of prejudices and misinformation and intolerance on many, many subjects, from the sciences to the arts. To picture him—someone less than mortal—as a Nobel judge, one who played a decisive role in crowning annual gods, was astonishing. I had always believed, without ever having thought of it much, that if there were Nobel Prize judges, they were the wisest elders of our age. Actually, I suspected, most people did not believe the Nobel Prizes were decided upon by judges at all, but rather selected at a meeting of deities on high Olympus or selected by some massive, invisible computing and judgment machine that could X-ray the earth's talented, its geniuses, and recommend the winners.

Intrigued by the contrast between what I had expected and what I found before me, I began to ask Dr. Hedin all about his functions on his Nobel committees, about how winners were nominated, sorted out, narrowed down, secretly discussed and debated, and about his own role and the roles of his fellow judges. Dr. Hedin sensed my excitement, and was pleased and expansive, and he rattled on at great length.

After I had left Dr. Hedin, I knew that I had stumbled upon something that should be written about—the truth about the Nobel Prize awards—the truth about those who gave and those who took—but I did not know what kind of story it was or could be, or in what form it might take final shape. I knew only that I wanted more of it. Immediately, I sought out several of Dr. Hedin's Nobel colleagues, scholarly Swedish judges on the Nobel Prize science and literature committees, who also lived in Stockholm. I found them as outspoken as Dr. Hedin. In discussing the Nobel awards, these other judges named names, spoke of the human frailties of the judges and the judged, revealed stupidities and brilliance in the selections, exposed politics and prejudices and petty vanities as well as honesty and wisdom and courage in the Nobel Prize voting.

When my interviews were done, I had a writer's treasure, I knew. I had no idea what to do with it.

Still in Stockholm, I did other work in the days that followed, but always bothered and nagged by this new material, and suddenly it was a Sunday. My wife and I slept most of the morning, and after we awakened, we had breakfast in our room. Outside, after a week of rain, the sun was shining at last. It was noon. I moved to the living room window and looked down across the Strömmen canal and idly watched and listened as the King's band played before his enormous Royal Palace across the way. The postcard grandeur of the scene, the outer unreality of it, struck me, and then I remembered my afternoon with Dr. Sven Hedin, my interviews with the other judges, and I understood that all these sights were façades, and that plainer, cruder, human events happened behind palace walls, behind academy walls, behind all walls where earth people dwelt. And that was the moment of conception. At once, I knew what must be done.

I turned from the window to my wife, who was still having coffee. "Sylvia," I said, "has anyone ever written a novel about the Nobel Prizes?"

From that moment, I was slave to an embryo, a brainchild, faceless, almost shapeless, that I would not be delivered of for a decade and a half. But it was to Dr. Hedin, and to several of his fellow judges, that I owed my inspiration for the idea, and some of the factual material, that I finally developed into a work of fiction, The Prize, a novel which was published in 1962.

I did not keep up with Dr. Hedin's career after I left Stockholm in 1946, but recently I wondered what had happened to him in the years that had followed our meeting. As far as can be learned, Dr. Hedin went on no more expeditions, either to Asia or to any other country. Instead, he remained in his Stockholm apartments, and continued to write and publish the volumes about his earlier expedition to northern China. When I had seen him, thirty-one volumes had been published. In the next eight years, Dr. Hedin produced eight more volumes. Also, in 1950, I am told, he published a memoir entitled Without Mission in Berlin. This, I presume, was the book he told me about in 1946, the one which he then intended to call "Germany's Last Years." His political views during these years remained unchanged.

In the eight years that he lived after our meeting, he also continued to cast his ballot for the Nobel Prizes in literature, physics, and chemistry. He was in those eight years one of the judges who elected such Nobel laureates as Sir Edward Appleton in physics, Dr. Arne Tiselius in chemistry, and André Gide, T. S. Eliot, William Faulkner, and Bertrand Russell in literature.

I have no knowledge about Dr. Hedin's relationship with his fellow Nobel judges, but I have my suspicions that it was not always the best. When Norway, which chooses the winner of the Nobel Peace Prize, gave its 1935 award to Carl von Ossietzky—a German national and early enemy of the Nazis, then in a concentration camp—Hitler was enraged. He announced that thereafter no German would be allowed to accept a Nobel Prize. Discussing that tense incident, Dr. Hedin had told me in 1946, "I went to Hitler to talk the matter over with him. I explained to him that Norway was solely responsible for that award, and that, after all, four out of five categories of the Nobel Prizes were given by Sweden. I pleaded with him to permit Germans to accept the Swedish-voted prizes. He would not relent." Relative to this, I found interesting a statement in a book written and endorsed by members of the Nobel Foundation of Stockholm, in 1951. Discussing the Ossietzky award, it said:

"In Germany there was violent resentment, and on January 31, 1937, Hitler issued a decree forbidding German nationals in the future to accept any Nobel Prize. The Swedish explorer Sven Hedin suggested in this connection that Norway should be deprived of the right to award the Peace Prize, and that this function should be entrusted to Sweden."

In these words written by August Schou, then Director of the Norwegian Nobel Peace Prize, one might detect a certain degree of asperity toward Dr. Hedin.

Almost to the end, Dr. Hedin's vigor remained, and he was in control of all his faculties. The year after I saw him, he even recovered the sight of one eye which had been blind for a half century.

He fell ill early in 1952 of a virus disease, and suffered from it through most of that year. In December, 1952, he died of a cerebral inflammation. He was eighty-seven years old.

I cannot say how widely or deeply Dr. Hedin was mourned. He had touched greatness once, but had been brought down—an Icarus who had ventured too close to the heat of savage conflict—because he had loved an alien land and its violent leaders too well and too long. The moral is self-evident: To love with abiding loyalty is not a virtue in itself, if one loves without discrimination.

THE MAN WHO HATED HEMINGWAY

WHEN I arrived in Madrid early one sunny morning last spring, the press association man was waiting for me outside the station beside his little German-made Opel. As I squeezed into the car I made the obligatory joke about a sardine can, and he laughed in the way all newspapermen laugh when they meet a magazine writer and think to themselves, So that's how smart you have to be to do it.

We went bumping down the Gran Vía, past the shining store windows with their endless offerings of women's furs and men's leather game sets, and then turning and turning up wide clean streets to the Ritz Hotel. A fat doorman in an impressive blue coat with brass buttons saluted me and took out the luggage.

The press association man, who was from Arizona and not homesick, was telling me that his wife sent him all the Andrews Sisters records by TWA, and they were months in coming. I sat half in the car, half out, listening to his story. When he finished, he asked if I would dine with him the next evening. I accepted his invitation with thanks, and started to go, but he put his hand on my shoulder. "Just one more thing," he said. "If I were you, I'd go up and see Olascoaga at the Subsecretariat of Education. He clears you for Foreign Office press credentials. Nothing to it. You get a card with your passport photo on it. And it's damn useful."

I thanked him again. But after he left, I promptly forgot about his advice.

The following evening the press association man called for me and said he was going to show me how the better-class working Spaniard eats. I went with foreboding. We drove deep into Madrid, to a dark side-street *tasca* where the fat proprietor sang out his menu. I had a thick vegetable soup, a slice of chicken in oil and a plate of *tirón,* a beige-colored gummy Spanish candy, for the equivalent of $1.40.

Since dinner in Madrid begins about ten in the evening, we didn't return to the hotel until one o'clock. Two soldiers, in long coats and short muskets, were walking back and forth. The press association man explained that they had guarded the Ritz ever since Communist underground members had heaved a bomb into the hotel's garden and disturbed some of the distinguished guests. Later I realized that this bombing didn't explain why draftees were also guarding banks, grocery stores and cafeterias about Madrid. I wondered about it until I learned that Franco had almost a million men under arms ("the largest army in Western Europe," an INS man told me) and he had to keep them busy.

As I left the car, the press association man said, "By the way, did you do what I told you?"

"Do what?"

"Those press credentials, remember? Did you get them from the Subsecretariat of Education? Well, you'd better. Let me tell you something. A state of war was declared in Spain in 1936, and that declaration has never been rescinded. There's still an official state of war in this country. That can affect you. Soon you'll be seeing the underground—"

I said I didn't know if I would.

"Sure you will, they all do, first thing."

As a matter of fact, he was right. I saw Republican and anarchist underground leaders within a week.

"You'll see them, and if Franco's police should catch you at it, meeting with those people, why, they could try you as an enemy of the state. But there's one loophole. Get yourself a press card. The card will prove you are a foreign correspondent and will say that you are free to go anywhere in Spain and see anyone, if it's related to your job. This permit isn't meant to include talking to members of the underground, but if you are caught with the Communists it gives you an excuse. Of course, they'll shoot your friends and boot you out of Spain, but it saves you from getting into more serious trouble. Look, those of us who stay on here keep our noses clean—we have to—and we have no problems. So you'd just better see Olascoaga and get that card."

I said thanks. I thought about it in bed that night, in a half-conscious dream: myself, hair mussed, shirt ripped, a kind of Reed, trapped by those booted Franco police. The next morning I phoned the American Embassy. The press attaché, Ted Maffitt—a bright, crisp fellow who had made an impression on me the very first day by telling me he had been offered $10,000 by a Spaniard for his 1946 Packard—said surely I must get press credentials, and he would arrange an appointment for me to get them.

"But let me ask you just one thing—have you ever written anything against Franco?"

I said no. I had done the usual anti-Fascist pieces on Hitler and Mussolini for *Ken* magazine, and once, in the army, had managed to retain in a Signal Corps orientation film some footage of Franco and the Fuehrer shaking hands, but beyond such minor sins I had been well-behaved.

"Okay," said Maffitt, "you're in. They can only object on the basis of your magazines, and that's not likely. They've been very friendly this past year. I'll call Olascoaga and fix you up."

The morning following, a Friday morning, after stopping at Cook's on the Avenida José Antonio for my mail, I took a taxi to the Subsecretariat of Education. The entrance was through a patio, squeezed between stores. I went up the wooden stairs and presented my calling card to a bulky attendant behind a table who was dressed like a Santa Fe conductor. He limped away, then returned and signaled me to follow.

In a moment we were in a small office, furnished with a green desk—barren except for a pile of foolscap—a swivel chair, a file cabinet, and a colored portrait of Francisco Franco on the wall.

"Señor de Olascoaga will meet you here," the attendant said. He indicated a chair. "Please."

I had been told that Señor de Olascoaga, a stumpy, twinkling man in his fifties, a laughing boy, would be cordial, not too inquisitive. I had only to exchange a few pleasantries with him, display my passport, my credentials from magazine editors, and then he would okay me and in a week I could pick up my press card in the Foreign Office across the city. I had sat alone for several minutes, staring up at the portrait of a flaccid Franco, when the door opposite suddenly opened. A tall, slender, well-dressed man stood in the doorway. He paused there a moment, looking at me. His hair was slicked flat, his eyes black and bright, his cheeks hollow, his thin line of mustache accenting his sensual lips. He smiled. It went on; it went off. He stepped across the room, hand out. "How do you do?"

"Señor de Olascoaga?" I asked, confused, rising and moving forward to meet him.

"No, I'm afraid not. I am the Marqués de Espinardo." His voice was high, fragile, his English correct and very British. "No, our friend Señor de Olascoaga was called out on business. I have been delegated to talk with you and review your application. Do sit down."

I made my way back to my chair, wondering, and he went on around the desk and settled his long frame into the swivel chair behind it. He put his bony fingers together, tilted the chair backward, and looked at me pleasantly. In Hollywood, I had once met a bogus and larcenous German count who was blond and said he was from Heidelberg, and who looked almost like this. The count got five years.

"I hope you have some time to talk," said the Marqués de Espinardo.

I said I did.

"I like to talk with English writers," he said easily. "I was educated at Sandhurst, you know, and I've read the works of a good many of you English writers."

"I come from Kenosha, Wisconsin," I said, "by way of Los Angeles, California, and my friends do not think I am an English writer—"

"An American, then. I was once in the United States, in New York, for two months. I wonder. Is New York the United States? Is it exactly like Kansas City? Or like Los Angeles? Could I write an authoritative book about America because I spent eight weeks talking to New Yorkers?"

"I'm not writing a book on Spain," I said, controlled.

He smiled indulgently. "Oh now, now—I was not jibing at you personally—I am speaking generally, of American writers and correspondents. I do believe it is a mistake to think you can interview ten or one hundred—even two hundred—Spaniards, and pretend to know how we live and how we think. Believe me, we are all different. Especially in Spain we are all different. Take me. I am a northern Basque."

I was surprised. I had been up in San Sebastián, among the Basques, and they are a very unsophisticated people. Except for a few eccentricities like believing their language was spoken by Adam and Eve and that they will win autonomy, they are a cheerful and uncomplicated race. Your average Basque is without tricks. I would have bet the marqués was a Castilian, Madrid Spanish, bruising easily, humorless, indirect, unhealthy, ingrown, too old, too devious.

"We Basques are more serious, more profound, not so silly as the Castilians here in Madrid. Those are distinctions one must know."

He was speaking more forcefully now, his tone of voice was flatter and of more substance, and his face was red. Suddenly he paused. He had been leaning against the desk. He let out his breath, and slowly lay back in the chair. He was thin again, devious, Castilian.

"I have read your American writers," he said. "I have read Hemingway. I loathe him."

I sat in silent wonder.

"Hemingway is a liar," he said, less cautiously, deciding I wasn't Hemingway's friend or a member of his school. "He is a fraud, a sensationalist. *For Whom the Bell Tolls* was an obviously cheap appeal for easy money. His other book on Spain, *Death in the Afternoon,* it is really too filthy to be reprinted here. We love everything on bullfighting, but that book is too filthy. In it he uses Spanish words that you Americans just don't understand. But they are words even a respectable Spanish prostitute would not dare use."

I was nettled by the pointless tirade. "I'm sorry you don't like Mr. Hemingway. Each to his own literary tastes. But at least Mr. Hemingway is permitted, in America, to write as he pleases."

The marqués cocked his head and looked at me more carefully. I could feel his bewilderment. He had judged me after the first minute—silent and too assenting. Now he was bewildered and, as a matter of fact, much more interested.

"I admit we have censorship in Spain, I admit it," he said slowly. "We do not ban all ideas and news, but we water them, certainly. And I will tell you why. In the old days, our press was yellow like yours. Everything ran to sensationalism. If there was a murder in Barcelona—"

In Madrid all the murdering is done in Barcelona.

"—if a severed head were found under a streetcar seat, reporters and photographers would rush up there, and then splash front pages with the most gruesome stories about it for weeks. This provoked fantastic ideas in the minds of unbalanced readers and also provoked a whole wave of murders and suicides. I have read medical books, and I know that sensational journalism is provocative. Today, under Franco, we ban such irritants, and so we have an orderly, peaceful country."

I made a wry face at this limping apology, and he became quite annoyed.

"But what I have said is true."

This time, I nodded, as one agrees with a lying child who belongs to someone else. He stared across the desk at me.

"You have as much censorship in the United States as we have in Spain. Oh yes, you do. Your Hollywood movies are censored by an office that sees the law is always triumphant and crime the loser. Why such censorship? For the good of the state? Yes, and we censor for the very same reason. I have been in England and I know the English make movies in which women wear décolleté gowns, exposing their naked breasts to the camera, but your prudish censors in America say these scenes might provoke American audiences. So you censor. Ours is no more restrictive than that."

I toyed with the idea of repeating the story I had heard of how Generalissimo Franco, a great movie fan, is always annoyed by a certain female musical comedy star because she wears tights and is so leggy, and how he always has her films censored for the public. I decided the story would inspire a long aimless discussion of movies, and I shelved it. I determined to bring up the specific business of my credentials.

"About my credentials—" I began.

The marqués was not listening. "I am disgusted with American writing. We in Spain regard America as the most superficial country on earth. Two of your ambassadors have concurred with me in that opinion. You Americans get all your distorted capsule knowledge from newspapers and magazines or from spoon-fed Book-of-the-Month Club selections. You do not read profoundly at all. Writers come here, without learning Spanish history, without cultural background, without a knowledge of economics, without understanding the causes for our present condition. The key to why we are as we are today rests in simple economics. Understand how Spain lives, that we are not self-sufficient and wealthy as you are, that we have not your material resources, understand where we get our clothes and metal and food, and you will understand present living conditions in Spain."

"I can't dispute that, Marqués," I said, "because I've been here less than a week and I haven't looked around yet—"

"How can you criticize us? I have heard about conditions in the United States. There are not enough shoes for people to wear. And the housing is terrible, terrible. I read a letter in *Life* magazine. An ex-serviceman says he cannot find meat to eat, clothes to wear, a home to live in. The only thing he finds everywhere is signs advising him to re-enlist in the army. He thinks it is a put-up job by your government. Why should you have a housing shortage? You have had no great destruction of your cities and villages as we have had. Why a shortage?"

I gave him some of the pat answers. And I added, "In a city like Los Angeles, people who came to go into the war industries now don't want to go home—"

"Ah yes, yes, we have exactly the same, slums in all our cities, composed of villagers who should go home now. But no. Here, they have the cinema, and they want to stay. We should force them to return to the farms where they would live better. Perhaps Spain and America have much in common after all. Perhaps language is the greatest obstruction to friendly relations. Perhaps it is that too many Americans believe that, since their Republicans are conservative rightists, our Spanish Republicans are exactly the same. Tell them it is not so. Tell them our Republicans are Communists, murderers. Tell them that and we can be friends."

He halted on a high, shrill note, and caught himself there and pulled himself down with embarrassment. He took out a handkerchief and touched his forehead daintily. I was glad to see the handkerchief was silk.

He pulled himself together and sat straight in the chair for the first time.

"Now then, about your credentials. You are writing for *The Saturday Evening Post, Reader's Digest, Collier's—*"

He stopped on the *Collier's*. It pushed a button in his memory. He dug his right hand into his coat pocket and extracted a folded piece of white paper. He half opened it, moving his lips as he read it to himself, and shoved it back into his pocket. "*Collier's?*" he said. "Perhaps you have heard of a girl named Martha Gellhorn?"

I felt I might as well tie the whole interview together. "She was married to Hemingway," I said.

"She writes worse trash for *Collier's* than Hemingway, and they print it. Last year I read an article by her, written from France about us, about Spanish refugee children in southern France. It was full of lies. It was worthy of a Communist. Is she a Communist? Why does she write that way?"

"We have a kind of press freedom in America," I said, "and she writes what she pleases to write, what she sees and thinks, and American magazines publish it if they like it."

The marqués was not satisfied. "Your magazines are inaccurate about Spain. They publish biased stories. They always write against us."

The ice was thin, but I was sick of the marqués and the whole credential opera. "Look," I said, "you just don't understand the American press. You should study it more closely. Almost every major magazine in the United States is against Communism, baits Russia, yet these same magazines publish pro-Russian articles when they get hold of a good one. If they could ever, ever, get an article from Spain which proved that there was one decent thing to say in support of General Franco, about the Falange party, about what you people are doing to Spain, why, they would publish it. Until they get such an article, I am afraid the American press must continue to print what you call biased stories."

I thought he might stand up there. He didn't. He sat a moment, looking down at the desktop, and then lifted his head, dug into his pocket and offered me a Chesterfield. I refused it.

"Well," he said, rising at last, "we have a long way to go to understand each other—our countries have, that is."

I laid my passport and papers on the desk. "You want to see these for my credentials, don't you?"

"Oh yes, certainly." He unscrewed his pen, made a few sprawling notes on a sheet of foolscap, after glancing at my papers.

I gathered up my things. He put his pen away, and pushed out his long hand. "This was a pleasant and instructive hour. Perhaps you will call upon me again. Yes, you must. We will have a real talk about American writers. Not Hemingway, but others. You will do that?"

"I certainly shall. Good day."

That evening, at the British-American Club, beneath the three framed portraits of the King and Queen of England, the President of the United States, and Francisco Franco, I sat over bourbon-and-sodas with several resident American correspondents. Although they knew everyone in the government, especially in the press department of the Foreign Office, not one of them had ever seen or even heard of the Marqués de Espinardo.

"Tall? Mustache? Sandhurst?" said the correspondent who had come into Madrid shortly after Franco. "Can't say I've ever heard of him. He's a new one. Most likely secret police. Oh, they still do that. As for press credentials, look, old man, you'll do better without them."

He paused, reflected a moment. "Espinardo, eh? He sounds like an improvement. At least he's read Hemingway."

WHAT HAS HAPPENED SINCE . . .

The preceding story was one result of my first visit to Spain. I had taken a train from Paris to the Spanish frontier in January of 1947, stayed in the Basque capital of San Sebastián briefly, then continued on by train to Madrid. A month later, in February, my wife and I agreed to depart from Spain by automobile, sharing the ride and the burden of driving with a pretty, young brunette, and free-lance American correspondent, named Rita Hume. We drove from Madrid to Zaragoza, and then on to Barcelona, and later went on to La Junquera, crossing out of Spain to visit Montpellier, Marseille, Cannes, Rapallo, and finally Rome.

The adventures on this ride eventually provided not me but my close friend, Zachary Gold, with the basis for a hilarious short story, his last before his untimely death in 1953. The innocent triangle of Rita, my wife Sylvia, and myself became Gold's "A Lady in No Distress" in *Woman's Home Companion* for September, 1952. However, there is a second sad postscript to the story: Rita Hume eventually married John Secondari, author of *Three Coins in the Fountain* and later a television network commentator, but short years after their marriage, Rita was killed in a motorcar accident in Europe.

During the time I spent in Spain, I wrote three magazine articles. One was about the independent, eccentric, and fascinating Basques of Spain. Another recounted my adventures in a small Spanish village south of Madrid, an impoverished village inhabited by brave but angry men who were anti-Franco. I had been taken there by Charles Gordian Troeller, publisher of Luxembourg's *L'Indépendent,* and his friend, a sweet, gentle, chubby Barcelona member of the anarchist underground who looked like Robert Benchley and was equally beloved wherever he went. I published this story in *The Saturday Evening Post*. Partially as a result of my story, but mainly because of further clandestine activities on their part, Troeller was eventually ousted from Spain, and the sweet anarchist gentleman was caught and executed. I was banned from Spain. However, apparently the passage of eighteen years has had its mellowing effect on the Falangist authorities, for now all of my books, fiction and nonfiction, have been or will be published in Spain, and several of my novels have achieved widespread popularity there.

The third article I wrote in Spain was "The Man Who Hated Hemingway." My journal reminds me that I met the Marqués de Espinardo on Friday, January 24, 1947, in Madrid. I was sufficiently impressed and irritated by the interview simply to sit down and write the preceding impression, although I had no periodical in mind.

Having always had affection for the story, I decided to include it in this collection. In preparing to do so, I wondered what had happened in the many years since to the Marqués de Espinardo. I did not know where to inquire, and then I remembered one press-association friend—a Spaniard who had worked for an American newspaper syndicate in Madrid—and I wrote to him. Here is his reply verbatim:

Dear Irving,

Please excuse me for the delay in writing, but I was awaiting replies to my inquiries for particulars about the Marqués of Espinardo. For many days I was trying to remember the family name of this Marqués, and I did not succeed. The only Espinardo I know is a little village in the Murcia Province. I contacted some friends for further information. They said the name was unknown down there. You know, the titles of nobility are common among Spanish officials these days, especially in the Foreign Ministry. But this one was a real mystery. One thing is certain: the Marqués was an official of the Spanish Foreign Ministry, since Olascoaga (who died several years ago) was not in the Ministry of Information and Tourism but in the Foreign Office itself.

It was difficult to identify the man, despite the very good description you give in your story. One thing is clear to me: the Marqués must have been, may still be, a Foreign Ministry intelligence official, because Olascoaga was Vice-Chief of the Oficina de Información Diplomática, and the Marqués was certainly a substitute for him. I don't think that the Marqués was an obvious secret policeman, as the correspondent in the British-American Club told you. Secret policemen are quite different in Spain, and they usually do not speak the fluent English your Hemingway-hater spoke. The Marqués was probably more important and less known to outsiders. I think you will not find out more about him.

If the marqués was still alive at the time, it is unlikely that he grieved at the news of Hemingway's suicide in Idaho on that early July morning in 1961. But I suspect that today the marqués enjoys little satisfaction from the disappearance of the corporeal Hemingway. For he must know that Hemingway, the artist, still lives.

Yes, Hemingway lives and will survive his mortal critics, be they a Spanish marqués or an American literary Brahmin. What I could not tell the Marqués de Espinardo in our conversation in 1947, is now known to the whole world.

As Hemingway wrote in *Death in the Afternoon:*

"The sun is very important. . . . The Spanish say, 'El sol es el mejor torero.' The sun is the best bullfighter, and without the sun the best bullfighter is not there. He is like a man without a shadow."

Today, more than ever, the sun shines on Ernest Hemingway, and as a consequence, his long shadow falls across, envelops, and obscures every marqués on earth.

» 19 «

THE INCREDIBLE
DR. BELL

ONE EVENING, about the turn of the last century, after enjoying a
weekend shoot in Scotland, a dozen guests sat around a dinner table discussing human monsters, famous murders, and unsolved crimes.
One of the guests, Dr. Joseph Bell, the eminent Edinburgh surgeon
and medical instructor, had the others wide-eyed with his deductive
acrobatics.

"The trouble with most people," he said, "is that they see, but do not
observe. Any really good detective ought to be able to tell, before a
stranger has fairly sat down, his occupation, habits, and past history
through rapid observation and deduction. Glance at a man and you find
his nationality written on his face, his means of livelihood on his hands,
and the rest of his story in his gait, mannerisms, tattoo marks, watch
chain ornaments, shoelaces and in the lint adhering to his clothes."

The guests were skeptical. One challenged Dr. Bell to give an example
of applied observation. Promptly, Dr. Bell obliged.

"A patient walked into the room where I was instructing the students,
and his case seemed to be a very simple one. I was talking about what
was wrong with him. 'Of course, gentlemen,' I happened to say, 'he has
been a soldier in a Highland regiment, and probably a bandsman.' I
pointed out the swagger in his walk, suggestive of the Highland piper;
while his shortness told me that if he had been a soldier, it was probably
as a bandsman. But the man insisted he was nothing but a shoemaker
and had never been in the army in his life. This was rather a floorer,
but being absolutely certain, I told two of the strongest clerks to remove
the man to a side room and strip him.

"Under his left breast I instantly detected a little blue D branded on his skin. He was an army deserter. That was how they used to mark them in the Crimean days. You can understand his evasion. However, this proved my first observation correct. He confessed having played in the band of a Highland regiment in the war against the Russians. It was really elementary, gentlemen."

Most of the guests were impressed. But one listener jocularly remarked, "Why, Dr. Bell might almost be Sherlock Holmes."

To which Dr. Bell snapped, "My dear sir, I *am* Sherlock Holmes."

Dr. Bell was not jesting. He was, indeed, the original Sherlock Holmes, the real-life inspiration for the immortal detective of fiction. "It is most certainly to you that I owe Sherlock Holmes," A. Conan Doyle wrote Dr. Bell in May, 1892. Thirty-two years later, still grateful to Dr. Bell, author Doyle publicly admitted, "I used and amplified his methods when I tried to build up a scientific detective who solved cases on their own merits."

Unlike the detective, Dr. Bell wore neither deerstalker cap nor ankle-length Inverness cape, and used neither magnifying glass nor cocaine. Where Sherlock Holmes was the eccentric bachelor in his cluttered rooms at No. 221B Baker Street, Dr. Bell was entirely the family man with a son, two daughters, and two sprawling multi-gabled homes of his own. Where Sherlock Holmes dwelt in a shadow world bounded by Moriarty and Watson, Dr. Bell was a surgeon whose courage won compliments from Queen Victoria, whose crusades for nurses earned the friendship of Florence Nightingale, whose classroom sorcery influenced five decades of Edinburgh University undergraduates ranging from A. Conan Doyle to Robert Louis Stevenson and Sir James Barrie.

However, the one unique thing which the detective and the doctor held in common overshadowed all their differences. Just as Sherlock Holmes was the foremost fictional practitioner of what he termed "the science of deduction and analysis," so his real-life model, Dr. Joseph Bell, was perhaps the most brilliant master of observation the world has seen in the last one hundred years.

Many of Dr. Bell's views on the science of observation became household words, after the character Sherlock Holmes mouthed them through sixty classic stories. "Let the inquirer begin," advised Sherlock Holmes, "by mastering more elementary problems. Let him, on meeting a fellow-mortal, learn at a glance to distinguish the history of the man, and the trade or profession to which he belongs. . . . By a man's finger-nails, by his coat-sleeve, by his boots, by his trouser-knees, by the callosities of his forefinger and thumb, by his expression, by his shirt-cuffs—by each of these things a man's calling is plainly revealed."

In story after story, Sherlock Holmes reiterated his rules for deduction and analysis. "It is a capital mistake to theorize before one has data. Insensibly one begins to twist facts to suit theories, instead of theories to suit facts. . . . You know my method. It is founded upon the observation of trifles. . . . It is a curious thing that a typewriter has really quite as much individuality as a man's handwriting. . . . I have frequently gained my first real insight into the character of parents by studying their children. . . . I always put myself in the other man's place, and, having first gauged his intelligence, I try to imagine how I should myself have proceeded under the same circumstances."

These rules merely echoed the real-life gospel of Dr. Joseph Bell. "I always impressed over and over again upon all my scholars the vast importance of little distinctions, the endless significance of the trifles," Dr. Bell once told a reporter. "The great majority of people, of incidents, and of cases resemble each other in the main and larger features. For instance, most men have apiece a head, two arms, a nose, a mouth, and a certain number of teeth. It is the little differences, in themselves trifles, such as the droop of the eyelid or what not, which differentiate men."

In an essay on crime, penned a half century ago, Dr. Bell wrote, "The importance of the infinitely little is incalculable. Poison a well at Mecca with the cholera bacillus, and the holy water which the pilgrims carry off in their bottles will infect a continent, and the rags of the victims of the plague will terrify every seaport in Christendom."

What were some of these "infinitely little" factors Dr. Bell regarded as important in observation? "Nearly every handicraft writes its sign-manual on the hands," contended Dr. Bell. "The scars of the miner differ from those of the quarryman. The carpenter's callosities are not those of the mason. . . . The soldier and sailor differ in gait. Accent helps you to district and, to an educated ear, almost to county. . . . With a woman, especially, the observant doctor can often tell, by noticing her, exactly what part of her body she is going to talk about."

While Dr. Bell felt that the development of observation was a necessity to doctors and detectives, he felt equally strongly that it was a thrilling sport for laymen. The vain Sherlock Holmes disagreed, holding little hope for the common man. "What do the public, the great unobservant public, who could hardly tell . . . a compositor by his left thumb, care about the finer shades of analysis and deduction?" bemoaned Sherlock Holmes. But Dr. Bell felt the unobservant public might care a good deal, once let in on the game.

Every man, argued Dr. Bell, can transform his world from one of monotony and drabness into one of excitement and adventure by developing his faculty of observation. For this reason—though once he complained in exasperation, "I am haunted by my double, Sherlock

Holmes!"—Dr. Bell heartily approved of A. Conan Doyle's detective stories that popularized his ideas. "Doyle shows how easy it is, if only you can observe, to find out a great deal as to the works and ways of your innocent and unconscious friends, and, by an extension of the same method, to baffle the criminal and lay bare the manner of his crime. . . . His stories make many a fellow who has before felt very little interest in his life and daily surroundings think that, after all, there may be much more in life if he keeps his eyes open." Once aware of the entertainment and instruction to be had from careful observation, the average man will find his workaday world much the richer. Like Sherlock Holmes, he will be able to detect from a man's hat that his wife does not love him, from a man's cane that he fears being murdered, from a man's pipe that he is muscular, left-handed, careless, and wealthy.

Throughout his life, Dr. Bell continued to amaze his circle with the observation game. "When the family traveled in a train," his surviving daughter, Mrs. Cecil Stisted, recalls, "he would tell us where all the other passengers in the carriage were from, where they were going to, and something of their occupations and their habits. All this without having spoken to them. When he verified his observations, we thought him a magician."

His students also thought him a magician. Years after Dr. Bell's death, A. Conan Doyle told an interviewer, "Dr. Bell would sit in his receiving room, with a face like a red Indian, and diagnose people as they came in, before they even opened their mouths. He would tell them their symptoms, and even give them details of their past life, and hardly ever would he make a mistake."

Inside the spired Royal Infirmary of Edinburgh, in the packed lecture amphitheater beneath the flickering gaslights, Dr. Bell daily tried to prove to his pupils that observation was not a form of magic but a science. According to one former pupil, Dr. Harold Emery Jones, writing in *Collier's* in 1904, Dr. Bell's standard demonstration of this, its running commentary given in a voice full of dry humor before each new group of medical students, involved taking up a tumbler filled with an amber-colored liquid. "This, gentlemen, contains a very potent drug," Dr. Bell would explain. "To the taste it is intensely bitter. Now I want to see how many of you gentlemen have educated your powers of perception. Of course, we might easily analyze this chemically, but I want you to test it by smell and taste; and, as I don't ask anything of my students which I wouldn't be willing to do myself, I will taste it before passing it around."

Dr. Bell would then dip his finger into the liquid, put the finger to his mouth, suck it, and grimace. He would then pass the tumbler around. Each student would dip his finger into the vile concoction, suck it, and promptly make a sour face. When the tumbler had made the rounds, Dr. Bell would gaze at the assembly and begin laughing. "Gentlemen," he would say, "I am deeply grieved to find that not one of you has developed this power of perception, which I so often speak about, for, if you had watched me closely, you would have found that, while I placed my forefinger in the bitter medicine, it was the middle finger which found its way into my mouth!"

In the Royal Infirmary wards, in the dispensaries, especially in the out-patient department where ailing citizens were brought forward by student clerks, Dr. Bell practiced what he preached. Glancing at a newcomer, Dr. Bell remarked, "A cobbler, I see." He explained to his students that "the inside of the knee of the man's trousers was worn; that was where the man had rested the lapstone, a peculiarity only found in cobblers." Another time, when a laborer appeared with a spinal complaint, Dr. Bell said to him, "Your back must ache badly, but carrying a heavy hod of bricks won't improve it." The laborer was astounded, and cannily inquired, "I'm no' saying ye're wrang, but wha' tell't ye I was a bricklayer to trade?" Dr. Bell replied by pointing to the laborer's peculiarly rough horny hands. On yet another occasion, Dr. Bell studied his visitor a moment, then announced to his students, "Gentlemen, I am not quite sure whether this man is a cork-cutter or a slater. I observe a slight callus, or hardening, on one side of his forefinger, and a little thickening on the outside of his thumb, and that is a sure sign he is either one or the other."

Once, when a tall weather-beaten patient entered the ward, Dr. Bell looked at him and said to his students, "Gentlemen, a fisherman. It is a very hot summer's day, yet the patient is wearing top-boots. No one but a sailor would wear them in this season. The shade of his tan shows him to be a coast sailor. A knife scabbard beneath his coat, the kind used by fishermen. And to prove the correctness of these deductions, I notice several minute fishscales adhering to his clothes and hands."

Students of Dr. Bell's would remember, for years after, some of the master's deductive feats. Dr. Harold Emery Jones recalled that Dr. Bell would summon his charges up front to try their own hand at observing. "What is the matter with this man, sir?" Dr. Bell once asked of a quaking student. "No, you mustn't touch him. Use your eyes, sir. Use your ears, use your brain, your bump of perception, and use your powers of deduction." At sea, the confused student blurted, "Hip-joint disease, sir." Dr. Bell scowled, shook his head. "Hip-nothing! The man's limp is not from his hip, but from his foot. Were you to observe closely, you would see that there are slits, cut by a knife, in those parts of the shoes where the pressure of the shoe is greatest against the foot. The man is a sufferer from corns, gentlemen, and has no hip trouble at all. But he has not come here to be treated for corns, gentlemen. His trouble is of a much more serious nature. This is a case of chronic alcoholism, gentlemen. The rubicund nose, the puffed, bloated face, the bloodshot eyes, the tremulous hands and twitching face muscles, with the quick, pulsating temporal arteries, all show this. These deductions, gentlemen, must however be confirmed by absolute and concrete evidence. In this instance my diagnosis is confirmed by the fact of my seeing the neck of a whiskey-bottle protruding from the patient's right-hand coat pocket . . . never neglect to ratify your deductions."

At one time, when young Doyle was Dr. Bell's student assistant, a patient entered and sat down. "Did you like your walk over the golf links today, as you came in from the south side of town?" inquired Dr. Bell. The patient replied, "Why yes, did your honor see me?" Dr. Bell had not seen him. "Conan Doyle could not understand how I knew," Dr. Bell related later, "but on a showery day such as that had been, the reddish clay at bare parts of the golf links adheres to the boot, and a tiny part is bound to remain. There is no such clay anywhere else." Years later, writing "The Five Orange Pips," A. Conan Doyle had Sherlock Holmes say to a visitor, "You have come up from the southwest, I see." The visitor replied, "Yes, from Horsham." And Holmes explained, "That clay and chalk mixture which I see upon your toe caps is quite distinctive."

But the most famous example of Dr. Bell's skill was the one A. Conan Doyle told in his autobiography. A civilian outpatient, a total stranger to Dr. Bell, came into his ward. In silence, Dr. Bell studied the visitor, then spoke:

"Well, my man, you've served in the army."

"Aye, sir."

"Not long discharged?"

"No, sir."

"A Highland regiment?"

"Aye, sir."

"A non-com officer?"

"Aye, sir."

"Stationed at Barbados?"

"Aye, sir."

Dr. Bell turned to his students. "You see, gentlemen, the man was a respectful man, but he did not remove his hat. They do not in the army, but he would have learned civilian ways had he been long discharged. He has an air of authority and he is obviously Scottish. As to Barbados, his complaint is elephantiasis, which is West Indian and not British."

Years after, A. Conan Doyle was still sufficiently impressed by this incident ("very miraculous until it was explained," he admitted) to reproduce it closely in his Sherlock Holmes story, "The Greek Interpreter."

A. Conan Doyle, after five years as a struggling medical student, graduated from Edinburgh University in 1881. He nailed up his oculist shingle and waited for patients. Six years later, he was still waiting. Lacking a practice, desperate for any kind of income, Doyle turned to writing. After one false start, and under the influence of Gaboriau and Poe, he decided to try a detective story. And for it he wanted a new kind of detective. "I thought of my old teacher Joe Bell, of his eagle face, of his curious ways, of his eerie trick of spotting details," Doyle recollected in his autobiography. "If he were a detective, he would surely reduce this fascinating but unorganized business to something nearer to an exact science. . . . It was surely possible in real life, so why should I not make it plausible in fiction? It is all very well to say that a man is clever, but the reader wants to see examples of it—such examples as Bell gave us every day in the wards. The idea amused me. What should I call the fellow?"

He called him Sherlock Holmes after an English cricketer named Sherlock and Oliver Wendell Holmes.

In describing the detective, Doyle again remembered his old instructor. Dr. Bell had been forty-four when Doyle last saw him. "He was thin, wiry, dark, with a high-nosed acute face, penetrating grey eyes, angular shoulders, and a jerky way of walking. His voice was high and discordant." With this as Doyle's model, Sherlock Holmes became the familiar tall, stooped, hawk-faced, intense, and inscrutable human bloodhound. His first appearance, in *Beeton's Christmas Annual*, with "A Study in Scarlet" in 1887, was inauspicious. But as a result, an American editor, three years later, ordered more Sherlock Holmes stories and the detective was on his way to literary immortality.

Sherlock Holmes's deductive tricks thrilled readers on both sides of the Atlantic. Each Holmes stunt was discussed and admired by fans everywhere. In "The Adventure of the Norwood Builder," when a frantic young man burst into the rooms on Baker Street and announced himself as John McFarlane, Sherlock Holmes lazily replied, "You mentioned your name, as if I should recognize it, but I assure you that, beyond the obvious facts that you are a bachelor, a solicitor, a Freemason, and an asthmatic, I know nothing whatever about you."

In "The Adventure of the Blue Carbuncle," after studying an unknown's seedy, hard felt hat, Holmes concluded, "That the man was highly intellectual is of course obvious upon the face of it, and also that he was fairly well-to-do within the last three years, although he has now fallen upon evil days. He had foresight, but has less now than formerly, pointing to a moral retrogression, which, when taken with the decline of his fortunes, seems to indicate some evil influence, probably drink, at work upon him. This may account also for the obvious fact that his wife has ceased to love him. . . . He has, however, retained some degree of self-respect. He is a man who leads a sedentary life, goes out little, is out of training entirely, is middle-aged, has grizzled hair which he has had cut within the last few days and which he anoints with lime-cream."

This fictional witchcraft, made so plausible by Doyle's deft pen, became an international fad. But very often an Edinburgh graduate would recognize from whom Doyle had derived this genius. In 1893, the year before his death, Robert Louis Stevenson, after meeting the "ingenious and very interesting" Sherlock Holmes in print for the first time, asked A. Conan Doyle in a letter from Samoa, "Only one thing troubles me. Can this be my old friend, Joe Bell?" A. Conan Doyle was quick to tell Stevenson, the press, and the world that the prototype for Sherlock Holmes was indeed Dr. Bell. As Doyle wrote to Dr. Bell, "I fear that one effect of your identity being revealed will be that you will have ample opportunity for studying lunatic letters, and that part at least of the stream that pours upon me will be diverted to you. You will hear alas from the youth in the south of Portugal, from the American lady with the curved spine, from the Liverpool merchant who burns to know who Jack the Ripper is, from many folks who believe that their neighbors are starving maiden aunts to death in hermetically sealed attics."

At first, Dr. Bell labeled pestering reporters "fiends" and pretended annoyance with A. Conan Doyle. But he was secretly pleased at being regarded as the original of Sherlock Holmes and at the wide publicity given his methods. Dr. Bell occasionally passed along suggestions for Holmes stories, some of which Doyle regarded as impractical. When Dr. Bell suggested in 1892 that Holmes joust with a germ murderer, Doyle replied, "I think that a fine thing might be done about a bacteriological criminal, but the only fear is lest you get beyond the average man, who won't be interested unless he thoroughly understands." However, Doyle was pleased with most of Dr. Bell's other suggestions. Once, Dr. Bell passed along his anecdote about the bandsman in the Highland regiment, who insisted that he was a shoemaker to hide the fact that he was a deserter. Doyle gratefully accepted it, writing, "The deserter-cobbler is admirable, and I wish I had a dozen more such cases. All you tell me is most useful." And in another letter to Dr. Bell, "Your sketch of the crime is capital. It wants some other red herring across the scent besides the ex-soldier, but there is the nucleus. I shall certainly, with your kind permission, avail myself of the idea."

Even though, in speaking of his Edinburgh mentor, A. Conan Doyle pointed out that "it was toward the detection of disease rather than of crime that his remarkable talents were directed," Dr. Bell could never resist dabbling in a first-class murder. This was his primary extracurricular activity. The Crown welcomed Dr. Bell's detecting genius. As an amateur detective, without official status, Dr. Bell worked hand in hand for twenty years with Sir Henry Littlejohn, professor of medical jurisprudence, and police surgeon to the city of Edinburgh. Dr. Bell's greatest success, in the years before he became known as Sherlock Holmes, was the part he played in the sensational Chantrelle case.

Eugene Chantrelle, a onetime Paris medical student, was a powerful, handsome man with mutton-chop whiskers. He had come to Edinburgh in 1866, to teach languages, and within a year had seduced a fifteen-year-old pupil named Elizabeth Dyer and been forced to marry her. The marriage was a singularly unhappy one. In moments of enthusiasm, Chantrelle, cursing, would beat his wife black-and-blue, boast that he would yet poison her, and then leave her alone while he made the rounds of the city's bordellos.

In October, 1877, fearing that his fragile wife might meet with an accident, Chantrelle thoughtfully insured her life for $5,000. Early one morning, about ten weeks later, the housemaid heard a moaning from one of the upstairs bedrooms. Rushing to Madame Chantrelle's room, the maid found her unconscious. Beside her bed were a partially filled glass of lemonade, some orange slices, and a few leftover grapes. After calling Monsieur Chantrelle, the maid ran out for a doctor. Returning, the maid found Chantrelle hurriedly stepping away from the window. The lemonade glass was empty, the orange slices and grapes gone. When the doctor arrived, Chantrelle told him he thought his wife had been overcome by a gas leakage. At once, the doctor sent a note to Sir Henry Littlejohn: "If you would like to see a case of coal-gas poisoning, come up here at once."

Littlejohn, accompanied by Dr. Bell, studied the bedroom and the ailing woman, and then removed her to the Royal Infirmary. There, after several hours, she died. Chantrelle was told she had died of narcotic poison. He protested, "But you know we have had an escape of gas!" Nevertheless, he was arrested for murder.

Littlejohn and Dr. Bell had indeed found evidences of poison. There were many green-brown vomit spots on her pillow, and two on her nightgown. These contained opium in solid form, mingled with grape seed fragments—matching a smaller portion of the same contents which were found in her alimentary canal. Checking with chemists, Dr. Bell found Chantrelle had recently purchased thirty doses of opium.

Chantrelle loudly insisted his wife had died accidentally from leaking gas. Investigating, the gas company located a broken gas pipe behind Madame's window shutter. The maid, claiming there had been no smell of gas in the room when she discovered the body but a faint smell when she returned to find Chantrelle moving away from the window, thought Chantrelle himself had wrenched the pipe loose to make the death appear accidental. To this, Chantrelle replied he could not have broken the pipe, since he did not even know it existed. Suspicious, Dr. Bell began snooping about, and finally located a gas fitter who admitted repairing the pipe behind the shutter for Chantrelle only a year before, while "Chantrelle watched with interest the operation." With this evidence, plus proof that Chantrelle had been in serious financial difficulties, the Crown brought the French schoolmaster to the dock. The trial lasted four days. The jury was out one hour and ten minutes. The verdict: "Guilty of murder as libelled."

On May 31, 1878, Chantrelle, gay dog to the last, started his long march. Recalling the scene, a former student of Dr. Bell's, Z. M. Hamilton, reported, "The morning of the execution, Chantrelle appeared on the scaffold beautifully dressed and smoking an expensive cigar. Dr. Littlejohn was there in accordance with his duty. Just before being pinioned, Chantrelle took off his hat, took a last puff on his cigar and, waving his hand to the police physician, cried out, 'Bye-bye, Littlejohn. Don't forget to give my compliments to Joe Bell. You both did a good job in bringing me to the scaffold!' "

A far more spectacular affair, if a less satisfactory one for Dr. Bell, was the celebrated Monson case. This case had its beginnings in 1890, when a London financier, Major Dudley Hambrough, hired a bankrupt young Oxford graduate named Alfred Monson to tutor his seventeen-year-old son Cecil for the Hants Militia. Three years later, having won Cecil's affection, Monson managed to insure him with the New York Mutual Assurance Company for $100,000, with Mrs. Monson designated as sole beneficiary. One early morning shortly thereafter, Monson and a companion took Cecil hunting in a nearby woods. A few hours later, Monson returned to announce calmly Cecil Hambrough was dead. Monson claimed that after they had separated, he had heard a shot and gone in its direction. "I then saw Hambrough at the bottom of the sunk fence on his left side, with his gun beside him. We lifted him up, and he was quite dead."

Everyone agreed the death was accidental. Cecil had doubtless stumbled and shot himself. After a brief time, Monson applied for the $100,000 insurance indemnity. The company replied that Cecil was a minor, and hence the policy was invalid. Monson admitted he knew that, but had hoped to bluff payment out of them anyway. Consequently, the company became suspicious, and a month later Sir Henry Littlejohn and Dr. Bell exhumed the body and re-examined the remains.

The two doctors found the skull had suffered a triangular wound, that it was shattered only locally, that there was no blackening or scorching of the skin from gunpowder. Re-enacting the crime, Dr. Bell showed that to produce such a wound the shot had to be fired nine feet from the body by a second party. Had Cecil killed himself, by either intent or accident, the gun would have been but two or three feet from his skull, would have blown his head apart, and blackened and scorched what was left of it.

Monson was indicted for murder. The Crown, using one hundred and ten witnesses, tried to show that Monson had earlier attempted to drown Cecil by boring a hole in a rowboat and, at a strategic moment, removing the plug. Failing in this attempt, he had shot Cecil from behind. In support of this contention, Dr. Bell, who was receiving much fanfare as the living Sherlock Holmes, went to the witness stand and testified, "Mr. Hambrough died in consequence of a gunshot wound, and I have not been able to make out any way by which the injury could have been done either designedly or accidentally by Mr. Hambrough himself."

However, the presiding judge, Lord Kingsburgh, was sitting at his first trial. In his reminiscences later, he admitted lying awake nights in "dull perspiration, turning things over and over." In his final charge, preferring a safe and sure verdict, he reminded the jury not to be swayed from objective justice by Monson's bad character. In a little over an hour, the jury announced, "Not Proven on both charges"—a quaint Scottish verdict meaning acquitted.

To his last days, Dr. Bell remained convinced that Monson was guilty. "He got off because it was Kingsburgh's first case," Dr. Bell told his wife. "Kingsburgh was afraid to start off with a death sentence." It pleased Dr. Bell to learn that Monson eventually wound up in prison for again attempting to defraud an insurance company.

Dr. Bell went after an impossible crime, as others attack difficult crossword puzzles. In 1888, when the fiendish, insane Jack the Ripper was prowling London's side streets, Dr. Bell cooperated with the police. Receiving a report detailing all the clues, Dr. Bell did most of his work on the case without leaving Edinburgh.

No one knew whether Jack the Ripper was male or female, but all agreed he was the greatest monster of modern times. His surgical slaughters, since celebrated in plays, movies, and novels, began in August of 1888, when a prostitute was found in a Whitechapel gutter with her throat slit and her body cold-bloodedly mutilated. The next month three more prostitutes were dissected. Miss Chapman, her head almost severed from her body, was found in the backyard of a tenement, her internal organs extracted and neatly laid at her feet. Miss Stride was killed on the lawn of a house in which a party was taking place (a man riding a pony cart interrupted the dissection, the pony shied, and the Ripper ran). Miss Eddowes was cut down in an alley, and when the killer finished he wiped his hands on her dress. The fifth was the worst. Mary Kelly, aged twenty-four, a beautiful prostitute, was found naked on her bed, her ears, nose, vital organs removed and arranged neatly around her corpse, with her bloody heart placed on the pillow. "The operator must have been at least two hours over his hellish job," stated Scotland Yard. "The madman made a bonfire of some old newspapers, and by this dim irreligious light, a scene was enacted which nothing witnessed by Dante, in his visit to the infernal regions, could have surpassed."

These were the five certain murders. There may have been three others. London was terrified, and everyone possessing a long-handled knife or a knowledge of anatomy was suspected. There was a Polish barber, seen running from a Ripper murder (the killings ceased when he moved to Jersey City). There was an insane Russian physician. There was an American sailor. There was an English doctor, who was found floating in the Thames after the last crime.

Bringing a friend of his into the investigation, Dr. Bell sifted the evidence. "There were two of us in the hunt," he said later, "and when two men set out to find a golf ball in the rough, they expect to come across it where the straight lines marked in their mind's eye to it, from their original positions, crossed. In the same way, when two men set out to investigate a crime mystery, it is where their researches intersect that we have a result." Dr. Bell and his friend made independent investigations. From the suspects brought in, Dr. Bell deduced the murderer, wrote his name on a strip of paper, placed it in a sealed envelope. His friend did likewise. They exchanged envelopes. In both, the same name occurred. At once, Dr. Bell communicated with Scotland Yard. A week later, the murders ended. If this was merely coincidental, or if Dr. Bell was in any way responsible, no one will ever know. But the murders did end—and Jack the Ripper was never arrested.

Despite all his publicity as the original of Sherlock Holmes, Dr. Bell abhorred the spotlight. He was a reticent man, and interviewers actually learned little about his background or his private life.

Joseph Bell, product of five generations of surgeons, was the eldest son of a devout and renowned physician. At the age of twenty-two, Bell took his medical degree at Edinburgh University, and two years later became house surgeon in the Royal Infirmary. His courage was amazing. On one occasion, at a time when diphtheria was a little-understood disease, an ailing child suffering from diphtheria was wheeled into surgery. After the operation, poison accumulated and, since there were no mechanical means for suction, the child was given little chance to live. Without a moment's hesitation Dr. Bell put his lips to the child's, sucked the poison from its throat, and saved its life. As a result, Dr. Bell himself caught diphtheria, which permanently impaired his voice. When the elderly Queen Victoria, visiting Edinburgh, heard the story, she personally congratulated Dr. Bell. "The dear old lady was so friendly," he reported afterward, "and I was not one bit flustered."

Dr. Bell devoted much of his medical career to crusading for nurses, and through this crusade he gained Florence Nightingale and Robert Louis Stevenson as two of his closest friends. At a time when nurses were little better than street women, with no interest whatsoever in their patients, Dr. Bell fought to bring dignity to the profession. Later, when nursing had become fashonable, Dr. Bell fought equally hard to keep out pretty girls who were primarily interested in wearing uniforms. Dr. Bell's only published book, brought out in 1906, was *Notes on Surgery for Nurses.*

Dr. Bell's wedded life was idyllic but short-lived. He married at the age of twenty-eight, and his wife Edith died nine years later. On her tombstone he had carved, "I thank my God upon every remembrance of you." He immersed himself in work, filled his home with friends, and grew into old age a crusty widower. He lost the Sherlock Holmes look, and a student remembers him toward the end as "a brisk Scotsman, rather under middle height, of compact but not stout build, and of energetic manner. He had a weathered, rather red, full face and iron-gray hair and eyebrows, with little tufts of iron-gray whiskers on each cheek." He walked with a limp, due to an old hunting fall, and his eye was so keen he could identify any bird on the wing. He liked to drive fast, never drank, and felt cigarettes made his feet grow cold.

In company, Dr. Bell expressed very definite opinions on all matters. "Hysterical people are generally liars," he would say. Or, "I have no patience with bigots. There is always some hypocrisy in conjunction with bigotry." Or, after visiting the remains of Wellington and Nelson, "I should not have liked to know them. One should not see a hero too near." He was Empire-minded, defending the Boer War to a friend: "You surely don't want us to be kicked out of South Africa. Once a nation begins to give in, it is a dying nation, and soon will be a dead one." He liked parables and Sir Walter Scott and pitied "poor Dreyfus." Like all amateur detectives, he regarded policemen as flatfoots. "You cannot expect the ordinary policeman to stand eight hours on his legs and then develop a great mental strength."

Above all, he had a sense of humor. When visitors begged him to recount tales of his deductive prowess, he enjoyed relating the story of his visit to a bedridden patient. "Aren't you a bandsman?" Dr. Bell asked, standing over the patient. "Aye," admitted the sick man. Dr. Bell turned cockily to his students. "You see, gentlemen, I am right. It is quite simple. This man had a paralysis of the cheek muscles, the result of too much blowing at wind instruments. We need only inquire to confirm. What instrument do you play, my man?" The man got up on his elbows. "The big drum, Doctor!"

Dr. Bell died in October, 1911, at the age of seventy-four. His funeral was impressive, attended by the Seaforth Highlanders, by a deputation of nurses, by endless influential medical men, and by swarms of poor people he had treated. He was dead, but he did not rest long.

A. Conan Doyle, before dying in 1930, became intensely interested in spiritualism. Doyle, who had once killed Sherlock Holmes and brought him back to life, now attempted to resurrect the prototype. One night at a seance, he announced that the late Dr. Bell had materialized and spoken to him. As proof, Doyle produced a spirit photograph of Dr. Bell attired in flowing hair and a long gown. When Dr. Bell's daughter, Mrs. Stisted, saw the photograph, she was furious.

"It looked nothing at all like Father," she says today. "And anyway, if he were going to return and appear before anybody, I am most sure he would appear before me!"

WHAT HAS HAPPENED SINCE . . .

The genesis of this story occurred during casual readings of long ago, in which I would occasionally find a hint that a real person, with astounding deductive skills, had inspired the creation of the fictional Sherlock Holmes. Later, Sir Arthur Conan Doyle's autobiography, *My Memories and Adventures,* confirmed that there had been such a living prototype of Sherlock Holmes. Doyle's book also informed me that the man's name was Dr. Joseph Bell, and he had been an instructor in medicine at the University of Edinburgh.

Sheer curiosity prompted me to begin investigating the life of this mysterious Dr. Bell. I was eager to learn all that I could about a human being possessing such remarkable gifts. The research was not easy. It required tracing many sources, across many years, to construct a full man on the skeletal frame of a name. Some progress was made when I discovered in a London rare-book shop a privately printed memoir entitled *Joseph Bell, an Appreciation* by Jessie Saxby. A major step was made after I learned that one of Dr. Bell's heirs, a daughter, Mrs. Cecil Stisted, was alive in Egerton, Kent, since Mrs. Stisted kindly shared with me personal reminiscences of her father, and loaned me his letters and scrapbooks. Other valuable information was obtained when I located some writings by Dr. Bell, and then tracked down and interviewed former students of his in such widely separated cities as Edinburgh, Calgary, Chicago.

As my research notes mounted, I think that I hoped to write a slender biographical book about Dr. Bell. But in the end I saw that while there was not enough background material to justify a book, there was quite enough for a thorough magazine article. So I wrote the article, instead. In abridged form, "The Incredible Dr. Bell" appeared as the lead story in *The Saturday Review of Literature* for May 1, 1948, and then was republished in the *Reader's Digest* for June, 1948.

Pleased by the favorable international response to the story, I wondered if I should attempt another book project I had long had in mind. For years, I had wanted to write a biographical collection with the subheading, "Lives of extraordinary people who inspired memorable characters in fiction," in which I would reveal who had actually been Robinson Crusoe, Emma Bovary, Dr. Jekyll and Mr. Hyde in real life. I decided to go ahead with the project. I did even more research on Dr. Bell, then expanded and developed my article further, and on this cornerstone of one chapter I built my first published book, *The Fabulous Originals*, which appeared in the United States in 1955. In the years after, my story of Dr. Bell continued to be widely circulated, since the article was included in an anthology, *The Saturday Review Gallery*, and my own book containing the Dr. Bell chapter was eventually published in England, Australia, Germany, and Spain.

Many persons who had known Dr. Bell, some of whom had assisted me in researching my story, wrote to me. One of these was Dr. Douglas Guthrie, lecturer on the history of medicine at the University of Edinburgh, who wrote me on October 10, 1955, after reading my chapter:

I at once turned the pages to read of "The Real Sherlock Holmes," and was so fascinated that I could not stop until I had finished that chapter. Although I am not quite such a Doyle "fan" as the folk who foster what they call The Sacred Canon in their societies, I am an unrepentant admirer of Sherlock Holmes and find him much better than any character in more modern thrillers. Perhaps the reason is, that I remember seeing Joseph Bell when I was a student, and I remember the eagerness with which the early Adventures in the Strand Magazine *were read, and the rush to buy each new number.*

You will be sorry to learn, if you have not heard already, of the death of Mrs. Cecil Stisted, of Egerton, Kent, about a year ago: the last remaining member of the family of Dr. Joseph Bell. Her son, Mr. Joseph Bell [Stisted], is still in the house, so far as I know.

Among those who also responded to my article, and then to my book chapter on Dr. Bell, although less appreciatively—in fact, most angrily— was Adrian Conan Doyle, son of the creator of Sherlock Holmes.

I do not know Adrian Conan Doyle, except as one who has dedicated a good deal of his life to perpetuating his father's image as the creator of Sherlock Holmes. The only biographical information I have on Adrian Conan Doyle is that which appears on the jacket of a book, *The Exploits of Sherlock Holmes*. In this volume, there are a dozen newly written Holmes stories, half contributed by Adrian Conan Doyle himself, and half done in collaboration with the estimable John Dickson Carr, but all based on tantalizing references to other Sherlock Holmes cases, made by Watson in Sir Arthur's own stories. From the book jacket, we learn that "Adrian Conan Doyle is the youngest son of Sir Arthur Conan Doyle, and his father's literary executor," that he had previously published a personal adventure story about deep-sea fishing off Africa, that he was raised in the Victorian tradition, and that "the son—like the father—has a lust for adventure, cherishes relics of the past and, above all, has the same sense of chivalry that so completely characterized Sherlock Holmes. Adrian Conan Doyle uses the very desk on which his father wrote."

I find this as impressive as I have always found Adrian Conan Doyle formidable. And it gives one a better understanding of what I shall now relate—what happened to me when Adrian Conan Doyle learned that I credited Dr. Joseph Bell with being the inspiration for the character of Sherlock Holmes.

Actually, I was neither the first nor the only one of Dr. Bell's champions to incur Adrian Conan Doyle's wrath. Four years before my story was published, Mrs. Stisted had chanced to display to the press some letters from Sir Arthur Conan Doyle to her father, which proved that Dr. Bell had been the real-life prototype of Sherlock Holmes. At once, Adrian Doyle entered his public defense of *his* father as being the prototype in the pages of the Edinburgh *Evening News:*

"It is neither my wish nor my intention to belittle the remarkable characteristics of Dr. Bell, nor to question the attributes of the doctor's influence upon my father. But it is my intention to rectify a most fallacious impression that Sherlock Holmes was, in fact, merely a literary reflect of Dr. Joseph Bell. My father's letters quoted by Mrs. Stisted open no fresh ground whatever, for as my father's old friends will agree, one of his most marked and lovable characteristics was the genuine pleasure that he derived in placing the major part of the credit for any of his successful adventures upon the shoulders of others rather than upon his own."

This sounded the warring note, although with gentlemanly and chivalrous restraint, out of respect (no doubt) to the sex and age of the enemy. It was almost the last time that Adrian Doyle would show such public restraint in dealing with the hosts of the Dr. Bell camp.

In 1943, the popular English biographer, Hesketh Pearson, published an unauthorized life entitled *Conan Doyle*. In it he wrote:

"There were living models for both Holmes and Watson. Doyle always declared that Dr. Joseph Bell, surgeon at the Edinburgh Infirmary, was the model for Sherlock Holmes, but Bell once confessed that Doyle owed 'much less than he thinks to me.' What happened, obviously, was that Bell stimulated Doyle's fancy, which, once released, far surpassed the original."

Hesketh Pearson then went on to describe, at length, Dr. Bell's deductive gifts, and several times referred to Sir Arthur Conan Doyle's debt to his old instructor. (I might add, here, that when Hesketh Pearson later read my story of Dr. Bell, he wrote me, "Though this isn't of the least importance . . . you call my Life of Doyle unauthorised. Actually the Doyle family, in the person of Adrian, gave me access to private material, which I acknowledged in the Note at the beginning; but of course the book was written quite independently and they disliked my honest treatment of their father, especially, I fancy, the way I deal with his spiritualism."

Whether it was the manner in which Pearson dealt with Sir Arthur's spiritualism, or simply his remark that Dr. Bell had "stimulated" the invention of Sherlock Holmes, or both reasons, the Pearson biography had a particularly inflammatory effect upon Adrian Doyle. In 1945, lance directed at Pearson, the youngest Doyle published a slender book, *The True Conan Doyle*, aimed, as the American jacket blurb stated, "against the self-styled biographers who wrote glibly and voluminously about Arthur Conan Doyle without ever having known him personally and without having access to the family documents." The jacket blurb then went on to state that Adrian Doyle's rebuttal had "created a furor among Conan Doyle enthusiasts." In his monograph, Adrian Doyle began:

"During the past year, I have been distressed by the number of letters that have reached me from both acquaintances and strangers in protest against an alleged 'biography' of my father by a Mr. Hesketh Pearson. As the majority of my correspondents were, naturally, under the impression that the manuscript was submitted to me before publication, I must assure them that that was not the case. In its portrayal of my father and his opinions, the book is a travesty."

Thirteen pages later, Adrian Doyle arrived at the peak of his counterattack:

"Mr. Hayden Coffin, the American journalist, has offered us interesting confirmation in his recent statement to the press that my father told him in a private interview in 1918 that—'If anyone is Holmes, then I must confess that it is I.' For half a century, a variety of writers and critics have, with insufficient knowledge, confused the public mind by placing all the credit, and not a minor part of that credit, for Sherlock Holmes at the feet of Dr. Joseph Bell, which is analogous to the ridiculous position that could arise if the plaudits due to a brilliant virtuoso were reserved only for the teacher who gave him the original music lessons. Conan Doyle was too great in himself to be annoyed by this misconception. Indeed, I know that he derived no small degree of amusement from it. And yet he threw out a clue when he wrote—'a man cannot spin a character out of his inner consciousness and make it really lifelike unless he has the possibilities of that character within himself.'

"Dr. Bell's remarkable characteristics brought to their full growth the deductive propensities latent in Conan Doyle. They did that, and they did no more. If the good doctor had been endowed with the power to create extraordinary gifts that were not already innate, then the Edinburgh University course of 1876-81 would have produced, among the many hundreds of students that passed under his aegis, a spate of incarnated Sherlock Holmes!"

This was the situation then—the lull before the real storm—when I published the most contemporary popular biography of Dr. Joseph Bell three years later. Adrian Doyle read my article in *The Saturday Review of Literature,* for he promptly wrote that publication:

"I have in my possession the inside facts of the correspondence and friendly association that linked my father and his old professor, Dr. Bell. I wish to place it on record that there is not a word of truth in Mr. Irving Wallace's statement that Dr. Bell made an assertion that he was Sherlock Holmes. On the contrary, he denied it most flatly, while on the other hand in 1918 my father put on record the fact that Sherlock Holmes was none other than himself."

More amused than irritated, I saw no point in heightening the conflict. I do not mean to sound lofty, not when facing so indomitable a combatant as Adrian Conan Doyle, Keeper of the Name, but I felt that my story of Dr. Bell, much of it based on documented facts from the Bell family, would withstand any doubts engendered in readers by the Youngest Son.

When the public reception accorded my Dr. Bell article encouraged me to expand upon it and include it as the initial biography in my first book, *The Fabulous Originals*, I foresaw no further difficulties with Adrian Doyle. I thought that, having had his say, he considered the matter closed. I was never more mistaken.

The English edition of *The Fabulous Originals* appeared throughout Great Britain in 1956, under the notable imprint of Longmans, Green & Co., Ltd. The English edition was widely and favorably received, and one major review, written by the renowned and respected Cyril Connolly, appeared under the heading "Borrowed From Life" in the *Sunday Times* of London. In his essay, Mr. Connolly considered the Dr. Bell chapter one of "the three most interesting studies in this book." He spoke of Conan Doyle's "obsession" with Dr. Bell. He went on:

"Conan Doyle envied the effortless, eccentric superman who was also an aesthete, while he waited in vain for patients in Portsmouth. . . . Dr. Bell practiced deduction and astounded his students. Conan Doyle created Sherlock Holmes from him, and when the fact was known Dr. Bell began to be consulted by Scotland Yard, grew more like Holmes and claimed to solve the mystery of Jack the Ripper."

In Geneva, Switzerland, Adrian Doyle read the Cyril Connolly review, and, clearly enraged, took down his rusty lance and charged off to defend the family honor. His immediate action was to fire off a stern communication for publication in Cyril Connolly's newspaper, the *Sunday Times*. In the *Sunday Times*, the son argued the case for his father as the real Sherlock Holmes and trusted this would put down "Mr. Wallace's ingenuous efforts to re-create a fairy tale."

Still brooding perhaps about the injustice done to his father's creativity, determined once and for all to rout and humiliate the Dr. Bell adherents, either Adrian Doyle or his relatives got in touch with their solicitors in Woburn Square, London. In January, 1957, Mark Longman, of Longmans, Green & Co., received a legal warning from the solicitors of "the family of the late Sir Arthur Conan Doyle." The solicitors—fearsomely named Vertue and Churcher, Amalgamated with Gush, Phillips, Walters and Williams—wrote that their clients were concerned about "certain totally false and damaging statements" in my story on Dr. Bell. What disturbed their clients most, the solicitors declared, was that I had claimed as a fact that A. Conan Doyle wrote Dr. Bell asking him for Sherlock Holmes plots and thanking him for those received. Unless I could provide tangible proof of A. Conan Doyle's doing this, I was being advised to publish an immediate retraction of my statement and offer my full apologies to the Doyle family. If I failed to provide either evidence or an apology, then the Doyle family was ready to take "action" to protect the value of their copyright and Sir Arthur's memory from fabricated writings calculated to damage it.

Learning of my position, the celebrated New York copyright attorney, Philip Wittenberg, checked the facts in the case and then volunteered to defend me against any legal action. He felt confident that the Doyle family did not have a sound case. While Wittenberg stood by, I wrote Longmans, Green & Co. in London:

I am enclosing all the evidence that I believe is necessary at this time. Sir Arthur Conan Doyle, in his autobiography, admitted that he had received "suggestions" for stories from Dr. Bell. And, in personal letters written to Bell, he confessed to using these suggestions for Sherlock Holmes stories. Also, in these letters, he requested that Bell send him more ideas for Sherlock Holmes plots. I am sending you copies of this correspondence.

Following the submission of this first preliminary evidence, the Doyle solicitors, Vertue and Churcher, Amalgamated with Gush, Phillips, Walters and Williams, were not heard from again. I felt I had silenced the Doyle family for all time. As before, I was mistaken, for I underestimated the wrath and energy of the Youngest Son.

In his Swiss retreat at 3 Quai Turrettini, Geneva, Adrian Conan Doyle was apparently contemplating his bent lance and sifting through a mass of clippings reviewing my book and its chapter on Dr. Bell. At last, Adrian Doyle took to his pen. If he could not have my neck in a court of law, he would have it in the court of public appeal. His letters went out to such diverse newspapers as the *Northern Echo*, Priestgate, Darlington; the *Bristol Evening World*, Bristol; and *The Bulletin and Scots Pictorial*, Glasgow.

While both J. L. H. Stisted, on behalf of Dr. Bell's family, and I had replied to Adrian Doyle in the *Sunday Times* of London, and felt our presentation of the facts sufficient, we were now shaken by the force and detail of Adrian Doyle's fresh and most determined assault. My time was valuable to me, and I saw no use in dredging up all the old facts once more. I felt any new defense I made would engage me, possibly unto eternity, with a seemingly tireless opponent.

But then I began to read what Adrian Doyle was writing to the British press in February and March of 1957, and I knew that I must rally my strength for one last battle. There was, after all, much at stake. Possibly more for me than for Adrian Doyle. For while the son was defending the integrity of a relative, I was defending my own integrity as an author.

I studied the letter that Adrian Doyle was sending to the press. The full version of Adrian Doyle's letter, as it appeared in the *Northern Echo*, February 5, 1957, read as follows:

Sir,

Owing to my absence abroad, it is only recently that my attention has been drawn to a book allegedly on the subject of Sherlock Holmes by a Mr. Irving Wallace.

I have never denied that Dr. Bell played a distinguished part in setting the model for Holmes's methods in my father's mind and in developing the latter's own powers for observation and deduction. But that was all. As this American author quotes an 1892 letter in which my father, with typical modesty, attempted to endow his old professor with the identity of Holmes, it is worth while to consider Bell's reply—"No, no, my dear Conan Doyle, you are yourself Sherlock Holmes, and well you know it."

The correctness of Bell's assertion was proved by later events, such as the Slater case, the Edalji case, the Missing Dane, etc. Mr. Wallace attempts to make play with the fact that Stevenson, when expressing his admiration for my father's writings, identified Bell from the Holmes-trick of deduction. Of course he did, for this was the very characteristic that first planted in my father's imagination the idea of developing his own type of detective. But what else did Stevenson write in 1894? "In the forefront of every battle for justice will be seen the white plume of Conan Doyle." It was a prophecy that came true.

It was Conan Doyle, not Bell, who created Sherlock Holmes, and it was Conan Doyle, to a far greater degree than Bell, who put into practice Holmes's methods for the solution of crime in real life. This fact was recognised almost from the first by such famous criminologists as Dr. Edmond Locard, H. Ashton-Wolfe, Dr. Katju, William J. Burns, and others, some of whom came to England for the express purpose of consulting him on difficult cases.

Though Mr. Wallace is ignorant of the real identity of Holmes, the police officials knew, certain criminals knew and so did those who wrote such letters to him as (I quote from the archives): "Sir Conan Doyle, you breaker of my shackles, you lover of truth for justice's sake"; or "I have had an extraordinary escape and I dread to think what might have happened. I don't know how to thank you sufficiently . . . for all you have done for me"; or "There are those who say you have not long to live. I won't answer for your safety a day."

We are now told that Bell played a leading part in the Chantrelle murder case, etc., and yet I am informed by an expert in criminological history that his name is not even mentioned in any of the documentations which are given in full in Notable British Trials. *It seems that the editors of England's most renowned encyclopaedia of crime have been startlingly remiss.*

Reasonable criticism one accepts, however much one may disagree with it, but I will not remain silent in the face of downright inventions about my father. There is not a word of truth in the assertion that he wrote "letter after letter to Bell, asking him, and thanking him, for plots." As curator of his records, which incidentally include many thousands of letters covering every period of his life, I am in a position to state that he corresponded very little with his old teacher.

In chasing the shadow rather than the substance, Mr. Wallace has missed a golden opportunity. Had he been a researcher, he would have found himself engrossed in my father's wonderful archives, where he might have learnt of the part that Holmes, or rather his "fabulous original," played behind the scenes of Britain's national life. Only a few weeks ago a learned professor who, at the instigation of a world-famous university, has been occupied with these very researches, preparatory to a fully documented 300,000-word standard reference work on my father, wrote to me: "In spite of Dickson Carr's fine Life of Sir Arthur, I did not realize the wide range of influence, all the more extraordinary because it was hidden, that your father wielded in national affairs during that critical period from the turn of the century until the end of the Great War." There, in the facts of that hidden influence functioning on a noble level and in his country's interests, we have the epitome of the living Holmes.

Yours etc.,
Adrian Conan Doyle

I knew that I could not permit this attack on my Dr. Bell story to go unchallenged. And so, marshaling my research notes, I replied to Adrian Doyle carefully and at length. I sent off my defense of Dr. Bell as prototype not only to the *Northern Echo*, where it appeared in full on March 27, 1957, but to every other British newspaper which I learned had published Adrian Doyle's attack. My letter, as it appeared in the *Northern Echo*, read as follows:

Sir,

Several months ago the Northern Echo *was kind enough to review my book,* The Fabulous Originals, *which concerned itself with unusual real persons who inspired the creation of memorable characters in fiction. Among the most notable of these was Dr. Joseph Bell, consulting surgeon to the Royal Infirmary of Edinburgh, whose remarkable talents inspired one of his students, Sir Arthur Conan Doyle, to invent Sherlock Holmes.*

Recently, I have been informed there appeared in your pages a letter, signed by Mr. Adrian Conan Doyle, taking strong exception to the facts in my book—facts unearthed after years of research and first-hand interviews. Since Mr. Doyle disparages my research, my biography of Dr. Bell, and the abilities of Dr. Bell himself, I feel it my duty to have my day in court.

While one must, indeed, admire Mr. Doyle's filial devotion, one cannot help but feel that this very devotion detracts from his objectivity. I have made the full case for Dr. Bell as the original of Sherlock Holmes in my book. I shall do no more than briefly summarise that case here.

1. The star witness in the case for Dr. Bell remains none other than the creator of Sherlock Holmes himself. A. Conan Doyle, in a letter to Dr. Bell dated May 7, 1892, frankly acknowledged the source of his inspiration. He admitted that he owed the creation of Holmes to his old instructor's teachings and to his demonstrations of deduction, inference and observation. A. Conan Doyle further acknowledged Dr. Bell as the prototype in interviews given to the press and in his autobiography.

2. Over a period of years I corroborated A. Conan Doyle's admission by correspondence or personal interviews with other students who, like Doyle, had studied under Dr. Bell in the Royal Infirmary of Edinburgh and who knew the role their mentor played in the creation of Sherlock Holmes. Among these were Dr. J. Gordon Wilson, Mr. Z. M. Hamilton, and Dr. Harold E. Jones. Even Robert Louis Stevenson, in 1893, after meeting the "ingenious and very interesting" Sherlock Holmes in print for the first time, asked A. Conan Doyle in a letter from Samoa, "Only one thing troubles me. Can this be my old friend Joe Bell?"

3. Though A. Conan Doyle's place in modern literature is secure, though he performed wonders in the Edalji and Slater cases, there are still those who have written that Doyle was "singularly unobservant." Dr. Bell, on the other hand, performed miracles of observation and deduction before his students, among them Doyle—and his investigations in the Chantrelle, Monson, and Jack the Ripper murder cases cannot be dismissed lightly. Mr. Adrian Doyle remains highly suspicious of Dr. Bell's detecting abilities, since an "expert" had informed him that the Notable British Trials edition of the Chantrelle murder made no mention of Dr. Bell. On the other hand, Mr. Adrian Doyle's "expert" neglected to inform him that many other English sources did give fair credit to Dr. Bell's role in this case, among them the late William Roughead, a leading editor of the Notable British Trials series.

With little relevance to the issue at hand, Mr. Adrian Doyle has made a spirited defence of his father's "hidden influence" in the affairs of England. I do not doubt this, and I never have. A. Conan Doyle is as admired and beloved in America as in his homeland. This, however, makes him no better a candidate for the prototype of Sherlock Holmes than Dr. Bell, who counted among his supporters Queen Victoria, Florence Nightingale—and Arthur Conan Doyle.

Mr. Adrian Doyle's untiring argument for his father as prototype and detective seems to me unnecessary. His father has his immortality as author of the Sherlock Holmes saga. It is enough. He does not require (nor, I feel sure, would he demand, were he alive) the additional honour of being the model for his own hero. Undoubtedly, were he alive today, he would repeat what he asserted more than a half-century ago—that Dr. Joseph Bell was the inspiration for Sherlock Holmes.

Yours etc.,
Irving Wallace

With the publication of my letter, there came silence and peace, and it was wonderful. This zany literary conflict about who was the real Sherlock Holmes ended in 1957, and has not been revived to this day. It is my hope that a mellower Adrian Conan Doyle has come to a closer understanding of what the Dr. Bell heirs feel and what I believe: that Sir Arthur Conan Doyle deserves all of the credit for being the creator of one of the greatest and most enduring characters of fiction, Sherlock Holmes, and that Sir Arthur's university instructor, Dr. Joseph Bell, deserves credit for having possessed extraordinary gifts that inspired the invention of Doyle's character.

I shall conclude with a summary of the controversy, written by the Marquis of Donegal in *The Sherlock Holmes Journal*, tenth issue, published by the Sherlock Holmes Society of London:

"There, for the moment, the matter rests. . . . Let us call the fair-minded layman's attention to Dr. Bell's preface to the 1893 Ward, Lock and Bowden edition of A *Study in Scarlet*.

"Obviously, Dr. Bell's modesty forbade him to lay direct claim to being the 'prototype.' But he writes:—(the italics are ours)

" 'Dr. Conan Doyle's *education as a student of medicine taught* him how to observe, and his practice . . . has been a splendid *training* for a man such as he is, *gifted* with eyes, memory and imagination.

" '*Trained* as he has been to *notice* and *appreciate* minute detail, Dr. Doyle saw how he could interest his intelligent readers. . . .'

"So, as Jonathan Small asked, in *The Sign of Four:*—'Is there any other point you would like to ask about?' "

DON'T CALL HER MADAM

THIS IS ABOUT SEX in Japan.

For five years now, week after week, the Tokyo radio has been promising elimination of the geisha girl. The most recent shortwave reports state that all geisha will soon become members of women's labor battalions.

I am here to say it will not come to pass.

In mobilizing their empire for a last-ditch stand in this Second World War, the Japanese leaders can go far. They can make their people eat dried seaweed, canned grasshoppers, bread baked of straw and green leaves. They can make their people give up telephones, warm kimonos, weekend vacations, autos, tobacco, foreign movies, romantic songs, dancing. They can eliminate formal wedding ceremonies. They can remove the sacred metal from a hundred thousand temples.

All this they can take away, and no trouble. But let them touch the geisha—and comes the revolution.

The reason, of course, is that in Japan sex is a special subject, kept apart from all others, as are Bushido, flower arrangement, Sendai chests, slave labor, and the emperor. I learned this in Tokyo a year before Pearl Harbor, when I visited Mr. Hidezo Kubo, known variously as President of the Shimbashi Geisha Guild and the yellow woman's John L. Lewis.

It was only in order to understand the nature of the Japanese better that I explored the subject of the geisha girl.

Japan is a man's world. The average wife is no more than a passive instrument for breeding. Romance and love in the Western sense do not warm the Japanese family hearth. But there is another guise for sex—or sexual stimulation. In Japan, the geisha girl alone represents a lofty world where flirtation and romance are raised to professional arts, mellowed and refined by centuries of practice. The geisha girl is sex in Japan. And she is there to stay.

I was first introduced to the geisha by a lanky, toothy Indian named V. Chockalingam, who was recommended to me as the one person who could show me the Tokyo not to be found in the guidebooks. He eked out a living by writing occasional dispatches for the United India Press. He spoke several Indian tongues, a perfect Japanese which he had learned while at his university, and English. He read banned books and argued world politics in the lobby of the Imperial Hotel.

It was Chock who took me, one Saturday night, first to the renowned Yoshiwara district of Tokyo. The Yoshiwara is a city within a city, where at least 6,000 of Japan's 70,000 licensed "one-night wives" or prostitutes —who are not geisha—are segregated. Most of them are in semislavery, each dwelling in a tiny cage-style house with barred windows. This system has had apologists. In an English-language guidebook published by the Hokuseido Press of Tokyo, an Englishman, George Caiger, writes of the Yoshiwara:

"In no other great city can ladies go through such a quarter in the sure knowledge that they will meet with no insult, and see no immodesty or vulgarity. . . . Vice is here robbed of its viciousness, for it is dignified, and, in the final analysis, a civilized handling of a universal problem."

I saw a nightful of this "civilized handling." We walked through the narrow streets, none more than six feet wide, flanked on either side, endlessly, by the miniature houses. Sometimes, I could observe the young ladies reading or sewing indoors. Other times, they stood at their windows and called "Ha-ro," a corruption of "Hello." Most of the girls were decorous, only a very few obscene.

We went into one of the larger houses, down the wooden corridors, past the sliding partitions. I met four or five of the girls. They were all in ruthless bondage—but all resigned to it. Most came from farms. There were frequent bad seasons on the farms, and if a father wished to survive, he would borrow perhaps $300 from the men of Yoshiwara, and turn over his fifteen-year-old daughter as security for the loan. The daughter would work off this debt with her body. After four or five years, the debt might be repaid, and then the daughter could return to the farm. But usually, she just remained.

Chock assured me, however, that the Yoshiwara was not the real sex story of Japan. The most important part of the story, he said, was the geisha. Everyone talked so much about the geisha that the subject was considered a cliché. "But no one's really covered it," he said. "And when you realize the geishas have one of the most powerful unions—"

"You mean they're organized?"

Chock nodded. "Best union in Japan. And I know the head man. His name is Hidezo Kubo, president of the Shimbashi Geisha Guild."

So I went with Chock to see Mr. Kubo.

>«

Hidezo Kubo was a slight, grayish, immaculate man attired in a Palm Beach suit. He was bald except for a thin semicircle of hair. He wore metal-rimmed spectacles and a quiet mustache. He was sixty-five years old.

He sat, in the best Little Napoleon manner, behind a massive, aseptic walnut desk. His large office contained two fat safes, three busts of Japanese war heroes, an old gramophone. Also, there was a microphone and switch. "It is our speaker system," Mr. Kubo explained. "It connects me with each of our four floors."

Mr. Kubo's sanctum was on the second floor of the guild's four-story modernistic building in the heart of Tokyo. From this office, Mr. Kubo, possessing the world's strangest and perhaps in ways most enviable job, controlled the daily doings of 280 first-rate geisha houses in the Shimbashi district of the island's capital. Mr. Kubo was, indeed, the middleman to end all middlemen.

In Tokyo, there were three million males. The love life of most of these males consisted largely of visiting the 13,793 geisha girls residing in 4,526 geisha houses located in Tokyo's fifty-four geisha districts—of which the most expensive and exclusive was Mr. Kubo's Shimbashi district.

Actually, Mr. Kubo's guild was a clearinghouse in sex. Whenever a male, or a group of males, desired female companionship, they phoned Mr. Kubo or any one of his eighty office employees. Then Mr. Kubo, in turn, advised his geisha to be prepared for visitors at their *machiai* or waiting house, that evening, or ordered them to be on hand at the *ryoriya* or restaurant.

"But, I must make one thing clear to you," said Mr. Kubo from behind his walnut desk, "and it is important. In fact, it is why I wished to see you even on a Sunday afternoon. It is that our geisha girls are *not* prostitutes —and our Shimbashi district is not a red-light district!"

I started to comment on this point, but he was just beginning his educational discourse. His spectacles wavered on his nose as he spoke.

"Oh, yes, it is unfortunately true," he continued, "that some of the third-rate geisha, in cheaper districts, who are unaccomplished in the traditional arts, have lowered themselves by becoming mere prostitutes.

These cheap geisha have given all geisha a bad name with foreigners.

"I do not say that every one of my eight hundred girls here is a virgin. After all, their virginity is a private matter, just as it is with American entertainers like your movie actresses in Hollywood. From what I have heard about your movie actresses, I would venture to say that our geisha use their bodies far less for purposes of advancement.

"The main point is this—our geisha do not make a living by romancing with guests. They make a living purely from reciting songs, dancing, playing the samisen, conversing wittily. Just last week, there was a professor here from one of your big American universities. He spent one night with our girls and left convinced they were not prostitutes."

I asked the professor's name. Mr. Kubo started to tell me, stopped, then wagged his head.

"No, I'd better not tell. Anyway, if the professor could be convinced, maybe you too will go home and help correct the impression in America that the geisha are prostitutes. In keeping with the New Order in Japan, and to lift the unfair stigma attached to the word geisha, we in the guild are planning to call our girls by a different name. Maybe that will help."

The geisha have had a long history in their struggle to rise above prostitution. In 1761, retired courtesans became the first geisha. For almost a century, they were nothing more than expensive *filles de joie*. Finally in 1830, the samurai, the specially privileged feudal-brutal knights of Japan, began patronizing and defending the geisha, and thus gave them respectability. After that, the geisha themselves made a fight to break away from outright prostitution. Those who preferred the life of the red light disappeared into Yoshiwara, while those who preferred to be entertainers enlisted in the rapidly rising Shimbashi. By 1890, the geisha were considered so chaste that if one of their number permitted herself a bed partner on company time, she was driven from the district, while her best kimono was taken from her and hung in disgraceful display from the center of the waiting house for all to see.

Mr. Kubo informed me further that there were six classes of geisha. His own charges fell into the upper two brackets. The first class was called *jimae*, and its young ladies owned their own private houses. The second class was called *wake*, and it included the young ladies who divided their incomes fifty-fifty with the house owners. In the third class were the girls called *schichisan*, who kept three-tenths of their earnings. "The rest," said Mr. Kubo, "are the lower-class geisha, who give us a bad name. We nickname them the pillow geisha. I do not have to explain."

All this anti-prostitution talk left me honestly befuddled, and still skeptical. I had been to three expensive geisha parties, two sponsored for me by the Japanese government, and another, quaintly enough, sponsored by the Japanse-American Friendship Society. Each of these parties ended with my friends, stimulated by potent sake, wandering off for the night with their respective first-class geisha.

But I suppose such activity, as Mr. Kubo insisted, was purely extracurricular. I recall reading a book, *Geisha Girl*, written by Mr. Aisabuto Akiyama, published in Yokohama. One passage explained:

"The geisha may be taken for an independent artist unique in nature providing her chastity be kept intact. It is, nevertheless, a deplorable fact that she is often deprived of her virtue by wanton guests who lay manifold nets over her in a way that makes it practically impossible to escape."

I asked Mr. Kubo if it was true that most girls were driven into the career of geisha because of economic necessity. "In this respect, I've heard it's just like Yoshiwara," I said.

Mr. Kubo bristled indignantly. "We have no slavery," he replied. "There are some cheap districts that give parents 500-yen loans and receive their daughters for five years to work off the loans, but that is mere prostitution again. Here, in Shimbashi, our district is so famous, so wealthy, so well patronized, that girls come to us of their own free will to audition. We study the new girls. Finally, we select fifty a year for qualities of appearance, voice, health, intelligence. Sometimes, we learn of a young geisha in Kobe or Osaka who is very popular, and we buy up her contract. But usually we depend upon developing new girls. We take them between twelve and twenty-one; most have attended high school, some have even gone to college. We teach them singing, dancing, conversation; we teach them to play the samisen, our traditional three-stringed instrument which resembles your guitar; and we teach them the drums, flute, cymbals.

"Here, in Shambashi, a geisha need develop only one of these talents well. If she becomes expert in it, she can make a good deal of money."

I wondered what a good deal of money might be.

"To hire one geisha from us for one hour's entertainment," said Mr. Kubo, "the customer must pay 4.40 yen, or one dollar in your American money. Out of this 4.40 yen, 79 sen goes to the restaurant where the geisha entertains, 36 sen goes to us here in the guild, and the remaining 3.25 to the geisha herself. If the geisha entertains two hours, her customer pays 6.50 yen—of which 1.30 goes to the restaurant, 42 sen to us, and the remaining 4.78 to her.

"Thus, if a geisha is well accomplished and popular, she earns from 700 to 800 yen a month. That is about $200 a month American money. An unpopular geisha would earn only one-tenth of that."

It wasn't until much later that I learned how impressive these earnings of a first-class geisha were—by Japanese standards they were fabulous, considering that the average Japanese girl in the cotton mill received exactly $5.88 *a month.*

Mr. Kubo had been mentioning the fees collected by his Geisha Guild, and I thought it time to inquire into the exact function of this guild.

"First let me explain how we came about," said Mr. Kubo. "At the turn of the century, there were five types of places frequented by geisha. There were restaurants, waiting houses, meat markets, fish stores, and houseboats. You have seen the big dry ditches through Tokyo? They used to be canals traveled by houseboats. Then, at the time of Premier Ito, the country was filled with revolt, with terror and assassination. Political refugees fled to these five different types of places, and while in hiding, while discussing and planning their future political action, they were entertained by the geisha. Finally, the government combined these five different places into two—Japanese-style restaurants and waiting houses. And the government established a Geisha Guild to transact all business between the individual geisha, and the establishments and their customers.

"The Shimbashi Guild is a subsidiary of the main guild. Its purpose is to keep the geisha from being exploited, to create better working conditions and higher wage minimums, to see that the geisha receives proper treatment, and to offer her services to the accredited restaurants and houses. The geisha is not at all mistreated. She has a voice. She can even strike—in fact, *has* gone on strike."

In one of the most incredible episodes in modern Japanese history, the traditional geisha went on strike. On February 26, 1937, Domei, the Japanese news agency, reported the first geisha strike:

"Declaring they were exploited by their management, which refused them the right to form a new trade union, some eighty geisha girls of Osaka have staged a spectacular walkout unparalleled in Japanese history. Leaving the gay quarters of Osaka, the strikers marched in a body up tortuous mountain slopes to the Gyokuzo Temple, where priests gave sanctuary to the valiant strikers in their little temple . . .

"There the strikers issued a manifesto declaring their determination to fight to the death to gain their twin demands—the right to form their own trade union and permission to select their own gentlemen friends. 'We are not cheap Japanese goods for sale to all comers at bargain rates,' they proclaimed."

By the end of the second day of the strike, the group of eighty geisha grew until it numbered three hundred. All night life in Osaka was halted. After two weeks, the chief of the Osaka police called an emergency conference, and around a table thirty angry employers and thirty triumphant geisha met and argued. In the end, the geisha got their special union, and won the right they still possess to accept or reject male companions offered them.

Mr. Kubo said that his own guild tried to improve the quality of geisha. Of course, he admitted, there was not much time for guidance and schooling. The girls often worked from six in the morning until nine at night at private parties in restaurants, and then from nine to midnight at the waiting houses. But every afternoon, the guild conducted a three-hour instruction period. If a girl had the time, she could attend daily, at a fee of only one yen a month. These classes could help her improve her classical dancing, or teach her to converse with more intelligence on politics and sports.

"Also," added Mr. Kubo, "once a year at our private theater, the Shimbashi Embujo, we put on a show. It gives visitors a chance to see how some of the girls have improved, and gives new stars publicity. The most popular hundred and twenty in this show receive diplomas of accomplishment, which you can see framed on the walls of the rehearsal rooms downstairs."

"Who are some of your most famous geisha?" I inquired.

"Generally, they are all famous," Mr. Kubo answered with a flash of levity. Then sobering, "We have one famous one, Kiharu, who speaks English."

I said that I had met her.

"Yes? She is charming. Don't you think so?" said Mr. Kubo. "Her father was a physician. He died and left his family poor. So Kiharu, who had studied singing and languages, became a geisha to support her family. She is twenty-six now, and the Foreign Office uses her always to entertain you American visitors. I now have five or six other young girls all studying English, so they can take care of American and British parties."

Mr. Kubo recalled some of the other famous Shimbashi geisha. There was Okoi, who had had a stockbroker and a wrestler for her lovers, and a Kabuki actor for a husband until he deserted her. Eventually, Okoi's talents attracted Prince Taro Katsura, Prime Minister of Japan, and he took her for his mistress. Throughout the Russo-Japanese War of 1904, Okoi was the confidante of the prime minister and his advisers. When the prime minister fell into disfavor after the war, his geisha mistress was equally condemned, and had to go into hiding. After Katsura died, Okoi retired to a nunnery, where she herself died in the mid-1940's.

An even more legendary Shimbashi geisha was the beautiful Ohana, who became the mistress of the late Prince Saionji, last of the elder statesmen and intimate adviser of Hirohito. At the time of the Versailles Peace Conference, Prince Saionji took his geisha to Paris with him, and

President Woodrow Wilson, charmed by her demeanor, presented her with a pearl necklace. There was considerable embarrassment later, when President Wilson learned of the young lady's occupation and position. "Today," said Mr. Kubo, "Ohana is retired. She is abbess of a nunnery near Tokyo. Of course, all our girls aspire to such fame. They all dream of growing up to be another Okichi—you know, like Cho-Cho-San in Puccini's *Madame Butterfly*."

Unlike Puccini's operatic geisha, Okichi was a real person, and her Lieutenant Pinkerton was also real and his name was Townsend Harris. He was the first United States consul general to the Japan which Admiral Perry had just opened to the West. To please the middle-aged Harris, Japanese officials took a leading eighteen-year-old geisha, Okichi, away from her carpenter sweetheart and introduced her to the American consul. Okichi, known for her comeliness and her singing, entranced the American, and she, in turn, found him attractive and eventually fell deeply in love with him. However, when new American officials arrived in Japan, Townsend Harris was forced to send away his geisha mistress temporarily. As he became busier and busier, she became lonelier and lonelier. Soon, she took to drinking, became an alcoholic, and Harris could do nothing but give her up. Some years after his death in Brooklyn, Okichi suffered a stroke and committed suicide.

"But it is Okichi's *Madame Butterfly* years that our girls choose to remember and envy," said Mr. Kubo.

Then, a little teasingly, Mr. Kubo asked me if I had met any of the male geisha. I had not, and I was unable to hide my amazement.

"We have many male geisha, or *hokan*, as we call them," said Mr. Kubo. "It will surprise you maybe to know we have one American citizen who is an official geisha working for the Asakusa Guild. He specializes in Japanese dancing and even has a male patron!"

After that, we discussed the future of the individual geisha, and Mr. Kubo was cheerful. He said that he lost as many as twenty-five girls a year to marriage. I later learned that this was an exaggerated figure. For while most of the geisha acquired generous patrons, few ever have the opportunity to marry those patrons. Most geisha are resigned to achieving, with good fortune, the role of *mekake* or "second wife." The best that the average geisha might hope for was ownership of her waiting house— and security.

It was already late, the Sunday afternoon almost gone, and I saw that it was time to leave. I looked at Chock, who had been interpreting for me, and Chock told me that he would like to ask a question of his own.

"I've been with a lot of geisha," said Chock. "Now I want you to tell me a secret, Mr. Kubo. What type of man do the girls like?"

Mr. Kubo answered this one in the stereotyped tradition of the best Hollywood press agent.

"Our girls like decent men," he said. "They have told me they like men who are clean, who are frank and goodhearted. I say to you that if a very rich munitions manufacturer comes to a geisha and puts all his indecent blood money before her, she will scorn him and turn to more decent men."

I had a faint suspicion that Mr. Kubo's reply had been colored by a personal antipathy toward munitions makers.

Mr. Kubo went on. "Our geisha have been with the most brilliant men in the world, so they are more intelligent than the average girls, and harder to please. The patrons of our girls almost fill Japan's *Who's Who*. Men of the cabinet like Prince Konoye, Matsuoka, Tojo, men like Mitsui, all have girls in Shimbashi. Politicians, nobility, intellectuals, they are all our customers. Only munitions makers, newly rich—"

There it was again.

"—rich on others' blood, they rarely come a second time, because our girls have nothing in common with them and are cold to them."

Before leaving, I thought it might be tactful to flatter Mr. Kubo with a few personal questions. So I asked how he got into this unique business.

"After the big 1923 earthquake disaster, I gave up my flour store, and organized several geisha houses," replied Mr. Kubo. "Today, I work from ten in the morning until eight at night, but I am not paid a penny. It is an honorary job. Some of my employees, however, make as much as 250 yen a month. My own money comes from several geisha houses I own. You may be interested to know, too, that I am a happily married man with five children. Yes, three of my sons are doctors, all of them today serving on the Chinese war front. Two of the sons are now lieutenants."

Mr. Kubo accompanied us downstairs, and then continued speaking while we pulled on our shoes.

He said to me, "I have enjoyed our talk very much. You will be sure to write they are not prostitutes. And by the way, I have a favor for you. I have one or two special girls. You may take them for a weekend to one of the resorts. They will wear Western-style dress. Usually our fee for a weekend with foreigners is high, but you are a friend—"

I said, "Thanks, Mr. Kubo, I'll take a rain check on that."

It's four years now, and I still have that rain check. I'm giving it to some of my buddies.

They intend to be in Mr. Kubo's vicinity very soon.

WHAT HAS HAPPENED SINCE...

It was in August, 1940, sixteen months before the Japanese attack on Pearl Harbor, that I was in Tokyo, researching and writing as a free-lance magazine contributor. I had just completed a fascinating interview, in a resort villa at the foot of Mount Fujiyama with ninety-year-old Mitsuru Toyama, head of a group of extremists and professional assassins known as the Black Dragon Society, and our talk had dealt mostly with the possibilities of war. But once back in Tokyo, I was tired of political interviews, eager to do something frivolous and diverting. I considered trying a story on the institution of the geisha, then decided that too many other writers had touched upon it in recent years. But when Chockalingam told me that the geisha girls had a union, I knew that this was my diverting subject after all, and with Chock I went to see Hidezo Kubo.

I meant to write the story at once, but more topical subjects kept me from it. And then, the following year I was married, and then, after another year I was in the army, and my notes on Mr. Kubo lay untouched in a drawer of my desk. But while I was in the Signal Corps, where every morning I received copies of monitored Japanese shortwave broadcasts, I came across the announcement that the Japanese were considering doing away with the geisha girl for the duration of the war. At once, my interview with Mr. Kubo came to mind, and on my first free Sunday away from the army base, I wrote the story. It appeared in the September, 1945, issue of *Tricolor* magazine, an attractive monthly then produced in New York but since become defunct.

In my story, I had doubted that the Japanese government, despite the pressures of war and austerity, would ever succeed in eliminating the geisha girl. I was proved right. Although the geisha unions were suspended, the geisha girl continued to exist in a limited fashion as one of Japan's few luxuries throughout the Second World War, and she survived that war and her homeland's defeat intact. Yet in the postwar years, numerous prophets of doom went on predicting the demise of the geisha, insisting that she would give way before the advent of the emancipated, Americanized, new Japanese woman. In November, 1958, *Time* magazine headlined a story "The Vanishing Geisha," which reported that nude shows and more stringent tax laws (that made a geisha party ineligible as a deductible business expense) were lessening the attraction of the geisha, and concluded, "The plain fact is that the stylized coquetry of the classic geisha is no longer fashionable. 'Frankly,' said one Japanese businessman last week, 'they have become a bore.'"

Curious to know if the geisha was on her way out—in fact, curious to know what had happened to the geisha in the two decades since I wrote about her and her improbable union—I began to investigate the situation in Tokyo today, with the assistance of Mrs. Keiko Akamatsu, the translator of several of my novels into Japanese. I am pleased to report that, while the situation of the geisha is not precisely what it was in 1940, she continues to survive, even to flourish, as a part of Japan's culture. Moreover, she is still unionized, perhaps more strongly than before, and the Shimbashi Geisha Guild has become more powerful than it was when I visited it.

At the present time, there are fifty-two geisha guilds in the city of Tokyo. They are still divided into six classes, and the Shimbashi Geisha Guild still remains in the "first-rate" class. There are 2,216 geisha houses in Tokyo today, half the number I found in 1940, and there are now 4,408 female geisha practicing their art, one-third the number I wrote about at an earlier time.

I learned that my old friend Hidezo Kubo, the managing director of the Shimbashi Geisha Guild whom I had interviewed in 1940, had stayed on in that job until 1945. There had then been some kind of disagreement between Kubo and his associates, and he had been forced to leave the guild and Tokyo itself. In the years that followed, he managed a single geisha house at To-no-sawa, in Hakone, Kanagawa Prefecture, and there he is said to have died in July, 1956.

Meanwhile, his Shimbashi Geisha Guild, closed down with all others toward the end of the war, was fully resurrected along more modern and enlightened lines in 1951. Kubo's old guild, I learned, had not been entirely devoted to the interests of the girls, had been "conspicuously feudalistic in character," and had existed "mainly for the convenience of its police contacts."

The new guild, headed by Mrs. Haru Shirohara, eighty-six years old, and Miss Shizu Nagai, an active and much desired geisha who would not give her age, is devoted strictly to the welfare of its 400 geisha girls who belong to seventy geisha houses in the district. The guild is strong, since it possesses an agreement with the Japanese Restaurant Association that permits only guild girls to work at parties in the *ryotei* or restaurants in the area.

The new guild manages almost everything for its girls. Before the war, parents sold their girls into the geisha world. This is now forbidden by law. Today, a potential geisha of twenty (eighteen years old, if she has her parents' permission) need only apply to the mistress of a geisha house that belongs to the guild. If she seems promising, she is trained in the arts of entertainment for one year, instead of the prewar minimum of ten years. If she passes an examination at the end of the year she agrees to pay the house mistress 25,000 yen, and then she is a full-fledged guild geisha, ready to work at union minimums.

The modern geisha usually spends her mornings sleeping, her afternoons perfecting her skills in the traditional songs and dances or in acquiring modern skills such as golf, tennis, bowling, Western dance steps, or reading for background in order to converse with male customers interested in discussing the Common Market, the New York Yankees, Red China's nuclear advances, or what not. In the evenings, the geisha works, spending time with customers in the private room of a restaurant from six o'clock until somewhere between ten o'clock and midnight.

The new guild sees that its member houses obtain proper employment for each girl. But it also takes care of each girl's continuing education, health, tax problems, social security insurance. Above all, the guild sees that its geisha girl member is not underpaid.

The standard pay for the services of a Shimbashi geisha girl is about 950 yen—almost three dollars—an hour. The greatest part of her income, however, comes from *oshugi*—tips—and these can often be generous. A really top-flight geisha girl, I am told, can earn 300,000 yen or $800 a month. However, all of this income is not profit. She has many expenses such as her guild fee, house commission, training tuition, and the upkeep of a kimono and obi wardrobe that may cost as much as 300,000 yen.

As before, my Shimbashi Geisha Guild informants were most sensitive about my questions concerning sex and the modern geisha girl. "Much to our bewilderment and regret," a guild official said, "foreigners are still often apt to mix up geisha and prostitutes. Even in 1940, few people went to visit a geisha merely to satisfy sexual desire. If a man wanted a girl, he would go to a *Kuruwa*, a licensed prostitution quarter like Yoshiwara, and enjoy an *oiran*, a high-class prostitute. Often, when a man visited such a prostitute, he would call a geisha to entertain him with dance and songs before he went to bed with the prostitute."

In 1956, I learned, the Prostitution Prohibition Law went into effect. The prostitute was outlawed, and 60,000 women were put out of business, as were 16,000 keepers of brothels. Since there are no longer any licensed prostitutes in Japan, and since the geisha is not supposed to traffic in sex, I wondered where the single Japanese male or errant married man found his illicit pleasures. Presumably, I would guess, he found them where his American counterpart found them, among emancipated single or married women, who also wanted pleasure, and not pay.

Still, I was not satisfied with what I heard. Did or did not any geisha have anything to do with professional sex? "That is a very delicate question," I was told. "But it can be said that many of the 'third-rate' geisha with poor artistic accomplishments were and are apt to degrade themselves easily under the name of love. There is a Japanese expression, '*daruma*-geisha,' to indicate that some of the geisha are very easy to roll over like a *daruma*—a traditional round-shaped doll. Yet, having a geisha as an object of such desire would be so expensive that most males might better enjoy playing with girls or hostesses of cabarets or saloons."

When I asked Mrs. Akamatsu, my translator, what she thought the future of the geisha to be, she replied:

"The problem is that the first-rate geisha is expensive. In prewar Japan, there were quite a number of customers who enjoyed and patronized geisha and their arts as such, and not for physical love or desire. Today, such customers are fewer in number, while there are an increasing number of wealthy people who have no eye or ear for traditional dances and music, and utilize the geisha only for business entertainment.

"In order for the geisha and their world to survive the ever-changing realities of the present in this country, they will have to concentrate on cultivating their art accomplishments so that they can claim to be retainers of the traditional cultural assets of Japan. Otherwise, with modernization, the social meaning of their existence will be lost.

"I think the challenge to the geisha world today must be more or less the same as the one faced by the Kabuki play. Their survival will depend on how they succeed in handing down the excellent cultural heritage of the nation while, at the same time, acting up to the tastes of contemporary people."

And then, Mrs. Akamatsu added:

"By the way, about the matter of calling the geisha union by the term of 'guild'—a Shimbashi Guild official felt that the term 'guild' suggested something very feudal, and that it was no longer a fit term for the present setup, and he suggested that you use 'Shimbashi Geisha Association' instead. Can you do this?"

Yes, I can. I will agree to call the girls members of a progressive association if, in turn, they will do something for me—never let me catch them in shirttails and slacks, dancing the cha-cha-cha or watusi, with bearded beatniks in a Tokyo discothèque.

»IV«

The
Sunday Gentleman
on Monday

» 21 «

THE CHAIR
IN THE OVAL OFFICE

I STOOD beside the vacant chair, stared down at it, and was strangely moved.

It was a black leather, high-backed, executive swivel chair, further padded in the seat with an ordinary striped cushion, and it rested behind the aged carved oak desk, known as the Buchanan desk, in the Oval Office of the White House in Washington, D.C. It was the chair that belonged to the President of the United States, who, that balmy mid-September afternoon nine weeks before a journey to Dallas, was John Fitzgerald Kennedy.

Someone had come up beside me. It was Pierre Salinger, press secretary to the President.

"Go on, sit down in it," he said. "You're here to write a novel about how it *feels* to be President, so sit down in it, and make believe, and I'm sure you'll find what you're after."

And so I sat down in President Kennedy's chair, and although I did not fit it for size, I knew instantly that Salinger was right. He had said that I would feel something, and I did. What I felt that moment, I have felt frequently in moments of the days since, and I believe that feeling will continue to recur until the day I die. It is a feeling I would wish for every American alive.

With my bulk occupying the chair in the Oval Office, I crossed my arms on the small green blotter that was centered on the desk and contemplated what was immediately before me. First, I saw a long desk lamp with a fluorescent light. On one side of it was a cluster of gadgets, knick-knacks, souvenirs, some reflecting personal high spots in the President's life, or the lives of his family, others obviously the gifts of visiting dignitaries from far lands. On the other side of the lamp were six books held upright, one of them written by the President himself. And then my eye was caught by something resembling a menu holder in which had been inserted a card bearing the typewritten heading THE PRESIDENT'S EN-GAGEMENTS, and beneath these words were typed the hours and appointments for that day.

At my right elbow lay a manila folder bulging with papers to be studied, and perhaps signed, and next to it was a green-matted writing board. At my left elbow stood a green telephone console with eight punch keys. Then I became aware of the other telephones—there were two or three—and the simple black one, such as most of us possess in our homes, which was described to me as "the famous hot line."

This was the immediate world before the President's chair. Beyond, and all about, there was more. Riding the swivel chair, I decided to let my gaze make one unbroken orbit of the President's office, a room first brought into use in 1909. To my left was the door to the President's engagements secretary's office. Then there was an open door with a chain across it, and behind the chain, in the tiled corridor, a Secret Service agent sat at a desk, a White House policeman standing beside him, and both were watching me, while engaging themselves in conversation.

Wheeling slowly, I could see, directly across the desk and the expanse of the quiet office, its cane back to me, the padded Presidential rocker, flanked by two upholstered sofas, each holding three extra pillows. And breaking the far wall was the fireplace, two three-masted ship models on its mantel, and a naval painting of the sea battle between the American *Bonhomme Richard* and British *Serapis* above. A door near the fireplace led to the tiny office of the President's personal secretary, an efficient, cautious, loyal woman married to a Veterans Administration officer.

Revolving slowly to the right, I could see through the three French doors, one of them open, that led onto the colonnaded walk along the magnificent Rose Garden. Beyond the garden, in a second-floor bedroom of the White House, above the hoary magnolia trees, President Kennedy lay dozing, taking his after-lunch nap. From studying his shaded window, my eyes dropped to two Secret Service agents, young, athletic, conservatively suited, their shoulder holsters hidden, at guard on the colonnaded walk.

I swung completely around to take in the rear of the Oval Office, behind the swivel chair. There was a table with a half-dozen newspapers—I could make out *The New York Times*, the Washington *Post*, the Baltimore *Sun*—and there was a metallic gray Dictaphone machine. On either side of the table rose a flag, one the American flag, the other the Presidential flag, and off through the three green-draped windows, I could see a police guardhouse, and past it, on the South Lawn, the putting green Eisenhower had used, and among the trees the swings, slides, and square white playhouse used by the Kennedy children.

I came around, and I was back where I had started.

My visual orbit had been fleeting, and yet, I sensed, for me it had been unforgettable. It had been an inspiration of my maturity.

There was activity now in the Oval Office. Several famous aides came poking in and out. A secretary crossed hastily. Then, more Secret Service agents. To all of this I was almost oblivious. Sitting in President Kennedy's chair, I tried to define my emotion.

I thought: This chair was, in a sense, manufactured by a group of wigged men who rode in buggies to a place in Philadelphia to declare their independence from tyranny and to declare a democracy of men where all would be equal under the law of God. Today, this chair had become the center of the world, the seat of freedom to which all Americans elevate one of their own to represent them in their continuing yearning for peace, security, absolute individual liberty.

I pushed myself out of that black leather chair, and once more stood beside it, staring down at it with feelings I had not known I still possessed. As we grow older—and I had enjoyed and suffered forty-seven years of living when I stood beside that chair—we become more cynical about our fellow men and their promises, more disenchanted by the possibilities of each new day, and often we are either too bruised by life's trials, or too worldly and sophisticated, for the old words and dreams we no longer believe can be true.

I'm not sure that I felt that way before that moment, but however I felt, it was not as I felt when I left the chair in the Oval Office. My skepticism about the wheeling and dealing in and around the White House, about the bartering and politics, about the gossip inevitably surrounding all our leaders and high places, had fallen away from me. I felt renewed by my vision of the goodness and purpose of our nation and its way of life. The meaning of the chair, Everyman's chair and no one's throne, was clear to me. My youthful patriotism, my belief in the rightness and practical possibilities of virtue in our system, was entirely restored.

As I slowly walked away from that chair, and from the Oval Office itself, I was moved by a powerful emotion. It was as if I knew that the community of men and women in which I lived, of which I was a part, the ones who made the chair in the Oval Office possible and gave it its meaning, was the best community yet devised by the mind of man, and could be better and would be better still and that I would do my part.

Suddenly, I felt less selfish, intolerant, narrow, helpless. Suddenly, I fully understood my citizenship, my allegiance to the cause of freedom, and my role in the community. I counted as an individual. My neighbors counted. Because that chair counted.

All of us, I thought, must make an effort to keep that chair in the White House not only a chair of strength and decision, but a chair of wisdom and justice. I wondered: What could be done by each of us? Participate in government, vote, I had long been taught. Good, I thought, but not good enough. And then I knew what was demanded of us—that *each* of us, in his way, must work as an individual to abolish hatred, violence, intolerance, hypocrisy, despair, inequality in the United States. To abolish these blights in our land, each of us, I knew, would have to abolish the evils within his own self.

And what else must be done? Well, I had come to Washington, D.C., to the White House, to the Oval Office in the West Wing, and finally to the President's chair because I wanted to write an intimate and difficult fictional book about the Presidency. At no time, before sitting in that chair, had I been certain I could or would write this book. But then, after rising from the chair, I knew that I must write it, and that I was ready to write it, at last. And so, for better or for worse, I wrote it, because I now believed in my fellow men and my country and our system more than I ever had before, and because I wanted to become better than I was, and perhaps move others as I had been moved.

The journey to that remarkable moment in the chair in the Oval Office was hesitant, roundabout, slow—yet adventurous. It consisted not of dramatic physical adventures such as certain people we read about have. It consisted of smaller inner adventures such as men who dream—or write—are more likely to have.

For me, it began on the midnight of a Saturday in June, 1963, as I was scanning the next morning's newspapers with all their calamitous news about civil rights strife in altogether too many of the fifty states of the United States. For several years I had wanted to write a novel about this racial conflict, and had considered and rejected a number of ideas. Now, suddenly, I sat up. I had the idea I had been searching for. I had it whole. It had come to me as a question: What would happen to all of us if a Negro congressman, because of a sudden accident and the law of succession, became President of the United States for an unexpired term? What would happen to the United States? How would the event affect nations and peoples abroad? What would happen to the Negro President himself? And to those whites, men and women, whose lives converged upon his life? To find the answers, I would have to write a work of fiction, a novel with a factual background, a novel to be called *The Man*. That was it, for me a story that must be told, if I could tell it—if I had the perception, sensitivity, stamina and, above all, the courage.

Uncertainly, I fumbled forward in the days and weeks that followed, trying to convert dream into reality. I researched in Los Angeles and New York. Under the shading umbrella of an outdoor café on the Champs-Élysées in Paris, I worked out the characters and story. In hotel rooms of Frankfurt and Juan-les-Pins I wrote scenes. By the time I reached Rome, I had come to a halt. I was not sure I could make the background— mainly scenes in the White House—authentic enough to be believable. Perhaps I did not fully understand its role in our lives.

In numerous visits to Washington in the past I had, as a plain tourist, taken the limited morning tour of the East Wing of the White House. But while what I had seen was impressive, I retained the memory of a museum. A real President worked in the downstairs West Wing offices, and lived as a human being in the upstairs second-floor apartments, both areas barred to tourists. To go forward, I knew that I must see what others could not see. My project hung in the balance.

I wrote to several friends in Washington, and asked how I could go about living inside, getting the real feel of the White House for a week or two. Soon, I had one reply from a friend in the State Department. At a reception given by Secretary of State Dean Rusk, this friend had run into the President's press secretary, Pierre Salinger, and he had relayed my wishes. Salinger had replied, "Tell Mr. Wallace I've read a couple of his books—and I'm looking forward to meeting him."

At once I wrote to Salinger and outlined my needs. He responded instantly: Come to Washington, call him, and he would do what he could.

On September 16, 1963, I arrived at the Pennsylvania Avenue entrance to the White House. After being cleared by two policemen, I walked up the curving driveway and entered the West Wing lobby or Reading Room, teeming with perhaps one hundred newspapermen. As I came in, Salinger, his amiable round face, cigar, white shirt visible in the midst of the reporters, was answering questions on the savage slaying of the children in that Birmingham church. Finishing, Salinger saw me, recognized me somehow, and called out, "See you in five minutes!"

In five minutes I was sitting across the desk from Salinger in his large, cluttered office. I explained the theme of my novel, and what I would need to go on. He challenged me on several points, but was otherwise intrigued by my idea. I told him, "I don't want to go through here as a tourist. I want to go through the offices and private apartments making believe I am President, which is what the hero of my novel will be." Salinger agreed to cooperate. Visiting the President's Oval Office and the rooms around it would not be difficult since President Kennedy usually napped or rested in his private quarters upstairs from two-thirty in the afternoon to four-thirty. However, visiting his private living quarters presented some obstacles. The Kennedys felt that their private living area should not be turned into a goldfish bowl. Still, Salinger thought that since I was writing fiction, something might be done.

We set up a series of appointments, and it was on the following afternoon that I made my first of a half-dozen visits to the President's Oval Office—and sat in that chair.

The inspiring moment in that chair was intensified by other intimate and electric moments that followed in the next days. First Salinger, then a White House policeman, took me on a complete visit to every portion of the ground floor of the White House itself. I saw the housekeeper's office, the private flower shop, the physician's office, the modern stainless-steel kitchen, the private movie projection room that has chairs for fifty people spaced over its blue carpet. Returning to the Oval Office—I counted thirty-three steps along an outdoor colonnaded walk to get there —the policeman said to me, "We'll all read whatever you write, you know. The Secret Service studies all novels about the White House. They want to know how much the book might tell the public about inside details of the layout here—in case some nut reads it, gets a notion on how to get into here and attempt to assassinate the President."

Later, having requested an interview with the President's personal secretary of eleven years, Mrs. Evelyn N. Lincoln, whose office was next door to the President's own, I was introduced to her. Mrs. Lincoln was nervous. Recently, I had occasion to remind Mrs. Lincoln of our interview. "I promised you," I wrote her, "that I would not use you as a character in my fiction—and I have not—but said that I wanted to know something of the routine of the President's personal secretary and would use that background—and I have used it. You will not, I am certain, recognize anything of yourself in that key fictional character in my book, Miss Edna Foster, but I am sure you will recognize, perhaps with a sigh, something of the pressure and travail of your recent position."

Memories now come to mind of our talk. Her gray electric typewriter, the television set behind her desk, the overflow of Presidential souvenirs on her shelves. Above all, I recall the magnified peephole built into her door, through which she could peek into the Oval Office to see if the President was occupied with visitors or alone. Mrs. Lincoln told me that a White House limousine which picked her up in front of her apartment at seven-thirty every morning deposited her here in the West Wing, where she often toiled until eight-thirty at night. She handled all of the President's *personal* letters, phone calls, and dates. "I don't know if I should tell you this," she said, "but I even get his suits for him, and see that they are sent to him on time. Of course, he has definite tastes, and orders what he wants, but I follow through."

The days that followed were a kaleidoscope of impressions of visits to every nook and cranny of the nation's first house. The most exciting of all was the early evening when President Kennedy's Negro valet, Preston, in a black suit and a white tie, escorted me through the rarely seen second-story apartments where the President and First Lady lived, shut off from the outside world. Little things, not big ones, remain in mind: the white match covers with "The President's House" imprinted in gold, in an ashtray in the Lincoln Bedroom, where Mrs. Rose Kennedy often slept; the leather-topped table behind a yellow sofa where the President worked in his living room late at night, while his wife curled up on the sofa and read beneath the brilliant Cezannes on the wall; the green pads on the white patio furniture outside on the Truman Balcony, where the President could stretch out during soft summer evenings, chatting off the record with Lyndon B. Johnson and Congressional leaders; the giant humidor in the President's bedroom where he kept his cigars.

As for President Kennedy himself, I saw him three times in those days —did not interview him, but rather, saw him in action and close up. The first occasion was a morning in the Cabinet Room, when he made some public remarks after the swearing in of new representatives to the eighteenth United Nations General Assembly. Afterward, he and Adlai Stevenson joked. I saw his remarks, later, in the official transcript, but not the jokes.

The next occasion was more memorable. I was invited to the Oval Office to watch President Kennedy deliver a television broadcast to the nation on the tax cut he so much wanted. It was to be, although none of us knew it at the time, his last national television address. I watched as his desk was cleared of its gadgets, a black curtain hung behind it for a backdrop, and two pillows placed on his chair (I asked if this was to make him taller, and I was told no, it was to make him more comfortable, because of his bad back). I watched him enter the office, much huskier than I had imagined, and he nodded and greeted me, and I returned his greeting. I watched him run through his first paragraph for still photographers, and after the photographers were shown out, the red lights on the big television cameras blinked on, and the speech was under way.

The third and last time I saw him, on a late afternoon, he was walking, alligator briefcase under his arm, across the lawn of the Rose Garden toward the huge helicopter squatting on its steel pad on the South Lawn, readying to fly to New York and the United Nations.

A few days later, I was back in Los Angeles, filled with the spirit of what I had seen, undramatic and yet more dramatic than anything I had ever witnessed, and I knew that I must write my book about all this, and could write it—and I did.

But there is one last part of the story to tell, so mystical, so strange, that I almost hesitate to recount it. Yet, tell it I must, for it is part of the whole adventure.

I had been writing my novel feverishly. At the end of the first chapter, my fictional Negro succeeds to the unexpired term of the dead fictional President. I wanted to show my fictional President, Douglass Dilman, sworn in by the Chief Justice, show him with his hand on the Bible, and I wondered to what passage he might open the Bible. My mind ranged across all the pertinent Bible quotations I could remember, and then fastened on one. I looked it up to be sure I had it right. And then I wrote it. Here is exactly what I wrote:

"She heard Eaton inquire of Senator Dilman, 'Do you wish this open on any particular passage?'

"She heard Dilman reply, 'Psalms 127:1.' Slowly, Eaton leafed through the book, and then he said, 'Is this it? "Except the Lord build the house, they labour in vain that build it: except the Lord keep the city, the watchman waketh but in vain."' He glanced inquiringly at Dilman, and Dilman swallowed, his Adam's apple bobbing, and said, 'Yes, sir, that is it.'"

One week later—it was noon, and I had just resumed work—my wife called from an appointment at her beauty parlor and cried out, "President Kennedy has been shot in Dallas!" With disbelief, I turned on my radio. An hour later, stunned with the nation and the world, I learned that he was dead.

All that shocking afternoon was a blur, and late that night, sitting on the edge of my bed, exhausted, numbed, I watched and heard the mournful television reports. Then, suddenly, a commentator was on, and he was saying that when the President was killed, his motorcade had been headed toward the Dallas Trade Mart, where he was to address a luncheon of the Dallas Citizens' Council. President Kennedy's speech had been prepared. It would never be delivered. The commentator felt that this last speech by John Fitzgerald Kennedy should be read now. So he read the speech, and when he reached the final paragraph, he read that the President had written that our generation was "the watchman on the walls of world freedom," and that we must forever exercise strength tempered by wisdom and restraint to achieve peace on earth. And then, the commentator read the President's last words of his last speech:

"That must always be our goal, and the righteousness of our cause must always underlie our strength. For as was written long ago: 'except the Lord keep the city, the watchman waketh but in vain.'"

I sat chilled. *Except the Lord keep the city, the watchman waketh but in vain.* Inspired by a chair in the Oval Office, I had written those words for a fictional President succeeding an imaginary dead President a week before. And here were the final words of our own President. The coincidence was as incredible and mysterious to me as the mystery of existence itself.

The life of the nation went on. We all went on. And months later, seeking another appropriate quotation for my book, I found one I had jotted on the back of a folded envelope as I had left the Oval Office. Now, firmly, I wrote it into my story, and it was the essence of all that I had learned from the vacant chair in the Oval Office—and perhaps, from the one who had filled it so well, so briefly. Writing, I had a white lawyer, the Negro President's best friend, say to him:

"The American people have finally learned what a great Kansas editor tried to teach them years ago, that liberty is the only thing you cannot have—unless you are willing to give it to others."

WHAT HAS HAPPENED SINCE...

This article was the last one I wrote after I won my freedom from being only a Sunday Gentleman.

For several years, the editors of the *Family Weekly,* a popular magazine supplement published in New York and distributed to subscribing newspapers throughout the United States, had been asking me if I would contribute a brief memoir to a series they had been running. The series was called "My Most Inspiring Moment," and a great number of renowned authors in the United States and Great Britain had already contributed to it.

Since I had noticed that most authors' inspiring moments fall into the pattern of recollections about an uplifting or edifying experience shared with their parents, or a brave handicapped friend, I did not feel that I could enhance the series with more of the same. And so I told the editors that if I should ever have an idea that was different and that absorbed me, I would contribute to their series.

I then forgot about the matter. However, the editors of *Family Weekly* did not. From time to time, they wrote to ask me if I had yet found an idea about which I wanted to write, and always I said that I had not, not yet. One such inquiry from them came some months after President Kennedy's assassination, at a period when I was finishing my writing of *The Man.* As usual, I replied that I had nothing in mind, not yet. But then, shortly after answering, suddenly, thinking of how my visit to the White House had inspired me to complete my novel, I realized with rising excitement that there *was* something I wanted to write about, something I burned to write about and have readers across the nation read.

Immediately, I picked up the telephone and spoke to the chief editor of *Family Weekly* in New York City, and sketched out the personal story I wanted to call "The Chair in the Oval Office." He was enthusiastic about it, and insisted upon my setting a delivery date so that he could schedule its publication in advance. I promptly made notes, but then became caught up in rewrites of my novel, and it was not until the summer of 1964 that I finally sat down to write this story. I wrote it in Paris, rewrote it in Cannes, and mailed it off. The editors accepted it, moved and pleased by it, and scheduled the story to be printed in the issue of their supplement that would appear in newspapers across the United States on the first anniversary of President Kennedy's death.

It did not appear in print on the first anniversary of President Kennedy's death. Nor did it appear in print in any issue of that supplement at any later date. Perplexed, I asked my literary agent what had happened. He in turn asked the editors what had happened. They were evasive. For "reasons" beyond their control, they had found that they could not publish it at all.

This was not a satisfactory answer, and I remained mystified until, on a visit to New York, I accidentally ran into one of the editors at a social gathering. I asked him bluntly what had happened to "The Chair in the Oval Office." He said, somewhat sadly, that the story had been suppressed. He said that when certain Southern newspaper publishers, who subscribed to and helped support the supplement, learned about the contents of my story, they protested. They did not intend to use it. As a result, the supplement's editors decided to withdraw the article.

This was the explanation given me. I do not know if it is the true one, or the entire one. I only know that a story so often solicited, and eagerly accepted, was inexplicably kept from being published—until its appearance now in this volume.

I am pleased to close this book with my White House adventure, because I feel that its point is more meaningful today than ever before: "Liberty is the only thing you cannot have—unless you are willing to give it to others."

John F. Kennedy understood this fully. I grieve over our loss of him for many reasons, but this is one of the major reasons, that he understood the definition of liberty fully and might have brought more of us to an understanding of it more swiftly had he lived. Yet, I suspect, the chair in the Oval Office of the White House will be better occupied in the future, to the benefit of all of us, because he sat there once, briefly.

Recently, in a London periodical, I came across W. H. Auden's

"Elegy for J.F.K." It seemed to me a fitting note upon which to conclude this story.

Why then? Why there?
Why thus, we cry, did he die?
The heavens are silent

What he was, he was;
What he is fated to become
Depends on us

Remembering his death,
How we choose to live
Will decide its meaning.

When a just man dies,
Lamentation and praise,
Sorrow and joy are one.

ACKNOWLEDGMENTS

THE publishers listed below gave their permission for me to reprint those of my articles which originally appeared in the pages of their publications in abridged form, as well as permission to reprint those articles of mine that they owned but had not published. I have listed the titles of the articles as they were used in their magazine publication. Where these original titles have been changed for this book, I have placed my new titles in parentheses.

Crowell-Collier Publishing Company, New York: "What's Krupp Up to Now?" ("Tycoon"), 1953; "The Seven Secret Cells of Spandau" ("The Seven Secret Prison Cells"), unpublished.

Curtis Publishing Company, Philadelphia: "The Man Who Swindled Goering," copyright 1947; "The Great Globe Trotter" ("Everybody's Rover Boy"), copyright 1947; "Nabob's Chariot" ("Millionaire's Chariot"), copyright 1947; "Adventure's Favorite Train" ("Intrigue Express"), copyright 1947; "Operation of the Last Resort" ("They Cut Away His Conscience"), copyright 1951.

Newspaper Magazines, Inc., New York: "The Chair in the Oval Office," unpublished.

Reader's Digest, Pleasantville, N. Y.: "France's Greatest Detective" ("Monsieur Bertillon"), 1950; "Frank Merriwell: Paragon of the Paperbacks" ("Paragon of the Paperbacks"), 1953; "Tourist's Bible," unpublished.